Lecture Notes in Computer Science 4789

Commenced Publication in 1973
Founding and Former Series Editors:
Gerhard Goos, Juris Hartmanis, and Jan van Leeuwen

Editorial Board

Michael Butler   Michael G. Hinchey
María M. Larrondo-Petrie (Eds.)

Formal Methods and Software Engineering

9th International Conference
on Formal Engineering Methods, ICFEM 2007
Boca Raton, FL, USA, November 14-15, 2007
Proceedings

 Springer

Volume Editors

Michael Butler
University of Southampton, School of Electronic and Computer Science
Highfield, Southampton, SO17 1BJ, UK
E-mail: m.j.butler@ecs.soton.ac.uk

Michael G. Hinchey
Loyola College in Maryland, Department of Computer Science
4501 N. Charles Street, Baltimore, MD 21210, USA
E-mail: mike.hinchey@usa.net

María M. Larrondo-Petrie
Florida Atlantic University, Department of Computer Science and Engineering
777 Glades Road SE-308, Boca Raton, FL 33431-0991, USA
E-mail: petrie@fau.edu

Library of Congress Control Number: 2007938401

CR Subject Classification (1998): D.2.4, D.2, D.3, F.3

LNCS Sublibrary: SL 2 – Programming and Software Engineering

ISSN   0302-9743
ISBN-10   3-540-76648-0 Springer Berlin Heidelberg New York
ISBN-13   978-3-540-76648-3 Springer Berlin Heidelberg New York

Springer is a part of Springer Science+Business Media

springer.com

© Springer-Verlag Berlin Heidelberg 2007
Printed in Germany

Typesetting: Camera-ready by author, data conversion by Scientific Publishing Services, Chennai, India
Printed on acid-free paper   SPIN: 12187614   06/3180   5 4 3 2 1 0

Preface

Formal methods for the development of computer systems have been extensively researched and studied. A range of semantic theories, specification languages, design techniques, and verification methods and tools have been developed and applied to the construction of programs of moderate size that are used in critical applications. The challenge now is to scale up formal methods and integrate them into engineering development processes for the correct construction and maintenance of computer systems. This requires us to improve the state of the art by researching the integration of methods and their theories, and merging them into industrial engineering practice, including new and emerging practice.

ICFEM, the International Conference on Formal Engineering Methods, aims to bring together those interested in the application of formal engineering methods to computer systems. Researchers and practitioners, from industry, academia, and government, are encouraged to attend and to help advance the state of the art. The conference particularly encourages research that aims at a combination of conceptual and methodological aspects with their formal foundation and tool support, and work that has been incorporated into the production of real systems.

This volume contains the papers presented at ICFEM 2007 held November 14–15, 2007 in Florida Atlantic University, Boca Raton, Florida. There were 38 submissions. Each submission was reviewed by four Program Committee members. The committee decided to accept 19 papers based on originality, technical soundness, presentation, and relevance to formal engineering and verification methods. We thank the Program Committee members and the other referees for their effort and professional work in the reviewing and selecting process. The program also includes contributions from the two keynote speakers: Jean-Raymond Abrial and Tom Maibaum. Professor Abrial gave a talk on a system development process with Event-B and the Rodin Platform while Professor Maibaum gave a talk on the challenges of software certification.

A workshop on the *verifiable file store mini-challenge* was held on November 13, 2007 co-located with ICFEM 2007. This workshop was organized by Jim Woodcock and Leo Freitas as part of the Grand Challenge in Verified Software.

ICFEM 2007 was jointly organized and sponsored by Florida Atlantic University, Loyola College in Maryland, and the University of Southampton and we would like to thank all those who helped in the organization. We used the Easychair system to manage the submissions, refereeing, paper selection, and proceedings production. We would like to thank the Easychair team for a very powerful tool.

August 2007

Michael Butler
Mike Hinchey
Maria M. Larrondo-Petrie

Conference Organization

Conference Chair

General Chair   Mike Hinchey (Loyola College in Maryland, USA)
Program Chairs   Michael Butler (University of Southampton, UK)
                     Maria M. Larrondo-Petrie (Florida Atlantic University,
                        USA)
Publicity Chair   Denis Gracanin (Virginia Tech, USA)

Program Committee

Keijiro Araki	Shriram Krishnamurthi	Mannu Satpathy
Farhad Arbab	Kung-Kiu Lau	Klaus-Dieter Schewe
David Basin	Rustan Leino	Kaisa Sere
Ana Cavalcanti	Michael Leuschel	Wuwei Shen
Jessica Chen	Xuandong Li	Marjan Sirjani
Yoonsik Cheon	Zhiming Liu	Ketil Stølen
Kai Engelhardt	Shaoying Liu	Sofiene Tahar
Eduardo B. Fernandez	Tiziana Margaria	Helen Treharne
Colin Fidge	Huaikou Miao	T.H. Tse
John Fitzgerald	Peter O'Hearn	Farn Wang
Marc Frappier	Michael Poppleton	Wang Yi
Marcelo Fabián Frias	Marie-Laure Potet	Jian Zhang
Uwe Glässer	Anders Ravn	Jin Song Dong
Joseph Kiniry	Davide Sangiorgi	Zhenhua Duan

Local Organization

Eduardo B. Fernandez
Michael VanHilst
Nelly Delessy-Gassant
Maureen Manoly
Colleen Glazer

External Reviewers

Rezine Ahmed	Neil Evans	Olga Grinchintein
Bernhard Aichernig	Bernd Fischer	Osman Hasan
Joachim Baran	Wan Fokkink	Felix Klaedtke
Achim D. Brucker	Amjad Gawanmeh	István Knoll

Linas Laibinis
Yuan Fang Li
Sotiris Moschoyiannis
Juan Antonio
  Navarro-Pérez
Joseph Okika
Gennaro Parlato
Daniel Plagge
Marta Plaska

Sampath Prahlad
Zongyan Qiu
S. Ramesh
Niloofar Razavi
Atle Refsdal
Ragnhild Kobro Runde
Mehrnoosh Sadrzadeh
Mayank Saksena
Corinna Spermann

Volker Stolz
Jan Stöcker
Jun Sun
Leonidas Tsiopoulos
Andrzej Wasowski
Mohamed Zaki
Miaomiao Zhang
Jianhua Zhao
Hui Liang

ICFEM Steering Committee

He Jifeng (East China Normal University, China)
Keijiro Araki (Kyushu University, Japan)
Jin Song Dong (National University, Singapore)
Chris George (UNU-IIST, Macao)
Mike Hinchey (Loyola College in Maryland, USA)
Shaoying Liu (Hosei University, Japan)
John McDermid (University of York, UK)
Tetsuo Tamai (University of Tokyo, Japan)
Jim Woodcock (University of York, UK)

Table of Contents

Invited Talks

A System Development Process with Event-B and the Rodin
Platform 1
    Jean-Raymond Abrial

Challenges in Software Certification 4
    Tom Maibaum

Security and Knowledge

Integrating Formal Methods with System Management 19
    Martin de Groot

Formal Engineering of XACML Access Control Policies in VDM++ 37
    Jeremy W. Bryans and John S. Fitzgerald

A Verification Framework for Agent Knowledge 57
    Jin Song Dong, Yuzhang Feng, and Ho-fung Leung

Embedded Systems

From Model-Based Design to Formal Verification of Adaptive
Embedded Systems 76
    Rasmus Adler, Ina Schaefer, Tobias Schuele, and Eric Vecchié

Machine-Assisted Proof Support for Validation Beyond Simulink 96
    Chunqing Chen, Jin Song Dong, and Jun Sun

VeSTA: A Tool to Verify the Correct Integration of a Component in a
Composite Timed System 116
    Jacques Julliand, Hassan Mountassir, and Emilie Oudot

Testing

Integrating Specification-Based Review and Testing for Detecting
Errors in Programs 136
    Shaoying Liu

Testing for Refinement in CSP 151
    Ana Cavalcanti and Marie-Claude Gaudel

Reducing Test Sequence Length Using Invertible Sequences............ 171
    Lihua Duan and Jessica Chen

Automated Analysis

Model Checking with SAT-Based Characterization of ACTL
Formulas... 191
  Wenhui Zhang

Automating Refinement Checking in Probabilistic System Design 212
  Carlos Gonzalia and Annabelle McIver

Model Checking in Practice: Analysis of Generic Bootloader Using
SPIN 232
  Kuntal Das Barman and Debapriyay Mukhopadhyay

Model Checking Propositional Projection Temporal Logic Based on
SPIN 246
  Cong Tian and Zhenhua Duan

Hardware

A Denotational Semantics for Handel-C Hardware Compilation 266
  Juan Ignacio Perna and Jim Woodcock

Automatic Generation of Verified Concurrent Hardware............... 286
  Marcel Oliveira and Jim Woodcock

Modeling and Verification of Master/Slave Clock Synchronization
Using Hybrid Automata and Model-Checking........................ 307
  Guillermo Rodriguez-Navas, Julián Proenza, and Hans Hansson

Concurrency

Efficient Symbolic Execution of Large Quantifications in a Process
Algebra... 327
  Benoît Fraikin and Marc Frappier

Formalizing SANE Virtual Processor in Thread Algebra 345
  Thuy Duong Vu and Chris Jesshope

Calculating and Composing Progress Properties in Terms of the
Leads-to Relation 366
  Arjan J. Mooij

Erratum

Challenges in Software Certification E1
  Tom Maibaum

Author Index... 387

A System Development Process with Event-B and the Rodin Platform

J.-R. Abrial

jabrial@inf.ethz.ch

Event-B is the name of a mathematical (set-theoretic) approach used to develop *complex discrete systems*, be they computerized or not.

The Rodin platform is an open tool set devoted to supporting the development of such systems. It contains a modeling database surrounded by various plug-ins: static checker, proof obligation generator, provers, model-checkers, animators, UML transformers, requirement document handler, etc. The database itself contains the various modeling elements needed to construct discrete transition system models: essentially variables, invariants, and transitions.

Formal Development. With the help of this palette, users can develop mathematical models and refine them. In doing so, they are able to reason, modify, and decompose their models before starting the effective implementation of the corresponding systems. Such an approach is well known and widely used in many mature engineering disciplines where reasoning on a abstract representation of the future system is routine. Just think of the usage of blueprints made by architects within a building construction process.

Technology Transfer. One of the main difficulties in transferring this technology is not that of its mastering by industry engineers (a common opinion shared by many analysts). It is rather, we think, the incorporation of this technology within the industrial *development process*. We believe that the above argument about the difficulty of mastering this technology is, in fact, a way of hiding (consciously or not) the one concerning the incorporation within the development process.

This Presentation. The aim of this presentation is to show that the Event-B technology can be put into practice. For this, we must follow a well defined development process. That process is precisely the one which has to be transferred to industry. The Rodin platform, in its final form, will be the supporting tool for achieving this.

Before describing the Event-B development process however, we make precise what we mean by an industrial development process in general terms.

Industrial Development Processes are now common practice among important critical system manufacturers (train signalling system companies, avionic and space companies, automotive manufacturers, power system designers, defense sector industries, etc.). A system development process contains the definition of the various milestones encountered in the system construction together with the precise definition of what is to be done between these milestones, by

M. Butler, M. Hinchey, M.M. Larrondo-Petrie (Eds.): ICFEM 2007, LNCS 4789, pp. 1–3, 2007.

whom, and within which delays. It also contains different ways of re-iterating on these milestones in case the process encounters some difficulties.

Usually, industrial managers are very reluctant to modify their development processes because: (1) it is part of their company culture and image, (2) it is difficult to define and make precise, and (3) it is even more difficult to have them accepted and followed by working engineers.

In order to know how to modify the development process due to the introduction of some formal method technology (Event-B and Rodin) in the construction of complex systems, it is clearly very important to understand that this process is aimed at obtaining systems which can be considered to be *correct by construction*. This presentation does not pretend to solve all related problems nor to give the key to a successful incorporation of formal methods in industry: it aims at providing the beginning of a systematic way of envisaging these matters.

Let us now briefly present the Event-B development process and show how the Rodin platform supports it.

Requirement Document. After the initial feasibility studies phase which is not subsequently modified, the second phase of the process is the writing of the *requirement document.* It must be pointed out that most of the time such documents are very poor: quite often, they just contain the pseudo-solution of a problem which, to begin with, is not stated. Our opinion is that it is very risky to proceed further with such poor documents. More precisely, we think that it is necessary to rewrite them very carefully in a systematic fashion. Each requirement must be stated by means of a short English statement which is well recognizable and clearly labelled according to some taxonomy to be defined for each project.

The Rodin platform in its final form will provide a plug-in able to support the gradual construction of such structured requirement documents, to retrieve them, and to form the initial basis of the necessary traceability.

Refinement Strategy. The next phase consists in defining a temporary *refinement strategy.* It contains the successive steps of the refined models construction. Clearly, it is out of the question to construct a unique model taking account of all requirements at once. Each such refinement step must give a reference to the precise requirements, stated in the previous phase, which are taken into account. A preliminary completion study can be performed (no requirements are forgotten). The refinement strategy in this phase is only temporary as it might be reshaped in further phases.

The Rodin platform in its final form will provide a plug-in able to support the writing of the refinement strategy and to check that it is correctly linked to the requirement document.

Refinements and Proofs. The next phase is divided up in many sub-steps according to the precise strategy defined in the previous phase. Each sub-step is made of the definition of the *formal refinement* which is performed, together with the corresponding *proofs.* It might be accompanied by some model-checking, model testing, as well as animations activities.

The three previous activities are very important to be performed at each refinement sub-step as they help figuring out that some requirements are impossible to achieve (or very costly), whereas some other had been simply completely forgotten. In other words, these activities help *validate the requirement document*. The outcome of these activities (checked or tested properties and model animations) can be seen and understood by the "client", who is then able to judge whether what has been formally modeled at a given stage indeed corresponds to what he had in mind. Notice that in each refinement sub-step, it might be found also that the previous refinement strategy was not adequate so that it has to be modified accordingly.

The Rodin platform provides the core elements able to support this central phase: modeling database, proof obligation generator, and provers. The surrounding plug-ins (model-checker, animator, UML translator) support the other requirement document validation activities

Decomposition. The next phase proceeds with the *decomposition* of the refined model obtained at the end of the previous one. In particular, this decomposition might separate that part of the model dealing with the external environment from that part of the system dealing with the hardware or software implementation. The latter part might be refined in the same way as it was done on the global model in the previous phase. This refinement/decomposition pair might be repeated a number of times until one reaches a satisfactory architecture.

The Rodin platform in its final form will provide plug-ins to support and prove that proposed decompositions are correct.

Code Generation. The final phase consists in performing the various hardware or software *automatic code generation*.

The Rodin platform in its final form will provide plug-ins to perform these translations.

As can be seen the incorporation of these phases within an existing development process is certainly not an easy task. An important point to take into account is the incorporation (and measurement) of the many proofs which have to be performed in order to be sure that the final system will be indeed "correct by construction".

Challenges in Software Certification

Tom Maibaum

Software Quality Research Laboratory and Department of Computing and Software
McMaster University
1280 Main St West, Hamilton ON, Canada L8S 4K1
tom@maibaum.org

Abstract. As software has invaded more and more areas of everyday life, software certification has emerged as a very important issue for governments, industry and consumers. Existing certification regimes are generally focused on the wrong entity, the development process that produces the artifact to be certified. At best, such an approach can produce only circumstantial evidence for the suitability of the software. For proper scientific evaluation of an artifact, we need to address directly the attributes of the product and their acceptability for certification. However, the product itself is clearly not enough, as we need other artifacts, like requirements specifications, designs, test documentation, correctness proofs, etc. We can organise these artifacts using a simple, idealised process, in terms of which a manufacturer's own process can be "faked". The attributes of this idealised process and its products can be modelled, following the principles of Measurement Theory, using the product/process modelling method first introduced by Kaposi.

1 Introduction

Software standards have been a concern amongst the software engineering community for the past few decades and they remain a major focus today as a way of introducing and standardising engineering methods into the software industry. Software certification, or at least certification of systems including software, has emerged as an important issue for software engineers, industry, government and society. One has only to point to the many stories of serious disasters where software has been identified as the main culprit and the discomfort that is being felt about this amongst members of these communities. Several organisations, including standards organizations and licensing authorities, have published guidance documents to describe how software should be developed to meet standards or certification criteria.

In this paper, we focus on the issues related to software certification and refer to standards only when relevant, though much could be said about the failures of software related standards to meet criteria characterising rigorous engineering standards. These licensing organisations, through their guidance documents, aim to establish a common understanding between software producers and certifiers (evaluators). The US Food and Drug Administration (FDA) is one of these organisations. The Common Criteria consortium, focusing on security properties of IT systems, is another. The FDA has published several voluminous guidance documents concerning the validation of medical software (as has The Common Criteria

M. Butler, M. Hinchey, M.M. Larrondo-Petrie (Eds.): ICFEM 2007, LNCS 4789, pp. 4–18, 2007.

consortium on security properties). However, these recommendations are not specified in an explicit and precise manner. In more detail, the FDA validation approach, as described in the FDA guidance document [6]:

- does not describe effectively the objects that are subject to assessment,
- does not specify the measurable attributes that characterize these objects, and
- does not describe the criteria on which the FDA staff will base their decision, in order to approve or reject the medical software and, therefore, does not describe the measurement procedures to be used to ascertain the values of the relevant attributes of the objects being assessed.

In fact, the focus of these documents is on the characteristics of a software development *process* that is likely to produce satisfactory software. It shares this approach and concern with almost all certification authorities' requirements (as well as those of standards organisations and approaches based on 'maturity', such as CMM [17]). This seems to miss the point of the aim of certification, namely to ascertain whether the *product*, for which a certificate is being sought, has appropriate characteristics. Certification should be a *measurement* based activity, in which an objective assessment of a product is made in terms of the values of measurable attributes of the product, using an agreed objective function. (This objective function, defined in terms of the measurable attributes of the product, is itself subjectively defined; but once agreed, its use is completely objective, predictable and, perhaps most importantly, repeatable.) After all, we are not going to be happy if an avoidable disaster is down to a product being faulty, even though the process that produced it was supposed to deliver a sound product. A process can never provide this guarantee, if it does not actually examine relevant qualities of the product being certified. Even if the process is one that gives us correctness by construction (in the sense used in formal methods), mere correctness is not enough to convince us of the acceptability of the product. (For example, the specification on which the correctness assertion is based may be faulty. Or not all requirements have been taken into account. See [15,22,23].)

Hence, our hypothesis, boldly stated, is that process oriented standards and certification regimes will never prove satisfactory as ways of guaranteeing software properties and providing a basis for licensing, and we have to develop a properly scientific, product based approach to certification.

2 Process Oriented Standards and Certification

The Food and Drug Administration (FDA) is a public agency in the United States of America concerned with the validation of medical device software or software used to design, develop, or produce medical devices in the United States. In response to the questions about FDA validation requirements, the FDA has expressed its current thinking about medical software validation through guidance documents [6.7.8]. These documents target both the medical software industry and FDA staff. According to the FDA, validation is an important activity that has to be undertaken throughout the software development lifecycle. In other words, it occurs at the beginning, end and even during stages of software development.

For example, the FDA guidance documents recommend validation to start early while the software is being developed. In this sense, the FDA guidance document [6] considers other activities; like planning, verification, testing, traceability, configuration management; as important activities which all together participate in reaching a conclusion that the software is validated.

In essence, the FDA validation approach is a generic approach. It appears in the form of recommendations to apply some software engineering practices. These practices are considered to be working hand by hand to support the validation process. The reason behind FDA taking such a generic approach is due to the 'variety of medical devices, processes, and manufacturing facilities' [6]. In other words, the nature of validation is significantly dependant on the medical device itself. Examples of such validation determinant factors are [6]: availability of production environment for validating the software, ability to simulate the production environment, availability of supportive devices, level of risk, any prerequisite regulations/approvals re validation, etc.

The recommendations in the FDA guidance documents aim to make it possible for the FDA to reach a conclusion that the software is validated. It applies to software [6]:

- used as a component, part, or accessory of a medical device;
- that is itself a medical device (e.g., blood establishment software);
- used in the production of a device (e.g., programmable logic controllers in manufacturing equipment);
- used in implementation of the device manufacturer's quality system (e.g., software that records and maintains the device history record).

Having reached the conclusion that the software is validated increases the level of confidence in the software and, accordingly, the medical device as well. In its guidance documents, the FDA recommends certain activities to be undertaken and certain deliverables to be prepared during the development of the medical software. These activities and deliverables are subject to validation. For instance, validating the Software Requirements Specification (SRS), a deliverable that contains all requirements, aims to ensure that there are no ambiguous, incomplete, unverifiable and technically infeasible requirements. Such validation seeks to ensure that these requirements essentially describe the user needs, and are sufficient to achieve the users' objectives. In the same manner, testing is another key activity that is thoroughly described in the guidance. On the other hand, the guidance points out some issues that are interrelated as a result of the nature of software. Examples of such issues are: frequent changes and their negative consequence, personnel turnover in the sense that software maintainers might have not be involved in the original development. Moreover, the FDA guidance stresses the importance of having well-defined procedures to handle any software change introduced. Validation in this context addresses the newly added software as well as already existing software. In other words, in addition to validating the newly added pieces (components) of code, the effect of these new pieces on the existing ones has to be checked. Such a check ensures that the new components have no negative impact on the existing ones. Furthermore, the guidance highlights the importance of having independence in the review process, in the sense that the personnel who participate in validating the software are not the ones who developed it.

These are mainly the kinds of issues which the FDA guidance documents address with regard to software validation. In terms of software development, the FDA approach does not favour any specific software development model. In other words, it leaves the choice of the approach to be used in developing the software to software producers themselves. This supports the fact that some organizations have there own policies, standards and development approaches that must be followed. Furthermore, it supports the fact that some approaches may well suit certain types of projects or software. Therefore, the FDA leaves the choice of the software development model to software producers, as long as it sufficiently describes the lifecycle of the software. However, it is explicitly required that validation occurs throughout all stages of the software development model (approach). In this context, the guidance states that the magnitude of validation effort, expressed in terms of the level of coverage, is relative to the complexity and the safety risk which the medical software introduces.

In summary, the FDA guidance documents attempt to prescribe very detailed guidance on the nature of the software process to be used. This focus on process is sometimes lost and the guidance documents go into details of the products of the process. However, the nature of the product is highly underdefined, at least in terms of the requirements of measurement, and nothing is said about how the evidence submitted to the FDA will be evaluated. These characteristics make the FDA's certification process lengthy, costly. subjective and, therefore, highly uncertain.

2.1 Faking It

We have been criticizing process oriented methods of certification on the basis that the evidence about the product is indirect and offers no proper guarantees of the kind we actually need. One might then ask whether process based ideas are of any use at all in certification activities. In order to answer such a question, we need to look at what evidence about the product is required to make a proper assessment of its certifiability. Before doing that in the next section, we will discuss an idea due to Parnas [26], though implicit in the work of Dijkstra and many others, about *faking* the software process. The main point Parnas was trying to make was that actual instances of a development process are likely to be imperfect. There is a lot of backtracking, correction and work arounds that do not conform to the process definition. However, at the end of the project, one can fake the ideal execution of the project, an execution in which there is no backtracking, no fixing, no work arounds, etc.

The problem with process based guidance for certification, as in that of the FDA [6,7] (see also [8]) or the Common Criteria [1,2,3,4,5], is that the prescription of the process 'mandates' (the FDA does not legally mandate!) many mechanisms and procedures that are purely to do with managing the imperfections of the process. So, for example, the FDA recommends the development and implementation of a configuration management plan, or a problem reporting plan. As a certifier, why should one care about configuration management during development? (In contrast, one might very well worry about configuration management of a product once it is out in the field.) What does it have to do with the properties of the product actually delivered for certification? Similar comments may be made about bug reporting and fixing mechanisms. The only thing that matters is the qualities of the final version of the product seeking certification. (Of course, if one knew that these matters were not handled well during development, then this might provide circumstantial evidence about the potential quality of the final product. This might then influence the certification authority to look more carefully at evidence about the product. But, this is a secondary effect and we leave it for future discussion.)

On the other hand, we need some products other than the one seeking certification as part of the evidence being assessed. An obvious example is a requirements specification. Other examples are: a design specification, a document describing validation of the design against the requirements, documents relating to testing, documents proving correctness, etc. We could organize these pieces of evidence, various products, in terms of some simple, idealized development process. One candidate for such an idealized process might be a simple version of the waterfall model well known from software engineering texts. In this version, there would be no backtracking, and every stage would have to be completed before moving on to the next one. And this is where the faking it comes in. Whatever actual process one follows, or does not follow, the onus is on the organization seeking certification for their product to map their documents/evidence onto the ideal model and its products. This gives the certification authority a standard product (consisting of the actual product and associated other products/evidence) to 'measure' and decide on certifiability. So, the certification authority should not 'mandate' any particular development process, or the necessity of having a configuration management plan, or whatever. This has the added benefit for the software developer that its internal processes are up to them, as long as they can effectively map their products onto the ones required by the much simpler, faked process. They can then manage their

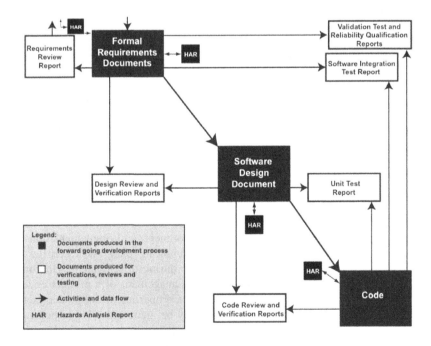

Fig. 1. The Ontario Hydro idealized development process [29]

process without having to undertake the difficult job of redemonstrating conformance to the process 'mandated' by the certification authority or standard.

Of course, the certification authority has to decide what evidence is required and design the idealized process to 'deliver' this evidence. Hence, there is a fine balance between the level of detail in the idealized process and the weight of evidence necessary to make the certification decision. Striking this fine balance is probably the most difficult job the certification authority has to perform. An example of this idea in action, though not mandated by the certification authority, is the model used in the Ontario Hydro redevelopment of the Darlington nuclear power station safety system [29]. See Figure 1.

This is a simplified version of the figure that actually appears in [29] and is clearly insufficient, as it, stands to prescribe a real development process.

3 Measurement and Product/Process Modelling

The "Product/process (P/p) methodology" was introduced by Myers and Kaposi in their book "A First Systems Book" [18,24]. The purpose of this section is to provide a brief overview of this methodology. (See [20,21] for a more detailed description.) The language supporting the methodology provides abstractions for the two main constructs of the method: *products* and *processes*.

The basics of the method are described in [18,24], as is the relationship of the method to Measurement Theory. (See also [27,12] on measurement.) What we are modelling in many engineering problems is some real (existing or yet to be built) process and its associated products, technical or administrative (or both). Either this process is in place and we are modelling what we observe or we are intending, via the model, to prescribe what we eventually intend to observe in the organisation. The observed or intended phenomenon is called the *empirical referent* (and is to our endeavours what specific physical phenomena are to physicists attempting to understand the world by building scientific theories/models).

The language we use for modelling processes has three basic constructs via which the empirical referent must be modelled: products, processes and, an artefact of the method, gates. The first of these, *product*, is used to model the entities manipulated by processes. A product is an 'instantaneous' entity, in that it represents the measurable attributes of the entity at a specific moment in time. On the other hand, a process is an entity that relates to behaviour and so represents a phenomenon taking place over time. Gates are, to some extent, an artefact of the method. Processes are modelled via 'single input, single output' transformers and so require products to be assembled (input from several preceding processes) and disassembled (to send parts of the output to separate subsequent processes).

One may recognise here strong relationships to business process modelling. Business process modelling is, of course, not a new subject! Many consultants make big money out of it! Our focus here is on the problem of modelling itself, with a particular focus on technical processes and requiring levels of detail in process definition which enable the methods and principles of measurement theory to be applied for the purposes of analysis, prediction and certification. A standard reference to approaches to business process modelling is [16].

The idea of characterising formally the process of software development is not new either. The early work of [25,19], etc is notable in this regard and relevant recent material on process modelling in software engineering can be found in [13]. The spirit of what we are attempting is very much in the style of [25], i.e., characterising processes as programs. We see the major difference as being the larger domain of processes being modelled, the much more powerful and expressive language being used and the focus on measurement and measurability. Also, software engineering has moved on since the time of this work and concepts such as patterns and software architecture enable a more sophisticated approach.

Fenton and Pfleeger defined **processes, in the context of software engineering,** in [12], as 'collections of software-related activities'. Hence the process usually has a time factor, i.e., it has a clear beginning and end. Attributes of the process are the inherent characteristics of the process. These attributes are meaningful descriptions over the process lifetime. Fenton and Pfleeger in [12] use the term "internal process attributes" to describe the attributes which can be measured directly by examining the process definition on its own. We will refer to these attributes as static attributes. Having identified these attributes, the evaluation procedure, used by a certifier, should consider the procedures used to measure each of these attributes. The evaluation may take place at predefined time checkpoints or even continue over a time interval.

In contrast, dynamic process attributes are those attributes that can only be measured with regard to the way the process relates to its environment, i.e., the behaviour of the process is the main concern of the measurement activity, rather than the process definition. The values of these process attributes are not meaningful outside their operating environment. Examples of such attributes are: quality and stability. The values of dynamic process attributes (external attributes in [12]) may depend on some values of the static process attributes.

On the other hand, Fenton and Pfleeger defined products in [12] as 'any artifacts, deliverables or documents that result from a process activity'. We will refer to a product as a deliverable of a process. In a sense, we will overload the word deliverable to mean any outcome of the process. Examples of deliverables (products) are: Software Requirements Specification (SRS) document, Software Design Specification document, software source code or some other intermediate outcome of the development prooocess. Products are atemporal in the sense that product attributes can be measured at any time instant (though the measured values may differ from one instant to another). The same notion of static and dynamic attributes is applicable to the deliverables (products). To be more concrete, the version number (as a static attribute) of the software (as a product) is related to the product itself. Whereas, reliability (as a dynamic attribute) of the software (as a product) is relative to the way in which the product (software) behaves in its operating environment. (There is a potentially very interesting discussion to be had here about a program or process being a *product*, e.g., the code, and a *process*, e.g., the behaviour the program describes. But, we will not go there in this document.)

To achieve objective judgment of the evaluation evidence (deliverables), attributes have to be specified for products. This involves two main points: defining the *measurement scale* for the attribute, i.e., its type, and an effective *measurement procedure* for ascertaining the value of the type. Once the deliverable's attributes are specified, an acceptability criterion for each attribute has to be established. Such a criterion will define the acceptable attribute values, from the point of view of the evaluation. Often, it is not the value of a specific attribute that determines the acceptability of the product, but the result of some utility function applied to some or all of the attribute measures of a product. Having both the measurement procedures and the acceptable values documented at the outset of any "deliverable (product) development" will facilitate the development, interim validation and the formal evaluation of these products. In the same manner, tools and machines that may be used in software production may have to be evaluated. Tools are considered as entities with attributes, exactly as for products (i.e., they are products), and hence their attributes have to be specified and 'measured'.

Having such a measurement framework defined will decrease the level of subjectivity in the evaluation activity. The FDA approach lacks such a measurement framework. The FDA approach has no explicit definition of what entities (processes or products) are to be measured. Hence the developers of the medical software and the evaluators from the FDA side share no common understanding about what evidence will be inspected, what attributes in this evidence will be measured, what values are acceptable and what values are not. Similar comments may be made about the Common Criteria, though a better attempt is made in identifying products of development processes and determining what the evaluator must do, though not necessarily providing specific enough criteria and procedures to do it.

(Motivated by the idea that processes and products are the key objects of measurement, Basili, Caldiera and Rombach in [11] developed the Goal-Question-Metric (GQM) approach to help engineers develop models based on these kinds of ideas. GQM is an engineering approach effective for the specification and the assessment of entities. The GQM model is hierarchical in the sense that it is layered into three main levels: the conceptual level (goals), the operational level (questions) and the quantitative level (metrics, i.e., measurement). At the conceptual level, goals specify the objectives to be achieved by measuring some objects (products or processes). At the operational level, questions (what, who and how) should be derived from each goal. Answers to these questions will determine whether the goals are being met or not. Finally, the quantitative level describes what type of data has to be collected for every question in addition to the measurement mechanism to ensure a quantitative answer for the assessment. The key advantage of the GQM is that it enables us to identify the key attributes along with their measurement scales and procedures. These attributes are the ones that are identified as being important for achieving the objectives and goals. Fenton and Pfleeger also considered process maturity models, such as CMM, to be used hand in hand with the GQM model. As the GQM helps to understand why we measure an attribute in a process, the process maturity model suggests whether or not we are capable of measuring the process in a practical way. Thus this supports the applicability of the GQM model. The main reason for considering this maturity model is that not all processes are at the same level of maturity, i.e., processes vary in terms of the visibility of input products and output products. The model is described in detail in [12]. In this context, we want to emphasize that processes with clearly defined input and output products are our main concern.)

4 The Common Criteria (CC) for Information Technology Security Evaluation: A Potential Model?

The Common Criteria (CC) for Information Technology (IT) Security Evaluation is an international standard for specifying and evaluating IT security requirements and products. This standard was developed as a result of a cooperation between six national security and standards organisations in the Netherlands, Germany, France, United Kingdom, Canada and the United States of America. This cooperation aims to define an international standard in order to replace the existing security evaluation criteria in those countries. (The consortium has been significantly expanded since its inception.) The main reason for considering the CC is the more systematic and consistent approach, as compared to the FDA, that the CC follows in specifying security requirements and evaluating their implementation. As we will illustrate, the CC falls into the trap of prescribing in detail development process standards, but, on the other hand, it does provide a semblance of being product and measurement oriented.

In the CC, IT security requirements can be classified into Security Functional Requirements (SFRs) and Security Assurance Requirements (SARs). SFRs are mainly concerned with describing the functionalities to be implemented by the final product, whereas SARs are concerned with describing the properties that the final product should possess. As per the CC terminology, the final product that has to be developed, and after that evaluated, is called the Target-Of-Evaluation (TOE). The TOE is defined in [1] as 'an IT product or system and its associated administrator and user guidance documentation that is the subject of an evaluation' [1]. The requirements that describe the TOE are specified in the Security Target (ST). The Security target is a document that is similar to an SRS document, in which functional requirements are specified using [2], and assurance requirements are specified using [3]. These requirements are categorized in [2] and [3], according to the CC taxonomy, into classes, families and components. A class describes the security focus of its members. In other words, families of the same class share the same security concern, but each has a security objective that supports that concern. Components in the same family share the security objective of their family, but differ in the level of rigour in which the security objective is handled.

For instance, the security focus of communication class (Class CFO: Communication), a security functional class defined in [2], is to 'assure the identity of a party participating in a data exchange' [2]. This class has two families with two different objectives, yet they share the same security concern (communication). Non-repudiation of origin (FCO NRO: Non-repudiation of origin) is the first family in this class, which aims to ensure that the 'originator cannot successfully deny having sent the information' [2]. The other family (FCO NRR: Non-repudiation of receipt) aims to ensure that the 'recipient cannot successfully deny receiving the information' [2]. Components in the same family solve the security problem as described by their family, but with different levels of rigour. In this sense, "non-repudiation of origin" has two components. The first component (FCO NRO.1 Selective proof of origin) solves the "repudiation of origin" problem in the sense that it requires the "relied-on security enforcer (software or hardware or, in the case of CC level 7, both)" to have entities 'with the capability to request evidence of the origin of information' [2]. On the other hand, the other component (FCO NRO.2 Enforced proof of origin) also solves the "repudiation of origin" problem, but it requires the "relied-on security enforcer (software or hardware or both)" to always "generate evidence of origin for transmitted information" [2].

In this context, CC part 2 [2] describes the following security functional classes with their families and components: security audit, communication, cryptographic support, user data protection, identification and authentication, security management, privacy, protection of the Toe Security Functionality (TSF), resource utilisation, and trusted path/channels. On the other hand, CC part 3 [3] describes the following security assurance classes with their families and components: Protection Profile (PP) evaluation, Security Target (ST) evaluation, development, guidance documents, life-cycle support, tests, vulnerability assessment, and composition. As previously described, components of the same family share the security objective of the family, but they differ in the level of rigour of the implementation of that objective. In other words, the level of rigour is essentially determined by the components that describe the level of confidence required for particular security issues. According to the CC, the Evaluation Assurance Level (EAL) determines the level of confidence required in the TOE. The CC defines seven evaluation assurance levels. These are [3]:

- EAL1: functionally tested
- EAL2: structurally tested
- EAL3: methodically tested and checked
- EAL4: methodically designed, tested and reviewed
- EAL5: semiformally designed and tested
- EAL6: semiformally verified design and tested
- EAL7: formally verified design and tested

Each evaluation assurance level requires certain components of particular assurance families to be implemented. The correspondence between the evaluation assurance level and the components of assurance families in a class appears in the following table as given in [3]. The "assurance class" column lists the security assurance classes as defined in CC part three (CC part 3: Security Assurance Requirements [3]). Each of these classes has security assurance families that share the security concern with other families in the same class. The assurance families of each class are listed under the "assurance family" column along the assurance class row. For instance, the "Development" assurance class (ADV) has ADV ARC, ADV FSP, ADV IMP, ADV INT, ADV SPM and ADV TDS as its assurance families. It is the CC convention for any family to start with the class symbol (ADV for DeVelopment Class) followed by an underscore ( ) and then a family symbol (ARC for security ARChitecture family, FSP for Functional SPecification family, IMP for IMPlementation representation family, INT for tsf INTernals family, SPM for Security Policy Modelling family and TDS for Toe DeSign family). The development class symbol (ADV) and all other assurances classes' symbols (AGD for Guidance Documents, ALC for Life Cycle, ASE for Security Target evaluation, ATE for TEsts and AVA for Vulnerability Assessment) start with the letter "A" in order to differentiate them from functional classes.

As described in the "evaluation assurance level summary" table below, each family has a set of components that share the same security problem but differ in the level of rigour of the solution. For example, ADV FSP family of the assurance class "development" has six components. As the table indicates, the first component (1) is necessary for evaluation assurance level one (EAL1). Whereas the second component (2) of the same family is necessary for evaluation assurance level two (EAL2). In the same manner, EAL5 and EAL6 both require the implementation of the fifth component (5) of this family, and so on. Finally, some cells in the table are left blank. This means that it is not required to implement any component from the given family in order to achieve that evaluation assurance level. Security functional and assurance requirements are specified in [2,3], respectively. They are specified in a generic way that enables customization.

Developing the security target starts with defining the level of confidence required in the product (software product in this case) as per the evaluation assurance levels. Having the level of confidence determined, the evaluation assurance level summary table imposes the specification and implementation of the security components in the ST and the TOE respectively. The requirements written in the security target, as taken from [2] and [CC 2006c], can then be customized to reflect some restrictions, such as organisation-specific or product-specific issues. Developing the security target using only the security functional requirements of [2] results in a CC part 2 conformant product. However, adding extra requirements to the security target, which are demonstrated to be needed by the ST developer, results in a CC part 2 extended product. The same concept applies to CC part 3 security assurance requirements.

We can observe that, though not cast in the terminology of product/process modelling, defining relevant attributes and measurement procedures, this looks very close to what we have been describing.

The security assurance requirements are organized into action elements for the developer, action elements for the content and presentation of the submitted deliverable, and action elements for the evaluator.

The taxonomy of the CC describes Security Assurance Requirements (SARs) in terms of action elements for the developer, action elements for the "content & presentation" of the submitted evaluation evidence and as action elements for the evaluator. Each evaluator action element in [3] corresponds to an action that is detailed into work units in the Common Evaluation Methodology [4], a companion document to the CC documents, which describes the way in which a product specified using the CC requirements is evaluated. The work units describe the steps that are to be undertaken by the testing laboratory in evaluating the ST, TOE and all other intermediate products. If these products passed the evaluation of a testing laboratory authorized by the CC, they would be submitted to the national scheme in that country to be certified.

In this context, the CC requires that the developer *shall* provide the TOE for testing. The TOE *shall* be suitable for testing and the evaluator *shall* examine sources of information to support the identification of potential vulnerabilities in the TOE. After that the evaluator *shall* conduct penetration testing to "confirm that the potential vulnerabilities cannot be exploited in the operational environment for the TOE" [3]. The CC uses the auxiliary verb *shall* to refer to mandatory work that has to be undertaken to ensure the correctness of evaluation and, accordingly, the verdicts assigned to products. On the other hand, the CC uses the auxiliary verb *should* to mean "strongly preferred".

Assurance class	Assurance Family	Assurance Components by Evaluation Assurance Level						
		EAL1	EAL2	EAL3	EAL4	EAL5	EAL6	EAL7
Development	ADV_ARC		1	1	1	1	1	1
	ADV_FSP	1	2	3	4	5	5	6
	ADV_IMP				1	1	2	2
	ADV_INT					2	3	3
	ADV_SPM						1	1
	ADV_TDS		1	2	3	4	5	6
Guidance documents	AGD_OPE	1	1	1	1	1	1	1
	AGD_PRE	1	1	1	1	1	1	1
Life-cycle support	ALC_CMC	1	2	3	4	4	5	5
	ALC_CMS	1	2	3	4	5	5	5
	ALC_DEL		1	1	1	1	1	1
	ALC_DVS			1	1	1	2	2
	ALC_FLR							
	ALC_LCD			1	1	1	1	2
	ALC_TAT				1	2	3	3
Security Target evaluation	ASE_CCL	1	1	1	1	1	1	1
	ASE_ECD	1	1	1	1	1	1	1
	ASE_INT	1	1	1	1	1	1	1
	ASE_OBJ	1	2	2	2	2	2	2
	ASE_REQ	1	2	2	2	2	2	2
	ASE_SPD		1	1	1	1	1	1
	ASE_TSS	1	1	1	1	1	1	1
Tests	ATE_COV		1	2	2	2	3	3
	ATE_DPT			1	2	3	3	4
	ATE_FUN		1	1	1	1	2	2
	ATE_IND	1	2	2	2	2	2	3
Vulnerability assessment	AVA_VAN	1	2	2	3	4	5	5

As an example, we include a small fragment of the CC that relates to testing:

ATE_FUN.1. Functional testing

Dependencies: ATE_COV.1 Evidence of coverage

Objectives: The objective is for the developer to demonstrate that the tests in the test documentation are performed and documented correctly.

Developer action elements:

ATE_FUN.1.1D. The developer shall test the TSF and document the results.

ATE_FUN.1.2D. The developer shall provide test documentation.

Content and presentation elements:

ATE_FUN.1.1C. The test documentation shall consist of test plans, expected test results and actual test results.

ATE_FUN.1.2C. The test plans shall identify the tests to be performed and describe the scenarios for performing each test. These scenarios shall include any ordering dependencies on the results of other tests.

ATE_FUN.1.3C. The expected test results shall show the anticipated outputs from a successful execution of the tests.

ATE_FUN.1.4C. The actual test results shall be consistent with the expected test results.

Evaluator action elements:

ATE_FUN.1.1E. The evaluator *shall confirm* that the information provided meets all requirements for content and presentation of evidence.

So, we are a long way from the ideal described in the product/process modelling approach, but we see elements of the approach in the above description. There are lacunae, such as a definition for "shall confirm", which is clearly referring to a (measurement) procedure that is supposed to determine whether "information provided meets all requirements for content and presentation of evidence".

5 Conclusions

Software certification is starting to appear on the agenda of various groups: governments, industry and consumers/citizens. Although it has existed as a requirement in some critical areas, the practice of certification still leaves a lot to be desired. Certification regimes tend to be focused on process oriented standards, expecting that good processes will produce artifacts with the right attributes for certification. But, at best, this is attempting to evaluate the worth of the artifact by using what lawyers might call circumstantial evidence. Lawyers and juries are rightly wary of convicting people for serious crimes based only on circumstantial evidence. This is more so when the crime involved is of a more serious nature, entailing more serious punishment. We should follow suit and be more and more wary of certification by circumstantial evidence when the artifact involved may have more serious consequences for society, individuals or organisations.

The concepts of measurement theory and the traditional engineering idea of modelling problems by using transfer functions, aka the product/process modelling ideas described above, provide a basis for defining much more rigorous standards for evidence and for the process of evaluating the evidence to make a certification decision.

There is much research to be done to enable us to put these ideas into action. Obvious questions include:

- Is there a generic notion of certification, valid across many domains?
- What, if anything, needs to be adapted/instantiated in the generic model to make it suitable for use in a particular domain?
- What simple process model is sufficient to enable the "faking" of real processes and providing a platform for evaluation by certification authorities?
- What is the difference between software quality, of a certain level, and certifiability?
- In what situations can we safely use process based properties as a proxy for product qualities?
- If we assume that both formal approaches and testing are necessary for demonstrating evidence of certifiability, what mix is to be used when? If we have levels of certifiability, as in the Common Criteria, how does this mix change with level?

- Since evaluating evidence about software is an onerous task, how can we assist an evaluator to perform their task by providing tools? (Amongst examples of such tools may be proof checkers (to check proofs offered in evidence), test environments (to re-execute tests offered in evidence), data mining tools to find "interesting" patterns in artifacts, etc.)

There are also cultural and political issues for software certification to deal with. Many software producers find the idea of software certificates anathema: witness the move in various jurisdictions to lower the liability of manufacturers from even the abysmal levels in place today. Governments are woefully ignorant of the dangers represented by the low levels (or non existent levels) of regulation in some industries, such as those producing medical devices, cars and other vehicles, financial services, privacy and confidentiality issues in many information systems, etc. However, the issue is much too large for us to ignore any longer.

Acknowledgements. The Natural Sciences and Engineering Research Council of Canada, McMaster University's Faculty of Engineering and the Department of Computing and Software provided support for this research. The work of the author's Masters student Marwan Abdeen contributed some material to this work. The author would like to thank many of his colleagues, in particular Alan Wassyng and Mark Lawford, for fruitful discussions about certification.

References

1. Common Criteria for Information Technology Security Evaluation, part 1: Introduction and general model, version 3.1, revision 1 (September 2006), http://www.commoncriteriaportal.org/public/files/CCPART1V3.1R1.pdf
2. Common Criteria for Information Technology Security Evaluation, part 2: Security Functional Requirements, version 3.1, revision 1 (September 2006), http://www.commoncriteriaportal.org/public/files/CCPART2V3.1R1.pdf
3. Common Criteria for Information Technology Security Evaluation, part 3: Security Assurance Requirements, version 3.1, revision 1(September 2006), http://www.commoncriteriaportal.org/public/files/CCPART3V3.1R1.pdf
4. Common Methodology for Information Technology Security Evaluation, version 3.1, revision 1 (September 2006), http://www.commoncriteriaportal.org/public/files/CEMV3.1R1.pdf
5. Common Criteria for Information Technology Security Evaluation, User Guide (October 1999), http://www.commoncriteriaportal.org/public/files/ccusersguide.pdf
6. General Principles of Software Validation; Final Guidance for Industry and FDA staff (January 2002), http://www.fda.gov/cdrh/comp/guidance/938.pdf
7. Guidance for the Content of Premarket Submissions for Software Contained in Medical Devices; Guidance for Industry and FDA staff (May 2005), http://www.fda.gov/cdrh/ode/guidance/337.pdf
8. Guidance on General Principles of Process Validation (May 1987) Reprinted (1993), http://www.complianceassociates.ca/pdf/Guide%20-%20Process%20Validation.pdf
9. Abdeen, M.M., Kahl, W., Maibaum, T.: FDA: Between Process & Product Evaluation, HCMDSS/MD PnP. IEEE Computer Society Press, Los Alamitos (2007)

10. Abdeen, M.M.: A Model for the FDA General Principles of Software Validation, Masters of Applied Science Thesis, Department of Computing and Software, McMaster University (2007)
11. Basili, V.R., Caldiera, G., Rombach, H.D.: The Goal Question Metric Approach, Encyclopedia of Software Engineering. Wiley & Sons Inc., Chichester (1994)
12. Fenton, N., Pfleeger, S.L.: Software Metrics: A Rigorous and Practical Approach, 2nd edn. PWS Publishing Co. (1997)
13. Finkelstein, A., Kramer, J., Nuseibeh, B.: Software Process Modelling and Technology. John Wiley, Chichester (1994)
14. Haeberer, A., Maibaum, T.: The Very Idea of Software Development Environments: A Conceptual Architecture for the ARTS Environment Paradigm. In: Redmiles, D., Nuseibeh, B. (eds.) ASE 1998, IEEE Computer Science Press, Los Alamitos (1998)
15. Haeberer, A., Maibaum, T.: Scientific Rigour, an Answer to a Pragmatic Question: A Linguistic Framework for Software Engineering. In: ICSE 2001, pp. 463–472. IEEE CS Press, Los Alamitos (2001)
16. Hammer, M., Champy, J.: Re-engineering the Corporation: A Manifesto for Business Revolution. Nicolas Brealey Publishing (1993)
17. Humphrey, W.: Managing the Software Process. Addison Wesley Professional, Reading (1989)
18. Kaposi, A., Myers, M.: Systems, Models and Measures. In: Formal Approaches to Computing and Information Technology, Springer, London (1994)
19. Lehman, M.: Process Models, Process Programs, Programming Support. In: Proceedings of 9th International Conference on Software Engineering, pp. 14–16. IEEE Computer Society Press, Los Alamitos (1987)
20. Maibaum, T.: The Mensurae Language: Specifying Business Processes. Technical Report, King's College London, Department of Computer Science (1999)
21. Maibaum, T.: An Overview of The Mensurae Language: Specifying Business Processes. In: Proc. Third Workshop on Rigorous Object-Oriented Methods, York University, BCS EWICS (2000)
22. Maibaum, T.: Mathematical Foundations of Software. Future of Software Engineering. In: ICSE 2000, pp. 161–172. IEEE CS Press, Los Alamitos (2000)
23. Maibaum, T.: The Epistemology of Validation and Verification Testing. In: Khendek, F., Dssouli, R. (eds.) TestCom 2005. LNCS, vol. 3502, pp. 1–8. Springer, Heidelberg (2005)
24. Myers, M., Kaposi, A.: A First Systems Book. Imperial College Press, London, UK (2004)
25. Osterweil, L.: Software Processes are Software Too. In: Proceedings of 9th International Conference on Software Engineering, pp. 2–13. IEEE Computer Society Press, Los Alamitos (1987)
26. Parnas, D.L., Clements, P.C.: A Rational Design Process: How and Why to Fake It. In: Proc. TAPSOFT Joint Conference on Theory and Practice of Software Development, pp. 25–29 (1985) Also published as University of Victoria/IBM Technical Report No. 3, 18 pgs (February 1985)
27. Roberts, F.: Measurement Theory, with Applications to Decision-Making, Utility and the Social Sciences. Addison-Wesley, Reading (1979)
28. Suppe, F.: The Structure of Scientific Theories. University of Illinois Press (1979)
29. Wassyng, A., Lawford, M.: Software Tools for Safety-Critical Software Development. International Journal of Software Tools for Technology Transfer, Special Section The Industrialisation of Formal methods: A View from Formal Methods 2003 8(4-5), 337–354 (2006)

Integrating Formal Methods with System Management

Martin de Groot

CSIRO, Australia

Abstract. Monitoring and fault diagnosis are core management tasks for deployed industrial systems. Diagnostic reasoning is closely related to reasoning about implementation correctness. A framework to support the integration of both reasoning tasks is introduced. Many well known formal methods for stepwise program refinement are shown to be compatible with the framework. Compatibility is achieved by treating a formal development as a hierarchical model of the implemented system and then adapting model-based reasoning techniques.

1 Background

This paper is an introduction to a novel framework for integrating formal developments with system management [8]. The framework grew out of an industry sponsored research program to investigate a practical problem which, despite its apparent simplicity, was never satisfactorily resolved by the engineers working for the sponsoring company. The practical problem was to build a general purpose 'alarms' or 'rules' module for telecommunications monitoring equipment. Such modules are components of many industrial systems. They are responsible for detecting, correlating and, occasionally, diagnosing error conditions from an array of performance metrics collected from the monitored system.

Initial investigations into this area revealed that expert systems had been used successfully for diagnosis in relatively static domains such as the human body [4,6], and also that they were unsuited to dynamic domains such as computer networks. Consequently, monitoring systems for the latter tend to offer very little high level analysis—generally providing only alarm collection, logging, display and categorisation facilities. This problem is known as the 'knowledge engineering bottleneck' in the artifical intelligence literature. It arises because accurate and detailed models (or knowledge bases) of non-trivial domains are inherently time consuming to develop and maintain. Because the industry sponsor was moving towards more formal software engineering methods—specifically the use of Z and object orientation—it was proposed that the resulting formal developments might be re-used as models for diagnostic reasoning.

The diagnostic framework that ultimately resulted from this project focused on two questions that have previously been explored by the author:

1. What is the relationship between reasoning about correct implementation and reasoning about observations of an implementation? [10]

M. Butler, M. Hinchey, M.M. Larrondo-Petrie (Eds.): ICFEM 2007, LNCS 4789, pp. 19–36, 2007.
© Springer-Verlag Berlin Heidelberg 2007

2. How can a formal development be described so that it is amenable to both reasoning about correctness and diagnostic reasoning? [9]

Only Question 1 is discussed below. The solution proposed is to view refinement as not only a 'correctness preserving' [15], but also as a 'fault preserving' transformation.

2   Formal Methods and Diagnostic Reasoning

The association between reasoning about correctness and reasoning about faults can be found in early formal methods literature. Floyd, for example, specifically defines a notion of program failure called a 'counterexample' [14]. Hoare's CSP programming model relies on a 'traces' function that, by exclusion, identifies all the sequences of events that a program should not participate in - the faults. However, there does not seem to be a programming model, with a rigorously defined semantics and refinement theory, that explicitly supports diagnostic reasoning.

Specification formalisms have been applied to fault detection under the guise of 'model-based testing' [13]. In this approach, the 'system under test' is formally modeled using, for example, VDM [11] or state charts [5]. Various algorithms have been proposed to then manipulate the model to generate a large number of significant test cases. The research to date on formal approaches to testing has focused on specification and largely ignored refinement or hierarchies of specifications.

'Model checking' is effectively another approach to fault detection employing formal specifications. There are now many model checking tools implementing a variety of languages and model checking (i.e. fault detection) techniques. SPIN [18] is a popular model checking tool in industry that uses temporal logic for specifications [27]. 'Alloy' is both a modeling language and the name of the associated model checking tool [19]. The Alloy language is a subset of Z.

Formal specification languages have also been used for fault diagnosis. Wotawa [28] describes applications and techniques to take VHDL output from a hardware design system and use it as the model for consistency based diagnosis. Papadopoulos [21] has developed a semi-automatic process for generating 'Safety Monitors' for complex dynamic systems. These monitors are real time applications that monitor, analyse, diagnose and, advise corrective action for, safety critical systems such as onboard aircraft fuel management. One of the supported input design document formats for the generation process is statecharts which can be produced by a design tool like Statemate [1].

There have been attempts to define novel process specification languages that explicitly support diagnosis of systems defined with that language. Riese [25] and Baroni et al. [3] are examples of proposals for different forms of communicating automata with built in diagnostic capacity. Both these proposals would require the redevelopment, or at least re-specification, of the target system. Recently Console et al. [7] proposed a more neutral process algebra that minimises the translation effort and also allows greater flexibility in the choice of diagnosis theory. Unfortunately, even with this more general modeling formalism the original development process is still completely separate from the modeling process. None of these proposals exploits the notion of refinement, or bisimulation, to build hierarchical models.

3   Model-Based Diagnosis

Model-based diagnosis (MBD) became well-defined in the 1980s. A good summary of the foundational issues in this area can be found in the canonical collection of articles by Hamscher et al. [16]. Reiter published a landmark paper describing: 'A theory of diagnosis from first principles' [24] (DFP) in 1987. DFP has become the standard definition of a form of MBD known as 'consistency-based' diagnosis. It is worthwhile briefly describing DFP here to convey an understanding of MBD to a software engineering audience.

Reiter develops a completely formal treatment of fault diagnosis. The 'first principles' in the title are predicates that form the model of the target system. The example system discussed at length is a digital circuit implementing a one bit adder which is a common example in the MBD literature.

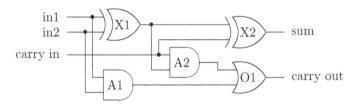

The components, and relations between components, are described using a set of consistent first order predicates called a 'system description', referred to as 'SD'. The following is a portion of SD for the adder that defines the first 'and' gate.

$$ANDG(x) \wedge \neg AB(x) \Rightarrow out(x) = and(in1(x), in2(x))$$
$$ANDG(A_1)$$
$$in1(X_1) = in1(A_1)$$
$$in2(X_1) = in2(A_1)$$
$$out(A_1) = in2(O_1)$$

A feature of component function definition is the use of a 'not abnormal' $(\neg AB)$ proviso. Fault detection is performed by verifying that the system description (SD) is consistent with the observation (OB) and the claim that all the components (c_i) are not faulty $(\neg AB)$. Hence the following set of predicates will be consistent if no fault is observed and inconsistent if faulty behaviour is observed.

$$SD \cup \{\neg AB(c_1), \neg AB(c_{2,}), ..., \neg AB(c_n)\} \cup OB$$

Diagnosis is performed by removing individual proviso predicates from the above statement to make the set of predicates consistent. A diagnosis (Δ) is a subset of the set of component labels corresponding to the removed provisos. A diagnosis of the system-component list-observation triple $(SD, COMP, OB)$ is a minimal set $\Delta \subseteq COMP$ such that:

$$SD \cup OB \cup \{AB(c) \mid c \in \Delta\} \cup \{\neg AB(c) \mid c \in COMP - \Delta\}$$

is consistent.

An observation of the adder is also a set of predicates, for example:

$$\{ in1(X_1) = 1 , \ in2(X_1) = 0 , \ in1(A_2) = 1 , \ out(X_2) = 1 , \ out(O_1) = 0 \}$$

A diagnosis is a minimal set (i.e. no other diagnosis is a subset) of component labels that make SD consistent with the observation. An example diagnosis for the above observation (OB) and the full adder (SD) is $\{X_2, O_1\}$ as it is minimal, and the derived set of predicates is consistent:

$$SD \cup OB \cup \{AB(c) \mid c \in \{X_2, O_1\}\} \cup \{\neg AB(c) \mid c \in COMP - \{X_2, O_1\}\}$$

Reiter offers proofs of computability results. DFP is generalisable to any system description language that is a form of 'default logic' [23]. One limitation is identified in the paper—DFP can only diagnose faults in discrete components. That means, for example, it would not be possible to produce the diagnosis that the adder circuit has been incorrectly wired together.

4   A General Diagnostic Framework

Reiter's classic theory of diagnosis identifies many elements of diagnostic reasoning: observations, system descriptions (SDs), faults, SD structure, and diagnosis. DFP is a diagnosis theory built upon a stylised first order predicate calculus. While predicate calculus is an important tool for formal software engineering methods, it cannot recreate many well known program specification formalisms.

In this section the core concepts of DFP are used as the basis of a more general diagnostic framework that is independent of the underlying specification formalism. This new framework is called 'Diagnosis from Formal Developments' or DFD. A small set of formal properties of DFD are labeled as 'Lemmas'. Proofs are given only for properties that do not follow immediately from definitions or previous lemmas.

4.1   Modalities

The foundation of DFD is a distinction between first class entities—things we want to reason about, and second class entities—things used to perform reasoning. These entities are known as 'system descriptions' (or 'SDs'), and 'observations'. Where possible they are visually distinguished by the use of upper and lower case respectively.

$$\text{SD} \mid \text{observation}$$

Examples of the SD/observation distinction familiar to formal methods practitioners would be: predicate/evaluation, set/element or program/pre-postcondition pair.

Relations between SDs and observations are termed 'modalities'. There are two 'core' modalities called 'concordance' and 'discordance'. Concordance contains desirable or mandated pairings between SDs and observations. The symbol associated with concordance is '$\multimap$' which is pronounced 'concords with'. Discordance contains the undesirable or prohibited pairings and has the symbol '$\rightarrowtail$'. Concordance and discordance are independently defined.

Examples of core modality pairings for the above list of formalisms follow.

$$x = y \multimap \{x \mapsto 1, y \mapsto 1\}$$
$$x = y \rightarrowtail \{x \mapsto 1, y \mapsto 2\}$$

$$\{a, b, c\} \multimap a$$
$$\{a, b, c\} \rightarrowtail x$$

$$\mathsf{y := x; z := (y + 1)} \multimap (x = 1, y = 1)$$
$$\mathsf{y := x; z := (y + 1)} \rightarrowtail (x = 1, z = 1)$$

Typographic conventions have been introduced in the above examples: evaluations are written as sets of maplets from variables to values, and; programs are in sans serif font.

4.2 Reasoning About SDs

Modalities can be used to define reasoning relations for SDs. The simplest reasoning relations are orderings induced by the core modalities. Concordance induces 'entails' ($\Subset$), while discordance induces 'breaks' ($\trianglelefteq$). Both orderings have a corresponding notion of equivalence. The inverse of breaking is called 'fixing'.

$$P \Subset Q \equiv (\forall\, ob \bullet P \multimap ob \;\Rightarrow\; Q \multimap ob)$$
$$P \mathrel{\underline{\Subset}} Q \equiv (P \Subset Q \;\wedge\; Q \Subset P)$$

$$P \trianglelefteq Q \equiv (\forall\, ob \bullet P \rightarrowtail ob \;\Rightarrow\; Q \rightarrowtail ob)$$
$$P \mathrel{\underline{\wedge}} Q \equiv (P \trianglelefteq Q \;\wedge\; Q \trianglelefteq P)$$

Concordance is also used to define a relation between sets of SDs and single SDs called 'consequence' ($\Vdash$).

$$PP \Vdash Q \equiv (\forall\, ob \bullet (\forall\, P : PP \bullet P \multimap ob) \Rightarrow Q \multimap ob)$$

An example DFD consequence is:

$$\{P1, P2\} \Vdash C$$

A Venn style diagram with a universe of observations (adapted from Struss [26]) illustrates the example consequence. The ovals indicate the set of concording observations for each SD.

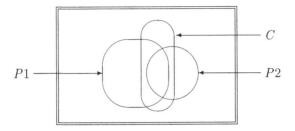

Like consequence in first order predicate calculus, DFD consequence is monotonic.

Lemma 1: Consequence monotonicity

$$(PP \Vdash C) \implies ((PP \cup \{Q\}) \Vdash C)$$

Discordance is used to define 'diagnoses' ($\updownarrow$) and 'diagnoses with a fault model' ($\Updownarrow$), where a fault model contrains diagnosis.

$$\Delta \updownarrow (S, ob) \equiv (\Delta \trianglelefteq S \,\wedge\, \Delta \not\to ob)$$
$$\Delta \Updownarrow (F, S, ob) \equiv (F \trianglelefteq \Delta \,\wedge\, \Delta \updownarrow (S, ob))$$

Another Venn style diagram illustrates both forms of DFD diagnosis. In this diagram the triangles enclose the set of discording observations for the associated SD. The solid point labeled 'ob' is a single observation.

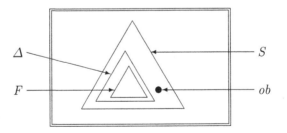

'ob' indicates a fault in 'S' as it is within 'S's set of discording observations. 'ob' does not discord with 'Δ', 'Δ' breaks 'S' and fixes 'F', hence 'Δ' is a valid diagnosis.

Diagnosis with fault models ($\Updownarrow$), and hence also diagnosis ($\updownarrow$), is monotonic with respect to target SD fixing.

Lemma 2: Fault diagnosis fix monotonicity

$$(P \trianglelefteq Q) \wedge (\Delta \Updownarrow (F, P, ob)) \implies (\Delta \Updownarrow (F, Q, ob))$$

4.3   Refinement

Formal software engineering often defines 'refinement' ($\sqsubseteq$) as a correctness preserving transformation [15]. DFD defines correctness preservation by reference to a set of modalities called a 'canon'. Where it cannot be determined by context, the canon is made explicit by prefixing it to the refinement symbol, yielding the following definition.

$$P \; canon. \sqsubseteq Q \equiv (\forall \odot : canon \bullet (\forall \; ob \bullet P \odot ob \;\Rightarrow\; Q \odot ob))$$

DFD refinement allows the definition of correctness in terms of any set of modalities. The next Venn style diagram shows the corresponding sets of observations for SDs 'P' and 'Q' with respect to two modalities - called '$grey$' and '$dash$'.

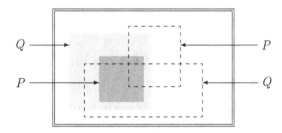

The role of the canon in DFD refinement is demonstrated with a short list of refinement statements consistent with the above modalities and SDs.

$$P \{grey\}. \sqsubseteq Q$$
$$P \{dash\}. \not\sqsubseteq Q$$
$$P \{grey, dash\}. \not\sqsubseteq Q$$
$$Q \varnothing. \sqsubseteq P$$

Including discordance as a canonic modality makes refinement a subset of fixing.

Lemma 3: Discordant refinement entails fixing

$$((\rightarrowtimes \in canon) \wedge (P \; canon. \sqsubseteq Q) \;\Rightarrow\; (P \trianglelefteq Q)$$

It follows from the definition of fixing, and from Lemmas 2 and 3, that both fault detection and diagnosis are monotonic with respect to refinement where discordance is canonic.

Lemma 4: Fault detection—discordant refinement monotonicity

$$((\rightarrowtimes \in canon) \wedge (P \; canon. \sqsubseteq Q) \wedge (P \rightarrowtimes ob)) \;\Rightarrow\; (Q \rightarrowtimes ob)$$

Lemma 5: Fault diagnosis—discordant refinement monotonicity

$$((\rightarrowtimes \in canon) \wedge (P \; canon. \sqsubseteq Q) \wedge (\Delta \updownarrow (F, P, ob)) \;\Rightarrow\; (\Delta \updownarrow (F, Q, ob)$$

5   DFD Diagnosis Example

To demonstrate DFD we return to the full adder discussed in Reiter's theory of diagnosis from first principles (DFP). The adder will be developed and diagnosed using DFD. Differences and similarities between the two diagnostic theories are clarified through this exercise.

5.1   Reasoning About the Adder

In order to reason about the adder, an instantiation of the DFD framework is required. Instances of DFD relations will be distinguished by prefixing an identifier to the corresponding symbol. Following from Reiter, the DFD instance encapsulates predicate calculus - identified by the prefix 'p'. Core modalities are defined in terms of models and anti-models of SD specification predicates.

$$S\,p.\!\multimap ob \equiv S \models ob$$
$$S\,p.\!\rightarrowtail ob \equiv \neg S \models ob$$

Defining core modalities in terms of satisfaction means that fixing is the inverse of entailment.

Lemma 6: Predicate entailment / breaking equivalence

$$P\,p.\!\Subset Q \ \equiv \ Q\,p.\!\trianglelefteq P$$

Proof

$$P\,p.\!\Subset Q$$

$\equiv$ {Definition of $p.\!\Subset$ and $p.\!\multimap$}
$(P \models ob) \Rightarrow (Q \models ob)$

$\equiv$ {Predicate calculus - definition of $\Rightarrow$}
$P \Rightarrow Q$

$\equiv$ {Predicate calculus - contraposition}
$\neg Q \Rightarrow \neg P$

$\equiv$ {Predicate calculus - definition of $\Rightarrow$}
$(\neg Q \models ob) \Rightarrow (\neg P \models ob)$

$\equiv$ {Definition of $p.\!\trianglelefteq$ and $p.\!\rightarrowtail$}
$Q\,p.\!\trianglelefteq P$

The refinement canon consists of just the negation of concordance, making refinement equivalent to reverse implication.

Lemma 7: Non-satisfaction refinement is reverse implication

$$P\,\{p.\!\not\multimap\}.\!\sqsubseteq Q \ \equiv \ P \Leftarrow Q$$

It follows from Lemmas 6 and 7 that this form of refinement is also equivalent to fixing.

Lemma 8: Non-satisfaction refinement is fixing

$$P\{p.\not\to\}.\sqsubseteq Q \;\equiv\; P\,p.\trianglelefteq Q$$

5.2   Developing the Adder

There is no explicit development process in Reiter's discussion. The design is simply presented in the form of the circuit diagram in Section 3. A slightly modified adder diagram is given here to facilitate a one-step predicate-based formal development.

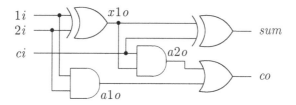

A table of variable names and uses clarifies the component specifications.

variable	content	DFP equivalent
$1i$	adder input 1	$in1(X_1), in1(A_2)$
$2i$	adder input 2	$in2(X_1), in2(A_1)$
ci	adder carry in	$in1(A_2), in2(X_2)$
$a1o$	and gate 1 output	$out(A_1), in2(O_1)$
$a2o$	and gate 2 output	$out(A_2), in1(O_1)$
$x1o$	xor gate 1 output	$out(X_1), in1(A_2), in1(X_2)$
sum	adder sum output	$out(X_2)$
co	adder carry output	$out(O_1)$

The DFD adder development has one step - refining the requirement (Req) into an implementation (Imp).

$$\begin{pmatrix} sum \Leftrightarrow ((1i \not\Leftrightarrow 2i) \not\Leftrightarrow ci) \\ \wedge\, co \Leftrightarrow ((1i \wedge 2i) \vee (ci \wedge (1i \not\Leftrightarrow 2i))) \end{pmatrix} \qquad \text{Req}$$

$$\{p.\not\to\}.\sqsubseteq \quad \begin{pmatrix} x1o \Leftrightarrow (1i \not\Leftrightarrow 2i) \\ \wedge\, sum \Leftrightarrow (x1o \not\Leftrightarrow ci) \\ \wedge\, a1o \Leftrightarrow (1i \wedge 2i) \\ \wedge\, a2o \Leftrightarrow (x1o \wedge ci) \\ \wedge\, co \Leftrightarrow (a1o \vee a2o) \end{pmatrix} \qquad \text{Imp}$$

The formal adder development can be verified.

Proof

$$\text{Req } \{p.\not\negmedspace\diagup\negmedspace\circ\}.\sqsubseteq \text{ Imp}$$

$\equiv$ {Lemma 7}
$$\text{Imp} \Rightarrow \text{Req}$$

$\equiv$ {Expand Imp, Req}
$$\Rightarrow \left(\begin{array}{l} x1o \Leftrightarrow (1i \not\Leftrightarrow 2i) \\ \wedge\, sum \Leftrightarrow (x1o \not\Leftrightarrow ci) \\ \wedge\, a1o \Leftrightarrow (1i \wedge 2i) \\ \wedge\, a2o \Leftrightarrow (x1o \wedge ci) \\ \wedge\, co \Leftrightarrow (a1o \vee a2o) \end{array} \right) \left(\begin{array}{l} sum \Leftrightarrow ((1i \not\Leftrightarrow 2i) \not\Leftrightarrow ci) \\ \wedge\, co \Leftrightarrow ((1i \wedge 2i) \vee (ci \wedge (1i \not\Leftrightarrow 2i))) \end{array} \right)$$

$\equiv$ {Expand sum, co}
$$\Rightarrow \left(\begin{array}{l} x1o \Leftrightarrow (1i \not\Leftrightarrow 2i) \\ \wedge\, sum \Leftrightarrow ((1i \not\Leftrightarrow 2i) \not\Leftrightarrow ci) \\ \wedge\, a1o \Leftrightarrow (1i \wedge 2i) \\ \wedge\, a2o \Leftrightarrow (x1o \wedge ci) \\ \wedge\, co \Leftrightarrow ((1i \wedge 2i) \vee ((1i \not\Leftrightarrow 2i) \wedge ci)) \end{array} \right) \left(\begin{array}{l} sum \Leftrightarrow ((1i \not\Leftrightarrow 2i) \not\Leftrightarrow ci) \\ \wedge\, co \Leftrightarrow ((1i \wedge 2i) \vee (ci \wedge (1i \not\Leftrightarrow 2i))) \end{array} \right)$$

$\equiv$ {Predicate calculus}
$$true$$

5.3   Monitoring the Adder

An observation of the adder, using binary numbers for truth values, that corresponds to the example in Reiter's paper is:

$$\texttt{adob1} \;\;\widehat{=}\;\; \{1i \mapsto 1, 2i \mapsto 0, ci \mapsto 1, sum \mapsto 1, co \mapsto 0\}$$

The observation 'adob1' indicates a fault with the adder as it discords with the requirement specification 'req'.

Proof

$$\texttt{req}\, p.\negmedspace\rightarrowtail\negmedspace\times \texttt{adob1}$$

$\equiv$ {Definition of $p.\negmedspace\rightarrowtail\negmedspace\times$}
$$\neg\texttt{req} \models \texttt{adob1}$$

$\equiv$ {Expand req; substitute variable values from adob1}
$$\neg((1 \Leftrightarrow ((1 \not\Leftrightarrow 0) \not\Leftrightarrow 1)) \wedge (0 \Leftrightarrow (1 \wedge 0) \vee (1 \wedge (1 \not\Leftrightarrow 0)))))$$

$\equiv$ {Predicate calculus}
$$true$$

Consistent with the definition of fixing and Lemma 8, the observation can be shown by a similar proof to discord with the implementation.

$$\texttt{imp } p. \rightarrow\!\!\!\!\times \texttt{ adob1}$$

Using a different observation, the benefits of using DFD, over Reiter's proposal, for hierarchical fault detection can be seen.

$$\texttt{adob2} \ \ \widehat{=} \ \ \{1i \mapsto 1, 2i \mapsto 0, x1o \mapsto 0\}$$

No fault is detected in the abstract requirement with the new observation.

$$\texttt{req } p. \not\rightarrow\!\!\!\times \texttt{ adob2}$$

However, a fault is detected using the more detailed implementation.

Proof

$$\texttt{imp } p. \not\rightarrow\!\!\!\times \texttt{ adob2}$$

$\equiv$ {Definition of $p. \not\rightarrow\!\!\!\times$}
$\quad \neg\texttt{imp} \models \texttt{adob1}$

$\equiv$ {Expand $\texttt{imp}$; substitute variable values from $\texttt{adob2}$}
$\quad \neg \left(\begin{array}{l} false \land (sum \Leftrightarrow ((1 \not\Leftrightarrow ci))) \land (a1o \Leftrightarrow 0) \land \\ (a2o \Leftrightarrow (x1o \land ci)) \land (co \Leftrightarrow (0 \lor (0 \land ci))) \end{array} \right)$

$\equiv$ {Predicate calculus}
$\quad true$

This example demonstrates how DFD fault detection may not yield false positives—only false negatives. That means a fault detected in an abstraction indicates there is definitely something wrong with the implemented system. In terms of a contract view of specification, a false negative by using an abstract SD is also helpful, as the observation does not indicate a breech of the original contract.

5.4 Diagnosing the Adder

Having detected a fault in the adder with observation 'adob1', a diagnosis for that scenario is determined. Following the pattern of DFP, diagnosis will be performed through selectively faulting components by removing them from the specification. The adder requirement effectively has two components—the sum and the carry calculators. Our first diagnosis of complete failure of the sum calculator is not valid.

Proof

$$(co \Leftrightarrow ((1i \land 2i) \lor (ci \land (1i \not\Leftrightarrow 2i)))) \, p.\updownarrow (\texttt{req}, \texttt{adob1})$$

$\equiv$ {Definition of $\updownarrow$}
$\quad (co \Leftrightarrow ((1i \land 2i) \lor (ci \land (1i \not\Leftrightarrow 2i)))) \, p.\triangleleft \ \texttt{req}$
$\quad \land (co \Leftrightarrow ((1i \land 2i) \lor (ci \land (1i \not\Leftrightarrow 2i)))) \, p. \not\rightarrow\!\!\!\times \texttt{adob1}$

$\equiv \{$Lemmas 7 and 8; predicate calculus$\}$
$\qquad (co \Leftrightarrow ((1i \wedge 2i) \vee (ci \wedge (1i \not\Leftrightarrow 2i)))) \, p.\not\times \mathbf{adob1}$

$\equiv \{$Definition of $\not\times\}$
$\qquad \neg(\neg(co \Leftrightarrow ((1i \wedge 2i) \vee (ci \wedge (1i \not\Leftrightarrow 2i)))) \models \mathbf{adob1}))$

$\equiv \{$Substitute observation variable values$\}$
$\qquad \neg\neg(0 \Leftrightarrow ((1 \wedge 0) \vee (1 \wedge (1 \not\Leftrightarrow 0))))$

$\equiv \{$Predicate calculus$\}$
$\qquad false$

By similar reasoning, faulting the carry calculator is also not a valid diagnosis.

$$(sum \Leftrightarrow ((1i \not\Leftrightarrow 2i) \not\Leftrightarrow ci)) \, p.\not\updownarrow (\mathbf{req}, \mathbf{adob1})$$

Faulting both components produces a valid, but trivial, diagnosis.

$$true \, p.\updownarrow (\mathbf{req}, \mathbf{adob1})$$

Consistent with Lemmas 2 and 8, the diagnosis of the requirement is a valid diagnosis of the implementation.

$$true \, p.\updownarrow (\mathbf{imp}, \mathbf{adob1})$$

Diagnoses in DFD is not restricted to faulting components by removing them from the SD. In the next example a fault model is used to guide the generation of diagnoses. The adder fault model implements logic gate failure as sticking at '1' - a common problem with CMOS technology. As a faulty component may even fail to fail, the fault model should be sufficiently non-deterministic to allow both faulty and functional behaviour.

$$\mathbf{fm1} \quad \widehat{=} \quad \begin{pmatrix} (1i \not\Leftrightarrow 2i) \Rightarrow x1o \\ \wedge (x1o \not\Leftrightarrow ci) \Rightarrow sum \\ \wedge (1i \wedge 2i) \Rightarrow a1o \\ \wedge (x1o \wedge ci) \Rightarrow a2o \\ \wedge (a1o \vee a2o) \Rightarrow co \end{pmatrix}$$

Because the trivial diagnosis ($true$) does not fix ($\trianglelefteq$) the fault model ($fm1$) it is excluded.

$$true \, p \not\Updownarrow (\mathbf{fm1}, \mathbf{req}, \mathbf{adob1})$$

A potential diagnosis can be produced by faulting the components identified in one of Reiter's diagnoses in accordance with the known faulty behaviour of gates sticking at 1.

$$\delta x2o1 \quad \widehat{=} \quad \begin{pmatrix} x1o \Leftrightarrow (1i \not\Leftrightarrow 2i) \\ \wedge (x1o \not\Leftrightarrow ci) \Rightarrow sum \\ \wedge a1o \Leftrightarrow (1i \wedge 2i) \\ \wedge a2o \Leftrightarrow (x1o \wedge ci) \\ \wedge (a1o \vee a2o) \Rightarrow co \end{pmatrix}$$

The new diagnosis (δx2o1) does not diagnose the requirement with the fault model (fm1) as neither the fault model nor the diagnosis break the requirement.

Proof

$$\delta\text{x2o1} \ p.\Updownarrow \ (\text{fm1}, \text{req}, \text{adob1})$$

$\equiv$ {Definition of $p.\Updownarrow$ and $p.\Uparrow$ }
$$(\text{fm1} \ p.\trianglelefteq \ \delta\text{x2o1}) \ \wedge \ (\delta\text{x2o1} \ p.\trianglelefteq \ \text{req}) \ \wedge \ (\delta\text{x2o1} \ p.\nrightarrow \text{adob1})$$

$\equiv$ {Lemmas 7 and 8}
$$(\delta\text{x2o1} \ \Rightarrow \ \text{fm1}) \ \wedge \ (\text{req} \ \Rightarrow \ \delta\text{x2o1}) \ \wedge \ (\delta\text{x2o1} \ p.\nrightarrow \text{adob1})$$

$\equiv$ {Predicate calculus}
$$true \ \wedge \ false \ \wedge \ (\delta\text{x2o1} \ p.\nrightarrow \text{adob1})$$

$\equiv$ {Predicate calculus}
$$false$$

Fault detection monotonicity in DFD means that, even though it is not a valid diagnosis for the requirement, 'δx2o1' may be a valid diagnosis for the implementation. The proof follows the pattern of previous proofs for the constituent relations, except this time the diagnosis breaks the SD.

$$\delta\text{x2o1} \ p.\Updownarrow \ (\text{fm1}, \text{imp}, \text{adob1})$$

6   Other Theories of Programming

The previous section demonstrated that predicate calculus is consistent with the DFD framework. In this section three more programming formalisms—relations, Hoare triples and weakest preconditions—are restated as forms of DFD. All three restatements as instances of DFD include proof that the relevant refinement ordering is also fix ordering. Consequently, formal developments using any of these theories of programming yield SDs suitable for hierarchical diagnostic reasoning.

6.1   Relations

Programs can be described as 'state transformers' or as 'relations on states'. The conventional programming model for the Z specification language is perhaps the most widely known example of a relational program semantics. Defining relations as an instantiation of DFD requires three modalities—the two core modalities and 'apply'. Relational SDs are relations on states, while observations are pairs of states.

$$R \ r.\multimapdotinv (d, r) \equiv (d, r) \in R$$

$$R \ \text{apply} \ (d, r) \equiv d \in \text{dom} \ R$$

$$R \ r.\rightarrowtail (d, r) \equiv (R \ \text{apply} \ (d, r) \ \wedge \ R \ r.\nrightarrow (d, r))$$

Orderings induced by the core modalities are:

$$P\, r.\Subset Q \equiv P \subseteq Q$$

$$P\, r.\trianglelefteq Q \equiv (d \in \mathrm{dom}\, P \ \wedge \ (d, r) \notin P) \ \Rightarrow \ (d \in \mathrm{dom}\, Q \ \wedge \ (d, r) \notin Q)$$

The standard form of relational refinement [22, p.221] as the conjunction of an 'applicability' and a 'correctness' condition can be induced from a canon consisting of discordance and the apply modality.

Lemma 9: Canonic relational refinement

$$P\, \{\mathrm{apply}, r.\!\rightarrowtail\}.\sqsubseteq Q \ \equiv \ (\mathrm{dom}\, P \ \subseteq \ \mathrm{dom}\, Q) \ \wedge \ ((\mathrm{dom}\, P \triangleleft Q) \ \subseteq \ P)$$

Proof

$$P\, \{\mathrm{apply}, r.\!\rightarrowtail\}.\sqsubseteq Q$$

$\equiv$ {Expand $\sqsubseteq$, apply and $r.\!\rightarrowtail$}
$d \in \mathrm{dom}\, P \ \Rightarrow \ d \in \mathrm{dom}\, Q$
$\wedge\, (d \in \mathrm{dom}\, P \ \wedge \ (d, r) \notin P) \ \Rightarrow \ (d \in \mathrm{dom}\, Q \ \wedge \ (d, r) \notin Q)$

$\equiv$ {Distribute implication over conjunction; Re-arrange antecedents}
$d \in \mathrm{dom}\, P \ \Rightarrow \ d \in \mathrm{dom}\, Q$
$\wedge\, (d, r) \notin P \ \Rightarrow \ (d \in \mathrm{dom}\, P \ \Rightarrow \ d \in \mathrm{dom}\, Q)$
$\wedge\, (d \in \mathrm{dom}\, P \ \wedge \ (d, r) \notin P) \ \Rightarrow \ (d, r) \notin Q$

$\equiv$ {Remove redundant implication}
$d \in \mathrm{dom}\, P \ \Rightarrow \ d \in \mathrm{dom}\, Q$
$\wedge\, (d \in \mathrm{dom}\, P \ \wedge \ (d, r) \notin P) \ \Rightarrow \ (d, r) \notin Q$

$\equiv$ {Re-arrange antecedents; Contraposition; Re-arrange antecedents}
$(d \in \mathrm{dom}\, P \ \Rightarrow \ d \in \mathrm{dom}\, Q) \ \wedge \ ((d \in \mathrm{dom}\, P \wedge (d, r) \in Q) \Rightarrow (d, r) \in P)$

$\equiv$ {Set theory}
$(\mathrm{dom}\, P \ \subseteq \ \mathrm{dom}\, Q) \ \wedge \ ((\mathrm{dom}\, P \triangleleft Q) \ \subseteq \ P)$

By Lemma 3, DFD relational refinement implies fixing.

Lemma 10: Relational refinement fixes

$$P\, \{\mathrm{apply}, r.\!\rightarrowtail\}.\sqsubseteq Q \ \Rightarrow \ P\, r.\trianglelefteq Q$$

6.2   Hoare Triples

Hoare triples [17] are the basis of a form of reasoning about program semantics known as 'Hoare logics'. A triple consists of a 'precondition', 'program' and 'postcondition', traditionally written it the following way:

$$\{pre\}P\{post\}$$

The above triple is valid if, starting in any state satisfying '*pre*', the program '*P*' terminates in a state satisfying '*post*', if it terminates. The semantics of a program can be understood as the set of all its valid triples. Instantiating DFD to replicate Hoare triples can be achieved by casting programs as SDs and pre-postcondition pairs as observations.

$$P\,h.\!-\!\circ(pre,post) \equiv \{pre\}P\{post\}$$
$$P\,h.\!-\!\!\times(pre,post) \equiv \{pre\}P\{\neg post\}$$

A distinguishing property of Hoare logics is the equivalence of entailment and fixing. This is the opposite of the case with DFD predicates as demonstrated in Lemma 6.

Lemma 11: Hoare entail / fix equivalence

$$P\,h.\!\in Q \quad \equiv \quad P\,h.\!\trianglelefteq Q$$

Proof

$$P\,h.\!\in Q$$

$\equiv$ {Definition of $h.\!\in$ and $h.\!-\!\circ$}
    $\{pre\}P\{post\} \Rightarrow \{pre\}Q\{post\}$

$\equiv$ {Substitute equivalent set of postconditions}
    $\{pre\}P\{\neg post\} \Rightarrow \{pre\}Q\{\neg post\}$

$\equiv$ {Definition of $h.\!\trianglelefteq$ and $h.\!-\!\!\times$}
    $P\,h.\!\trianglelefteq Q$

It follows from Lemma 11 that DFD refinement for Hoare triples can make both, or either, core modalities canonic and still reproduce the standard form of refinement for Hoare triples.

Lemma 12: Hoare DFD refinement

$$P\,\{h.\!-\!\circ, h.\!-\!\!\times\}.\!\sqsubseteq Q \quad \equiv \quad \{pre\}P\{post\} \Rightarrow \{pre\}Q\{post\}$$

Proof

$$P\,h.\!\in Q$$

$\equiv$ {Definition of $h.\!\in$ and $h.\!-\!\circ$}
    $\{pre\}P\{post\} \Rightarrow \{pre\}Q\{post\}$

$\equiv$ {Substitute equivalent set of postconditions}
    $\{pre\}P\{\neg post\} \Rightarrow \{pre\}Q\{\neg post\}$

$\equiv$ {Definition of $h.\!\trianglelefteq$ and $h.\!-\!\!\times$}
    $P\,h.\!\trianglelefteq Q$

6.3   Weakest Preconditions

Dijkstra proposed [12] a form of Hoare logic that relies on a 'weakest precondition' calculation function usually called 'wp'. This function calculates the predicate describing the largest set of starting states from which a program is guaranteed to terminate in a state satisfying a given postcondition. As with Hoare triples, observations are described with pre-postcondition pairs.

$$P\ w.\multimap(pre, post) \equiv pre \subseteq wp(P, post)$$
$$P\ w.\rightarrowtail(pre, post) \equiv pre \subseteq wp(P, \neg post\}$$

By following a similar proof to Lemma 11, entailment and fix orderings can be shown to be equivalent.

Lemma 13: Weakest precondition entail - fix equivalence

$$P\ w.\in Q \quad \equiv \quad P\ w.\trianglelefteq Q$$

Being a Hoare logic, the canon contains both core modalities. The resultant refinement ordering is consistent with Dijkstra's definition.

Lemma 14: Weakest precondition refinement

$$P\ \{w.\multimap, w.\rightarrowtail\}.\sqsubseteq Q \quad \equiv \quad wp(P, post) \subseteq wp(Q, post)$$

Proof

$$P\ \{w.\multimap, w.\rightarrowtail\}.\sqsubseteq Q$$

$\equiv$ {Definition of $w.\multimap$ and $w.\rightarrowtail$; Lemma 12}
$\quad\ pre \subseteq wp(P, post) \Rightarrow pre \subseteq wp(Q, post)$

$\equiv$ {Set theory}
$\quad\ wp(P, post) \subseteq wp(Q, post)$

7   Extending DFD

Unlike other theories of MBD, DFD does not require a separate modeling phase. A development carried out within any programming formalism that is consistent with DFD can be immediately re-used as the diagnostic model of the implemented system. The only requirement for consistency with the framework is that refinement is a failure preserving transformation. This requirement has been shown to be satisfied by many well known forms of refinement.

The above discussion should highlight the need to extend the DFD framework to exploit decomposition. Refinement calculi [2,20] include many rules for the introduction of structure into programs. It would be very helpful to allow components to be labeled and explicitly identified in diagnoses. Adding this facility to DFD is complex and requires, amongst other things, a formalisation of formal developments themselves.

Another area for extension of DFD is to look at process algebras. Process algebras often rely on a notion of bisimulation, rather than refinement, to perform step-wise development. Given that bisimulation basically equates to observational equivalence, it seems likely that bisimulation would preserve failures.

References

1. ilogix.com. Accessed (February 2007)
2. Back, R.J.R., von Wright, J. (eds.): Refinement Calculus: A Systematic Introduction. Springer, New York (1998)
3. Baroni, P., Lamperti, G., Pogliano, P., Zanella, M.: Diagnosis of large active systems. Artificial Intelligence 110(1), 135–183 (1999)
4. Bratko, I., Mozetič, I., Lavrač, N.: KARDIO: A Study in Deep and Qualitative Knowledge for Expert Systems. MEM Press, Cambridge, Massachusetts (1989)
5. Chow, T.S.: Testing design modeled by finite-state machines. IEEE Transactions on Software Engineering 3(3), 178–187 (1978)
6. Compton, P., Edwards, G., Kang, B., Lazarus, L., Malor, R., Preston, P., Srinivasan, A.: Ripple down rules: Turning knowledge acquisition into knowledge maintenance. Artificial Intelligence in Medicine 4, 463–475 (1992)
7. Console, L., Picardi, C., Ribaudo, M.: Process algebras for systems diagnosis. Artif. Intell. 142(1), 19–51 (2002)
8. de Groot, M.: Reasoning about Designs: A framework for coupling formal developments and system management. PhD thesis, University of New South Wales, Sydney, NSW (August 2006)
9. de Groot, M., Robinson, K.: Modular refinement and model building. In: Proceedings of the 7th Algebraic Methods and Software Technology, Springer, Heidelberg (1997)
10. de Groot, M., Robinson, K.: Correctness in refinement developments. In: Proceedings of Formal Methods Pacific 1998, pp. 117–132. Springer, Heidelberg (1998)
11. Dick, J., Faivre, A.: Automating the generation and sequencing of test cases from model-based specifications. In: Larsen, P.G., Woodcock, J.C.P. (eds.) FME 1993. LNCS, vol. 670, pp. 268–284. Springer, Heidelberg (1993)
12. Dijkstra, E.W.: A Discipline of Programming. Prentice-Hall, Englewood Cliffs (1976)
13. El-Far, I.K., Whittaker, A.: Model-based software testing. In: Marciniak, J.J. (ed.) Encyclopedia of Software Engineering, Wiley, Chichester (2001)
14. Floyd, R.W.: Assigning meanings to programs. In: Symposium in Applied Mathematics. Mathematical Aspects of Computer Science, pp. 19–32. American Mathematical Society, Providence, RI (1967)
15. Gerhart, S.: Correctness preserving program transformations. In: Proc. 2nd ACM Conference on Programming Languages, ACM Press, New York (1975)
16. Hamscher, W., Console, L., de Kleer, J.: Readings in Model-based Diagnosis. Morgan Kaufmann, San Mateo, CA (1992)
17. Hoare, C.A.R.: An axiomatic basis for computer programming. Communications of the ACM 12 (1969)
18. Holzmann, G.J.: The model checker SPIN. IEEE Transactions on Software Engineering 23(5) (1997)
19. Jackson, D.: Automating first-order relational logic. In: Proc. ACM SIGSOFT Foundations of Software Engineering, ACM Press, New York (2000)
20. Morgan, C.C.: Programming from Specifications. Prentice Hall, Englewood Cliffs (1994)
21. Papadopoulos, Y.: Model-based system monitoring and diagnosis of failures using statecharts and fault trees. Reliability Engineering and System Safety 81, 325–341 (2003)

22. Potter, B., Sinclair, J., Till, D.: An Introduction to Formal Specification and Z. Prentice Hall, Englewood Cliffs (1991)
23. Reiter, R.: A logic for default reasoning. Artificial Intelligence 13, 81–132 (1980)
24. Reiter, R.: A theory of diagnosis from first principles. Artificial Intelligence 32, 57–95 (1987)
25. Riese, M.: Model-Based Diagnosis of Communication Protocols. PhD thesis, Swiss Federal Institute of Technology, Lausanne, Switzerland (1993)
26. Struss, P.: What's in SD? Towards a theory of modeling for diagnosis. In: Hamscher, w., Console, L., de Kleer, J. (eds.) Readings in Model-based Diagnosis, pp. 419–449. Morgan Kaufmann, San Mateo, CA (1992)
27. Vardi, M.Y., Wolper, P.: Reasoning about infinite computations. Information and Computation 115, 1–37 (1994)
28. Wotawa, F.: Debugging VHDL designs using model-based reasoning. Artificial Intelligence in Engineering 14(4), 331–351 (2000)

Formal Engineering of XACML Access Control Policies in VDM++

Jeremy W. Bryans and John S. Fitzgerald

School of Computing Science
Newcastle University
NE1 7RU, UK
{Jeremy.Bryans,John.Fitzgerald}@newcastle.ac.uk

Abstract. We present a formal, tool-supported approach to the design and maintenance of access control policies expressed in the eXtensible Access Control Markup Language (XACML). Our aim is to help developers evaluate the consequences of policy decisions in complex situations where security requirements change and access decisions may depend on the external dynamic environment. The approach applies the model-oriented specification language from the Vienna Development Method (VDM++). An executable formal model of XACML access control is presented in VDM++. The use of the model to analyse and revise both policies and requirements on the environment is illustrated through an example. An approach to the practical problem of analysing access control in virtual organisations with dynamic membership and goals is proposed.

1 Introduction

For a multi-user computer system to be secure, the developer must ensure that the people or systems using it are only allowed to perform legitimate actions. The functionality that achieves this is often separated out into a distinct *access control policy* which defines the response to access requests. In many situations, the response given to a request depends on the environment in which the request is evaluated. For example, a request may be disallowed outside of regular working hours, and so each time the request is made a clock will need to be consulted. Such policies are termed *context-sensitive* (also context-aware or dynamic). Context-sensitivity adds complexity to the development and validation of access control policies. They often need to satisfy requirements from different domains, for example legal, technical and commercial. Conformance with each of these sets of requirements must be checked any time the access control policy is modified. Modern virtual organisations are composed of separate agents, each with their own access control policies. They often work to volatile functional requirements and so policies need to be updated accurately and quickly.

The goal of our current work is to assist the access control policy developer by providing rapid feedback on design decisions. Formal techniques are well suited to this task because of the breadth and rigour of analysis that they afford. However,

M. Butler, M. Hinchey, M.M. Larrondo-Petrie (Eds.): ICFEM 2007, LNCS 4789, pp. 37–56, 2007.
© Springer-Verlag Berlin Heidelberg 2007

our goal is pragmatic, so it is vital that formal techniques for policy design are relevant to industry practice. Our specific aims are therefore to support policy analysis in an existing and widely-used access control framework (rather than to propose a new formalism), to focus on methods that can be supported by tools, and to exploit the benefits of formal approaches but provide a low technical barrier to their use by integrating with current and emerging industry practice.

The contribution of this paper is to provide a semantics for XACML in a language (VDM++) which is executable and has strong tool support (VDMTools.) Consistent with the lessons of previous industrial applications of VDM++ we emphasise modelling and analysis code verification and pay special attention to using the strong tool support for model validation by testing. The intention behind this approach to provide entry-level access to formal methods technology without requiring users to learn advanced modelling and analysis techniques at the outset.

We approach this by focussing on a substantial subset of the OASIS standard eXtensible Access Control Markup Language (XACML), providing a formal semantics for it in the formal specification language of VDM++ [10]. The semantics is similar in structure to XACML and includes environments, enabling analysis of context-sensitive policies. The semantic model can be executed directly using the VDMTools interpreter, providing a basis for testing and analysing proposed policies and environments. Test suites may be run against these interpreted models, providing rapid feedback to the developer.

Section 2 contains a brief overview of access control, and Section 3 gives an overview of semantics for XACML policies in VDM++. The validation and evolution of policies using the formal model are illustrated in Section 4. The application of the model in the volatile environment of dynamic virtual organisations is outlined in Section 5. We conclude by comparing related work and identifying potential improvements to the coverage of the formal model and the range of analyses supported.

2 Context-Sensitive Access Control in XACML

This section gives a simplified overview of XACML [16], pointing out how it is used to describe context-sensitive access control policies. XACML provides a *policy language* for describing access control policies and a *request language* for interrogating these policies.

Access control systems that implement XACML have the abstract structure shown in Figure 1. A request to perform an operation on SYS (the system under access control) is forwarded to the *Policy Enforcement Point* (PEP). The PEP translates the request into the XACML request language and passes it on to the *handler*. In XACML a request is a triple containing multiple subjects, actions and resources. However, we will follow [7] and [6] in restricting request triples to contain a single subject, action and resource. We assume that the PEP is defined to break any compound request into a set of requests and submit them singly, then combine the results in whatever way the developer chooses.

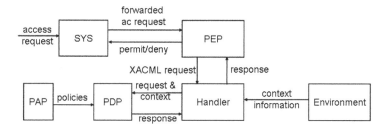

Fig. 1. XACML overview

The handler forwards the request, together with any relevant information from the context, to the *Policy Decision Point* (PDP). The PDP retrieves the relevant policies from the *Policy Access Point* (PAP), which contains all the access control policies for SYS. The PDP then evaluates the relevant access control policies in the context and sends the response to the handler. The result is returned to the PEP where it is enforced as either permission or denial. The decision of how to enforce the result returned by the PDP is in general application-dependent and is not in the scope of our current formalisation.

The PAP may contain a number of arbitrarily nested policies. When faced with a request, each policy must produce a single result, so a parent policy contains an algorithm for combining the responses of all the child policies into a single result. Policies may also contain a *target* – a set of subjects, resources, and actions denoting the limits of the applicability of the policy. A policy is applied to a request if the request *matches* the policy target, i.e. if the request subject, resource and action are in the set of policy target subjects, resources and actions respectively. If a request does not match the policy target – i.e. it relates to a subject, resource or action outside the policy target – the policy will generate the result *"not applicable"*. If the target is not present in the policy every request will match.

The lowest-level policies contain sets of rules, together with a combining algorithm. Like policies, rules in XACML may contain a target. They will also contain an effect (permit or deny). Optionally, they may also contain a *condition*.

A *condition* is the part of a policy which is *context-sensitive*. It is a Boolean function, and may range over the subject, resource and action of the request as well as arbitrary environment variables. If a request matches a rule target the condition of the rule is evaluated. Evaluating the condition will involve consulting the environment of the system. If the condition evaluates to true the effect of the rule will be returned (which may be either permit or deny). If the condition evaluates to false the rule will return not applicable. If the condition cannot be evaluated (perhaps because some system-level environmental information is missing) the rule will return *indeterminate*. Finally, if the request did not match the rule target *not applicable* is returned.

If several rules return a result for a request, the results are combined using a *rule-combining-algorithm*. The ones considered in this paper are *denyOverrides*, which will deny a request if a single rule denies it, and *permitOverrides*, which will permit a request if a single rule permits it.

As an example, consider the access control policy for a document management system designed to control access to documents within a chemical engineering plant. Documents are held on a central database and access must be carefully controlled. Each document must be reviewed after it is written. Suppose the initial stages of a project involve two documents – the hazard analysis and the production plan. We begin by developing the access control policy needed for these early stages. Suppose the developer is initially given two rules to implement:

1. The hazard analysis must be signed off before anyone may write to the production plan.

2. An author of a document cannot be the reviewer of that document.

An outline of a possible XACML realisation of the first rule is:

```
<Rule RuleId="hazanBeforePPRule" Effect="Deny">
  <Description> Deny PP write before haz_an signed off </Description>
  <Target>
    <Subjects><AnySubject/></Subjects>
    <Resources>...ProductionPlan...</Resources>
    <Actions>...write...</Actions>
  </Target>
  <Condition FunctionId="...:function:not">
    <Apply FunctionId="...signed-off">...haz_an...</Apply>
  </Condition>
</Rule>
```

The effect (to deny access) is in the top line, the target of the rule tells us that the rule is about write requests on the production plan and finally the rule has a condition (which will vary according to the precise context.) If a request is made to write to the production plan the rule must be able to check if the hazard analysis has been signed off. The second rule, requires that it be possible to check authorship of any document.

The structure available in the environment to answer the context-related queries may vary in each case. The documents may be in XML format, with "signed-off" and "authorship" fields, or the information may be recorded separately in a database. The policy developer will not necessarily know in advance which of these alternative implementations to assume. It is therefore important that the developer can model the environment abstractly, without requiring a particular implementation, but ensuring that the abstract model of the environment will have all the relevant behaviours that the real environment may exhibit.

3   A Semantics for XACML

This section introduces the VDM++ formalism, then presents a semantics for XACML in terms of an executable formal model in VDM++.

3.1   The VDM++ Formalism and Tools

The model is expressed in VDM++ [10], the object-oriented extension of the Vienna Development Method (VDM) specification language [13,1]. For a detailed introduction to VDM and its support tools the reader is referred to [8] and the VDM portal [17]. VDM++ models are composed of class definitions, each of which may contain local state specified by typed instance variables. Type definitions are given in terms of abstract basic types including token types for representing structureless values. Complex types are constructed using record and union constructors, set, sequence and mapping types. Type membership is restricted by invariants. Functionality in each class is expressed in terms of operations that may modify the values of the instance variables and auxiliary functions that do not affect the local state. Operations and functions may be specified implicitly by means of postconditions, or explicitly. In either case, restrictions on their domains are expressed by logical preconditions. Constants may also be declared (as values). In our work on XACML, we remain within an executable subset of the modelling language, allowing our models of access control policies to be readily analysed using the VDMTools interpreter.

VDM++ benefits from strong tool support and a record of industrial use [9]. The existing tool set (VDMTools) includes a syntax and type checker, an interpreter for executable models, test scripting and coverage analysis facilities, program code generation and pretty-printing. These have the potential to form a platform for tools specifically tailored to the analysis of access control policies in an XACML framework. Advanced static analysis for VDM models includes automatic proof obligation generation and automated proof support is under development.

An access control policy in XACML can be thought of as a data structure based on a set of complex data types. The XACML standard is a description of these data types and of the evaluation functions over them. VDM++, with its separation of data types and functionality, is an appropriate language to describe access control policies. VDM++ also allows a clear encapsulation of functionality within classes, which makes it particularly suitable for describing the architectural model of an access control environment.

3.2   A Model of XACML

This section gives an overview of a formal model of access control in VDM++. Throughout this section and Section 4 we use the interchange syntax of VDM++. The extracts are drawn from the full VDM++ model[1].

Fig. 2 is an informal class diagram showing the structure of the VDM++ model. The structure of the model closely reflects that of XACML. The Request class describes requests that a user may make. Policies are represented in objects of the PAP class; individual rules may include conditions that are expressed in expressions of the FExp class. The Evaluator collects together the functionality of the XACML handler and Policy Decision Point. It evaluates a request with

---

[1] Available at *http://homepages.cs.ncl.ac.uk/jeremy.bryans/VDMPPacmodel/*

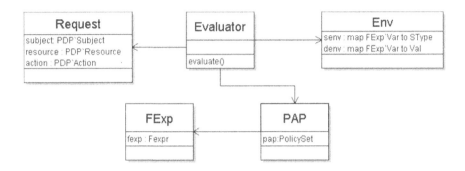

Fig. 2. Overview of the VDM++ model

respect to a `PAP` policy in an environment (an instance of the `Env` class). We briefly consider each of the main classes in turn.

Policy Model. The policy model is described in the Policy Access Point (PAP) class. In the VDM++ model, objects from the PAP class contain a single instance variable `pap` of type `PolicySet`. A `PolicySet` contains an optional `Target`, a set of elements from `Policy` and `PolicySet`, and the name of the policy combining algorithm (of type`CombAlg`).

```
PolicySet :: target : [Target]
          components : set of (Policy|PolicySet)
        policyCombAlg : CombAlg;

Target :: subjects : set of Subject
          resources : set of Resource
            actions : set of Action;

Policy :: target : [Target]
             rules : set of Rule
       ruleCombAlg : CombAlg;

CombAlg = <denyOverrides> | <permitOverrides>;

Rule :: target : [Target]
        effect : Effect
          cond : [FExp]
```

A `policy` contains an `Target` (optional, indicated by the `[..]`), a set of `Rules`, and a combining algorithm name. The enumerated values `<denyOverrides>` and `<permitOverrides>` act as pointers to the appropriate algorithms, defined in the `Evaluator` class. Other possible combining algorithms are given in the XACML Standard [16], but for simplicity we will model only these two here. Both these algorithms may be applied to both policies and rules; a slight modification would allow us to include algorithms which only apply to either policies or rules. The `effect` of the rule is the value returned by the rule when a request is evaluated against it. It can be one of the enumerated values `<Permit>`, `<Deny>`, `<Indet>` or `<NotApplicable>`. The condition `cond` may contain an expression of the class `FExp`.

Dynamic Context. The context in which the rules are evaluated is given by the environment, which contains two mappings. `senv` represents a static environment mapping expression variables to types, and `denv` represents a dynamic environment mapping expression variables to values.

```
senv : map FExp'Var to SType;
denv : map FExp'Var to Val
```

The `senv` component contains a record of the types of the variables in the dynamic component. This allows us to type check expressions evaluated within this environment. The dynamic component of the environment contains the values of each the variables. The abstract syntax of values is given below.

```
Val = AtomicVal | StructuredVal;
AtomicVal = bool | int | <Indet>;
StructuredVal = BoolArray | IntArray | VarArray;
BoolArray = map FExp'Var to bool;
IntArray = map FExp'Var to int;
VarArray = map FExp'Var to (map FExp'Var to bool)
```

An XACML implementation must provide support for arbitrary run time environments, whereas in our approach we build a simpler abstract model of the environment that manifests the behaviour necessary to test the rules and policies that we design. For this reason our syntax of expressions is currently less expressive than that offered by XACML. However, it is readily extensible.

Atomic values may be Boolean or integer, as well as the special value `Indet` used to model situations where the environment fails to return a result. A `BoolArray` is a map from variables to Booleans and an `IntArray` is a map from variables to integers. A `VarArray` is a map to `BoolArrays`.

Condition Expressions. The syntax of expressions and the structure of the environment are closely related. Objects from the FExp class are used to build the conditions that form the context-sensitive part of rules. Each object is an expression. In general, an environment and a request may need to be provided in order to fully evaluate an expression, as it may contain references to elements in both of them. An ordinary expression is one which only uses variable names declared in the environment, and a full expression also uses the reserved terms `requester` or `resource`. Before a full expression is evaluated, these are instantiated with the name of the request subject and resource. Ordinary (non-full) expressions take one of the following forms:

```
Expr = Var | Unary | Infix | Literal | ArrayLookup | VarArrayLookup;

Unary :: op : <NOT>
         body : Expr;
```

```
Infix :: left  : Expr
             op  : <AND>|<OR>|<LT>
          right : Expr;

ArrayLookup :: aname : Var
               index : Var;

VarArrayLookup :: aname  : Var
                  index1 : Var
                  index2 : Var
```

A `Var` expression is a record with a single token field, and a `Literal` may be a Boolean literal or an integer literal. Expressions may be negated using the `Unary` type. `Infix` expressions may be conjunctions or disjunctions of Boolean expressions, and integer expressions may be combined using less-than. Expressions may also look up values in environment `Arrays`. An `ArrayLookup` contains the name of the array and the index to be looked up. A `VarArrayLookup` contains the name of a `VarArray` and two indices. The first index is the name of the Boolean array to be looked up, and the second is the name of the index to be addressed within the Boolean array.

The syntax of full expressions (not shown here) extends the above by including `requester` and `resource` as uninstantiated variables.

```
UnVar :: <requester>|<resource>
```

These may be used in the same way as instantiated variables, so full expressions contain `Var|UnVar` where `Var` appears above.

Evaluating Requests. The `Evaluator` class describes the evaluation of requests, combining the functionality of the XACML handler and Policy Decision Point.

As indicated in Section 2, we restrict requests to a single `subject`, `resource`, and `action`. In the VDM++ these are instance variables of the `Request` class. The `Subject`, `Resource` and `Action` types are drawn from the PAP class but could be pulled out into a separate unit.

```
subject  : PAP'Subject;
resource : PAP'Resource;
action   : PAP'Action
```

The Evaluator class contains four instance variables: a `PAP`, an environment `Env`, a `request` and the instantiation mapping `inst`. The `inst` mapping will map the reserved terms `requester` and `resource` to the actual requester and resource in the access control request triple. This allows `requester` and `resource` in any of the conditions in the `PAP` to be bound to the current request `subject` and `resource`. The constructor takes a request, a PAP and an environment, and instantiates `Inst` from the request. The operation `evaluate` then returns the effect of evaluating the request `req` against the PAP `pap` in the environment `env`.

```
pap : PAP;                        -- an object of class PAP
env : Env;                        -- an object of class Env
req : Request;                    -- an object of class Request
inst: Inst := mk_Inst({|->});     -- the instantiation mapping
```

The evaluate operation (below) invokes the appropriate evaluator on the basis of the combining algorithm.

```
public evaluate: () ==> PAP'Effect
evaluate() ==
  if (pap.GetpolicyCombAlg() = <denyOverrides>) then
    return(evaluatePAPDenyOverrides())
  elseif (pap.GetpolicyCombAlg() = <permitOverrides>) then
    return(evaluatePAPPermitOverrides())
  else
    return(<NotApplicable>)
```

The tree of policies is traversed and each policy combines the results of the sub-components of that policy using the stated combining algorithm. At the level of single rules, the effect of the rule is returned if there is no condition or the condition evaluates true in the current environment. Otherwise the rule returns <NotApplicable> if the condition evaluates false and <Indet> if the condition can not be evaluated (e.g. if a variable reference in the condition does not point to a variable in the environment).

```
evaluateRule : PAP'Rule ==> PAP'Effect
evaluateRule(rule) ==
  if targetmatch(rule.target) then
      if rule.cond = nil
      then return(rule.effect)
      else
        cases (rule.cond).Evaluate(req,env):
                  true    -> return(rule.effect),
                  false   -> return(<NotApplicable>),
                <Indet> -> return(<Indet>)
        end
  else
    return(<NotApplicable>)
```

4   Validating Access Control Policies Using the Model

Our overall aim is to support the design and evolution of context-sensitive access control policies. In particular, we wish to provide rapid feedback on the characteristics of policies, or on the effects of changing policies, before they are implemented. The formal model of XACML presented in Section 3 can provide a basis for this form of evaluation.

The XACML model is written in the executable subset of VDM++. Initialised with an environment and a proposed policy, a set of test requests can be evaluated by direct execution of the semantic model on the VDMTools interpreter.

Based on the outcome of such an evaluation, the designer may choose to modify either or both of the policy and the environment. For example, a policy might be modified to add specific constraints, or the environment might have to be extended in order to include external information required to facilitate a new rule. The designer has an eye to the data that can be obtained from the environment as well as the content of the policy itself. This process of test and modification can go through several iterations, eventually yielding a model policy and environment. The policy can be implemented in a real XACML Policy Access Point. The environment model specifies the external data that must be obtainable from the real environment in order for the policy to behave correctly.

This section illustrates the process of iterative development using the executable semantics of XACML. Using the simple example introduced in Section 2, we first show an initial encoding of two elementary rules in an access control policy and then illustrate the testing and subsequent modification of the policy. Throughout we show how policies and tests are represented in VDM++, but in practice we expect the user of a tool based on the semantic model to access it through a more friendly interface.

4.1   Designing Rules

Consider first the implementation of the two rules given in Section 1, namely

> 1. The hazard analysis must be signed off before anyone may write to the production plan.
> 2. An author of a document can not be the reviewer of that document.

The developer begins by defining, in VDM++, a sample environment in which the rules will be exercised. From the example rules, necessary elements in the environment will include names for the two documents in question (haz_an for the hazard analysis and pp for the production plan) and the names of the two relevant actions (write and review). To fully specify an example environment, in which different subjects will have different privileges, the names of some subjects (here Anne and Bob) are included. All these are defined in VDM++ as variables from the class FExp.

```
haz_an : FExp'Var = mk_FExp'Var(mk_token("hazard_analysis")),
pp     : FExp'Var = mk_FExp'Var(mk_token("production_plan")),

write  : FExp'Var = mk_FExp'Var(mk_token("write")),
review : FExp'Var = mk_FExp'Var(mk_token("review")),

Anne   : FExp'Var = mk_FExp'Var(mk_token("Anne")),
Bob    : FExp'Var = mk_FExp'Var(mk_token("Bob"))
```

To construct the environment, we consider the two rules. Rule 1 contains a reference to hazard analysis being signed off. Since this will change over the course of the document lifetime, it must be possible when the policy is being evaluated to determine it from the environment. The developer does not need to know at this stage the way in which the environment stores this information, merely that it must be available. One possibility open to the developer is to include a Boolean variable to indicate whether or not the document is signed off. This is a straightforward solution, but if the policy expands, an environment with a large number of such Boolean variables could become complex to maintain and update. This becomes more important when we come to test the policy in environments with different values. We therefore add a variable called `signed_off`, of type `BoolArray`, to the environment. It is instantiated in the dynamic environment `denv` as a mapping from documents to Booleans. In the example environment given we populate it with the map {`haz_an |-> true, pp |-> false`}.

```
signed_off : FExp'Var = mk_FExp'Var(mk_token("signed_off")),

env : Env = new Env({...
                    signed_off |-> <BoolArray>},
                  {...
                    signed_off |->
                      {haz_an |-> true, pp |-> false}})
```

Rule 1 applies to any subject trying to write to the production plan, so we introduce a symbol `all_subjects` to represent the set of all subjects in the rule target. This is initialised to {`Anne,Bob`} and allows us to change the set of test subjects without having to change the rule target. The XACML convention is that if the target field is empty it applies to all possible subjects; we allow the developer to use that convention but retain `all_subjects` for clarity.

```
all_subjects : set of PAP'Subject = {Anne,Bob},

hazanBeforePPRule: PAP'Rule =
 mk_PAP'Rule(
   mk_PAP'Target(all_subjects,{pp},{write}), <Deny>,
               new FExp(mk_FExp'FUnary(<NOT>,
                   mk_FExp'FArrayLookup(signed_off,haz_an))))
```

In order to evaluate Rule 2, it must be possible at any time to determine the authorship of any document. To support this, a mapping `author` is added to the environment as a `VarArray` which has type `map Var to (map Var to bool)`. It is instantiated in the dynamic environment as a map from documents to people to Booleans:

```
author : FExp'Var = mk_FExp'Var(mk_token("author")),

environment1 : Env = new Env({author     |-> <VarArray>,
                              signed_off |-> <BoolArray>},
      {author |-> {haz_an |-> {Anne |-> false, Bob |-> true},
                   pp     |-> {Anne |-> true, Bob |-> false}},
       signed_off |-> {haz_an |-> true, pp |-> false}})
```

Rule 2 itself is a separation of duty constraint applying to all requests to `review` a document, and denying any author the ability to review their own document.

This demonstrates the need to vary the result of a rule evaluation depending on the relationship between the requester and the resource. It therefore makes use of both the `resource` and `requester` reserved words. In order to evaluate the effect of this rule, the evaluator must instantiate both of these variables via the `inst` mapping.

```
requester : FExp'UnVar = mk_FExp'UnVar(<requester>),
resource  : FExp'UnVar = mk_FExp'UnVar(<resource>),

reviewRule : PAP'Rule =
   mk_PAP'Rule(mk_PAP'Target(all_subjects,{haz_an,pp},{review}),
         <Deny>,
      new FExp(mk_FExp'FVarArrayLookup(author,resource,requester)))
```

Following the XACML structure, these two rules are combined in a policy within a PAP. Both the policy and the PAP have a `denyOverrides` rule combining algorithm, so, unless a request is specifically permitted by the rules, it will be denied. Formally:

```
CompanyPolicy : PAP'Policy =
 mk_PAP'Policy(mk_PAP'Target(all_subjects,{haz_an,pp},{review,write}),
       {hazanBeforePPRule,reviewRule},
        <denyOverrides>),

pap : PAP =  new PAP({CompanyPolicy}, <denyOverrides>)
```

4.2   Testing and Modifying Rules

To build confidence in the design of the policy, a number of tests are created. Each test is a single request which may be made of the policy. The developer evaluates the policy with respect to these tests, and decides if the results of the tests correspond to his or her understanding of the requirements. The testing process can be repeated in several environments.

For example, we might define a second test environment (`environment2`) in which authorship of each of the documents is as in `environment1`, but `haz_an` has not been signed off:

```
environment2 : Env = new Env({author    |-> <VarArray>,
                             signed_off |-> <BoolArray>},
                {author |-> {haz_an |-> {Anne |-> false, Bob |-> true},
                             pp     |-> {Anne |-> true, Bob |-> false}},
                 signed_off |-> {haz_an |-> false, pp |-> false}})
```

Table 1 shows the results of evaluating various test requests in each of these two environments. At this stage the two given rules have been designed, but it is clear that we are some way from a comprehensive access control policy.

The kind of error that is usually highlighted in this way is *policy incompleteness* – there are legitimate requests for which the policy has no rule. These are the requests for which the policy returns `<NotApplicable>`.

We could use this approach to highlight inconsistencies between rules within a policy by applying the same set of tests to two different rules. Note, however,

Table 1. Results of request evaluation in two environments

Request	Environment 1	Environment 2
`Request(Anne,haz_an,{write})`	`<NotApplicable>`	`<NotApplicable>`
`Request(Anne,haz_an,{review})`	`<NotApplicable>`	`<NotApplicable>`
`Request(Bob,haz_an,{write})`	`<NotApplicable>`	`<NotApplicable>`
`Request(Bob,haz_an,{review})`	`<Deny>`	`<Deny>`
`Request(Anne,pp,{write})`	`<NotApplicable>`	`<Deny>`
`Request(Anne,pp,{review})`	`<Deny>`	`<Deny>`
`Request(Bob,pp,{write})`	`<NotApplicable>`	`<Deny>`
`Request(Bob,pp,{review})`	`<NotApplicable>`	`<NotApplicable>`

that an inconsistency – one rule returns `Permit>` where another returns `<Deny>` – is not necessarily a cause for concern. It is relatively common in access control policies to have general rule with specific exceptions, and the combining algorithm takes care of the resolution.

In Table 1 no permission is given for any requests: they are all either denied or out of scope of the policy, returning the effect `<NotApplicable>`. This highlights a choice for the developer: what is to be the default behaviour of the Policy Enforcement Point if `<NotApplicable>` is returned from the policy evaluation? The two choices are *permit-biased* and *deny-biased*. If the PEP is permit-biased it will permit requests for which the policy returns `<NotApplicable>`, and rules must be designed to deny all requests that should be forbidden. An alternative is a *deny-biased* PEP, which treats `<NotApplicable>` as `<Deny>`. In this case a policy must be designed to permit all requests which are to be allowed.

If the developer wishes to make the behaviour of the policy independent of the style of the PEP, they must ensure that the policy does not return `<NotApplicable>` for any requests which match the policy target. In this example, we pursue this latter option. This is done by including a general permission rule (`permitRule`) in the policy. This permits any requests to write and review the two documents. When combined with the other rules using `<denyOverrides>`, this means that requests not specifically denied by the other rules in the policy will be permitted. The `permitRule` has no expression in the condition clause, because it is not conditional on any aspect of the environment:

```
permitRule: PAP'Rule = mk_PAP'Rule(mk_PAP'Target(
            all_subjects,{pp,haz_an},{write,review}),
            <Permit>,nil)
```

The `CompanyPolicy` is altered to include the new rule:

```
CompanyPolicy : PAP'Policy =
   mk_PAP'Policy(mk_PAP'Target(all_subjects,{haz_an,pp},{review,write}),
       {hazanBeforePPRule,reviewRule,permitRule},
          <denyOverrides>)
```

Testing these three rules in each of our environments has the anticipated results: each `<NotApplicable>` is set to `<Permit>` (Table 2).

Table 2. Test results for policy independent of PEP bias

Request	Environment 1	Environment 2
Request(Anne,haz_an,{write})	\<Permit\>	\<Permit\>
Request(Anne,haz_an,{review})	\<Permit\>	\<Permit\>
Request(Bob,haz_an,{write})	\<Permit\>	\<Permit\>
Request(Bob,haz_an,{review})	\<Deny\>	\<Deny\>
Request(Anne,pp,{write})	\<Permit\>	\<Deny\>
Request(Anne,pp,{review})	\<Deny\>	\<Deny\>
Request(Bob,pp,{write})	\<Permit\>	\<Deny\>
Request(Bob,pp,{review})	\<Permit\>	\<Permit\>

4.3 Environment Modification

Another problem highlighted by the test results is that requests by both Anne and Bob to write to haz_an, and by Bob to review haz_an, are permitted, even though it has been signed off. This is an inadequacy of the rules as given, which do not cover that explicitly. To deal with this, we could propose a rule which refuses any action on a document after it has been signed off, for example:

```
NoActionAfterSignoffRule : PAP'Rule =
    mk_PAP'Rule(mk_PAP'Target(all_subjects,{haz_an,pp},{review,write}),
            <Deny>,
        new FExp(mk_FExp'FArrayLookup(signed_off,resource)))
```

Let us assume that, through analysing the test results, the developer realises a further requirement

3. For each document, writing and reviewing phases must not overlap.

Implementing this rule will require a new environment variable, a Boolean array (completed). For each document, this is to be set to true when the writing phase is over and it is ready for review. The following two rules will keep the writing and reviewing phases separate:

```
NoWriteIfCompletedRule : PAP'Rule =
    mk_PAP'Rule(mk_PAP'Target(all_subjects,{haz_an,pp},{write}),
            <Deny>,
        new FExp(mk_FExp'FArrayLookup(completed,resource))),

NoReviewUntilCompletedRule : PAP'Rule =
    mk_PAP'Rule(mk_PAP'Target(all_subjects,{haz_an,pp},{review}),
            <Deny>,
        new FExp(mk_FExp'FUnary(<NOT>,
            mk_FExp'FArrayLookup(completed,resource))))
```

These three rules can be combined into a separate policy:

```
CompletionPolicy : PAP'Policy =
    mk_PAP'Policy(mk_PAP'Target(all_subjects,{haz_an,pp},{write,review}),
        {NoWriteIfCompletedRule,NoReviewUntilCompletedRule,
        NoActionAfterSignoffRule},
        <denyOverrides>)
```

Table 3. Test results in environment augmented with separated phases

Request	Environment 1	Environment 2
Request(Anne,haz_an,{write})	<Deny>	<Permit>
Request(Anne,haz_an,{review})	<Deny>	<Deny>
Request(Bob,haz_an,{write})	<Deny>	<Permit>
Request(Bob,haz_an,{review})	<Deny>	<Deny>
Request(Anne,pp,{write})	<Permit>	<Permit>
Request(Anne,pp,{review})	<Deny>	<Deny>
Request(Bob,pp,{write})	<Permit>	<Permit>
Request(Bob,pp,{review})	<Deny>	<Deny>

This new policy can then be added to the PAP:

```
pap : PAP =
  new PAP({CompanyPolicy,CompletionPolicy}, <denyOverrides>)
```

A value for the mapping can be added to the dynamic part of each test environment. In this case we add {completed |-> {haz_an |-> false, pp |-> false}}. Testing the new PAP in the two environments gives the results shown in Table 3. In Environment 1, the only requests now permitted are requests by Anne and Bob to write to pp. In Environment 2 there is an inconsistency. Requests to write to both haz_an and pp are allowed. This has happened because haz_an has been signed off without being completed. This inconsistency would be unacceptable in the implementation, and an appropriate safeguard would need to be put in place. However, modelling such an inconsistent environment is valuable, because doing so can help to identify environmental assumptions made by the policy.

5   An Application: Access Control Design for Virtual Organisations

We have proposed a semantic model of XACML which serves as a tool for the iterative development of access control policies. One of our motivations for addressing this topic formally has been the need to develop and maintain access control policies for virtual organisations. In this section, we show how the formal model can be used in this domain.

Virtual organisations (often called dynamic coalitions or virtual enterprises) are opportunistic collaborations that form around business needs and opportunities. Examples include coalitions of companies involved in designing, assessing and manufacturing a new chemical compound or agencies collaborating in an emergency relief scenario. Members of virtual organisations are agents, each having their own resources and policies for controlling access to them. However, within a coalition, some additional access is given to other coalition members in order to achieve the coalition's goal. The members agree a joint workflow for the common task, and adapt their individual access control policies if necessary to accommodate the workflow.

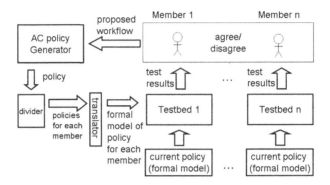

Fig. 3. Evolution of access control policies in virtual organisations

Virtual organisations evolve in real time as members join and leave, and as workflows are modified to adapt to changing business goals. At each step in the evolution, each member must make a trade-off between the risks and the benefits of modifying their access control policies to deal with the changed workflow or coalition membership. A source of complexity in this process is the need to determine the consistency of policy modifications with the member's own policies.

The executable formal model can be used to assist trade-off analysis by providing designer feedback on potential policy modifications. The process is illustrated in Fig. 3. An Access Control policy generator (which could be an off-the-shelf tool such as [5]) generates access control requirements from a workflow. These are split into sub-policies, one for each coalition member. These sub-policies represent the access policy that each member needs to deliver in order to satisfy the needs of the coalition. The translator (as demonstrated in [4] for context-free XACML) now translates the proposed policies into VDM++. These are then combined with the formal model of the current access control policy thus, for each member, giving a formal model of the new policy each member must enforce if they accept the workflow.

Each coalition member now has to decide independently if the proposed adaptions to their current policy are acceptable. They are faced with two questions: first, "What access privileges to my resources need to be granted to other members in the course of executing this workflow?" and second, "Will adding these new privileges to my existing access control policy violate my own security policy?"

These questions can be answered using the VDMTools interpreter. The tests are derived from the member's own information security policy (a high-level description of the company information security policy). Deriving these tests will take understanding and insight (although it need only be done when the information security policy changes) but performing them and understanding the results should be more straightforward, especially if the results are presented through a GUI interface.

Any failures are presented to the decision maker. If any member decides that the policy is unacceptable, they can do more than simply signal disapproval. For every test that fails they may use the formal model to investigate precisely why it failed, and which particular parts of the access control policy were invoked. They can use this information to propose alternative workflows to the collaboration. Once all members agree on a workflow, they add the new access control policy to their current policies and may then begin to execute the workflow.

As an example, consider the scenario developed earlier, but suppose that company A outsources the hazard analysis to company B, thus forming a style of coalition. Further, suppose that legislation requires that the author of the hazard analysis verify that the production plans implement any recommendations made. However, when a workflow capturing these requirements is proposed and tested by both companies, the first company discovers that the production plan is classified as commercially sensitive, and as such only company employees may see it. The onus is now the first company to propose a new workflow. Note that the tool highlights the issue but it does not enforce a particular solution.

6   Concluding Remarks

We have presented a VDM++ model for a substantial subset of XACML and shown how this can be used for developing context-sensitive access control policies. The utility of the approach has been demonstrated on a small but realistic example development of an access control policy fragment, showing how VDM-Tools can be used to analyse prototype policies and provide rapid feedback to the developer. In particular, the modelling and testing process helps to drive out requirements on both the policy and environment to be implemented. We have also outlined the value of the formal model in the development and evolution of access control policies in virtual organisations.

Current research addresses a variety of semantic models of context-sensitive access control policies. Constraint logic programming in Datalog has been used in several formalisations of access control in general(e.g. [6]) and of specific policy languages such as SecPAL [2]. Few, if any, of these formalisations deal directly with XACML. The policy modelling formalism RW [18] may be translated to XACML. Its semantics permit model checking with respect to a goal involving a combination of reading and manipulating propositional variables. Model checking of access control policies derived from XACML has also been demonstrated in Alloy [11], where the authors present several ordering relations between policies and use these to specify policy properties. Event systems have been proposed as a semantic model for dynamic access control policies in [15], where the authors show how to prove that an access control policy refines a given event system specification. A Haskell semantics of XACML 1.1 [12] covers more of the expression part of the language than we have done here for XACML 2.0, our focus being on the exploitation of the model in the policy design process.

The goal of our current work is to assist the access control policy developer by providing rapid feedback on design decisions. How far have we gone towards achieving this? Our approach has a formal basis but the goal is pragmatic and this has led to the use of a tool-supported model-oriented formalism and a test-based approach to model exploration. The use of a model-oriented formalism such as VDM++ makes it relatively easy to build a formal model that has a very similar structure to the XACML framework, easing translation of the validated policy model into its implementation. The model-oriented formalism also makes validation by testing straightforward. We have made this a priority as we wish to support evolution of models that may already have legacy test sets and we also want to have a low technical barrier to the use of the formal model.

The formal model that we have developed is expressed in a notation that will not be familiar to the majority of security engineers. It would be preferable if users could invoke the model through a tailor-made interface that allows the definition of XACML rules, policies and environments and allows the execution of the model on test requests. It is straightforward to construct such an interface using the VDMTools API, allowing the model to be exercised directly by the user without them having to face the formalism directly.

Not all of the XACML Standard [16] is so far modelled, but many of the remaining extensions are technically straightforward, including the extension to cover the remaining four policy combination algorithms and a capability for the policy developer to define their own combination algorithms. Requests can be extended to encompass sets of subjects, resources and actions. When returning an effect to the PEP, an XACML policy may also return *obligations* which must be carried out by the PEP in addition to enforcing the effect. Such obligations can modify the environment. For example, a policy might permit a user to log on if the number of unsuccessful attempts is suitably small, and oblige the PEP to increment this number with every denied request. Allowing the policy to modify its own environment directly will allow us to model the ability of a user to modify other users' access rights.

Currently our policy validation approach is based on testing. We would like to extend this to include the possibility of proving that policies meet key information security objectives. Automating this would utilise on proof technology for VDM which is currently being developed.

As remarked in Section 5, the semantics and tool developed so far allow the decision maker to see the implications of changes to access control policies. We are deliberately neutral about the surrounding processes which are the province of domain experts. These include the determination of environment models and the negotiation of resolutions to defects in policies for particular applications. The synthesis of specifications based on explicit assumptions about the surrounding computational and real-world environments [14] is an area of active research. The development of a tools framework for more domain-specific policy design is a natural next step for evaluating and tuning the formal engineering approach.

We would like to extend the work done so far to allow the user to explore the consequences of access control decisions on information flow in virtual organisations. In [3] we present a way of formally modelling a range of virtual organisations in order to investigate information flow properties between the members. Combined with the work presented here, this would allow the decision maker to ask "what-if" questions based on possible future scenarios. Here again, an intuitive interface, via the tool API, will be important.

Acknowledgments. We are grateful for support from the GOLD project and particularly Panos Periorellis. We are also grateful to our colleagues from Dstl, in particular Tom McCutcheon, Helen Phillips and Olwen Worthington. We acknowledge the many helpful comments of the anonymous reviewers.

References

1. Andrews, D.J. (ed.): Information technology – Programming languages, their environments and system software interfaces – Vienna Development Method – Specification Language – Part 1: Base language. International Organization for Standardization, International Standard ISO/IEC 13817-1 (December 1996)
2. Becker, M.Y., Fournet, C., Gordon, A.D.: SecPAL: Design and semantics of a decentralized authorisation language. Technical Report MSR-TR-2006-120, Microsoft Research (September 2006)
3. Bryans, J.W., Fitzgerald, J.S., Jones, C.B., Mozolevsky, I.: Formal modelling of dynamic coalitions, with an application in chemical engineering. In: 2nd International Symposium on Leveraging Applications of Formal Methods, Verification and Validation (ISoLA), IEEE Computer Society Press, Los Alamitos (2006) Also available as Technical Report CS-TR-981, Newcastle University, UK (to appear)
4. Bryans, J.W., Fitzgerald, J.S., Periorellis, P.: Model based analysis and validation of access control policies. Technical Report CS-TR-976, Newcastle University, School of Computing Science (July 2006)
5. Domingos, D., Rito-Silva, A., Veiga, P.: Authorization and access control in adaptive workflows. In: Snekkenes, E., Gollmann, D. (eds.) ESORICS 2003. LNCS, vol. 2808, pp. 23–38. Springer, Heidelberg (2003)
6. Dougherty, D.J., Fisler, K., Krishnamurthi, S.: Specifying and reasoning about dynamic access-control policies. In: Proceedings of the International Joint Conference on Automated Reasoning (August 2006)
7. Fisler, K., Krishnamurthi, S., Meyerovich, L.A., Tschantz, M.C.: Verification and change-impact analysis of access-control policies. In: ICSE 2005, pp. 196–205. ACM Press, New York (2005)
8. Fitzgerald, J.S., Larsen, P.G.: Modelling Systems: Practical Tools and Techniques in Software Development. Cambridge University Press, Cambridge (1998)
9. Fitzgerald, J.S., Larsen, P.G.: Triumphs and challenges for the industrial application of model-oriented formal methods. In: 2nd International Symposium on Leveraging Applications of Formal Methods, Verification and Validation (ISoLA), IEEE Computer Society Press, Los Alamitos (2006) Also available as Technical Report CS-TR-999, Newcastle University, UK (to appear)
10. Fitzgerald, J.S., Larsen, P.G., Mukherjee, P., Plat, N., Verhoef, M.: Validated Designs for Object-oriented Systems. Springer, Heidelberg (2004)
11. Hughes, G., Bultan, T.: Automated verification of access control policies. Technical Report 2004-22, University of California, Santa Barbara (2004)
12. Humenn, P.: The formal semantics of XACML, available at
    http://lists.oasis-open.org/archives/xacml/200310/pdf00000.pdf
13. Jones, C.B.: Systematic Software Development using VDM. International Series in Computer Science. Prentice-Hall, Englewood Cliffs (1990)
14. Jones, C.B., Hayes, I.J., Jackson, M.A.: Deriving specifications for systems that are connected to the physical world. In: Woodcock, J. (ed.) Essays in Honour of Dines Bjørner and Zhou Chaochen on the Occasion of their 70th Birthdays. LNCS, vol. 4700, pp. 364–390. Springer, Heidelberg (2007)

15. Méry, D., Merz, S.: Event systems and access control. In: Gollmann, D., Jürjens, J. (eds.) 6th International Workshop on Issues in the Theory of Security, Vienna, Austria, IFIP WG 1.7, Vienna University of Technology, pp. 40–54 (2006)
16. OASIS: eXtensible Access Control Markup Language (XACML) version 2.0. Technical report, OASIS (February 2005)
17. Overture Group: The VDM Portal (2007), http://www.vdmportal.org
18. Zhang, N., Ryan, M.D., Guelev, D.: Synthesising verified access control systems through model checking. Journal of Computer Security (in print, 2007)

A Verification Framework for Agent Knowledge

Jin Song Dong[1], Yuzhang Feng[1,*], and Ho-fung Leung[2]

[1] National University of Singapore
[2] The Chinese University of Hong Kong
{dongjs,fengyz}@comp.nus.edu.sg
lhf@cuhk.edu.hk

Abstract. One of the challenges for designing multi-agent systems is how to capture and reason about agent knowledge and knowledge evolution in a highly abstract and modular way. Hence it is very desirable to have a generic framework in which such systems can be conveniently specified and the properties verified under one umbrella. As a classical reasoning support, the model checking technique has proved to be applicable for systems of reasonable size. However current model checkers for epistemic logics suffer from the state explosion problem and their inability to handle infinite state problems. Prototype Verification System (PVS) is an environment for the development of formal specifications. It integrates a highly expressive specification language and a well supported theorem prover. In this paper, we demonstrate our attempt towards mechanizing epistemic logic reasoning by building a formal, sound and complete verification framework in PVS for reasoning about a spectrum of (dynamic) epistemic logics.

1 Introduction

The area of multi-agent systems is traditionally concerned with formal representation of the mental state of autonomous agents in a distributed setting. For this purpose, many modal logics have been developed and investigated. Among them epistemic logic, the logic of knowledge, is one of the most studied and has grown to find diverse applications such as artificial intelligence in computer science and game theory in economics [8,17].

Epistemic logic typically deals with what agents consider possible given their current information. This includes knowledge about facts as well as higher-order information about information that other agents have. Public announcement logic [21] extends normal epistemic logics with modal operator for public announcement. These logics can be perceived as a basis not only for specification languages of a particular spectrum of multi-agent systems, but also for mechanized machine-aided reasoning.

Recently some state-of-the-art model checkers [9,20,26] have been developed for automated verification of epistemic properties. However such approaches suffer from some major drawbacks. Firstly, the system to be verified has to be fully

---

* Corresponding author.

M. Butler, M. Ilinchey, M.M. Larrondo-Petrie (Eds.): ICFEM 2007, LNCS 4789, pp. 57–75, 2007.
© Springer-Verlag Berlin Heidelberg 2007

specified even if the property only concerns with a fragment of the system. Secondly, as the sizes of the states and relation are exponential to the number of proposition of the system, the model checkers suffer from what is known as the state explosion problem. The task of representing and verifying against all possible computations of a system may not be problematic for small examples, but may become unfeasible for realistic multi-agent systems. Lastly and perhaps most importantly, these model checkers deal with *finite* state systems only. But we are often faced with infinite states as the number of agents is neither fixed nor known in advance. Consequently the properties are often beyond the expressiveness of epistemic logic and hence cannot be verified by model checkers.

In this paper we explore a complementary approach. In the specification language of a well established interactive theorem prover, we build a reasoning framework which consists of (1) logic-level proof systems for deriving logic theorems, (2) theorem sets for storing the logic-level theorems, (3) object-level reasoning systems for application modelling and verification, and (4) reasoning rule sets for the object-level reasoning system. With this separation of concerns between the logic meta-level and application object-level, we are able to not only derive all valid formulae of a logic but also specify multi-agent applications and perform verification under one umbrella.

Other than obtaining a sound and complete reasoning system, many other advantages arise from using this translation approach. Firstly we can exploit the well supported theorem prover for the purpose of doing proofs in the multi-agent logic. Secondly as we are able to quantify over functions, we obtain the generality and power of higher-order logic. Thirdly, theories in PVS can be easily extended and reused. This means that we can extend our framework to support other epistemic logics with minimal effort. At the same time, system developers can easily select the suitable reasoning system to specify and verify the system being developed. Lastly we can utilize the power of proof strategies in PVS for proof automation.

The rest of the paper is organized as follows. In Section 2, we provide a brief overview of some well accepted epistemic logics, some model checker for epistemic logics, and Prototype Verification System. We describe our reasoning framework in detail in Section 3. An example will be used to explain the proof process and how we use proof strategies to enhance automation in Section 4. Section 5 concludes the paper.

2   Overview

2.1   Epistemic Logic

In computer science, it is often useful to reason about modes of truth. Modal logic, or (less commonly) intensional logic is the branch of logic that deals with sentences that are qualified by modalities such as can, could, might, may, must, possibly, and necessarily, and others. A formal modal logic represents modalities using modal sentential operators. The basic set of modal operators are usually given to be $\square$ and $\lozenge$. In alethic modal logic (i.e. the logic of necessity and possibility) $\square$ represents necessity and $\lozenge$ possibility.

When applied to knowledge representation and reasoning about multi-agent systems, the specific type of modal logics is called epistemic logic. For example each of many interacting agents may have different knowledge about the environment. Furthermore, each agent may have different knowledge about the knowledge of other agents. The formula $\square\varphi$ is read as: it is known that φ.

In the context of epistemic logic, one can view worlds that are possible for an agent in a world as epistemic alternatives, that are compatible with the agent's information in that world. The formal semantics will be introduced later in Section 2.2.

Epistemic Logic K. Epistemic logic K is the weakest epistemic logic that does not have any 'optional' formula schemes. It is based on a set of atomic propositions and a set of agents. It just contains propositional logic and all instances of formula scheme K. Here the operator K has exactly the same properties as $\square$.

Definition 1. *Let $\mathcal{P}$ be the set of atomic propositions, and $\mathcal{A}$ a set of agents. The language of the logic, $\mathcal{L}_K$ is defined by the following grammar.*

$$\phi ::= \top \mid \bot \mid p \mid \neg\phi \mid \phi \wedge \phi \mid \phi \vee \phi \mid \phi \rightarrow \phi \mid \phi \leftrightarrow \phi \mid K_a\phi$$

where $p \in \mathcal{P}$ and $a \in \mathcal{A}$. $K_a\phi$ means that 'agent a knows that ϕ holds'.

Epistemic Logic $KT45$. Also known as $S5$, $KT45$ is probably one of the most well known epistemic logics. Having the same language as logic K, $KT45$ adds three axioms:

- Truth: The agent knows only true things.
- Positive Introspection: If an agent knows something, he knows that he knows it.
- Negative Introspection: If the agent does not know something, he knows that he does not know it.

Epistemic Logic $KT45^n$. When reasoning about the knowledge of a group of agents, it becomes useful to reason not just about knowledge of an individual agent, but also about the knowledge of the group. Epistemic logic $KT45^n$ which is also known as $S5C$ extends $KT45$ by providing support for shared knowledge and common knowledge among a set of agents.

Definition 2. *The language of the logic, $\mathcal{L}_{KT45^n}$ is defined by the following grammar.*

$$\phi ::= \top \mid \bot \mid p \mid \neg\phi \mid \phi \wedge \phi \mid \phi \vee \phi \mid \phi \rightarrow \phi \mid \phi \leftrightarrow \phi \mid K_a\phi \mid E_G\phi \mid C_G\phi$$

where $E_G\phi$ (shared knowledge) means that every agent in the group G knows ϕ and $C_G\phi$ (common knowledge) means that every agent in G knows about ϕ

and every agent knows that every agent knows ϕ, etc. It captures a higher state of knowledge and can be thought of as an infinite conjunction $E_G\phi \wedge E_G E_G\phi \wedge E_G E_G E_G\phi \wedge ...$

First studied by Lewis [14], the notion common knowledge has received much attention in the area of economics and computer science after Aumann's seminal result [3]. The inclusion of common knowledge for a group of agents adds much more complexity to the task of reasoning about multi-agent systems. As a result, many previous reasoning systems of epistemic logic have left out the notion of common knowledge. We will discuss more on this in Section 5.

Epistemic Logic PAL and PAL-C. The knowledge of an agent is more complex than a collection of static data; it evolves typically as a result of agent communication. Dynamic epistemic logics analyze changes in both basic and higher-order information. A public announcement in public announcement logic (PAL) [21] is an epistemic update where all agents commonly know that they learn that a certain formula holds. Public announcement logic with common knowledge (PAL-C) extends PAL with support for common knowledge.

Definition 3. *The language of the logic, $\mathcal{L}_{\mathsf{PAL}}$ is defined by the following grammar.*

$$\phi ::= \top \mid \bot \mid p \mid \neg\phi \mid \phi \wedge \phi \mid \phi \vee \phi \mid \phi \rightarrow \phi \mid \phi \leftrightarrow \phi \mid K_a\phi \mid [\phi]\phi$$

The language of the logic, $\mathcal{L}_{\mathsf{PAL\text{-}C}}$ is defined by the following grammar.

$$\phi ::= \top \mid \bot \mid p \mid \neg\phi \mid \phi \wedge \phi \mid \phi \vee \phi \mid \phi \rightarrow \phi \mid \phi \leftrightarrow \phi \mid K_a\phi \mid E_G\phi \mid C_G\phi \mid$$
$$[\phi]\phi$$

where $[\varphi]\psi$ means that 'ψ holds after every announcement of φ'.

There have been various discussions of the equivalence and translations between $S5$ and PAL [4,10]. Every formula in the language of public announcement logic without common knowledge is equivalent to a formula in the language of epistemic logic.

Theorem 1. *For any arbitrary atomic proposition p and PAL formulae φ, ψ and χ, the following hold.*

$$
\begin{array}{rcl}
[\varphi]p & \leftrightarrow & (\varphi \rightarrow p) \\
[\varphi](\psi \wedge \chi) & \leftrightarrow & ([\varphi]\psi \wedge [\varphi]\chi) \\
[\varphi](\psi \rightarrow \chi) & \leftrightarrow & ([\varphi]\psi \rightarrow [\varphi]\chi) \\
[\varphi]\neg\psi & \leftrightarrow & (\varphi \rightarrow \neg[\varphi]\psi) \\
[\varphi]K_a\psi & \leftrightarrow & (\varphi \rightarrow K_a[\varphi]\psi) \\
[\varphi][\psi]\chi & \leftrightarrow & [\varphi \wedge [\varphi]\psi]\chi
\end{array}
$$

These results conveniently provide us with a rewrite system that allows us to eliminate announcement from the logical language. In other words PAL is a syntactical extension to $S5$ and is equivalent to $S5$. However when common knowledge is added, an equivalence cannot be formulated, thus creating complexity for reasoning with common knowledge in dynamic epistemic logic.

2.2   Semantics

Typically the semantics of various epistemic logics are given using the idea of *possible worlds* and *Kripke structures*.

Definition 4. *Given a set of atomic propositions $\mathcal{P}$ and a set of agents $\mathcal{A}$, a Kripke model is a structure $\mathcal{M} = \langle \mathcal{S}, \mathcal{R}, \mathcal{V} \rangle$, where*

- *$\mathcal{S}$ is a set of states or possible worlds. It is sometimes also called the domain $\mathcal{D}(\mathcal{M})$ of $\mathcal{M}$.*
- *$\mathcal{R} : \mathcal{A} \to \mathcal{S} \times \mathcal{S}$ is a function, which maps from each agent $a \in \mathcal{A}$ to its possibility relation. Intuitively, $(s, t) \in \mathcal{R}(a)$ if agent a cannot differentiate between s and t.*
- *$\mathcal{V} : \mathcal{P} \to 2^{\mathcal{S}}$ is an evaluation function that for every $p \in \mathcal{P}$ yields the set of states in which p is true.*

Epistemic formulae are interpreted on epistemic states $(\mathcal{M}, s)$ consisting of a Kripke model $\mathcal{M} = \langle \mathcal{S}, \mathcal{R}, \mathcal{V} \rangle$ and a state $s \in \mathcal{S}$.

Definition 5. *Given a model $\mathcal{M} = \langle \mathcal{S}, \mathcal{R}, \mathcal{V} \rangle$ we have that a formula φ is true in $(\mathcal{M}, s)$, written as $\mathcal{M}, s \models \varphi$, as follows:*

$$
\begin{array}{lll}
\mathcal{M}, s \models p & \textit{iff} & s \in \mathcal{V}(p) \\
\mathcal{M}, s \models (\varphi \wedge \psi) & \textit{iff} & \mathcal{M}, s \models \varphi \text{ and } \mathcal{M}, s \models \psi \\
\mathcal{M}, s \models \neg \varphi & \textit{iff} & \text{not } \mathcal{M}, s \models \varphi \\
\mathcal{M}, s \models K_a \varphi & \textit{iff} & \text{for all } t \text{ such that } (s, t) \in \mathcal{R}(a),\ \mathcal{M}, t \models \varphi \\
\mathcal{M}, s \models E_G \varphi & \textit{iff} & \text{for all } a \text{ such that } a \in G,\ \mathcal{M}, t \models K_a \varphi \\
\mathcal{M}, s \models C_G \varphi & \textit{iff} & \text{for all } t \text{ such that } (s, t) \in T^*,\ \mathcal{M}, t \models \varphi, \\
\mathcal{M}, s \models [\varphi]\psi & \textit{iff} & \mathcal{M}, s \models \varphi \text{ implies } \mathcal{M}|\varphi, s \models \psi
\end{array}
$$

where T^* is the reflexive transitive closure of $\bigcup_{a \in G} \mathcal{R}(a)$ and the model $\mathcal{M}|\varphi = \langle \mathcal{S}', \mathcal{R}', \mathcal{V}' \rangle$ is defined by restricting $\mathcal{M}$ to those worlds where φ holds. So $\mathcal{S}' = [\![\varphi]\!]$, $\mathcal{R}' = \mathcal{R}(a) \cap [\![\varphi]\!]^2$ and $\mathcal{V}'(p) = \mathcal{V}(p) \cap [\![\varphi]\!]$, where $[\![\varphi]\!] = \{ s \in \mathcal{S} \mid \mathcal{M}, s \models \varphi \}$.

When $\mathcal{M}, s \models \varphi$ for all $s \in \mathcal{D}(\mathcal{M})$, we write $\mathcal{M} \models \varphi$. If $\mathcal{M} \models \varphi$ for all Kripke models $\mathcal{M}$, we say that φ is valid. If for formula φ there is a state $(\mathcal{M}, s)$ such that $\mathcal{M}, s \models \varphi$, we say that φ is satisfied in $(\mathcal{M}, s)$.

Kripke semantics makes our epistemic logic *intensional*, in the sense that we give up the property of extensionality, which dictates that the truth of a formula is completely determined by the truth of its sub-formulae.

2.3   A Classical Example

Now we present a classical example of epistemic logics, the Three Wise Men problem [16], which captures the knowledge and the reasoning process of a typical agent in a multi-agent environment. We take the following problem specification as in [8].

> *There are three wise men. It is common knowledge that there are three red hats and two white hats. The king puts a hat on each of them so that*

*they cannot see their own hat, and asks each one **in turn** if they know the colour of the their hats. Suppose the first man says he does not know; then the second says he does not know either. It follows that the third man must be able to tell his hat is red.*

We can formalize the problem as follows, very similar to the formalization in [12], only adding public announcement features. Let p_i be the proposition meaning that the wise man i has a red hat; so $\neg p_i$ means that he has a white hat. Let Γ be the set of formulae

$$\{ C(p_1 \vee p_2 \vee p_3),$$
$$C(p_1 \rightarrow K_2 p_1), C(\neg p_1 \rightarrow K_2 \neg p_1), C(p_1 \rightarrow K_3 p_1), C(\neg p_1 \rightarrow K_3 \neg p_1),$$
$$C(p_2 \rightarrow K_1 p_2), C(\neg p_2 \rightarrow K_1 \neg p_2), C(p_2 \rightarrow K_3 p_2), C(\neg p_2 \rightarrow K_3 \neg p_2),$$
$$C(p_3 \rightarrow K_1 p_3), C(\neg p_3 \rightarrow K_1 \neg p_3), C(p_3 \rightarrow K_2 p_3), C(\neg p_3 \rightarrow K_2 \neg p_3)\}$$

We want to prove

$$\Gamma \vdash [\neg (K_1 p_1 \vee K_1 \neg p_1)][\neg (K_2 p_2 \vee K_2 \neg p_2)]K_3 p_3$$

2.4   Reasoning about Epistemic Logics - The Model Checking Approach

As the semantics of epistemic logic are given in Kripke structures, model checking is a natural method of verifying epistemic properties [11,6,23,27]. MCK [9], which deals with the logic of knowledge and both linear and branching time using BDD based algorithms, MCMAS [20], which handles knowledge and branching time using BDD based algorithm, and DEMO [26], which is an explicit state model checker based on a dynamic epistemic logic, are three recent state-of-the-art epistemic model checkers. Some of these model checkers support logics beyond PAL-C. For example DEMO supports both public and private announcement.

Though the model checking technique is advantageous over theorem proving for its automation, it has some drawbacks. For one, the system to be verified has to be fully specified even if the property only concerns with a fragment of the system. It is even worse for the case of DEMO in which all states and accessibility relations have to be manually specified. The sizes of the states and relation are exponential to the number of proposition of the system. For another, while model checking technique provides a fully automated mechanism for verifying properties of a system, it suffers from what is known as the state explosion problem. The task of representing and verifying against all possible computations of a system may not be problematic for small examples, but may become unfeasible for realistic multi-agent systems. The last and most important drawback is that these model checkers only deal with finite state systems, but in many cases the state space is infinite due to arbitrary number of agents involved.

Hence in this work we take a different and complementary approach. We encode the epistemic logics in an expressive specification language and perform the reasoning in a well supported theorem prover in a user-guided fashion. However for simplicity, our current framework allows only public announcement and leaves out private announcement to future work.

2.5 PVS

Prototype Verification System (PVS) is an integrated environment for the development of formal specifications. The primary purpose of PVS is to provide formal support for conceptualization and debugging in the early stages of design of a hardware or software system. The distinguishing feature of PVS is its synergistic integration of a highly expressive specification language and powerful theorem-proving capabilities.

The PVS specification language augments classical higher-order logic with a sophisticated type system with predicate subtypes and dependent types, and with parameterized theories and a mechanism for defining abstract data types. PVS specifications are organized into theories, which define data types, axioms, theorems and conjectures that can be reused by other theories. The ability to allow specifications to be built in hierarchy and reused makes it easier to specify, reason about and extend systems with multi-level architectures.

PVS has a powerful interactive theorem prover [18]. The basic deductive steps in PVS are large compared with many other systems; there are atomic commands for induction, quantifier reasoning, automatic condition rewriting, simplification, etc. User-defined proof strategies can be used to enhance the automation.

The prover maintains a proof tree. The users' goal is to construct a complete proof tree, in which all leaves (proof goals) are recognized as true. The proof goals in PVS are represented as sequents which consist of a list of formulae called the antecedents and a list of formulae called the consequents. The formal interpretation of a sequent is that the conjunction of the antecedents implies the disjunction of the consequents.

3   Reasoning Framework

The system architecture of our reasoning framework is depicted in Fig. 1. Based on the encoding of the logic formulae, the framework primarily consists of four components, namely *Proof Systems*, *Theorem Sets*, *Reasoning Systems* and *Reasoning Rule Sets*. A solid arrow from a component B to a component A indicates that A imports B. A dotted arrow from a component A to a component B represents dataflow from A to B.

In addition, because of the relationship between the epistemic logics, we organize the encodings for each epistemic logic in a hierarchical fashion too, as shown in Fig. 2. So we have in effect established a two-dimensional hierarchy – *horizontal* hierarchy among different components for a particular logic and *vertical* hierarchy among different logics. As a result, system developers can easily select and reuse the desired system environment for specification and reasoning.

In this section, we explain the functionalities of each individual component and how they are used with each other as a system. Due to space limitations, the full PVS specification is not completely shown, but can be found online[1].

---

[1] http://www.comp.nus.edu.sg/~fengyz/PVSFramework

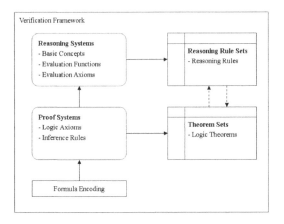

Fig. 1. Framework Architecture

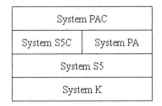

Fig. 2. Logic Hierarchy

The logic formulae are encoded using the PVS abstract datatype construct as shown below. The PVS abstract datatype mechanism is useful because it automatically generates theories containing axioms and definitions. The datatype declaration simply specifies the ways a logic formula can be constructed. For example the ninth line specifies that a formula can be constructed by using a *constructor* k and two arguments where the first is of type AGENT and the second is a palc_formula. k? is a *recognizer* for formulae constructed in this way. agent and sub are accessors for the arguments.

```
palc_formula[AGENT: TYPE]: DATATYPE
BEGIN
    base: base?
    knot(sub: palc_formula): knot?
    kand(left: palc_formula, right: palc_formula): kand?
    kor(left: palc_formula, right: palc_formula): kor?
    kif(left: palc_formula, right: palc_formula): kif?
    kiff(left: palc_formula, right: palc_formula): kiff?
    k(agent: AGENT, sub: palc_formula): k?
    e(agents: set[AGENT], sub: palc_formula): e?
    c(agents: set[AGENT], sub: palc_formula): c?
    pa(inner: palc_formula, outer: palc_formula): pa?
END palc_formula
```

Type-checking the datatype specification automatically generates two PVS theory files which contain axioms and definitions over the logic formulae. An example is shown below. It defines what is meant by two k? formulae being equivalent.

```
palc_formula_k_extensionality: AXIOM FORALL (k?_var: (k?), k?_var2: (k?)):
    agent(k?_var) = agent(k?_var2) AND sub(k?_var) = sub(k?_var2)
        IMPLIES k?_var = k?_var2;
```

3.1 Proof Systems

A logic is a set of formulae. An axiomatization is a syntactic way to specify a logic: it gives a core set of formulae, called axioms, and inference rules, from which all other valid formulae in the logic can be derived.

Definition 6. *Let* $\boldsymbol{X}$ *be an axiomatization of an arbitrary logic with axioms* $A_1, \ldots, A_n$ *and derivation rules* $R_1, \ldots, R_m$. *Then a derivation for a formula* φ *within* $\boldsymbol{X}$ *is a finite sequence* $\varphi_1, \ldots, \varphi_k$ *of formulae such that* $\varphi_k = \varphi$ *and every* φ_i *in the sequence is an instance of one of the axioms* $A_1, \ldots, A_n$, *or the result of the application of one of the rules* $R_1, \ldots, R_m$ *to some formulae* φ_j *where* $j < i$. *If there is a derivation for* φ *in* $\boldsymbol{X}$, *we write* $\boldsymbol{X} \vdash \varphi$, *or if the system* $\boldsymbol{X}$ *is clear from the context, we just write* $\vdash \varphi$. *We also say that* φ *is a theorem of* $\boldsymbol{X}$.

We want to construct a framework that can be used to reason about an arbitrary model. On the one hand, we need to be sure that our system is complete; all valid formulae can be proved. On the other hand, we want the base model to be as concise as possible. Hence we encode the axiomatizations, obtaining completeness at minimal cost.

In our architecture, the *Proof Systems* component captures the axiomatizations of various epistemic logics. Because some axiomatizations extend some others, we utilize the reuse facilities of PVS by storing each sub-component in a separate theory and using the IMPORTING clause to capture the extensional relationship. In effect, we construct a hierarchy of proof systems following the relationships among various logics.

The basic axiomatization $\boldsymbol{K}$ for the epistemic logic K is comprised of the axioms A_1 and A_2, together with the derivation rules R_1 and R_2 as given below.

$A_1\ \varphi$	φ is any propositional tautology
$A_2\ (K_a\varphi \wedge K_a(\varphi \rightarrow \psi)) \rightarrow K_a\psi$	K-axiom
$R_1 \vdash \varphi, \vdash \varphi \rightarrow \psi \Rightarrow\ \vdash \psi$	Modus Ponens
$R_2 \vdash \varphi \Rightarrow\ \vdash K_a\varphi$	K-Necessitation

The encoding of the axiomatization for the logic K is shown below. In this encoding, derives is defined as a function from a palc_formula to a boolean value. Formally $derives(\varphi)$ holds if and only if φ is a theorem in the system, that is $\vdash \varphi$. The two logic axioms and the two derivation rules are specified as PVS axioms.

```
systemK[AGENT: TYPE] : THEORY
BEGIN
    IMPORTING palc_formula_adt[AGENT]
    derives: [palc_formula -> bool]
    tautology: [palc_formula -> bool]
    pro_tauto: AXIOM FORALL (p: palc_formula): tautology(p) IMPLIES derives(p)
    k_axiom : AXIOM FORALL (p1,p2: palc_formula),(a: AGENT):
        derives(kif(kand(k(a,p1),k(a,kif(p1,p2))),k(a,p2)))
    modus_ponens : AXIOM FORALL (p1,p2: palc_formula):
        derives(p1) AND derives(kif(p1,p2)) IMPLIES derives(p2)
    k_necessitation: AXIOM FORALL (p: palc_formula),(a: AGENT):
        derives(p) IMPLIES derives(k(a,p))
END systemK
```

With the axioms and derivation rule, the proof systems can be proved to be sound and complete. We adopt the soundness and completeness results of [25] and omit the proof here. For space limitation, we also skip the discussions on encoding of axiomatization of the logic $S5$, $S5C$, PAL and PAL-C which are available online[2].

As we have discussed in Section 2.1, the logic PAL is as expressive as the logic $S5$. Furthermore it has been shown that the computation complexity of PAL coincide with that of epistemic logic S5 [15]. But the logical language of public announcement is a convenient specification tool to express this particular sort of dynamics of multi-agent systems. In fact it has been shown that there are properties that can be expressed exponentially more succinctly in PAL than in $S5$. Hence in our framework, PAL is *not* encoded as S5. Being an essentially syntactical extension to $S5$, the proof system of PAL is encoded by extending that of $S5$ with additional axioms based on the equivalence. The purpose of doing so, like the purpose of having PAL with the existence of $S5$, is to provide the users with flexibility and convenience to specify the systems. Furthermore it establish a higher level of reasoning by providing axioms and theorems on the public announcement operator rather than simply the K operator.

3.2   Theorem Sets

This component contains a set of theorem sets, one for each of the proof systems. Each theorem set contains the theorems that have been proved in the corresponding proof system. In other words, these theorems can be applied to any arbitrary model expressed in the logic. The importing relationships among the theorem sets are the same. Such structure makes the access to a particular logic with its proof system and theorems easier. It should be noted that, although the proof systems are complete, these theorem sets are by no means complete. It initially contains some basic and commonly used theorems such as the axioms in the axiomatization. These theorems can be used (and hence do not need to be proved again) with the derivation rules for proving new theorems which are then added back into the theorem set. Therefore the size of the theorem set grows with the use of the system. It should be emphasized that the proof systems being complete ensures that all valid formulae can be proved as theorems.

---

[2] http://www.comp.nus.edu.sg/~fengyz/PVSFramework

3.3   Reasoning Systems

As compared with the proof systems which aim at proving general theorems at logic level, the reasoning systems build an environment for reasoning about concrete object-level models. This component evaluates a formula on a given model. We specify the reasoning system for logic K below.

```
reasonerK : THEORY BEGIN
    Agent : TYPE
    IMPORTING systemK[Agent]
    Knowledge : TYPE = palc_formula
    eval : [Knowledge -> bool]
    knot_ax : AXIOM FORALL (k:Knowledge):
        eval(knot(k)) IMPLIES NOT eval(k)
    kand_ax : AXIOM FORALL (k1,k2:Knowledge):
        eval(kand(k1,k2)) IMPLIES (eval(k1) AND eval(k2))
    kor_ax : AXIOM FORALL (k1,k2:Knowledge):
        eval(kor(k1,k2)) IMPLIES (eval(k1) OR eval(k2))
    kif_ax : AXIOM FORALL (k1,k2:Knowledge):
        eval(kif(k1,k2)) IMPLIES (eval(k1) IMPLIES eval(k2))
    kiff_ax : AXIOM FORALL (k1,k2:Knowledge):
        eval(kiff(k1,k2)) IMPLIES (eval(k1) IFF eval(k2))
END reasonerK
```

Agent is defined as an uninterpreted type and is passed down to the proof systems as a type parameter. *Knowledge* is defined as a type equivalent to logic formulae. Given a model every piece of knowledge should have a truth value at any time. Therefore we define a *evaluation function* eval. More formally, for a formula φ of a given model, $eval(\varphi)$ holds if and only if the formula φ evaluates to true in the model. We have defined five logical connectives for knowledge corresponding to the logical negation, conjunction, disjunction, implication and equivalence. The advantage of doing this is that we can easily compose new knowledge from existing ones. As a result we need to define a set of evaluation axioms which map the logical connectives for knowledge to their logic counterparts straightforwardly.

We maintain the hierarchical structure of the whole verification framework. However the reasoning systems for different logics do not differ a lot because much of the difference is reflected in the underlying proof systems and theorem sets. We still specify the reasoning systems in separate theories for consistency. The reasoning systems of $S5$ and PAL are the same as that of K. The reasoning system of PAL-C is the same as that of $S5C$. So we only describe the reasoning system for $S5C$ below.

```
reasonerS5C: THEORY
BEGIN
    IMPORTING reasonerS5, systemS5C[Agent]
    e_ax: AXIOM FORALL (g: set[Agent]),(k1: Knowledge):
        eval(e(g,k1)) IFF FORALL (a: Agent): member(a,g) IMPLIES eval(k(a,k1))
    c_ax: AXIOM FORALL (g: set[Agent]),(k1: Knowledge):
        eval(c(g,k1)) IFF eval(e(g,k1)) AND eval(c(g,e(g,k1)))
END reasonerK
```

We define evaluation axioms for modal connectives for shared knowledge and common knowledge. As we have discussed earlier, C is in fact an infinite conjunction of E. As PVS only allows finite conjunctions we model the evaluation function for the common knowledge connective using a recursive definition. During the reasoning process we can choose the extent to which we expand the axiom.

3.4 Reasoning Rule Sets

Definitions and evaluation functions alone are not sufficient to prove the properties efficiently. The last component of the framework is the *Reasoning Rule Sets*. They are encoded based on the reasoning systems. In other words, they are applied when reasoning about actual models. Therefore their aims are not to make the system complete, but to achieve a higher degree of automation by abstracting certain amount of underlying model from the reasoning process. The reasoning rule sets are constructed hierarchically, similar to the other three components. Each reasoning rule set of a logic initially contains the (non-inherited) axioms from the corresponding proof systems. For example the encoding of the reasoning rule set for $S5$ is shown below.

```
reasoningRuleS5: THEORY
BEGIN
    IMPORTING reasonerS5, reasoningRuleK
    Truth : THEOREM FORALL (k:Knowledge),(a:Agent): eval(K(a,k)) IMPLIES eval(k)
    Positive_Introspection : THEOREM FORALL (k:Knowledge),(a:Agent):
        eval(K(a,k)) IMPLIES eval(K(a,(K(a,k))))
    Negative_Introspection : THEOREM FORALL (k:Knowledge),(a:Agent):
        eval(knot(K(a,k))) IMPLIES eval(K(a,(knot(K(a,k)))))
END reasoningRuleS5
```

The way of encoding for the reasoning rules is slightly different from the corresponding axiom in the proof system, mainly because they are used for different purposes. The ones in proof systems are for deriving other theorems whereas the ones here are applied to a particular model for evaluation of formulae. Hence there are two ways to construct the reasoning rules. Firstly new reasoning rules can be derived from existing ones. Secondly new reasoning rules for a logic can be obtained by translating theorems from the corresponding theorem set. Theorems in the theorem set are of the form

   FORALL Q: derives(F)

where Q is a set of bound variables and F is formula in the corresponding logic. We do not change the quantifier or the bound variables and translate only the quantified formula. The translated formula is

   FORALL Q: F'

where F' uses the evaluation function eval. We have implemented a simple translation program which works recursively on the propositional structure of the formula[3].

3.5 Framework Workflow

Having described the components, we explain the framework methodology depicted in Fig. 3. When the framework is first used, the theorem sets and reasoning

---

[3] Algorithm available at http://www.comp.nus.edu.sg/~fengyz/PVSFramework

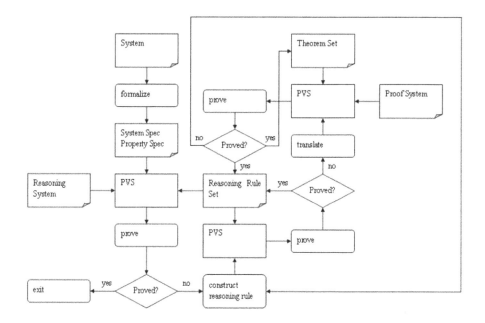

Fig. 3. Framework Workflow

rule sets contain the initial theorems and reasoning rules. Subsequently,

1. Given a *system*, formalize it using an appropriate epistemic logic to produce the *system specification*. Specify the property to be proved about system.
2. With the appropriate *reasoning system* and *reasoning rule set*, try to prove the property. If the property is proved, exit.
3. Construct a reasoning rule which may help prove the property.
4. Try to prove the new reasoning rule in PVS based on the existing reasoning rules in the *reasoning rule set*. If the rule is proved, add it to the *reasoning rule set* and go to step 2. Otherwise translate it into theorem format.
5. Try to prove the translated theorem in *proof system* based on existing theorems in the *theorem set*. If successful, add the theorem to the theorem set and the reasoning rule to the reasoning rule set and go to step 2. Otherwise go to step 3.

In effect, the user keeps trying to prove the property with reasoning rules which can be proved by using either the existing reasoning rules or the existing theorems. In the process the reasoning rule set and the theorem set are incrementally constructed.

4   Example

As an example of how to use the framework, we now illustrate with the running example, Three Wise Men problem. The procedures follow the workflow explained in Section 3.5.

4.1   Formalizing the System

We can formalize the problem in our reasoning framework as shown in Fig. 4. As we can see the specification is a direct translation of the model in Section 2.3.

```
twm: THEORY BEGIN
    IMPORTING reasonerPAC
    IMPORTING reasoningRulePAC
    m1,m2,m3: Agent
    p1,p2,p3: (base?)
    g: set[Agent] = {a : Agent | a = m1 OR a = m2 OR a = m3}
    init: AXIOM eval(c(g,kor(kor(p1,p2),p3)))
    init_m1: AXIOM
        eval(c(g,kif(p1,k(m2,p1)))) AND eval(c(g,kif(knot(p1),k(m2,knot(p1))))) AND
        eval(c(g,kif(p1,k(m3,p1)))) AND eval(c(g,kif(knot(p1),k(m3,knot(p1))))) 
    init_m2: AXIOM
        eval(c(g,kif(p2,k(m1,p2)))) AND eval(c(g,kif(knot(p2),k(m1,knot(p2))))) AND
        eval(c(g,kif(p2,k(m3,p2)))) AND eval(c(g,kif(knot(p2),k(m3,knot(p2)))))
    init_m3: AXIOM
        eval(c(g,kif(p3,k(m2,p3)))) AND eval(c(g,kif(knot(p3),k(m2,knot(p3))))) AND
        eval(c(g,kif(p3,k(m1,p3)))) AND eval(c(g,kif(knot(p3),k(m1,knot(p3)))))
    conclude: THEOREM
        eval(pa(knot(kor(k(m1,p1),k(m1,knot(p1)))),
                pa(knot(kor(k(m2,p2),k(m2,knot(p2)))),k(m3,p3))))
END twm
```

Fig. 4. Three Wise Men specification

As we are going to use the logic PAL-C for reasoning, we import the reasoning system `reasonerPAC` and the reasoning rule set `reasoningRulePAC`. We first define the three wise men as agents and define three pieces of ground knowledge p1, p2 and p3 each of which corresponds to the proposition meaning that the i-th man is wearing a red hat. Then the negation of them mean that the i-th man is wearing a white hat. For ease of specifying the system we define the group of agents g containing the three agents. The fact that initially it is commonly known that at least one of them is wearing a red hat (implied from the fact that there are two white hats and three red hats) is captured by the axiom `init`. The fact that the colour of one's hat is known to the others is captured by the three axioms `init_1`, `init_2` and `init_3`. Then `conclude` is the property we want to prove, that is, after the first two men declared their ignorance about the colour of their hat, the third knows his hat is red. Formally this is

$$[\neg (K_1 p_1 \vee K_1 \neg p_1)][\neg (K_2 p_2 \vee K_2 \neg p_2)] K_3 p_3$$

4.2   Constructing and Proving Reasoning Rules

The PVS prover cannot prove the property automatically. Hence according to the workflow we need to construct some reasoning rules. There are 9 reasoning rules that we need for proving the property. Some of these reasoning rules are from the original reasoning rule set, while others cannot be proved directly from other reasoning rules. Therefore we input them into the translation program to

obtain the corresponding theorems and then prove them in the proof system
PAC. For space limitation, simple proofs for the lemmas are omitted.

Let φ, φ_1, φ_2, ψ and ω be arbitrary formulae, p a ground proposition, B an
arbitrary set of agents, and a an agent in B then the following lemmas hold.

Lemma 1. $\vdash C_B\varphi \rightarrow K_a\varphi \wedge C_B K_a\varphi$.

Lemma 2. $\vdash [\varphi \wedge [\varphi]\psi]\omega \rightarrow [\varphi][\psi]\omega$.

Lemma 3. $\vdash (\varphi \rightarrow K_a[\varphi]\psi) \rightarrow [\varphi]K_a\psi$.

Lemma 4. $\vdash (\varphi \rightarrow p) \rightarrow [\varphi]p$.

Lemma 5. $\vdash \varphi \wedge [\varphi]\neg \psi \rightarrow \neg [\varphi]\psi$.

Lemma 6. $\vdash \varphi \wedge [\varphi]K_a\psi \rightarrow K_a[\varphi]\psi$.

Lemma 7. $\vdash [\varphi](\psi \wedge \omega) \rightarrow [\varphi]\psi \wedge [\varphi]\omega$.

Lemma 8. $\vdash (\varphi_1 \rightarrow \varphi_2) \rightarrow (K_a\varphi_1 \rightarrow K_a\varphi_2)$.

Lemma 9. $\vdash K_a\varphi_1 \rightarrow (K_a\varphi_2 \rightarrow K_a(\varphi_1 \wedge \varphi_2))$.

With the reasoning rules, it is now sufficient to prove the property. For space
limitation, we would not show the proof details such as proof commands used in
this proof. The proof tree can be found in the appendix. To improve readability
and save space in the proof tree, $\neg K_1p_1 \wedge \neg K_1\neg p_1$ is renamed to φ_1 and
$\neg K_2p_2 \wedge \neg K_2\neg p_2$ to φ_2 in some parts of the proof without loss of correctness.

An observation is that a generalized version of the problem, where there are
n wise men and the last would know that he has a red hat if the first $n - 1$
had declare their ignorance, presents an infinite state system. It is even beyond
the expressiveness of the epistemic logics to represent such system, let alone to
prove the property using the current model checkers. However it is possible by
using induction in theorem provers.

4.3 Proof Strategies

PVS proof strategies provide an accessible means of increasing the degree of
automation available to PVS users. A proof strategy is intended to capture
patterns of inference steps. A defined proof rule is a strategy that is applied in a
single atomic step so that only the final effect of the strategy is visible and the
intermediate steps are hidden from the user. PVS provides strong support for
writing strategies. Therefore being able to use proof strategies to increase the
degree of automation is a major motivation for using PVS.

To illustrate how proof strategies can be useful, consider the proof fragment
we have discussed in the Three Wise Men example shown in Fig. 5.

This figure represents the situation whereby there are n antecedent formulae
and 1 consequent formula, all of which are of the form $K_a\varphi$. We want to simulate

$$[\text{K}] \frac{\neg\, p_2, \neg\, p_3, p_1 \vee p_2 \vee p_3 \vdash p_1}{K_1 \neg\, p_2, K_1 \neg\, p_3, K_1(p_1 \vee p_2 \vee p_3) \vdash K_1 p_1}$$

Fig. 5. Proof Fragment for K elimination

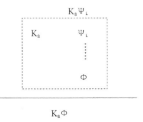

Fig. 6. K introduction in natural deduction

```
(defstep k_elim ()
    (try (try (forward-chain "k_collect")
              (then (hide -2) (try (forward-chain -1)
                                   (then (hide -2) (k_elim))
                                   (then (fail) (fail)))))
         (skip))
         (kand_collapse)
         (skip))
    "k box: eliminating k operator" "k box: eliminating k operator")

(defstep kand_collapse ()
    (try (forward-chain "kand_ax")
         (then (hide -2) (kand_collapse))
         (skip))
    "collapsing kand clause" "collapsing kand clause")
```

Fig. 7. Proof Strategy Examples

the effect of dashed boxes in natural deduction (as shown in Fig. 6) by stripping away K_a, so that the sequent can be simplified.

The naive method would be to first apply the k_collect reasoning rule $n-1$ times to merge the antecedent formulae into one and then apply the kbox rule to remove the K operator and then apply evaluation axioms $n-1$ times to break the single antecedent formula into n antecedent formulae. The problem is that in the general case the number of antecedent formulae is not fixed. It is desired that we can achieve the effect with a single proof command regardless of the number of antecedent formulae. The proof strategies are shown in Fig. 7.

5   Conclusion

In this paper we presented a formal hierarchical framework for specifying and reasoning about agent knowledge. We encoded a hierarchy of epistemic logics K, $S5$, $S5C$, PAC and PAL-C in the PVS specification language. The framework mainly consists of four components: *Proof Systems* for the ability to completely derive theorems of a particular logic, *Theorem Sets* for storing the theorems derived from the proof systems, *Reasoning Systems* for evaluating a formula of a concrete model, and *Reasoning Rule Sets* for storing reasoning rules for better proof automation. *Proof Systems* and *Theorem Sets* work on the meta-level while *Reasoning Systems* and *Reasoning Rule Sets* work on the object level. We demonstrated the idea by solving the classical Three Wise Men problem.

Some researchers have done related work along a similar line. Kim and Kowalski used meta-reasoning with common knowledge based on a Prolog implementation to solve the same Three Wise Men puzzle [13]. Compared with their work, our approach has the advantage of being able to quantify over agent, knowledge and even functions, i.e., offering higher-order logic benefits. In [5], Basin *et al.* presented a theoretical and practical approach to the modular natural deduction presentation of a class of modal logics using Isabelle [19]. In [22], the sequent calculus of classical linear logic $KDT4_{lin}$ is coded in the higher order logic using the proof assistant COQ [7] with two-level meta-reasoning. These two pieces of work include neither the common knowledge operator nor the public announcement operator which adds much complexity to the reasoning process. A similar approach to our work was taken by Arkoudas and Bringsjord in [2]. Instead of encoding the logic and the axiomatization, they encode the sequent calculus for a epistemic logic in Athena [1], an interactive theorem prover too, and reason about the reasoning process in the logic. Two other major differences are that their work did not provide support for public announcement operators and that they did not comment on the completeness of their system.

The framework we have proposed achieves a higher space bound than the current state-of-the-art model checkers for epistemic logic, at the expense of automation. The user has to select one from a set of rules that is applicable in some stage of the reasoning process. This requires much human expertise. Currently the reasoning rules are simply collected in a set which grows with the use of the system. A better rule management will be able to categorize the rules according to some criteria such as the type of formula involved, the number of premises or the number of bound variables. Another area we would like to explore further is the use of PVS proof strategies. We have demonstrated how proof strategies can improve the degree of automation. PVS strategies can provide much stronger support than what we have illustrated. It is envisioned that proof strategies can be constructed to produce different proof heuristics with which we can further improve the reasoning methodology. Lastly a language extension has recently been proposed [24] which adds assignment operator to languages for epistemic actions, so that change of knowledge and change of facts can be combined in specifications of multi-agent system dynamics. To incorporate the notion of actions, state-based formalisms could be appropriate.

Acknowledgement

This work has been supported by ARF grant Rigorous Design Methods and Tools for Intelligent Autonomous Multi-Agent Systems (R-252-000-201-112). The authors also wish to thank Dr Hans P. van Ditmarsch for the valuable discussions on the topic.

References

1. Arkoudas, K.: Athena. http://www.cag.csail.mit.edu/~kostas/dpls/athena/
2. Arkoudas, K., Bringsjord, S.: Metareasoning for multi-agent epistemic logics. In: Leite, J.A., Torroni, P. (eds.) CLIMA 2004. LNCS (LNAI), vol. 3487, pp. 50–65. Springer, Heidelberg (2005)
3. Aumann, R.J.: Agreeing to disagree. The Annals of Statistics 4(6), 1236–1239 (1976)
4. Baltag, A., Moss, L.S., Solecki, S.: The logic of public announcements, common knowledge, and private suspicions. In: Proceedings of the 7th conference on theoretical aspects of rationality and knowledge, pp. 43–56 (1998)
5. Basin, D., Matthews, S., Viganò, L.: A modular presentation of modal logics in a logical framework. In: Ginzburg, J., Khasidashvili, Z., Vogel, C., Lévy, J.-J., Vallduví, E. (eds.) The Tbilisi Symposium on Logic, Language and Computation: Selected Papers, pp. 293–307. CSLI Publications, Stanford, CA (1998)
6. Benerecetti, M., Giunchiglia, F., Serafini, L.: Model checking multiagent systems. Journal of Logic and Computation 8(3), 401–423 (1998)
7. Coquand, T., Huet, G.: The calculus of constructions. Information and Computation 76(2-3), 95–120 (1988)
8. Fagin, R., Halpern, J.Y., Moses, Y., Vardi, M.Y.: Reasoning about knowledge. MIT Press, Cambridge, Mass. (1995)
9. Gammie, P., van der Meyden, R.: Mck: Model checking the logic of knowledge. In: Alur, R., Peled, D.A. (eds.) CAV 2004. LNCS, vol. 3114, pp. 479–483. Springer, Heidelberg (2004)
10. Gerbrandy, J.: Bisimulations on Planet Kripke. PhD thesis, University of Amsterdam (1999)
11. Halpern, J.Y., Vardi, M.Y.: Model checking vs. theorem proving: A manifesto. In: Allen, J., Fikes, R.E., Sandewall, E. (eds.) KR 1991, pp. 325–334. Morgan Kaufmann Publishers, San Mateo, CA (1991)
12. Huth, M., Ryan, M.: Logic in Computer Science: Modelling and Reasoning about Systems. Cambridge University Press, Cambridge (1999)
13. Kim, J.-S., Kowalski, R.A.: An application of amalgamated logic to multi-agent belief. In: Proceedings MetaLogic 1990, pp. 272–283 (1990)
14. Lewis, D.K.: Convention: A Philosophical Study. Harvard University Press, Cambridge, MA (1969)
15. Lutz, C.: Complexity and succinctness of public announcement logic. In: Proceedings of the 5th international joint conference on Autonomous agents and multiagent systems, pp. 137–143 (2006)
16. McCarthy, J.: Formalization of common sense. In: Lifschitz, V. (ed.) Ablex (1990)
17. Meyer, J.-J.C., Hoek, W.V.D.: Epistemic Logic for AI and Computer Science. Cambridge University Press, New York (1995)
18. Owre, S., Rushby, J.M., Shankar, N.: PVS: A prototype verification system. In: Kapur, D. (ed.) CADE-11. LNCS, vol. 607, pp. 748–752. Springer, Heidelberg (1992)
19. Paulson, L.C.: Isabelle. LNCS, vol. 828. Springer, Heidelberg (1994)
20. Penczek, W., Lomuscio, A.: Verifying epistemic properties of multi-agent systems via bounded model checking. In: AAMAS 2003, pp. 209–216. ACM Press, New York (2003)

21. Plaza, J.A.: Logics of public communications. In: Emrich, M.L., Pfeifer, M.S., Hadzikadic, M., Ras, Z.W. (eds.) Proceedings of the 4th International Symposium on Methodologies for Intelligent Systems, pp. 201–216 (1989)

22. Sadrzadeh, M.: Modal linear logic in higher order logic, an experiment in coq. In: Basin, D., Burkhart, W. (eds.) Proceedings of Theorem Proving in Higher Order Logics, Rome, Italy, pp. 75–93 (2003)

23. van der Hoek, W., Wooldridge, M.: Model checking knowledge and time. In: Proceedings of the 9th International SPIN Workshop on Model Checking of Software, pp. 95–111. Springer, London (2002)

24. van Ditmarsch, H.P., van der Hoek, W., Kooi, B.P.: Dynamic epistemic logic with assignment. In: Proceedings of the fourth international joint conference on Autonomous agents and multiagent systems, New York, NY, USA, pp. 141–148 (2005)

25. van Ditmarsch, H.P., van der Hoek, W., Kooi, B.P.: Dynamic Epistemic Logic. Springer, Heidelberg (2006)

26. van Eijck, J.: Dynamic epistemic modelling. CWI Technical Report SEN-E0424, Centrum voor Wiskunde en Informatica, Armsterdam (2004)

27. Wooldridge, M., Fisher, M., Huget, M.-P., Parsons, S.: Model checking multi-agent systems with mable. In: AAMAS 2002, pp. 952–959. ACM Press, New York (2002)

Appendix. Proof Tree for Three Wise Men Puzzle

$$
\cfrac{
\cfrac{
\cfrac{
\cfrac{
\cfrac{
\cfrac{
\cfrac{
\cfrac{
\cfrac{
\cfrac{
\cfrac{
\cfrac{
\cfrac{
\cfrac{
\cfrac{
\cfrac{
\cfrac{
\cfrac{
\cfrac{
\cfrac{
p_1 \vee p_2 \vee p_3, \neg p_3, \neg p_2 \vdash p_1,
}{K_1(p_1 \vee p_2 \vee p_3), K_1 \neg p_3, K_1 \neg p_2 \vdash K_1 p_1,} {\scriptstyle [\text{k\_elim}]}
}{K_1(p_1 \vee p_2 \vee p_3), \neg p_i \rightarrow K_j \neg p_i, \neg p_3, \neg p_2 \vdash K_1 p_1,}
}{K_1(p_1 \vee p_2 \vee p_3), \neg p_i \rightarrow K_j \neg p_i, \neg K_1 p_1, \neg K_1 \neg p_1, \neg p_3 \vdash p_2}
}{K_1(p_1 \vee p_2 \vee p_3), \neg p_i \rightarrow K_j \neg p_i, \neg K_1 p_1 \wedge \neg K_1 \neg p_1, \neg p_3 \vdash p_2}
}{K_1(p_1 \vee p_2 \vee p_3), \neg p_i \rightarrow K_j \neg p_i, \neg p_3 \vdash (\neg K_1 p_1 \wedge \neg K_1 \neg p_1) \rightarrow p_2}
}{K_1(p_1 \vee p_2 \vee p_3), \neg p_i \rightarrow K_j \neg p_i, \neg p_3 \vdash [\neg K_1 p_1 \wedge \neg K_1 \neg p_1] p_2} {\scriptstyle [\text{Lem. 4}]}
}{K_2 K_1(p_1 \vee p_2 \vee p_3), K_2(\neg p_i \rightarrow K_j \neg p_i), K_2 \neg p_3 \vdash K_2 [\neg K_1 p_1 \wedge \neg K_1 \neg p_1] p_2} {\scriptstyle [\text{k\_elim}]}
}{K_2 K_1(p_1 \vee p_2 \vee p_3), K_2(\neg p_i \rightarrow K_j \neg p_i), \neg p_i \rightarrow K_j \neg p_i, \neg p_3 \vdash K_2 [\neg K_1 p_1 \wedge \neg K_1 \neg p_1] p_2}
}{K_2 K_1(p_1 \vee p_2 \vee p_3), K_2(\neg p_i \rightarrow K_j \neg p_i), \neg p_i \rightarrow K_j \neg p_i, \neg K_2 [\neg K_1 p_1 \wedge \neg K_1 \neg p_1] p_2 \vdash p_3}
}{K_2 K_1(p_1 \vee p_2 \vee p_3), K_2(\neg p_i \rightarrow K_j \neg p_i), \neg p_i \rightarrow K_j \neg p_i, \varphi_1, \neg K_2 [\varphi_1] p_2, \neg K_2 [\varphi_1] \neg p_2 \vdash p_3} {\scriptstyle [\text{Lem. 5,6}]}
}{K_2 K_1(p_1 \vee p_2 \vee p_3), K_2(\neg p_i \rightarrow K_j \neg p_i), \neg p_i \rightarrow K_j \neg p_i, \varphi_1, [\varphi_1] \neg K_2 p_2, [\varphi_1] \neg K_2 \neg p_2 \vdash p_3} {\scriptstyle [\text{Lem. 7}]}
}{K_2 K_1(p_1 \vee p_2 \vee p_3), K_2(\neg p_i \rightarrow K_j \neg p_i), \neg p_i \rightarrow K_j \neg p_i, \varphi_1, [\varphi_1](\varphi_2) \vdash p_3}
}{K_2 K_1(p_1 \vee p_2 \vee p_3), K_2(\neg p_i \rightarrow K_j \neg p_i), \neg p_i \rightarrow K_j \neg p_i, \varphi_1 \wedge [\varphi_1] \varphi_2 \vdash p_3}
}{K_2 K_1(p_1 \vee p_2 \vee p_3), K_2(\neg p_i \rightarrow K_j \neg p_i), \neg p_i \rightarrow K_j \neg p_i \vdash \varphi_1 \wedge [\varphi_1] \varphi_2 \rightarrow p_3}
}{K_2 K_1(p_1 \vee p_2 \vee p_3), K_2(\neg p_i \rightarrow K_j \neg p_i), \neg p_i \rightarrow K_j \neg p_i \vdash [\varphi_1 \wedge [\varphi_1] \varphi_2] p_3} {\scriptstyle [\text{Lem. 4}]}
}{K_3 K_2 K_1(p_1 \vee p_2 \vee p_3), K_3 K_2(\neg p_i \rightarrow K_j \neg p_i), K_3(\neg p_i \rightarrow K_j \neg p_i) \vdash K_3 [\varphi_1 \wedge [\varphi_1] \varphi_2] p_3} {\scriptstyle [\text{k\_elim}]}
}{K_3 K_2 K_1(p_1 \vee p_2 \vee p_3), K_3 K_2(\neg p_i \rightarrow K_j \neg p_i), K_3(\neg p_i \rightarrow K_j \neg p_i), \varphi_1 \wedge [\varphi_1] \varphi_2 \vdash K_3 [\varphi_1 \wedge [\varphi_1] \varphi_2] p_3}
}{K_3 K_2 K_1(p_1 \vee p_2 \vee p_3), K_3 K_2(\neg p_i \rightarrow K_j \neg p_i), K_3(\neg p_i \rightarrow K_j \neg p_i) \vdash \varphi_1 \wedge [\varphi_1] \varphi_2 \rightarrow K_3 [\varphi_1 \wedge [\varphi_1] \varphi_2] p_3} {\scriptstyle [\text{Lem. 3}]}
}{K_3 K_2 K_1(p_1 \vee p_2 \vee p_3), K_3 K_2(\neg p_i \rightarrow K_j \neg p_i), K_3(\neg p_i \rightarrow K_j \neg p_i) \vdash [\varphi_1 \wedge [\varphi_1] \varphi_2] K_3 p_3} {\scriptstyle [\text{Lem. 2}]}
}{K_3 K_2 K_1(p_1 \vee p_2 \vee p_3), K_3 K_2(\neg p_i \rightarrow K_j \neg p_i), K_3(\neg p_i \rightarrow K_j \neg p_i) \vdash [\varphi_1][\varphi_2] K_3 p_3} {\scriptstyle [\text{Lem. 1}]}
}{C(p_1 \vee p_2 \vee p_3), C(p_i \rightarrow K_j p_i), C(\neg p_i \rightarrow K_j \neg p_i) \vdash [\varphi_1][\varphi_2] K_3 p_3}
$$

From Model-Based Design to Formal Verification of Adaptive Embedded Systems[*]

Rasmus Adler[1], Ina Schaefer[2], Tobias Schuele[3], and Eric Vecchié[3]

[1] Fraunhofer Institute for Experimental Software Engineering (IESE),
Kaiserslautern, Germany
Rasmus.Adler@iese.fraunhofer.de
[2] Software Technology Group, Department of Computer Science,
University of Kaiserslautern, Germany
inschaef@informatik.uni-kl.de
[3] Reactive Systems Group, Department of Computer Science,
University of Kaiserslautern, Germany
{schuele,vecchie}@informatik.uni-kl.de

Abstract. Adaptation is important in dependable embedded systems to cope with changing environmental conditions. However, adaptation significantly complicates system design and poses new challenges to system correctness. We propose an integrated model-based development approach facilitating intuitive modelling as well as formal verification of dynamic adaptation behaviour. Our modelling concepts ease the specification of adaptation behaviour and improve the design of adaptive embedded systems by hiding the increased complexity from the developer. Based on a formal framework for representing adaptation behaviour, our approach allows to employ theorem proving, model checking as well as specialised verification techniques to prove properties characteristic for adaptive systems such as stability.

1 Introduction

Many embedded systems autonomously adapt at runtime to changing environmental conditions by up- and downgrading their functionality according to the current situation. Adaptation is particularly important in safety-critical areas such as the automotive domain to meet the high demands on dependability and fault-tolerance. For this reason, adaptation has become state-of-the-art in antilock braking, vehicle stability control and adaptive cruise control systems. For example, if the sensor measuring the yaw rate of a car fails, the vehicle stability control system may adapt to a configuration, where the yaw rate is approximated by steering angle and vehicle speed. In this way, it can be guaranteed that the system is still operational even if some of the components fail in order to provide a maximum degree of safety and reliability. However, adaptation significantly complicates the development of embedded systems. One reason for

---

[*] This work has been supported by the Rheinland-Pfalz Cluster of Excellence 'Dependable Adaptive Systems and Mathematical Modelling' (DASMOD).

M. Butler, M. Hinchey, M.M. Larrondo-Petrie (Eds.): ICFEM 2007, LNCS 4789, pp. 76–95, 2007.

this is that in the worst case the number of configurations a system can adapt to is exponential in the number of its modules. Moreover, for ensuring system correctness it is not sufficient to consider each configuration separately but the adaptation process as a whole has to be checked.

A promising approach to deal with the increased complexity posed by adaptation is model-based design. As a major advantage, model-based design allows to focus on the needs of each phase in the design process and to model the required concepts as close as possible to the intuition by capturing them in an accurate and understable manner. Regarding the development of adaptive systems, model-based design supports the validation and verification of adaptation behaviour before the actual funtionality is implemented. The integration of formal verification into the development process is important to rigorously prove that the adaptation behaviour meets critical requirements such as stability.

In this paper, we propose an integrated framework for model-based design and formal verification of adaptive embedded systems. The modelling concepts of our approach hide the complexity at system level by fostering modular design and independent specification of functionality and adaptation behaviour. In this way, the designer can concentrate on the adaptation behaviour during early phases of the design process without having to consider implementation specific details. The design can then be refined successively by adding the intended functionality.

In order to formally reason about adaptive embedded systems, we propose a framework that captures the semantics of the modelling concepts at a high level of abstraction. Using this framework, the models as well as the desired properties can be formulated in a semantically exact manner. This is particularly important regarding the application of different verification techniques: Firstly, it is possible to embed the models into a representation suitable for a theorem prover and to verify the specified properties directly, e.g. by means of induction. Secondly, properties frequently occurring in the verification of adaptive system can be checked by automatic techniques such as symbolic model checking.

However, many systems encountered in practice are not directly amenable to formal verification by model checking due to their huge state space. To solve this problem, our formal framework allows to perform transformations on the models in order to reduce verification complexity. For example, data abstraction techniques may be employed to reduce the state space. The separation between functionality and adaptation behaviour is thereby maintained, which allows to consider purely functional, purely adapative and combined aspects. As the models in our framework have a clear semantics, it can be guaranteed by means of a theorem prover that the applied transformations are property preserving.

For certain properties, it is often advantageous to apply specialised verification methods, as standard model checking procedures are not always as efficient as possible. This is the case for stability of the adaptation process, one of the most important properties in adaptive systems, as adaptations in one component may trigger further adaptations in other components, which may lead to unstable configurations. However, in embedded systems, which are usually subject to certain real-time constraints, it must be guaranteed that a system stabilises after a bounded number of adaptation steps. To this end, we propose an approach that allows to verify stability of adaptive systems more efficiently than using standard model checking procedures.

To illustrate our approach, we use a building automation system as running example. The system consists of four modules: an occupancy detection, a light control, a lamp and an alarm system. The functionality is as follows: The light in a room is controlled according to the room occupancy. If the room is unoccupied, the lamp is switched off. Otherwise, the lamp is adjusted according to the current illuminance of the room. Additionally, an alarm is raised if the room is occupied without authorisation. Each module has a number of configurations for maintaining its functionality in case of failures. For instance, the module *Occupancy Detection* uses data from a camera, a motion detector, and transponders to determine occupancy of the room. When the camera is defect, the module adapts from camera-based to motion-based occupancy detection.

The rest of this paper is structured as follows: In Section 2, we introduce the concepts for modelling adaptive embedded systems and present the underlying formal framework. In Section 3, we address some aspects of adaptive system verification with a focus on stability. In Section 4, we describe the implementation of our approach. Finally, we discuss related work (Section 5) and conclude with an outlook to future work (Section 6).

2   Modelling Adaptive Embedded Systems

2.1   Concepts for Modelling Adaptation Behaviour

The objective of our modelling concepts called MARS (Methodologies and Architectures for Runtime Adaptive Systems) is the explicit modelling of adaptation behaviour, which is a prerequisite for its validation and verification. These concepts have been successfully applied in industry and academia for several years and provide a seamlessly integrated approach for the development of adaptive systems [21]. The major difficulty in modelling adaptation behaviour are complex interdependencies between the modules of a system. To solve this problem, we employ the concept 'separation of concerns' by separating functional from adaptation behaviour and the concept 'divide and conquer' by defining the adaptation behaviour modularly within the modules. Based on these concepts, it is possible to hide the complexity at system level from the developer.

A system consists of a set of modules that communicate with each other by passing signals via ports. This is a common notion found in various modelling languages and complies with the definition of architecture description languages by Taylor et al. [10]. In contrast to non-adaptive modules, our modules have several functional behaviours in order to support different degradation levels.

Quality Descriptions. A modular definition of adaptation behaviour is indispensible for handling the enormous complexity of most systems. For this reason, we establish a quality flow in the system making such modular definitions possible. Besides the actual data, each signal has an additional quality description. To this end, signals are typed by datives (extended data type for adaptive systems) that do not only describe which data values a signal may take, but also how the quality of this data can be described. Hence, a dative consists of a data type and a quality type. The former describes the type of data values like integers or real numbers. The quality type provides type-specific quality information, because a general purpose quality information like the relative error is not reasonable in many cases, e.g. for Boolean signals. Since the quality is part of the type definition, module designers are able to define the adaptation behaviour solely on the basis of quality descriptions available at a module's local interface. Additionally, they define how the current quality of the provided signals is determined.

In order to define the quality of a functional value of a signal, it is necessary to know which behavioural variant has been used to determine a value. In the first place, a quality type is defined by a set of possible modes. A developer using a signal knows the deficiencies associated with a certain mode and decides how a module must adapt in order to compensate for these deficiencies. Additionally, mode attributes can be used to describe the signal quality more precisely using mode-specific characteristics. Consequently, a mode is described by the mode itself and a set of mode attributes.

As an example, Figure 1 shows the definition of the dative *occupancy*. Its quality type contains five modes: The mode *camera* refers to a camera-based occupancy detection and mode *motion* indicates that the occupancy is derived from the detected motions. A deficiency associated with mode *motion* is that only movements are detected instead of actual persons in the room. As the quality of motion-based occupancy detection strongly depends on the reaction point of the motion sensor, the mode attribute *reactionpoint* is attached to the mode *motion*. In the example, *reactionpoint* represents the sensitivity of the motion sensor.

Modules. Based on datives, developers can modularly define the adaptation behaviour of single modules using two extensions made to conventional modules.

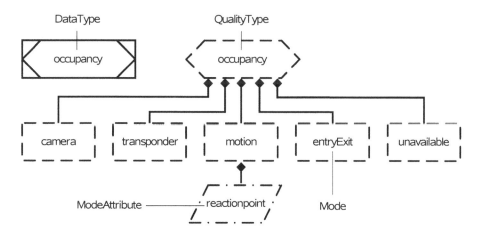

Fig. 1. Example for the definition of a dative

First, the behaviour specification is not directly assigned. Several configurations can be assigned to a module, each of them representing one behaviour variant. Second, in addition to the input/output interface, we define a required/provided interface. This distinction is used for describing the direction of the quality flow. This is not always identical to the direction of the data flow between two connected module ports. Although the connection is typed by one dative, the data part of the dative flows from an output port of one module to an input port of another module, while the quality flows from a provided port to a required port. This can for instance be the case for an actuator where a data value is propagated to the actuator while the actuator's status is conveyed to the functional unit via the signal's quality. The interface of a module is defined by a set of input signals, a set of output signals, a set of required signals and a set of provided signals.

Configurations. A module can be in one of several configurations, each of them representing one behavioural variant. A module is thus defined by its interface and a set of configurations. In our running example, the module *OccupancyDetection* can be in one of five configurations, depending on how occupancy of a room is determined. For instance, *CameraDetection* is the configuration, where the occupancy is derived from a camera image. A configuration is defined by the following elements: (1) a specification of the associated behavioural variant, (2) a guard defining under which conditions the configuration can be activated, (3) a priority and (4) an influence defining how the quality of the provided signals is determined.

A guard is a Boolean expression. If the guard evaluates to true at run time, the configuration can be activated. Operands of guards are quality descriptions of required signals. A guard defines which signals are required in which mode and which values the mode attributes may have. For instance, the guard of the configuration *MotionDetection* in module *OccupancyDetection* defines that the required quality of the signal *detected_motion* has to be in mode 'available'. Additionally, it could be enforced that the mode attribute *reactionpoint* is in a certain range. Often, guards of several configurations are satisfied at the same time. Therefore, an unambiguous priority is assigned to each configuration. At run time, the configuration with the highest priority is activated and the associated behaviour is executed. Influence rules describe how the quality of the provided signals is determined. Each influence rule consists of an influence guard and an influence function. The influence guard refines the configuration guard and defines a condition under which the respective influence function is applied. The influence function assigns the appropriate mode to each provided signal and calculates the mode attributes. For instance, configuration *MotionDetection* has only one influence rule whose influence function assigns the quality of signal *occupancy* to mode *motion*.

2.2   Formal Representation of Modelling Concepts

In this subsection, we show how the modelling concepts of MARS can be formally represented by Synchronous Adaptive Systems (SAS), which constitute the

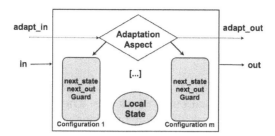

Fig. 2. Separation of functional and adaptation behaviour in an SAS module

basis for formal verification of adaptive embedded systems [16]. SAS capture the semantics of adaptation behaviour at a high level of abstraction bridging the gap between the modelling concepts and their formal representation. The modularity provided by MARS is represented by composing synchronous adaptive systems from a set of modules. Each module comprises a set of predetermined behavioural configurations it may adapt to. SAS maintain the separation of adaptive and functional behaviour. This is accomplished by defining an adaptation aspect on top of the different functional configurations. The active configuration is determined by the adaptation aspect. SAS are assumed to be open systems with input provided by the environment. Furthermore, they are modelled synchronously as their simultaneously invoked actions are executed in true concurrency. Figure 2 depicts the intuitive notion of a module.

For the definition of SAS syntax, we assume a set of distinct variable names *Var* and a set of values *Val* that can be assigned to these variables. The formal definition of modules is based on state transition systems.

Definition 1 (Module and Adaptation). *An SAS module m is a tuple $m = (in, out, loc, init, confs, adaptation)$ with*

- *$in \subseteq Var$, the set of input variables, $out \subseteq Var$, the set of output variables, $loc \subseteq Var$, the set of local variables and $init : loc \rightarrow Val$ their initial values*
- *$confs = \{(guard_j, next\_state_j, next\_out_j) \mid j = 1, ..., n\}$ the configurations of the module, where*
  - *$guard_j$: the Boolean closure of constraints on $\{adapt\_in, adapt\_loc\}$ determining when configuration j is enabled with $adapt\_in$ and $adapt\_loc$ as defined below*
  - *$next\_state_j$: $(in \cup loc \rightarrow Val) \rightarrow (loc \rightarrow Val)$ the next state function for configuration j*
  - *$next\_out_j$: $(in \cup loc \rightarrow Val) \rightarrow (out \rightarrow Val)$ the output function for configuration j*

The adaptation aspect is defined as a tuple $adaptation = (adapt\_in, adapt\_out, adapt\_loc, adapt\_init, adapt\_next\_state, adapt\_next\_out)$, where

- *$adapt\_in \subseteq Var$ is the set of adaptation in-variables, $adapt\_out \subseteq Var$ the set of adaptation out-variables, $adapt\_loc \subseteq Var$ the set of adaptation local state variables and $adapt\_init : adapt\_loc \rightarrow Val$ their initial values*

- $adapt\_next\_state : (adapt\_in \cup adapt\_loc \rightarrow Val) \rightarrow (adapt\_loc \rightarrow Val)$ the adaptation next state function
- $adapt\_next\_out : (adapt\_in \cup adapt\_loc \rightarrow Val) \rightarrow (adapt\_out \rightarrow Val)$ the adaptation output function

The module concept of MARS is represented by SAS modules where module ports are mapped to input and output variables. The dative associated with a port is modelled by a set of variables: one functional variable for the functional data, an adaptive variable for each mode and additional adaptive variables for mode attributes. In the running example, the module *OccupancyDetection* is represented by an SAS module. The input signal *motion_detected* is split into two variables, a functional variable *motion_detected* and an adaptive variable *motion_detected_quality* carrying the mode of the signal. A configuration in a module is represented by an SAS configuration, where the configuration guard is mapped to an SAS configuration guard and the priority to the configuration index. The configuration behaviour is expressed by the *next_output* function of the configuration. So, the configuration *MotionDetection* in module *Occupancy-Detection* is represented by an SAS configuration with a guard expressing that the adaptive variable *motion_detected_quality* must have the value 'available'. The influence function of a configuration is represented using the *adapt_next_out* function of the SAS module's adaptation aspect. In our example the adaptive output variable *occupancy_quality* corresponding to the quality part of the signal *occupancy* is assigned to the mode *motion* by the *adapt_next_out* function if the configuration *MotionDetection* is used. Since MARS concepts currently do not use state variables, the respective parts of SAS remain unused.

An SAS is composed from a set of modules that are interconnected via their own and the system's input and output variables. For technical reasons, we assume that all system variable names and all module variable names are disjoint. Whereas for module ports in MARS it is defined whether a quality is required or provided, quality and data flow in SAS are completely decoupled using separate adaptive connections. Hence, provided ports are mapped to adaptation output variables and required ports are mapped to adaptation input variables. A module can trigger adaptations in other modules via adaptive connections.

Definition 2 (SAS). *A synchronous adaptive system S is a tuple*

$$S = (M, input_a, input_d, output_a, output_d, conn_a, conn_d),$$

where

- $M = \{m_1, \ldots, m_n\}$ *is a set of SAS modules with* $m_i = (in_i, out_i, loc_i, init_i, confs_i, adaptation_i)$
- $input_a \subseteq Var$ *are adaptation inputs and* $input_d \subseteq Var$ *functional inputs to the system*
- $output_a \subseteq Var$ *are adaptation outputs and* $output_d \subseteq Var$ *functional outputs from the system*

- $conn_a$ is a function connecting adaptation outputs to adaptation inputs, system adaptation inputs to module adaptation inputs and module adaptation outputs to system adaptation outputs, i.e. $conn_a : \bigcup_{j,k=1,\ldots,n}(adapt\_out_j \cup input_a) \rightarrow (adapt\_in_k \cup output_a)$, where $conn_a(input_a) \subseteq adapt\_in_k$
- $conn_d$ is a function connecting outputs of modules to inputs, system inputs to module inputs and module outputs to system outputs, i.e. $conn_d : \bigcup_{j,k=1,\ldots,n}(out_j \cup input_d) \rightarrow (in_k \cup output_d)$, where $conn_d(input_d) \subseteq in_k$.

The semantics of SAS is defined in a two-layered approach. We start by defining the local semantics of single modules similar to standard state-transition systems. From this, we define global system semantics. A local state of a module is defined by a valuation of the module's variables, i.e. input, output and local variables and their adaptive counterparts. A local state is initial if its functional and adaptation variables are set to their initial values and input and output variables are undefined. A local transition between two local states evolves in two stages: First, the adaptation aspect computes the new adaptation local state and the new adaptation output from the current adaptation input and the previous adaptation state. The adaptation aspect further selects the configuration with the smallest index that has a valid guard with respect to the current input and the previous functional and adaptation state. The system designer should ensure that the system has a built-in default configuration 'off' which becomes applicable when no other configuration is. The selected configuration is used to compute the new local state and the new output from the current functional input and the previous functional state.

Definition 3 (Local States and Transitions). *A local state s of an SAS module m is a variable assignment:*

$$s : in \cup out \cup loc \cup adapt\_in \cup adapt\_out \cup adapt\_loc \rightarrow Val$$

A local state s is called initial iff $s|_{loc} = init$, $s|_{adapt\_loc} = adapt\_init$ and $s|_V = undef$ for $V = in \cup out \cup adapt\_in \cup adapt\_out$.[1] An SAS module performs a local transition between two local states s and s', written $s \rightsquigarrow s'$, iff the following conditions hold:

$$s'|_{adapt\_loc} = adapt\_next\_state(s'|_{adapt\_in} \cup s|_{adapt\_loc})$$
$$s'|_{adapt\_out} = adapt\_next\_out(s'|_{adapt\_in} \cup s|_{adapt\_loc})$$
$$\forall\ 0 < j < i\,.\,s'|_{in} \cup s|_{loc} \cup s'|_{adapt\_in} \cup s|_{adapt\_loc} \not\models guard_j$$
$$s'|_{in} \cup s|_{loc} \cup s'|_{adapt\_in} \cup s|_{adapt\_loc} \models guard_i$$
$$s'|_{loc} = next\_state_i(s'|_{in} \cup s|_{loc})\ and\ s'|_{out} = next\_out_i(s'|_{in} \cup s|_{loc})$$

The state of an SAS is the union of the local states of the contained modules together with an evaluation of the system inputs and outputs. A system state is initial if all states of the contained modules are initial and the system input and output is undefined. A transition between two global states is performed in

---

[1] For a function f and a set M, $f|_M = \{(x, f(x)) \mid x \in M\}$ is the restriction of f to the domain M.

three stages. Firstly, each module reads its input either from another module's output of the previous cycle or from the system inputs in the current cycle. Secondly, each module synchronously performs a local transition. Thirdly, the modules directly connected to system outputs write their results to the output variables.

Definition 4 (Global States and Transitions). *A global state σ of an SAS consists of the local states $\{s_1, \ldots, s_n\}$ of the contained modules, where s_i is the state of $m_i \in M$, and an evaluation of the functional and adaptive inputs and outputs, i.e. $\sigma = s_1 \cup \ldots \cup s_n \cup ((input_a \cup input_d \cup output_a \cup output_d) \to Val)$. A global state σ is called initial iff all local states s_i for $i = 1, \ldots, n$ are initial and the system inputs and outputs are undefined. Two states σ and σ' perform a global transition, written $\sigma \to_{glob} \sigma'$, iff*

- *for all $x, y \in Var \setminus (input_d \cup input_a)$ with $conn_d(x) = y$ or $conn_a(x) = y$ it holds that $\sigma'(y) = \sigma(x)$, for all $x \in input_a$ and $y \in Var$ with $conn_a(x) = y$ it holds that $\sigma'(y) = \sigma'(x)$ and for all $x \in input_d$ and $y \in Var$ with $conn_d(x) = y$ it holds that $\sigma'(y) = \sigma'(x)$*
- *for all $s_j \in \sigma$ and for all $s_j' \in \sigma'$ it holds that $s_j \rightsquigarrow s_j'$*
- *for all $x \in Var$ and $y \in output_d$ with $conn_d(x) = y$ it holds that $\sigma'(y) = \sigma'(x)$ and for all $x \in Var$ and $y \in output_a$ with $conn_a(x) = y$ it holds that $\sigma'(y) = \sigma'(x)$*

A sequence of global states $\sigma^0 \sigma^1 \sigma^2 \ldots$ of an SAS is a path if σ^0 is an initial global state and for all $i \geq 0$ we have $\sigma^i \to_{glob} \sigma^{i+1}$. The set $Paths(SAS) = \{\sigma^0 \sigma^1 \sigma^2 \ldots \mid \sigma^0 \sigma^1 \sigma^2 \ldots$ is a path$\}$ constitutes the SAS semantics.

3   Verification

The properties to be verified for adaptive embedded systems can be classified according to whether they refer to adaptive, functional or both aspects. Moreover, one can distinguish between generic properties that are largely independent of the application and application specific properties. In the following, we will concentrate on generic properties of the adaptation behaviour.

As specification languages, we use the temporal logics CTL (computation tree logic) and LTL (linear time temporal logic) [6,18]. In both CTL and LTL, temporal operators are used to specify properties along a given computation path. For example, the formula $F\varphi$ states that φ eventually holds and $G\psi$ states that ψ invariantly holds. In CTL, every temporal operator must be immediately preceded by one of the path quantifiers A (for all paths) and E (at least one path). Thus, $AG\varphi$ and $EF\psi$ are CTL formulae stating that φ invariantly holds on all paths and ψ eventually holds on at least one path, respectively. LTL formulae always have the form $A\varphi$, where φ does not contain any path quantifiers. None of these two logics is superior to the other, i.e., there are specifications that can be expressed in LTL, but not in CTL, and vice versa. However, both are subsumed by the temporal logic CTL* [6,18].

SAS models can be verified directly by embedding them into a semantic representation of an interactive theorem prover such as Isabelle/HOL [12]. As a major advantage, interactive theorem provers do not suffer from the state explosion problem, as many properties can be verified without having to enumerate all possible states. On the other hand, it is often more convenient to employ automatic verification methods such as model checking, since using a theorem prover can be rather tedious. In the remainder of this section, we will therefore focus on the application of standard and specialised model checking procedures for the verification of SAS models.

3.1 System Transformations

As mentioned in the introduction, SAS models are usually not directly amenable to model checking due to their complexity. Sources of complexity are for instance unbounded data domains, the size of arithmetic constants or the mere size of the model. In order to reduce the runtime of the verification procedures, we perform a number of transformations on SAS models transparent to the user [2]. These transformations are formally verified to be property preserving using Isabelle/HOL.

To deal with unbounded data domains or large constants, we apply the concept of data domain abstraction [5]. Data values from a large or infinite domain are thereby mapped to a smaller finite domain using a homomorphic abstraction function, provided that the domain abstraction is compatible with the operations of the system. Alternatively, one may apply abstract interpretation based techniques [7] that overapproximate the effect of certain operations in the abstracted system and yield a conservative abstraction of the system behaviour. Hence, properties to be verified are abstracted such that an abstracted property implies the original property. As an example, consider a system input ranging over the integers. The integer domain may be reduced to the abstract domain $\{low, high\}$ such that an integer value v is mapped to low iff $v < 50$ and to $high$ iff $v \geq 50$. A constraint on the input like $input \geq 50$ is subsequently transformed to $input = high$ without loosing precision due to the suitably chosen abstraction.

Moreover, we restrict the model to those parts that are relevant for verifying the property under consideration. This means that we first remove all variables that are declared but never used in the model. Furthermore, we perform an analysis which variables of the system model and which associated parts influence the considered property. Unnecessary parts of the model can safely be removed. This technique is known as cone of influence reduction [6] in model checking of Boolean circuits.

SAS models also support reasoning about purely adaptive, purely functional or combined aspects of system models by separating functional from adaptive behaviour. Since model checking tools do in general not have any means to distinguish between functionality and adaptation, the generation of different verification problems from SAS models alleviates verification complexity. For purely adaptive properties, we generate verification output containing only the adaptive part of the models, i.e. adaptive variables and the associated transition functions.

Together with a system transformation, we provide a formal proof that the transformation is property preserving. This means that for a given SAS and a given property, the transformed system satisfies the transformed property if the original property is true in the original system. Our approach is based on translation validation techniques previously applied in compilers. We use a correctness criterion based on property preservation by simulation for the universal fragment of CTL*. We prove in the interactive theorem prover Isabelle/HOL [12] that for each transformation the transformed system simulates the original system and that the transformed property can be concretised to imply the original one. Then, validity of the transformation is established (cf. [2]).

3.2   Verification of Generic Properties by Model Checking

Most of the generic properties can be expressed in CTL, which allows us to employ standard model checking techniques. To verify such properties, we translate the reduced SAS model to the input description of the model checker. First of all, we want to verify that no module gets stuck in the default configuration 'off'. This can be expressed by the CTL formula $\mathsf{AG}(c = \mathit{off} \to \mathsf{EF}\, c \neq \mathit{off})$, where c stores the current configuration. The next specification is even stronger and asserts that every module can reach all configurations at all times: $\mathsf{AG}(\bigwedge_{i=1}^{n} \mathsf{EF}\, c = \mathit{config}_i)$. If this specification holds, the system is deadlock-free and no configuration is redundant. Moreover, a module must always be in one of the predefined configurations such that no inconsistent states can be reached: $\mathsf{AG}(\bigvee_{i=1}^{n} c = \mathit{config}_i)$.

Many application specific properties can also be verified using standard model checking techniques. On the one hand, these properties are concerned with the adaptation behaviour resulting from the concrete combination of different modules. As an example, one may verify that adaptation in one module leads to a particular configuration in another module after a certain number of cycles. If, for instance, the camera in the building automation system fails, the module *OccupancyDetection* will switch to configuration *MotionDetection* in the next cycle. On the other hand, application specific properties address the functionality of a system. For example, in the building automation scenario, one may verify that the occupancy of the room is determined correctly indepedent of the used configurations and the order of their activation.

3.3   Verification of Stability

As mentioned in the introduction, one of the most important properties of adaptation is stability [15]. Since adaptation in the considered class of systems is not controlled by a central authority, adaptation in one module may trigger further adaptations in other modules. While *finite* sequences of adaptations are usually intended, cyclic dependencies between the modules may lead to an *infinite* number of adaptations, which results in an unstable system. For this reason, it is important to verify that the configurations of a module eventually stabilise if the inputs do not change.

As stability can be expressed in LTL (but not in CTL), it can be verified using standard model checking procedures for LTL. However, model checking procedures for temporal logic formulae are not always as efficient as specialised verification procedures for certain properties. In particular, there are more efficient ways to check stability, as we will show in this section. Before we go into detail, we briefly describe the μ-calculus, which we will use as the basis of our approach. More detailed information on the μ-calculus can be found in [6,18].

In order to define the syntax and semantics of the μ-calculus, we need the notion of Kripke structures. In our implementation (see Section 4), SAS models are first translated to synchronous programs, which can then be compiled to symbolic descriptions of Kripke structures.

Definition 5 (Kripke structures). *Given a set of variables $\mathcal{V}$, a Kripke structure $\mathcal{K}$ is a labelled transition system $(\mathcal{S}, \mathcal{I}, \mathcal{R}, \mathcal{L})$, where $\mathcal{S}$ is the set of states, $\mathcal{I} \subseteq \mathcal{S}$ is the set of initial states, $\mathcal{R} \subseteq \mathcal{S} \times \mathcal{S}$ is the transition relation, and $\mathcal{L} : \mathcal{S} \to \mathscr{P}(\mathcal{V})$ is the labelling function that maps each state to a set of variables.*

The predecessors and successors of a set of states are used to define the semantics of the μ-calculus:

Definition 6 (Predecessors and Successors). *Given a Kripke structure $\mathcal{K} = (\mathcal{S}, \mathcal{I}, \mathcal{R}, \mathcal{L})$, the predecessors and successors of a set of states $Q \subseteq \mathcal{S}$ are defined as follows:*

- $\mathsf{pre}_\exists^{\mathcal{R}}(Q) := \{ s \in \mathcal{S} \mid \exists s' \in \mathcal{S}.(s, s') \in \mathcal{R} \wedge s' \in Q \}$
- $\mathsf{pre}_\forall^{\mathcal{R}}(Q) := \{ s \in \mathcal{S} \mid \forall s' \in \mathcal{S}.(s, s') \in \mathcal{R} \to s' \in Q \}$
- $\mathsf{suc}_\exists^{\mathcal{R}}(Q) := \{ s' \in \mathcal{S} \mid \exists s \in \mathcal{S}.(s, s') \in \mathcal{R} \wedge s \in Q \}$
- $\mathsf{suc}_\forall^{\mathcal{R}}(Q) := \{ s' \in \mathcal{S} \mid \forall s \in \mathcal{S}.(s, s') \in \mathcal{R} \to s \in Q \}$

Definition 7 (Syntax of the μ–Calculus). *Given a set of variables $\mathcal{V}$, the set of μ–calculus formulae Form_μ is defined as follows with $x \in \mathcal{V}$ and $\varphi, \psi \in \mathsf{Form}_\mu$:*

$$\mathsf{Form}_\mu := x \mid \varphi \wedge \psi \mid \varphi \vee \psi \mid \Diamond \varphi \mid \Box \varphi \mid \overleftarrow{\Diamond} \varphi \mid \overleftarrow{\Box} \varphi \mid \mu x.\varphi \mid \nu x.\varphi$$

Intuitively, a modal formula $\Diamond \varphi$ holds in a state iff φ holds in at least one successor state, and $\Box \varphi$ holds iff φ holds in all successor states. The operators $\overleftarrow{\Diamond}$ and $\overleftarrow{\Box}$ refer to the past (predecessors) instead of to the future (successors). Finally, the operators μ and ν denote least and greatest fixpoints, respectively. In order to define the semantics of the μ-calculus, we denote the subset of states satisfying a formula $\varphi \in \mathsf{Form}_\mu$ by $[\![\varphi]\!]_\mathcal{K}$.

Definition 8 (Semantics of the μ–Calculus). *Given a Kripke structure $\mathcal{K} = (\mathcal{S}, \mathcal{I}, \mathcal{R}, \mathcal{L})$, the semantics of the μ–calculus is defined as follows, where $\mathcal{K}_x^Q$ is the Kripke structure obtained from $\mathcal{K}$ by changing the states $s \in \mathcal{S}$ such that $x \in \mathcal{L}(s)$ holds iff $s \in Q$ holds:*

$[\![x]\!]_\mathcal{K} := \{ s \in \mathcal{S} \mid x \in \mathcal{L}(s) \}$ *for all* $x \in \mathcal{V}$

$[\![\varphi \wedge \psi]\!]_\mathcal{K} := [\![\varphi]\!]_\mathcal{K} \cap [\![\psi]\!]_\mathcal{K}$ $\qquad\qquad$ $[\![\varphi \vee \psi]\!]_\mathcal{K} := [\![\varphi]\!]_\mathcal{K} \cup [\![\psi]\!]_\mathcal{K}$

$[\![\Diamond \varphi]\!]_\mathcal{K} := \mathsf{pre}_\exists^{\mathcal{R}}([\![\varphi]\!]_\mathcal{K})$ $\qquad\qquad$ $[\![\Box \varphi]\!]_\mathcal{K} := \mathsf{pre}_\forall^{\mathcal{R}}([\![\varphi]\!]_\mathcal{K})$

$[\![\overleftarrow{\Diamond} \varphi]\!]_\mathcal{K} := \mathsf{suc}_\exists^{\mathcal{R}}([\![\varphi]\!]_\mathcal{K})$ $\qquad\qquad$ $[\![\overleftarrow{\Box} \varphi]\!]_\mathcal{K} := \mathsf{suc}_\forall^{\mathcal{R}}([\![\varphi]\!]_\mathcal{K})$

$[\![\mu x.\varphi]\!]_\mathcal{K} := \bigcap \{ Q \subseteq \mathcal{S} \mid [\![\varphi]\!]_{\mathcal{K}_x^Q} \subseteq Q \}$ $\qquad$ $[\![\nu x.\varphi]\!]_\mathcal{K} := \bigcup \{ Q \subseteq \mathcal{S} \mid Q \subseteq [\![\varphi]\!]_{\mathcal{K}_x^Q} \}$

The satisfying states of fixpoint formulae can be computed by fixpoint iteration: The states $[\![\mu x.\varphi]\!]_{\mathcal{K}}$ satisfying a least fixpoint formula $\mu x.\varphi$ are obtained by the iteration $Q_{i+1} := [\![\varphi]\!]_{\mathcal{K}_x^{Q_i}}$ starting with $Q_0 := \emptyset$. For greatest fixpoint formulae, the iteration starts with $Q_0 := \mathcal{S}$. In both cases, the sequence Q_i is monotonic (increasing for least fixpoints and decreasing for greatest ones).

An important characteristic of a μ-calculus formula is its *alternation-depth*, which is roughly speaking the number of interdependent fixpoints. For example, the formula $\mu y.\Box(\nu x.((y \vee \varphi) \wedge \Box x))$ has alternation-depth two, since the inner fixpoint depends on the outer one. A formula that does not contain interdependent fixpoints is *alternation-free*.[2] The importance of the alternation-depth stems from the fact that the complexities of all known model checking algorithms for the μ-calculus are exponential in it [18]. Regarding the above formula, this means that for each iteration of the outer fixpoint formula, the inner one has to be reevaluated.

Let us now return to the problem of stability checking. Suppose that φ_{in} holds iff the inputs of an SAS are stable for one unit of time. Moreover, let φ_{so} hold iff the state variables and the outputs are stable for one time unit. Then, the SAS is stable iff the LTL formula $\Phi :\equiv \mathsf{AG}(\mathsf{G}\varphi_{in} \rightarrow \mathsf{FG}\varphi_{so})$ holds. However, simply checking Φ by means of standard model checking procedures for LTL is not optimal, since the resulting μ-calculus formula is not alternation-free. The proof is based on the fact that Φ is equivalent to $\mathsf{A}(\mathsf{FG}\varphi_{in} \rightarrow \mathsf{FG}\varphi_{so})$. Given that φ_{in} holds on all states, we obtain the formula $\mathsf{AFG}\varphi_{so}$. This formula can be translated to the μ-calculus formula $\mu y.\Box(\nu x.((y \vee \varphi_{so}) \wedge \Box x))$ [13,18], which has has alternation-depth two (see above). In the following, we propose a solution that does not require the computation of interdependent fixpoints and turns out to be more efficient in practice. For that purpose, we need the notion of paths of a Kripke structure:

Definition 9 (Paths). *A path* $\pi \colon \mathbb{N} \rightarrow \mathcal{S}$ *of a Kripke structure* $\mathcal{K} = (\mathcal{S}, \mathcal{I}, \mathcal{R}, \mathcal{L})$ *is an infinite sequence of states such that* $(\pi(i), \pi(i+1)) \in \mathcal{R}$ *holds for all* $i \in \mathbb{N}$. *The set of all paths originating in a state* $s \in \mathcal{S}$ *is denoted by* $\mathsf{Paths}_{\mathcal{K}}(s)$.

We assume that the set of variables $\mathcal{V}$ consists of a set of input variables $\mathcal{V}_{in}$ and a set of state and output variables $\mathcal{V}_{so}$ such that $\mathcal{V}_{in} \cap \mathcal{V}_{so} = \emptyset$ holds. Moreover, we say that a path is steady w.r.t. a set of variables iff none of the variables changes its value after some point of time.

Definition 10 (Steadiness). *Given a Kripke structure* $\mathcal{K} = (\mathcal{S}, \mathcal{I}, \mathcal{R}, \mathcal{L})$, *a path* $\pi \colon \mathbb{N} \rightarrow \mathcal{S}$ *is steady from time* $k \in \mathbb{N}$ *w.r.t. a set of variables* $V \subseteq \mathcal{V}$ *iff the following holds:*

$$\mathsf{steady}_{\mathcal{K}}(\pi, k, V) :\Leftrightarrow \forall i \geq k.\mathcal{L}(\pi(i)) \cap V = \mathcal{L}(\pi(i+1)) \cap V$$

---

[2] As every CTL formula can be translated to an alternation-free μ-calculus formula [6,18], there is no need for specialised verification procedures in order to check the generic properties described in Subsection 3.2.

$\mathcal{L}(s_i)$: a b ab a ab

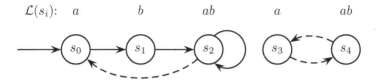

Fig. 3. Example for a Kripke structure

As an example, consider the Kripke structure shown in Figure 3 (dashed lines represent transitions of the restricted transition relation $\mathcal{R}'$ defined below). Since b holds on states s_1 and s_2, the path $s_0, s_1, s_2, s_2, \ldots$ is steady w.r.t. the set $\{b\}$ from time one. In contrast, the path $s_3, s_4, s_3, \ldots$ is not steady w.r.t. $\{b\}$, as b holds on state s_4, but not on state s_3.

Having defined the notion of steadiness, stability of a state and a Kripke structure can now be rephrased as follows:

Definition 11 (Stability). *Given a Kripke structure $\mathcal{K} = (\mathcal{S}, \mathcal{I}, \mathcal{R}, \mathcal{L})$, a state $s \in \mathcal{S}$ is stable iff we have:*

$$\mathsf{stable}_\mathcal{K}(s) :\Leftrightarrow \forall \pi \in \mathsf{Paths}_\mathcal{K}(s).\mathsf{steady}_\mathcal{K}(\pi, 0, \mathcal{V}_\mathsf{in}) \to \exists i \in \mathbb{N}.\mathsf{steady}_\mathcal{K}(\pi, i, \mathcal{V}_\mathsf{so})$$

Moreover, $\mathcal{K}$ is stable iff every reachable state of $\mathcal{K}$ is stable.

Consider again the Kripke structure of Figure 3 and assume that $\mathcal{V}_\mathsf{in} = \{a\}$ and $\mathcal{V}_\mathsf{so} = \{b\}$ holds. Then, the states s_0, s_1, and s_2 are stable as all paths originating in these states are either not steady w.r.t. $\mathcal{V}_\mathsf{in}$ or steady w.r.t. $\mathcal{V}_\mathsf{so}$. Since the path $s_3, s_4, s_3, \ldots$ is steady w.r.t. $\mathcal{V}_\mathsf{in}$ but not w.r.t. $\mathcal{V}_\mathsf{so}$, s_3 and s_4 are not stable.

In order to formulate stability as a μ-calculus formula without interdependent fixpoints, we first restrict the transition relation to those paths that are steady w.r.t. $\mathcal{V}_\mathsf{in}$ and do not contain any self-loops, i.e., we construct a Kripke structure $\mathcal{K}' = (\mathcal{S}, \mathcal{I}, \mathcal{R}', \mathcal{L})$ with

$$\mathcal{R}' := \{(s, s') \mid (s, s') \in \mathcal{R} \wedge s \neq s' \wedge \mathcal{L}(s) \cap \mathcal{V}_\mathsf{in} = \mathcal{L}(s') \cap \mathcal{V}_\mathsf{in}\}.$$

Then, it remains to check whether the paths of $\mathcal{K}'$ are steady w.r.t. $\mathcal{V}_\mathsf{so}$. As $\mathcal{R}'$ does not contain any self-loops, a path π is steady from time k iff $\pi(k)$ has no successors. Thus, a state $s \in \mathcal{S}$ is stable iff all paths originating in s are finite. In the μ-calculus, this can be expressed by the formula $\nu x.\Diamond x$, which holds in a state $s \in \mathcal{S}$ iff there exists at least one infinite path originating in s. Consequently, a Kripke structure $\mathcal{K}$ is stable iff $[\![\nu x.\Diamond x]\!]_{\mathcal{K}'}$ does not contain any reachable states. The latter are exactly the set $[\![\mu x.\chi_\mathcal{I} \vee \overleftarrow{\Diamond} x]\!]_\mathcal{K}$, where $\chi_\mathcal{I}$ is the characteristic function of $\mathcal{I}$, i.e., $[\![\chi_\mathcal{I}]\!]_\mathcal{K} = \mathcal{I}$. This leads to the following theorem:

Theorem 1. *A Kripke structure $\mathcal{K} = (\mathcal{S}, \mathcal{I}, \mathcal{R}, \mathcal{L})$ is stable iff $[\![\mu x.\chi_\mathcal{I} \vee \overleftarrow{\Diamond} x]\!]_\mathcal{K} \cap [\![\nu x.\Diamond x]\!]_{\mathcal{K}'} = \emptyset$ holds.*

As both fixpoint formulae are independent of each other, they can be evaluated separately, which significantly reduces the total number of fixpoint iterations.

In fact, if a Kripke structure is not stable, we do not even have to compute all reachable states. Given that the formula $\nu x.\Diamond x$ has already been evaluated, the fixpoint iteration for the least fixpoint formula can be aborted when a state is encountered that belongs to $[\![\nu x.\Diamond x]\!]_{\mathcal{K}'}$.

For the Kripke structure of Figure 3, we obtain $[\![\mu x.\chi_{\mathcal{I}} \vee \overleftarrow{\Diamond} x]\!]_{\mathcal{K}} = \{s_0, s_1, s_2\}$ with $\mathcal{I} = \{s_0\}$ and $[\![\nu x.\Diamond x]\!]_{\mathcal{K}'} = \{s_3, s_4\}$. Hence, the Kripke structure is stable.

4   Implementation and Experimental Results

4.1   Modelling Environment and Formal Representation

We integrated the MARS modelling concepts into the Generic Modelling Environment GME[3] [9], a tool for computer-aided software engineering, and developed a GME meta model for representing the MARS modelling concepts. Based on this meta model, concrete examples like our running example (see Figure 4) can be instantiated. GME automatically produces a model representation in XML format which is used as input for validation and verification as well as for code generation.

Besides formal verification of adaptation behaviour, MARS currently offers two further analyses for its validation. First, we support the simulation of adaptation behaviour and the visualisation of reconfiguration sequences using adaptation sequence charts ASC [21]. Second, it is possible to perform a probabilistic analysis of the adaptation behaviour [1]. For this purpose, the adaptation behaviour model is transformed into an equivalent hybrid component fault tree. The probability that a configuration of a module is activated can then be derived from the failure rates of sensors and actuators.

After the adaptation behaviour of a model has been successfully validated and verified, the functional behaviour can be integrated into the model. When the behaviour of the whole system is completely specified, code generation is possible. For simulation and code generation, we use MATLAB-Simulink,[4] the de facto standard in industrial development of embedded systems.

Moreover, we implemented a tool called AMOR (Abstract and MOdular verifieR) that reads XML output generated by GME and translates it to a formal representation based on SAS. SAS models are internally represented as immutable terms using Katja [11]. Additionally, we implemented the transformations described in Subsection 3.1 in order to make the models amenable to formal verification using model checking. The correctness of the transformations is established by automatically generating proof scripts for Isabelle/HOL [12]. AMOR also supports the translation of SAS models into a semantical representation of Isabelle/HOL, so that SAS models can be directly verified using theorem proving techniques. Alternatively, AMOR is able to generate code for symbolic model checkers. The generated code may contain only adaptive behaviour (for the verification of purely adaptive properties) or both adaptive and functional behaviour (for the verification of combined properties).

---

[3] http://www.isis.vanderbilt.edu/projects/gme/

[4] http://www.mathworks.com

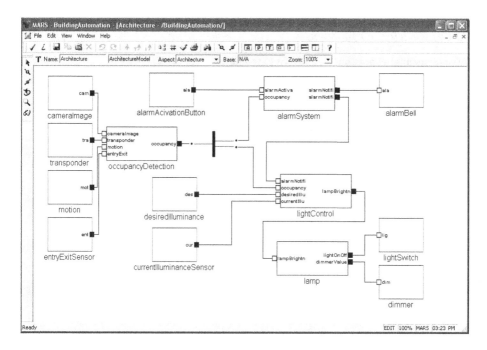

Fig. 4. Top level view of building automation example in GME

4.2   Verification

As model checking back-end, we use the Averest[5] framework, a set of tools for
the specification, implementation and verification of reactive systems [19]. In
Averest, a system is given in the synchronous programming language Quartz,
which is well-suited for describing adaptive systems obtained from SAS models.
In particular, as both are based on a synchronous semantics, SAS modules can be
easily mapped to threads in Quartz. Moreover, causality analysis of synchronous
programs can be used to detect cyclic dependencies that may occur if the quality
flow generated by an output is an input of the same module. Specifications can
be given in temporal logics as well as in the μ–calculus. To check stability, we
implemented the method described in Subsection 3.3 in Averest.

4.3   Evaluation of the Building Automation System

To evaluate our approach, we modelled the building automation example with
MARS, translated it to an SAS model using AMOR and generated a Quartz
program from this model. The resulting system contains 108 variables and has
approximately 1.5×10^{20} reachable states. As the first step, we checked the
generic specifications described in Subsection 3.2 for each module using Averest's
symbolic model checker. Each of these specifications could be checked in less

---

[5] http://www.averest.org

than one second. For example, we verified the following CTL formulae for the *OccupancyDetection* module:

$\mathsf{AG}(\texttt{occupancyDetection} = \texttt{off} \to \mathsf{EF}(\texttt{occupancyDetection} \neq \texttt{off}))$

$\mathsf{AG}(\mathsf{EF}(\texttt{occupancyDetection} = \texttt{camera}) \wedge \mathsf{EF}(\texttt{occupancyDetection} = \texttt{transponder}) \wedge$
$\quad \mathsf{EF}(\texttt{occupancyDetection} = \texttt{motion}) \wedge \mathsf{EF}(\texttt{occupancyDetection} = \texttt{entryExit}) \wedge$
$\quad \mathsf{EF}(\texttt{occupancyDetection} = \texttt{off}))$

$\mathsf{AG}(\texttt{occupancyDetection} = \texttt{camera} \vee \texttt{occupancyDetection} = \texttt{transponder} \vee$
$\quad \texttt{occupancyDetection} = \texttt{motion} \vee \texttt{occupancyDetection} = \texttt{entryExit} \vee$
$\quad \texttt{occupancyDetection} = \texttt{off})$

Additionally, we checked five application specific (functional) properties. For instance, the following formula states that if the light is available and the desired brightness is greater than zero then the light will be switched on ($\mathsf{AX}\varphi$ holds iff φ holds on all paths at the next point of time):

$$\mathsf{AG}(\texttt{lightQuality} = \texttt{available} \wedge \texttt{lampBrightness} > 0 \to \mathsf{AX}(\texttt{light} = \texttt{on}))$$

The application specific properties could also be checked in a few seconds, but the construction of the transition relation required significantly more time compared to the generic properties (92s instead of approx. 1s). This indicates that the separation of adaptive from functional behaviour considerably accelerates verification. As the second step, we checked stability of the system with LTL model checking and with the approach described in Subsection 3.3. LTL model checking requires a total number of 39 fixpoint iterations and takes 130s, whereas our approach only performs 9 iterations in less than one second.

5   Related Work

There are various approaches that integrate model-based design and formal verification in the development of *non*-adaptive systems. Most of them use an intermediate representation that aims at closing the gap between modelling and verification. The Rhapsody UML Verification Environment [17] supports the verification of UML models using the VIS model checker via an intermediate language called SMI. The authors of [22] propose an approach linking xUML, an executable subset of UML, and the SPIN model checker. They also propose transformations on the intermediate layer but do not prove them correct, since the intermediate representation has no formal semantics. The IF Toolset [3] integrates modelling in UML and SDL (Specification and Description Language) with different verification tools using the IF intermediate language. IF also supports a number of techniques to reduce the state space, e.g. elimination of irrelevant parts of a model, but the transformations are not explicitly verified. Furthermore, none of these approaches considers adaptation.

With respect to adaptive system development, most approaches concentrate either on modelling or on verification aspects. There are various approaches focussing on modelling self-managed dynamic software architectures; for a survey, consult [4]. However, only few of them deal with *predetermined dynamic software reconfiguration* [21] and consider the overall development process of adaptive embedded systems. The method described in [14] addresses the modelling of reconfiguration but omits verification aspects completely. In [24], the authors introduce a method for constructing and verifying adaptation models using Petri nets. However, specifying adaptation behavior using Petri nets is not an intuitive way to design complex industry sized systems like the ESP (Electronic Stability Program). Moreover, the notion of adaptivity is more coarse-grained than in our work, since it is restricted to three fixed types of adaptation.

Regarding verification of adaptive systems, linear time temporal logic is extended in [23] with an 'adapt' operator for specifying requirements on the system before, during and after adaptation. An approach to ensure correctness of component-based adaptation was presented in [8], where theorem proving techniques are used to show that a program is always in a correct state in terms of invariants. Initial work on the verification of MARS models can be found in [20]. In contrast to [20], the work presented in this paper supports the verification of both adaptive and functional aspects. Furthermore, the formal representation introduced in this work bridges the gap between modelling and verification techniques and integrates formal verification into the development process in a way transparent to the user. Additionally, [20] does not discuss specialised verification procedures for properties characteristic for adaptive systems such as stability.

6   Conclusion and Future Work

Although dynamic adaptation significantly complicates system design, it is frequently used as cost-efficient solution to increase dependability in safety-critical embedded systems. In this paper, we have presented an integrated framework for model-based development of adaptive embedded systems that supports intuitive modelling as well as efficient formal verification. It provides the developer with a user-friendly modelling method for specifying the system's adaptation behaviour and its interface to functional behaviour. It further allows to formally represent the semantics of the specified models close to the introduced modelling concepts. This enables us to express crucial system properties in a semantically exact manner. Based on the formal model, these properties can be verified using interactive theorem proving, symbolic model checking and specialised verification methods for adaptive embedded systems.

We are currently extending the modelling concepts for adaptation behaviour by integrating a configuration transition management. Moreover, we are working on additional techniques to reduce verification complexity for the application of model checking such as predicate abstraction. Additionally, we plan to support the development of distributed adaptive systems, where adaptation can be used to compensate for the failure of whole components.

References

1. Adler, R., Förster, M., Trapp, M.: Determining configuration probabilities of safety-critical adaptive systems. In: UbiSafe 2007, IEEE Computer Society Press, Los Alamitos (2007)
2. Blech, J.O., Schaefer, I., Poetzsch-Heffter, A.: Translation validation for system abstractions. In: RV 2007, Vancouver, Canada (2007)
3. Bozga, M., Graf, S., Ober, I., Ober, I., Sifakis, J.: The IF toolset. In: Bernardo, M., Corradini, F. (eds.) Formal Methods for the Design of Real-Time Systems. LNCS, vol. 3185, pp. 237–267. Springer, Heidelberg (2004)
4. Bradbury, J.S., Cordy, J.R., Dingel, J., Wermelinger, M.: A survey of self-management in dynamic software architecture specifications. In: WOSS 2004, pp. 28–33. ACM Press, Newport Beach, USA (2004)
5. Clarke, E.M., Grumberg, O., Long, D.E.: Model checking and abstraction. ACM Transactions on Programming Languages and Systems (TOPLAS) 16(5), 1512–1542 (1994)
6. Clarke, E.M., Grumberg, O., Peled, D.A.: Model Checking. MIT, London, England (1999)
7. Dams, D., Gerth, R., Grumberg, O.: Abstract interpretation of reactive systems. ACM Trans. Program. Lang. Syst. 19(2), 253–291 (1997)
8. Kulkarni, S.S., Biyani, K.N.: Correctness of component-based adaptation. In: Crnković, I., Stafford, J.A., Schmidt, H.W., Wallnau, K. (eds.) CBSE 2004. LNCS, vol. 3054, pp. 48–58. Springer, Heidelberg (2004)
9. Ledeczi, A., Maroti, M., Bakay, A., Karsai, G., Garrett, J., Thomason, C., Nordstrom, G., Sprinkle, J., Volgyesi, P.: The generic modeling environment. In: WISP 2001, Budapest, Hungary, IEEE Computer Society Press, Los Alamitos (2001)
10. Medvidovic, N., Taylor, R.N.: A classification and comparison framework for software architecture description languages. IEEE Transactions on Software Engineering 26(1) (2000)
11. Michel, P.: Redesign and enhancement of the Katja system. Technical Report 354/06, University of Kaiserslautern (October 2006)
12. Nipkow, T., Paulson, L.C., Wenzel, M.: Isabelle/HOL. LNCS, vol. 2283. Springer, Heidelberg (2002)
13. Niwiński, D.: Fixed points vs. infinite generation. In: LICS 1988, pp. 402–409. IEEE Computer Society Press, Washington, DC. (1988)
14. Rawashdeh, O.A., Lumpp Jr., J.E.: A technique for specifying dynamically reconfigurable embedded systems. In: IEEE Conference Aerospace, IEEE Computer Society Press, Los Alamitos (2005)
15. Schaefer, I., Poetzsch-Heffter, A.: Towards modular verification of stabilisation in self-adaptive embedded systems. In: Datta, A.K., Gradinariu, M. (eds.) SSS 2006. LNCS, vol. 4280, pp. 584–585. Springer, Heidelberg (2006)
16. Schaefer, I., Poetzsch-Heffter, A.: Using abstraction in modular verification of synchronous adaptive systems. In: Workshop on Trustworthy Software, Saarbrücken, Germany (2006)
17. Schinz, I., Toben, T., Mrugalla, Chr., Westphal, B.: The Rhapsody UML Verification Environment. In: SEFM, pp. 174–183 (2004)
18. Schneider, K.: Verification of Reactive Systems – Formal Methods and Algorithms. Texts in Theoretical Computer Science (EATCS Series). Springer, Heidelberg (2003)

19. Schneider, K., Schuele, T.: Averest: Specification, verification, and implementation of reactive systems. In: ACSD 2005, St. Malo, France (2005)
20. Schneider, K., Schuele, T., Trapp, M.: Verifying the adaptation behavior of embedded systems. In: SEAMS 2006, Shanghai, China, pp. 16–22. ACM Press, New York (2006)
21. Trapp, M., Adler, R., Förster, M., Junger, J.: Runtime adaptation in safety-critical automotive systems. In: SE 2007, ACTA, Innsbruck, Austria (2007)
22. Xie, F., Levin, V., Kurshan, R.P., Browne, J.C.: Translating software designs for model checking. In: FASE, pp. 324–338 (2004)
23. Zhang, J., Cheng, B.H.C.: Specifying adaptation semantics. In: WADS 2005, pp. 1–7. ACM, St. Louis, USA (2005)
24. Zhang, J., Cheng, B.H.C.: Model-based development of dynamically adaptive software. In: ICSE 2006, Shanghai, China, pp. 371–380. ACM Press, New York (2006)

Machine-Assisted Proof Support for Validation Beyond Simulink

Chunqing Chen, Jin Song Dong, and Jun Sun

School of Computing
National University of Singapore
{chenchun,dongjs,sunj}@comp.nus.edu.sg

Abstract. Simulink is popular in industry for modeling and simulating embedded systems. It is deficient to handle requirements of high-level assurance and timing analysis. Previously, we showed the idea of applying Timed Interval Calculus (TIC) to complement Simulink. In this paper, we develop machine-assisted proof support for Simulink models represented in TIC. The work is based on a generic theorem prover, Prototype Verification System (PVS). The TIC specifications of both Simulink models and requirements are transformed to PVS specifications automatically. Verification can be carried out at interval level with a high level of automation. Analysis of continuous and discrete behaviors is supported. The work enhances the applicability of applying TIC to cope with complex Simulink models.

Keywords: Simulink, Real-Time Specifications, Formal Verification, PVS.

1   Introduction

Simulink [18] is popular in industry for modeling and simulating embedded systems. It is deficient to handle requirements of high-level assurance and timing analysis. Formal methods have been increasingly applied to the development of embedded systems because of their rigorous semantics and powerful verification capability [15]. Previously, we showed the idea of applying Timed Interval Calculus (TIC) [10], a formal notation of real-time systems to complement Simulink [5]: an automatic translation from Simulink models to TIC specifications preserves the functional and timing aspects; important timing requirements can hence be formally validated by the well-defined TIC reasoning rules and the strong support of mathematical analysis in TIC.

Currently, the validation is accomplished by hand. When verifying complex Simulink models, it becomes difficult to ensure the correctness of each proof step and to manage all proof details manually. Thus, developing machine-assisted proof support is necessary and important to ease the analysis beyond Simulink.

Simulink models usually involve continuous dynamics, and important timing requirements often concern behavior over arbitrary (infinite) intervals. These features make the automated verification of Simulink models challenging. An

M. Butler, M. Hinchey, M.M. Larrondo-Petrie (Eds.): ICFEM 2007, LNCS 4789, pp. 96–115, 2007.

approach, i.e., model checking [6] has successfully handled finite state transition systems with its fully automatic proving process. Nevertheless the discretization abstraction of infinite state transition systems can decrease the accuracy when analyzing properties of continuous dynamics (e.g., space distance [22]). On the other hand, theorem proving [4] can directly deal with infinite state transition systems with powerful proof methods (e.g. mathematical induction). Higher order theorem proving systems such as PVS [24], HOL [11], and Isabelle [23] support expressive input forms and automated proof capabilities (e.g., automated linear arithmetic reasoning over natural numbers). A recently developed NASA PVS library [1] formalizes and validates integral calculus based on the work [8] that supports elementary analysis. The library has been successfully used to verify a practical aircraft transportation system [21] which involves complex continuous behavior. In this paper, we apply PVS as a framework to encode and verify the TIC models generated from Simulink. The NASA PVS library allows us to rigorously represent and analyze continuous Simulink models.

We firstly construct the TIC denotational semantic models and validate the TIC reasoning rules in PVS. Based on the encoding, we define a collection of PVS *parameterized types* which correspond to the TIC library functions of Simulink library blocks. The TIC specifications are automatically transformed into PVS specifications. The transformation preserves the hierarchical structure. We define a set of rewriting rules to simplify the proving process and keep certain detailed TIC semantic encodings transparent to users. Hence we can formally validate Simulink models at interval level with a high grade of automation: powerful proving capability (including automatic type checking) of PVS guarantees the correctness of each reasoning step; proofs at low level can be automatically discharged, mainly by the decision procedures on sets and the propositional simplifications over real numbers in PVS. We have successfully validated continuous and hybrid systems represented in Simulink against safety and bounded liveness requirements.

The rest of the paper is organized as follows. In section 2, we brief the work on representing Simulink models in TIC followed by an introduction of PVS. The encoding of the primary TIC semantics and reasoning rules is presented in Section 3. Section 4 defines the library of PVS parameterized types. In the next section, the transformation strategy is illustrated with a non-trivial hybrid control system. Section 6 shows the benefits of the rewriting rules and the facilities of our approach by formally validating the control system in PVS. Related works are discussed in section 7. Section 8 concludes the paper with future work.

2   Background

2.1   Simulink in Timed Interval Calculus (TIC)

A Simulink [18] model is a wired block diagram that specifies system behavior by a set of mathematical functions over time. A block can be either an elementary block or a wired block diagram for a sub-model. An *elementary block* denotes a primitive mathematical relationship over its inputs and outputs. Elementary blocks are generated from a rich set of Simulink *library blocks* by using the parameterization method. A *wire* depicts the dependency relationship between connected blocks. The source (destination) block can write (read) values to (from) a wire according to its *sample time* which is the execution rate of an elementary block during simulation. Simulink adopts *continuous time* as the unifying domain to support various systems (continuous, discrete or hybrid). Note that discrete systems behave piecewise-constantly continuously in Simulink.

Example 1. A brake control system is used as a running example to explain our idea and illustrate the results. The system aims to prevent a vehicle from over speeding by automatically enabling a brake device to decelerate the vehicle in time. The Simulink model is shown in Figure 1: each square box is an elementary library block, and each ellipse denotes an interface. The model consists of three subsystems, namely, subsystem *plant* depicting the physical speed behavior, subsystem *sensor* discretizing the speed, and subsystem *brake* controlling the brake device status based on the sensed speed. More details are provided in Section 5 where we translate the system with its requirements into PVS specifications, and here we select subsystem *sensor* to describe our previous work. The subsystem contains three components: two denote the interface (i.e., *speedS* and *speedR*), and block *detector* created from Simulink library block *ZeroOrderHold* stores the input value at each sample time point (the sample time is 1 second in the example) and keeps it till the next sample time point. Its simplified content is available in Figure 2.

We applied the Timed Interval Calculus (TIC) [10] to formally represent the Simulink denotational semantics, and developed a tool to automatically translate Simulink models into TIC specifications. The translation preserves the functional and timing aspects as well as the hierarchical structure [5].

TIC is set-theory based and reuses the Z [30] mathematical and schema notations. It extends the work in [17] by defining *interval brackets* to abstract time

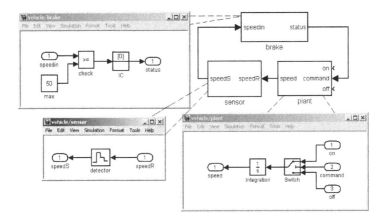

Fig. 1. The brake control system with its subsystems in Simulink

points and specifies properties at interval level. *Time domain* ($\mathbb{T}$) is non-negative real numbers, and *intervals* are continuous ranges of time points. In addition, α, ω, δ are *interval operators* in TIC to return the infimum, supremum and length of an interval. Note that they can be used to explicitly access endpoints. *Timed traces* defined in TIC are total functions of time to depict physical dynamics, and integration and differentiation have been rigorously defined in [9]. Each pair of interval brackets denotes a set of intervals during which an enclosed predicate holds at *all* time points. There are four *basic interval types* according to the endpoint inclusion. When the involvement of endpoints is unspecified, a *general interval type* is defined to cover all types of intervals. Hence system behavior can be modeled by predicates as relations over intervals. To manage the TIC specifications, *TIC schemas* are adopted: a TIC schema groups a collection of variables in the declaration part and constrains the relationships among the variables at the interval level in the predicate part. A set of well-defined TIC reasoning rules captures properties over sets of intervals and is used to verify complex systems.

We defined a set of *TIC library functions* to capture the denotational semantics of Simulink library blocks, i.e., mathematical functions between their inputs and outputs over time. Each TIC library function accepts a collection of arguments that correspond to Simulink library parameters, and returns a TIC schema that specifies the functionality of an instantiated library block. For example, function *ZOH* shown in Figure 2 preserves the sample time value (i.e., variable *st*) and describes the discrete execution in each sample time intervals (where interval brackets   represent a set of *left-closed, right-open* intervals).

The translation from Simulink models into TIC specifications is in a bottom-up manner. Elementary blocks are translated into TIC schemas by applying appropriate TIC library functions to relevant Simulink parameters. For example, schema *vehicle_sensor_detector* below is constructed by passing the sample time value to the *ZOH* function. Note that symbol "_" is used to retain the hierarchical order in Simulink models (*vehicle_sensor_detector* indicates that block *detector* is a component of system *sensor* which is a subsystem of system *vehicle*). Simulink diagrams are converted into TIC schemas. Specifically, the schemas declare each component as an instance of a TIC schema that represents the corresponding component, and each wire is expressed by an equation that consists of variables from the declaration. For example, schema *vehicle_sensor* in Figure 2 captures its three components and the connections.

2.2 Prototype Verification Systems (PVS)

PVS [24] is an integrated environment for formal specification and formal verification. The specification language of PVS is based on the classic typed, higher-order logic. Built-in types in PVS include *Boolean, real numbers, natural numbers* and so on. Standard predicate and arithmetic operations, such as conjunction (AND) and addition ($+$) on these types are also defined in PVS. Types can be defined starting from the built-in types using the type constructions. For example, *record* types are of the form $[\#a_1 : t_1, \ldots, a_n : t_n\#]$, where the a_i are named

```
Block {
  BlockType        SubSystem
  Name             "sensor"
  System {
    Block {
      BlockType    Inport
      Name         "speedR" }
    Block {
      BlockType    ZeroOrderHold
      SampleTime   "1"
      Name         "detector"}
    Block {
      BlockType    Outport
      Name         "speedS" }
    Line {
      SrcBlock     "speedR"
      DstBlock     "detector" }
    Line {
      SrcBlock     "detector"
      DstBlock     "speedS" }}}
```

$$ZOH : \mathbb{T} \to \mathbb{P}[In_1, Out : \mathbb{T} \to \mathbb{R};\ st : \mathbb{T}]$$

$$\forall t : \mathbb{T} \bullet ZOH(t) = [In_1, Out : \mathbb{T} \to \mathbb{R};\ st : \mathbb{T} \mid$$
$$st > 0 \wedge st = t \wedge$$
$$(\exists k : \mathbb{N} \bullet \alpha = k * st \wedge \omega = (k+1) * st) =$$
$$(Out = In_1(\alpha))]$$

$$vehicle\_sensor\_detector \,\widehat{=}\, ZOH(1)$$

$$\underline{\quad vehicle\_sensor \quad\quad\quad\quad}$$
$$speedR, speedS : \mathbb{T} \to \mathbb{R}$$
$$detector : vehicle\_sensor\_detector$$

$$\mathbb{I} = (speedR = detector.In1)$$
$$\mathbb{I} = (detector.Out = speedS)$$

Fig. 2. The *sensor* subsystem in Simulink and TIC

record accessors and the t_i are types. Elements of a record can be referenced by using the projection functions: 'a_i for instance.

Functions in PVS are total, and partial functions are supported by *predicate subtype* and *dependent types* which restrict the function domain. In addition, functions in PVS can share the same name as long as the types of their parameters are different. PVS specifications are organized into *theories*, which usually contain type declaration, axioms and lemmas. A theory can be reused in other theories by means of the *importing* clause.

The PVS theorem prover offers powerful primitive proof commands that are applied interactively under user guidance. Proofs are performed within a *sequent calculus* framework. A proof obligation consists of a list of assumptions $A_1, \ldots, A_n$ as *antecedents* and a list of conclusions $B_1, \ldots, B_m$ as *consequents*. It denotes that the conjunction of the assumptions implies the disjunction of the conclusions.

Primitive proof commands deal with propositional and quantifier rules, induction, simplification and so on. Users can introduce proof *strategies* which are constructed from the basic proof commands to enhance the automation of verification in PVS.

PVS contains many built-in theories as libraries which provide much of the mathematics needed (e.g. *real numbers* and *set*) to support verification. Recently, the NASA PVS library[1] extends the existing PVS libraries by providing means of modeling and reasoning about hybrid systems. The library formalizes the mathematical element analysis such as *continuity*, *differentiation* and *integration*, and contains many lemmas and theorems for manipulating these notations.

---

[1] It is available at http://shemesh.larc.nasa.gov/fm/ftp/larc/PVS-library/pvslib.html

3 Primitive Encoding of TIC

We construct the TIC denotational semantic model in PVS in a bottom up fashion. Each subsection below corresponds to a PVS theory. Complex theories can hence reuse the simple ones. The encoding forms a foundation to generate PVS specifications for TIC specifications and support TIC verification by formalizing and validating all TIC reasoning rules in PVS[2].

Time and Interval. The Time domain is represented by the PVS built-in type, i.e., *nnreal* for nonnegative real numbers. `Time: TYPE = nnreal`.

An interval is a tuple made up by two elements: The first specifies the interval type, i.e., `InterVal_Type: TYPE = {OO, CO, OC, CC}` (e.g., CO indicates that the interval type is left-closed, right-open). The second is a pair which denotes the starting point (*stp*) and the ending point (*etp*).

```
GenInterVal: TYPE = [invt: Interval_Type, {stp: Time, etp: Time | stp <= etp}]
```

The *general* interval type (*II*) captures the relation between basic interval types and endpoints. For example, when the interval is both-closed ($gi'1 = CC$), its ending point can equal the starting point ($gi'2'1 <= gi'2'2$ where symbols '1 and '2 are the projection operators of PVS for accessing a tuple). Note that when an interval is *general*, it can be one of the four basic interval types. We apply the *predicate subtype* mechanism of PVS to define basic interval types (e.g. the type of left-closed, right-open intervals, *COInterVal* is given below).

```
II: TYPE = { gi : GenInterVal | (gi'1 = CC and (gi'2)'1 <= (gi'2)'2) or
      ((gi'1 = OO or gi'1 = OC or gi'1 = CO) and (gi'2)'1 < (gi'2)'2)};
COInterVal: TYPE = {i: II | i'1 = CO}
```

Timed Trace and Interval Operators. The type of timed traces is a total function from time to real number. The interval operators, α, ω, and δ are functions from interval to time (We show the encoding of α here due to the size limit, and variable *i* is a variable of type *II*).

```
Trace: TYPE = [Time -> real];
ALPHA(i): Time = (i'2)'1;   % i: var II
```

Expressions and Predicates. Though time and intervals are abstracted in TIC specifications for concise modeling, they need to be explicitly accessible when interpreting expressions and predicates in PVS.

A basic element of TIC can have different types. Specifically, it can be a timed trace, an interval operator, or a constant. To *unify* different types into one type during the encoding, function *LIFT* is defined in the way which accepts three kinds of parameters (where the second and third parameters are the time and intervals respectively) and returns real numbers. Note that this is accomplished

---

[2] The complete PVS specifications of the TIC semantics and the reasoning rules are available at http://www.comp.nus.edu.sg/~chenchun/PVSTIC

by the *overloading* mechanism of PVS. For example, a timed trace is evaluated at a given time point while a constant is unchanged regardless of the time points and intervals.

```
LIFT(x)(t, i): real = x;        % t : var Time, x: var real
LIFT(tr)(t, i): real = tr(t);   % tr : var Trace
LIFT(tm)(t, i): real = tm(i);   % tm : var Term
```

Expressions in TIC are constructed by applying mathematical operators (including calculus operators, e.g., "$\int$") to the basic elements and other sub-expressions. As time and intervals are required by the *LIFT* function, they are passed down to the constituent sub-expressions. The *propagation* stops when all the sub-expressions are primitive elements. Similarly way is applied to analyze predicates which are formed from applying mathematical relation over expressions or predicate logic on constituent sub-predicates. We show below the type declarations of the expressions and predicates, a subtraction expression, and a disjunctive predicate:

```
TExp: TYPE = [Time, II -> real];
-(el, er)(t, i): real = el(t, i) - er(t, i);   % el, er: var TExp
TPred: TYPE = [Time, II -> real];
or(pl, pr)(t, i): bool = pl(t, i) or pr(t, i); % pl, pr: var TPred;
```

An important feature of TIC is that the elemental calculus operations are supported, in particular *integration* and *differentiation*. Their definitions are formalized precisely in the NASA PVS library, and hence we can directly represent them in PVS. For example, the integral operation of TIC encoded below uses function *Integral* from the NASA PVS library where expressions *el* and *er* denote the bounded points of an integral.

```
TICIntegral(el, er, tr)(t, i): real = Integral(el(t, i), er(t, i), tr);
```

Quantification in TIC is supported in PVS by defining a *higher-order function* from the range of the bounded variable to the quantified predicate. For example, if the range of the bounded variable is natural numbers, and then the type of the quantification is from natural numbers to TIC predicate. Note that the following representation adopts the existence quantifier (*EXISTS*) of PVS directly.

```
QuaPred: TYPE = [nat -> TPred]; qp: var QuaPred;
exNat(qp)(t, i): bool = EXISTS (k: nat): (qp(k)(t, i))
```

TIC Expressions. A TIC expression is either formed by the interval brackets or a set operation on other TIC expressions. We present the way of encoding the interval brackets and concatenation operation below as they are defined special in TIC. Other TIC expressions can be constructed by using the PVS *set* theory.

In TIC, a pair of interval brackets denotes a set of intervals during which an enclosed predicate holds *everywhere*. Firstly function *t_in_i* detects if a time point is within an interval according to the interval type. Next, function *Everywhere?* checks whether a predicate is true at all time points within an interval. Lastly the set of desired intervals is formed by using the set constructor in PVS. For example, the definition of the interval brackets ($\llbracket\,\rrbracket$) which return a set of general intervals is shown below:

```
t_in_i(t, i): bool = (i'1 = 00 and t > (i'2)'1 and t < (i'2)'2) or
  (i'1 = OC and t > (i'2)'1 and t <= (i'2)'2) or
  (i'1 = CO and t >= (i'2)'1 and t < (i'2)'2) or
  (i'1 = CC and t >= (i'2)'1 and t <= (i'2)'2);
Everywhere?(pl, i): bool = forall t: t_in_i(t, i) => pl(t, i);
AllS(pl): PII =  {i | Everywhere?(pl, i)}; % PII: TYPE = setof[II];
```

In TIC, concatenations are used to model sequential behavior over intervals. A concatenation requires the connected intervals to meet *exactly*, i.e., no gap and no overlap. Note that there are eight correct ways to concatenate two intervals based on the inclusion of their endpoints. Here we just consider one situation that a set of left-closed, right-open intervals is the result of linking two sets of left-closed, right-open intervals: the absence of gap is guaranteed by the equivalence of the connected endpoints (i.e., the ending point of *co*1 equals the starting point of *co*2), and the overlap is excluded by restricting the types of the connected endpoints (i.e., *co*1 is right-open while *co*2 is left-closed).

```
concat(cos1, cos2): PCC = {c : COInterVal |    % cos1 is a set of CO intervals
  exists (co1 : cos1), (co2: cos2):            % cos2 is a set of CO intervals
    OMEGA(co1) = ALPHA(co2) and ALPHA(co1) = ALPHA(c) and OMEGA(co2) = OMEGA(c)}
```

Based on the above encoding, we can formalize and validate the TIC reasoning rules in PVS. They capture the properties of sets of intervals and the concatenations and used to verify TIC specifications at the level of intervals. We have checked all rules stated in [10, 2], and hence they can be applied as proved lemma when verifying TIC specifications of Simulink models in PVS in the following sections.

4   Constructing PVS Library Types

Simulink library blocks create elementary blocks by instantiating parameters specific values. Similarly, we previously defined a set of TIC library function to represent the library blocks. To be specific, an instantiation of a library block is modeled as an application of a TIC library function. In this section, we construct a library of PVS parameterized types for the TIC library functions. In this way we produce concise PVS specifications for Simulink elementary blocks, and keep a clear correspondence of mathematical functions denoted in different notations.

A TIC library function accepts a set of parameters and returns a TIC schema, where the inputs, outputs and relevant parameters of an elementary block are defined as variables with their corresponding types, and the functional and timing aspects are captured by constraints among the variables.

We represent each TIC library function by a PVS *parameterized* type, which declares a type based on parameters. The parameters are the ones of a TIC library function, and the declared type is a *record type*. The record type models a generated schema by a TIC library function: variables are the *record accessors*;

and each predicate is represented by a constraint restricting the type domain of
an associated accessor which is used to construct a set of records. Note that there
are two categories of schema predicates: one indicates the relations between the
declared variables and the TIC function parameters (or constants); the other
captures the relations between variables denoting the inputs and outputs of
Simulink blocks. For the first category of predicates, they constrain the domains
of the corresponding variables; and the predicates of the second category restrict
the domains of the outputs.

Taking TIC library function *ZOH* from Section 2.1 as an example, the PVS
library type, *ZOH* below represents a record type that contains three accessors,
i.e. *st*, *In*1 and *Out*. The TIC predicates constrain the type domains of relevant
accessors. To be specific, the first two predicates (that belong to the first category) are the criteria for assigning sample time value correctly, and the last
predicate (which satisfies the second category) is used to express the behavior
of timed trace *Out*. Note that the PVS library type closes to the TIC library
function in terms of the structure (where operator "o" is a function composition
defined in PVS).

```
ZOH (t: Time): TYPE = [# st : {temp: Time | temp > 0 AND temp = t},
   In1: Trace,
   Out: {temp: Trace |
      COS(exNat(lambda(k: nat): LIFT(ALPHA) = LIFT(k) * LIFT(st) AND
                                LIFT(OMEGA) = (LIFT(k) + LIFT(1)) * LIFT(st)))
      = COS(LIFT(temp) = (LIFT(In1) o LIFT(ALPHA)))} #]
```

Continuous library blocks are important in Simulink modeling. They are
directly represented in TIC with the well-defined operators [9] on elementary
analysis. Using the recently developed NASA PVS library, these features can be
preserved in PVS. For example, a continuous Simulink library block *Integrator*
that performs an integration operation over its input is modeled formally in the
TIC library function *Integrator*:

$$Integrator : \mathbb{R} \to \mathbb{P}[IniVal : \mathbb{R}; \ In_1 : \mathbb{T} \to \mathbb{R}; \ Out : \mathbb{T} \nrightarrow \mathbb{R}]$$

$$\forall init : \mathbb{R} \bullet Integrator(init) =$$
$$[IniVal : \mathbb{R}; \ In_1 : \mathbb{T} \to \mathbb{R}; \ Out : \mathbb{T} \nrightarrow \mathbb{R} \mid IniVal = init \land$$
$$Out(0) = IniVal \land \mathbb{I} = \{\!|Out(\omega) = Out(\alpha) + \int_\alpha^\omega In_1|\!\}]$$

Operator $\nrightarrow$ in the TIC specification indicates that the output is continuous.
We retain this feature explicitly by function *continuous* from the NASA PVS
library (specifically, *continuous(temp)* in the set constraint below). Note that
PVS variable *fullset* denotes all valid intervals and maps to the TIC symbol, $\mathbb{I}$.

```
Integrator (init: real): TYPE = [# IniVal: {temp: real | temp = init},
   In1: Trace,
   Out: {temp: Trace | temp(0) = IniVal and continuous(temp) and
      fullset = AllS((LIFT(temp) o LIFT(OMEGA)) = (LIFT(temp) o LIFT(ALPHA)) +
                     TICIntegral(LIFT(ALPHA), LIFT(OMEGA), In1))}           #]
```

We found it useful to formalize functions as type declarations instead of conventional functions, although the second seems more intuitive. The reason is that

type information is available to the PVS prover, and hence we can minimize the number of type correctness conditions generated which are side effects of proof steps during the type checking in PVS. The benefit has also been investigated by Stringer-Calvert et al. [27]. They applied PVS to prove Z refinements for a compiler development. Their work focused on supporting partial functions of Z in PVS, however the way of handling schemas was missing. As we will show in the following sections, representing schemas as record types can facilitate both transformation and verification of TIC specifications.

5   Transformation of TIC Specifications

In this section, we present a strategy to transform TIC specifications which represent both Simulink models and requirements. The transformation preserves the hierarchical structure and has been implemented in Java for the automation.

5.1   Transforming TIC Schemas of Simulink Models

A Simulink model is a wired block diagram, and a block can be another wired block diagram. This hierarchical structure modeling feature eases the challenge of handling large scale systems. In the TIC specifications of Simulink models, using schemas as types is the way to preserve the hierarchical structure. When verifying these TIC specifications in PVS, it is important and necessary to retain the same hierarchical structure: on the one hand, we can support large scale systems in PVS, on the other hand the diagnostic information obtain at the level of PVS can be reflected back to the level of Simulink. The goal is achieved by using the record type of PVS as illustrated below.

The TIC specifications of Simulink models are TIC schemas and can be classified into two groups. One group represents the elementary blocks, and each schema is formed by an application of a TIC library function with relevant Simulink parameters. The transformation of this type of schemas is direct because of the PVS library types defined in the previous section. Namely, each schema is converted to a PVS record type which is an application of an appropriate PVS library type (i.e., the parameterized record type). The selection criterion is the name of the TIC library function by the one-to-one relationship between the TIC library functions and the PVS library types. For example, schema *vehicle_sensor_detector* of elementary block *detector* in Figure 1 is transformed to the following PVS specification:

$$vehicle\_sensor\_detector \mathrel{\widehat{=}} ZOH(1)$$

```
vehicle_sensor_detector: TYPE = ZOH(1);
```

The other group represents (sub)diagrams. A schema of this group models the diagram components in the declaration part and the connections in the predicate part. Taking the brake control system (see Figure 1) as an example, the whole system is made up of three subsystem, where each is represented by a variable of schema type, and the wires between components are expressed as equalities in terms of intervals.

$$
\begin{array}{|l|}
\hline
\_\,vehicle \rule[-0.5ex]{0pt}{2ex}\\
\hline
\quad plant : vehicle\_plant;\ \ sensor : vehicle\_sensor;\ \ brake : vehicle\_brake\\
\hline
\quad \mathbb{I} = \llbracket plant.speed = sensor.speedR \rrbracket\\
\quad \mathbb{I} = \llbracket sensor.speedS = brake.speedin \rrbracket\\
\quad \mathbb{I} = \llbracket brake.status = plant.command \rrbracket\\
\hline
\end{array}
$$

Similar to the way of dealing with the first group, each schema is transformed into a PVS record type. However, the difference is that the predicates constrain *all* accessors together rather then *some* accessors. The main reason is that unlike Simulink elementary blocks which denote relationships between inputs and outputs, the predicates of Simulink diagrams denote the connections among components, and it is thus difficult to determine which accessor should be constrained, especially when the wires form a cycle. For example, if we adopt the previous way, one possible PVS specification of schema *vehicle* is below:

```
vehicle: TYPE = [# plant: vehicle_plant,
  sensor: {temp: vehicle_sensor |
       fullset = AllS(LIFT(temp'speedR) = LIFT(plant'speed))},
  brake: {temp: vehicle_brake |
       fullset = AllS(LIFT(temp'speedin) = LIFT(sensor'speedS) AND
       fullset = AllS(LIFT(temp'status) = LIFT(plant'command))}     #]
```

It is not hard to observe that above PVS specification forces a dependency relation among three subsystems, and the correspondence between the PVS type declaration and the TIC library function is loose. To solve the problem, we apply the *predicate subtype* mechanism of PVS to define a set of records which represent the schema variables as accessors and satisfy the restrictions denoted by the schema predicates. In this way the transformed PVS specifications follow closely the schemas. Regarding the previous example, the schema is converted to the following PVS type declaration:

```
vehicle: TYPE = { temp: [#
  plant: vehicle_plant, sensor: vehicle_sensor, brake: vehicle_brake #] |
  fullset = AllS(LIFT(temp'plant'speed) = LIFT(temp'sensor'speedR)) AND
  fullset = AllS(LIFT(temp'sensor'speedS) = LIFT(temp'brake'speedin)) AND
  fullset = AllS(LIFT(temp'brake'status) = LIFT(temp'plant'command))     }
```

We remark that representing TIC schemas by the PVS record types supports the popular modeling technique in Z that uses schemas as types. As shown in the above PVS specification, the projection function (') acts like the selection operator (.) in Z to access a component. We remark that our way is different from Gravell and Pratten [12] who discussed some issues on embedding Z into both PVS and HOL. They interpreted Z schemas as Boolean functions of record types and it is thus difficult to handle the case where schemas declared as types.

5.2   Transforming Requirements

Requirements are predicates formed from the TIC specifications of Simulink models. They are directly converted into PVS *theorem* formulas based on the PVS specifications of the TIC schemas. With the primitive encoding of TIC semantics mentioned in Section 3, the way of transforming requirements is similar to the one analyzing schema predicates explained in the previous section. Below we skip details of the transformation due to the page limit, and provide the transformed PVS specifications of two requirements of the brake control system. They are used to illustrate the verification of TIC specifications in the next section.

One requirement checks the computational accuracy of the sensed speed. Namely, at any time the sensor should measure the speed within an accuracy of 10 meters/second. The TIC predicate and the translated PVS specification (where the used PVS variables such as *plant* can be found in Appendix B) are given below respectively.

$Approximation == \forall\, v : vehicle \bullet \mathbb{I} = \{t | v.sensor.speedS - v.plant.speedR| \leq 10\}$

```
Approximation: THEOREM forall (v: vehicle): fullset =
  AllS(LIFT(v'sensor'speedS) - LIFT(v'plant'speed) <= LIFT(10) AND
      LIFT(v'sensor'speedS) - LIFT(v'plant'speed) >= LIFT(-10));
```

Another requirement concerns the response time within which the brake device should respond. To be specific, if an interval of which the length is more than 1 second and during which the speed in the plant is not less than 50 meters/second, the brake must be enabled within 1 second and keep on till the end. The requirement is represented by the TIC predicate followed by the transformed PVS specifications:

$$Response == \forall\, v : vehicle \bullet \{v.plant.speed \geq 50 \wedge \delta > 1\} \subseteq$$
$$\{\delta < 1\} \frown \{v.brake.status = 1\}$$

```
Response: THEOREM forall (v: vehicle): subset?(
  CCS(LIFT(v'plant'speed) >= LIFT(50) AND LIFT(DETLA) > LIFT(1)),
  concat( COS(LIFT(DELTA) < LIFT(1)),
         CCS(LIFT(v'brake'status) = LIFT(1))));
```

We have demonstrated the strategy to automatically transform system design and requirements into PVS specifications. Important issues about different ways to represent TIC schemas have been discussed as well. The transformation preserves the hierarchical structure denoted in TIC specifications. In other words, systems specified in three notations (i.e. Simulink, TIC, and PVS) share the same viewpoint of structure. This feature improves the traceability when analyzing systems in different formalisms, for example, verifying TIC specifications in PVS can follow a similar proving procedure in TIC.

6   Validation Beyond Simulink in PVS

After transforming system designs and requirements into PVS specifications, we can formally verify Simulink models at the interval level (by the encoded TIC reasoning rules) with a high grade of automation (by powerful proving support of PVS). In this section, we first define and validate a set of rewriting rules dedicated for Simulink modeling features to make verification more automated, followed by an illustration of verifying the brake control system to show that our developed tool supports the validation beyond Simulink such as dealing with open systems and checking timing properties.

6.1   Rewriting Rules for Simulink

Wires in Simulink models are represented by equations in TIC. Each equation consists of two timed traces that denote the connected block ports. When verifying TIC specifications in PVS, it is often to replace one timed trace by another when they both are in an equation. However, the substitution could be tedious in PVS since we need to expand the TIC semantic encoding thoroughly to make both time and interval explicitly for allowing the PVS prover to automatically discharge the proof obligation. To simplify the process as well as keep the detailed encoding transparent to users, we define a set of rewriting rules to easily handle the replacement of two equivalent timed traces. For example, rule *BB_ge_sub* substitutes two timed traces *tr1* and *tr2* over an inequality at the interval level.

```
BB_ge_sub: LEMMA forall (tr1, tr2, tr3: Trace):
   fullset = AllS(LIFT(tr1) = LIFT(tr2)) =>
   AllS(LIFT(tr1) > LIFT(tr3)) = AllS(LIFT(tr2) > LIFT(tr3));
```

Time domain of discrete systems in Simulink is decomposed into a sequence of left-closed, right-open intervals. We can hence define rewriting rules to facilitate the analysis of the discrete Simulink models. For example, rule *CO_to_All* states that for a predicate that is interval operator free[3], if it holds on *all* sample intervals (a *sample interval* is a left-close, right-open interval of which the endpoints are a pair of adjacent sample time points.), it is true in *any* interval. We remark that the rule is useful to check safety requirements of discrete systems.

```
st: var Time; tp: TPred;
CO_to_All: LEMMA st > 0 AND No_Term?(tp) =>
   subset?(COS(exNat( lambda(k: nat): LIFT(ALPHA) = LIFT(k) * LIFT(st) AND
                                      LIFT(OMEGA) = (LIFT(k) + LIFT(1)) * LIFT(st))),
           COS(tp))
   => fullset = AllS(tp);
```

6.2   Reasoning About the Brake Control System

The brake control system is *open* as the exact function of the acceleration change is difficult to known. Simulink can check functional behavior for just closed systems by simulation. Moreover, timing requirements are difficult to specify in Simulink. In the following, we show how our approach can formally validate the nontrivial system with a high level of automation.

---

[3] We define PVS function *No_Term?* to check if the predicate is dependent on the interval endpoints or interval length.

Adding Environment Assumptions. When analyzing open physical environment, it is often that the exact functions of environment variables is unknown while loose information is available such as the ranges of environment inputs. The loose information can be easier modeled as constraints in TIC than in Simulink, and we can hence check the open systems represented in Simulink with the new constraints. For example, the range of the acceleration (the output of block *switch* in Figure 1) is known as below: input port *on* which denotes the value when the brake is enabled has a range between -10 and 0 $meters/second^2$; input port *off* which indicates the acceleration when the brake is disabled has a range from 0 to 10 $meters/seond^2$. The loose information is thus expressed by the following TIC predicate as well as the corresponding PVS specification.

$$InputAssump == \forall\, v : vehicle \bullet$$
$$\mathbb{I} = [\![-10 \leq v.plant.on \leq 0]\!] \wedge \mathbb{I} = [\![0 \leq v.plant.off \leq 10]\!]$$

```
InputAssump: LEMMA FORALL (v: vehicle):
        fullset = AllS(LIFT(v'plant'on) >= LIFT(-10) AND
                       LIFT(v'plant'on) <= LIFT(0))
    AND fullset = AllS(LIFT(v'plant'off) >= LIFT(0) AND
                       LIFT(v'plant'off) <= LIFT(10))
```

Checking the Approximation Requirement. The requirement concerns the functional behavior. It involves the analysis of continuous dynamics (e.g., the vehicle speed is the integration of the acceleration.), and it requires the checking over *all* types of intervals. The reasoning process is sketched below[4]:

1. We apply the rewriting rule, i.e., *CO_to_All* to reduce the type of intervals to be checked. Namely, we only need to observe the behavior over the sample intervals instead of all types of intervals. This is motivated by the discrete components, i.e., block *detector* is discrete in the *sensor* subsystem.
2. By the functionality of block *detector* (specified by the *ZOH* type defined in Appendix A) and the connection within the *vehicle* system and its *sensor* subsystem, we need to compare the output value of subsystem *plant* at the beginning of a sample interval and other values at *all* time points in the sample interval. The PVS *skolemization instantiation* mechanism allows to replacing all time points by an arbitrarily fixed time point, so we can just analyze the output values within a both-closed interval formed by two time points, i.e., the beginning endpoint and the fixed time point.
3. Since variable *speed* of subsystem *plant* is the output of continuous block *integration*, the analysis of continuous dynamics is needed. Based on the assumption of the environment encoded early, we can apply a lemma from the NASA PVS library to show that the difference of the speed at two specific time points mentioned in Step 2 is between -10 and 10. The lemma named *Integral_bound* relates the bound of the integration of a function and the bound of the function over a closed interval.

---

[4] The complete verification of both requirements in PVS is available at `http://www.comp.nus.edu.sg/~chenchun/brakecontrol`

```
Integral_bound: LEMMA a < b AND Integrable?(a,b,f) AND
           (FORALL (x: Closed_interval(a,b)): m <= f(x) AND f(x) <= M )
      IMPLIES m*(b-a) <= Integral(a,b,f) AND Integral(a,b,f) <= M*(b-a)
```

In the above analysis, the rewriting rules and the powerful proving capability of PVS facilitate the verification, and the NASA PVS library enhances the capability of our tool to handle continuous dynamics.

Checking the Response Requirement. Verifying Simulink models against timing requirements is non-trivial: the models usually involve continuous dynamics; and the timing requirements often investigate system behavior over arbitrary (infinite) intervals. Here we demonstrate how a typical timing requirement, *response* requirement of the brake control system can be validated.

The requirement involves all three subsystems, where subsystem *sensor* acts as a converter to pass the sensed speed to the brake. Note that the detector updates its output only at sample time points. The verification thus becomes nontrivial as each endpoint of an arbitrary interval may not be a sample time point. We adopt the *proof by exhaustion* method to solve the difficulty. An informal proof procedure is given below:

Firstly, we show that any arbitrary interval can be classified into one of *finite* cases. The following lemma, *Endpoints_general_form* states that given a positive sample time (ST), the interval endpoints can be expressed in a uniform format. The lemma has been checked correctly in PVS. Therefore we can group all intervals into *four* cases according to the values assigned to variables n and q (either 0 or positive real number).

```
Endpoints_general_form: LEMMA FORALL (i: II):
   EXISTS (m, p: nat), (n, q: nnreal): n < ST AND q < ST AND
     ALPHA(i) = m * ST + n AND OMEGA(i) = p * ST + q;
```

Next, we check that the validity of the *response* requirement in all cases. We consider the case where the intervals consist of multiple sample intervals as the basic case, as variables n and q are 0. Other types of intervals from the left three cases can be formed by appending an interval which lasts less than one sample time to the front or the back of a multiple sample intervals.

Lemma *Mult_Sample_Intervals* is defined specially for the basic case, and it facilitates the analysis over other three cases. The lemma allows a proof over a multiple sample intervals to be accomplished by reasoning about sub-proofs over every constituent sample interval. To be specific, the lemma checks the consequence relation between two predicates $(tp1$ and $tp2)$ which both are interval operator free. Note that by the skolemization instantiation method of PVS, we can only check the proof over one sample interval instead of every sample interval, and hence reduce the complexity of proving the lemma correctness.

```
Mult_Sample_Intervals: LEMMA No_Term?(tp1) AND No_Term?(tp2) AND x < y =>
    ((FORALL (k: {n: nat | x <= n AND n < y}):
        subset?( COS( tp1 AND LIFT(ALPHA) = LIFT(k) * LIFT(ST) AND
                      LIFT(OMEGA) = LIFT(k) * LIFT(ST)), COS(tp2)))
   => subset?( COS( tp1 AND LIFT(ALPHA) = LIFT(x) * LIFT(ST) AND
                    LIFT(OMEGA) = LIFT(y) * LIFT(ST)), COS(tp2)));
```

We remark that the lemma is generic to be applied to other systems which involve *periodical* behavior. For example, it can check the *exportable interval properties* defined in Interval Temporal Logic [20] which is a linear-time temporal logic with a discrete model of time.

The verification of the requirement is nontrivial: initial proof without using auxiliary lemmas takes more than 1000 steps. The complexity can be reduced by half after applying five proved lemmas: Four of five represent the validity of the requirement over four cases mentioned above according to lemma *Endpoints_general_form*, and the fifth captures the behavior over the primitive interval (i.e., the requirement holds everywhere in the interval of which the starting point is a sample time point and the interval length is not longer than one sample time). The reason for the decrease is that using lemmas we can save proof steps in many repeated sub-proofs.

Besides the method, proof by exhaustion, used here, we have also applied other powerful methods, such as *proof by contradiction* and *proof by induction* to verify safety requirements of continuous and hybrid Simulink models.

7 Related Works

Recently, there are a number of works on reasoning about Simulink models. Meenakshi et al. [19] used a model checker to analyze single-rate discrete Simulink models. Tripakis et al. [29] applied synchronous programming language *Lustre* to support multi-rate discrete Simulink models. Tiwari et al. [28] discretizing differential equations denoted by Simulink models into difference equations to construct discrete transition systems. Different from theirs our approach can directly represent and analysis continuous Simulink models. Gupta et al. [13] developed a tool to increase the modeling capability of Simulink. The tool emphasized on checking functional behavior which is also the main concern of the works mentioned previously, and hence timing analysis lack support. Jersak et al. [16] translated Simulink models into SPI models for timing analysis, although the translation abstracts the functional aspect. In contrast, our approach supports the validation over functional and timing behavior.

There were two preliminary works on supporting TIC using theorem provers. Dawson and Goré [7] validated TIC reasoning rules in Isabelle/HOL [23]. But the encoding of TIC semantics is incomplete, and it is hence difficult to support verification of TIC in general. Cerone [2] described many axioms on interpreting TIC expressions and predicates. However, the interpretation of the *concatenation* operator differed from the original [10], and his work dealt with just five reasoning rules. Our approach encoded the complete TIC semantics and handled all TIC reasoning rules in PVS. Some researchers have investigated the machine-assistant proof for a similar formal notation, Duration Calculus (DC) [31]. Skakkebaek and Shankar [26] developed a proof checker upon PVS, and Heilmann [14] applied Isabelle to support the mechanized proof. Chakravorty and Pandya [3] digitized a subclass of DC (i.e. Interval Duration Calculus) into another subclass for just discrete systems. As DC and its extensions [33, 32] describe systems behavior without explicit reference to absolute time, they are limited to represent the constraints which are relevant to the values of interval endpoints. For example, the function of Simulink library block *Zero Order Hold* relies on specific sample time points. We remark that continuous behavior which is usually involved in Simulink models lacks of support in above works on TIC and DCs. For example, the *integral* function is either ignored or captured by a few axioms of limited properties. This is different from ours, as our approach can handle the analysis of continuous behavior.

8   Conclusion

In this paper, we extended our previous work which applied TIC to capture functional and timing aspects of Simulink diagrams as well as preserve the hierarchical structure. We developed a tool based on PVS to support the machine-assisted proofs for the Simulink models represented in TIC. A strategy has been implemented in Java to automatically transform the TIC specifications to PVS specifications. The transformed PVS specifications follow closely the hierarchical structured denoted by TIC specifications. Hence we can relate the diagnostic information of validation at the level of PVS to the level of Simulink.

We define a set of rewriting rules to simply the proving process and capture special characteristics of Simulink modeling. With the support of the NASA PVS library, we can directly analyze continuous dynamics which are usually involved in Simulink models. Validation in our framework can be carried out at the interval level with a high grade of automation. Open systems which are not checkable in Simulink can be reasoned about by specifying assumptions in TIC. Powerful mathematical proof methods (e.g. proof by induction) are useful to verify timing requirements (of safety and bounded liveness) beyond Simulink.

Currently, we are enhancing our framework in several directions. One is to develop graphical user interface (GUI) on top of the framework so as to facilitate the usability of our framework: transformation or proving can be executed by clicking buttons, and systems modeled in different notations can be shown in a better layout with colors to highlight the correspondence. Another is to improve the automation of the validation. Though verification of complex Simulink models is challenging, we are constructing more rewriting rules for special features of specific domain (e.g. hybrid control systems, the primary domain of Simulink modeling), and developing more PVS strategies to simplify the proving process. Extending the framework to support real-time systems development [25] of other formal notations is also one of our goals in the future.

Acknowledgements

We thank Ricky W. Butler for the help on using the NASA PVS library in the beginning. We are also grateful for the valuable comments from Anders P. Ravn, Chenchao Zhou, and Jeremy Dawson about the related work..

References

1. Butler, R.W.: Formalization of the integral calculus in the pvs theorem prover. Technical report, NASA Langley Research Center, Hampton, Virginia (October 2004)
2. Cerone, A.: Axiomatisation of an interval calculus for theorem proving. Electr. Notes Theor. Comput. Sci. 42 (2001)
3. Chakravorty, G., Pandya, P.K.: Digitizing interval duration logic. In: Ball, T., Jones, R.B. (eds.) CAV 2006. LNCS, vol. 4144, pp. 167–179. Springer, Heidelberg (2006)
4. Chang, C.-L., Lee, R.C., Lee, R.C.-T.: Symbolic Logic and Mechanical Theorem Proving. Academic Press, Inc., London (1997)
5. Chen, C., Dong, J.S.: Applying Timed Interval Calculus to Simulink Diagrams. In: Liu, Z., He, J. (eds.) ICFEM 2006. LNCS, vol. 4260, pp. 74–93. Springer, Heidelberg (2006)
6. Clarke, E.M., Grumberg, O., Long, D.E.: Model checking and abstraction. ACM Trans. on Prog. Lang. and Sys.s 16(5), 1512–1542 (1994)
7. Dawson, J.E., Goré, R.: Machine-checking the timed interval calculus. In: Sattar, A., Kang, B.-H. (eds.) AI 2006. LNCS (LNAI), vol. 4304, pp. 95–106. Springer, Heidelberg (2006)
8. Dutertre, B.: Elements of mathematical analysis in PVS. In: von Wright, J., Harrison, J., Grundy, J. (eds.) TPHOLs 1996. LNCS, vol. 1125, pp. 141–156. Springer, Heidelberg (1996)
9. Fidge, C.J., Hayes, I.J., Mahony, B.P.: Defining differentiation and integration in Z. In: ICFEM 1998, pp. 64–73 (1998)
10. Fidge, C.J., Hayes, I.J., Martin, A.P., Wabenhorst, A.: A Set-Theoretic Model for Real-Time Specification and Reasoning. In: Jeuring, J. (ed.) MPC 1998. LNCS, vol. 1422, pp. 188–206. Springer, Heidelberg (1998)
11. Gordon, M.J.C., Melham, T.F.: Introduction to HOL: A theorem proving environment for higher order logic. Cambridge University Press, Cambridge (1993)
12. Gravell, A.M., Pratten, C.H.: Embedding a formal notation: Experiences of automating the embedding of z in the higher order logics of pvs and hol. In: Grundy, J., Newey, M. (eds.) TPHOLs 1998. LNCS, vol. 1479, pp. 73–84. Springer, Heidelberg (1998)
13. Gupta, S., Krogh, B.H., Rutenbar, R.A.: Towards formal verification of analog designs. In: ICCAD 2004, pp. 210–217 (2004)
14. Heilmann, S.T.: Proof Support for Duration Calculus. PhD thesis, Department of Information Technology, Technical University of Denmark (1999)
15. Henzinger, T.A., Sifakis, J.: The embedded systems design challenge. In: Misra, J., Nipkow, T., Sekerinski, E. (eds.) FM 2006. LNCS, vol. 4085, pp. 1–15. Springer, Heidelberg (2006)
16. Jersak, M., Cai, Y., Ziegenbein, D., Ernst, R.: A transformational approach to constraint relaxation of a time driven simulation model. In: Futatsugi, K., Mizoguchi, F., Yonezaki, N. (eds.) ISSS 2003. LNCS, vol. 3233, pp. 137–142. Springer, Heidelberg (2004)
17. Mahony, B.P., Hayes, I.J.: A case-study in timed refinement: A mine pump. IEEE Transactions on Software Engineering 18(9), 817–826 (1992)
18. The MathWorks. Simulink - Simulation and Model-based Design - Using Simulink Version 6 (2004)
19. Meenakshi, B., Bhatnagar, A., Roy, S.: Tool for translating simulink models into input language of a model checker. In: Liu, Z., He, J. (eds.) ICFEM 2006. LNCS, vol. 4260, pp. 606–620. Springer, Heidelberg (2006)

20. Moszkowski, B.C.: A complete axiomatization of interval temporal logic with infinite time. In: LICS 2000, pp. 241–252 (2000)
21. Muñoz, C., Carreño, V., Dowek, G.: Formal analysis of the operational concept for the Small Aircraft Transportation System. In: REFT 2006, pp. 306–325 (2006)
22. Muñoz, C., Carreño, V., Dowek, G., Butler, R.W.: Formal verification of conflict detection algorithms. I. Jour. on Soft. Tools for Tech. Trans. 4(3), 371–380 (2003)
23. Nipkow, T., Paulson, L.C., Wenzel, M.: Isabelle/HOL — A Proof Assistant for Higher-Order Logic. Springer, Heidelberg (2002)
24. Owre, S., Rushby, J.M., Shankar, N.: PVS: A Prototype Verification system. In: Kapur, D. (ed.) CADE-11. LNCS, vol. 607, pp. 748–752. Springer, Heidelberg (1992)
25. Rischel, H., Cuéllar, J., Møk, S., Ravn, A.P., Wildgruber, I.: Development of safety-critical real-time systems. In: Bartosek, M., Staudek, J., Wiedermann, J. (eds.) SOFSEM 1995. LNCS, vol. 1012, pp. 206–235. Springer, Heidelberg (1995)
26. Skakkebæk, J.U., Shankar, N.: Towards a duration calculus proof assistant in pvs. In: Langmaack, H., de Roever, W.-P., Vytopil, J. (eds.) FTRTFT 1994. LNCS, vol. 863, pp. 660–679. Springer, Heidelberg (1994)
27. Stringer-Calvert, D.W.J., Stepney, S., Wand, I.: Using pvs to prove a z refinement: A case study. In: Jones, C.B. (ed.) FME 1997. LNCS, vol. 1313, pp. 573–588. Springer, Heidelberg (1997)
28. Tiwari, A., Shankar, N., Rushby, J.M.: Invisible Formal Methods for Embedded Control Systems. Proceedings of the IEEE 91(1), 29–39 (2003)
29. Tripakis, S., Sofronis, C., Caspi, P., Curic, A.: Translating discrete-time simulink to lustre. Trans. on Embedded Computing Sys. 4(4), 779–818 (2005)
30. Woodcock, J., Davies, J.: Using Z: Specification, Refinement and Proof. Prentice Hall International, Englewood Cliffs (1996)
31. Zhou, C.C., Hoare, C.A.R., Ravn, A.P.: A calculus of durations. Information Processing Letters 40, 269–276 (1991)
32. Zhou, C.C., Li, X.S.: A mean value calculus of durations. In: A classical mind: essays in honour of C. A. R. Hoare, Prentice-Hall International, Englewood Cliffs (1994)
33. Zhou, C.C., Ravn, A.P., Hansen, M.R.: An extended duration calculus for hybrid real-time systems. In: Hybrid Systems, pp. 36–59. Springer, Heidelberg (1993)

A   PVS Library Types of the Brake Control System

```
ZOH(t: Time): TYPE = [# st: {temp: Time | temp > 0 and temp = t}, In1: Trace,
    Out: {temp: Trace | COS(exNat(lambda (k: nat): LIFT(ALPHA) = LIFT(k) * LIFT(st) AND
                                      LIFT(OMEGA) = (LIFT(k) + LIFT(1)) * LIFT(st)))
                = COS(LIFT(temp) = (LIFT(In1) o LIFT(ALPHA)))} #]

Integrator(x: real): TYPE = [# IniVal: {temp: real | temp = x}, In1: Trace,
    Out: {temp: Trace| temp(0) = IniVal AND
                    AllTrue((LIFT(temp) o LIFT(OMEGA)) = (LIFT(temp) o LIFT(ALPHA))
                                    + TICIntegral(LIFT(ALPHA), LIFT(OMEGA), In1)) AND
                    continuous(temp)} #]

Switch_G(t: Time, x: real): TYPE = [# st: {temp: Time | temp = t},
    TH: {temp: real | temp = x}, In1, In2, In3: Trace,
    Out: {temp: Trace |
      IF st = 0 THEN AllS(LIFT(In2) > LIFT(TH)) = AllS(LIFT(temp) = LIFT(In1)) AND
                AllS(LIFT(In2) <= LIFT(TH)) = AllS(LIFT(temp) = LIFT(In3))
      ELSE COS(exNat(lambda (k: nat): LIFT(ALPHA) = LIFT(k) * LIFT(st) AND
                                      LIFT(OMEGA) = (LIFT(k) + LIFT(1)) * LIFT(st)))
          = COS( ((LIFT(In2) o LIFT(ALPHA)) > LIFT(TH) =>
                LIFT(temp) = (LIFT(In1) o LIFT(ALPHA)))
              AND ((LIFT(In2) o LIFT(ALPHA)) <= LIFT(TH) =>
                LIFT(temp) = (LIFT(In3) o LIFT(ALPHA))))
      ENDIF} #];
```

```
Relation_GE(t: Time): TYPE = [# st: {temp: Time | temp = t}, In1, In2: Trace,
   Out: {temp: BTrace |
     IF st = 0 THEN AllS(LIFT(In1) >= LIFT(In2)) = AllS(LIFT(temp) = LIFT(1)) AND
                    AllS(LIFT(In1) < LIFT(In2)) = AllS(LIFT(temp) = LIFT(0))
     ELSE COS(exNat(lambda (k: nat): LIFT(ALPHA) = LIFT(k) * LIFT(st) AND
                                     LIFT(OMEGA) = (LIFT(k) + LIFT(1)) * LIFT(st)))
         = COS( ((LIFT(In1) o LIFT(ALPHA)) >= (LIFT(In2) o LIFT(ALPHA))=>
                  LIFT(temp) = LIFT(1))
                AND
                ((LIFT(In1) o LIFT(ALPHA)) < (LIFT(In2) o LIFT(ALPHA)) =>
                  LIFT(temp) = LIFT(0)))
     ENDIF}  #];

InitCond(t: Time, x: real): TYPE = [# st: {temp: Time | temp = t},
   IniVal: {temp: real | temp = x}, In1: Trace,
   Out: {temp: Trace |
          IF st = 0 THEN subset?(AllS(LIFT(ALPHA) = LIFT(0)),
                                 AllS((LIFT(temp) o LIFT(0)) = LIFT(IniVal)))
                     AND  subset?(AllS(LIFT(ALPHA) > LIFT(0)),
                                 AllS(LIFT(temp) = LIFT(In1)))
          ELSE COS(LIFT(ALPHA) = LIFT(0) AND LIFT(OMEGA) = LIFT(st)) =
               COS(LIFT(temp) = LIFT(IniVal))
            AND COS(exNat1(lambda (k: posint): LIFT(ALPHA) = LIFT(k) * LIFT(st) AND
                                     LIFT(OMEGA) = (LIFT(k) + LIFT(1)) * LIFT(st)))
               = COS(LIFT(temp) = (LIFT(In1) o LIFT(ALPHA)))
          ENDIF}  #];

Constant(x: real): TYPE = [# IniVal: {IniVal: real | IniVal = x},
   Out: {temp: Trace| AllTrue(LIFT(temp) = LIFT(IniVal))}  #];
```

B   Transformed PVS Specifications of the Brake Control System

For subsystem *brake*:

```
vehicle_brake_max: TYPE = Constant(50);
vehicle_brake_check: TYPE = Relation_GE(0);
vehicle_brake_IC: TYPE = InitCond(0, 0);
vehicle_brake: TYPE = {temp: [# speedin, status: Trace,
     max: vehicle_brake_max, check: vehicle_brake_check, IC: vehicle_brake_IC #] |
        fullset = AllS(LIFT(temp'speedin) = LIFT(temp'check'In1)) AND
        fullset = AllS(LIFT(temp'max'Out) = LIFT(temp'check'In2)) AND
        fullset = AllS(LIFT(temp'check'Out) = LIFT(temp'IC'In1)) AND
        fullset = AllS(LIFT(temp'IC'Out) = LIFT(temp'status))}
```

For subsystem *sensor*:

```
vehicle_sensor_detector: TYPE = ZOH(1);
vehicle_sensor: TYPE = {temp: [# speedS, speedR: Trace,
     detector: vehicle_sensor_detector #] |
        fullset = AllS(LIFT(temp'speedR) = LIFT(temp'detector'In1)) AND
        fullset = AllS(LIFT(temp'detector'Out) = LIFT(temp'speedS))}
```

For subsystem *plant*:

```
vehicle_plant_Integration: TYPE = Integrator(0);
vehicle_plant_Switch: TYPE = Switch_G(0, 0);
vehicle_plant: TYPE = {temp: [# on, off, command, speed: Trace,
     Switch: vehicle_plant_Switch, Integration: vehicle_plant_Integration #] |
        fullset = AllS(LIFT(temp'on) = LIFT(temp'Switch'In1)) AND
        fullset = AllS(LIFT(temp'command) = LIFT(temp'Switch'In2)) AND
        fullset = AllS(LIFT(temp'off) = LIFT(temp'Switch'In3)) AND
        fullset = AllS(LIFT(temp'Switch'Out) = LIFT(temp'Integration'In1)) AND
        fullset = AllS(LIFT(temp'Integration'Out) = LIFT(temp'speed))}
```

For whole system *vehicle*:

```
vehicle: TYPE = { temp: [# plant: vehicle_plant, sensor: vehicle_sensor,
     brake: vehicle_brake #] |
        fullset = AllS(LIFT(temp'plant'speed) = LIFT(temp'sensor'speedR)) AND
        fullset = AllS(LIFT(temp'sensor'speedS) = LIFT(temp'brake'speedin)) AND
        fullset = AllS(LIFT(temp'brake'status) = LIFT(temp'plant'command))}
```

VeSTA: A Tool to Verify the Correct Integration of a Component in a Composite Timed System[*]

Jacques Julliand, Hassan Mountassir, and Emilie Oudot

LIFC - Laboratoire d'Informatique de l'Université de Franche-Comté
16, route de Gray, 25030 Besançon Cedex, France
Tel.: +33 (0)3 81 66 66 51, Fax: +33 (0)3 81 66 64 50
{julliand,mountass,oudot}@lifc.univ-fcomte.fr

Abstract. VeSTA is a push-button tool for checking the correct integration of a component in an environment, for component-based timed systems. By correct integration, we mean that the local properties of the component are preserved when this component is merged into an environment. This correctness is checked by means of a so-called divergence-sensitive and stability-respecting timed τ-simulation, ensuring the preservation of all linear timed properties expressed in the logical formalism MITL (Metric Interval Temporal Logic), as well as strong non-zenoness and deadlock-freedom. The development of the tool was guided by the architecture of the OPEN-KRONOS tool. This allows, as additional feature, an easy connection of the models considered in VeSTA to the OPEN-CAESAR verification platform, and to the OPEN-KRONOS tool.

Keywords: τ-simulation, integration of components, timed systems, preservation of linear-time properties.

1 Motivations

Model-checking is an attractive automatic verification method to ensure the correctness of models of systems. However, it is well-known that this method has difficulties to handle large-sized models, in particular when treating models involving timing constraints. Component-based modeling is a method often used to model timed systems. First, it consists in decomposing the system into a set of sub-systems, called components. Next, each component is modeled and the interactions between them are specified. The complete model is obtained by putting together all these components with respect to their interactions. With such a modeling, two kinds of properties can be checked to ensure the correctness of the model: global properties concerning the behavior of the complete model, and local properties concerning the behavior of one or some components. For both kind of properties, verification by model-checking is usually performed on

---

[*] This work has been partially funded by the ANR-06-SETI-017 TACOS project (Trustworthy Assembling of Components: from requirements to specification). VeSTA is available at the following URL: http://lifc.univ-fcomte.fr/~oudot/VeSTA

M. Butler, M. Hinchey, M.M. Larrondo-Petrie (Eds.): ICFEM 2007, LNCS 4789, pp. 116–135, 2007.

the complete model, and thus can become difficult if the size of the model is too large.

We propose to use an alternative method for the verification of local properties of the components: integration of components. Integration of components is an incremental development method. It consists, for a local property L of a component C, in checking L only on C. Model-checking is here applicable due to the generally small size of the components. Obviously, L has to be preserved when C is integrated in an environment E. When using the classic parallel composition operator $\|$ between components, the preservation of local safety properties of C on $C\|E$ is ensured for free. This is not the case for local liveness properties.

Simulation relations are a way to ensure preservation of properties. They have already been used in the untimed case for this purpose. For instance, [1] defines the refinement of transition systems as a kind of τ-simulation, which ensures the preservation of LTL properties. In the timed case, a time-abstracting simulation is defined in [2], but does not preserve timed properties. Timed simulation is defined in [3], but does not consider the possible internal activity of the systems (internal activity is a main barrier for the preservation of liveness properties). A timed ready simulation is defined in [4], but does not allow to preserve liveness properties. To our knowledge, there is no simulation relation for timed systems, which handles internal activity of the systems, and also preserves liveness properties. Therefore, we defined in [5] a *divergence-sensitive and stability-respecting (DS) timed τ-simulation* for timed components expressed as timed automata [6] and proved it can ensure the preservation of all linear timed properties which can be expressed in the logical formalism MITL [7], thus in particular linear liveness and bounded liveness properties. Strong non-zenoness and deadlock-freedom are also preserved by the relation. That is, if C simulates $C\|E$ with respect to this relation, all linear local timed properties of C are preserved on $C\|E$.

The tool VeSTA (**Ve**rification of **S**imulations for **T**imed **A**utomata) was developed to automate the verification of the DS timed τ-simulation. More precisely, VeSTA considers component-based timed systems, developed incrementally by integration of components, where each component is modeled as a timed automaton. It allows to check that local properties of a component (or group of components) of the system are preserved during its integration with other components of this system. The architecture of the tool was inspired by the one of the OPEN-KRONOS tool [8]. Thus, as OPEN-KRONOS, VeSTA benefits of libraries which provide an efficient symbolic representation for networks of timed automata. This choice also allows to connect the models considered in VeSTA to OPEN KRONOS, and also to the verification platform OPEN-CAESAR[9].

The structure of the paper is the following. In section 2, we recall some background on timed systems, i.e., on the formalisms which are used in VeSTA for the modeling of timed systems and their properties. This section also introduces the divergence-sensitive and stability-respecting timed τ-simulation, and its preservation abilities. Section 3 presents the tool VeSTA: its architecture, the algorithms which are implemented and its graphical user interface. In section 4, we illustrate the interest of VeSTA by using it to verify incrementally properties of a case study concerning a production cell. Section 5 presents some additional features of the tool. Finally, section 6 contains the conclusion and exhibits some future developments for VeSTA.

2   Incremental Verification of Timed Systems

We present here the preliminary notions that we consider concerning component-based timed systems. First, we introduce timed automata which we use to model timed components, and the composition operator we use to assemble these components. Then, we present the simulation relation we defined for timed automata and recall previous results concerning the properties that it preserves during incremental development, and in particular, during integration of components.

2.1   Modeling Timed Systems

Since their introduction in [6], timed automata are amongst the most studied models for timed systems. They are finite automata with real-valued variables called clocks, to model time elapsing.

Clock valuations and clock constraints. Let X be a set of clocks. A clock valuation over X is a mapping $v : X \to \mathbb{R}^+$, associating to each clock in X a value in $\mathbb{R}^+$. We note $\mathbf{0}$ the valuation assigning the value 0 to each clock in X. Given a clock valuation v and $t \in \mathbb{R}^+$, $v + t$ is the valuation obtained by adding t to the value of each clock in v. Given $Y \subseteq X$, the dimension-restricting projection of v on Y, written $v|_Y$, is the valuation over Y only containing the values in v of clocks in Y. The reset in v of the clocks in Y, written $[Y := 0]v$, is the valuation in which all clocks in Y are reset to zero, while the value of other clocks remains unchanged.

A clock constraint over X is a set of clock valuations over X. The set $\mathcal{C}_{df}(X)$ of diagonal-free clock constraints[1] over X is defined by the following grammar:

$$g ::= x \sim c \mid g \wedge g \mid true$$

where $x \in X$, $c \in \mathbb{N}$ and $\sim \in \{<, \leq, =, \geq, >\}$. Diagonal-free clock constraints do not allow comparison between clocks such as $x - y \sim c$. Note that a clock constraint defines a convex X-polyhedron. We note **zero** the X-polyhedron defined by $\bigwedge_{x \in X} v(x) = 0$. The dimension-restricting projection and reset operation can be directly extended to clock constraints. The backward diagonal projection of the X-polyhedron ζ defines a X-polyhedron $\swarrow\zeta$ such that $v' \in \swarrow\zeta$ if $\exists t \in \mathbb{R}^+ \cdot v' + t \in \zeta$. The forward diagonal projection of ζ defines a X-polyhedron $\nearrow\zeta$ such that $v' \in \nearrow\zeta$ if $\exists t \in \mathbb{R}^+ \cdot v' - t \in \zeta$. Given $c \in \mathbb{N}$, the extrapolation of ζ w.r.t. c, written $\text{Approx}_c(\zeta)$, is the smallest polyhedron $\zeta' \supseteq \zeta$ defined intuitively

---

[1] We restrict ourselves to this kind of clocks constraints to ensure the correctness of the construction of the symbolic representation of TA [10].

as follows: lower bounds of ζ greater than c are replaced by c, and upper bounds greater than c are ignored. All these operations preserve convexity.

Timed Automata. Let *Props* be a set of atomic propositions. A timed automaton (TA) over *Props* is a tuple $A = \langle Q, q_0, \Sigma, X, T, \text{Invar}, L \rangle$ where Q is a finite set of locations, $q_0 \in Q$ is the initial location, Σ is a finite alphabet of names of actions, X is a finite set of clocks, $T \subseteq Q \times \mathcal{C}_{df}(X) \times \Sigma \times 2^X \times Q$ is a finite set of edges, Invar is a function mapping to each location a clock constraint called its invariant and L is a labelling function mapping to each location a set of atomic propositions over *Props*. Each edge is a tuple $e = (q, g, a, r, q')$ where q and q' are the source and target locations, g is a clock constraint defining the guard of the edge, a is the label of the edge and r is the set of clocks to be reset by the edge. We use the notation $\text{label}(e)$ to denote the label a of the edge e. Examples of TA can be found in section 4.

Semantics. The semantics of a TA A is an infinite graph $\mathcal{G}(A)$ in which states are pairs (q, v), where q is a location of A and v a clock valuation over the clocks of A, such that $v \in \text{Invar}(q)$. The transitions of this graph can be either discrete or time transitions. Consider a state (q, v). Given an edge $e = (q, g, a, r, q')$ of A, $(q, v) \xrightarrow{e} (q', v')$ (where $v' = [r := 0]v$) is a discrete transition in $\mathcal{G}(A)$ if $v \in g$ and $v' \in \text{Invar}(q')$. We call (q', v') a discrete successor of (q, v). Time transitions have the form $(q, v) \xrightarrow{t} (q, v + t)$ where $t \in \mathbb{R}^+$ and $v + t \in \text{Invar}(q)$. We say that $(q, v + t)$ is a time successor of (q, v).

Symbolic representation. Due to the dense nature of time, the semantic graph of a TA has an infinite number of states. To perform algorithmic analysis for TA, a finite representation of this state space is needed. The symbolic representation currently used is based on the notion of zones, and leads to a symbolic graph called *simulation graph*. A zone (q, ζ) is a set of (semantic) states of a TA, such that they have the same discrete part q and the set of their valuations forms a convex polyhedron ζ. Given a zone $z = (q, \zeta)$, we note $\text{disc}(z)$ the discrete part q of z, and $\text{poly}(z)$ its polyhedron ζ. The transitions of a simulation graph are labelled by discrete actions (intuitively time elapses inside zones, and thus there are no transitions labelled by time delays). The following operations allow to compute the transitions of a simulation graph: $\text{time-succ}(z)$ and $\text{time-pred}(z)$ represent respectively the set of time successors and predecessors of some state in z, while $\text{disc-succ}(e, z)$ and $\text{disc-pred}(e, z)$ represent the set of discrete successors of some state in z, by taking transition e. The operation $\text{post}(e, z, c)^2$ computes the successor zone of z by taking transition e, with respect to a constant $c \in \mathbb{N}$ (in general, this constant is the greater constant appearing in the constraints of the TA), while the operation $\text{pre}(e, z)$ computes the predecessor zone of z by transition e.

---

[2] The operation post is used to compute the simulation graph. The use of the operator Approx_c in its definition ensures the termination of the construction of the simulation graph. More details can be found in [8].

$$\texttt{time-succ}(z) \overset{def}{=} \{s' \mid \exists s \in z, t \in \mathbb{R}^+ \ s \overset{t}{\rightarrow} s'\}$$

$$\texttt{time-pred}(z) \overset{def}{=} \{s \mid \exists s' \in z, t \in \mathbb{R}^+ \cdot s \overset{t}{\rightarrow} s'\}$$

$$\texttt{disc-succ}(e, z) \overset{def}{=} \{s' \mid \exists s \in z \cdot s \overset{e}{\rightarrow} s'\}$$

$$\texttt{disc-pred}(e, z) \overset{def}{=} \{s \mid \exists s' \in z \cdot s \overset{e}{\rightarrow} s'\}$$

$$\texttt{post}(e, z, c) \overset{def}{=} \texttt{Approx}_c(\texttt{time-succ}(\texttt{disc-succ}(e, z)))$$

$$\texttt{pre}(e, z) \overset{def}{=} \texttt{disc-pred}(e, \texttt{time-pred}(z))$$

Consider a TA $A = \langle Q, q_0, \Sigma, X, T, \texttt{Invar}, L \rangle$ and $c \in \mathbb{N}$ a constant greater or equal to the greatest constant appearing in a constraint of A. The simulation graph of A with respect to c, written $SG(A, c)$, is a tuple $\langle Z, z_0, \Sigma, \mathcal{E} \rangle$ where Z is the finite set of states of the graph (i.e., a set of zones) and $z_0 = (q_0, \nearrow \texttt{zero} \cap \texttt{Invar}(q_0))$ is the initial zone. The set $\mathcal{E} \subseteq Z \times T \times Z$ of transitions is defined as follows: given a zone z and an edge $e \in T$, if $z' = \texttt{post}(e, z, c) \neq \emptyset$, then z' is a zone of the graph and $z \overset{e}{\rightarrow} z'$ is a transition of the graph.

Classic parallel composition operator for TA. We consider timed systems modeled in a compositional framework. Each component is modeled as a TA, and components are put together with some parallel composition operator. We consider here the classic parallel composition operator for TA. This operator, written $\|$, operates between TA with disjoint sets of clocks. It is defined as a synchronized product where synchronizations are done on actions with identical labels. Other actions interleave and time elapses synchronously between all the components. Formally, let us consider two TA $A_i = \langle Q_i, q_{0_i}, \Sigma_i, X_i, T_i, \texttt{Invar}_i, L_i \rangle$ for $i = 1, 2$, such that $X_1 \cap X_2 = \emptyset$. The parallel composition of A_1 and A_2, written $A_1 \| A_2$, creates a new TA which set of clocks is $X_1 \cup X_2$ and which labels are $\Sigma_1 \cup \Sigma_2$. The set Q of locations consists of pairs (q_1, q_2) where $q_1 \in Q_1$ and $q_2 \in Q_2$. The initial location is the pair (q_{0_1}, q_{0_2}). The invariant of a location (q_1, q_2) is $\texttt{Invar}(q_1) \wedge \texttt{Invar}(q_2)$, and its label is $L(q_1) \cup L(q_2)$. The set T of edges is defined by the following rules:

Interleaving:
$$\frac{(q_1, q_2) \in Q \ , \ (q_1, g_1, a, r_1, q_1') \in T_1 \ , \ a \notin \Sigma_2}{((q_1, q_2), g_1, a, r_1, (q_1', q_2)) \in T}$$

$$\frac{(q_1, q_2) \in Q \ , \ (q_2, g_2, a, r_2, q_2') \in T_2 \ , \ a \notin \Sigma_1}{((q_1, q_2), g_2, a, r_2, (q_1, q_2')) \in T}$$

Synchronization:
$$\frac{(q_1, q_2) \in Q, \ (q_1, g_1, a, r_1, q_1') \in T_1 \ , \ (q_2, g_2, a, r_2, q_2') \in T_2}{((q_1, q_2), g_1 \wedge g_2, a, r_1 \cup r_2, (q_1', q_2')) \in T}$$

2.2   Simulation Relations to Preserve Properties

Recall that we are interested in developing incrementally component-based timed systems, by integration of components. The major issue when using such a method is to ensure preservation of already checked local properties of a component, when integrating it in an environment. We defined in [5] a divergence-sensitive and stability-respecting (DS) timed τ-simulation, which ensures the preservation of linear timed properties, in particular safety, liveness and bounded-liveness ones.

Consider a component C to be integrated in an environment E, using the parallel composition operator $\|$, where each component is modeled as a timed automaton. This integration leads to a composite automaton $C\|E$, which contains new clocks and new actions comparing to C. New clocks are the clocks of E, and new actions are internal actions of E which do not synchronize with an action of C. In $C\|E$, we consider such actions as being non-observable and rename them by τ. The DS timed τ-simulation is defined between the traces of $C\|E$ and C and is characterized by (i) if $C\|E$ can make an action of C after some amount of time, then C could also make this action after the same amount of time (clauses 1 and 2 of Definition 1), (ii) internal actions of the environment E (called τ) stutter (clause 3 of Definition 1). Note that this definition actually corresponds to the classic notion of τ-simulation, that we extend to handle time. We also add two criteria to the definition of this simulation, namely divergence-sensitivity and stability-respect. Divergence-sensitivity ensures that internal actions τ of E will not take the control forever, and stability-respect guarantees that the integration of C in E will not create new deadlocks.

In order to avoid too many definitions, we remained concise in the presentation of the simulation and focus here directly on its symbolic formal definition, which is the one implemented in the tool VeSTA. More details, as well as the definition at the semantic level, can be found in [5]. However, the following technical points used in Definition 1 must be clarified. The predicate `free`, used in the clause *stability-respect*, was defined in [8]. Informally, given a location q of a timed automaton, $\mathtt{free}(q)$ is the set of all valuations (of states with q as discrete part) from which a discrete transition can be taken after some time elapsed. The formal definition is: $\mathtt{free}(q) = \bigcup_{e=(q,g,a,r,q')\in T} \swarrow (g \cap ([r := 0]\mathtt{Invar}(q')))$.The predicate `src_val`, used in the clause *strict simulation* is defined formally as follows: $\mathtt{src\_val}(z, e, z') = \mathtt{poly}(\mathtt{pre}(e, z') \cap z)$. It represents the valuations of the subset of states in z which lead to states in the zone z' by taking transition e and letting time elapse.

Definition 1 (Symbolic DS timed τ-simulation). *Let $SG_1 = \langle Z_1, z_{0_1}, \Sigma_1, \mathcal{E}_1 \rangle$ and $SG_2 = \langle Z_2, z_{0_2}, \Sigma_1 \cup \{\tau\}, \mathcal{E}_2 \rangle$ be two simulation graphs, obtained respectively from two TA A_1 and A_2. The symbolic DS timed τ-simulation $\mathcal{Z}_{ds}$ is the greatest binary relation included in $Z_2 \times Z_1$, such that $z_2 \mathcal{Z}_{ds} z_1$ if:*

1. *Strict simulation:*
   $$z_2 \xrightarrow{e_2} z_2' \wedge \mathtt{label}(e_2) \in \Sigma_1 \Rightarrow \exists z_1' \cdot (z_1 \xrightarrow{e_1} z_1' \wedge \mathtt{label}(e_1) = \mathtt{label}(e_2) \wedge$$
   $$\mathtt{src\_val}(z_2, e_2, z_2')\!\downarrow_{X_1} \subseteq \mathtt{src\_val}(z_1, e_1, z_1') \wedge z_2' \, \mathcal{Z}_{ds} \, z_1').$$

2. *Equality of delays and of common clocks valuations:* $\mathtt{poly}(z_2)\!\downarrow_{X_1} \subseteq \mathtt{poly}(z_1)$.

3. *τ-transitions stuttering:* $z_2 \xrightarrow{e_2} z_2' \wedge \mathtt{label}(e_2) = \tau \Rightarrow z_2' \, \mathcal{Z}_{ds} \, z_1$.

4. *Stability respect:* $(\mathtt{poly}(z_2)\backslash\mathtt{free}(\mathtt{disc}(z_2)))\!\downarrow_{X_1} \subseteq \mathtt{poly}(z_1)\backslash\mathtt{free}(\mathtt{disc}(z_1))$.

5. *Divergence sensitivity: SG_2 does not contain any non-zeno τ-cycles. A non-zeno τ-cycle is a cycle which only contains transitions labelled by τ and in which the total time elapsed goes to infinity (i.e., time diverges).*

We extend this relation to simulation graphs. Consider two simulation graphs SG_1 and SG_2, which initial zones are respectively z_{0_1} and z_{0_2}. We say that SG_1 simulates SG_2 with respect to $\mathcal{Z}_{ds}$, written $SG_2 \preceq_{\mathcal{Z}_{ds}} SG_1$, if $z_{0_2} \mathcal{Z}_{ds} z_{0_1}$.

Preservation abilities. The DS timed τ-simulation preserves all properties which can be expressed with the logic MITL (Metric Interval Temporal Logic) [7], as well as strong non-zenoness and deadlock-freedom. Formal proofs can be found in [5]. MITL is a linear timed logic, which can be viewed as the timed extension of the linear (untimed) logic LTL [11] and in which temporal operators are constrained by a time interval. Strong non-zenoness is a specific essential property of timed systems. A TA is said to be strongly non-zeno if time can diverge along each path of its semantic graph. Note that the timed τ-simulation, without divergence-sensitivity and stability-respect criteria, preserves all safety properties.

Composability. Composability is an essential property for integration of components. Indeed, it expresses that a component automatically simulates its integration with other ones. Formally, given components C and E, it means that C simulates its integration with E, i.e., the composition $C\|E$. Thus, composability can ensure the preservation of local properties of C for free (properties preserved depends on the notion of simulation which is considered).

The composability property is guaranteed with the timed τ-simulation (without divergence-sensitivity and stability-respect), when integration is achieved with the classic parallel omposition operator. This implies that safety properties are preserved for free during this integration process. However, this is not the case when considering the divergence-sensitivity and stability-respect criteria. Composability does not automatically hold. To ensure this property, the DS timed τ-simulation has to be checked algorithmically. Therefore, we implemented this verification in a tool named VeSTA.

3   The Tool Vesta

VeSTA considers component-based timed models consisting of a set of components (modeled as timed automata) which interact using the classic parallel composition operator $\|$. Therefore, it provides graphical and textual editors to capture these elements. Then, VeSTA can automatically generate composite systems, made up by parallel composition of chosen components with respect to the given interactions.

The main feature of VeSTA is to check if local properties of a component are preserved when it is merged into an environment, by checking if this component simulates the composite system obtained by this merging. The simulation can be checked either in a "general way", i.e., to ensure preservation of all the local properties of a component, or "partially", i.e., for some specific given properties. This partial verification is presented in details in section 5.1. In both cases, if the simulation is not checked successfully, the tool reports the error found as well as a graphical diagnostic consisting of the trace of the composite system which is not simulated by any traces of the component, and the trace of the component it had to correspond to.

3.1   Architecture of Vesta

VeSTA was developed using both C and Java languages. Java is used for the graphical user interface, which is described in the next section, and C for the core of the tool, which is described below. The architecture of VeSTA is shown in Fig. 1. The models considered consist of three kinds of elements: the set of components (saved in .aut files) and possibly their local properties (prop) in the case of partial verification, the types of the variables used in the components and the interactions between components (sync). From this modeling, VeSTA can automatically generate composite systems by using the classic parallel composition operator between the components (.exp files). Compositions can also have local properties.

To get an efficient representation of this model, VeSTA is based on SMI[3] (Symbolic Model Interface). SMI is a powerful library providing efficient representation for finite-state models, by building an equivalent symbolic representation using decision diagrams. Note that our choice was guided by the functioning of the OPEN-KRONOS tool [8], which is already based on SMI.

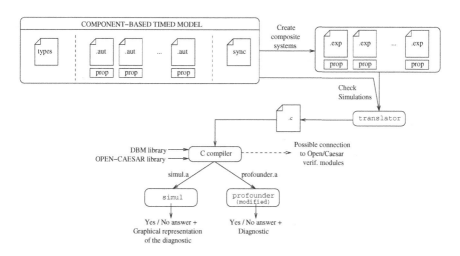

Fig. 1. Structure of VeSTA

The core of the tool consists of two modules: `translator` and `simul`, taking as input two components, which can be composite systems (.exp files): one corresponding to a component C to be integrated in an environment E, and the other to the composite system $C\|E$ obtained after having integrated C in E.

---

[3] http://www-verimag.imag.fr/~async/SMI/index.shtml

translator creates a file .c which implements data structures and functions to generate a symbolic graph (the so-called simulation graph) for each input component. The way data structures and functions are created for $C\|E$ allows it to be connected to the different modules of OPEN-CAESAR. When this file is created, it is compiled and linked to OPEN-CAESAR and DBM libraries (DBM libraries allow to manipulate the timing constraints of the model). Then, an executable simul is created and run to check the stability-respecting timed τ-simulation. The divergence-sensitivity part is checked thanks to an adaptation of an algorithm of the module PROFOUNDER [12] of OPEN-KRONOS. This algorithm, as well as the one implemented in simul, is presented in the next section.

3.2   Algorithms

The DS timed τ-simulation is checked in two phases. The divergence-sensitive part (i.e., clause 5 of Def. 1) is checked independently with an adaptation of an algorithm of the module PROFOUNDER, which is part of the OPEN-KRONOS tool. Then, the stability-respecting timed τ-simulation is checked in the module simul (i.e., clauses 1 to 4 of Def. 1). Thus, VESTA uses two main algorithms to check the DS timed τ-simulation: one for divergence-sensitivity, and the other for the stability-respecting timed τ-simulation.

Adaptation of the module Profounder to check divergence-sensitivity.
For this verification, we use the algorithm called *full DFS* (*full Depth First Search*) defined in [8,12]. This algorithm was first designed to test the emptiness of a timed Büchi automaton, in the case of a persistent acceptance condition (i.e., from one point on, the automaton only visits accepting states). The algorithm thus consists in detecting non-zeno cycles in the automaton such that they only contain accepting states. For this, it visits all the paths of the simulation graph of the automaton, and puts them in a stack. The exploration of a path stops when reaching a state which is already in the stack (this means that an elementary cycle is found). It only remains to check that the cycle is non-zeno and only contains accepting states.

Algorithm 1 presents the adaptation of this algorithm to detect non-zeno τ-cycles, instead of non-zeno accepting cycles, in a simulation graph $SG = \langle Z, z_0, \Sigma, \mathcal{E}\rangle$, where the alphabet Σ contains the action τ. When a cycle is detected, we test if it is non-zeno and if all the transitions of the cycle are labelled by τ. The procedures Top, Push and Pop are classic operations on stacks, allowing to get the top of a stack, and to add and remove an element in the stack. The procedure Part(Stack, e) gets all the elements of the stack Stack added after the element e. The procedure Next(Stack, e) gets the element following e in Stack (i.e. the element added after e). The procedure non_zeno is defined as in [8] and performs a syntactic test to check if a path is non-zeno. This test consists in checking that, in the cycle, there exists a clock x which is reset at a point i of the cycle, and that x has a lower bound at a point j of the cycle. Intuitively, this allows to ensure that at least one time unit elapses at each loop in the cycle.

ALGORITHM 1. A *full DFS* TO CHECK DIVERGENCE-SENSITIVITY

```
divergence_sensitivity(SG){
    Stack := {z₀}
    return non_zeno_τ_cycles()
}


non_zeno_τ_cycles(){
    z := top(Stack)
    cycle := false
    while ∃ z ⟶ᵉ z' ∈ 𝓔 and cycle = false
        if z' ∉ Stack then
            Push(z', Stack)
            cycle := non_zeno_τ_cycles()
            Pop(Stack)
        else
            if ∀z₁ ∈ Part(Stack, z'), ∃z₁ ⟶ᵀ Next(Stack, z₁) ∈ 𝓔
                                    and non_zeno(Part(Stack, z')) then
                return true
    end while

    return cycle
}
```

Note that a classic DFS is generally not sufficient to detect non-zeno τ-cycles. Indeed, this search can miss cycles. For instance, consider a simulation graph with four states (and, to simplify only τ-transitions), such that there is a zeno τ-cycle visiting the following states: $1 \rightarrow 2 \rightarrow 3 \rightarrow 1$, and a non-zeno one $1 \rightarrow 4 \rightarrow 2 \rightarrow 3 \rightarrow 1$. A simple DFS would explore the path $1 \rightarrow 2 \rightarrow 3 \rightarrow 1$ and find this zeno cycle, which is not retained for divergence-sensitivity checking. Then, the search would explore the path $1 \rightarrow 4 \rightarrow 2$, and stop since the state 2 has already been visited. Thus, the non-zeno cycle is missed. The full DFS would not have missed this cycle since it explores all cycles. However, the drawback of this algorithm is its worst-case complexity: exponential in the size of the simulation graph [12]. The problem exposed above with a simple DFS comes from zeno cycles. For strongly non-zeno simulation graphs (i.e., which do not contain any zeno path), a simple DFS (linear in the size of the graph) is sufficient.

Checking the stability-respecting timed τ-simulation in the module simul. Algorithm 2 checks the symbolic stability-respecting timed τ-simulation between two simulation graphs $SG_1 - \langle Z_1, z_{0_1}, \Sigma_1, \mathcal{E}_1 \rangle$, with set of clocks X_1, and $SG_2 = \langle Z_2, z_{0_2}, \Sigma_1 \cup \{\tau\}, \mathcal{E}_2 \rangle$. Formally, it checks that $SG_2 \preceq_{Z_{ds}} SG_1$, without the divergence-sensitivity clause. This verification is in $\mathcal{O}((|Z_1| + |\mathcal{E}_1|) \times (|Z_2| + |\mathcal{E}_2|))$. The algorithm is cut in four parts, the main one being verification Z_{ds}. A procedure verif_Z_and_stability_respect performs a joint depth-first search of SG_2 and SG_1, and at each step of the search, it checks clauses 1 to 4 of Def. 1. A set Visited records the already visited pairs of zones in relation, and a stack Stack contains the currently checked pairs of zones. This stack also allows to return diagnostics when the verification fails.

ALGORITHM 2. VERIFICATION OF THE SYMBOLIC DS TIMED τ-SIMULATION

```
verification_𝒵ds(SG₂, SG₁){
    if (divergence_sensitivity(SG₂)) then
        return false
    else
        Stack := {(z₀₂, z₀₁)}
        Visited := ∅
        return verif_𝒵_and_stability_respect()
}

verif_𝒵_and_stability_respect(){
    simul_ok := true
    (z₂, z₁) := top(Stack)
    if delays_equality(z₂, z₁) ∧ stab_respect(z₂, z₁) then
        while ∃ a transition z₂ →ᵉ² z₂' in ℰ₂ and simul_ok = true
            if label(e₂) ∈ Σ₁ then
                if ∃z₁ →ᵉ¹ z₁' s.t. label(e₁) = label(e₂) ∧
                    strict_simulation(z₁, e₁, z₁', z₂, e₂, z₂') = true then
                    if (z₂', z₁') ∉ Visited and (z₂', z₁') ∉ Stack
                        Push((z₂', z₁'), Stack)
                        simul_ok := verif_𝒵_and_stability_respect()
                        Pop(Stack)
                else
                    return false
            else
                if (z₂', z₁) ∉ Visited and (z₂', z₁) ∉ Stack then
                    Push((z₂', z₁), Stack)
                    simul_ok := verif_𝒵_and_stability_respect()
                    Pop(Stack)
        end while
    else
        return false

    if simul_ok = true then Visited := Visited ∪ {(z₂, z₁)}
    return simul_ok
}

strict_simulation (z₁, e₁, z₁', z₂, e₂, z₂'){
    return (src_val(z₂, e₂, z₂')⌋ₓ₁ ⊆ src_val(z₁, e₁, z₁'))
}

stab_respect (z₂, z₁){
    return (poly(z₂)\free(disc(z₂)))⌋ₓ₁ ⊆ poly(z₁)\free(disc(z₁))
}

delays_equality (z₂, z₁){
    return (poly(z₂)⌋ₓ₁ ⊆ poly(z₁))
}
```

3.3   Graphical User Interface

The GUI of VeSTA is shown in Fig. 2. The tree on the left is an explorer to
navigate between the elements of the model, the generated assembling of components, and the results of already checked preservations (i.e., simulations). The
bottom-right part is a log window, displaying informations such as syntax errors
or summarized results of preservation checkings. The top-right part is the main
element of the GUI, with five tabs:

- the *Types* tab displays the types of the variables used in the model,
- the *Interactions* tab shows the interactions between the components,
- the *Basic Components* tab contains all the components of the model,
- the *Composite Components* tab contains the assembling of components,
- the *Simulations* tab contains results for each already checked preservation.

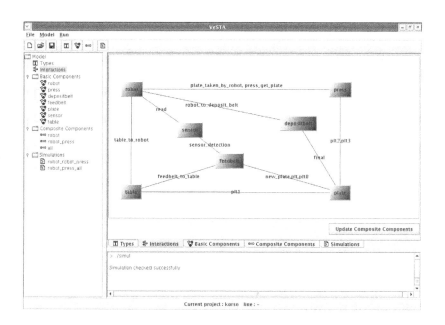

Fig. 2. Graphical User Interface of VeSTA

The menubar and toolbar provide buttons to treat a new model. They allow to create new components, import components from another model, choose
components to put together and automatically create the assembling, and check
simulations. The interactions between components can be created graphically via
the *Interactions* tab. Components (i.e. timed automata[4]) are described through
a textual editors, with a simple language which consists in giving the invariant

---

[4] Actually, VeSTA considers *extended* timed automata, which can be equiped with
boolean, bounded-integer and enumerative-type variables. However, the use of these
variables is restricted to a local use for the components (no shared variables).

of each location, and the transitions of the component (name, source and target location, guard, reset and, possibly, update of some variables).

4   Vesta in Practice: Incremental Verification of a Production Cell

The tool VeSTA allowed us to show the interest of incremental development by integration of components, formalized by the DS timed τ-simulation, in comparison to a direct verification on the complete model of the system. We present in this section a case study concerning a production cell[5]. This case study was developed by FZI (the Research Center for Information Technologies, in Karlsruhe) as part of the Korso project. The goal was to study the impact of the use of formal methods when treating industrial applications. Thus, this case study was treated in about thirty different formalisms. We treated it with timed automata, as it was in [14].

Presentation of the case study. The production cell contains six devices, as shown in Fig. 3: a feed-belt equipped with a sensor, a deposit-belt, an elevating-rotary table, a two-arms robot and a press. It also contains one or several pieces to be treated. Our modeling of the cell follows the one of [14].

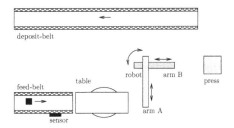

Fig. 3. The Production Cell Example

Description of the production cell. A simplified functioning of the cell is the following. Pieces arrive on the feed-belt. The sensor detects when a piece is introduced in the cell, and sends a message to the robot to inform that the piece is going to be available. When it arrives at the end of the belt, it is transferred to the table, which goes up and turns until being in an adequate position to give to the robot the possibility to take it. The robot turns 90° so that its arm A can pick the piece up, and then puts it in the press which processes it. When the treatment is finished, the piece is taken by the arm B of the robot, which transports it to the deposit-belt where it is evacuated. The behavior of each device depends on timing constraints and is modeled by a timed automaton. In the sequel, we focus particularly on local properties concerning the robot, and

---

[5] The detailed results for this case study, as well as other experimentations, can be found in [13].

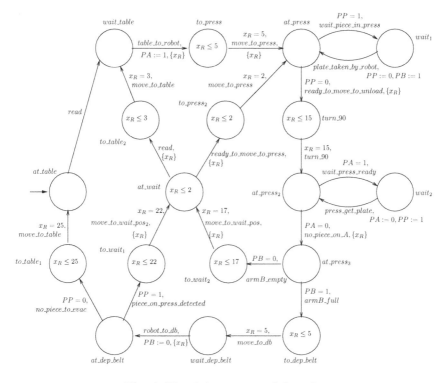

Fig. 4. Timed Automaton of the robot

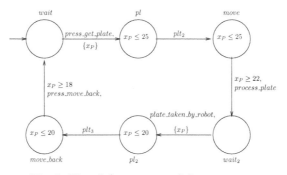

Fig. 5. Timed Automaton of the press

the assembling robot‖press. Fig. 4 and 5 show respectively the timed automata modeling the robot and the press.

Some local properties. We identified seven main properties of the robot: two safety properties (called P_1 and P_2), two liveness (response) properties (P_3 and

P_4) and three bounded liveness properties (P_5, P_6 and P_7)[6]. We also identified a main liveness property (P_8) ensuring the correct functioning of the robot and the press when they are put together. We express these properties in MITL[7].

Our objective is to compare direct verification and incremental verification by integration of components, for MITL properties. The first method consists in assembling all the components, and then to check properties P_1 to P_8 on the complete model obtained. The second method consists in checking these properties locally only on the components they concern, and then to ensure they are preserved when these components are integrated in their environment. That is, properties P_1 to P_7 are checked on the robot component, and property P_8 on the assembling robot‖press. Then, the preservation of P_1 to P_7 must be ensured when the robot component is integrated with the press component. The preservation of P_8 must be guaranteed when this assembling is integrated with all the other components of the system. In this way, each locally checked property will hold on the complete model, since preservation is checked thanks to the DS timed τ-simulation, which is a preorder, and thus, is a transitive relation.

Experimental results for the production cell. First note that VeSTA is not a model-checker. Thus to check the properties locally and globally, we used the model-checker KRONOS[15]. KRONOS is a verification tool for timed systems which performs TCTL model-checking [16]. TCTL is a logical formalism that allows to express branching-time properties. Even if we do not consider branching-time properties, we can use it for this example since the MITL properties we consider can also be expressed in TCTL[8]. It turns out that the local and global verification of all the properties, achieved with KRONOS, succeeded. VeSTA allows to ensure the preservation of locally established properties. Therefore, it is first used to check that the local properties of the robot are preserved when it is combined with the press, and then that the property of the assembling robot‖press is preserved when these components are integrated with the rest of the components of the cell and one piece. In both cases, the verification succeeded, and thus, the preservation of the MITL properties P_1 to P_8 is guaranteed (as well as the preservation of strong non-zenoness and deadlock-freedom).

Fig. 6 presents the results obtained on the example, by comparing incremental verification by integration of components to direct verification. We compared the time consumed to perform this direct verification on the whole model (column "Global Verification") and the time spent to achieve incremental verification, i.e., local verification and preservation checking. It turns out that, even if the computation times are still acceptable, direct verification consumes much more time (almost 20 seconds) than incremental verification when preservation is achieved with VeSTA (less than one second).

---

[6] Under some conditions, safety properties express that *something bad will not happen*, liveness ones that *something expected will eventually happen* and bounded liveness ones that *something expected will eventually happen within some bounded delay*.

[7] The detailed expressions of these properties can be found in [13].

[8] To our knowledge, there is no tool performing MITL model-checking.

Property	Global Verification (KRONOS)	Local Verification (KRONOS)	Preservation checking (VeSTA)
P_1 (safety)	0.01	< 0.001	
P_2 (safety)	0.01	< 0.001	
P_3 (liveness)	0.98	< 0, .001	
P_4 (liveness)	15.79	0.04	0.05
P_5 (bounded liveness)	0.68	< 0.001	
P_6 (bounded liveness)	0.48	< 0.001	
P_7 (bounded liveness)	0.7	< 0.001	
P_8 (liveness)	0.93	0.02	0.46
Total	19.58	0.06	0.51

Fig. 6. Comparison of the local and global verification times (in seconds)

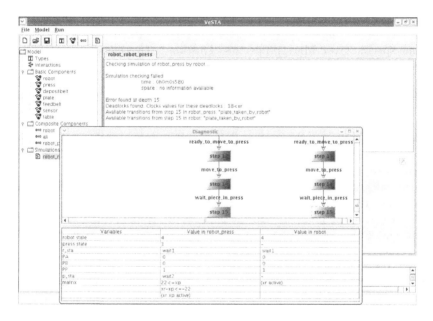

Fig. 7. Diagnostic provided by VeSTA

Diagnostics. In section 3, we stated that VeSTA has the ability to provide diagnostics when the verification of the DS timed τ-simulation (and thus of the preservation) fails. To show this functionality, we slightly modify the automaton of the press. We add a guard (for instance $x_p \leq 40$) to the transition *plate_taken_by_robot*, which means that the press expects to be unloaded by the robot at most 40 time units after having received a piece. This modification prevents the preservation from being established, when integrating the robot with the press. Indeed, adding this guard introduces a deadlock in the assembling press‖robot, which did not exist in the robot component alone. Thus, deadlock-freedom is obviously not preserved. Moreover, MITL properties P_3 to P_7 are also not preserved since non-introduction of deadlocks is precisely one of the conditions which define the DS timed τ-simulation (clause *stability-respect*), and thus, which ensure the preservation of MITL properties. Note that properties P_1 and P_2 are still preserved since they are safety properties and, therefore, their preservation does not need neither stability-respect, nor divergence-sensitivity. The graphical diagnostic provided by VESTA helps detecting where the deadlock is introduced, by showing the trace of the assembling robot‖press where the deadlock appears, and the corresponding trace of the component robot that had to simulate it, with respect to the DS timed τ-simulation. Fig. 7 shows how diagnostics are displayed in VESTA.

5   Additional Features

The main functionality of VESTA is to check the DS timed τ-simulation, using exactly algorithms 1 and 2. In addition, VESTA proposes an interesting additional feature, consisting in verifying partially the relation to ensure the preservation of some specific given MITL properties. This kind of verification, as well as the motivations, are explained below.

5.1   Partial Verification of the Preservation

Let us go back to the second version of the production cell example, in which we modified the guard of the edge *plate_taken_by_robot* in the automaton of the press. As we explained, the deadlock introduced in the assembling robot‖press prevents ensuring the preservation of all the properties which can be expressed for the robot, since the verification of the simulation fails. However, the specified local properties of the robot may be preserved. For this reason, we improved VESTA by giving the possibility to the user to specify the properties to preserve, and to check the preservation only for these properties (instead of a "global preservation"). This is what we call *partial verification of the preservation*.

Thus, the objective of such a verification is to guarantee the preservation of specified local properties of a component, rather than the preservation of all the properties which could be potentially specified. Until now, this functionality is only available for response properties of the form $\Box(p \Rightarrow \Diamond q)$. The reasoning for this kind of verification is the following. In most cases, the verification of the simulation fails due to an introduction of deadlocks (i.e., the clause *stability-respect* of the simulation does not hold). Consider now a component C, a local property $L = \Box(p \Rightarrow \Diamond q)$ of C and an environment E in which C must be integrated. A path π in $C\|E$, in which a deadlock is introduced comparing to the path of C which simulates it, makes the verification of the preservation fail. However, if this path π does not concern L, then the preservation should be guaranteed.

Let us detail how this partial verification is achieved, for a response property of the form $\Box(p \Rightarrow \Diamond q)$. To ensure the preservation of such a property, we must guarantee that, when p is encountered in a path π, this path is not *cut* (by the introduction of a deadlock) before q is reached. Thus, the partial verification consists in checking this non-introduction of deadlock (i.e., the clause *stability-respect*) only for the states of π located between the state satisfying p, and the

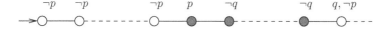

○ No verification of stability-respect and divergence-sensitivity

● Verification of stability-respect and divergence-sensitivity

Fig. 8. Partial verification for a property of the form $\Box(p \Rightarrow \Diamond q)$

one satisfying q. Fig. 8 illustrates the principle of this verification for this kind of property. A path is represented, and the states on which stability-respect must be checked are put in grey. Note also that divergence-sensitivity must also be checked for these states, to ensure that the path is not cut by means of the introduction of an infinite sequence of non-observable actions. The verification for divergence-sensitivity consists in checking that these states are not part of a non-zeno cycle only containing non-observable actions.

Thus, VeSTA gives the possibility to specify the local properties of C, of the form $\Box(p \Rightarrow \Diamond q)$, which must be preserved, and to verify the simulation only to guarantee the preservation of these properties. Note that, contrary to the classic verification, this partial verification does not guarantee the preservation of strong non-zenoness and deadlock-freedom.

5.2   Connection to Other Platforms and Tools

Another interesting point of VeSTA is the following. Recall that the way the tool was designed was inspired by the OPEN-KRONOS tool. In particular, the syntax used to describe the components, and the symbolic representation of these models, is identical to the one in OPEN-KRONOS. Thus, a direct consequence of this design choice is that models considered in VeSTA can be connected to the OPEN-KRONOS tool. Connection to the OPEN-CAESAR verification platform is also possible as another direct consequence, since this connection was already available from OPEN-KRONOS models.

The connection to OPEN-KRONOS is particularly interesting. Indeed, the ability to connect VeSTA models to OPEN-KRONOS could allow to check MITL properties directly on the models considered in VeSTA. Recall that, now, we use the tool KRONOS to perform model-checking, since there exist no tools for MITL model-checking. Thus, as KRONOS is a TCTL model-checker, we are restricted to MITL properties which can also be expressed in TCTL. Moreover, VeSTA models must be translated into KRONOS syntax. The OPEN-KRONOS tool can perform reachability analysis, but can also test timed Büchi automata (TBA) emptiness. MITL properties can be translated into TBA which recognize the same language. Thus, with a translator from MITL to TBA (such translators do not exist yet) and an implementation of the composition of TA with TBA (see [8] to get more details about this special composition), it would be possible to directly connect VeSTA models of components to OPEN-KRONOS, perform MITL model-checking on these components, and then check with VeSTA the preservation of these properties during the integration of these components.

6   Conclusion and Further Developments

In this paper, we presented the tool VeSTA, which allows (i) to model incrementally a component-based timed system, by integration of components, and (ii) to ensure the preservation of established local properties of the components on the complete model, instead of performing a direct verification of these properties on this complete model. Timed components are modeled as timed automata, and integration is achieved thanks to the classic parallel composition operator for timed automata. Preservation is checked by means of a divergence-sensitive and stability-respecting timed τ-simulation. Precisely, a successful verification of this relation ensures the preservation of all linear timed properties expressed with the logic MITL, strong non-zenoness and deadlock-freedom.

The first results obtained for incremental verification by integration of components, using VeSTA for the preservation part, are encouraging. On the production cell case study of [14], it turns out that a direct verification consumes almost 20 seconds of computation time, while the incremental one based on preservation needs less than one second. Other experiments showed that VeSTA can handle models up to 400000 symbolic states. Beyond this number, we had not enough memory for the verification of the preservation to be run to completion (on a PC with 1Gb memory). Nevertheless, this number has to be relativized with respect to the number of clocks of the model, which is a direct cause of great memory consumption: 15 clocks for the model from which we obtained this upper bound. Thus, further improvements will be dedicated to handle this limitation, by implementing abstractions such as the *active-clock reduction* [17,18], allowing to ignore clocks in states where they are inactive.

Another further development concerns the partial verification of the DS timed τ-simulation. The objective of such a verification is to check preservation only for the local properties which are specified for the components, instead of ensuring the preservation of all properties which could potentially be expressed. Until now, this partial verification is only available for response properties of the form $\Box(p \Rightarrow \Diamond q)$. It seems interesting to extend this kind of verification to other patterns of liveness and bounded-liveness properties. Moreover, this kind of verification could optimize computation times. Indeed, recall that partial verification consists, in particular, in checking the stability-respecting part of the simulation only on some specific states, instead of checking it systematically. As stability-respect is checked by means of high-cost operations, such as polyhedra complementation, it is essential to avoid as much as possible to check this clause. Thus, generalizing partial verification could lead to better performances in terms of computation times to check preservation.

ADDITIONAL INFORMATIONS. More informations on VeSTA can be found in its complete documentation and user guide at the following URL:
`http://lifc.univ-fcomte.fr/publis/papers/pub/2006/RT2006-01.pdf`.

Acknowledgments. We would like to thank Stavros Tripakis for having sent to us the distribution of OPEN-KRONOS, particularly the module PROFOUNDER and some (useful !) source files. Thanks also for the time spent answering questions.

References

1. Bellegarde, F., Julliand, J., Kouchnarenko, O.: Ready-simulation is not Ready to Express a Modular Refinement Relation. In: Maibaum, T.S.E. (ed.) ETAPS 2000 and FASE 2000. LNCS, vol. 1783, pp. 266–283. Springer, Heidelberg (2000)
2. Henzinger, M., Henzinger, T., Kopke, P.: Computing simulations on finite and infinite graphs. In: FOCS 1995, pp. 453–462 (1995)
3. Tasiran, S., Alur, R., Kurshan, R., Brayton, R.: Verifying Abstractions of Timed Systems. In: Sassone, V., Montanari, U. (eds.) CONCUR 1996. LNCS, vol. 1119, pp. 546–562. Springer, Heidelberg (1996)
4. Jensen, H., Larsen, K., Skou, A.: Scaling up Uppaal: Automatic verification of real-time systems using compositionnality and abstraction. In: FTRTFT 2000, pp. 19–30. Springer, London, UK (2000)
5. Bellegarde, F., Julliand, J., Mountassir, H., Oudot, E.: On the contribution of a τ-simulation in the incremental modeling of timed systems. In: Proc. of FACS'05. Volume 160 of ENTCS., Macao, Macao, Elsevier (2005) 97–111
6. Alur, R., Dill, D.: A theory of timed automata. Theoretical Computer Science 126, 183–235 (1994)
7. Alur, R., Feder, T., Henzinger, T.: The benefits of relaxing punctuality. Journal of the ACM 43, 116–146 (1996)
8. Tripakis, S.: The analysis of timed systems in practice. PhD thesis, Universite Joseph Fourier, Grenoble, France (1998)
9. Garavel, H.: OPEN/CAESAR: An Open Software Architecture for Verification, Simulation and Testing. In: Steffen, B. (ed.) ETAPS 1998 and TACAS 1998. LNCS, vol. 1384, Springer, Heidelberg (1998)
10. Bouyer, P.: Untameable Timed Automata! In: Alt, H., Habib, M. (eds.) STACS 2003. LNCS, vol. 2607, pp. 620–631. Springer, Heidelberg (2003)
11. Pnueli, A.: The temporal logic of programs. In: Proceedings of the 18th IEEE Symposium on Foundations Of Computer Science, pp. 46–77. IEEE Computer Society Press, Los Alamitos (1977)
12. Tripakis, S., Yovine, S., Bouajjani, A.: Checking Timed Büchi Automata Emptiness Efficiently. Formal Methods in System Design 26, 267–292 (2005)
13. Bellegarde, F., Julliand, J., Mountassir, H., Oudot, E.: Experiments in the use of τ-simulations for the components-verification of real-time systems. In: SAVCBS 2006, Portland, Oregon, USA, ACM, New York (2006)
14. Burns, A.: How to verify a safe real-time system: The application of model-checking and timed automata to the production cell case study. Real-Time Systems Journal 24, 135–152 (2003)
15. Yovine, S.: KRONOS: A verification tool for real-time systems. Journal of Software Tools for Technology Transfer 1, 123–133 (1997)
16. Alur, R., Courcoubetis, C., Dill, D.: Model-Checking in Dense Real-time. Information and Computation 104, 2–34 (1993)
17. Daws, C., Yovine, S.: Reducing the number of clock variables in timed automata. In: RTSS 1996, IEEE Computer Society Press, Los Alamitos (1996)
18. Daws, C., Tripakis, S.: Model checking of real-time reachability properties using abstractions. In: Steffen, B. (ed.) ETAPS 1998 and TACAS 1998. LNCS, vol. 1384, pp. 313–329. Springer, Heidelberg (1998)

Integrating Specification-Based Review and Testing for Detecting Errors in Programs*

Shaoying Liu

Hosei University, Japan
sliu@hosei.ac.jp

Abstract. Review and testing are the most practical verification techniques that complement each other, and their effectiveness can be enhanced by utilizing formal specifications. In this paper, we describe a verification method that integrates specification-based review and testing for detecting errors of programs in three phases. First, inspection is used to check whether all the relevant conditions defined in a specification are implemented in the corresponding program and whether there are any errors that may prevent the program from normal termination. Second, testing is carried out to detect errors through dynamic executions of the program and to build a useful relation between the specification and the program. Finally, walkthrough analysis is performed to check whether every functional scenario defined in the specification is correctly implemented by the traversed execution paths in the program and whether any untraversed paths exist and are desired. We present an example to show how our method is applied in practice.

1   Introduction

Specification-based testing (SBT) has been well researched under different names, such as specification-based testing, model-based testing, and functional testing or black-box testing, and its scientific nature and tool supportability have been significantly improved when formal specifications are employed [1, 2]. An obvious advantage of SBT over implementation-based (or structural) testing is that tests can be performed without the need to analyze program structures. However, this advantage may not be achieved if the program under test does not run normally (e.g., crash or infinite loops in execution). It is often the case that large-scale programs do not run normally just after being developed according to our industrial partners in Japan. In this case, even formal specifications may not help very much for testing. To tackle this problem, review can play an effective role.

Software review is a static analysis technique commonly used in industry for software quality assurance [3]. It usually includes two specific techniques: inspection [4] and walkthrough [5]. The purpose of inspection is to detect and identify software product anomalies, including software element errors (e.g., lack

---

* This work is supported by the Ministry of Education, Culture, Sports, Science and Technology of Japan under Grant-in-Aid for Scientific Research (No. 18500027).

M. Butler, M. Hinchey, M.M. Larrondo-Petrie (Eds.): ICFEM 2007, LNCS 4789, pp. 136–150, 2007.

of statements updating loop conditions) and deviations from required standards and specifications. Walkthrough is aimed at understanding a software product, through which software anomalies can be revealed and the conformance of software products to standards and specifications can be evaluated. The feature of review is that human reviewers read through and analyze review targets (i.e., the documents under review), and the determination of errors depends upon reviewer's judgements. Unfortunately, review techniques used in practice offer neither precise rules for reviewers to make judgements nor precise technical procedures for systematically carrying out reviews [6]. Over the last several years, we have been concentrating on research on specification-based review techniques [7, 8] in order to tackle this problem. We have established a rigorous inspection method that facilitates the reviewer to check whether every functional scenario defined in a formal specification is properly implemented in the corresponding program. However, the method may meet challenges in associating functional scenarios in the specification with the corresponding execution paths in the program and in detecting run-time errors.

Our experience suggests that both review and testing are necessary and they complement each other in program verification. We believe that an integration of review and testing can enhance their advantages and avoid their disadvantages. The question is how to make such an integration so that the integrated technique can be rigorous, systematic, effective, and easy to be supported by software tools.

In this paper we describe an integrated method that combines specification-based review and testing techniques. A specification provides precise guidelines and references for review and testing, while review and testing are used at different phases to check the program for different purposes. First, inspection is used to check whether all the relevant conditions defined in the specification are implemented in the corresponding program and whether there are any errors that may prevent the program from normal termination. Second, testing is carried out to detect errors through dynamic executions of the program and to build a useful relation between the specification and the program. Finally, walkthrough analysis is performed to check whether every functional scenario defined in the specification is correctly implemented by the traversed execution paths in the program and whether any untraversed paths exist and are desired. We applied our method to verify an Automated Teller Machine (ATM) software system based upon its formal specification in SOFL [9], an extension of VDM for practicality, and the result shows that the method is effective in detecting errors. Since the whole application is too large to fit into the paper, we choose only one of the operations of the system as an example to explain how our method is applied in practice.

The rest of the paper is organized as follows. Section 2 describes the goal of program verification and Section 3 discusses the integrated method for fulfilling the goal. Section 4 presents an example to illustrate how the method is used. Section 5 overviews the related work. Finally, Section 6 concludes the paper and points out future research directions.

2 The Goal of Verification

In this section, we discuss the goal of program verification using our integrated method. Conceptually, we use the format $S(S_{iv}, S_{ov})[S_{pre}, S_{post}]$ to denote the specification of an operation S, where S_{iv} is the set of all the input variables whose values are not changed by the operation, S_{ov} is a set of all the output variables whose values are produced or updated by the operation, and S_{pre} and S_{post} are the pre- and postconditions of S, respectively. In addition, we adopt the following convention for our discussions throughout this paper:

- If a variable x is used as both an input and an output, then we use $\tilde{x}$ to denote the input value of x and x (i.e., itself) to denote the output value of x. Thus, $\tilde{x} \in S_{iv}$ and $x \in S_{ov}$.

Definition 1. *The program P refines the specification S iff*
$$\forall_{\tilde{\sigma} \in \Sigma} \cdot S_{pre}(\tilde{\sigma}) \Rightarrow S_{post}(\tilde{\sigma}, P(\tilde{\sigma})).$$

In the quantified expression, S is perceived as an abstraction of P, which generally defines a relation between the initial state $\tilde{\sigma}$ before the execution of P and the final state σ $(= P(\tilde{\sigma}))$ after the execution of P. P is treated as a function mapping the initial state $\tilde{\sigma}$ to the final state σ. The program P refines the specification S iff for any initial state $\tilde{\sigma}$ satisfying the precondition S_{pre}, the final state σ resulting from the execution of P satisfies the postcondition S_{post}.

It is well-known that trying to use all the initial states satisfying the precondition S_{pre} to test the program P is not realistic due to the state explosion problem. Therefore, we try to make use of human judgments for help. For this purpose, it is important that the specification provides precise guidelines and references for human to carry out an effective verification. To this end, we require the specification S to be well-formed, as defined below. But for this definition, we first need to introduce a concept called *functional scenario form*.

Definition 2. *Let $S_{post} \equiv (C_1 \wedge D_1) \vee (C_2 \wedge D_2) \vee \cdots \vee (C_n \wedge D_n)$, where each C_i ($i \in \{1, ..., n\}$) is a predicate called a* guard condition *that contains no output variable in S_{ov} and D_i a defining condition that contains at least one output variable in S_{ov} but no guard condition. Then, a (functional) scenario f_s of S is a conjunction $\tilde{S}_{pre} \wedge C_i \wedge D_i$, and the expression $(\tilde{S}_{pre} \wedge C_1 \wedge D_1) \vee (\tilde{S}_{pre} \wedge C_2 \wedge D_2) \vee \cdots \vee (\tilde{S}_{pre} \wedge C_n \wedge D_n)$ is called a* functional scenario form *(FSF) of S.*

where $\tilde{S}_{pre} = S_{pre}[\tilde{\sigma}/\sigma]$ denotes the predicate resulting from substituting the initial state $\tilde{\sigma}$ for the final state σ in the precondition S_{pre}. We treat a conjunction $\tilde{S}_{pre} \wedge C_i \wedge D_i$ as a scenario because it defines an independent function: when $\tilde{S}_{pre} \wedge C_i$ is satisfied by the initial state (or intuitively by the input variables), the final state (or the output variables) is defined by the defining condition D_i. Note that in the pre- and postconditions of a specification, we treat a relation (e.g., $x > y$) and a *strict quantified predicate* as an atomic predicate. A strict quantified predicate is a quantified predicate whose body does not contain any atomic predicate unrelated to its bound variables. For example, $\forall_{x \in X} \cdot y > x$ is a strict quantified predicate, while $\forall_{x \in X} \cdot y > x \wedge t \geq 0$ is not, because it contains the atomic predicate $t \geq 0$ that is not related to the bound variable x. These concepts are useful for transforming a specification into an FSF, and an algorithm for such a transformation is already made available in our previous publication [7].

Note that simply treating a disjunctive clause in the disjunctive normal form of a postcondition as a functional scenario is not necessarily correct in supporting our verification method. For example, let $x > 0 \wedge (y = x \vee y = -x) \vee x \leq 0 \wedge y = x + 1$ be the postcondition of an operation whose precondition is assumed to be *true*, where x is the input and y the output. It states that when $x > 0$, y is defined either as x or as $-x$ (the specifier does not care which definition will be implemented). In this case, if we convert it into the disjunctive normal form $x > 0 \wedge y = x \vee x > 0 \wedge y = -x \vee x \leq 0 \wedge y = x + 1$, and treat each of the two disjunctive clauses $x > 0 \wedge y = x$ and $x > 0 \wedge y = -x$ as an individual functional scenario, respectively, and require the existence of corresponding execution paths in the program to implement both of them, we may not find a satisfactory answer in the program, since the programmer may decide to implement only clause $x > 0 \wedge y = x$ as a refinement of $x > 0 \wedge (y = x \vee y = -x)$.

Definition 3. *Let an FSF of specification S be* $(\tilde{S}_{pre} \wedge C_1 \wedge D_1) \vee (\tilde{S}_{pre} \wedge C_2 \wedge D_2) \vee \cdots \vee (\tilde{S}_{pre} \wedge C_n \wedge D_n)$ *where* $(n \geq 1)$. *Then, S is said to be well-formed iff*
$$(\forall_{i,j \in \{1,...,n\}} \cdot (i \neq j \Rightarrow (C_i \wedge C_j \Leftrightarrow false)) \wedge (\tilde{S}_{pre} \Rightarrow (C_1 \vee C_2 \vee \cdots \vee C_n \Leftrightarrow true))$$

We call a specification S satisfying this condition *well-formed* specification. A well-formed specification ensures that every pair of the guard conditions in its FSF are exclusive, and the disjunction of all the guard conditions under the precondition of the specification constitutes a tautology. Assume every defining condition D_i $(i \in \{1, ..., n\}$ in the FSF of a specification is satisfiable, the well-formedness of the specification guarantees its feasibility: for any initial state satisfying the precondition, there exists a final state that satisfies the postcondition. This is because for any initial state $\tilde{\sigma}$, there must exist a guard condition C_i such that $C_i(\tilde{\sigma})$ holds. Since its corresponding defining condition D_i is assumed to be satisfiable, there must exist a final state σ such that $D_i(\tilde{\sigma}, \sigma)$. Let us consider the operation Conditional_Swap as an example. Suppose its specification is given as follows:

$Conditional\_Swap \ ([\tilde{x}, \tilde{y}], \{x, y\})$
$\qquad [x \geq 0,$
$\qquad \tilde{x} \leq \tilde{y} \wedge y = \tilde{x} \wedge x = \tilde{y}$
$\qquad \vee$
$\qquad \tilde{x} > \tilde{y} \wedge y = \tilde{y} \wedge x = \tilde{x}$
$\qquad] \ ,$

where $Conditional\_Swap_{iv} = \{\tilde{x}, \tilde{y}\}$ is the input variable set, $Conditional\_Sqrt_{ov} = \{x, y\}$ is the output variable set, $x \geq 0$ is the precondition, and $\tilde{x} \leq \tilde{y} \wedge y = \tilde{x} \wedge x = \tilde{y} \vee \tilde{x} > \tilde{y} \wedge y = \tilde{y} \wedge x = \tilde{x}$ is the postcondition, and all the variables involved are of real type. The FSF of the operation specification is:

$$\tilde{x} \geq 0 \wedge \tilde{x} \leq \tilde{y} \wedge y = \tilde{x} \wedge x = \tilde{y} \vee$$
$$\tilde{x} \geq 0 \wedge \tilde{x} > \tilde{y} \wedge y = \tilde{y} \wedge x = \tilde{x}$$

where $\tilde{x} \leq \tilde{y}$ and $\tilde{x} > \tilde{y}$ are two guard conditions, and $y = \tilde{x} \wedge x = \tilde{y}$ and $y = \tilde{y} \wedge x = \tilde{x}$ are two defining conditions. Obviously, the specification is well-formed because the specification satisfies the condition in Definition 3. It is also feasible because each of the two defining conditions are satisfiable.

A well-formed and feasible specification forms a basis for applying our integrated method. As far as the issue of how to achieve a well-formed and feasible specification is concerned, many techniques available in the literature can help, such as specification animation [10] or testing [11, 12]. In this paper, we concentrate only on the problem of how to verify a program against its well-formed and feasible specification.

3   The Method for Verification

This section focuses on the discussion of the integrated verification method with which we can fulfill the goal of program verification defined in the previous section. The fundamental idea of the method is to analyze and test whether every functional scenario defined in a specification is correctly implemented in its corresponding program. The purpose of the method is not aimed at achieving this goal (simply because it is almost impossible in practice), but at detecting as many errors as possible by trying to take the way leading to the goal. The question is how to carry out the verification so that we can find more errors. As we mentioned before in this paper, our experience suggests that integration of review and testing can be an effective solution. The principle of the integration is summarized as the following three phases:

Phase 1. Carry out an inspection of the program based on both the functional scenarios in the specification and some standards.

Phase 2. Conduct a testing of the program based on the functional scenarios in the specfciation.

Phase 3. Carry out a walkthrough analysis of the traversed execution paths based on the functional scenarios in the specification.

The first phase tries to prepare for the phase 2 by creating a situation where the program can run normally. The phase 2 tries to test the program and meanwhile link functional scenarios in the specification to the corresponding traversed paths in the program. The resulting association between scenarios and paths will serve as an effective guideline for the phase 3. The third phase tries to go through entire paths that have been traversed during the phase 2 to analyze whether more potential errors still remain. We discuss the details of each phase of the three, respectively, next.

3.1   Inspection

The task of the inspection phase is twofold. One is to check whether every guard condition, including all the variables and their relations involved, of a functional scenario in the specification is properly implemented in the program. If this is not the case, it indiates a possibility that some functional scenario is not correctly implemented in the program because every scenario defines a conditional behavior in terms of a guard condition and a defining condition. Another task is to reveal errors that prevent the program from running normally. In order to systematically guide the inspector to effectively perform an inspection, we need to make a checklist that contains appropriate questions. In our method, a checklist contains the following questions:

- Is the precondition of the specification properly implemented in the program?
- Is the guard condition of every functioanl scenario in the specification implemented properly in the program?
- Is the defining condition of every functioanl scenario in the specification implemented properly in the program?
- Is every guard condition of a conditional or loop statement in the program satisfiable?
- Is there any variant in the body of every loop statement to ensure the termination of the statement?

When applying this checklist to a specific specifiaction and program, a specalized checklist will be derived from this general checklist. Each question on the specalized checklist is concerned with a specific inspection target. For example, to inspect the program implementing the specification *Conditional_Swap*, we need to raise the following specific questions on the checklist:

- Is the precondition $x \geq 0$ properly implemented?
- Is the guard condition $\tilde{x} \leq \tilde{y}$ properly implemented?
- Is the guard condition $\tilde{x} > \tilde{y}$ properly implemented?
- ......

For the sake of space, we omit the other relevant questions on the checklist. This point will be illustrated with an exmaple in Section 4.

3.2   Testing

Testing in our method is aimed at fulfilling two tasks. One is to dynamically check whether the behavior defined by each functional scenario in the specification is correctly implemented by the program. In theory, there should be a set of execution paths in the program that are responsible for the implementation of each scenario in the specification if the program does refine the specification, so the major issue to address here is how to generate test cases based on each scenario so that all the corresponding paths will be traversed at least once. As is well known, even when a path is traversed once, it does not however guarantee no error remaining on the path. To find more errors on the path, more tests are needed, but this can be costly or impossible due to practical constraints (e.g., time). In our method we adopt a *scenario-based walkthrough analysis* to find more potential errors on paths for cost-effectiveness, as described in detail in the next subsection. For such an analysis, we need clearly understand which paths in the program are responsible for implementing which functional scenario in the specification. Testing can be used as a technique to find out such information. So another task of testing in our method is to link functional scenarios in the specification to execution paths in the program. To this end, we put forward the following criterion for test case generation from the specification.

Criterion 1. *Let S be a specification and its FSF be $(\tilde{S}_{pre} \wedge C_1 \wedge D_1) \vee (\tilde{S}_{pre} \wedge C_2 \wedge D_2) \vee \cdots \vee (\tilde{S}_{pre} \wedge C_n \wedge D_n)$ where $(n \geq 1)$. Let T be a test set generated based on S. Then, T is said to satisfy the scenario-coverage (or to cover all the scenarios) of S iff $\forall_{i \in \{1,...,n\}} \exists_{t \in T} \cdot \tilde{S}_{pre}(t) \wedge C_i(t)$.*

A test set T, which is a collection of test cases, satisfies the scenario-coverage iff for any functional scenario in the FSF of the specification S, there exists some test case in T such that it satisfies both the precondition of S and the guard condition of the scenario. Such a test set T ensures that the corresponding execution paths of every scenario are tested. However, since many execution paths may be needed to implement a single scenario in the specification, the test set T may not guarantee to traverse all the paths for a given scenario. For example, suppose the following program segment is used to implement the scenario $\tilde{x} \geq 0 \wedge \tilde{x} \leq \tilde{y} \wedge y = \tilde{x} \wedge x = \tilde{y}$ of the specification *Conditional_Swap*:

```
S1
  if (x <= y)
   if (x < y)
      int q;
      q = x;
      x = y;
      y = q;
  S2 ,
```

then there are two paths implementing the scenario: $[S1, x <= y, x < y, int q, q = x, x = y, y = q, S2]$ and $[S1, x <= y, !x < y, S2]$, where $S1$ represents the program segment written before the first *if* statement and $S2$ denotes the program segment after the assignment $y = q$, and $!x < y$ means $x < y$ does not hold. If we generate a test set $T = \{(10, 6), (2, 8)\}$, obviously it meets the Criterion 1, and therefore covers every scenario defined in the specification, but it does not ensure that every path implementing the scenario given above, because the path $[S1, x <= y, !x < y, S2]$ is not traversed by the test. In order to ensure that every execution path (in terms of *statement and condition coverage*) is covered, we need to expand the test set T by creating more test cases. This process continues until all the execution paths are traversed at least once. The question here is how to proceed to create more test cases.

We take a *gradual dividing* method for the selection of more test cases. Let $(\tilde{S}_{pre} \wedge C_i \wedge D_i)$ $(i \in \{1, ..., n\})$ be any scenario of the specification S. Then, by this method we divide the sub-domain defined by the conjunction $\tilde{S}_{pre} \wedge C_i$ into smaller sub-domains, say $\Sigma_1, \Sigma_2, ..., \Sigma_q$ $(q > 1)$, and select a test case from each sub-doman Σ_j $(j \in \{1, 2, ..., q\})$ to expand the test set T. Continuously applying this method until all the execution paths are traversed. The challenge here lies in providing a general rule for deciding the sub-domains for a given sub-domain like the one defined by $\tilde{S}_{pre} \wedge C_i$, because the structure of the sub-domain is undecidable due to various possibilities in the content of the predicate $\tilde{S}_{pre} \wedge C_i$. Since the main purpose of testing in our verification method is to ensure that all the execution paths are traversed and linked to scenarios in the specification, our experience shows that chooseing values for input variables with longer "distance" can be more effective than values with shorter "distance" [13]. For example, the sub-domain defined by $\tilde{x} \geq 0 \wedge \tilde{x} \leq \tilde{y}$ of the scenario of the specification *Conditional_Swap* mentioned above can be divided into the following two sub-domains: $\tilde{x} \geq 0 \wedge \tilde{x} < \tilde{y}$ and $\tilde{x} \geq 0 \wedge \tilde{x} = \tilde{y}$ in order to cover the two obvious cases. When generating specific values for $\tilde{x}$ and $\tilde{y}$ as test cases, the two pairs of values $(\tilde{x} = 5, \tilde{y} = 10000)$ and $(\tilde{x} = 10000, \tilde{y} = 5)$ would be more effective than the two pairs of values $(\tilde{x} = 5, \tilde{y} = 10)$ and $(\tilde{x} = 10, \tilde{y} = 5)$. This is because, for example, if $\tilde{x} < \tilde{y}$ is refined into the guard condition $\tilde{x} + 6 < \tilde{y}$ in implementation, the former two pairs of values make the condition evaluate to *true* and *false* once, respectively, while the latter two pairs of values make the condition evaluate only to *false* twice.

3.3   Walkthrough

The testing phase can help traverse all relevant execution paths and detect the corresponding errors on those paths, but it does not guarantee the detection of all the errors on those paths by a limited number of executions. This is a typical limitation of testing: testing can only find the presence of bugs, but not their absence. To overcome this weakness of testing, we adopt a specification-based review technique in our verification method that allows the reviewer to perform a walkthrough analysis to find more potential errors on the tested paths. The walkthrough can also facilitate the reviewer to analyze the execution paths that are not traversed at all during the testing phase. There may be two possibilities for the test phase not to traverse some paths. One is the lack of sufficient test cases within the required schedule for testing. Another possibility is that the program may have some paths irrelevant to the functions defined in the specification or have errors that prevent the paths from being traversed (e.g., the guard condition of a *while* loop is a contradiction).

Let us treat a specification S as a set of its all scenarios and a program P as a set of its all execution paths. Then, the relation between S and P in general can be reflected by a function from S to the power set of P, based on which a walkthrough analysis is performed.

Definition 4. *Let specification S denote a set of functional scenarios $\{f_1, f_2, ..., f_n\}$ and program P denote a set of execution paths $\{p_1, p_2, ..., p_m\}$. Then, we define M as the following function:*

$$M : S \rightarrow power(P)$$
$$\forall_{f \in S} \exists_{q \in power(P)} \cdot M(f) = q$$

In this definition, f_i ($i \in \{1, ..., n\}$) denotes a scenario $\tilde{}S_{pre} \wedge C_i \wedge D_i$ of S; $power(P)$ denotes the power set of P; and $M(f) = q$ ($q \subseteq P$) means that the set of paths q correctly implements the scenario f. A formal interpretation of this equation is given as follows.

Definition 5. *Let $f \in S$ be a scenario and $q \in power(P)$ be a set of paths. Then, $M(f) = q$ iff the following condition holds:*

$$\forall_{\tilde{}\sigma, \sigma \in \Sigma} \cdot (\exists_{p \in q} \cdot \sigma = p(\tilde{}\sigma)) \Rightarrow f(\tilde{}\sigma, \sigma)$$

where a path p is treated as a partial function from states to states. A set of paths q is said to correctly implement a scenario f, denoted as $M(f) = q$, iff any final state σ produced by a single path p in the path set q based upon an initial state $\tilde{}\sigma$ satisfies the scenario f (considering f as a predicate that may contain both initial and final state variables).

Note that there is a possibility that the range of M does not fully cover the set $power(P)$ because P may be an extension rather than a refinement of S (albeit this situation may not be desired and need to be corrected ultimately). Therefore, there may be a subset of P that does not implement any scenario in the specification. We name this special subset ω; that is, $\omega \in power(P)$. Note that $\omega = \{\}$ is possible (if P is a correct refinement of S).

A walkthrough analysis is adopted in our integrated method to check whether a program P refines its specification S. If the walkthrough analysis is successful (i.e., it confirms that P refines S), it will increase the confidence in the correctness of P with respect to S; otherwise, it will help to find errors for correction or improvement. A definition of P refining S in terms of M is given as follows.

Definition 6. *Let specification S denote a set of functional scenarios $\{f_1, f_2, ..., f_n\}$ and program P denote a set of execution paths $\{p_1, p_2, ..., p_m\}$. Then, P refines S iff*

$$(\forall_{f \in S} \exists_{q \in power(P)} \cdot M(f) = q) \wedge (\forall_{p \in P} \exists_{f \in S} \cdot p \in M(f))$$

Program P refines specification S iff for any scenario in S there exists a set of execution paths in P that correctly implements the scenario and every execution path in P contributes to the implementation of some scenario in S. This definition is a specialization of the refinement concept defined in Definition 1. This is the goal to achieve by our integrated verification method and the final responsibility falls onto the "shoulder" of the walkthrough analysis phase.

The testing phase has prepared for a walkthrough analysis in two ways. One is that it clearly establishs the correspondance between a scenario in the specifiaction and some paths in the program. Another preparation is that test cases for testing the implementation of each scenario are already generated. The walk-through analysis will make good use of these prepared results in such a manner that some of the test cases are used by the reviewer to help the analysis of all the paths for each scenario.

When carrying out a walkthrough analysis of a path p in the program against the corresponding scenario f in the specification, the reviewer chooses some test case, which satisfies the guard condition of the scenario under review, and then uses the test case to manually "execute" the corresponding path for the analysis of the potential behavior. During the walkthrough process, the reviewer should also keep asking questions concerning each statement or condition on the path, such as "what is this statement/condition for?" and "why is this statement/condition here?", and the programmer (or the person responsible) tries to explain to the reviewer. During this "question time", errors are expected to be found.

4   An Example

We have applied our integrated method to the verification of an Automated Teller Machine (ATM) software system developed by a group of senior students at Hosei University in our recent project. Since the verification of the entire system is too large to fit in this paper, we choose only one operation called *Change_Password* as an example to explain how our method can be used in practice. Considering our expertise in formal specification language, we wrote the operation specification in the Structured Object-Oriented Formal Language (SOFL) [9]. Since SOFL is an extension of VDM-SL toward engineering friendly practice, our method can also be applied to VDM-SL and other model-oriented notations (e.g., Z, B), as well as their variations (e.g., VDM++, Alloy).

The specification of the operation *Change_Password* is given as follows:

process $Change\_Password(id, old\_pass, new\_pass: int)$
ext *wr* $result\_message: string$
     wr $accounts: set\ of\ Account$
pre $true,$
post $let\ R = Find\_Account(id, old\_pass, \tilde{\ }accounts)\ in$
            $R.found = true\ \wedge$
            $(1000 \le new\_pass \le 9999\ \wedge$
            $accounts =$
                $Modify\_Account(\tilde{\ }accounts, R.account, new\_pass)\ \wedge$
            $result\_message =$
                $"Your\ password\ has\ been\ successfully\ changed."$
                       $\vee$
            $\neg 1000 \le new\_pass \le 9999 \wedge accounts = \tilde{\ }accounts\ \wedge$
            $result\_message = "Your\ new\ password\ is\ unacceptable.")$
                       $\vee$
            $R.found = false \wedge accounts = \tilde{\ }accounts\ \wedge$
            $result\_message = "Your\ id\ or\ pass\ is\ wrong."$
end_process

where *int* denotes the integer type, and the two functions *Find_Account* and *Modify_Account* are defined as follows:

function *Find_Account*(*id, pass*: *int*,
$\qquad\qquad\qquad$ *accounts*: *set of Account*): *FoundAccount*
post $\qquad\qquad$ $(\exists_{a \in accounts} \cdot a.id = id \wedge a.pass = pass \Rightarrow$
$\qquad\qquad\qquad$ $Find\_Account = mk\_FoundAccount(a, true))$
$\qquad\qquad\qquad\qquad\qquad\qquad \wedge$
$\qquad\qquad$ $((\neg\exists_{a \in accounts} \cdot a.id = id \wedge a.pass = pass) \Rightarrow$
$\qquad\qquad\qquad$ $Find\_Account = mk\_FoundAccount(nil, false))$
end_function
function *Modify_Account*(*accounts*: *set of Account, account*: *Account*,
$\qquad\qquad\qquad$ *new_pass*: *int*): *set of Account*
pre $\qquad\qquad$ $account \in accounts$
post $\qquad\qquad$ $Modify\_Account = (accounts \setminus \{account\}) \cup$
$\qquad\qquad\qquad$ $\{modify(account, pass \rightarrow new\_pass)\}$

end_function,

where the composite type *Account* and *FoundAccount* are defined as follows, respectively.

$Account =$ **composed of**
$\qquad\qquad$ *id*: *int*
$\qquad\qquad$ *pass*: *int*
$\qquad\qquad$ *balance*: *nat0*
$\qquad\qquad$ *amount_available* : *nat0*
$\qquad\qquad$ **end**
$FoundAccount =$ **composed of**
$\qquad\qquad\qquad$ *account*: *Account*
$\qquad\qquad\qquad$ *found*: *bool*
$\qquad\qquad\qquad$ **end**

where *nat0* denotes the natural number type including 0.

The operation *Change_Password* takes the user's identification number *id*, old password *old_pass*, and a new password *new_pass*, and updates the customer's account in the account set, denoted by *accounts*, by replacing the old password with the new password. However, if the input *id* or *old_pass* is not correct, an error message is provided. The following is an FSF of the *Change_Password* specification.

$R = Find\_Account(id, old\_pass, \tilde{\ }accounts) \wedge$
$R.found = true \wedge 1000 \leq new\_pass \leq 9999 \wedge$
$accounts = Modify\_Account(\tilde{\ }accounts, R.account, new\_pass) \wedge$
$result\_message = "Your \ password \ has \ been \ successfully \ changed."$
$\qquad\qquad\qquad\qquad \vee$

$R = Find\_Account(id, old\_pass, \tilde{}accounts) \wedge$
$R.found = true \wedge \neg 1000 \leq new\_pass \leq 9999 \wedge$
$accounts = \tilde{}accounts \wedge$
$result\_message = "Your\ new\ password\ is\ unacceptable."$

$$\vee$$

$R = Find\_Account(id, old\_pass, \tilde{}accounts) \wedge R.found = false \wedge$
$accounts = \tilde{}accounts \wedge$
$result\_message = "Your\ id\ or\ pass\ is\ wrong."$

Note that in the FSF, we have converted conjunctions like $true \wedge P$ into P for simplicity. The FSF consists of three scenarios, each of which is one of the three disjunctive clauses in the FSF. The conditions

(1) $R = Search\_Account(id, pass, \tilde{}accounts) \wedge$
$\quad R.found = true \wedge 1000 \leq new\_pass \leq 9999,$
(2) $R = Search\_Account(id, pass, \tilde{}accounts) \wedge$
$\quad R.found = true \wedge \neg 1000 \leq new\_pass \leq 9999,$
(3) $R = Search\_Account(id, pass, \tilde{}accounts) \wedge R.found = false$

are three guard conditions of the three scenarios, respectively, and the rest parts are their defining conditions, respectively. According to Definition 3, this specification is well-formed. The specification is implemented as a method in Java as follows, where each line of the code is assigned a number for reference in discussions.

```
0 public void Change_Password (int id, old_pass, new_pass) {
1 FoundAccount R = new FoundAccount();
2 R = Find_Account(id, old_pass, accounts);
3 if (R.found = true) {
4 if (1000 <= new_pass && new_pass < 999) {
5 accounts = Modify_Account(accounts, R.account, new_pass);
6 result_message = "Your password has been successfully changed."; }
7 else result_message = "Your new password is unacceptable."
8 }
9 else result_message = "Your id or pass is wrong.";
10 }
```

We first carried out an inspection to confirm that each of the three guard conditions and each of the three defining conditions defined in the specifiaction are implemented in the program. For example, the guard condition of the first scenario (appearing as the first disjunctive clause in the FSF) above is implemented by the statements on lines 2, 3, and 4 in the program, and the defining condition of the same scenario is implemented by the statements on lines 5 and 6. We found no other errors by inspection that could prevent the program from running normally.

After the inspection, we generated a test set to test the program. This test helped us to find no error, but build the correspondance relation between the

Table 1. A test for the program Change_Password

Test cases				Execution paths
id	old_pass	new_pass	$\tilde{}\,accounts$	
6942	5190	2901	$\{(2319, 5492, 200, 100),$	$\{path_1\}$
			$(6942, 5190, 300, 100)\}$	
2319	5492	389	$\{(2319, 5492, 200, 100),$	$\{path_2\}$
			$(6942, 5190, 300, 100)\}$	
3187	5291	9147	$\{(4018, 2391, 100, 2000)\}$	$\{path_3\}$

scenarios in the specification and the execution paths in the program. Table 1 shows all the test cases generated and the corresponding paths traversed. where $path_1$, $path_2$, and $path_3$ denote the following execution paths:

$path_1 = [1, 2, 3, 4, 5, 6, 8, 10]$
$path_2 = [1, 2, 3, 4, 7, 8, 10]$
$path_3 = [1, 2, 3, 9, 10]$.

Finally, we conducted a walkthrough analysis of the three paths against their corresponding scenarios. As a result, we found an error in line 4 on $path_1$ and $path_2$. The error is that the condition $new\_pass < 9999$ should be $new\_pass <= 9999$ according to the specification, but this error could not be found by the test, since none of the three new passwords in the test cases is 9999.

5   Related Work

While formal specification-based testing techniques have been well researched, specification-based review and its integration with testing techniques are not widely explored yet.

Bernot *et al* set up a theoretical foundation and a tool support for specifciation-based testing, explaining how a formal specification can serve as a basis for test case generation and as an oracle for test result evaluation [1]. Dick and Faivre proposed to transform pre- and postconditions into a disjunctive normal form (DNF) and then to use it as the basis for test case generation [14]. Stocks and Carrington suggested to define test template as the basis for test case generation and to divide a large test template into smaller templates for generating more detailed test cases [2]. Offutt and Liu investigated how to effectively generate test cases based on SOFL specifiactions [15] and finite state machine-based formal specifications [16], and discussed the advantages and weakness of the existing specification-based testing techniques.

As far as specification-based review is concerned, an early idea of using formal specifications to help the inspection of programs was described by Parnas and his colleagues in [17]. The technique, known as Document Driven Inspection (DDI), was developed to tackle structured programs. Using the DDI technique, the inspector needs to document the program to be inspected as a set of *displays*.

Each display consists of three elements: formal specification, program, and a list of invoked subroutines. However, the DDI technique is focused on the issue of how to derive a formal document from a given structured program, but not much on how the formal document is utilized to systematically guide inspections of programs. In order to address this issue and to make formal specification benefical to software review in industry, we have conducted an intensive research on specification-based review over the last five years. We established a systematic method for inspecting programs based on formal operation specifications in pre- and postconditions in [7]. The fundamental principle underlying the method is to inspect whether every functional scenario defined in a specification is correctly implemented in the program. We have also carried out a case study for the assessment of the method and constructed a prototype tool for the method [8].

During our research on specifiaction-based review and testing techniques, we found that both techniques are complementary rather than one can replace another, as explained in Section 1. Compared to the existing work mentioned above, the integrated method described in this paper has taken advantages of specification-based review and testing and avoided their disadvantages. We believe that our method can be more cost-effective in detecting errors than the existing review or testing approaches based on our experience so far, but further rigorous studies are needed to clarify this point in the future.

6   Conclusion and Future Work

We have described an integrated method for verifying programs. The method combines the specifiaction-based review and testing in three phases: inspection, testing, and walkthrough analysis. Each phase prepares for the next one and helps find errors from a different angle. We have presented an example to show how the method is applied to verify the program of an operation called *Change_Password* in an ATM system against its formal specification. As future research, we plan to carry out several empirical studies on the application of the method to large-scale programs for the assessment of its effectiveness and to build a software tool for the method to enhance its usability and efficiency.

References

[1] Bernot, G., Gaudel, M.C., Marre, B.: Software testing based on formal specifications: a theory and a tool. Software Engineering Journal, 387–405 (November 1991)
[2] Stocks, P., Carrington, D.: A Framework for Specification-Based Testing. IEEE Transactions on Software Engineering 22(11), 777–793 (1996)
[3] IEEE. 1028-1997 IEEE Standard for Software Reviews. IEEE Computer Society (1997)
[4] Wheeler, D.A., Brykczynski, B., Meeson, R.N.: Software Inspection: An Industry Best Practice. IEEE Computer Society Press, Los Alamitos (1996)
[5] Menachem, M.B., Marliss, G.S.: Software Quality: Producing Practical, Consistent Software. International Thomson Computer Press (1997)

[6] Heyer, T.: Semantic Inspection of Early UML Designs. IEEE Transactions on Software Engineering 28(4), 413–430 (2002)

[7] Liu, S., Nagoya, F., Chen, Y., Goya, M., McDermid, J.A.: An Automated Approach to Specification-Based Program Inspection. In: Lau, K.-K., Banach, R. (eds.) ICFEM 2005. LNCS, vol. 3785, pp. 421–434. Springer, Heidelberg (2005)

[8] Nagoya, F., Liu, S., Chen, Y.: A Tool and Case Study for Specification-Based Program Review. In: COMPSAC 2005, Edinburgh, Scotland, July 25-28, pp. 375–380. IEEE Computer Society Press, Los Alamitos (2005)

[9] Liu, S.: Formal Engineering for Industrial Software Development Using the SOFL Method. Springer, Heidelberg (2004)

[10] Liu, S., Wang, H.: An Automated Approach to Specification Animation for Validation. Journal of Systems and Software 80, 1271–1285 (2007)

[11] Liu, S.: Verifying Consistency and Validity of Formal Specifications by Testing. In: Wing, J.M., Woodcock, J., Davies, J. (eds.) Proceedings of the World Congress on Formal Methods in the Development of Computing Systems, Toulouse, France. LNCS, pp. 896–914. Springer, Heidelberg (1999)

[12] Miller, T., Strooper, P.: A Framework and Tool Support for the Systematic Testing of Model-Based Specifications. ACM Transactions on Software Engineering and Methodology 12(4), 409–439 (2003)

[13] Liu, S., Chen, Y.: A Relation-Based Method Combining Functional and Structural Testing for Test Case Generation. Journal of Systems and Software (to appear, 2007)

[14] Dick, J., Faivre, A.: Automating the Generation and Sequencing of Test Cases from Model-based Specifications. In: Larsen, P.G., Woodcock, J.C.P. (eds.) FME 1993. LNCS, vol. 670, pp. 268–284. Springer, Heidelberg (1993)

[15] Offutt, A.J., Liu, S.: Generating Test Data from SOFL Specifications. Journal of Systems and Software 49(1), 49–62 (1999)

[16] Offutt, A.J., Liu, S., Abdurazik, A., Ammann, P.: Generating Test Data from State-Based Specifications. Journal of Software Testing, Verification and Reliability 13, 25–53 (2003)

[17] Parnas, D.L., Madey, J., Iglewski, M.: Precise Documentation of Well-Structured Programs. IEEE Transactions on Software Engineering 20(12), 948–976 (1994)

Testing for Refinement in CSP

Ana Cavalcanti[1] and Marie-Claude Gaudel[2]

[1] University of York, Department of Computer Science
York YO10 5DD, UK
[2] LRI, Université de Paris-Sud and CNRS
Orsay 91405, France

Abstract. CSP is a well-established formalism for modelling and verification of concurrent reactive systems based on refinement. Consolidated denotational models and an effective tool have encouraged much work on algebraic reasoning and model checking. Testing techniques based on CSP, however, have not been widely explored, and in this paper we take a first step by instantiating Gaudel et al's theory of formal testing to CSP. We identify the testability hypothesis that we consider necessary to use CSP models as a basis for testing. We also define test sets that we prove to be exhaustive with respect to traces and failures refinement, and consider optimisations, inputs and outputs, and selection strategies. Our results are proved in terms of the CSP denotational models; they are a sound foundation for the development of test-generation techniques.

1 Introduction

It is well accepted that formal specifications can be useful bases for software testing; we refer to [6,11,2,3,1,17] among many other pioneering papers and surveys. In spite of that, testing based on CSP [26,16], which is a popular formal notation for specification and verification of concurrent systems, has not been widely explored. In this paper, we establish the foundations of CSP-based testing by instantiating a well-established theory of formal testing.

Even though it has been recognised for a while that formal models can bring much to software testing, embedding implementation testing within a formal framework is far from being obvious. In this case, we test a system: a system is not a formula, even if it can be (partially) described as such. Thus, testing is related to, but very different from proof of correctness based on the program text using, for example, an assertion technique. Similarly, testing is different from model checking, where verifications are based on a known model of the system: when testing, the model corresponding to the system under test is unknown. If it was known, testing would not be necessary... Moreover, it is sometimes difficult to observe the state of the system under test [6,12,17]. These points have been successfully circumvented in several testing methods that are based on formal specifications (or models) and on conformance relations that precisely state what it means for a system under test to satisfy a specification [7,8,9,31,14,13,20,18].

The gap between systems and models is generally taken into account by explicit assumptions on the systems under test [6,1,17] that are called "testability

M. Butler, M. Hinchey, M.M. Larrondo-Petric (Eds.): ICFEM 2007, LNCS 4789, pp. 151–170, 2007.
© Springer-Verlag Berlin Heidelberg 2007

hypotheses" in [1] or "test hypotheses" in [4]. Such assumptions are fundamental in the proof that the success of the test set derived from the specification establishes the conformance relation. Moreover, they provide hints on complementary tests or proofs that may be necessary to ensure this equivalence.

CSP provides, in addition to a formal semantics of communicating processes, formal definitions of notions of refinement similar to the conformance relations used in specification-based testing or model-based testing. Peleska and Siegel [24,25] have already studied and applied CSP-based testing. They have not, however, addressed the issue of the gap between the system under test and the CSP model that it defines. The practical test sets they propose in [25] are inspired by, but not in direct correspondence with, their theoretical definitions.

Schneider [27] defines a partition that classifies refusable and non-refusable events, and high-level and low-level events, for the purposes of modelling security applications in CSP. In that work, two conformance relations based on testing are defined, and Schneider shows how model checking can be used to establish such relations. In our work, on the other hand, we are interested in refinement.

More recently, CSP has been used to formalise a notion of conformance traditionally associated with input-output labelled transition systems [22]. This work goes well beyond ours, in that it provides a technique and a tool for generation and selection of tests based on the use of FDR, the CSP refinement model checker. Our definition of a test case, however, is similar to theirs. We believe that the results on exhaustiveness of test sets and factorisation that we present here are relevant to further justify some of the definitions in [22].

The work in [29] recognises the potential impact of the assumptions about the interaction of a system with its environment on refinement; it aims at supporting the validation of (implicit) assumptions. For that, mutation testing techniques are applied to a CSP model of the system, and the mutants that satisfy the properties of interest are used as a basis for the clarification of requirements.

In this paper, we state the testability hypotheses that are associated with the use of CSP. Moreover, we formalise accurately the kind of observations (traces and refusals) that must be done when performing test experiments derived from a CSP specification. It leads to a novel formulation of the tests and of their verdicts. We give algebraic proofs that getting the right observations when running these tests is equivalent to establishing traces or failures refinement.

In the next section, we give a brief introduction to CSP, and in Section 3 we discuss the consequences of using a process algebra as a basis for testing. In Section 4, we introduce our testability hypotheses and their consequences, and in Section 5, we give our exhaustive test sets. In the next three sections, we discuss possible optimisations of our tests, test selection criteria, and the issues raised by inputs and outputs. Proofs of our results can be found in [5]. We conclude in Section 9 with a summary, and a discussion of related and future work.

2   A Few Things on CSP

Here we briefly recall the syntax of CSP, and some important points of its semantics and notions of refinement. More information can be found in [26].

2.1   Main CSP Operators

In CSP, a system is modelled as a process that can interact with its environment via a number of events. CSP models describe a collection of processes and their patterns of interactions. The unit of interaction is an event which processes perform and on which they may synchronise; the *occurrence* of events is atomic. The set of (external) events of a process P is denoted αP.

There are two basic processes: *STOP* is a deadlocked process, and *SKIP* is the terminating process. The process $a \to P$ can perform an event a and then behave as P. The external choice, $P_1 \;\square\; P_2$, is initially prepared to behave either as P_1 or as P_2, with the choice being made on occurrence of the first event. Nondeterminism is modelled by an internal choice, $P_1 \;\sqcap\; P_2$, which is a process that can arbitrarily choose to behave as either P_1 or P_2.

Processes can also be combined in sequence, using the operator ; , or in parallel. CSP provides a number of operators for parallelism; here we use the alphabetised parallelism: $P_1 \;[\![\, A \,]\!]\; P_2$, which executes P_1 and P_2 concurrently, requiring that they synchronise on events that are in the set A.

Events can be external, that is, observable and controllable by the environment, or internal. Using the hiding operator, like in $P \setminus A$, we define a process that behaves like P, but whose events in the set A are internal.

A simple example, which we use later on, is given below: a process $Counter_2$ that counts from 0 to 2, and is defined in terms of the processes C_1 and C_2.

$$Counter_2 = add \to C_1$$
$$C_1 = add \to C_2 \;\square\; sub \to Counter_2$$
$$C_2 = sub \to C_1$$

The events in $\alpha\,Counter_2 = \{add, sub\}$ model requests to add or subtract.

In CSP, inputs and outputs are not primitive concepts; they are modelled using events whose names are composite. A classical example is a copying process *Replicator*, which takes an input x from a channel c and sends it back.

$$Replicator = c?x \to c!x \to C$$

If we assume that the type of x is the rather small set $\{0, 1, 2\}$, then we have the events $c.0$, $c.1$, and $c.2$. In this case, the above definition of *Replicator* is just an abbreviation for the following definition in terms of these basic events.

$$Replicator = (c.0 \to c.0 \to C) \;\square\; (c.1 \to c.1 \to C) \;\square\; (c.2 \to c.2 \to C)$$

An input $c?x \to P(x)$ is an abbreviation for a possibly infinite external choice over processes $c.v \to P(v)$, for all possible values v for x. An output event $c!e$, on the other hand, is just another name for $c.v$, where v is the value of e.

2.2   Semantics and Refinement

There are three well-established semantic models of CSP: the traces, the (stable) failures, and the failures-divergences models. The traces model characterises a process P by its set $traces(P)$ of traces: finite sequences of events which it can perform. It is a subset of $((\alpha P) \cup \{ \checkmark \})^*$; A^* is the set of finite sequences of elements of A. The special event $\checkmark$ records termination. The empty trace is $\langle \rangle$. The set of all events, except only for $\checkmark$, is Σ; the set including $\checkmark$ is denoted $\Sigma^\checkmark$. In the sequel, we sometimes consider traces as processes: the finite trace $a_1, a_2, \ldots$ corresponds to the process $a_1 \to a_2 \to \ldots \to SKIP$.

As usual we write P/s to describe the behaviour of the process P after one of its traces s, and $initials(P/s)$ for the set of events performable by P after s. In fact, $initials$ is defined for any process P [26, page 197], and can be characterised in terms of its traces as $initials(P) = \{ a : \Sigma^\checkmark \mid \langle a \rangle \in traces(P)$.

For a trace s of a process P and a subset $A = \{ a_1, \ldots, a_n \}$ of αP, the pair (s, A) is a failure for P if, and only if, after performing s, P may refuse all events of A: in other words, $P \, [\![\alpha P]\!] \, (s; (a_1 \to P_1 \square \ldots \square a_n \to P_n)$ may deadlock just after s. For $Counter_2$, the set of failures includes the following elements.

$(\langle \rangle, \{ sub \}), (\langle \rangle, \emptyset), (\langle add \rangle, \emptyset),$
$(\langle add, add \rangle, \{ add \}), (\langle add, add \rangle, \emptyset), (\langle add, sub \rangle, \{ sub \}), (\langle add, sub \rangle, \emptyset),$
$(\langle add, add, sub \rangle, \emptyset), \ldots$

The set $failures(P)$ containing all failures of P is subset closed: for instance, if P may deadlock when the choice among the events $\{ a, b \}$ is proposed by its environment after a trace s, it may deadlock as well if only a or b is proposed. The traces of P can be defined from its failures: $traces(P) = \{ t : \Sigma^{\checkmark *} \mid (t, \emptyset) \in failures(P) \}$.

The set $divergences(P)$ is the set of traces of P that lead to divergent behaviour, that is, an infinite sequence of internal events, plus all the extensions of those traces. The canonical semantics of CSP is given by the failures-divergences model; it represents a process P by the two sets $failures(P)$ and $divergences(P)$.

Here, we assume that specifications and systems are divergence free. A divergent specification is necessarily a mistake. Also, when testing, divergences raise problems of observability; generally, it is not possible to distinguish a divergent from a deadlocked system using testing. Therefore, we identify divergence with deadlock in the models of the systems under test, so that the models are divergence free; most authors circumvent the problem of observability in this way. If the system under test is divergent, the divergence is detected as a (probably forbidden) deadlock and reported as such by the verdict of the tests.

We consider two refinement relations between CSP processes: traces and failures refinement. A process P is trace-refined by a process Q, that is $P \sqsubseteq_T Q$, if, and only if, $traces(Q) \subseteq traces(P)$. For failures refinement, $P \sqsubseteq_F Q$, we require that $failures(Q) \subseteq failures(P)$, that is, Q refines P with respect to failures if, and only if, all its possible traces are traces of P, and Q may refuse a set of events and deadlock after a trace only if P may.

The first refinement relation is restrictive: it states that there are no observable behaviours of the refined process that are not behaviours of the original process. It accepts the idle process $STOP$ as a trace refinement of any other process. The second refinement relation is still restrictive on traces, but prescriptive on acceptances: it states that the refined process can only refuse to do something when the original process may refuse the same thing in the same situation. In this case, there are forbidden behaviours and mandatory behaviours.

For divergence-free processes, failures refinement as described above corresponds to the refinement relation in the canonical model of CSP: failures-divergences refinement, which is defined as follows.

$$P \sqsubseteq_{FD} Q \mathrel{\widehat{=}} \mathit{failures}(Q) \subseteq \mathit{failures}(P) \wedge \mathit{divergences}(Q) \subseteq \mathit{divergences}(P)$$

In CSP, failures refinement is defined for the stable-failures model, and not for the failures-divergences model as above. In the stable-failures model, a process is represented by its set of traces and its set of failures, that is, we have a separate record of the traces, independent of the failures. This is because, in this model, failures are only recorded for stable states, so that traces that lead to divergence are not in any of the failures. For the stable-failures model, failures refinement requires subset inclusion of both traces and failures.

In the absence of divergence, however, the failures in the stable-failures model are exactly those of the failures-divergences model, which contain a failure for all traces of the process [26, page 215]. In this case, failures inclusion, as required above in our definition of failures refinement, implies traces inclusion. In summary, for divergence-free processes, our definition of failures refinement is equivalent to the standard definition of failures refinement in CSP.

Furthermore, since the set of divergences of divergence-free processes are empty, failures-divergences refinement corresponds to failures refinement. In summary, our definition of failures refinement is the notion of refinement in the canonical model of CSP, when we are restricted to divergence-free processes.

3   Process-Algebra Based Testing

Given a specification SP and a system under test (SUT), any testing activity is, explicitly or not, based on a satisfaction relation (also called conformance relation): SUT sat SP. The subject of the test is an executable system. A system is a dynamic entity. It raises tricky issues such as observability and controllability, and is sometimes submitted to peculiar physical constraints. The only way to observe it is to interact via some specific (and often limited) interface.

To test a system against a process specification, we need tests (more exactly tester processes) built on the same alphabet of events as the specification (possibly enriched by some special symbols). The execution of a given test consists in running it and the SUT in parallel.

The verdict about the success or not of a test execution depends on the observations that can be made, and it is based on the satisfaction relation. Most testing methods based on process algebras consider that two kinds of observations are possible: external events, and deadlock (that is, refusal of some external events). Deadlock is observed via time-out mechanisms: it is assumed that if the SUT does not react after a given time limit, it is blocked.

The tests are derived from the specification on the basis of the satisfaction relation, and often on the basis of some additional knowledge of the SUT and of its operational environment called *testability hypothesis*. One advantage of such a formal framework is that it makes it possible to define test sets that are unbiased and valid: they accept any *SUT* satisfying the specification and the testability hypothesis, and they reject any *SUT* that does not. Such test sets are called *exhaustive* in [12] or *complete* by other authors [3].

Exhaustive test sets are often infinite, or too large to be used in practice, but they are used as references for selecting finite, practical, test subsets according to a variety of criteria, such as additional hypotheses on the *SUT* [1], coverage of the specification [6,17], or test purposes [10].

4   Testing Versus Refinement: Testability Hypotheses

Work on testing processes is traditionally based on labelled transition systems or finite state machines. To recast these results for CSP, the obvious route is to consider its operational semantics. However, there is a formal link between the operational and the denotational semantics of CSP. The main concepts usually associated with the operational semantics, like sets of initials and refusals, are also defined in terms of the denotational semantics.

This is most convenient to establish a relationship between testing and refinement. The definitions of refinement based on the denotational semantics are very simple: just subset inclusion, as presented above. It is fortunate that we are able to discuss testing notions based on the usual operational notions, but that we have a clear link to the denotational semantics. This simplifies the proofs, and allows for a formal algebraic style. When considering test criteria and test selection, though, it is necessary to refer to the operational semantics. For instance, the most popular selection criterion is transition coverage: explicit notions of states and transitions are needed to formulate it.

The refinement relations presented in Section 2.2 are natural candidates for CSP-based testing. They are, however, relations between *CSP* process, and the *SUT* is not a *CSP* process. A classical way of overcoming this difficulty is to assume that *the SUT behaves like some unknown CSP process*; this is our first testability hypothesis. With this assumption, we can then require that this process is a refinement of the *CSP* specification. We define that a system P behaves like a CSP process Q to mean that, in any environment, running P or running Q yields the same set of observations. If P and Q were both CSP processes, then behavioural equivalence would be characterised as refinement in both directions, but P is not a CSP process; it is a system.

In more detail, if SUT_{CSP} denotes the unknown *CSP* process that behaves as the *SUT*, we can consider the satisfaction relation $SP \sqsubseteq_F SUT_{CSP}$ based on failures refinement. In the sequel, we write *SUT* instead of SUT_{CSP} when there is no ambiguity. The use of failures refinement as a satisfaction relation has been studied in different frameworks, with various names and notations since the original definition of testing equivalence in [21]; *testing preorder*, *failure preorder*, $\leq_{te}$, *red*, *conf* are examples of the terminology that has been adopted.

The testability hypothesis requires that events of the specification abstract operations are perceived as atomic and of irrelevant duration in the SUT. It is necessary to ensure in some way that this requirement is fulfilled, for example, by developing wrappers, or performing some complementary proofs or tests.

It is interesting to note that, similarly, testing methods based on Finite State Machine (FSM) descriptions assume that the SUT behaves as an FSM with the same number of states as the specification, or a known number of states [17]. Likewise, methods based on IO-automata or IO-Transition Systems assume that the SUT behaves as an IO-automata: it is input-enabled, that is, always ready to accept any input [31]. Analogously, methods based on algebraic specifications assume that the SUT behaves as a many-sorted algebra [1].

Our second testability hypothesis is related to nondeterminism in the SUT and its influence on the verdict after test executions. This hypothesis, sometimes called the *complete testing assumption*, postulates that *there is some known integer k such that, if a test experiment is performed k times, then all possible behaviours are observed*. The issue of the number of test executions is a classical problem in black-box testing of nondeterministic systems. Its choice is generally based on empirical knowledge of the system, as, for example, its level of internal parallelism that may give rise to nondeterminism, and the length of the test. Without such hypotheses, it is hopeless to get a meaningful conclusion after a test campaign. For some hints, see [13], and for recent variants, see [15].

An example is an SUT that reads the system *clock*, and based on whether the time is an odd or an even number, performs the *even* or *odd*. Using the first testability hypothesis, we assume that it behaves like the CSP process below.

$$CReader = clock?t \rightarrow \textbf{if} \ even(t) \, \textbf{then} \ (even \rightarrow SKIP) \, \textbf{else} \ (odd \rightarrow SKIP)$$

If we cannot observe the *clock*, then the behaviour of the SUT is more accurately described by the CSP process $CReader \setminus \{\!|clock|\!\}$, which, using the algebraic laws of CSP, we can show to be equal, in the failures-divergences model, to the nondeterministic process $even \rightarrow SKIP \sqcap odd \rightarrow SKIP$. Such SUT does not satisfy, according to the semantics of nondeterminism in CSP, our second testability hypothesis: no SUT that behaves like a nondeterministic CSP process does, since nondeterminism in CSP is modelled as a completely arbitrary choice, with no guarantee of balanced behaviour for any value of k. Extra knowledge of the performance of the SUT, and of the system *clock*, however, may allow us to conclude that, if the system is executed, for instance, sixty times in a single minute, it is guaranteed to read an even and an odd time at least once.

Such considerations are beyond what we aim at formalising in this paper. For the above example, for instance, we can say that $CReader \setminus \{\!|clock|\!\}$ is not an accurate model of the SUT. The extra knowledge of the performance of the SUT and of the clock means that we know that it actually behaves like a deterministic, in the sense of CSP, process whose description requires the formalisation of a notion of time, and properties of the clock. In other words, we accept the restriction imposed by the second testability hypothesis that, in the CSP sense, the SUT is deterministic, but point out that determinism may come from the observation of events that are not necessarily expected to be in the alphabet of the specification. In our example, these events are, for instance, the passage of time and the system clock.

These considerations are not relevant for works based, for example, on finite state machines, where nondeterminism is not necessarily arbitrary. In CSP, nondeterminism captures a notion of abstraction relevant for system development, and, therefore, refinement. If there is any factor that allows us to make any conclusion about the balance of nondeterministic behaviour, this means that, in the CSP sense, the system is not really nondeterministic.

5   Tests and Exhaustive Test Sets

Failures refinement can be expressed in terms of traces refinement and a well-studied satisfaction relation [3]: the *conf* conformance relation (cf. Proposition 3.13.1 in [30]). For CSP processes P and Q, *conf* can be defined as follows.

$$Q \; conf \; P \cong \forall \, t : traces(P) \cap traces(Q) \bullet Ref(Q, t) \subseteq Ref(P, t)$$
$$\text{where } Ref(P, t) \cong \{ \, X \mid (t, X) \in failures(P) \, \}$$

The above definition of $Ref(P, t)$ is compatible with the definition of $refusals(P)$ in CSP, for the process P/t [26, pages 94,197].

The following theorem establishes the relationship between failure refinement, traces refinement, and *conf*; its simple proof is in [5].

Theorem 1. $(P \sqsubseteq_F Q) \Leftrightarrow (P \sqsubseteq_T Q \land Q \; conf \; P)$

This theorem justifies the suggestion in [30] that traces refinement and *conf* can be checked separately. In this section we first study how to test a system with respect to traces refinement (that is, trace containment), and then address testing against *conf* (that is, refusal containment). These two kinds of testing are suitable for the detection of different types of faults. Testing against traces refinement makes it possible to detect forbidden behaviours, and testing against *conf* makes it possible to detect forbidden deadlocks.

5.1   Testing Against Traces Refinement

Since trace refinement prescribes that $traces(SUT) \subseteq traces(SP)$, but not the reverse, a testing strategy does not need to test that a SUT can execute the traces of SP. It is sufficient to test it against those traces in $\alpha(SP)^{\checkmark *}$ that are not traces of SP and to check that they are refused. Moreover, it is sufficient to consider the minimal prefixes of forbidden traces that are forbidden themselves. For example, if after a trace abc, the event d is forbidden, then $abcda$, and $abcdb$, for example, are also forbidden, but we only need to consider $abcd$. On the other hand, if abd is also forbidden, we also check that it is refused.

Formally, we define a test set that proposes to the SUT the following traces.

$$\{ s \frown \langle \, a \, \rangle \mid s \in traces(SP) \land a \notin initials(SP/s) \}$$

For one test execution, the verdict is as follows. If the trace s, followed by a deadlock is observed, then the test execution is said to be a *success*. If $s \frown a$

is observed, we have a *failure*. If a strict prefix of *s* followed by a deadlock is observed, then the test execution is *inconclusive*; the trace *s* has not been executed by the *SUT*, and this is acceptable for traces refinement.

As mentioned in Section 4, if the *SUT* is nondeterministic, then several executions of the same test must be performed and a global verdict is reached based on such a set of executions. When the *SUT* is known to be deterministic, there is no need for several executions of any of the tests, and the *SUT* passes a test as soon as the verdict is either successful or inconclusive, and not a failure.

When the *SUT* is nondeterministic, the following global verdict for several executions of the same test is recorded. If there is one execution with a failure verdict, the *SUT* does not pass the test. If for all the test executions the verdict is either success or inconclusive, the *SUT* passes the test.

The idea of basing the test set on the pairs (s, a) where $s \in traces(SP)$ and $a \notin initials(SP/s)$ is inspired by the work of Peleska and Siegel [24], where it is proved that based on this set of pairs, it is possible to detect all violations of traces refinement, and that this is the minimal set of pairs with this property. The notions of test and verdict that we present below, however, are slightly different, and also, we give an algebraic proof of the exhaustivity of the test set.

As mentioned in Section 3, a test execution is a run of the *SUT* and a test process *T* in parallel; we describe this in CSP as $(SUT \parallel\!\![\alpha SP]\!\!\parallel T)\backslash\alpha SP$. The synchronisation set, which is the interface of the system as defined in the specification, is hidden; so, the external events of *SUT* are internal in a test execution. This means that synchronisation between the *SUT* and the test proceeds immediately, and cannot be affected by the test execution environment.

On the other hand, this also means that direct observation of traces is not possible in such test executions. Thus, we introduce three special events, *pass*, *fail*, and *inc*, in the alphabet of the test in order to perform on-the-fly verdict. Using these events, we have a very direct characterisation in CSP of the verdict of a single test execution as described above.

For a finite trace $s = a_1, a_2, \ldots, a_n$ and an event a, we define a *CSP* test process $T_T(s, a)$ as $inc \rightarrow a_1 \rightarrow \ldots inc \rightarrow a_n \rightarrow pass \rightarrow a \rightarrow fail \rightarrow STOP$. Formally, we can describe it as shown below.

$$T_T(\langle\rangle, a) = pass \rightarrow a \rightarrow fail \rightarrow STOP$$
$$T_T(\langle\checkmark\rangle, a) = pass \rightarrow a \rightarrow fail \rightarrow STOP$$
$$T_T(\langle b\rangle \frown s, a) = inc \rightarrow b \rightarrow T_T(s, a)$$

Extending *s* with *a* is supposed to lead to an invalid trace; and the test aims at ruling it out. The event $\checkmark$, it if happens, is final [26, page 143], and only marks termination. So, no event should occur after it.

The execution of a test *T* for a given *SUT*, against a specification *SP*, is described by the *CSP* process below.

$$Execution^{SP}_{SUT}(T) = (SUT \parallel\!\![\alpha SP]\!\!\parallel T)\backslash\alpha SP$$

The verdict is given by the last event observed (*pass*, *fail*, or *inc*) before deadlock.

Depending on the precision required for the verdict and on some knowledge of the SUT, it is possible in some cases to use only one or two events among $pass$, $fail$, and inc. If the SUT is deterministic, for instance, there are no inconclusive verdicts, and inc can be eliminated. In fact, in our case, since we are testing for absence of forbidden traces, we can eliminate inc in this way. If any prefix of a tested trace is observed, the test is successful (due to the prefix closure of the sets of traces and the definition of trace refinement). Our use of the three events, however, gives a direct model of verdict for a single test execution.

We now define an exhaustive test set for trace refinement.

$$Exhaust_T(SP) = \{\ T_T(s, a) \mid s \in traces(SP) \wedge a \notin initials(SP/s)\ \}$$

Testing of termination is covered because it is signalled by the event $\checkmark$ that is explicitly included in the traces. As an example, we consider the process $Counter_2$ from Section 1. The set $Exhaust_T(Counter_2)$ contains the following tests.

$T_T(\langle\ \rangle, sub) = pass \rightarrow sub \rightarrow fail \rightarrow STOP$
$T_T(\langle add, add\rangle, add) = inc \rightarrow add \rightarrow inc \rightarrow add \rightarrow pass \rightarrow add \rightarrow fail \rightarrow STOP$
$T_T(\langle add, sub\rangle, sub) = inc \rightarrow add \rightarrow inc \rightarrow sub \rightarrow pass \rightarrow sub \rightarrow fail \rightarrow STOP$
$T_T(\langle add, add, sub, add\rangle, add) =$
    $inc \rightarrow add \rightarrow inc \rightarrow add \rightarrow inc \rightarrow sub \rightarrow inc \rightarrow add \rightarrow pass \rightarrow add \rightarrow fail \rightarrow STOP$
$T_T(\langle add, add, sub, sub\rangle, sub) = \ldots$

This is, of course, an infinite set since the set $traces(Counter_2)$ is infinite.

The next theorem establishes that an SUT that does not fail any of the tests in $Exhaust_T(SP)$ is a traces refinement of SP. Its proof can be found in [5]. For a trace t, we use $last(t)$ to refer to its last event.

Theorem 2 (Exhaustivity of $Exhaust_T$). *Given two CSP processes, SUT and SP, $SP \sqsubseteq_T SUT$ if, and only if*

$$\forall\ T_T(s, a) : Exhaust_T(SP);\ t : traces(Execution_{SUT}^{SP}(T_T(s, a))) \bullet last(t) \neq fail$$

As mentioned in Section 3, on the basis of this exhaustive test set, it is possible to design selection and optimisation strategies for getting finite test sets.

5.2   Testing Against Refusals

In this section we address the problem of testing whether an SUT behaves as a CSP process SUT_{CSP} that satisfies SUT_{CSP} *conf* SP. The definition of *conf* requires us to check that, after performing one of their common traces, the failures of SUT are failures of SP as well. For that we check that, after every trace s of SP, the SUT cannot refuse all events in a set A accepted by SP.

This is achieved by executing the test described by the CSP process corresponding to the trace s followed by an external choice among the events in A. Basically, a test execution proposes to the SUT the traces of the CSP process $s; (\Box\ a \in A \bullet a \rightarrow STOP)$ where $s \in traces(SP)$ and $(s, A) \notin failures(SP)$. The verdict of one execution of such a test is as follows. If s, followed by a deadlock is observed, the test execution is said to be a *failure*. If a trace $s \frown a$, with $a \in A$ is observed the result of the test is said to be a *success*. If a strict prefix of s followed by a deadlock is observed, the test execution is said to be *inconclusive*; the trace s has not been executed by the SUT during this test execution.

Using the same events *inc*, *pass*, and *fail* that modelled the verdict of test executions concerned with traces refinement, we define the test for a trace $s = a_1, a_2, \ldots, a_n$ of SP and a set A such that $(s, A) \notin failures(SP)$, or in other words, $A \notin Ref(SP, s)$ as follows.

$$T_F(s, A) = inc \rightarrow a_1 \rightarrow inc \rightarrow a_2 \rightarrow inc. \ldots a_n \rightarrow fail \rightarrow (\square\, a \in A \bullet a \rightarrow pass \rightarrow STOP)$$

It can be formally defined as follows.

$$T_F(\langle\,\rangle, A) = fail \rightarrow (\square\, a \in A \bullet a \rightarrow pass \rightarrow STOP)$$
$$T_F(\langle\, a \,\rangle \frown s, A) = inc \rightarrow a \rightarrow T_F(s, A)$$

Termination is not a special case here: every set is refused after a trace ending by $\checkmark$. If s ends in $\checkmark$, then there is no A that does not belong to the failures of SP [26, page 192], and so we do not need to define $T(\langle\checkmark\,\rangle, A)$.

When the SUT is nondeterministic, the global verdict for several executions of the same test is just as before. If there is one execution with a failure verdict, the SUT does not pass the test. If for all the test executions the verdict is either success or inconclusive, it passes the test. However, it is not necessary to consider all these tests because as soon as $(s, A) \notin failures(SP)$, then $\forall A' \supset A \bullet (s, A') \notin failures(SP)$. If the SUT passes the test for A, it will in principle pass the test for A'; the only concern would be with nondeterminism. On the other hand, if the SUT fails the test for A, it may pass the test for A', which offers more choices, but a problem has already been identified.

Thus for each trace s, it is sufficient to consider a subset of the sets A' such that (s, A') are not in $failures(SP)$; namely we consider the set $\mathcal{A}_s$ of sets $A_1, \ldots, A_m$ of events such that for all A_i, $(s, A_i) \notin failures(SP)$, and for all $(s, A) \notin failures(SP)$ there is $A_i \in \mathcal{A}_s$ such that $A \supseteq A_i$. These are the minimal acceptance sets of SP. In the case of a deadlock, there is no A such that $(s, A) \notin failures(SP)$, and in this case $\mathcal{A}_s$ is empty. Precisely, we propose the following exhaustive minimal test set for refusal containment.

$$Exhaust_{conf}(SP) = \{\, T_F(s, A) \mid s \in traces(SP) \wedge A \in \mathcal{A}_s \,\}$$

where $\mathcal{A}_s = min_{\subseteq}(\{\, A \mid (s, A) \notin failures(SP) \,\})$. For a set $\mathcal{S}$ of sets, we define $min_{\subseteq}(\mathcal{S}) = \{\, S \mid \overline{S} \in \mathcal{S} \wedge \neg\, \exists S' \bullet S' \in \mathcal{S} \wedge S' \subset S \,\}$.

For the process $Counter_2$, we have the following minimal acceptances.

For $\langle\,\rangle$, we have $\{\, add \,\}$
For $\langle\, add \,\rangle$, we have $\{\, add \,\}, \{\, sub \,\}$
For $\langle\, add, add \,\rangle$, we have $\{\, sub \,\}$
For $\langle\, add, sub \,\rangle$, we have $\{\, add \,\}$
For $\langle\, add, add, sub \,\rangle$, we have $\{\, add \,\}, \{\, sub \,\} \ldots$

For each trace, there can be several refusal sets, and similarly, several sets of minimal acceptances. In the exhaustive test set, we have the following tests.

$$T_F(\langle\,\rangle, \{\,add\,\}) = fail \rightarrow add \rightarrow pass \rightarrow STOP$$
$$T_F(\langle\,add\,\rangle, \{\,add\,\}) = inc \rightarrow add \rightarrow fail \rightarrow add \rightarrow pass \rightarrow STOP$$
$$T_F(\langle\,add\,\rangle, \{\,sub\,\}) = inc \rightarrow add \rightarrow fail \rightarrow sub \rightarrow pass \rightarrow STOP$$
$$T_F(\langle\,add, add\,\rangle, \{\,sub\,\}) = inc \rightarrow add \rightarrow inc \rightarrow add \rightarrow fail \rightarrow sub \rightarrow pass \rightarrow STOP$$
$$T_F(\langle\,add, sub\,\rangle, \{\,add\,\}) = inc \rightarrow add \rightarrow inc \rightarrow sub \rightarrow fail \rightarrow add \rightarrow pass \rightarrow STOP$$
$$T_F(\langle\,add, add, sub\,\rangle, \{\,add\,\}) =$$
$$inc \rightarrow add \rightarrow inc \rightarrow add \rightarrow inc \rightarrow sub \rightarrow fail \rightarrow add \rightarrow pass \rightarrow STOP$$
$$T_F(\langle\,add, add, sub\,\rangle, \{\,sub\,\}) =$$
$$inc \rightarrow add \rightarrow inc \rightarrow add \rightarrow inc \rightarrow sub \rightarrow fail \rightarrow sub \rightarrow pass \rightarrow STOP$$
$\ldots$

The exhaustive test set is enough to establish conformance: an SUT for which none of the test executions deadlock after a $fail$ is in conformance with SP according to $conf$; a proof is found in [5].

Theorem 3 (Exhaustivity of $Exhaust_{conf}$). *Given two CSP processes SUT and SP, $(SUT\ conf\ SP)$ if, and only if,*

$$\forall\ T_F(s, A) : Exhaust_{conf}(SP); \ (t, B) : failures(Execution_{SUT}^{SP}(T_F(s, A))) \bullet$$
$$last(t) \neq fail \vee B \neq \{\,inc, pass, fail\,\}$$

This theorem is similar, up to the notation, to Proposition 4.5, proved by Tretmans in [30, page 85]. The main difference there is that $initials(SP/s)$ was added to the minimal set of acceptance sets for technical reasons: the test set was defined by induction, starting from the empty trace, and all the successors of the state before the last one must appear at each induction step in order to get all the traces at the next step.

There is also a similar result by Peleska and Siegel in [24], with a rather different formulation of the sets of acceptance sets to be considered. In their theoretical work, deadlock observations are characterised in terms of maximal traces. This is not accurate for nondeterministic systems, since in the traces model a prefix of a maximal trace may be included just because it is a prefix of a possible trace, or because the system may deadlock after that prefix. It is well known that the traces model is not enough to characterise failures. In practice, one uses timeout to conclude that there is a deadlock, but in the theoretical work, this must be expressed in terms of the failures model. In the test derivation method that has been applied to several industrial systems [25], though, Peleska and Siegel handle deadlock adequately.

5.3 Running Tests Against Systems

The two last theorems are about CSP processes, namely a specification SP, an unknown process SUT_{CSP} such that the system under test behaves like it, and some tests. They state some equivalence between, on the one hand, a conformance relation between SP and SUT_{CSP}, and, on the other hand, some properties of the traces of the parallel composition of SUT_{CSP} with the tests. These theorems are fundamental for stating practical properties on testing the SUT.

In practice, for every test in $Exhaust_T$ and $Exhaust_{conf}$, it is trivial to obtain some tester program (in any suitable language for interacting with the SUT, for instance TTCN, Concert C, ...), that behaves like the CSP test. When performing one test experiment of the SUT with the tester program corresponding to a test t, we define that SUT $passes_1$ t if the verdict as defined in the previous section is not a failure. Now, from the second testability hypothesis, for any test t, there is an integer k that prescribes the number of experiments that must be performed with t. We define that SUT $passes$ t if there is no failure observed when performing k experiments with t. We also define that SUT $passes$ TS when SUT passes all the tests in a test set TS.

Theorem 2 above allows to say that, under the testability hypotheses, an SUT passes all the tests of $Exhaust_T(SP)$ if and only if $SP \sqsubseteq_T SUT_{CSP}$. In a more mathematical form we have:

$$Testability\ Hypotheses \implies (SUT\ passes\ Exhaust_T(SP) \Leftrightarrow SP \sqsubseteq_T SUT_{CSP})$$

Similarly, Theorem 3 and Theorem 1 allow us to say that under the testability hypotheses, an SUT passes all the tests of $Exhaust_T(SP)$ and $Exhaust_{conf}(SP)$ if, and only if, $SP \sqsubseteq_F SUT_{CSP}$.

$$Testability\ Hypotheses \implies$$
$$(SUT\ passes\ Exhaust_T(SP) \cup Exhaust_{conf}(SP) \Leftrightarrow SP \sqsubseteq_F SUT_{CSP})$$

Of course the set of experiments described above, that is, the SUT passing an exhaustive test set, is not realistic since the test sets are infinite. This leads to the problem of selecting a finite subsets of these experiments. This can be done by enriching the hypotheses on the SUT with so-called selection hypotheses, keeping the same kind of properties as above: under the testability hypotheses and the selection hypotheses, the SUT passes the selected test set if and only if it is a refinement of SP. Some hints on test selection are given later in Section 7.

6   Factorisation

The tests in $Exhaust_T$ can be factorised, taking advantage of the fact that the set of traces of a process is prefix-closed. This factorisation decreases the number of inconclusive executions, although it may result in some adaptive tests, originally called adaptive checking sequences [17]. They were introduced for dealing with a nondeterministic SUT. Instead of submitting a preset sequence of events to the SUT, a tree of possible behaviours is submitted to it, allowing a test to follow and reveal the nondeterministic choices of the SUT.

In the case of traces refinement testing, for a trace s, we define a factorised test $Fact_T^{SP}(s)$ which, after each of the events of s proposes to the SUT an external choice between the continuation of the trace and those events forbidden after the prefix of the trace executed so far. It is formally defined as follows, in terms of the function $Fact_{tr}^{SP}(s, dt)$ that takes as an extra parameter the trace dt that has already been executed.

$Fact_T^{SP}(s) = Fact_{tr}^{SP}(s, \langle \rangle)$

$Fact_{tr}^{SP}(\langle \rangle, dt) = TFail^{SP}(dt)$
$Fact_{tr}^{SP}(\langle a \rangle ^\frown s, dt) = TFail^{SP}(dt) \;\square\; inc \to a \to Fact_{tr}^{SP}(s, dt ^\frown \langle a \rangle)$

$TFail^{SP}(s) = pass \to \;\square\; a^f \notin initials(SP/s) \bullet a^f \to fail \to STOP,$
$$provided \; \overline{initials(SP/s)} \neq \emptyset$$
$TFail^{SP}(s) = STOP,$ otherwise

The function $TFail^{SP}(s)$ defines the CSP process that proposes all the invalid extensions of s according to SP.

For $Counter_2$, we have that $Fact_T^C(\langle add, add, sub, add \rangle)$ is the following test.

$pass \to sub \to fail \to STOP$
$\square$

$inc \to add \to inc \to add \to \left(\begin{array}{l} pass \to add \to fail \to STOP \\ \square \\ inc \to sub \to inc \to add \to pass \to add \to fail \to STOP \end{array} \right)$

This factorised test subsumes three tests in the set $Exhaust_T(Counter_2)$, namely, $T_T(\langle \rangle, sub)$, $T_T(\langle add, add \rangle, add)$, and $T_T(\langle add, add, sub, add \rangle, add)$.

The factorised tests, however, have a problem concerning coverage of behaviours, since the choices are no more under the control of the test and can be biased. For example, in the above factorised test, after the SUT performs the trace $\langle add, add \rangle$, there is a choice between the testing events $pass$ and inc that is left up not to the test, but to the environment of the test execution. It is an external choice over events that are not in the alphabet of the SUT.

For the non-factorised tests, the environment of a test execution can be a simple process that is prepared to accept interaction on any of the events inc, $pass$, and $fail$, at any moment. Even in such a liberal environment, it is guaranteed that the interaction with the SUT defined by the trace that corresponds to the test is attempted in the test execution.

If the test is factorised, though, the environment of the test execution is offered choices between $pass$ and inc events, whenever there is a possibility, according to the specification, of extending the trace or deadlocking. To ensure coverage, both choices should be tried; in a simple environment like that described above, there is no such guarantee, and more care is needed in its design.

A related concern arises when there are several possibilities of failure. By way of illustration, we consider that the alphabet of $Counter_2$ includes a third event $mult$, which is always refused; the definition of $Counter_2$ remains that presented in Section 2. In this case, the factorised test takes the following shape.

$pass \to ((sub \to fail \to STOP) \;\square\; (mult \to fail \to STOP))$
$\square$
$inc \to add \to \dots$

In this case, in the beginning, if the environment of the test execution chooses to synchronise on $pass$, it then has no control over the choice between sub and *mult*: these events are not in its alphabet. The test is not making a choice, but rather offering it to the *SUT*. If the *SUT* can perform any of them, the mistake is going to be detected, but it is not possible to determine which of the mistaken events are possible, since the *SUT* is not forced to perform any of them.

If the *SUT* can perform one of the mistaken events, the test execution will indicate a *fail*, but it will not be clear which of the choices was made; it is a choice internal to the test execution. If the *SUT* can perform both *sub* and *mult* due to an internal nondeterminism, the second testability hypothesis guarantees that, after running the factorised test a certain number of times, both nondeterministic choices will be made, but again the test executions will not indicate when this has happened. If the *SUT* offers *sub* and *mult* in an external choice, in the test execution, the choice becomes nondeterministic, and even though the testability hypothesis guarantees that all choices will be made, there is no way, again, of identifying the reason of the problems that will be indicated.

On the other hand, if the non-factorised tests *pass* $\rightarrow$ *sub* $\rightarrow$ *fail* $\rightarrow$ *STOP* and *pass* $\rightarrow$ *mult* $\rightarrow$ *fail* $\rightarrow$ *STOP* are used instead, given the testability hypothesis, the verdict is more precise. If only one of the mistaken events can be performed by the *SUT*, only the test that offers that event will signal a *fail*. If the *SUT* can perform both *sub* and *mult* due to an internal nondeterminism, then the testability hypothesis guarantees that, after running each test a certain number of times, the nondeterministic behaviour will be revealed. Therefore, the executions for both tests will reveal a failure, and it will be observed that both mistakes are possible. If, on the other hand, the *SUT* can perform both *sub* and *mult* due to an external choice, then the individual non-factorised tests will make the choice and reveal the individual problems straightaway.

An even more factorised test can be defined. The automaton that defines set of traces of the so-called *canonical tester* [3] can be visualised as the tree formed by the traces of *SP* decorated at each node by a choice between the forbidden events after the traces from the root to the node. Such events lead to a failure verdict followed by *STOP*. In this case, there is no need for an inconclusive verdict, but the problem of coverage discussed above arises also with valid continuations of the trace. In this case, not only the environment cannot control the initial choice of mistaken events that are to be tried, that is, the choice between *sub* and *mult*, but it also cannot control whether the initial valid traces to be attempted are $\langle$ *add*, *add* $\rangle$ or $\langle$ *add*, *sub* $\rangle$, for example.

For this reason, the factorisation that we propose above is not the canonical tester. It provides some optimisation, in that it joins all the tests based on traces that are associated by the prefix relation, but it does not joint all the tests.

Several authors [3,30,24] have studied the minimisation and factorisation of the exhaustive test set for the *conf* relation. Brinksma in [3], and later on Tretmans in [30], provide some ways of building some canonical tester, that is, some nondeterministic tester process whose behaviour contains all the tests in $Exhaust_{conf}(SP)$. The factorisation is less obvious than for traces refinement since all acceptable sets must be attempted after a given trace. It leads to highly nondeterministic testers. In practice, this formulation raises issues of coverage of the test set, as discussed above for $Exhaust_T(SP)$.

7   Test Selection and Derivation

A testing strategy can be formalised as a way of selecting some finite subset of an exhaustive test set. The choice of such a strategy corresponds to stronger hypotheses on the system under test than the testability hypotheses discussed in Section 4. Such hypotheses are called selection hypotheses in [1]. Weak selection hypotheses lead to large test sets. Strong selection hypotheses lead to smaller, more practicable test sets, with the risk that they may not be fulfilled.

Various selection hypotheses can be formulated and combined depending on some knowledge of the program, some coverage criteria of the specification and ultimately cost considerations. For instance, a *regularity hypothesis* uses a size function on the tests and has the form, for a given exhaustive test set: " if the subset of the exhaustive test set made up of all the tests of size less than or equal to a given limit is passed, then the exhaustive test set is as well".

For $Exhaust_T$ and $Exhaust_{conf}$, an obvious candidate for a size function on tests such as $T_T(s, a)$ and $T_F(s, A)$ is the length of the trace s. Given the precise way in which these tests are specified in subsections 5.1 and 5.2, it is straightforward to implement test generators corresponding to these selection hypotheses. It must be noted, however, that regularity hypotheses are not always a good choice in practice. For instance, in [9], Dong and Frankl report cases where such a strategy failed to detect important faults.

A popular criterion for model-based testing (using finite state machines or labelled transition systems) is transition coverage. The corresponding selection hypothesis is a so-called *uniformity hypothesis*. Such hypotheses are common in software testing. They assume that the system behaves uniformly on some test subsets. Thus it is enough to have only one test from each of these subsets.

In the case of transition coverage, it can be reworded as: "if a subset of the exhaustive test set that exercises all the transitions is passed, then the exhaustive test set is as well". Given a finite model, it is quite feasible to develop a generator that yields a set of paths satisfying this criteria (see for instance [6,17]). One justification of this selection hypothesis is that in model-based testing, there is a testability hypothesis similar to our first one: the SUT behaves like a finite model. Since such models have no memory, the execution of a transition is independent of the way in which it has been reached, and it is sufficient to exercise it once, checking that the output (if any) is correct, and that the arrival state in the SUT is equivalent to the arrival state in the model.

The framework that we have developed so far for CSP-based testing is based on its denotational semantics. As mentioned in Section 4, to consider selection strategies based on states or transitions, we need to work with the finite labelled transition systems derived from CSP specifications using its operational semantics. A brute-force way of transposing transition coverage into our framework could be to select one subset of $Exhaust_T$ (resp., in $Exhaust_{conf}$), such that the set of the traces s that originate the selected $T_T(s, a)$ (resp., $T_F(s, A)$) ensures the coverage of all the transitions of this labelled transition system.

However, coverage of transitions is not just exercising the transitions, but, importantly, checking that the arrival state after each transition in the SUT is a right one: it accepts or refuses events that are compatible with the conformance relation. Here the conformance relations are derived from the notions of refinement, namely, $SP \sqsubseteq_T SUT_{CSP}$ and SUT_{CSP} $conf$ SP. These relations rely on traces, as they appear in the form of the tests, in both cases. In our testing approach, these traces correspond to full paths from the initial state, and transitions are not considered individually. Thus it is not clear that transition coverage is an adequate selection criteria for the approach of CSP-based testing that is presented here. Starting from the exhaustive test sets we have defined, new uniformity hypotheses must be investigated in order to propose pertinent selection strategies. This is the subject of future work.

8   Inputs and Outputs

So far, we have considered events, with no distinction between inputs and outputs. This distinction is extremely important in testing. The choice of inputs is under the control of the tester. The outputs are under the control of the SUT and provide the information for stating the verdict.

If we consider again our small *Replicator* example given in Section 2, for example, we observe that $Exhaust_T(Replicator)$ contains the following tests.

$$T_T(\langle c.0 \rangle, c.1) = inc \to c.0 \to pass \to c.1 \to fail \to STOP$$
$$T_T(\langle c.0 \rangle, c.2) = inc \to c.0 \to pass \to c.2 \to fail \to STOP$$
$$T_T(\langle c.1 \rangle, c.0) = inc \to c.1 \to pass \to c.0 \to fail \to STOP$$
$$T_T(\langle c.0, c.0, c.0 \rangle, c.1) =$$
$$\quad inc \to c.0inc \to c.0 \to inc \to c.0 \to pass \to c.1 \to fail \to STOP$$
$$\dots$$

Instead of inputs or outputs, we have specific events $c.0$, $c.1$, and $c.2$. The same applies for the tests in $Exhaust_{conf}$. We proved that these sets are enough to indicate mistaken implementations, but this is under our first testability hypothesis: that the SUT can be accurately described as a CSP process. It raises an issue related to input and output that is not directly captured in CSP: that of origin of data communication.

As described in Section 2, in CSP, inputs and outputs are only syntactic sugar for synchronisations on events with composite names. For example, the process *BReplicator* defined below is not at all different from *Replicator* itself.

$$BReplicator = (c?x \to c!x \to BReplicator) \,\square\, (c!0 \to c!0 \to BReplicator)$$

We could say that it is a process that, instead of waiting for an input, may decide to output 0, twice. Its CSP model, however, is exactly as that of *Replicator*, since $c!0 \to c!0 \to Replicator$ is a choice already offered by the input.

If we are concerned with checking that an implementation does not decide to make progress without duly waiting for input from the environment, this CSP approach to modelling is not appropriate. In [26, page 302], Roscoe mentions the possibility of introducing the notion of input and output as a basic concept in CSP, by making outputs undelayable events, in much the same way that the termination event ✓ is undelayable. Much of the work on this has been carried out in the context of security and timed applications.

In particular, Schneider [27] defines "may" and "must" tests in the context of a partition of events that classifies refusable and non-refusable event, but also high-level and low-level events, for the purposes of security applications. Schneider is interested in new conformance relations, rather than refinement, and on the use of model checking, rather than testing.

An interesting line for future work is the extension of CSP to include delayable and non-delayable events as suggested in [26], and analyse how results on testing based on input-output labelled transitions systems [31], and on other similar formalisms [19], can be cast in this new version of CSP.

By taking inputs and outputs into account, we are likely to be able to factorise some of the tests that are based on the several traces generated by the implicit choice associated with a CSP input.

9   Conclusions

In this paper we have established a solid foundation for model-based testing using CSP. We have characterised the relevant testability hypotheses, and discussed their consequences. We have concentrated on testing for traces and failures refinement, but discussed the issues raised by divergence. We have proposed exhaustive test sets; the algebraic proofs of exhaustiveness are directly based on the definition of the semantics of CSP. We have considered some possible optimisations of our tests, with the observation, however, that optimisations raise issues of controllability. Finally, we have indicated the challenges imposed by inputs and outputs, and test selection based on labelled transition systems.

In [25], Peleska and Siegel present a pioneering work on CSP-based testing. They define and study two extra relations, divergence refinement and robustness. However, they point out divergent specifications are not very useful, and it is not clear how they handle divergent implementations. Their test executions do not hide the events of the specification, and so they allow interference from the environment in the interaction between the test and the *SUT*. Their tests use only one extra event; it characterises success. In the absence of a success, they do not reveal if the test is inconclusive or a failure. They define may and must tests; we do not make this distinction because we are able to give an inconclusive verdict. Using the three events *pass*, *inc*, and *fail*, we have a very direct model of the verdict. Their definitions of tests are based on traces, but assume the possibility of infinite traces, as described in the operational semantics. For these, their tests are not well-defined CSP processes. Since we base our work on the denotational semantics, we have a natural characterisation of the set of finite traces that are relevant for a partial, but widely accepted characterisation of CSP processes: its canonical failures-divergences model.

The failures-divergences model that we adopt here is in direct correspondence with the UTP model of CSP processes. We expect to be able to recast our results in the UTP easily, and pave the way to consider more sophisticated concurrent languages that include constructs from other programming paradigms. In particular, we are interested in a combination of CSP and Z [28] that is adequate for refinement called *Circus* [23].

The next step in our work plans, however, is the characterisation of test selection and generation techniques. We plan to use the CSP model checker to provide some empirical results on test generation and selection that will guide further work on *Circus*.

Acknowledgments

We are grateful to the Royal Society of London, who supported our collaboration through funding for a Short Visit to the UK and an International Joint Project.

References

1. Bernot, G., Gaudel, M.-C., Marre, B.: Software Testing Based on Formal Specifications: A theory and a tool. Software Engineering Journal 6(6), 387–405 (1991)
2. Bougé, L., Choquet, N., Fribourg, L., Gaudel, M.-C.: Test set generation from algebraic specifications using logic programming. Journal of Systems and Software 6(4), 343–360 (1986)
3. Brinksma, E.: A theory for the derivation of tests. In: Protocol Specification, testing and Verification VIII, North-Holland, pp. 63–74 (1988)
4. Brinksma, E., Tretmans, J.: Testing Transition Systems: An Annotated Bibliography. In: Cassez, F., Jard, C., Rozoy, B., Dermot, M. (eds.) MOVEP 2000. LNCS, vol. 2067, pp. 187–195. Springer, Heidelberg (2001)
5. Cavalcanti, A.L.C., Gaudel, M.-C.: Testing for Refinement in CSP – Extended version.Technical report 1473, LRI, Università de Paris-Sud (2007), http://www.lri.fr/Rapports-internes/
6. Chow, T.S.: Testing Software Design Modeled by Finite-State Machines. IEEE TSE SE-4(3), 178–187 (1978)
7. Dauchy, P., Gaudel, M.-C., Marre, B.: Using Algebraic Specifications in Software Testing: a case study on the software of an automatic subway. Journal of Systems and Software 21(3), 229–244 (1993)
8. Dick, J., Faivre, A.: Automating the generation and sequencing of test cases from model-based specifications. In: Larsen, P.G., Woodcock, J.C.P. (eds.) FME 1993. LNCS, vol. 670, pp. 268–284. Springer, Heidelberg (1993)
9. Dong, R.K., Frankl, P.G.: The ASTOOT approach to testing object-oriented programs. ACM ToSEM 3(2), 103–130 (1994)
10. Fernandez, J.-C., Jard, C., Jéron, T., Viho, G.: An Experiment in Automatic Generation of Conformance Test Suites for Protocols with Verification Technology. Science of Computer Programming 29, 123–146 (1997)

11. Gannon, J., McMullin, P., Hamlet, R.: Data abstraction implementation, specification and testing. ACM ToPLaS 3(3), 211–223 (1981)
12. Gaudel, M.-C.: Testing can be formal, too. In: Mosses, P.D., Schwartzbach, M.I., Nielsen, M. (eds.) CAAP 1995, FASE 1995, and TAPSOFT 1995. LNCS, vol. 915, pp. 82–96. Springer, Heidelberg (1995)
13. Gaudel, M.-C., James, P.J.: Testing algebraic data types and processes: a unifying theory. Formal Aspects of Computing 10(5-6), 436–451 (1998)
14. Helke, S., Neustupny, T., Santen, T.: Automating Test Case Generation from Z Specifications with Isabelle. In: Till, D., Bowen, J.P., Hinchey, M.G. (eds.) ZUM 1997. LNCS, vol. 1212, pp. 52–71. Springer, Heidelberg (1997)
15. Hierons, R.M.: Testing from a Nondeterministic Finite State Machine Using Adaptive State Counting. IEEE Transactions on Computers 53(10), 1330–1342 (2004)
16. Hoare, C.A.R.: Communicating Sequential Processes. Prentice-Hall, Englewood Cliffs (1985)
17. Lee, D., Yannakakis, M.: Principles and methods of testing finite state machines - A survey. Proceedings of the IEEE 84, 1090–1126 (1996)
18. Legeard, B., Peureux, F., Utting, M.: Controlling test case explosion in test generation from B formal models. The Journal of Software Testing, Verification and Reliability 14(2), 81–103 (2004)
19. Lestiennes, G.: Contributions au test de logiciel basé sur des spécifications formelles. PhD thesis, Université de Paris-Sud (2005)
20. Machado, P., Sannella, D.: Unit Testing for CASL Architectural Specifications. In: Diks, K., Rytter, W. (eds.) MFCS 2002. LNCS, vol. 2420, pp. 506–518. Springer, Heidelberg (2002)
21. De Nicola, R., Hennessy, M.C.B.: Testing equivalences for processes. Theoretical Computer Science 3(1-2), 83–133 (1984)
22. Nogueira, S.: Automatic Test Case Generation from CSP Specifications Master's thesis (in Portuguese)
23. Oliveira, M.V.M., Cavalcanti, A.L.C., Woodcock, J.C.P.: A UTP Semantics for Circus. Formal Aspects of Computing (2007)
24. Peleska, J., Siegel, M.: Test automation of safety-critical reactive systems. In: Gaudel, M.-C., Woodcock, J.C.P. (eds.) FME 1996. LNCS, vol. 1051, Springer, Heidelberg (1996)
25. Peleska, J., Siegel, M.: Test automation of safety-critical reactive systems. South African Computer Journal 19, 53–77 (1997)
26. Roscoe, A.W.: The Theory and Practice of Concurrency. Prentice-Hall, Englewood Cliffs (1998)
27. Schneider, S.: Concurrent and Real-time Systems: The CSP Approach. Wiley, Chichester (2000)
28. Spivey, J.M.: The Z Notation: A Reference Manual, 2nd edn. Prentice-Hall, Englewood Cliffs (1992)
29. Srivatanakul, T., Clark, J.A., Stepney, S., Polack, F.: Challenging formal specifications by mutation: a CSP security example. In: 10th Asia-Pacific Software Engineering Conference, pp. 340–350. IEEE Computer Society Press, Los Alamitos (2003)
30. Tretmans, J.: A formal approach to conformance testing. PhD thesis, University of Twente, Enschede, The Netherlands (1992)
31. Tretmans, J.: Test Generation with Inputs, Outputs, and Quiescence. In: Margaria, T., Steffen, B. (eds.) TACAS 1996. LNCS, vol. 1055, pp. 127–146. Springer, Heidelberg (1996)

Reducing Test Sequence Length Using Invertible Sequences

Lihua Duan and Jessica Chen

School of Computer Science, University of Windsor
Windsor, Ont. Canada N9B 3P4
{duan1,xjchen}@uwindsor.ca

Abstract. Conformance testing has been extensively studied in the context where the desired behavior of the *implementation under test* is modeled in terms of finite state machines. An essential issue in FSM-based conformance testing is to generate from a given finite state machine a test sequence that is both effective in detecting the faults in the *implementation under test* and efficient in terms of its length. In this paper, we consider test sequences satisfying the test criterion of the U-method as they have been proved to have high fault detectability. We present our solution to reduce the length of such a test sequence by maximizing the overlap among the test segments through the use of *invertible sequences*.

Keywords: conformance testing, finite state machine, test sequence, UIO sequence.

1   Introduction

Conformance testing has been a great helper for us to gain enough confidence in the correctness of our final software products with respect to the expectation. In most of the cases, the *implementation under test* (IUT) is *stateful* in the sense that it reacts differently (e.g. by giving different outputs) to the same input provided at different time of the execution. To conduct conformance testing, we assume that we have the formal description of our expectation in terms of some structural models such as (input/output) *labelled transition systems (LTSs)*, and *Finite State Machines (FSMs)*. Such models are suitable for specifying the expected behavior of the IUT at different *states* during the execution. We adopt here FSM specification for the IUT. Different from the formal verification approach, the IUT is treated here as a *black box* from which we can only observe its input/output behavior.

One of the challenging issues in FSM-based conformance testing is how to generate an efficient and effective input/output sequence from a given FSM specification. Various approaches have been explored in this regard according to different test criteria: we generate from the specification FSM input sequences called either *test sequence* as in the T-method [1] and the U-method [2,3,4] or *checking sequence* as in the D-method [5,6,7] and the W-method [8]. See [9,10] for comprehensive surveys on this topic.

M. Butler, M. Hinchey, M.M. Larrondo-Petrie (Eds.): ICFEM 2007, LNCS 4789, pp. 171–190, 2007.

According to the T-method [1], the corresponding path of the generated test sequence in the specification FSM M should contain each transition in M at least once. Although most of the time the T-method yields a test sequence of much shorter length compared to those generated by other methods, it does not have a good fault detection capability [11]. The most rigorous criterion is expressed in *checking sequence* as used in the W-method [8] and the D-method [5,6,7]. Under certain circumstances, a checking sequence can distinguish M from any implementation FSM not equivalent to M. The high price for it is a much longer length of the checking sequence.

As a compromise between the above two approaches, the U-method (see e.g. [2,3,4]) turns out to be a popular choice. According to the U-method , the corresponding path of the generated test sequence in the specification FSM M should contain each transition in M with only its ending state in the implementation FSM *verified*. Unlike a checking sequence, such a test sequence does not have full support for fault coverage. However, it has a much shorter length compared to a checking sequence and the study of [11,12] shows that its effectiveness in detecting faults in the IUT is quite satisfactory.

To *verify* a state s in the implementation FSM, we usually apply to the IUT an input sequence called *UIO sequence for* s which, according to the specification FSM, should produce an output sequence that is unique among all output sequences we observe when we apply this input sequence to different states of the IUT. A *test segment* of transition t is t followed by a path in this FSM induced by applying a UIO sequence of the ending state s of t at s in order to verify this state in the implementation FSM. Thus, the path induced by applying U-sequence [13], i.e., a test sequence satisfying the test criterion in the U-method, should contain at least one test segment of transition t for all t in M [2,3,4,14,15,16].

Traditionally, U-sequence generation was achieved by generating one or multiple UIO sequences for each state and simply connecting each test segment using some so called *transfer sequences*. This method has been greatly improved with the observation that one test segment ρ of transition t may be used to verify the ending state s of another transition t' via some possibly empty transfer sequence ρ' (from s to the starting state of ρ). The appearance of these choices of test segments introduces additional overlap among test segments, which very often leads to possible U-sequences of shorter length. Here, the transfer sequence ρ' concatenated by t should be an *invertible sequence* [15] in the sense that there is no other transition sequence ending at the ending state of t with the same input/output sequence as that of ρ' concatenated by t.

The optimization problem of generating a minimal-length U-sequence or checking sequence from a given specification FSM is very hard in general. Much of existing work reduces this problem to the *Rural Postman Problem (RPP)* [2,7,17,18,19]. This is based on the fact that quite some sophisticated heuristics for solving CPP have been proposed in the literature (see e.g. [20]).

Suppose we are given a UIO sequence for each state of the specification FSM. In this paper, we consider the problem of reducing the lengths of U-sequences by making use of invertible sequences to maximize the overlaps among the test segments. Our solution is, again, obtained by reducing the problem to RPP. Our experimental results show that the proposed method outperforms the existing work in the literature.

Similar to many other pieces of research work in this field, the results presented here apply only to specifications given in *deterministic* FSMs. Consequently, the testing technique is developed for *integration testing* and *system testing* on those implementations executed by a single thread/process and for *unit testing* on each sequentially executed component of a distributed system.

The rest of the paper is organized as follows. Section 2 gives the terminology and notation used in this paper followed by an example. In Section 3, we give a brief literature review on recent improvements on U-sequence generation via the overlap among test segments. This leads to our problem description and the proposed method. In Section 4 and 5, we present a polynomial-time algorithm for finding minimal-length invertible sequences and an optimal solution for finding a minimal-length proximate test path. Then we compare our work with the other approaches in the literature on the optimization problem of generating minimal-length U-sequences (Section 6). In Section 7, we present our experimental results, and in Section 8, we compare the present work with a broader range of related work. This is followed by our conclusion in Section 9.

2   Preliminaries

In this section, we introduce terminology and notation on FSMs and digraphs, together with an example.

2.1 n-Port Finite State Machines

FSMs have been widely used to model sequential circuits, lexical analysis systems, communications protocols, and more generally, distributed systems. The definition of FSM has been generalized into n-port FSM to describe the abstract behavior of distributed systems with n different *interfaces* called *ports*.

An *n-port finite state machine* (simply called FSM below) is defined as $M = (S, X, Y, \delta, \lambda, s_0)$ where

- S is a finite set of states of M;
- $s_0 \in S$ is the initial state of M;
- $X = \bigcup_{i=1}^{n} X_i$, where X_i is the input alphabet of port i, and for simplicity, we assume that $X_i \cap X_j = \emptyset$ for $i, j \in \{1, 2, \ldots, n\}$, $i \neq j$;
- $Y = \prod_{i=1}^{n}(Y_i \cup \{-\})$, where Y_i is the output alphabet of port i, and $-$ means null output;
- δ is a transition function that maps $S \times X$ to S, i.e., $\delta: S \times X \to S$;
- λ is an output function that maps $S \times X$ to Y, i.e., $\lambda: S \times X \to Y$.

Note that each $y \in Y$ is a vector of outputs, i.e., $y = \langle y^1, y^2, \ldots, y^n \rangle$ where $y^i \in Y_i \cup \{-\}$ for $i \in \{1, 2, \ldots, n\}$.

We extend *input symbols* and *output symbols* of the transition function δ and output function λ to *strings* as follows: For input $x_1, \ldots, x_k \in X$, output $y_1, \ldots, y_k \in Y$, and $s_1, \ldots, s_{k+1} \in S$, if $\lambda(s_i, x_i) = y_i$ and $\delta(s_i, x_i) = s_{i+1}$ for $i \in [1, k]$, then $\lambda(s_1, x_1 \ldots x_k) = y_1 \ldots y_k$, $\delta(s_1, x_1 \ldots x_k) = s_{k+1}$.

A *transition* of an FSM is a triplet $t = (s_i, s_j, x/y)$, where $s_i, s_j \in S$, $x \in X$, and $y \in Y$ such that $\delta(s_i, x) = s_j$, and $\lambda(s_i, x) = y$. s_i and s_j are called the *starting state* and the *ending state* of t respectively. The input/output pair x/y is called the *label* of the transition. By definition, an FSM M is *deterministic*.

We keep the "slow environment" assumption used in the literature. That is, whenever an input reaches the system, the system will always prompt the output for it before the second input can reach the system. Furthermore, the inputs and the outputs are abstract symbols. The discussions on data types and complicate data structures in the inputs and outputs are beyond the scope of this paper.

We will use standard definitions of *path* and *transition tour* on FSMs. The label of a path ρ, denoted as $label(\rho)$, is the sequence of input/output pairs of the transitions in ρ. Let $\rho = t_1 t_2 \ldots t_k$ $(k \geq 1)$ be a tour. We say $\rho' = t_j, \ldots, t_k, t_1, \ldots, t_{j-1}$ is a path obtained by *breaking* ρ at t_j such that ρ' starts with transition t_j, and *ends* with transition t_{j-1}.

When $\rho \neq \epsilon$, we use $start(\rho)$ and $end(\rho)$ to denote the starting state of ρ and the ending state of ρ respectively. Also, we use $in(\rho)$ to denote the *input portion* of the concatenated labels of ρ.

Let $\chi = x_1 \ldots x_k$ be an input sequence. $\rho = (s, \delta(\chi), \chi/\lambda(s, \chi))$ is a path *induced by applying χ at state* $s \in S$.

Let ρ_1, ρ_2 be two paths in M. When $end(\rho_1)$ and $start(\rho_2)$ are the same state, we use $\rho_1 \rho_2$ to denote the *concatenation* of ρ_1 and ρ_2. For clarity, sometimes we also use $\rho_1 @ \rho_2$ for $\rho_1 \rho_2$. If $\rho = \rho_1 @ \rho_2 @ \rho_3$, we say ρ_2 is *contained in* ρ, denoted as $\rho_2 \in \rho$, where ρ_1, ρ_3 might be null path. Similarly, we use $\sigma_1 @ \sigma_2$ or $\sigma_1 \sigma_2$ to represent the concatenation of σ_1 and σ_2 when they are both input sequences or both input/output sequences.

Let ρ_1 and ρ_2 be two paths, and ρ the (maximum) common part of the suffix of ρ_1 and the prefix of ρ_2. When $\rho \neq \epsilon$, there is an *overlap* between ρ_1 and ρ_2. More precisely, we say ρ_1 *overlaps with* ρ_2.

Like in quite some other work on FSM-based conformance testing, we assume that the given specification FSM M is minimal. Given an FSM $M = (S, X, Y, \delta, \lambda, s_0)$, a UIO sequence of a state s is an input sequence such that the corresponding output sequence obtained by applying this input sequence at s in M is unique from those obtained by applying this input sequence at any other state. We use UIO_i to denote the UIO sequence for state s_i.

Most of the algorithms for test sequence generation are based on some well-known algorithms in graph theory applied to the directed graph of a given FSM: Each FSM M has a graph representation $G = (V, E)$, in which a state of M is represented by a vertex of V and a transition of M is represented by an edge of E. We use G_M to denote the graph representation of FSM M, where state s_i is represented by vertex v_i, and transition from s_i to s_j with input x and output y is represented by edge $(v_i, v_j, x/y)$.

The *distance* from vertex v_i to vertex v_j in G is the length of a shortest walk from v_i to v_j. The *diameter* of G is the longest distance in G, i.e., $max\{distance(v_i, v_j) \mid v_i, v_j \in V\}$. An FSM M is *strongly connected* if the digraph that represents M is strongly connected. Given a strongly connected graph $G = (V, E)$, a *Postman Tour* of G is a tour which contains every edge of E at least once. The *Chinese Postman Problem (CPP)* is to find the minimum-cost Postman Tour in a strongly connected digraph. Given a strongly connected $G = (V, E)$ and $E_1 \subseteq E$, a *Rural Postman Tour* is a tour which contains each edge in E_1 at least once. The *Rural Chinese Postman Problem (RPP)* is to find a Rural Postman Tour with minimum cost. CPP has a polynomial time solution while RPP is in general NP-hard. We will present our results in terms of strongly connected FSMs. A brief discussion on how to apply the proposed method to general FSMs is given in the Conclusion.

2.2   An Example

As an example, we present here a protocol for establishing service connection, which is commonly used in peer-to-peer systems. In this protocol, any participant, upon receiving a request from its user, can initiate a connection with any other peer participant by issuing a *connection request*. The connection will not be established until the confirmations from all peer participants are received. Each confirmation represents the permission from another participant. For simplicity, we consider such a protocol with two participants.

Note that the *connection requests* can be issued concurrently by both participants. That is, the two participants may issue the requests at about the same time. Consequently, it is possible that each participant receives a *connection request* from the other participant right after it has sent out its own request and yet before it receives the confirmation from its partner. In this case, in order to establish a connection, each participant should respond to the request from its partner as well as receive the confirmation from its partner for its own request.

The specification FSM $M_0 = (S, X, Y, \delta, \lambda, s_0)$ of a participant in this protocol is shown in Figure 1. M_0 has two ports: U and L. Port U represents the interface of the participant with the external users of the service; and port L represents the interface of the participant with the other participant. To distinguish the service primitives at different ports, we explicitly associate the source or destination of the messages to the symbolic representations of these messages. The service primitives and their symbolic representations for each participant in this protocol are listed below.

- *IntFromU*: user's intension for establishing a service connection;
- *ReqToL*: message to request the partner to establish connection;
- *RspFromL*: response from the partner for service connection;
- *ConfToU*: confirmation of the service connection to the user;
- *ReqFromL*: request from the partner for service connection;
- *PerReqToU*: request for the user's permission for service connection;

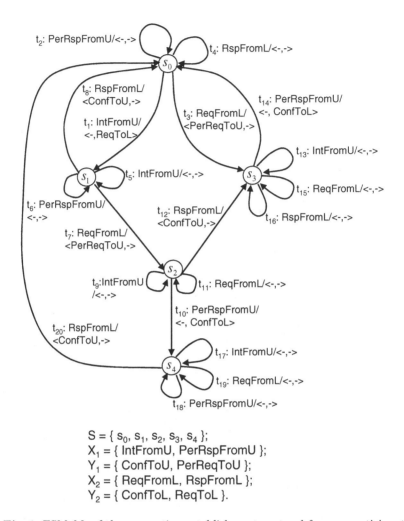

$S = \{ s_0, s_1, s_2, s_3, s_4 \};$
$X_1 = \{ \text{IntFromU, PerRspFromU} \};$
$Y_1 = \{ \text{ConfToU, PerReqToU} \};$
$X_2 = \{ \text{ReqFromL, RspFromL} \};$
$Y_2 = \{ \text{ConfToL, ReqToL} \}.$

Fig. 1. FSM M_0 of the connection establishment protocol for one participant

- *PerRspFromU*: user's permission for a service connection;
- *ConfToL*: confirmation of the service connection to the partner.

The input and output alphabet at port U is X_1 and Y_1, respectively; and the input and output alphabet at port L is X_2 and Y_2, respectively.

Suppose process A is a participant of this connection establishment protocol modeled by M_0. I/O pair $IntFromU/\langle -, ReqToL \rangle$ means that upon receipt of message $IntFromU$, A will send a request to its partner for the connection establishment. I/O pair $ReqFromL/\langle PerReqToU, - \rangle$ represents that when A receives message $ReqFromL$, it will send a request to its user asking for permission.

Table 1 shows the shortest UIO sequences for each state.

Table 1. UIO sequences for each states in M_0

states	UIO sequence
s_0	IntFromU
s_1	ReqFromL @ RspFromL
s_2	RspFromL @ PerRspFromU
s_3	PerRspFromU @ RspFromL
s_4	ReqFromL @ RspFromL @ PerRspFromU

3   Problem Description

Suppose that we have a UIO sequence for each state of an FSM M. As we mentioned in the Introduction, a *test segment* for a transition $t = (s_i, s_j, x/y)$ of M is a path obtained by concatenating t and the path ρ *induced* by applying a UIO sequence of s_j at s_j. This path ρ is used to *verify* the ending state of t in the implementation FSM. A test sequence is a *U-sequence* if it is the input portion of a path that contains the test segments of all the transitions in M. The optimization problem of generating a minimal-length U-sequence is reduced in general to the RPP [2] by connecting test segments using *transfer sequences*.

A more recent result along this approach makes use of the *invertible transitions* in the specification FSM. The notion of *invertible transition* was first introduced in [14][1]. A transition $(s_i, s_j, x/y)$ is *invertible* if it is the only transition entering state s_j with input x and output y. In the example FSM M_0, t_1, t_2, t_3 are invertible transitions while t_8 and t_{20} are not because both t_8 and t_{20} end at s_0 with the same label $RspFromL/\langle ConfToU, -\rangle$.

The existence of invertible transitions in existing protocol descriptions has been the major source of the recent success in reducing the lengths of the generated U-sequences. This is based on the following observation ([3,14]):

A) If t is an invertible transition and UIO_i is a UIO sequence of $end(t)$, then the input sequence $in(t) @ UIO_i$ is a UIO sequence for $start(t)$.

Suppose that t is an invertible transition, and $t\sigma$ is a test segment for t in the sense that σ is a path induced by applying the UIO sequence of state $end(t)$ at $end(t)$. Now if t' is a transition adjacent to t (i.e. $end(t') = start(t)$), then path $t't\sigma$ is a test segment for t'. As $t't\sigma$ contains test segments for both t' and t, we say there is an overlap between test segment $t't\sigma$ and test segment $t\sigma$. By using invertible transitions, the overlap between test segments is increased. It follows that the length of the generated U-sequence can be reduced.

Some heuristic algorithms have been proposed in [3,14] to maximize the use of invertible transitions to reduce the lengths of the U-sequences. In doing so, the notion of *invertible transition* is extended to that of *invertible sequence* [15]. A path ρ is an *invertible sequence* if it is the only path with label $label(\rho)$ that ends

---

[1] A similar notion called *non-converging edge* was defined on the digraphs that represent the FSMs ([3]).

at $end(\rho)$. That is, for any path ρ', $start(\rho) \neq start(\rho')$ implies $end(\rho) \neq end(\rho')$ or $label(\rho) \neq label(\rho')$. Clearly, when the length of an invertible sequence is 1, it is actually an *invertible transition*.

Similar to A), we have the following result [15]:

A') If ρ is an invertible sequence and UIO_i is a UIO sequence of $end(\rho)$, then the input sequence $in(\rho)@UIO_i$ is a UIO sequence of $start(\rho)$.

Note that the additional UIO for $start(\rho)$ obtained from A') may be longer than the given UIO sequence for $start(\rho)$. For the example in Figure 1, $t_{10}t_{20}$ is an invertible sequence ending at s_0. We know that $UIO_0 = IntFromU$ and $UIO_2 = RspFromL@PerRspFromU$. By using invertible sequence $t_{10}t_{20}$, we have another UIO sequence for s_2:

$$UIO_2' = PerRspFromU@RspFromL@IntFromU.$$

Although this newly found UIO sequence is longer than the given one, it may help to reduce the *total* length of a U-sequence since the test segment it produced has an *overlap* with other test segment(s). Let us use ρ_i to denote the test segment formed by concatenating t_i and the path induced by applying the originally given UIO sequence of $end(t_i)$ at $end(t_i)$. Consider the two test segments for transitions t_9 and t_{20} in M_0. We have $\rho_9 = t_9t_{12}t_{14}$ and $\rho_{20} = t_{20}t_1$. Using transfer sequence $t_1t_7t_{10}$ to connect these two test segments, we get

$$\rho = t_9t_{12}t_{14}t_1t_7t_{10}t_{20}t_1$$

which is a path containing both test segments. The length of ρ is 8. If we use the UIO sequence derived according to A'), one of the test segments for t_9 is $\rho_9' = t_9t_{10}t_{20}t_1$ which contains ρ_{20}. In this case, ρ_9' can be used to verify both t_{20} and t_9 and its length is only 4. With this observation, a heuristic algorithm was given in [15] to use the invertible sequences to reduce the length of U-sequences.

As from A) an optimal solution was derived for finding a minimal-length U-sequence in the special case when *all* transitions in M are invertible, now with A'), we would like to do the same for general FSMs which may contain both invertible transitions and non-invertible ones. This leads to the following proposal:

a') Determine a minimal-length path $\varrho = t_0\sigma_1t_1\sigma_2t_2\ldots\sigma_kt_k\sigma_0$, where for $0 \leq i \leq k$, σ_it_i is an invertible sequence and for each $t \in M$, there exists i $(0 \leq i \leq k)$ such that $t_i = t$. Without loss of generality, we assume t_0 is a transition starting from the initial state s_0.

b') Obtain ρ by remove σ_0 from ϱ and append path ρ' induced by applying the UIO sequence of $end(t_k)$ at state $end(t_k)$.

Then, we would like to use $in(\rho@\rho')$ as the desired U-sequence. Formally, we introduce the notion of *proximate test path*.

Definition 1 (proximate test path). *Let M be a given FSM. Suppose t_i is a transition in M and σ_i is a path in M $(0 \leq i \leq k)$. A proximate test path of M is $\varrho = t_0\sigma_1t_1\sigma_2t_2\ldots\sigma_kt_k\sigma_0$ such that:*

- t_0 is a transition starting from the initial state s_0;
- $\forall i \in \{0, \ldots, k\}$, $\sigma_i t_i$ is an invertible sequence;
- $\forall t \in M$, $\exists i$ $(0 \leq i \leq k)$ such that $t = t_i$.

With the notion of *proximate test path*, the correctness of using $in(\rho @ \rho')$ as the desired U-sequence is guaranteed by the following theorem:

Theorem 1. *Let* $M = (S, X, Y, \delta, \lambda, s_0)$ *be a minimal and strongly connected FSM. Let* $\varrho = t_0 \sigma_1 t_1 \sigma_2 t_2 \ldots \sigma_k t_k \sigma_0$ *be a proximate test path of* M, *where* t_i *is a transition and* σ_i *is a path in* M *such that* $\sigma_i t_i$ *is an invertible sequence for* $1 \leq i \leq k$. *If* $\mathrm{end}(t_k) = s_m$, *then* $in(t_0 \sigma_1 t_1 \sigma_2 t_2 \ldots \sigma_k t_k) @ \mathrm{UIO}_m$ *is a U-sequence.*

This result is straightforward from existing statements about invertible sequences given in [15].

According to this theorem, our problem is to generate minimal-length proximate test path in a given FSM. This is achieved in two steps:

i) search for a minimal-length invertible sequence starting from a given state and ending with a given transition;
ii) with the invertible sequences from i), generate a minimal-length proximate test path.

We present our result in the next two sections.

4   Minimal-Length Invertible Sequences

To find the optimal solution of minimal-length proximate test path, we need to have a shortest invertible sequence from any given state in the specification FSM M and ending with any given transition. The existence of such an invertible sequence is guaranteed by the following proposition.

Proposition 1. *Let* $M = (S, X, Y, \delta, \lambda, s_0)$ *be a minimal and strongly connected FSM with UIOs for each state. For any state* s_k *and any transition* $t = (s_i, s_j, x/y)$ *in* M, *there exists an invertible sequence starting from* s_k *and ending with* t.

Proof. Let ρ_k denote the path induced by applying UIO_k at s_k. Since M is strongly connected, there exists a path ρ from $end(\rho_k)$ to s_i. Below we prove $\rho' = \rho_k @ \rho @ t$ is an invertible sequence.

We prove by contradiction. Suppose ρ' is not an invertible sequence. Then there exists a path $\rho'' \neq \rho'$ such that $end(\rho'') = end(\rho')$ and $label(\rho'') = label(\rho')$. Since M is deterministic, we can deduce $start(\rho')$ and $start(\rho'')$ are different from $end(\rho'') = end(\rho')$ and $label(\rho'') = label(\rho')$. $label(\rho'') = label(\rho')$ implies the prefix of $label(\rho'')$ of length $|UIO_i|$ is the same as the prefix of $label(\rho')$ with the same length. It follows that UIO_i will produce the same output sequence on two different states s_i and $start(\rho'')$. This contradicts the definition of UIO_i. Thus, ρ' is an invertible sequence. In other words, there exists an invertible sequence starting from s_k and ending with t.

1: **Input:** FSM $M = (S, X, Y, \delta, \lambda, s_0)$, and transition $t = (r_1, r_2, x/y)$ in M.
2: **Output:** for each $s \in S$, a minimal-length invertible sequence starting from s and ending with t.

3: **Algorithm:**
4: $S_u := S$; $\Omega := \{x/y\}$; $\Omega' := \emptyset$; $\pi(x/y) := \{r_1\}$; mark$(x/y, r_1) :=$ true; $\Gamma := \emptyset$;
5: **for** all $s_1 \neq r_1$ s.t. there exists transition $(s_1, r_2, x/y)$ **do**
6:     $\pi(x/y) := \pi(x/y) \cup \{s_1\}$; mark$(x/y, s_1) :=$ false;
7: **end for**
8: **if** $|\pi(x/y)| = 1$ **then**
9:     $\Gamma := \{(r_1, x/y)\}$; $S_u := S_u - \{r_1\}$;
10: **end if**
11: **while** $S_u \neq \emptyset$ **do**
12:     **for** any $\omega \in \Omega$, $s, s_2 \in S$, s.t. $s \in \pi(\omega)$ and mark$(\omega, s) =$ true and there exists transition $(s_2, s, x'/y')$ for some x', y' **do**
13:         $\Omega' := \Omega' \cup \{x'/y'@\omega\}$; mark$(x'/y'@\omega, s_2) :=$ true;
14:         **if** $\pi(x'/y'@\omega)$ not defined **then**
15:             $\pi(x'/y'@\omega) := \{s_2\}$
16:         **else**
17:             $\pi(x'/y'@\omega) := \pi(x'/y'@\omega) \cup \{s_2\}$;
18:         **end if**
19:         **for** all $s_3 \neq s_2$ **do**
20:             **if** there exists transition $(s_3, s_4, x'/y')$ where $s_4 \in \pi(\omega)$ **then**
21:                 $\pi(x'/y'@\omega) := \pi(x'/y'@\omega) \cup \{s_3\}$;
22:                 **if** mark$(\omega, s_4) =$ true **then**
23:                     mark$(x'/y'@\omega, s_3) :=$ true;
24:                 **else**
25:                     mark$(x'/y'@\omega, s_3) :=$ false;
26:                 **end if**
27:             **else if** $s_2 \in S_u$ **then**
28:                 $\Gamma := \Gamma \cup \{(s_2, x'/y'@\omega)\}$;
29:                 $S_u := S_u - \{s_2\}$;
30:             **end if**
31:         **end for**
32:     **end for**
33:     $\Omega := \Omega'$; $\Omega' := \emptyset$;
34: **end while**
35: **for** all $(s, \omega) \in \Gamma$, output the path induced by applying the input of ω at s;

Fig. 2. Algorithm 1. Find minimal-length invertible sequences ending with a given transition.

Now that we know an invertible sequence from a given state and ending with a given transition is guaranteed, we consider how to obtain a *shortest* one. Figure 2 shows the algorithm to find a minimal-length invertible sequence starting from any state $s \in S$ and ending with a given transition $t = (r_1, r_2, x/y)$. The information of the result of this algorithm is kept in Γ: A pair $(s, \omega) \in \Gamma$ means that the path induced by applying the input of input/output sequence ω at s is a desired minimal-length invertible sequence ending with t.

Basically, we start from transition t and search backward for states from which there exists an invertible sequence of length k and ending with t. We start with $k = 1$ and increase this length with each iteration of the *while*-loop. For $k = 1$, if t is the only transition entering r_2 with x/y, then t is an invertible sequence and $(r_1, x/y)$ is added to Γ (line 9). Since k is increased one by one, it is guaranteed that for each state s, among all invertible sequences that start from s and end with t, we will hit a minimal-length one first. Of course, once we have found a state s we want (together with the input/output sequence ω of length k), we exclude s from consideration. For this purpose, we use S_u for the set of states from which the desired minimal-length invertible sequences have not yet been found.

We keep the information about the useful paths of length k in order to calculate the invertible sequences of length $k + 1$. Note that all potential invertible sequences to be considered depend only on certain length-k paths ending at r_2. These paths can be categorized into two groups: a) those ending with t; b) those not ending with t but ending at r_2 and sharing a same label as some path from category a). The information about length-k paths is represented by the following Ω, π, and *mark*:

- Ω is a set of input/output sequences (of length k) so that for any $\omega \in \Omega$, there exists $s \in S$ such that applying the input of ω in s will end at r_2. Apparently, we have $\Omega := \{x/y\}$ at the beginning. Ω' temporally records all the possible input/output sequences to be considered in the next iteration of the *while*-loop (line 11). These sequences share the same length which is that of those in Ω increased by 1. At the end of each iteration of the *while*-loop, the value of Ω' is assigned to Ω.
- π describes the correspondence between an input/output sequence $\omega \in \Omega$ and a subset S' of states such that applying the input of ω at any state in S' will yield the output of ω and will end at r_2. For example, for $x/y \in \Omega$, we have $r_1 \in \pi(x/y)$; if there exists transition $(s_1, r_2, x/y)$, then s_1 should be added into $\pi(x/y)$. See Figure 3.
- We use $mark(\omega, s) = true$ and $mark(\omega, s) = false$ to denote that the path induced by applying the input of ω at s is in group a) and b) respectively. For example, $mark(x/y, r_1) := true$. If there exists transition $(s_1, r_2, x/y)$ and $s_1 \neq r_1$, since this transition ends at r_2 but is not t, we have $mark(x/y, s_1) := false$.

Suppose $\omega \in \Omega$, $s \in \pi(\omega)$, and we find a transition $t' = (s_2, s, x'/y')$ in M (see Figure 3). Path $\rho = (s_2, r_2, x'/y'@\omega)$ is an invertible sequence if it is the only path entering r_2 with label $x'/y'@\omega$. The latter can be determined by checking if t' is the only transition entering some state in $\pi(\omega)$ with label x'/y'.

If the biggest length of the given UIO sequences is l and the *diameter* of digraph G_M of M is d, by the proof of Proposition 1, we know an invertible sequence starting from s and ending with t exists and its length is no longer than $(l + d)$. It follows that the number of iterations of the *while*-loop is no greater than $(l + d)$.

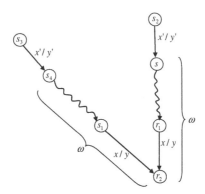

Fig. 3. An illustration for Algorithm 1

Within each iteration of the *while*-loop, the algorithm basically checks if it is possible to add a transition to an already known path to form an invertible sequence. No more than $|V| \times |X|$ transitions will be checked during each iteration. Thus, in the worse case, this algorithm requires $O((|V| \times |X|)^{(l+d)})$ time for execution. It is worth noticing that in practice this algorithm will terminate very soon. In the best case when all transitions are invertible, this algorithm is similar to the search of a spanning tree rooted at r_2 with minimal depth in digraph G'_M obtained by reversing the directions of the edges in G_M.

Below we prove the correctness of Algorithm 1.

Proposition 2. *Let $M = (S, X, Y, \delta, \lambda, s_0)$ be a minimal and strongly connected FSM with a UIO sequence for each state.*

1) *Let ρ and ρ' be two invertible sequences which start from a same state $s \in S$ and end with a same transition t in M. If ρ is produced by Algorithm 1, then $|\rho| \le |\rho'|$;*
2) *Algorithm 1 always terminates.*

Proof. According to the way Algorithm 1 works, the search of invertible sequences goes in such a way that the path with length $(m + 1)$ is searched only after all the candidate paths for the desired invertible sequences with length m are checked, and we only record the first occurrence of a desired invertible sequence for each state $s \in S$ into Γ. Thus, the invertible sequence we found is one of the shortest. As a consequence, $|\rho| \le |\rho'|$.

Since there exists a UIO sequence for each state in M, by Proposition 1, we know that there exists an invertible sequence starting from any given state $s \in S$ and ending with t. So by searching step by step with the increase of the length of the paths considered, we will eventually find all the shortest invertible sequences we need. Therefore, Algorithm 1 always terminates.

5   Minimal-Length Proximate Test Path

With the given shortest invertible sequences starting from each state of M and ending with each transition of M, now we show how to use graph theory to find the minimal-length proximate test path.

Let M be the given finite state machine. We first construct an *augmentation digraph of* M, denoted by G_M^*. $G_M^* = (V^*, E^*)$ is defined as follows:

- $V^* = \{v_t^1, v_t^2 \mid$ for any transition t in $M\}$
- $E^* = E_1 \cup E_2$, where

  - $E_1 = \{(v_t^1, v_t^2, t) \mid$ for any transition t in M $\}$
  - $E_2 = \{(v_{t_1}^2, v_{t_2}^1, \rho) \mid$ for any t_1, t_2 in M, $t_1 \neq t_2$, $\rho@t_2$ is a minimal-length invertible sequence starting from $end(t_1)$ and ending at $t_2\}$. Note that ρ may be a null path, denoted by ϵ.

For each transition t in M, i) there are two vertices in V^* representing states $start(t)$ and $end(t)$ respectively; and ii) there is an edge in E_1 representing this transition t. Note that in the case when $start(t)$ and $end(t)$ are the same state, we still have two separate vertices v_t^1 and v_t^2 in V^*.

Edges in E_2 are used to connect the edges in E_1. According to Proposition 1, it is always possible to find an invertible sequence starting from any given state and ending with any given transition. Let t_1 and t_2 be any two transitions in M, Algorithm 1 can compute the minimal-length invertible sequence staring with $end(t_1)$ and ending with t_2, so there is an edge from $v_{t_1}^2$ to $v_{t_2}^1$ for any t_1 and t_2 in M. Thus, G_M^* is strongly connected.

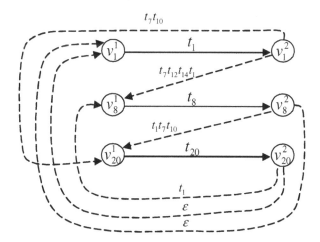

Fig. 4. Part of the constructed graph $G_{M_0}^*$ for finding the minimal-length proximate test path ϱ for M_0. Edges in E_1 and E_2 are shown in solid arrows and dashed arrows respectively.

Figure 4 shows part of the constructed graph $G_{M_0}^*$ for finding the minimal-length proximate test path ϱ for M_0. Here, for simplicity, we consider three transitions in M_0: t_1, t_8, and t_{20}. The edges in E_1 corresponding to these three transitions are: (v_1^1, v_1^2, t_1), (v_8^1, v_8^2, t_8), and $(v_{20}^1, v_{20}^2, t_{20})$. Now we show how the edges in E_2 are constructed. Transitions t_8 and t_{20} both end at s_0, and the shortest invertible sequence starting from s_0 and ending with t_1 is t_1. So the edges from v_8^2 and v_{20}^2 to v_1^1 is assigned label ϵ. Similarly, transition t_1 ends at s_1 and the shortest invertible sequence starting from s_1 and ending with t_8 is $t_7 t_{12} t_{14} t_1 t_8$. So we assign $t_7 t_{12} t_{14} t_1$ as the label of the edge from v_1^2 to v_8^1.

Since the above constructed G_M^* is strongly connected, we can find a minimal-cost RPP tour in it that contains each edge in E_1 at least once. The cost of each edge in G_M^* is defined as the length of its label. In particular, the cost of edges with label ϵ is 0.

Now, we derive the minimal-length proximate test path as follows:

a. Find a minimum-cost RPP tour ρ^* in G_M^* such that $\forall e \in E_1$, $e \in \rho^*$;
b. Let ρ' be the walk derived by breaking ρ^* at an edge $e \in E_1$ such that the label of e is a transition starting from the initial state s_0;
c. Concatenate the labels of the edges in ρ' (removing ϵ) to form a path ϱ in M.

Then ϱ is the desired minimal-length proximate test path.

To find a minimum-cost ρ^*, we can choose among various sophisticated heuristics proposed in the literature for RPP (see e.g. [20]). Polynomial time algorithm exists under the condition that for any $e = (v_i^1, v_i^2, t_i) \in E_1$, there exists $e' = (v_j^2, v_i^1) \in E_2$ for some j, such that $label(e') = \epsilon$. This is the case in particular when all transitions in M are invertible, and the problem is reduced to CPP.

For the example shown in Figure 1, the derived minimal-length proximate test path is:

$$\varrho = t_1 t_5 t_6 t_7 t_9 t_{10} t_{17} t_{18} t_{19} t_{19} t_{20} t_1 t_7 t_{11} t_{12} t_{13} t_{15} t_{16} t_{14} t_3 t_{14} t_2 t_4 t_1 t_8.$$

Note that t_1 and t_8 are the first transition and the last transition to be tested in ϱ respectively. Since t_8 is connected to t_1 with a *null* path, a test sequence can be derived by appending to $in(\varrho)$ the UIO sequence of state $end(\varrho)$, namely $IntFromU$. Thus, the generated test sequence $in(\varrho)@IntFromU$ is of length 26.

Now we prove that the above solution is sound.

Theorem 2. *Let M be a minimal and strongly connected FSM. Suppose that ϱ is a path in M derived by the proposed algorithm. Then,*

- *A. ϱ is a proximate test path; and*
- *B. for any ϱ', ϱ' is a proximate test path implies $|\varrho| \leq |\varrho'|$.*

Proof. First, we prove that ϱ is a proximate test path. Let ρ^* be an RPP tour in G_M^* that contains each edge in E_1 at least once, and let ρ' be a walk derived by breaking ρ^* at an edge $e \in E_1$ such that $label(e)$ is a transition starting from the initial state s_0. According to the way we construct G_M^*, ρ' has the following form:

$$\rho' = e_{1,0}e_{2,1}e_{1,1}e_{2,2}\ldots e_{2,k}e_{1,k}e_{2,0}$$

where $e_{1,i} \in E_1$ and $e_{2,i} \in E_2$ ($0 \leq i \leq k$). Since for any edge $e_{1,i}$ in E_1, $label(e_{1,i})$ is a transition in M, let $t_i = label(e_{1,i})$. Similarly, since for any edge $e_{2,i}$ in E_2, $label(e_{2,i})$ is a path in M, let $\sigma_i = label(e_{2,i})$. For $e_{2,i}e_{1,i}$ in ρ' ($0 \leq i \leq k$), its label $\sigma_i@t_i$ is a shortest invertible sequence starting from $end(t_l)$ and ending with t_i. Here $l = i - 1$ for $1 \leq i \leq k$ and $l = k$ for $i = 0$. Then, ϱ has the form of $\varrho = t_0\sigma_1t_1\sigma_2t_2\ldots\sigma_kt_k\sigma_0$ where we know that $\forall i \in \{0,\ldots,k\}$, σ_it_i is an invertible sequence. Furthermore, for any transition t in M, there exists an edge in E_1 whose label is t. So, from the fact that ρ^* contains each edge in E_1 at least once, we can conclude that for any t in M, $\exists i \in \{0,\ldots,k\}$ such that $t = t_i$ and $t_i \in \varrho$. Therefore, ϱ is a proximate test path.

Now we prove that B. holds. Since ϱ' is a proximate test path, ϱ' is in the form $\varrho' = t_0'\sigma_1't_1'\sigma_2't_2'\ldots\sigma_h't_h'\sigma_0'$ for some h, such that $\forall i \in \{0,\ldots,h\}$, $\sigma_i't_i'$ is an invertible sequence and for any $t \in M$, there exists some $i \in \{0,\ldots,h\}$ such that $t_i' = t$.

For each t_i', there exists a corresponding edge in E_1 such that its label is t_i'. We use $f(t_i')$ to denote the edge in E_1 of G_M^* and whose label is t_i'. Similarly, we use $f'(t_i')$ to denote the edge starting from the ending vertex of $f(t_i')$ and ending at the starting vertex of $f(t_i')$ in E_2 of G_M^*. Here $l = i - 1$ for $1 \leq i \leq h$ and $l = h$ for $i = 0$. Since the label of the walk obtained by concatenating $f'(t_i')$ and $f(t_i')$ is a shortest invertible sequence, we have $|label(f'(t_i'))@t_i'| \leq |\sigma_i'@t_i'|$. By replacing $\sigma_i't_i'$ with $label(f'(t_i'))@t_i'$ for all $0 \leq i \leq h$, we obtain a tour ϱ'' and $|\varrho''| \leq |\varrho'|$. Since ϱ is a path derived by RPP tour in G_M^* which has the minimum cost, we have $|\varrho| \leq |\varrho''|$. Thus, $|\varrho| \leq |\varrho'|$.

6   Comparisons with Other Methods

The following proposition shows that when using a transfer sequence σ to connect transition t_i and transition t_j such that $\sigma@t_j$ is a shortest invertible sequence starting from $end(t_i)$ and ending with t_j, the overlap between the test segments for these two transitions is maximized.

Proposition 3. Let $M = (S, X, Y, \delta, \lambda, s_0)$ be a minimal and strongly connected FSM. Let t_i and t_j be any two transitions in M. If σt_j is a shortest invertible sequence starting from state $end(t_i)$ and ending with t_j, and $t_j\varrho$ is a test segment for t_j, then $\rho = t_i@\sigma@t_j@\varrho$ is a shortest path that contains the test segment for t_i and ends with test segment $t_j\varrho$.

Proof. Let ρ' be any path that contains the test segment for t_i and ends with $t_j\varrho$. We have $\rho' = \rho_0@t_i@\sigma'@t_j@\varrho$, where ρ_0 is a possibly null path in M.

First, we prove that $\sigma'@t_j$ is an invertible sequence. Suppose $\sigma'@t_j$ is not an invertible sequence. There exists another path γ ending at $end(t_j)$ with the same label as that of $\sigma'@t_j$. Then $\gamma@\varrho$ forms a path ending at $end(\varrho)$ with the same label of path $\sigma'@t_j@\varrho$. It follows that $\sigma'@t_j@\varrho$ is not an invertible sequence. On the other hand, ρ' starts with the test segment of t_i, i.e., $\sigma'@t_j@\varrho$ starts with the path induced by applying a UIO sequence of $end(t_i)$ at $end(t_i)$. As we know, if an input sequence χ_1 is a UIO sequence, then $\chi_1@\chi_2$ is a UIO sequence for any input sequence χ_2. It follows that $in(\sigma'@t_j@\varrho)$ is a UIO sequence for $end(t_i)$. As proved in [15], the path induced by applying a UIO sequence of some state s at s is an invertible sequence. Thus $\sigma'@t_j@\varrho$ is an invertible sequence. This contradicts the previous conclusion that $\sigma'@t_j@\varrho$ is *not* an invertible sequence. Therefore, $\sigma'@t_j$ is an invertible sequence.

Since $\sigma'@t_j$ is an invertible sequence starting from $end(t_i)$ and ending with t_j while $\sigma@t_j$ is a *shortest* invertible sequence starting from $end(t_i)$ and ending with t_j, we have that $|\sigma@t_j| \leq |\sigma'@t_j|$. As a consequence, $|t_i@\sigma@t_j@\varrho| \leq |\rho_0@t_i@\sigma'@t_j@\varrho|$.

Thus, $\rho = t_i@\sigma@t_j@\varrho$ is a shortest path that contains the test segment for t_i and ends with $t_j\varrho$.

Proposition 3 suggests that for any given U-sequence χ generated by the approaches proposed in the literature (e.g. [2,14,15,16]), we can further reduce its length while preserving its satisfiability of U-sequence. This length reduction is performed by replacing certain sub-paths of the corresponding path induced by applying χ at s_0 with the *shortest invertible sequences*.

More precisely, let ρ be the path induced by applying χ at s_0. Since ρ contains each test segment at least once, we let $\rho = \varrho_1 t_1 \sigma_2 t_2 \dots \sigma_k t_k \sigma_{k+1} \varrho_2$, where i) ϱ_1 and ϱ_2 are (possibly *null*) transfer sequences; ii) for any t in M, there exists i ($1 \leq i \leq k$) such that $t_i = t$; and iii) each t_i ($1 \leq i \leq k$) is followed by a UIO of $end(t_i)$ in ρ. Since t_i ($1 \leq i \leq k$) is followed by a UIO of $end(t_i)$ in ρ, similar as in the proof of Proposition 3, we know $\sigma_{i+1} t_{i+1}$ is an invertible sequence for $1 \leq i \leq k-1$. Thus, we can derive $\rho' = \varrho_1 t_1 \sigma'_2 t_2 \dots \sigma'_k t_k \sigma'_{k+1} \varrho_2$ from ρ by replacing σ_i with σ'_i, where $\sigma'_i@t_i$ is a *shortest* invertible sequence starting from $end(t_{i-1})$ and ending with t_i for $2 \leq i \leq k+1$. Clearly, $|\rho'| \leq |\rho|$. Hence, we can use test sequence $in(\rho')$ instead of χ.

Note that ρ' is a proximate test path, and further reduction on ρ' is still possible by, for example, applying RPP algorithm on G^*_M as we did in this paper.

7   Experimental Results

Now we evaluate the performance of the proposed approach in terms of the lengths of the U-sequences generated from part of the specifications of several widely-used protocols: the *two-phase commit protocol* (2PC) with recovery scheme; the *ISDN BRI D-channel signaling protocol* specified in ITU-T Q.931; and the aforementioned connection establishment protocol (specified as M_0) used in peer-to-peer systems.

The two-phase commit protocol ensures that a transaction in a distributed database system can only be committed without invoking any inconsistency among distributed components (*all-or-nothing*). We suppose that transactions

Table 2. Comparison on the lengths of the generated U-sequences

specification	approach in [2]	approach in [3,14]	our approach
2PC-participant	72	56	50
2PC-coordinator	42	32	31
Q.931-network side	109	96	83
P2P connection establishment	72	31	26

are to be committed simultaneously by two participants with an additional process, the coordinator, to coordinate this activity.

The ISDN BRI D-channel signaling protocol is a network layer protocol describing the procedure for establishing, maintaining, and clearing basic circuit-switched voice connections between the user and the network interface in a *Integrated Services Digital Network*. Here, we consider the network part of the specification at the originating end.

The lengths of the U-sequences generated by our method and two other related approaches in the literature are shown in Table 2. Clearly, the lengths of the U-sequences are reduced by using our approach. This length reduction is achieved by making use of the shortest invertible sequences to maximizing the overlap among test segments.

8   Related Work

We have introduced our problem in Section 3 together with some closely related work. In Section 7 we have presented our experimental results to compare our method with two others along the same line. All these pieces of work fall into the category of testing deterministic systems in the sense that the given specification is deterministic.

Testing techniques developed for deterministic systems cannot be applied to concurrent/distributed systems due to the non-determinism involved. However, as we have mentioned in the Introduction, they can be applied to *unit testing* on each sequentially executed component. An interesting point is that if we can derive from deterministic testing that components I_1 and I_2 are trace equivalent to their respective specification P_1 and P_2, then under certain circumstances we know $I_1||I_2$ is a correct implementation of $P_1||P_2$ without performing further *integration testing* or *system testing* which involves nondeterministic system specifications. Of course, even for the deterministic systems, to establish trace equivalence between an implementation and its specification is a hard issue, very often resulting in lengthy (or even infinite) test sequences. Thus, while testing deterministic system plays an important role in the unit testing, we are equally interested in testing parallelly executed systems in general, which raises two major challenges: *nondeterminism* and *state explosion*.

The main issues in conformance testing of non-deterministic systems are discussed in the literature (e.g. [21,22,23]). To reduce the state explosion problem, a remarkable approach is to adopt model checking tools to help generating test sequences or test suites so that the advanced state space reduction techniques incorporated into the model checkers can be automatically employed into the testing techniques [24,25,26].

9   Conclusion

Invertible sequence is a key to obtaining a larger pool of test segments with significant overlap among them. This provides us with a possibility of reducing the length of U-sequences. An essential problem here is how to find a minimal-length proximate test path. In this paper we have presented an optimal solution to this problem.

The assumption of strong connectivity guarantees a test sequence tour can be generated. When the specification FSM is not strongly connected, a minimal-length proximate test path in each strongly connected component of the specification FSM can be generated by applying the proposed approach on the component. In this case, instead of a single test sequence, a set of test sequences will be generated from the given specification FSM.

When the IUT has more than one interface, our solution is directly applicable if the IUT is tested in a local test architecture. With a distributed test architecture, *controllability problems* [27] arise. If we want to generate *synchronizable* proximate test path to avoid controllability problems, the shortest invertible sequences should be synchronizable. Algorithm 1 can be tailored as follows to achieve this:

- construct a digraph $G' = (V', E')$, where $V' = \{v'_i \mid t \in M\}$ and $E' = \{(v'_i, v'_j) \mid t_i, t_j$ form a *synchronizable pair of transitions* $\}$;
- modify Algorithm 1 to find a minimal-length invertible sequence from any two vertices in V'.

Acknowledgments

This work is supported by the Natural Sciences and Engineering Research Council of Canada under grant number RGPIN 209774.

References

1. Naito, S., Tsunoyama, M.: Fault detection for sequential machines by transition tours. In: Proc. of 11th IEEE Fault Tolerant Computing Symposium, pp. 238–243. IEEE Computer Society Press, Los Alamitos (1981)
2. Aho, A.V., Dahbura, A., Lee, D., Uyar, M.: An optimization technique for protocol conformance test generation based on UIO sequences and Rural Chinese Postman Tours. IEEE Trans. Comm. 39(11), 1604–1615 (1991)
3. Miller, R.E., Paul, S.: On the generation of minimal length conformance tests for communications protocols. IEEE/ACM Transactions on Networking 1(1), 116–129 (1993)

4. Sabnani, K.K., Dahbura, A.: A protocol test generation procedure. Computer Networks and ISDN Systems 4(15), 285–297 (1988)

5. Gonenc, G.: A method for the design of fault detection experiments. IEEE Trans. Computers 19(6), 551–558 (1970)

6. Hennie, F.C.: Fault detecting experiments for sequential circuits. In: Proc. of 5th Ann. Symp. Switching Circuit Theory and Logical Design, pp. 95–110 (1964)

7. Ural, H., Wu, X., Zhang, F.: On minimizing the lengths of checking sequences. IEEE Transactions on Computers 46(1), 93–99 (1997)

8. Chow, T.S.: Testing software design modeled by finite-state machines. IEEE Trans. Software Eng. SE-4(3), 178–187 (1978)

9. Lai, R.: A survey of communication protocol testing. Journal of Systems and Software 62, 21–46 (2002)

10. Lee, D., Yannakakis, M.: Principles and methods of testing finite state machines — a survey. Proceedings of The IEEE 84(8), 1090–1123 (1996)

11. Sidhu, D.P., Leung, T.K.: Formal methods for protocol testing: A detailed study. IEEE Transactions on Software Engineering 15(4), 413–426 (1989)

12. Motteler, H., Chung, A., Sidhu, D.: Fault coverage of UIO-based methods for protocol testing. In: Proc. of IFIP TC6/WG6.1 6th International Workshop on Protocol Test Systems, pp. 21–33 (1994)

13. Chen, J., Duan, L.: Conditions for avoiding controllability problems in distributed testing. In: Liu, Z., He, J. (eds.) ICFEM 2006. LNCS, vol. 4260, pp. 460–477. Springer, Heidelberg (2006)

14. Hierons, R.M.: Extending test sequence overlap by invertibility. The Computer Journal 39(4), 325–330 (1996)

15. Hierons, R.M.: Testing from a finite state machine: extending invertibility to sequences. The Computer Journal 40(4), 220–230 (1997)

16. Yang, B., Ural, H.: Protocol conformance test generation using multiple UIO sequence with overlapping. In: ACM SIGCOMM 1990, pp. 118–125. ACM Press, New York (1990)

17. Chen, J., Hierons, R.M., Ural, H., Yenigun, H.: Eliminating redundant tests in a checking sequence. In: Khendek, F., Dssouli, R. (eds.) TestCom 2005. LNCS, vol. 3502, pp. 146–158. Springer, Heidelberg (2005)

18. Hierons, R.M., Ural, H.: Reduced length checking sequences. IEEE Transactions on Computers 51(9), 1111–1117 (2002)

19. Tekle, K.T., Ural, H., Yalcin, M.C., Yenigun, H.: Generalizing redundancy elimination in checking sequences. In: Yolum, p., Güngör, T., Gürgen, F., Özturan, C. (eds.) ISCIS 2005. LNCS, vol. 3733, pp. 915–926. Springer, Heidelberg (2005)

20. Eiselt, H.A., Gendreau, M., Laporte, G.: Arc routing problems, part II: the Rural Postman Problem. Operations Research 43, 399–414 (1995)

21. Hierons, R.M.: Testing from a non-deterministic finite state machine using adaptive state counting. IEEE Transactions on Computers 53(10), 1330–1342 (2004)

22. Luo, G., Bochmann, G., Petrenko, A.: Test selection based on communicating non-deterministic finite state machines using a generalized Wp-method. IEEE Transactions on Software Engineering 20, 149–162 (1994)

23. Tretmans, J.: Conformance testing with labelled transition systems: Implementation relation and test generation. Computer Networks and ISDN Systems 29, 49–79 (1996)

24. Ammann, P.E., Black, P.E., Majurski, W.: Using model checking to generate tests from specifications. In: ICFEM 1998, pp. 46–54. IEEE Computer Society Press, Los Alamitos (1998)

25. Vries, R.d., Tretmans, J.: On-the-fly conformance testing using SPIN. International Journal on Software Tools for Technology Transfer 2(4), 382–393 (2000)
26. Hong, H.S., Ural, H.: Using model checking for reducing the cost of test generation. In: Grabowski, J., Nielsen, B. (eds.) FATES 2004. LNCS, vol. 3395, pp. 110–124. Springer, Heidelberg (2005)
27. Sarikaya, B., Bochmann, G.V.: Synchronization and specification issues in protocol testing. IEEE Transactions on Communications 32, 389–395 (1984)

Model Checking with SAT-Based Characterization of ACTL Formulas*

Wenhui Zhang

Laboratory of Computer Science
Institute of Software, Chinese Academy of Sciences
P.O. Box 8718, Beijing 100080, China
zwh@ios.ac.cn

Abstract. Bounded semantics of LTL with existential interpretation and that of ECTL (the existential fragment of CTL), and the characterization of these existentially interpreted properties have been studied and used as the theoretical basis for SAT-based bounded model checking [2,18]. This has led to a lot of successful work with respect to error detection in the checking of LTL and ACTL (the universal fragment of CTL) properties by satisfiability testing. Bounded semantics of LTL with the universal interpretation and that of ACTL, and the characterization of such properties by propositional formulas have not been successfully established and this hinders practical verification of valid universal properties by satisfiability checking. This paper studies this problem and the contribution is a bounded semantics for ACTL and a characterization of ACTL properties by propositional formulas. Firstly, we provide a simple bounded semantics for ACTL without considering the practical aspect of the semantics, based on converting a Kripke model to a model (called a k-model) in which the transition relation is captured by a set of k-paths (each path with k transitions). This bounded semantics is not practically useful for the evaluation of a formula, since it involves too many paths in the k-model. Then the technique is to divide the k-model into submodels with a limited number of k-paths (which depends on k and the ACTL property to be verified) such that if an ACTL property is true in every such model, then it is true in the k-model as well. This characterization can then be used as the basis for practical verification of valid ACTL properties by satisfiability checking. A simple case study is provided to show the use of this approach for both verification and error detection of an abstract two-process program written as a first order transition system.

1 Introduction

Bounded semantics of LTL with existential interpretation (called existential LTL hereafter) and that of ECTL (the existential fragment of CTL), and the characterization of these existentially interpreted properties have been studied and used as the theoretical basis for SAT-based bounded model checking [2,18]. This has lead to a lot of successful work with respect to error detection in the checking of LTL and ACTL (the

---

* Supported by the National Natural Science Foundation of China under Grant No. 60573012 and 60421001, and the National Grand Fundamental Research 973 Program of China under Grant No. 2002cb312200.

M. Butler, M. Hinchey, M.M. Larrondo-Petrie (Eds.): ICFEM 2007, LNCS 4789, pp. 191–211, 2007.

universal fragment of CTL) properties by satisfiability testing [1]. It is considered as a complementary technique to BDD-based model checking [3,5] for combating the state explosion problem, esp. for effective error detection [19].

Bounded semantics of LTL with the universal interpretation and that of ACTL, and the characterization of such properties by propositional formulas have not been successfully established and this hinders practical verification of valid universal properties by satisfiability checking. Bounded semantics of existential LTL and that of ECTL, and the characterization of such properties are consistent with the fact that the witness of the properties can be searched within a fragment of the valid paths. For witness of existential LTL properties φ, one path of the form $u \cdot v^\omega$ is sufficient. In some cases, a finite path u may be sufficient, while in the general case, it is sufficient to find a finite path $u \cdot v$ such that there is a transition from the last element of v to the first element of v, and show that $u \cdot v^\omega \models \varphi$ holds. For an ECTL property, a witness may consist of several paths. Some may need to have a loop, while others may not need to have a loop. For simplicity, we assume that all these paths are of the same length. A path of length $k + 1$ is called a k-path (a path with k transitions). Then the number of k-paths needed for witnessing an ECTL formula depends on the number k and the structure of the formula. For instance, for $EGEF\varphi$ with φ being a propositional formula, the number of k-paths needed is $k + 1$.

The problem of characterization of universally interpreted properties lies in that it looks difficult to reason about all involved paths of a model, since the number of such paths is too big. This paper studies this problem and the contribution is a bounded semantics for ACTL and a characterization of ACTL properties by propositional formulas. Firstly, we provide a simple bounded semantics for ACTL without considering the practical aspect of the semantics, based on converting a Kripke model to a model (called a k-model) in which the transition relation is captured by a set of k-paths (each path with k transitions). Although this bounded semantics is not practically useful for the evaluation of a formula, it serves as the basis for further development. Then the technique is to divide the k-model into submodels with a limited number of k-paths (which also depends on k and the ACTL property to be verified) such that if an ACTL property is true in every such model, then it is true in the k-model as well. This characterization can then be used as the basis for practical verification of valid ACTL properties by satisfiability checking. A simple case study is provided to show the use of this approach for both verification and error detection of an abstract two-process program written as a first order transition system.

The contents of this papers is as follows. Section 2 presents background knowledge on CTL. Section 3 presents a bounded semantics for ACTL. Section 4 presents a further development of the bounded semantics of ACTL. Section 5 presents a characterization of the problem for model checking ACTL properties by propositional formulas. Section 6 presents the verification approach and a case study to show the use of this characterization for verification of abstract programs with respect to ACTL properties and for error detection of incorrect abstract programs. Section 7 proposes a combined verification approach in light of a discussion with respect to related work. Finally, we present concluding remarks in Section 8.

2   Computation Tree Logic (CTL)

Computation tree logic is a propositional branching-time temporal logic [10] introduced by Emerson and Clarke as a specification language for finite state systems. In this section, preliminary knowledge on CTL, including the syntax and the semantics of CTL and the definition of ACTL and ECTL, is presented.

Let AP be a set of proposition symbols. The set of CTL formulas is defined as follows:

- Every member of AP is a CTL formula.
- The logical connectives of CTL are: $\neg$, $\wedge$, and $\vee$.
  If φ and ψ are CTL formulas, then so are $\neg\varphi$, $\varphi \wedge \psi$, and $\varphi \vee \psi$.
- The temporal operators are
  $EX, ER, EU, AX, AR,$ and AU.
  If φ and ψ are CTL formulas, then so are:
  $EX\ \varphi, E(\varphi\ R\ \psi), E(\varphi\ U\ \psi), AX\ \varphi, A(\varphi\ R\ \psi),$ and $A(\varphi\ U\ \psi)$.

In addition to the logical connectives, $\varphi \rightarrow \psi$ may be used as an abbreviation of $\neg\varphi\vee\psi$. In addition to the temporal operators, $AF\varphi, AG\varphi, EF\varphi, EG\varphi$ may be used as abbreviations of respectively $A(true\ U\ \varphi)$, $A(false\ R\ \varphi)$, $E(true\ U\ \varphi)$, and $E(false\ R\ \varphi)$.

A model for CTL formulas is a Kripke structure $M = \langle S, T, I, L \rangle$ where S is a set of states, $T \subseteq S \times S$ is a transition relation which is total, $I \subseteq S$ is a set of initial states and $L : S \rightarrow 2^{AP}$ is a labeling function that maps each state of S to a set of propositions that are assumed to be true at that state. A sequence $\pi = \pi_0\pi_1\cdots$ of S is a path of M, if $T(\pi_i, \pi_{i+1})$ holds for all $i \geq 0$.

Definition 1. *Let M be a model, s a state, p a proposition symbol, φ and ψ CTL formulas. $M, s \models \varphi$ denotes that φ is true at the state s in M. Let π be a path of M. The relation $\models$ is defined as follows:*

$M, s \models p$ iff
$p \in L(s)$
$M, s \models \neg\varphi$ iff
$M, s \not\models \varphi$
$M, s \models \varphi \wedge \psi$ iff
$(M, s \models \varphi)$ and $(M, s \models \psi)$
$M, s \models \varphi \vee \psi$ iff
$(M, s \models \varphi)$ or $(M, s \models \psi)$
$M, s \models EX\varphi$ iff
$\exists \pi.(\pi_0 = s \wedge M, \pi_1 \models \varphi)$
$M, s \models E(\varphi U \psi)$ iff
$\exists \pi.(\pi_0 = s \wedge \exists k \geq 0.(M, \pi_k \models \psi \wedge \forall j < k.(M, \pi_j \models \varphi)))$
$M, s \models E(\varphi R \psi)$ iff
$\exists \pi.(\pi_0 = s \wedge (\forall j \geq 0.(M, \pi_j \models \psi) \vee$
$\exists k \geq 0.((M, \pi_k \models \varphi) \wedge \forall j \leq k.(M, \pi_j \models \psi))))$

$$M, s \models AX\varphi \text{ iff}$$
$$\forall \pi.(\pi_0 = s \rightarrow M, \pi_1 \models \varphi)$$

$$M, s \models A(\varphi U\psi) \text{ iff}$$
$$\forall \pi.(\pi_0 = s \rightarrow \exists k \geq 0.(M, \pi_k \models \psi \wedge \forall j < k.(M, \pi_j \models \varphi)))$$

$$M, s \models A(\varphi R\psi) \text{ iff}$$
$$\forall \pi.(\pi_0 = s \rightarrow (\forall j \geq 0.(M, \pi_j \models \psi)\vee$$
$$\exists k \geq 0.((M, \pi_k \models \varphi) \wedge \forall j \leq k.(M, \pi_j \models \psi))))$$

A CTL formula is in negation normal form (NNF), if the symbol $\neg$ is applied only to proposition symbols. Every formula can be transformed into an equivalent formula in NNF.

The sublogic ACTL is the subset of CTL formulas that can be transformed into NNF formulas not containing the temporal operators EX, EF, EG, EU, ER. Dually, the sublogic ECTL is the subset of CTL formulas that can be transformed into NNF formulas not containing the temporal operators AX, AF, AG, AU, AR.

Definition 2. *Let φ be an ACTL formula. φ is true in M, denoted $M \models \varphi$, iff φ is true at all initial states of M.*

3   Bounded Semantics of ACTL

Since every ACTL formula can be transformed into an equivalent formula in NNF, we only consider formulas of the form $\varphi \vee \psi$, $\varphi \wedge \psi$, $AX\varphi$, $A(\varphi R\psi)$, $A(\varphi U\psi)$ constructed from propositions and the negation of propositions. Therefore, in the following, a formula refers to such an ACTL formula unless otherwise stated. In this section, a bounded semantics of ACTL is presented. One of the particular aspects of this semantics is the use of the condition $eqs(\pi)$ for stating that there are same (or equal) states appearing in different positions in the path π. Note that in the semantics of existential LTL and that of ECTL, a condition indicating that there is a transition from the last state of π to some state already in π is used [2,18]. This condition is not useful for the construction of the bounded semantics for ACTL. The reason is that we need the property of $eqs(\pi)$ stated below for reasoning about the correctness of Lemma 1 and Lemma 2. Details are explained in the sequel.

For simplicity, we fix the model under consideration to be $M = \langle S, T, I, L \rangle$, and in the sequel, M refers to this model, unless otherwise stated. Let $k \geq 0$. A k-paths of M is a path $\pi = \pi_0 \cdots \pi_k$ of M where $\pi_i \in S$ for $i = 0, ..., k$ and $(\pi_i, \pi_{i+1}) \in T$ for $i = 0, ..., k - 1$. The k-model for M is a structure $M_k = \langle S, Ph_k, I, L \rangle$ where Ph_k is the set of all different k-paths of M. Let $|\pi|$ be the length of π. We have the following definition of $eqs(\pi)$.

$$eqs(\pi) := \bigvee_{i=0}^{|\pi|-1} \bigvee_{j=i+1}^{|\pi|-1} \pi_i = \pi_j.$$

If π is a prefix of π', then $eqs(\pi) \rightarrow eqs(\pi')$.

Definition 3 (Bounded Semantics of ACTL). *Let M_k be the k-model of M, s a state, p a proposition symbol, φ and ψ ACTL formulas. $M_k, s \models_k \varphi$ denotes that φ is true at*

the state s in M_k. Let $\pi = \pi_0 \cdots \pi_k$ be a path in Ph_k. Let $[n]$ denote the set $\{0, ..., n\}$.
The relation $\models_k$ is defined as follows:

$M_k, s \models_k p$ *iff*
$p \in L(s)$
$M_k, s \models_k \neg p$ *iff*
$p \notin L(s)$
$M_k, s \models_k \varphi \wedge \psi$ *iff*
$(M_k, s \models_k \varphi)$ *and* $(M_k, s \models_k \psi)$
$M_k, s \models_k \varphi \vee \psi$ *iff*
$(M_k, s \models_k \varphi)$ *or* $(M_k, s \models_k \psi)$
$M_k, s \models_k AX\varphi$ *iff*
$k \geq 1$ *and* $\forall \pi.(\pi_0 = s \rightarrow M_k, \pi_1 \models_k \varphi)$
$M_k, s \models_k A(\varphi U \psi)$ *iff*
$\forall \pi.(\pi_0 = s \rightarrow \exists i \in [k].(M_k, \pi_i \models_k \psi \wedge \forall j \in [i-1].(M_k, \pi_j \models_k \varphi)))$
$M_k, s \models_k A(\varphi R \psi)$ *iff*
$\forall \pi.(\pi_0 = s \rightarrow ((eqs(\pi) \wedge \forall j \in [k].(M_k, \pi_j \models_k \psi)) \vee$
$\exists i \in [k].((M_k, \pi_i \models_k \varphi) \wedge \forall j \in [i].(M_k, \pi_j \models_k \psi))))$

For the soundness of this definition, we need to know that if $M, s \models \varphi$ then there is a finite $k \geq 0$ such that $M_k, s \models_k \varphi$, and vice versa.

Let k_M be the number of reachable states of M. For $k' = k_M$, since $k' \geq 1$ and $eqs(\pi)$ are satisfied for every $\pi \in Ph_{k'}$, we have $M, s \models \varphi$ implies $M_{k'}, s \models_{k'} \varphi$ by restricting every path in M to be k'-path. On the other hand, an infinite path π of M has a k'-path as its prefix. A property is true on π, if it is true on such a prefix, unless it is a global property, i.e., a property of the form $A(\varphi R \psi)$ such that φ does not hold in any state of π and ψ must hold in all states of π, and therefore a prefix is not sufficient for showing the truth of $\varphi R \psi$. Assume this situation occurs and $A(\varphi R \psi)$ holds in the bounded semantics. We want to show that $\varphi R \psi$ also holds on such a path π. For the first, the situation implies that ψ is true on every state of every k'-path of which the set of states is a subset of that of π. For the second, the set of states of all these k'-paths with the start state π_0 covers the set of states of π. These two conditions guarantee that ψ is true on every state of π and therefore $\varphi R \psi$ holds on π. Summing up the above discussion, we have $M_{k'}, s \models_{k'} \varphi$ implies $M, s \models \varphi$. On the other hand, paths in a k-model with more than k_M transitions can be shortened to paths with k_M transitions[1] without affecting the satisfiability of ACTL formulas in the model. Formally, we have

Lemma 1. *Let $k \geq k_M$. $M, s \models \varphi$ iff $M_k, s \models_k \varphi$.*

This assures in some sense the soundness of the semantics, in addition, we need to have some kind of continuity of the truth values of $M_k, s \models_k \varphi$ for a sequence of values of k. Fortunately, the property of $eqs(\pi)$ allows us to prove that if an ACTL property holds on the k-model, it also holds on the $(k+1)$-model (which is a model with longer paths). Formally:

---

[1] The number of reachable states for k_M is an over-approximation. A smaller number is usually sufficient. The least such number is called the completeness threshold, Computation of such numbers has been studied in e.g. [13].

Lemma 2. *If $M_k, s \models_k \varphi$, then $M_{k+1}, s \models_{k+1} \varphi$.*

This means that if $M_k, s \models_k \varphi$ holds for $k = k_M$, then there is a $k' \leq k$ such that for all $k'' \geq k'$, $M_{k''}, s \models_{k''} \varphi$ holds, and for all $k'' < k'$, $M_{k''}, s \models_{k''} \varphi$ does not hold. Combining Lemma 1 and Lemma 2, we obtain

Theorem 1 (Soundness). $M, s \models \varphi$ *iff there is some* $k \leq k_M$ *such that* $M_k, s \models_k \varphi$.

Definition 4. *Let φ be an ACTL formula. φ is true in the k-model M_k, denoted $M_k \models_k \varphi$, iff φ is true at all initial states of the model M_k.*

Following Theorem 1 and Lemma 2, we have the following theorem.

Theorem 2. $M \models \varphi$ *iff there is some* $k \leq k_M$ *such that* $M_k \models_k \varphi$ *holds.*

4   Refining the Bounded Semantics

The bounded semantics of ACTL is not directly useful as a method for checking whether an ACTL formula holds in the model, since the number of k-paths in the k-model is large. An over-approximation of the number is $(k_M)^{k+1}$, while the exact number is difficult to compute. In the case of ECTL, if a witness exists, we only need to find a small subset (depends on k and the property to be verified) of k-paths in the k-model to certify the existence of a witness. in the case of ACTL, the number of involved k-paths for certification of the property is necessarily large. The technique is then to divide the k-model into submodels with a limited number of paths (which also depends on k and the property to be verified) and prove that if such an ACTL property is true in every such model, then it is true in the k-model as well. The details are explained in the sequel. We first define the concept of submodels.

Definition 5 (Submodels). *Let $M_k = \langle S, Ph_k, I, L \rangle$ be the k-model of M. $M_k' = \langle S, Ph_k', I, L \rangle$ is a submodel of M_k, if $Ph_k' \subseteq Ph_k$. We write $M_k' \leq M_k$ for this relation.*

Similarly, if M_k' and M_k'' are two submodels, $M_k' \leq M_k''$ iff $Ph_k' \subseteq Ph_k''$. The number of k-paths in a submodel M_k' is denoted by $|M_k'|$. We call a submodel M_k' with n k-paths a (k, n)-submodel. Note that in a (k, n)-submodel, we do not require the n k-paths in the submodel be different.

A state s in a submodel M_k' satisfies a formula φ, denoted by $M_k', s \models_k \varphi$, is defined just like the definition of $M_k, s \models_k \varphi$ (cf. Definition 3), except that $\forall \pi$ means $\forall \pi \in Ph_k'$ instead of $\forall \pi \in Ph_k$. We have the following property of submodels.

Proposition 1. *If $M_k' \leq M_k''$, then $M_k'', s \models_k \varphi$ implies $M_k', s \models_k \varphi$.*

Based on this proposition, we obtain:

Proposition 2. *Let M_k', M_k'' be respectively a (k, n)-submodel and a (k, m)-submodel. If $M_k', s_1 \not\models_k \varphi$ or $M_k'', s_2 \not\models_k \psi$, then there is a $(k, max(m, n))$-submodel M_k''' such that $M_k''', s_1 \not\models_k \varphi$ or $M_k''', s_2 \not\models_k \psi$.*

We may combine submodels. Let M_k', M_k'' be two submodels. Then $M_k' \cup M_k''$ is the submodel M_k^* with $Ph_k^* = Ph_k' \cup Ph_k''$ and the other components remain the same.

Proposition 3. *Let M_k', M_k'' be two submodels. If $M_k', s_1 \not\models_k \varphi$ and $M_k'', s_2 \not\models_k \psi$, then $M_k' \cup M_k'', s_1 \not\models_k \varphi$ and $M_k' \cup M_k'', s_2 \not\models_k \psi$.*

A consequence of this proposition is that if there is a (k, n)-submodel M_k' and a (k, m)-submodel M_k'' such that $M_k', s_1 \not\models_k \varphi$ and $M_k'', s_2 \not\models_k \psi$, then there is a $(k, m + n)$-submodel M_k''' such that $M_k''', s_1 \not\models_k \varphi$ and $M_k''', s_2 \not\models_k \psi$.

In the following, we analyze how many paths are needed in submodels such that we can conclude if an ACTL property is true in every such submodel of the k-model, then it is true in the k-model. Let φ be a propositional formula.

For every s, if for every $(k, 0)$-submodel M_k' (there is actually only one $(k, 0)$-submodel), $M_k', s \models_k \varphi$ holds, then $M_k, s \models_k \varphi$.

This is because propositional property does not depend on k-paths[2]. This fact serves as the basis for reasoning about composed formulas. Suppose that we have now the following two assumptions (which are needed for the following inductive construction):

1. For every s, if for every (k, n)-submodel M_k', $M_k', s \models_k \varphi$ holds, then $M_k, s \models_k \varphi$.
2. For every s, if for every (k, m)-submodel M_k'', $M_k'', s \models_k \psi$ holds, then $M_k, s \models_k \psi$.

We then consider the composed ACTL formulas. Let $z = max(m, n)$. According to Proposition 1 and the two assumptions, we have, for every s,

- if for every (k, z)-submodel M_k''', $M_k''', s \models_k \varphi$ holds, then $M_k, s \models_k \varphi$.
- if for every (k, z)-submodel M_k''', $M_k''', s \models_k \psi$ holds, then $M_k, s \models_k \psi$.

Combining these two statements, we obtain:

For every s, if for every $(k, max(m, n))$-submodel M_k^*, $M_k^*, s \models_k \varphi \wedge \psi$ holds, then $M_k, s \models_k \varphi \wedge \psi$.

For disjunction, we consider the validity of $M_k, s \models_k \varphi \vee \psi$. Suppose that $M_k, s \models_k \varphi \vee \psi$ does not hold. Then none of $M_k, s \models_k \varphi$ and $M_k, s \models_k \psi$ holds. According to assumption 1 and assumption 2, there is a (k, n)-submodel M_k' such that $M_k', s \not\models_k \varphi$ and there is a (k, m)-submodel M_k'', such that $M_k'', s \not\models_k \psi$. Combining these two submodels, we obtain a $(k, m + n)$-submodel M_k''' such that $M_k''', s \not\models_k \varphi$ and $M_k''', s \not\models_k \psi$. Then $M_k''', s \not\models_k \varphi \vee \psi$. By turning the direction of reasoning, we obtain:

For every s, if for every $(k, m + n)$-submodel M_k^*, $M_k^*, s \models_k \varphi \vee \psi$ holds, then $M_k, s \models_k \varphi \vee \psi$.

---

[2] The number of different (k, n)-submodels is limited by m^n where m is the number of different k-paths.

For temporal formulas of the form $AX\varphi$, suppose that $M_k, s \models_k AX\varphi$ does not hold. Then there is a k-path $P_1 = \pi_0\pi_1\cdots\pi_k$ with $\pi_0 = s$ such that $M_k, \pi_1 \models_k \varphi$ does not hold. According to assumption 1, there is a (k, n)-submodel M_k' such that $M_k', \pi_1 \not\models_k \varphi$. Extending M_k' with P_1, we obtain a $(k, n + 1)$-submodel M_k'' such that $M_k'', s \not\models_k AX\varphi$. By turning the direction of reasoning, we obtain

> For every s, if for every $(k, n + 1)$-submodel M_k^*, $M_k^*, s \models_k AX\varphi$ holds, then $M_k, s \models_k AX\varphi$.

For temporal formulas of the form $A(\varphi U\psi)$, suppose that $M_k, s \models_k A(\varphi U\psi)$ does not hold. Then there is a k-path $P_1 = \pi_0\pi_1\cdots\pi_k$ with $\pi_0 = s$ such that either (1) $M_k, \pi_i \models_k \psi$ does not hold for all $0 \leq i \leq k$ or

- (2a) $M_k, \pi_0 \models_k \psi$ does not hold, and
- (2b) for each $j < k$, if $M_k, \pi_i \models_k \varphi$ holds for all $0 \leq i \leq j$, then $M_k, \pi_{j+1} \models_k \psi$ does not hold.

According to assumption 1 and assumption 2,

- With condition (1), there is a (k, m)-submodel M_k^i such that $M_k^i, \pi_i \not\models_k \psi$ for each $0 \leq i \leq k$.
  According to Proposition 3, we may combine the $k + 1$ submodels, and obtain that there is a $(k, (k+1)m)$-submodel M_k^* such that $M_k^*, \pi_i \not\models_k \psi$ for each $0 \leq i \leq k$.
- With condition (2a), there is a (k, m)-submodel M_k^0 such that $M_k^0, \pi_0 \not\models_k \psi$.
- With condition (2b), for each $j < k$, there is a (k, n)-submodel $M_k'^i$ such that $M_k'^i, \pi_i \not\models_k \varphi$ for some $0 \leq i \leq j$, or there is a (k, m)-submodel M_k^{j+1} such that $M_k^{j+1}, \pi_{j+1} \not\models_k \psi$.
  According to Proposition 2, we obtain that for each $j < k$, there is a $(k, max(m, n))$-submodel M_k'' such that $M_k'', \pi_i \not\models_k \varphi$ for some $0 \leq i \leq j$, or $M_k'', \pi_{j+1} \not\models_k \psi$.
  According to Proposition 3, we obtain that there is a $(k, k \cdot max(m, n))$-submodel $M_k'^*$ such that for each $j < k$, $M_k'^*, \pi_i \not\models_k \varphi$ for some $0 \leq i \leq j$, or $M_k'^*, \pi_{j+1} \not\models_k \psi$.

Since condition (2a) and condition (2b) are to be satisfied at the same time, we need a $(k, k \cdot max(m, n) + m)$-submodel to cover condition (2). Since condition (1) is an alternative to condition (2), and $(k + 1) \cdot m \leq (k, k \cdot max(m, n) + m)$, a $(k, k \cdot max(m, n) + m)$-submodel is sufficient to cover both conditions. Take the path P_1 into consideration, we have a $(k, k \cdot max(m, n) + m + 1)$-submodel M_k^{**} such that $M_k^{**}, s \models_k A(\varphi U\psi)$ does not hold. By turning the direction of reasoning, we obtain

> For every s, if for every $(k, k \cdot max(m, n) + m + 1)$-submodel M_k^*, $M_k^*, s \models_k A(\varphi U\psi)$ holds, then $M_k, s \models_k A(\varphi U\psi)$.

Similar arguments can be applied to temporal formulas of the form $A(\varphi R\psi)$. Because the semantics of $A(\varphi R\psi)$ involves the condition $eqs(\pi)$, an analysis of $eqs(\pi)$ is needed. Otherwise, the reasoning is similar to that of the case of $A(\varphi U\psi)$.

Suppose that $M_k, s \models_k A(\varphi R\psi)$ does not hold. Then there is a k-path $P_1 = \pi_0\pi_1\cdots\pi_k$ with $\pi_0 = s$ such that

- (1) $eqs(\pi)$ does not hold or $M_k, \pi_j \models_k \psi$ does not hold for some $0 \le j \le k$, and
- (2) for each $j \le k$, if $M_k, \pi_i \models_k \psi$ holds for all $0 \le i \le j$, then $M_k, \pi_j \models_k \varphi$ does not hold.

Condition (1) can be divided into 2 subcases: (1a) $eqs(\pi)$ does not hold and (1b) $eqs(\pi)$ holds. According to assumption 1 and assumption 2,

- With condition (1b), we have that $M_k, \pi_j \models_k \psi$ does not hold for some $0 \le j \le k$. Then there is a (k, m)-submodel M'_k such that $M'_k, \pi_j \not\models_k \psi$ for some $0 \le j \le k$.
- With condition (2), for each $j \le k$, there is a (k, m)-submodel M'^i_k such that $M'^i_k, \pi_i \not\models_k \psi$ for some $0 \le i \le j$, or there is a (k, n)-submodel M^j_k such that $M^j_k, \pi_j \not\models_k \varphi$.

Then there is a $(k, (k + 1) \cdot max(m, n))$-submodel M''_k such that for each $j \le k$, $M''_k, \pi_i \not\models_k \varphi$ for some $0 \le i \le j$, or $M''_k, \pi_j \not\models_k \varphi$.

Applying the similar argument as that in the case of $A(\varphi U \psi)$, we obtain that in case $eqs(\pi)$ holds (i.e., we have condition (1b) and condition (2)), there is a $(k, (k + 1) \cdot max(m, n) + m + 1)$-submodel M^*_k such that $M^*_k, s \not\models_k A(\varphi R \psi)$. In case $eqs(\pi)$ does not holds, there is a $(k, (k + 1) \cdot max(m, n) + 1)$-submodel M'''_k such that $M'''_k, s \not\models_k A(\varphi R \psi)$. According to Proposition 1, there is a $(k, (k + 1) \cdot max(m, n) + m + 1)$-submodel M^*_k such that $M^*_k, s \not\models_k A(\varphi R \psi)$ also in the this case. Therefore, by turning the direction of reasoning, we obtain

For every s, if for every $(k, (k + 1) \cdot max(m, n) + m + 1)$-submodel M^*_k, $M^*_k, s \models_k A(\varphi R \psi)$ holds, then $M_k, s \models_k A(\varphi R \psi)$.

The above reasoning leads to the following definition of the necessary number of paths in such submodels.

Definition 6. *Let φ be an ACTL formula. $n_k(\varphi)$ is defined as follows.*

$$
\begin{array}{ll}
n_k(p) & = 0 \; if \; p \in AP \\
n_k(\neg p) & = 0 \; if \; p \in AP \\
n_k(\varphi \wedge \psi) & = max(n_k(\varphi), n_k(\psi)) \\
n_k(\varphi \vee \psi) & = n_k(\varphi) + n_k(\psi) \\
n_k(AX\varphi) & = n_k(\varphi) + 1 \\
n_k(A(\varphi R \psi)) & = (k + 1) \cdot max(n_k(\varphi), n_k(\psi)) + n_k(\psi) + 1 \\
n_k(A(\varphi U \psi)) & = k \cdot max(n_k(\varphi), n_k(\psi)) + n_k(\psi) + 1
\end{array}
$$

For verifying φ, we divide the k-model into submodels with $n_k(\varphi)$ paths This leads to the following lemma.

Lemma 3. $M_k, s \models_k \varphi$ iff for every $(k, n_k(\varphi))$-submodel M^*_k, $M^*_k, s \models_k \varphi$ holds.

This lemma can be proved by structural induction on φ based on the above analysis. Combining Theorem 1, we obtain

Theorem 3. $M, s \models \varphi$ iff there is some $k \le k_M$ such that for every $(k, n_k(\varphi))$-submodel M^*_k, $M^*_k, s \models_k \varphi$ holds.

Similar to Definition 4, we can define the relation $M_k^* \models_k \varphi$ for a submodel M_k^* and a formula φ. Then we obtain

Theorem 4. $M \models \varphi$ *iff there is some $k \leq k_M$ such that for every $(k, n_k(\varphi))$-submodel M_k^*, $M_k^* \models_k \varphi$ holds.*

5   SAT-Based Characterization of ACTL

Let $k \geq 0$. Let N_k be the number of different k-paths of M. Let $u_{i,0}, ..., u_{i,k}$ be a finite sequence of state variables for each $i \in \{1, ..., N_k\}$. The sequence $u_{i,0}, ..., u_{i,k}$ is intended to be used as a representation of a path of M_k.

Definition 7. *Let $k \geq 0$.*

$$P_k(i) := \bigwedge_{j=0}^{k-1} T(u_{i,j}, u_{i,j+1})$$

Every assignment to the set of state variables $\{u_{i,0}, ..., u_{i,k}\}$ satisfying $P_k(i)$ represents a valid k-path of M. The sequence $u_{i,0}, ..., u_{i,k}$ is then called a symbolic path of M_k. Let a be an assignment to $u_{i,0}, ..., u_{i,k}$ for $i \in \{1, ..., N_k\}$. Then the value assigned to $u_{i,j}$, denoted $a(u_{i,j})$, represents a state of M. Conversely, for each state $s \in S$ of M, we use $u(s)$ to represent that u has already been assigned a value representing the state s. The difference between a state variable u and $u(s)$ is that the latter has a fixed assignment and therefore cannot be assigned new values.

Definition 8 (Transition Relation). *Let $k \geq 0$. Let $0 \leq b \leq N_k$.*

$$[[M]]_k^b := \bigwedge_{i=1}^{b} P_k(i)$$

This is a collection of $P_k(l)$ for $l = 1, ..., b$. Let $p \in AP$ be a proposition symbol and $p(u)$ represent the propositional formula representing the states in which p is true according to L of M. State it differently, we have that $p(u)$ is true when u is assigned the truth value representing a state s such that p holds on s. Let $e_k(i)$ denote that there are same states appearing in different positions in path $P_k(i)$. Formally,

$$e_k(i) := \bigvee_{x=0}^{k-1} \bigvee_{y=x+1}^{k} u_{i,x} = u_{i,y}.$$

This definition corresponds to the definition of $eqs(\pi)$ for a k-path $\pi = u_{i,0} u_{i,1} \cdots u_{i,k}$.

Definition 9 (Translation of ACTL formulas). *Let $k \geq 0$. Let u be a state variable and φ be an ACTL formula. The encoding $[[\varphi, u]]_k^b$ is defined as follows.*

$$
\begin{aligned}
[[p, u]]_k^b &= p(u) \\
[[\neg p, u]]_k^b &= \neg p(u) \\
[[\varphi \vee \psi, u]]_k^b &= [[\varphi, u]]_k^b \vee [[\psi, u]]_k^b \\
[[\varphi \wedge \psi, u]]_k^b &= [[\varphi, u]]_k^b \wedge [[\psi, u]]_k^b \\
[[AX\varphi, u]]_k^b &= \bigwedge_{i=1}^{b}(u = u_{i,0} \rightarrow [[\varphi, u_{i,1}]]_k^b) \\
[[A(\varphi R\psi), u]]_k^b &= \bigwedge_{i=1}^{b}(u = u_{i,0} \rightarrow \\
&\qquad \bigvee_{j=0}^{k}([[\varphi, u_{i,j}]]_k^b \wedge \bigwedge_{t=0}^{j}[[\psi, u_{i,t}]]_k^b) \vee \bigwedge_{j=0}^{k}[[\psi, u_{i,j}]]_k^b \wedge e_k(i)) \\
[[A(\varphi U\psi), u]]_k^b &= \bigwedge_{i=1}^{b}(u = u_{i,0} \rightarrow \bigvee_{j=0}^{k}([[\psi, u_{i,j}]]_k^b \wedge \bigwedge_{t=0}^{j-1}[[\varphi, u_{i,t}]]_k^b))
\end{aligned}
$$

where $[[\varphi, u_{i,j}]]_0^b$ *denotes false for* $j > 0$.

$[[\varphi, u_{i,j}]]_0^b$ may occur when $k = 0$. We may only consider the cases with $k \geq 1$ in the definition. But we choose to allow $k = 0$ for avoiding situations where we may need to explicitly mention $k = 0$ as a special case.

Definition 10. $[[M, \varphi, u]]_k^b := [[M]]_k^b \rightarrow [[\varphi, u]]_k^b$.

$[[M, \varphi, u(s)]]_k^b$ encodes $M'_k, s \models \varphi$, in the sense that a model of $[[M, \varphi, u(s)]]_k^b$ satisfying $[[M]]_k^b$ yields a (k, b)-submodel M'_k such that $M'_k, s \models \varphi$. This means that if there is no falsifying assignments, then every (k, b)-submodel M'_k satisfies $M'_k, s \models \varphi$. On the other hand, a falsifying assignment of $[[M, \varphi, u(s)]]_k^b$ yields a (k, b)-submodel M''_k such that $M''_k, s \not\models \varphi$.

Lemma 4. $[[M, \varphi, u(s)]]_k^b$ *is valid iff for every* (k, b)-*submodel* M'_k, $M'_k, s \models \varphi$.

According to Lemma 3, we obtain $M_k, s \models \varphi$ iff $[[M, \varphi, u(s)]]_k^{n_k(\varphi)}$ is valid. Then with Theorem 1, we obtain

Theorem 5. $M, s \models \varphi$ *iff there is some* $k \leq k_M$ *such that* $[[M, \varphi, u(s)]]_k^{n_k(\varphi)}$ *is valid.*

Definition 11. $[[M, \varphi]]_k^b := I(u) \wedge [[M]]_k^b \rightarrow [[\varphi, u]]_k^b$.

$I(u)$ restricts the potential values of u to be the initial states of M. $[[M, \varphi]]_k^b$ is valid iff for each s of the initial states, $[[M]]_k^b \rightarrow [[\varphi, u(s)]]_k^b$ is valid. According to Lemma 4 and Lemma 3, we obtain $M_k \models \varphi$ iff $[[M, \varphi]]_k^{n_k(\varphi)}$ is valid. Then with Theorem 2, we obtain

Theorem 6. $M \models \varphi$ *iff there is some* $k \leq k_M$ *such that* $[[M, \varphi]]_k^{n_k(\varphi)}$ *is valid.*

6   Bounded Verification and Case Study

Bounded verification of valid ACTL properties can be based on theorem 6. For minimizing the number of propositions used in the SAT formulas, we base the verification on the following corollary where the variable u (implicitly) in Theorem 6 is replaced by $u_{1,0}$ which is already in $[[M]]_k^n$ (when $n \geq 1$). Let

$$[[M, \varphi]]_k^* := I(u_{1,0}) \wedge [[M]]_k^{n_k(\varphi)} \rightarrow [[\varphi, u_{1,0}]]_k^{n_k(\varphi)}.$$

Corollary 1. $M \models \varphi$ *iff there is a* $0 \leq k \leq k_M$ *such that* $[[M, \varphi]]_k^*$ *is valid.*

The verification approach is as follows. For a given model M and an ACTL formula φ,

- Start with $k = 0$;
- If $[[M, \varphi]]_k^*$ is valid, report that the property holds;
- Increase k, if $k \leq k_M$, go to the first "if"-test;
- Report that the property does not hold.

6.1 Case Study

We first present the tool for the case study. There are mainly two steps for the verification: one is the generation of a CNF formula and the other is the checking of the formula. The tool first converts the Boolean representation of the initial state and the transition relation of the abstract program and the property (to be checked) to the CNF formula and then call the satisfiability checker BOSCH[3] for checking the CNF formula. If the formula is satisfiable, an assignment that makes the formula satisfiable is presented. This can be used for error detection as demonstrated in Section 6.3.

We now present the abstract program (this is taken from [23] in which the program was used for the illustration of the verification of LTL properties) and the properties to be verified. Let a, b be variables of enumeration type which have respectively the domain $\{s_0, ..., s_3\}$ and $\{t_0, ..., t_3\}$. Let x, y, t be variables of Boolean type. The program consists of two processes: A and B with the following specification in a first order transition system [17]:

Process A:	
$a = s_0$	$\longrightarrow (y, t, a) := (1, 1, s_1)$
$a = s_1 \wedge (x = 0 \vee t = 0)$	$\longrightarrow (a) := (s_2)$
$a = s_2$	$\longrightarrow (y, a) := (0, s_3)$
$a = s_3$	$\longrightarrow (y, t, a) := (1, 1, s_1)$
Process B:	
$b = t_0$	$\longrightarrow (x, t, b) := (1, 0, t_1)$
$b = t_1 \wedge (y = 0 \vee t = 1)$	$\longrightarrow (b) := (t_2)$
$b = t_2$	$\longrightarrow (x, b) := (0, t_3)$
$b = t_3$	$\longrightarrow (x, t, b) := (1, 0, t_1)$

Let the initial state be $a = s_0 \wedge b = t_0 \wedge x = y = t = 0$. We consider two properties:

- A liveness property: process A or process B will at some future point (including the current one) pass a critical region, i.e. $AF(a = s_3 \vee b = s_3)$.
- A mixed property: at any point, process A or process B will at some future point (including the current one) pass a critical region, i.e. $AGAF(a = s_3 \vee b = s_3)$.

Let boolean variables a_0 and a_1 represent the variable a such that $a_0 = i \wedge a_1 = j$ meaning $a = s_{2i+j}$, and b_0 and b_1 represent b such that $b_0 = i \wedge b_1 = j$ meaning $b = t_{2i+j}$. Then each state is represented by a tuple $(a_0, a_1, b_0, b_1, x, y, t)$.

---

[3] A tool based on DPLL and developed based on parts of the code of a tool presented in [25].

Let $V = \{a_0, a_1, b_0, b_1, p, q, r\}$. The system can be represented by boolean formulas as follows:

$I(a_0, a_1, b_0, b_1, x, y, t)$
$\equiv x = 0 \wedge y = 0 \wedge t = 0 \wedge a_0 = 0 \wedge a_1 = 0 \wedge b_0 = 0 \wedge b_1 = 0$
$T(a_0, a_1, b_0, b_1, x, y, t, a_0', a_1', b_0', b_1', x', y', t')$
$\equiv a_0 = 0 \wedge a_1 = 0 \wedge y' = 1 \wedge t' = 1 \wedge a_1' = 1 \wedge same(V \setminus \{y, t, a_1\}) \vee$
$\quad a_0 = 0 \wedge a_1 = 1 \wedge (x = 0 \vee t = 0) \wedge a_0' = 1 \wedge a_1' = 0 \wedge same(V \setminus \{a_0, a_1\}) \vee$
$\quad a_0 = 1 \wedge a_1 = 0 \wedge y' = 0 \wedge a_1' = 1 \wedge same(V \setminus \{y, a_1\}) \vee$
$\quad a_0 = 1 \wedge a_1 = 1 \wedge y' = 1 \wedge t' = 1 \wedge a_0' = 0 \wedge same(V \setminus \{y, t, a_0\})$
$\quad b_0 = 0 \wedge b_1 = 0 \wedge x' = 1 \wedge t' = 0 \wedge b_1' = 1 \wedge same(V \setminus \{x, t, b_1\}) \vee$
$\quad b_0 = 0 \wedge b_1 = 1 \wedge (y = 0 \vee t = 1) \wedge b_0' = 1 \wedge b_1' = 0 \wedge same(V \setminus \{b_0, b_1\}) \vee$
$\quad b_0 = 1 \wedge b_1 = 0 \wedge x' = 0 \wedge b_1' = 1 \wedge same(V \setminus \{x, b_1\}) \vee$
$\quad b_0 = 1 \wedge b_1 = 1 \wedge x' = 1 \wedge t' = 0 \wedge b_0' = 0 \wedge same(V \setminus \{x, t, b_0\}) \vee loop\_action$

where $same(X)$ represents $v_1' = v_1 \wedge \cdots \wedge v_n' = v_n$ for the set of propositions $X = \{v_1, ..., v_n\}$, and loop_action is a transition enabled if none of the other transitions is applicable, and the effect of this transition is that the values of the state variables are kept unchanged in the next state.

The formula $(a = s_3 \vee b = t_3)$ is the same as the following.

$$(a_0 = 1 \wedge a_1 = 1 \vee b_0 = 1 \wedge b_1 = 1)$$

Let us denote this formula by ψ. Then the two properties are as follows.

$$(1)\ M \models AF\psi$$
$$(2)\ M \models AGAF\psi$$

6.2   Checking Correctness

For $M \models AF\psi$, we want to know whether $[[M, AF\psi]]_k^*$ is valid for some k. We check the satisfiability of the negation of $[[M, AF\psi]]_k^*$ for $k = 0, 1, 2, ...$, until the formula is unsatisfiable, or the completeness threshold k_M is reached. By making trivial simplifications, transforming the formula into CNF format, and using the tool BOSCH for satisfiability checking, we obtain that the CNF formula is satisfiable for $k = 0, 1, 2, 3$ and it is unsatisfiable for $k = 4$. This proves $M \models AF\psi$. Table 1 shows the experimental data of this verification on a Sun Blade 1000 with 750 MHz and 512 MB. The number of variables includes the number of variables representing the states and that of auxiliary variables used in the transformation of the formula into CNF. The time used by BOSCH for satisfiability checking is negligible.

For $M \models AGAF\psi$, we check the satisfiability of the negation of $[[M, AGAF\psi]]_k^*$ for $k = 0, 1, 2, ...$. We obtain that it is satisfiable for $k = 0, 1, ..., 9$ and it is unsatisfiable for $k = 10$. This proves $M \models AGAF\psi$. Table 2 shows the experimental data of this verification for $k = 0, 3, 6, 9, 10$. The time is that (in seconds) used by BOSCH for satisfiability checking.

Table 1. Experimental data for verification of $AF\psi$

Property	k	Variables	Clauses	Time	SAT
$AF\psi$	0	9	14	0.0	yes
	1	26	157	0.0	yes
	2	43	302	0.0	yes
	3	60	449	0.0	yes
	4	77	598	0.0	no

Table 2. Experimental data for for verification of $AGAF\psi$

Property	k	Variables	Clauses	Time	SAT
$AGAF\psi$	0	23	25	0.0	yes
	3	185	1000	0.0	yes
	6	410	2146	0.1	yes
	9	698	3463	0.2	yes
	10	808	3940	5.0	no

6.3   Error Detection

Suppose that we have an erroneous program where the transition rule

$$a = s_1 \wedge (x = 0 \vee t = 0) \rightarrow (a) := (s_2)$$

is wrongly written as

$$a = s_1 \wedge (x = 0 \vee t = 1) \rightarrow (a) := (s_2).$$

Then the two properties do not hold in this modified program. Let us denote this program (its equivalent Kripke structure) by M'. Then we need to check the properties up to the threshold $k_{M'}$. With Proposition 2, we may use an over approximation of $k_{M'}$. For instance, we may use 17, which is the number of reachable states of M', as the over approximation.

The inputs to the satisfiability checker are satisfiable with each k up to and including 17, and this certifies that the properties do not hold in this program, i.e.

$$M' \not\models AF\psi$$
$$M' \not\models AGAF\psi$$

Table 3 and Table 4 show the experimental data of error detection with respect to the properties $AF\psi$ and $AGAF\psi$ with $k = 0, 4, 8, 12, 16, 17$, respectively.

For error location, the path information produced by BOSCH can be used for the analysis of the problem of the program. For the property $AGAF\psi$, the path information is shown in Table 5, where $a = s_i$ iff $a_0 = i/2 \wedge a_1 = i\%2$ and $b = t_i$ iff $b_0 = i/2 \wedge b_1 = i\%2$. By looking at the path information, we find two paths. The first path has a loop at state 06 (the sixth state in the path) and the second path has a loop at state 02. The first path satisfies $AF\psi$ and the second one does not. Further, we can relate the first state of the second path to the first state of the first path, and this means that the second

Table 3. Experimental data for error detection w. r. t. $AF\psi$

Property	k	Variables	Clauses	Time	SAT
$AF\psi$	0	9	14	0.0	yes
	4	77	598	0.0	yes
	8	145	1214	0.0	yes
	12	213	1862	0.0	yes
	16	281	2542	0.0	yes
	17	298	2717	0.0	yes

Table 4. Experimental data for error detection w. r. t. $AGAF\psi$

Property	k	Variables	Clauses	Time	SAT
$AGAF\psi$	0	23	25	0.0	yes
	4	253	1363	0.0	yes
	8	595	3005	0.2	yes
	12	1049	4951	0.4	yes
	16	1615	7201	0.9	yes
	17	1774	7811	1.1	yes

Table 5. Path information for error detection w. r. t. $AGAF\psi$

Path	State	a_0	a_1	b_0	b_1	x	y	t
1	00	0	0	0	0	0	0	0
1	01	0	1	0	0	0	1	1
1	02	1	0	0	0	0	1	1
1	03	1	1	0	0	0	0	1
1	04	1	1	0	1	1	0	0
1	05	1	1	1	0	1	0	0
1	06	0	1	1	0	1	1	1
1	07	1	0	1	0	1	1	1
1	08	1	1	1	0	1	0	1
1	$09 = 06$	0	1	1	0	1	1	1
1	$\cdots$							
2	01	0	1	0	0	0	1	1
2	02	0	1	0	1	1	1	0
2	$03 = 02$	0	1	0	1	1	1	0
2	$\cdots$							

path starts at the first state of the first path, and this path has an execution sequence that looks like a deadlock. By analyzing the program, we know that there is a deadlock (not ending with a state satisfying ψ) and therefore the program does not satisfy $AGAF\psi$.

6.4 Complexity and Discussion

The complexity of $[[M, \varphi]]_k^*$ depends on M, k and $n_k(\varphi)$. For a given k, the number of propositional variables involved in $[[M, \varphi]]_k^*$ is $(k + 1) \cdot n_k(\varphi)$ where $n_k(\varphi) =$

$2^{O(\log(k)\cdot|\varphi|)}$. This means that the number of propositional variables could be exponential in the length (in practice, in the nesting depth of AR and AU) of φ. We expect that for practical applications, the nesting depth of AR and AU of a formula is small. Then the efficiency depends very much on k which is bounded by the number of reachable states (or more accurately, the diameter) of M.

When a small k is sufficient for the verification, the advantage of this approach is clear. In such cases, it could be much more efficient than BDD based approaches. we provide an example illustrating this advantage.

Let $p_0, ..., p_{n-2}, q, r$ be variables of the domain $\{0, 1\}$ and $\oplus$ be the function: addition modulo 2. Let the system be consist of n processes. A, B and C_i for $i = 0, ..., n-3$ (each is a sequential process which executed in parallel to each other with the interleaving semantics) with the following specification:

$$A : r = r \oplus 1; p_0 = p_0 \oplus 1$$
$$B : p_{n-2} = p_{n-2} \oplus 1; q = q \oplus 1$$
$$C_i : p_i = p_i \oplus 1; p_{i+1} = p_{i+1} \oplus 1; q = q \oplus 1$$

Let the initial state be $p_i = 0$ and $q = r = 1$.

Let $\varphi = AXA(qU(p_0 \vee p_2 \vee \cdots \vee p_{n-2}))$ for an even number n. For verifying $\varphi(n)$, we first transform the problem to CNF formula, then use zChaff, an implementation of the Chaff algorithm [16] for verification. For $n = 4, 6, 8, 10, 12$, the property is verified when k reaches respectively $2, 3, 4, 5, 6$. The verification times by zChaff for $n = 4, 6, 8, 10, 12$ are shown in Table 6.

For comparison, we have carried out the same verification task using SMV (release 2.5.4.3), an implementation of the symbolic model checking technique [15]. The verification times for $n = 4, 6, 8, 10, 12$ are shown in Table 7.

Table 6 and Table 7 show clear advantage of using this bounded verification approach over the BDD based verification approach for this example.

Table 6. Experimental data for verification by zChaff

Property	k	Time (s)	Variables	Clauses	SAT
$\varphi(4)$	2	0.01	139	1254	no
$\varphi(6)$	3	0.03	278	4077	no
$\varphi(8)$	4	0.11	465	9522	no
$\varphi(10)$	5	0.42	700	18456	no
$\varphi(12)$	6	1.15	983	31746	no

Table 7. Experimental data for verification by SMV

Property	Time (s)	BDD nodes	Memory (KB)
$\varphi(4)$	0.06	6092	1245.184
$\varphi(6)$	0.96	14545	1376.256
$\varphi(8)$	12.97	111981	2949.120
$\varphi(10)$	192.01	888025	15335.424
$\varphi(12)$	6596.34	6135235	99287.040

6.5 Summary

The case study shows that this approach can be used to both verification of correct properties and error detection, and the comparison has illustrated that when a small k is sufficient for the verification, the advantage is clear. In such cases, it could be much more efficient than BDD based approaches. For error detection, in addition to identifying that there is an error, error paths may also be produced. Creating and analyzing tree-like counter examples have also been studied in many papers including [8,20]. In our work, the counterexample may be created and presented as a set of k-paths. Although we may use this approach for error detection, it needs to reach a completeness threshold for k. This is usually not very efficient. This approach can be combined with that presented in [18] for error detection. This is to be discussed in the next section.

7 A Combined Verification Approach

Bounded model checking based on SAT (satisfiability checking) has first been introduced as a complementary technique to BDD-based symbolic model checking of LTL properties [2]. This idea has then been used for checking ACTL properties [18]. The characterization, denoted here by $[[\varphi, u_{i,j}]]_k^{*,b}$, is based on a bounded semantics for ECTL and the encoding of ECTL formulas as follows.

$$
\begin{aligned}
[[p, u]]_k^{*,b} &= p(u) \\
[[\neg p, u]]_k^{*,b} &= \neg p(u) \\
[[\varphi \vee \psi, u]]_k^{*,b} &= [[\varphi, u]]_k^{*,b} \vee [[\psi, u]]_k^{*,b} \\
[[\varphi \wedge \psi, u]]_k^{*,b} &= [[\varphi, u]]_k^{*,b} \wedge [[\psi, u]]_k^{*,b} \\
[[EX\varphi, u]]_k^{*,b} &= \bigvee_{i=1}^{b}(u = u_{i,0} \wedge [[\varphi, u_{i,1}]]_k^{*,b}) \\
\hline
[[EG\varphi, u]]_k^{*,b} &= \bigvee_{i=1}^{b}(u = u_{i,0} \wedge \bigwedge_{j=0}^{k}[[\varphi, u_{i,j}]]_k^{*,b} \wedge \bigwedge_{j=0}^{k} T(u_{i,k}, u_{i,j})) \\
[[E(\varphi U\psi), u]]_k^{*,b} &= \bigvee_{i=1}^{b}(u = u_{i,0} \wedge \bigvee_{j=0}^{k}([[\psi, u_{i,j}]]_k^{*,b} \wedge \bigwedge_{t=0}^{j-1}[[\varphi, u_{i,t}]]_k^{*,b}))
\end{aligned}
$$

where $[[\varphi, u_{i,j}]]_0^{*,b}$ denotes $false$ for $j > 0$. Define

$$[[M, \varphi]]_k^{*,b} := I(u) \wedge [[M]]_k^b \wedge [[\varphi, u]]_k^{*,b}.$$

Let $f_k(\varphi)$ be the sufficient number[4] of paths for a witness (if there is any) of the ECTL formula φ. According to this encoding, we have the following theorem [18].

Theorem 7. *Let φ be an ACTL formula. $M_k \not\models_k \varphi$ iff there is some $k < k_M$ such that $[[M, \neg\varphi]]_k^{*,f_k(\neg\varphi)}$ is satisfiable.*

This theorem can be used as a basis for efficient error detection with SAT-based model checking. The procedure for verification of a given model M against an ACTL formula φ could be as follows:

---

[4] The computation of $f_k(\varphi)$ is referred to the paper [18].

- Start with $k = 0$;
- If $[[M, \neg\varphi]]_k^{*,f_k(\neg\varphi)}$ is satisfiable, report "the property does not hold";
- Increase k, if $k < k_M$, go to the first "if"-test;
- Report that the property holds.

This can also be used for verification of valid properties. However, it is not efficient for this purpose, since one has to reach the condition with $k = k_M$. Theorem 7 and Theorem 6 can be combined to avoid the use of the completeness threshold k_M.

Corollary 2. *Let φ be an ACTL formula. $M_k \models_k \varphi$ if there is some $k \leq k_M$ such that $[[M, \varphi]]_k^{n_k(\varphi)}$ is valid or for all $k \geq 0$, $[[M, \neg\varphi]]_k^{*,f_k(\neg\varphi)}$ is unsatisfiable. $M_k \not\models_k \varphi$ if $[[M, \varphi]]_k^{n_k(\varphi)}$ is not valid for each $k \geq 0$ or there is some $k < k_M$ such that $[[M, \neg\varphi]]_k^{*,f_k(\neg\varphi)}$ is satisfiable.*

The procedure for the verification of a given model M against an ACTL formula φ could then be as follows:

- Start with $k = 0$;
- If $[[M, \varphi]]_k^{n_k(\varphi)}$ is valid, report "the property holds";
- If $[[M, \neg\varphi]]_k^{*,f_k(\neg\varphi)}$ is satisfiable, report "the property does not hold";
- Increase k, go to the first "if"-test;

The procedure based on Corollary 2 is guaranteed to terminate with a report on whether the property holds. In theory, there is still a completeness threshold that may be reach in some cases of the satisfiability checking. Even in such cases, the advantage is that we do not need to know the completeness threshold for which the cost for the calculation is high [1,13] and an over-approximation can be quite large.

The complexity of the procedure depends on the number of variables involved in the encoding. For a given k and an ACTL formula φ, the number of variables needed is $k^{O(|\varphi|)}$. The efficiency depends on whether there is a small k which is sufficient to certify or falsify the property. The part $O(|\varphi|)$ is small when there are few levels of nesting temporal operators (which is often the case in the practical property specification and verification).

Related Works. There has not been lack of motivation and work for proving properties based on SAT. Related works include, for instance, SAT-based analysis of partial correctness assertions [11,12], SAT-based proof of safety properties by using induction [21], conservative abstraction with counter example guided refinement [9], and interpolation based transition relation approximation for generating facts relevant with respect to given properties [14]. Proving simple liveness properties based on SAT was also considered in [1]. Recently, SAT-based verification of valid general LTL and ACTL properties has been considered in [23,24]. The idea is to verify a model of a particular length (as short as possible) and to generate a propositional formula that is unsatisfiable if the model is unsatisfiable with respect to the given property. However the condition in these approaches is only a sufficient condition, not a sufficient and necessary condition, such that there are valid LTL and ACTL properties that cannot be verified by using these approaches alone.

8   Concluding Remarks

Model checking has been considered as one of the most practical applications of the theoretical computer science in the verification of concurrent systems. The practical applicability of explicit state model checking, introduced in [6,7], is limited by the state explosion problem which could be caused by for instance, the representation of currency of operations by their interleaving. Therefore much effort has been put into the research aiming at minimizing models. Binary Decision Diagram (BDD) based on symbolic techniques has significantly improved the practical applicability of model checking by compactly representing transition relations and system states [4,3,5]. Although this is a great success, it has not solved the state explosion problem. For many problems, there is no polynomial size representation with BDD.

For combating this problem, bounded model checking based on SAT (satisfiability checking) has been introduced as a complementary technique to BDD-based symbolic model checking of LTL and ACTL properties in respectively 1999 and 2002 [2,18]. The basic idea is to search for a counter example of a particular length (as short as possible) and to generate a propositional formula that is satisfied iff such a counter example exists. This idea is similar to that for searching finite models [22] for which we search for counter models of given sizes until we find one.

Prasad, Biere and Gupta pointed out in a survey paper [19] in 2005 that, currently, the strength of SAT-based verification techniques lies primarily in falsification. This is a remark on verification related to general temporal properties. For simple properties, there has been a lot of work and report of success, for instance, for proving simple safety and liveness properties [21,9,14,1]. Recently, SAT-based verification of valid general LTL and ACTL properties has been considered in [23,24]. However these approaches are based on semantics with existential interpretation and the condition in these approaches is not a sufficient and necessary condition, such that there are valid LTL and ACTL properties that cannot be verified by using these approaches.

This work has provided a bounded semantics for ACTL, and based on this semantics, a refinement has been developed. Then a characterization of ACTL properties by propositional formulas and an approach is presented for the verification of ACTL formulas such that a sufficient and necessary condition is provided. This means that all ACTL properties can either be verified or falsified by using this approach, with the emphasis on verification. For practical application, falsification using this approach depends on a completeness threshold which is not very efficient, and therefore a proposal for combining this approach with the approach based on the bounded semantics for ECTL is suggested for avoiding the use of such a completeness threshold.

Acknowledgments. The author thanks anonymous referees for their constructive critics that helped improving this paper.

References

1. Biere, A., Cimmatti, A., Clarke, E., Strichman, O., Zhu, Y.: Bounded Model Checking. Advances in Computers 58. Academic Press, London (2003)
2. Biere, A., Cimmatti, A., Clarke, E., Zhu, Y.: Symbolic Model Checking without BDDs. In: Cleaveland, W.R. (ed.) ETAPS 1999 and TACAS 1999. LNCS, vol. 1579, pp. 193–207. Springer, Heidelberg (1999)
3. Burch, J.R., Clarke, E.M., McMillan, K.L., Dill, D.L., Hwang, J.: Symbolic model checking: 10^{20} states and beyond. In: LICS 1990, pp. 428–439 (1990)
4. Bryant, R.: Graph based algorithms for boolean function manipulation. IEEE Transaction on Computers 35(8), 677–691 (1986)
5. Bryant, R.: Binary decision diagrams and beyond: enabling technologies for formal verification. In: CAD 1995, pp. 236–243 (1995)
6. Clarke, E.M., Emerson, E.A.: Synthesis of synchronization skeletons for branching time temporal logic. In: Kozen, D. (ed.) Logics of Programs. LNCS, vol. 131, Springer, Heidelberg (1981)
7. Clarke, E.M., Emerson, E.A., Sistla, A.P.: Automatic verification of finite-state concurrent systems using temporal logic specifications. ACM Transactions on Programming Languages and Systems 8(2), 244–263 (1986)
8. Clarke, E.M., Jha, S., Lu, Y., Veith, H.: Tree-Like Counterexamples in Model Checking. In: LICS 2002, pp. 19–29 (2002)
9. Das, S., Dill, D.L.: Successive Approximation of Abstract Transition Relations. In: LICS 2001, pp. 51–60 (2001)
10. Emerson, E.A., Clarke, E.M.: Using Branching-time Temporal Logics to Synthesize Synchronization Skeletons. Science of Computer Programming 2(3), 241–266 (1982)
11. Frias, M.F., Galeotti, J.P., Pombo, C.L., Aguirre, N.: DynAlloy: upgrading alloy with actions. In: Inverardi, P., Jazayeri, M. (eds.) ICSE 2005. LNCS, vol. 4309, pp. 442–451. Springer, Heidelberg (2006)
12. Frias, M.F., Pombo, C.L., Baum, G.A., Aguirre, N., Maibaum, T.S.E.: Reasoning about static and dynamic properties in alloy: A purely relational approach. ACM Trans. Softw. Eng. Methodol. 14(4), 478–526 (2005)
13. Kroening, D., Strichman, O.: Efficient Computation of Recurrence Diameters. In: Zuck, L.D., Attie, P.C., Cortesi, A., Mukhopadhyay, S. (eds.) VMCAI 2003. LNCS, vol. 2575, pp. 298–309. Springer, Heidelberg (2002)
14. Jhala, R., McMillan, K.L.: McMillan. Interpolation and SAT-Based Model Checking. In: Hunt Jr., W.A., Somenzi, F. (eds.) CAV 2003. LNCS, vol. 2725, pp. 1–13. Springer, Heidelberg (2003)
15. McMillan, K L.: Symbolic Model Checking. Kluwer Academic Publishers, Dordrecht (1993)
16. Moskewicz, M.W., Madigan, C.F., Zhao, Y., Zhang, L., Malik, S.: Chaff: Engineering an Efficient SAT Solver. In: DAC 2001 (2001)
17. Peled, D.A.: Software Reliability Methods. Springer, Heidelberg (2001)
18. Penczek, W., Wozna, B., Zbrzezny, A.: Bounded Model Checking for the Universal Fragment of CTL. Fundamenta Informaticae 51, 135–156 (2002)
19. Prasad, M.R., Biere, A., Gupta, A.: A survey of recent advances in SAT-based formal verification. STTT 7(2), 156–173 (2005)
20. Shoham, S., Grumberg, O.: A Game-Based Framework for CTL Counterexamples and 3-Valued Abstraction-Refinement. In: Hunt Jr., W.A., Somenzi, F. (eds.) CAV 2003. LNCS, vol. 2725, pp. 275–287. Springer, Heidelberg (2003)
21. Sheeran, M., Singh, S., lmarck, G.S.: Checking Safety Properties Using Induction and a SAT-Solver. In: Johnson, S.D., Hunt Jr., W.A. (eds.) FMCAD 2000. LNCS, vol. 1954, pp. 108–125. Springer, Heidelberg (2000)

22. Zhang, J.: Problems on the generation of finite models. In: Bundy, A. (ed.) CADE-12. LNCS, vol. 814, pp. 753–757. Springer, Heidelberg (1994)
23. Zhang, W.: SAT-based verification of LTL formulas. In: Brim, L., Haverkort, B., Leucker, M., van de Pol, J. (eds.) FMICS 2006 and PDMC 2006. LNCS, vol. 4346, pp. 277–292. Springer, Heidelberg (2007)
24. Zhang, W.: Verification of ACTL properties by bounded model checking. In: Moreno Díaz, R., Pichler, F., Quesada Arencibia, A. (eds.) EUROCAST 2007. LNCS, vol. 4739. Springer, Heidelberg (2007)
25. Zhang, W., Huang, Z., Zhang, J.: Parallel Execution of Stochastic Search Procedures on Reduced SAT Instances. In: Ishizuka, M., Sattar, A. (eds.) PRICAI 2002. LNCS (LNAI), vol. 2417, pp. 108–117. Springer, Heidelberg (2002)

Automating Refinement Checking in Probabilistic System Design

C. Gonzalia and A. McIver

Dept. Computer Science, Macquarie University, NSW 2109 Australia
{carlos,anabel}@ics.mq.edu.au

Abstract. Refinement plays a crucial role in "top-down" styles of verification, such as the refinement calculus, but for probabilistic systems *proof of refinement* is a particularly challenging task due to the combination of probability and nondeterminism which typically arises in partially-specified systems.

Whilst the theory of probabilistic refinement is well-known [18] there are few tools to help with establishing refinements between programs.

In this paper we describe a tool which provides partial support during refinement proofs. The tool essentially builds small models of programs using an algebraic rewriting system to extract the overall probabilistic behaviour. We use that behaviour to recast refinement-checking as a *linear satisfiability problem*, which can then be exported to a linear arithmetic solver.

One of the major benefits of this approach is the ability to generate counterexamples, alerting the prover to a problem in a proposed refinement.

We demonstrate the technique on a small case study based on Schneider et al.'s Tank Monitoring [26].

Keywords: Probabilistic systems, probabilistic verification, algebraic rewriting system for probability, refinement, linear satisfiability.

1   Introduction

The generally-accepted semantics for probabilistic programs [10] is based on Markov Decision Processes (MDPs) [5], and incorporates probability and nondeterminism. That model is the basis for several refinement-style formalisms such as pGCL [18], probabilistic action systems [27,9,16], and probabilistic extensions to the B-method [12]. Whilst the theory of probabilistic-program refinement is well understood, there is little mechanised support to aid in its practical application, except in some specialised situations [11,2]. Our principal purpose in this paper is to address that problem, by providing partial support to automate the task of checking refinement for finite instances of systems, with the ability to provide counterexamples in cases where the proposed refinement fails.

The background to this work lies in *proof-based*- rather than *algorithmic* styles of verification such as model checking. The strengths of probabilistic model

M. Butler, M. Hinchey, M.M. Larrondo-Petrie (Eds.): ICFEM 2007, LNCS 4789, pp. 212–231, 2007.

checking lie in its detailed numerical calculation of various performance measures, on the other hand, even though it is restricted to the treatment of finite-state systems, there is normally no compensating version of "counterexample support" as for standard model checking systems.

In contrast a proof-based method uses mathematical reasoning to show that an implementation satisfies (or does not satisfy) a particular specified property or behaviour. It is more general than model checking but normally requires significant prover-guided intervention. Moreover the combination of arithmetic and predicates over program variables necessary in probabilistic systems poses significant practical challenges for automation [2]. Refinement — in which the behaviour of a specification program must be shown to match that of an implementation — is particularly difficult to verify, and moreover it is known that the staple "first order" rule [7] used in the standard B-toolkit, for example, does not carry over to probabilistic systems, except for a restricted class of refinements [12].

In this paper we propose a technique based on the algebra of probabilistic programs to reduce "iteration-free" programs to semantically equivalent form which allows probabilistic behaviour — on which refinement is ultimately judged — to be compared directly between programs. The actual comparison is formulated as the satisfaction of linear constraints, which is then exported to a linear arithmetic solver.

Whilst restricted to iteration-free programs, the technique is general enough to treat finite instances of arbitrary such programs, and appeal to invariant-style rules will typically promote an iteration-free refinement to one which even includes iteration [17,19]. However even proofs of refinements between small, but intricate programs, are often tricky to get right, and our aim is to support that part of the verification task.

A particular benefit of this approach is the possibility of generating counterexamples in the event that a putative refinement does not hold, and this is not something which other tools for probabilistic systems can currently supply. Moreover in certain cases where the system is "data independent" [15] even the ban on arbitrary variable types can sometimes be lifted.

Our specific contributions are:

1. The theoretical formulation of refinement as a linear satisfiability problem (Sec. 4 and Sec. 5);
2. An implementation of a refinement checker between two probabilistic programs, which are restricted to being iteration-free and having variables of finite type (Sec. 6);
3. A small case study based on Schneider et al. 's Tank Monitoring system [26] (Sec. 7);
4. A data-independent style theorem for generalising the automated refinement checking to a class of probabilistic programs for Tank Monitoring (Sec. 7.1).

We begin in Sec. 2 with a review of probabilistic program semantics, and end with a brief summary of other work on related topics and describe some areas for future research.

Notation. Function application is represented by a dot, as in $f.x$. We use an abstract state space S. (In our programming language a state is defined by a mapping from program variables to values.) We denote the set of discrete probability distributions over S by $\overline{S}$ (that is the sub-normalised functions from S into the real interval $[0,1]$, where function f is sub-normalised if $\sum_{s:\,S} f.s \leq 1$). We use δ_s for the point distribution such that $\delta_s.s' = 1$ if and only if $s' = s$, and otherwise is 0.

We often use functions or relations between reals "lifted" pointwise to real-valued functions. Examples include $\leq$ (no more than) and $\sqcap$ (minimum).

2 Probabilistic Program Semantics

When programs incorporate probability, their properties can no longer be guaranteed "with certainty", but only "up to some probability". For example the program

$$flip \;\; \hat{=} \;\; x := 0 \;\;_{2/3}\oplus\; x := 1 \;, \tag{1}$$

sets the real-valued variable x to 0 only with probability 2/3, and to 1 with probability 1/3. In practice this means that if the statement were executed a large number of times, and the final values of x tabulated, roughly 2/3 of them would record x having been set to 0 (up to well-known statistical confidence [8]).

The language pGCL [18] was developed to express such programs and to derive their probabilistic properties by extending the classical assertional style of programming to include a probabilistic choice operator [23]. Programs in pGCL are modelled (operationally) as functions (or transitions) which map *initial states* in S to (sets of) probability distributions over *final states* — the program at (1) for instance has a single transition which maps any initial state to a (single) final distribution; we represent that distribution as a function d, evaluating to 2/3 when $x = 0$ and to 1/3 when $x = 1$.

Central to verification is the notion of abstraction, by which programs' detailed behaviour may be specified by abstracting from much of the intermediate computation steps required to achieve some intended goal. As for standard programming we use *nondeterminism* to enable the specification of several possible "result distributions". For example the program

$$flip' \;\; \hat{=} \;\; x := 0 \;\;_{1/2}\oplus\; x := 1 \;\;\;\sqcap\;\;\; x := 0 \tag{2}$$

specifies two result distributions, which we have put together with nondeterministic choice. Thus at the extremes, *flip'* may behave either as a fair coin, or a completely biased coin, always setting x to 0. But *flip'* specifies much more: the intention of nondeterminism is to abstract from all resolution strategies, amongst them being both Boolean- and probabilistic choices. For example one of the outcomes specified by (2) is an implementation in which the choice is resolved by a probability e.g. $_{2/3}\oplus$. Thus we say

$$flip' \;\; \sqsubseteq \;\; (x := 0 \;\;_{1/2}\oplus\; x := 1)\;_{2/3}\oplus\;(x := 0) \;\; = \;\; flip \;, \tag{3}$$

where the refinement follows by replacing the $\sqcap$ in (2) with $_{2/3}\oplus$, and the right-hand side equality holds by the standard rules of probability theory [8] (i.e. in the middle expression at (3), the "event x is set to 0" happens with probability $2/3 \times 1/2 + 1/3 = 2/3$, which is expressed more succinctly by *flip*).

More generally we define the semantics of probabilistic programs as sets of result distributions, where following Morgan et al.[18] we restrict the result sets of the semantic functions according to an underlying order on the state space. That order has been set out in detail elsewhere [1], and we review it briefly in Sec. 4 to follow. An innovation, however, is to distinguish specially "miraculous" or infeasible behaviour from ordinary behaviour — miracles are used in program semantics to simplify calculations [23,22], or to model "guarded commands" [16]. In the semantics, miracles will be associated with a special introduced state $\top$, and our program model is defined over the *probabilistic power domain* [14] based on the underlying (flat) domain $(S^\top, \sqsubseteq)$, where $S^\top$ is S conjoined with the special state $\top$, and the order $\sqsubseteq$ is constructed so that $\top$ dominates all (proper) states in S, which are otherwise unrelated.

Definition 1. *The space of probabilistic programs[1] is given by $(\mathcal{L}S, \sqsubseteq)$ where $\mathcal{L}S$ is the set of functions from $S^\top$ to the power set of $\overline{S^\top}$, restricted to subsets which are* convex *closed with respect to $\sqsubseteq$. (All programs are $\top$-preserving mapping $\top$ to $\{\delta_\top\}$, and indeed $\delta_\top$ is always an outcome.) The order between programs is defined*

$$P \sqsubseteq P' \quad \text{iff} \quad (\forall s \colon S \cdot P.s \supseteq P'.s) .$$

(A set C is Convex *closed if whenever $d, d' \in C$, then so is $\lambda \times d + (1-\lambda) \times d'$ for any $0 \le \lambda \le 1$.[2])*

In Fig.1 we set out the semantics for pGCL, a variation of Dijkstra's GCL with several extensions and modifications. They are miracles, probability, and parallel [16], with the last restricted to programs operating over distinct state spaces and, in-line with standard MDP-style semantics [24], and can be understood as first resolving all the nondeterminism in either operand, followed by any probabilistic choice. All the other programming features have been defined previously elsewhere, and (apart from probabilistic choice) have interpretations which are merely adapted to the real-valued context. For example nondeterminism, as explained above, is interpreted *demonically* and can be thought of as being resolved by a "demon", providing guarantees on all program behaviour, such as is expected for total correctness. *Probabilistic choice*, on the other hand, selects the operands at random with weightings determined by the probability parameter p.

We also use the following short-hand expressions. Given a (finite) family $\mathcal{I}$ of commands we write $\sqcap_{i:\mathcal{I}} C_i$ for the generalised (nondeterministic) choice

---

[1] This particular "Lamington" model was first suggested by Carroll Morgan [21].

[2] Strictly speaking, we should also include "up-closure" and "Cauchy-closure" in our definition [18], but they are naturally implied by convex closure in the iteration-free context which allows miracles.

identity	skip.s	$\hat{=}$	$\lceil \{\delta_s\} \rceil$,
top	magic .s	$\hat{=}$	$\{\delta_\top\}$,
composition	$(P; P').s$	$\hat{=}$	$\{\sum_{u:\,S^\top}(d.u) \times d'_u \mid d \in P.s; d'_u \in P'.u\}$,
choice	$(if\ B\ then\ P\ else\ P').s$	$\hat{=}$	$if\ B.s,\ then\ P.s,\ otherwise\ P'.s$
probability	$(P\ {}_p\oplus P').s$	$\hat{=}$	$\lceil \{d\ {}_p\oplus d' \mid d \in P.s; d' \in P'.s\} \rceil$,
nondeterminism	$(P\ \sqcap\ P').s$	$\hat{=}$	$\lceil \{d \mid d \in (P.s \cup P'.s)\} \rceil$,
parallel	$(P \mid P').s$	$\hat{=}$	$\lceil \{d \otimes d' \mid d \in P.s \wedge d' \in P'.s)\} \rceil$, ‡
iteration	lt P tl	$\hat{=}$	$(\nu X \cdot P; X \sqcap 1)$.

In the above definitions s is a state in S and $\lceil K \rceil$ is the smallest up-, convex- and Cauchy-closed subset of distributions containing K. (Note up- and Cauchy-closed are normally implied by convex closure.) Given distributions d and d' over disjoint state spaces, their composition $d \otimes d'$ is defined as the normal product distribution between independent random events [8]. Programs are denoted by P and P', and the expression $(\nu X \cdot f.X)$ denotes the greatest fixed point of the function f — in the case of iteration the function is the $\sqsubseteq$-monotone program-to-program function $\lambda X \cdot (P; X \sqcap 1)$. All programs map $\top$ to $\{\delta_\top\}$. The parallel operator at ‡ is only defined between programs which act over disjoint state spaces.

Fig. 1. Semantics of probabilistic programs [18]

over the family, and $\bigoplus_{i \in \mathcal{I}} C_i @ p_i$ for the generalised probabilistic choice (where $\sum_{i \in \mathcal{I}} p_i = 1$). In cases where we need to be more explicit, we also use a list

$$[C_0\ @p_0, C_1\ @p_1, \ldots, C_k\ @p_k] , \qquad (4)$$

for the generalised probabilistic choice, where each C_i is executed with probability p_i. For assignments to variables v, we use $v :\in Pred$ for the generalised nondeterministic choice over any value from its type that satisfies the predicate *Pred*.

In this paper we are interested in the refinement-oriented style of verification, and in the next section we illustrate it for probabilistic programs by a small example.

3   Probabilistic Verification as a Refinement Problem

In this section we consider as an illustration the following problem, originally attributed to Dijkstra [3]. Given a biased coin

$$coin(x) \quad \hat{=} \quad x := 0\ {}_{1/3}\oplus x := 1 , \qquad (5)$$

in which the variable x is set to 0 with probability $1/3$ and to 1 with probability $2/3$, devise a strategy of such coin flips which effectively generates a fair coin.

The underlying idea of the solution is based on the following observation: if two such biased coins are flipped independently $coin(x); coin(y)$, then the chance that $x = 0 \wedge y = 1$ is *the same* as the chance that $x = 1 \wedge y = 0$. Intuition now implies that if we flip coins independently in pairs until $x \neq y$, then overall we should observe a fair distribution of the events $x = 0 \wedge y = 1$ and $x = 1 \wedge y = 0$. If our intuition is correct then the iteration *pairs* given at Fig.2 should be a refinement of the simple assignment *fair*, also at Fig.2:

$$fair \quad \sqsubseteq \quad pairs \ . \tag{6}$$

Observe that the specification program *fair* makes a fair probabilistic choice between two simultaneous assignments to x and y which distinguish the two possible cases satisfying $x \neq y$. The program *pairs*, on the other hand uses the iteration construct to define a loop, which makes pairs of independent coin flips by calling (5) independently twice. Whilst the general iteration construct in Fig.1 allows an arbitrary number of steps, the following coercion, defined

$$[x \neq y] \quad \hat{=} \quad \text{if } (x \neq y) \text{ then skip else magic} \ ,$$

forces the iteration to continue only until the desired condition has been established. Overall, if the refinement at (6) is valid then the only possible final results of the iteration *pairs* is to set the variables x and y in the pattern prescribed by *fair*.

$$pairs \ \hat{=} \ (\text{lt} \ \text{if } (x = y) \text{ then } coin(x); coin(y) \text{ else skip } \ \text{tl}); [x \neq y]$$

$$fair \ \hat{=} \text{ if } (x = y) \text{ then } (x, y := \ 0, 1) \ _{1/2} \oplus (x, y := \ 1, 0) \text{ else skip}$$

The program *pairs* effectively implements an arbitrary finite number of paired flips, terminating when x is not equal to y.

Fig. 2. Making a biased flip fair

Whilst the specification is quite straightforward, more difficult is the actual verification. As usual with iterative designs however proof may be delegated to the satisfaction of an invariant-style argument based on the iteration body. Here the appropriate rule is given by

$$w \sqsubseteq z; w \quad \wedge \quad [G]; w = [G] \quad \Rightarrow \quad w \sqsubseteq (\text{lt } z \text{ tl}); [G] \tag{7}$$

and is proved elsewhere for probabilistic programs [17,19]. The idea of the rule is that if the overall required behaviour specified by w and stopping condition G is an invariant of the iteration body z (the left-hand side of (7)) then it must be the case that the result of the iteration is indeed specified by w (the right-hand side of (7)).

For our example, this means that verification of (6) follows provided that the following refinement holds:

$$fair \quad \sqsubseteq \quad \text{if } (x = y) \text{ then } coin(x); coin(y) \text{ else skip } ; \ fair \ . \tag{8}$$

Whilst this refinement may be proved very easily "by hand" using effectively elementary probability theory we are interested in providing automated support more generally, for cases in which there are many such refinements to be proved [25,17], or where many small proof rules are required to demonstrate it. In these situations support either in the form of a proof, or concrete evidence that the refinement does not hold is very valuable in the verification task.

In the next section we show how to turn the problem of demonstrating refinements like (8) into a linear-programming problem, which can be exported to an automated "solver".

4   Refinement as a Linear Satisfiability Problem

To see the relevance of linear satisfiability to the refinement problem, we must first consider how distributions over a finite (discrete) state space (of size N) can be considered as points in an N-dimensional Euclidean space, and that the definition of the semantics of refinement given at Def. 1 corresponds to whether one convex polyhedron is contained in another. We begin by illustrating the ideas with a specific state space of size 3, and then go on to set out the general mathematical framework.

Let d be a result-distribution of a program operating over a state space of size 3, so that $S \mathrel{\hat{=}} \{s_0, s_1, s_2\}$.[3] Thus d can be thought of as a function $d : S \to [0, 1]$, and indeed may be represented by a 3-tuple (d_0, d_1, d_2), where $d_i \mathrel{\hat{=}} d.s_i$. In this notation, we can easily visualise d as a point in 3-dimensional Euclidean space, where the Cartesian axes are labelled s_0, s_1, s_2.

In general, of course, when nondeterminism is present the result set will consist of a number of distributions, giving a set of points. Fortunately the semantics guarantees that the set satisfies certain regularity conditions, in particular that it corresponds to a convex polyhedron.

For example if we consider the program

$$P \quad \mathrel{\hat{=}} \quad x := s_0 \; {}_{0.5}\!\oplus x :\in \{s_0, s_1, s_2\} , \qquad (9)$$

where x is either set to s_0 with probability 0.5, or (also with probability 0.5) to the nondeterministic choice over s_0, s_1, or s_2. When the result distributions are encoded as triples, and depicted graphically, the result is a triangular set of points P depicted at Fig.3. Note however that the three points $a \mathrel{\hat{=}} (1, 0, 0)$, $b \mathrel{\hat{=}} (1/2, 1/2, 0)$ and $c \mathrel{\hat{=}} (1/2, 0, 1/2)$, corresponding respectively to the the the three refinements $(x := s_0)$, $(x := s_0 \; {}_{0.5}\!\oplus x := s_1)$ and $(x := s_0 \; {}_{0.5}\!\oplus x := s_2)$, can between them generate all the other points in the set by *convex combinations*. Here a convex combination of a, b and c is an expression of the form $\lambda_0 \times a + \lambda_1 \times b + \lambda_2 \times c$, such that the $\lambda_i \geq 0$ and their sum is 1; the set generated by such a finite set of points is called the *convex hull*. Now, given any point d', we can decide whether it lies inside P or not, by considering only convex sums of a, b and c.

---

[3] For this example we do not deal with miraculous behaviour, but the general theory later does account for it.

For example the point z given by $(3/4, 1/8, 1/8)$, illustrated in Fig.3 is contained in P since

$$z = \frac{1}{2}a + \frac{1}{4}b + \frac{1}{4}c \; .$$

On the other hand point $y = (0, 1/2, 1/2)$ is not contained in P, and indeed it cannot be expressed as a convex combination of a, b and c, since any such combination must have representation (d_0, d_1, d_2) with $d_0 > 0$.[4]

> *Thus we have discovered the important fact, that any point may be determined to be inside, or outside of P by determining whether or not it can be expressed as a convex combination of the extreme points a, b and c.*

As we shall see, the problem of discovering whether or not a point can be expressed as a convex combination of a set of given points is equivalent to a linear satisfiability problem, and indeed can be exported directly to a satisfiability solver.

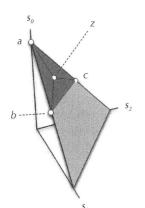

The dark triangle comprises the set P of result distributions generated by program P at (9). The large triangle is the set of (proper) distributions, i.e. the set of tuples (d_0, d_1, d_2) such that $d_0 + d_1 + d_2 = 1$.

Note that point z can be expressed as a convex combination of the extreme points a, b and c.

Fig. 3. The result of program P as a convex set

Finally we note that we can extend this idea to deciding whether one convex set A generated as the convex hull of a finite set of points $\{a_0, \ldots, a_k\}$ is contained inside another B generated by $\{b_0, \ldots, b_n\}$, by observing that $A \subseteq B$ if and only if each $a_i \in B$. This last condition can now be treated as above for each point a_i.

For example, consider program Q defined,

$$Q \; \hat{=} \; (x := s_0 \; \sqcap \; x := s_1)_{\,0.5} \oplus (x := s_0 \; \sqcap \; x := s_2) \; . \qquad (10)$$

Note that Q's result set Q is determined by four extreme points. They are a, b and c as for P, but also $d \; \hat{=} \; (0, 1/2, 1/2)$ corresponding to Q's refinement $x :=$

---

[4] A more general characteristic of non-containment of a point d in a convex set A is given later.

$s_1 \; _{0.5} \oplus x := s_2$. Thus we see immediately that $\mathsf{P} \subset \mathsf{Q}$, since a, b and c are all members of P, but as mentioned above, d does not lie in P. Thus we deduce that

$$Q \;\sqsubseteq\; P \;\not\sqsubseteq\; Q \;.$$

In general the refinement problem between two programs with result sets A and B over a finite state space is determined by whether $\mathsf{A} \subseteq \mathsf{B}$, and may be formalised as follows. Note that we use $cc.T$ to be the convex closure of a set T of points in some N-dimensional space.

Theorem 1. *Let* $\mathsf{A} \;\hat{=}\; cc.\{a_0, \ldots, a_k\}$. *The point b lies in A exactly when the following linear constraints defined by scalars λ_i are satisfiable.*

$$\lambda_i \geq 0 \;, \quad 0 \leq i \leq k \;,$$
$$\lambda_0 \times a_0 + \cdots + \lambda_k \times a_k \;\geq\; b \;,$$
$$\lambda_0 + \cdots + \lambda_k \leq 1 \;.$$

Here the order $\geq$ is the normal order on scalars lifted pointwise to tuples of reals.[5]

This result can be applied in general to check whether $cc.Q \subseteq cc.P$, for two finitely-generated sets of points P and Q. We simply apply Thm. 1 to each point in $q \in Q$.

The above satisfiability problem only partially solves the problem of proving refinements between programs, since it assumes that the semantics of a program is immediately available. That is an unlikely scenario in normal program development, where only the program text is available. In the next section we turn to the question of extracting semantics from program texts, so that Thm. 1 may be applied directly.

5   Normal Form for Non-iterating Programs

The semantics of programs set out at Def. 1 implies that operationally any program is equivalent to one in which all the nondeterminism is resolved first, followed by probabilistic choice. In this situation the result distributions, which ultimately determine the behaviour of the program, are immediately accessible. If the whole result set can be generated from a finite number of final distributions (by convex closing) then, as explained above, the problem of refinement checking may be reduced to a linear satisfiability problem.

Unfortunately the semantics of a program is not normally readily available. For example the program $prog_0$ defined,

$$prog_0 \;\;\hat{=}\;\; (y := 0 \;_{0.5} \oplus\; y := 1); ((y := y{+}1 \;\sqcap\; \mathsf{skip}) \;_{0.4} \oplus\; y := 2) \;, \qquad (11)$$

does not have distributions which can be simply "read off" immediately, since the initial probabilistic assignment must be modified by the subsequent demonic

---

[5] See http://www.comp.mq.edu.au/~anabel/ICFEM07.pdf for a detailed proof.

and probabilistic choices before the final result distributions may be computed. In contrast the result distributions are readily available in the program $prog_1$, defined

$$prog_1 \quad \hat{=} \quad \begin{aligned} &(y := 1 \,_{0.1}\oplus\, y := 2) \,\sqcap\, (y := 1 \,_{0.4}\oplus\, y := 2) \,\sqcap\, \\ &(y := 0 \,_{0.1}\oplus\, y := 2) \,\sqcap\, ((y := 0 \,_{0.5}\oplus\, y := 1) \,_{0.4}\oplus\, y := 2)\,, \end{aligned}$$
(12)

because the nondeterminism simply chooses between four possible probabilistic assignments, and these form the extreme points of the convex hull. Programs complying with that general syntactic shape — namely a nondeterministic choice selecting between probabilistic assignments — are said to be in "normal form", whose definition appears below at Def. 3. Since the definition is language specific however, we first fix our language to one which excludes iteration.

Definition 2. *We say that a program P constructed from the operators at Fig.1 is* iteration-free *if it contains no (syntactic) iterations. Thus it only contains nondeterminism, assignments, Boolean and probabilistic choices, and sequential composition (as well as possibly miraculous statements).*

Whilst iteration-free programs are not general enough to express most programs of interest, refinement between programs with iteration often follows from refinements between loop bodies, as illustrated in Sec. 3.

Now returning to iteration-free programs, we can now define their normal form: a program is said to be in *normal form* if it is the nondeterministic choice over probabilistic assignment statements.

Recall that we use generalised choice $\sqcap_{i\in\mathcal{I}}P_i$ for the nondeterministic choice over a finite index set $\mathcal{I}$, and occasionally $\bigoplus_{i\in\mathcal{I}}P_i@p_i$ for the generalised probabilistic choice with weights p_i (sometimes using the more convenient list form introduced above). Finally, for convenience, we allow the p_i to be real-valued functions from the state into $[0,1]$. We note that this can be used to encode Boolean choice, since (if B then P else Q) can be written as $P\,_{\overline{B}}\oplus\,Q$, where $\overline{B}$ is the characteristic function which returns 1 on states that satisfy B and 0 otherwise. To see that this is a valid encoding, compare an execution of $P\,_{\overline{B}}\oplus\,Q$ with (if B then P else Q) from an initial state s_0 which satisfies B. In both cases, P will be executed (with probability 1), since in the first case $\overline{B}.s_0 = 1$ (so that P is selected with probability 1), whereas in the latter case $B.s_0 = true$ determines also that P is executed.

Definition 3. *A program is said to be in* normal form *if it is of the form*

$$\sqcap_{i\in\mathcal{I}}P_i\,,$$

where $\mathcal{I}$ is a finite index set, and each P_i is a probability distribution (possibly depending on the state) over (deterministic) assignments to variables.

It turns out that all iteration-free programs have an equivalent formulation in normal form, and moreover that there is a decision procedure for converting programs to their normal forms, based on a set of algebraic rules. In Fig.4 we

(i) $(P_p \oplus Q)_q \oplus R = [P @p \times q, Q @(1-p) \times q, R @(1-p) \times (1-q)]$ ⎫
(ii) $(P \sqcap Q)_p \oplus R = (P_p \oplus R) \sqcap (Q_p \oplus R)$ ⎬ *Probability moves inwards*

(iii) $(P \sqcap Q); R = P; R \sqcap Q; R$ ⎫ *Operators distribute from the right*
(iv) $(P_p \oplus Q); R = P; R_p \oplus Q; R$ ⎬

(v) $(y := x); (P_p \oplus Q) = (y := x); P_{p'} \oplus (y := x); Q$ ⎫ *Assignments move from left*
(vi) $(y := x); (P \sqcap Q) = (y := x); P \sqcap (y := x); Q$ ⎬

Here y is defined by the program variables, and x can be some (deterministic) function of the state (i.e. program variables).

Note in rule (v), if the probability p is dependent on the state then p' is the result of "applying the assignment"; how that is done is set out elsewhere [18].

Finally, we have only given the rules for the binary form of the various choices — similar rules hold for generalised choices with respect to finite index sets.

Fig. 4. Rules for rewriting a program to equivalent normal form

set out what they are, and in the next lemma we show that they are sufficient to reduce all iteration-free programs to (semantically equivalent) normal form.

Lemma 1. *Let P be an iteration-free program. The algebraic rules set out at Fig.4 are sufficient to convert P into equivalent normal form.*[6]

We can see Lem. 1 in action by rewriting $prog_0$ above at (11) to $prog_1$ at (12). We reason as follows.

$$(y := 0 \,_{0.5}\oplus y := 1); ((y := y+1 \sqcap \mathsf{skip})\,_{0.4}\oplus y := 2)$$

$=$ $(y := 0; ((y := y+1 \sqcap \mathsf{skip})\,_{0.4}\oplus y := 2)$ Fig.4 (iv)
         $_{0.5}\oplus$
         $y := 1; ((y := y+1 \sqcap \mathsf{skip})\,_{0.4}\oplus y := 2))$

$=$ $((y := 0; y := y+1) \sqcap y := 0))\,_{0.4}\oplus y := 0; y := 2$ Fig.4 (v) and (vi)
         $_{0.5}\oplus$
         $((y := 1; y := y+1 \sqcap y := 1)\,_{0.4}\oplus y := 1; y := 2))$

$=$ $(y := 1 \sqcap y := 0))\,_{0.4}\oplus y := 2$ simplify assignments
         $_{0.5}\oplus$
         $((y := 2 \sqcap y := 1)\,_{0.4}\oplus y := 2))$

$=$ $[(y := 1 \sqcap y := 0) @0.2,\ y := 2 @0.6,\ (y := 2 \sqcap y := 1) @0.2]$.   Fig.4 (i)

From here we now apply rule Fig.4 (ii) twice, one for each nondeterministic choice, to obtain the nondeterministic choice over four probabilistic assignments:

$[y := 1 @0.2, y := 2 @0.8] \sqcap [y := 1 @0.4, y := 2 @0.6,] \sqcap$
$[y := 0 @0.2, y := 2 @0.8] \sqcap [y := 0 @0.2, y := 1 @0.2, \sqcap y := 2 @0.6]$,

---

[6] See http://www.comp.mq.edu.au/~anabel/ICFEM07.pdf for a detailed proof.

finally revealing $prog_1$, by converting each list to equivalent expressions using the binary probabilistic choice operator.

The normal-form reduction illustrated here involves many re-writing rules; in the next section we describe how that procedure may be automated, together with how the resulting normal form may be used to implement a refinement-checking program based on the Yices SMT solver [4].

6   Automating Refinement Checking

In this section we discuss the design and implementation of our software tool for automatic refinement checking of probabilistic programs. While this tool is working well for that core purpose, the reader should keep in mind that it is currently being improved and extended considerably. The source and various scripts which make up the tool are available elsewhere [6].

The tool consists of three core modules. The first part is the *normal-form analyser* and takes as input an iteration-free program text, and reduces it to equivalent normal form, implementing a rewriting system based on the algebraic rules set out at Fig.4.

The second part is the *distribution generator* and takes a normal-form and extracts its finite number of result distributions, which captures the precise semantic probabilistic and nondeterministic behaviour of the program.

The final part is the *refinement checker* which is implemented using the Yices SMT-solver [4]. The input for this part consists of two sets of distributions computed separately using the normal-form analyser and the distribution generator for two programs P and Q. The results are then used to generate satisfiability constraints defined by Thm. 1 in the Yices input syntax that can be passed to the Yices solver. The result of this part is either a report that the P is indeed refined by Q, or that it is not, together with a distribution in Q's result set that does not lie in P's result set.

In Fig.5 we give a graphical overview of how these three parts fit together, with some supplementary details and examples in the following sections.

6.1   Implementation Details

The lexical analysis and parsing of pGCL programs expressed as strings is implemented using the Moscow ML[7] versions of Lex/Yacc that come with the distribution. As usual with the application of such standard compiler tools, this makes for efficient and sound implementation of those two steps. The final product is a representation of the pGCL program as an algebraic data type. We have completely avoided the use of what few imperative features are available in the Moscow ML language, which in our opinion enhances the development and maintainability of the code base for our tool.

---

[7] We chose Moscow ML because it is the implementation environment for HOL and we intend in the future to link our tool with the existing formalisations of pGCL done in HOL [13].

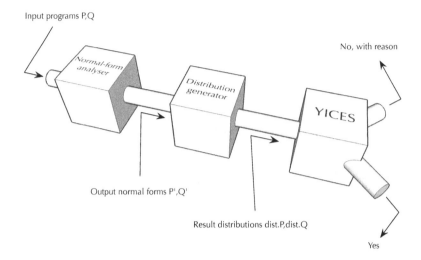

Input programs P,Q

Normal-form analyser

Distribution generator

No, with reason

YICES

Output normal forms P',Q'

Result distributions dist.P,dist.Q

Yes

Fig. 5. Modular design of the refinement checking tool to test $P \sqsubseteq Q$

The conversion of a pGCL program so represented to its normal form is carried out by a set of functions carefully designed to reflect the rewrite rules discussed in Sec. 5. When it is presented with a pGCL program, the analyser would first normalize the subprograms under its main construction, and then based on what this construction is, apply rewrite rules to push any operators that break normal form to their proper places. The correctness of such rewrites depends fundamentally on the assumption that the subprograms are already normalized, as is the case in our code. The result is again an internal representation of a pGCL program in algebraic data type form.

The production of pGCL normal forms following these rewrite rules is usually efficient enough to present the user with a result in a few seconds at most. However, the nature of the rules is such that a lot of subexpression duplication would be performed on even relatively uncomplicated programs, and so in some cases the answer may take many minutes to be produced. This happens in cases where a probabilistic choice with many branches is composed with a Boolean or a demonic choice. In the particular case of the composition with a Boolean choice, the subexpressions actually become all distinct, so this seems an unavoidable issue with the rules as implemented at the moment. An improvement on either the shape of the rules or their implementation (which at the moment reflects them in a very straightforward way) is a goal of our future work.

The probability distribution analysis takes as input one pGCL program in normal form in internal representation, and proceeds to follow its structure while applying the semantic meaning of pGCL constructions as discussed in Sec. 5. The result will be a list of distributions, each represented in turn as a list of state-probability pairs. Each state is a typical environment, that is, a list of variable-value pairs. At some intermediate points during the computation, Moscow ML library types for maps and sets are used to help make the generation of the distributions be more concise and readable.

Finally, given such a list of distributions, we implemented a procedure to generate a set of concrete linear constraints in the Yices syntax as set out in Thm. 1. Since each of the distributions is represented as an $|S|$-tuple, each constraint on the tuples must be expressed equivalently as $|S|$-individual linear constraints. The Yices solver then takes each of the satisfiability problems and reports either that it is not solvable, or that it is and in that case produces an example which sets out the exact convex combination of specification distributions needed to express the corresponding implementation distribution.

Thus overall, if Yices reports satisfiability of all these linear problems, then we know that refinement holds, and if at least one of these problems is unsatisfiable, then refinement fails to hold.

6.2   Some Examples

We illustrate now the production of normal forms and probability distributions of our tool with a few examples. The programs to be used as such are quite simple but still illustrate important aspects of the tool use, and have been mentioned already in preceding sections. The syntax is pretty close to the mathematical notation used before, but altered according to restrictions on possible textual inputs of the implementation compiler. Demonic choice is ^, and multi-branch probabilistic choice is of the shape @{n1: p1, ..., nm: pm} where the n are the numerical probabilities and the p the subprograms of each branch.

Example 1: $prog_0$ defined at (11)

```
@{0.5: y:=0, 0.5: y:=1}; @{0.4: y:=y+1 ^ y:=y, 0.6: y:=2}
```

For this program we obtain as its normal form:

```
@{0.2: y:=0; y:=y+1, 0.3: y:=0; y:=2, 0.2: y:=1; y:=y+1, 0.3: y:=1; y:=2} ^
@{0.2: y:=0; y:=y+1, 0.3: y:=0; y:=2, 0.2: y:=1; y:=y, 0.3: y:=1; y:=2} ^
@{0.2: y:=0; y:=y, 0.3: y:=0; y:=2, 0.2: y:=1; y:=y+1, 0.3: y:=1; y:=2} ^
@{0.2: y:=0; y:=y, 0.3: y:=0; y:=2, 0.2: y:=1; y:=y, 0.3: y:=1; y:=2}
```

And as the probability distributions of final states:

```
[[([("y", 0)], 0.0), ([("y", 1)], 0.2), ([("y", 2)], 0.8)],
 [([("y", 0)], 0.0), ([("y", 1)], 0.4), ([("y", 2)], 0.6)],
 [([("y", 0)], 0.2), ([("y", 1)], 0.0), ([("y", 2)], 0.8)],
 [([("y", 0)], 0.2), ([("y", 1)], 0.2), ([("y", 2)], 0.6)]]
```

Each line of the above is a separate distribution, in which each program state (represented as an environment, that is a list of pairs identifier/value) is associated with its probability of being the final state of the program.

Example 2: $prog_1$ defined at (12)

```
@{0.2: y:=1, 0.8: y:=2} ^ @{0.2: y:=0, 0.8: y:=2} ^ @{0.4: y:=1, 0.6: y:=2} ^
@{0.2: y:=0, 0.2: y:=1, 0.6: y:=2}
```

$Tank(N):$ $flow :\in \{0, 1, \ldots, N\}$

$Sensor(x):$ $x := flow _{0.9} \oplus x :\in \{0, 1, \ldots N\}$

$3Monitor:$ if$(a = b \lor a = c)$ then $rflow := a$ else $rflow := b$

$3System(N):$ $Tank(N);$
              $Sensor(a) \mid Sensor(b) \mid Sensor(c);$
              $3Monitor$

$Spec(N, p):$ $Tank(N);$
              $rflow := flow _p \oplus rflow :\in \{0, 1, \ldots N\}$

Fig. 6. The Tank Monitoring System [26]

The normal form is:
```
@{0.2: y:=1, 0.8: y:=2} ^ @{0.2: y:=0, 0.8: y:=2} ^ @{0.4: y:=1, 0.6: y:=2} ^
@{0.2: y:=0, 0.2: y:=1, 0.6: y:=2}
```

The probability distributions of final states are four, one for each following line:

```
[[([("y", 0)], 0.0), ([("y", 1)], 0.2), ([("y", 2)], 0.8)],
 [([("y", 0)], 0.2), ([("y", 1)], 0.0), ([("y", 2)], 0.8)],
 [([("y", 0)], 0.0), ([("y", 1)], 0.4), ([("y", 2)], 0.6)],
 [([("y", 0)], 0.2), ([("y", 1)], 0.2), ([("y", 2)], 0.6)]]
```

Observe here that, as expected, the set of result distributions are the same for $prog_0$ and $prog_1$.

7   Case Study: Tank Monitoring

In this section we illustrate the technique with a small case study based on Schneider et al.'s "tank monitoring".

The scenario is a tank filled by a pump which causes the rate of flow to vary between a low and a high thresholds. The flow of water is monitored by a number of sensors, which have a small chance of error. The results of the sensors are gathered by a central monitoring system which then combines them to make an estimate of the actual flow. In our case study we wish to explore the extent of the fault tolerance in the tank monitoring system, and in particular how the design of the monitoring system is able overall to reduce the margin of error below that of individual sensor reports.

In Fig.6 we set out the main components in the system. The *Tank* is modelled simply by a variable *flow* which is chosen nondeterministically from a range of values. Each *Sensor* is modelled by a variable which is either set to the current value of *flow*, or nondeterministically to any value between the low and the high threshold, with the chance of error set at 10%.

We study first the case of using three sensors — *3Monitor* is also set out at Fig.6 — it describes a system which bases its estimate *rflow* on the majority of the three reports. Notice how the *3Monitor* cannot refer directly to *flow* itself, but only the reports of the three sensors.[8] The specification $Spec(N, p)$ is that the *3System*(N) containing *3Monitor* will set the estimated value *rflow* to the true value *flow* with probability p, to be specified.

Case 1: **Finding counterexamples.** A counterexample to a refinement problem $P \sqsubseteq Q$ is any behaviour of Q which lies outside those specified by P. In this context it is any result distribution in Q which cannot be expressed as a linear combination of distributions in P.

In this first example we (as it turns out, optimistically) specify a required success probability of $p = 0.98$, thus we want to check the refinement

$$Spec(N, p) \quad \sqsubseteq \quad 3System(N) , \tag{13}$$

for all values of N. Our implemented refinement checker however must have all parameters defined initially, thus we try a small example with $N \mathrel{\hat{=}} 1$. For this small instance the checker reports a counterexample in the form of a distribution:

$$[rflow = 0 \wedge flow = 0 \ @0.972, \quad rflow = 1 \wedge flow = 0 \ @0.028] ,$$

which corresponds to a 0.972 chance that at least two out of the three sensors in *3System*(N) correctly report the flow.

Thus our specification was indeed too strong: if we weaken it to allow a more generous probability of failure, the checker verifies the refinement

$$Spec(1, 0.972) \sqsubseteq 3System .$$

Case 2: **Proving refinements.** Whilst the counterexample provides useful diagnostic information, better would be a general proof that (13) for some value of p, and for all values of N. Fortunately for some classes of system, including this one, the above check that $Spec(1, 0.972) \sqsubseteq 3System(1)$ implies the more general refinement for all values of N. That is because *3System*(N) is "data independent", and thus the general case follows from exhaustive analysis of some finite instance; we explain how in the next section.

7.1 A Data-Independence Lemma

A system is said to be *data independent* (with respect to a datatype X) "if and only if it cannot perform any operations involving values of type X, but it can only input such values, store them, output them, and perform equality tests between them" [15]. An informal inspection of *3System*(N) indicates that it does not do anything with the input values, except for assigning them to variables and making comparisons. Next we show how that intuition can be formalised to promote the finite check to a general proof of (13).

---

[8] In the original description, the median value is selected — but this reduces to the "majority value within some pre-set tolerance".

Lemma 2. *Let p be any real lying in the interval $[0,1]$. The following implication holds.*

$$Spec(1,p) \sqsubseteq 3System(1) \quad \Rightarrow \quad (\forall N : \mathbb{N} \cdot Spec(N,p) \sqsubseteq 3System(N)) \ .$$

Proof. Define programs

$$T_k \quad \hat{=} \quad flow :\in \{k, k+1\}$$

$$S_k(x) \quad \hat{=} \quad x := flow_{0.9} \oplus x :\in \{k, k+1\}$$

$$3System_k \quad \hat{=} \quad T_k \ ; \ (S_k(a)|S_k(b)|S_k(c)) \ ; \ 3Monitor \ .$$

Next we note some simple properties of our definitions.

- $Tank(N) = \sqcap_{0 \le k < N} T_k$ *(by distributivity of $\sqcap$);*
- $Sensor(x) = \sqcap_{0 \le k < N} S_k(x)$ *(by distributivity of $\sqcap$);*
- $3System(N) = \sqcap_{0 \le k < N} 3System_k$ *(above two properties);*
- $3System(1) = 3System_0$.

Next we note that $Spec(N,p) \sqsubseteq Spec(1,p)$, so that the hypothesis implies that $Spec(N,p) \sqsubseteq 3System(1)$; moreover by change of variable we must also have that $Spec(N,p) \sqsubseteq 3System(k)$. The result now follows.

Case 3: **Exploring numerical relationships between system parameters.**
    Our final example shows how the results of the distribution generator can be used to explore the effect of varying the parameters which define the system.

    In our case study so far, inspection of the distributions computed by the normal-form analyser suggests that the success rate of 0.972 is the greatest lower bound for the success probability of the monitor with 3 sensors. Our final experiment establishes a numerical relationship between the number of sensors and the probability that the monitor reports the correct value for the flow.

    Consider now the system which has $k+1$ sensors (where k is an odd number greater than 2). Define

$$kSystem(1) \ \hat{=} \quad Tank(1); Sensor(a_0)|\dots|Sensor(a_k); rflow := \mathsf{maj}(a_0 \dots a_N) \ .$$

where the reported value given by $\mathsf{maj}(a_0 \dots a_N)$ is just the majority of the values reported by the sensor. The table below gives the probability that the monitor reports the correct value of the flow for different numbers of sensors. The probabilities were computed from the distributions generated by the normal form analyser and distribution generator.

Number	3	5	7	9	11	13
Success prob	0.972	0.9914	0.9972	0.9991	0.9997	0.9999

    This experiment shows that having more than about five sensors does not appreciably improve the chance of success — thus the overall benefits of more sensors can be compared to the cost of installation.

8   Further Work and Conclusions

In this paper we have shown how the theoretical analysis of refinement can be used to reduce the problem of refinement checking to a linear satisfiability problem. We have also shown how an algebraic rewriting system may be used to extract the satisfiability formulation directly from the program text. We have demonstrated the technique with an implementation, ultimately exporting the problem to the Yices solver.

One of the main benefits of this system is the possibility to generate counterexamples in the case that a putative refinement does not hold. Production of counterexamples is not normally available in other tools for probabilistic verification.

One drawback of the currently-implemented system, is that for some combinations of probability and Boolean choices, the application of the rewriting rules is very inefficient; choosing a more efficient order of rule application would significantly improve that situation, and that is currently being investigated.

This work has suggested a number of topics for future research.

1. The current implementation in Yices produces a distribution as the counterexample, but this is not very helpful to the developer as it does not provide any hint as to how the problem arose. Reformulating the counterexample in a way that could indicate the place in the program which is at fault would be more useful.
2. Our Case 3 in the Tank Monitoring example could certainly be performed more efficiently using the model checker PRISM, for example, and an alternative approach would be to use the output from the normal-form analyser to obtain an efficient translation of the original code into PRISM for performance-style analysis. This would provide a nice way to combine refinement-style systems with probabilistic model checking.

There are other automated tools for investigating refinement, but they are only valid for a restricted class of refinements [12,2]. Meanwhile other tools for optimising action-system-style designs have also been implemented [9], but these systems do not check for general refinements.

Other systems which use an abstract specification, principally for analysis, include probabilistic abstract interpretation [20].

References

1. McIver, A., Weber, T.: Towards automated proof support for probabilistic distributed systems. In: Sutcliffe, G., Voronkov, A. (eds.) LPAR 2005. LNCS (LNAI), vol. 3835, Springer, Heidelberg (2005)
2. Celiku, O., McIver, A.: Compositional specification and analysis of cost-based properties in probabilistic programs. In: Fitzgerald, J.A., Hayes, I.J., Tarlecki, A. (eds.) FM 2005. LNCS, vol. 3582, pp. 107–122. Springer, Heidelberg (2005)
3. Dijkstra, E.: Making a fair roulette from a possibly biased coin. Information Processing Letters 36, 193 (1990)

4. Dutertre, B., de Moura, L.: A fast linear-arithmetic solver for DPLL(T)*. In: Ball, T., Jones, R.B. (eds.) CAV 2006. LNCS, vol. 4144, pp. 81–94. Springer, Heidelberg (2006)
5. Filar, J., Vrieze, O.J.: Competitive Markov Decision Processes: Theory, Algorithms, and Applications. Springer, Heidelberg (1996)
6. Gonzalia, C.: Source and scripts for the normal form analyser and distribution generator www.ics.mq.edu.au/~carlos
7. Gries, D., Prins, J.: A new notion of encapsulation. In: Symposium on Language Issues in Programming Environments, ACM Press, New York (1983)
8. Grimmett, G.R., Welsh, D.: Probability: an Introduction. Oxford Science Publications (1986)
9. Hallerstede, S., Butler, M.: Performance analysis of probabilistic action systems. Formal Aspects of Computing 16(4), 313–331 (2004)
10. He, J., Seidel, K., McIver, A.K.: Probabilistic models for the guarded command language. Science of Computer Programming 28, 171–192 (1997)
11. Hoang, T.S., Morgan, C.C., McIver, A., Robinson, K.A., Jin, Z.D: Refinement in probabilistic B: Foundation and case study. In: Treharne, H., King, S., Henson, M.C., Schneider, S. (eds.) ZB 2005. LNCS, vol. 3455, pp. 252–273. Springer, Heidelberg (2005)
12. Hoang, T.S.: The Development of a Probabilistic B-Method and a Supporting Toolkit. PhD thesis, School of Computer Science and Engineering (2005)
13. Hurd, J., McIver, A.K., Morgan, C.C.: Probabilistic guarded commands mechanised in HOL. In: Theoretical Computer Science, pp. 96–112 (2005)
14. Jones, C., Plotkin, G.: A probabilistic powerdomain of evaluations. In: Proceedings of the IEEE 4th Annual Symposium on Logic in Computer Science, pp. 186–195. IEEE Computer Society Press, Los Alamitos (1989)
15. Lazic, R.: A Semantic Study of Data Independence with Applications to Model Checking. PhD thesis, Programming Research Group (1999)
16. McIver, A.: Quantitative refinement and model checking for the analysis of probabilistic systems. In: Misra, J., Nipkow, T., Sekerinski, E. (eds.) FM 2006. LNCS, vol. 4085, pp. 131–146. Springer, Heidelberg (2006)
17. McIver, A., Cohen, E., Morgan, C.: Using probabilistic kleene algebra for protocol verification. In: Schmidt, R.A. (ed.) RelMiCS/AKA 2006. LNCS, vol. 4136, Springer, Heidelberg (2006)
18. McIver, A., Morgan, C.: Abstraction, Refinement and Proof for Probabilistic Systems. In: Technical Monographs in Computer Science, Springer, New York (2004)
19. Meinicke, L., Hayes, I.J.: Reasoning algebraically about probabilistic loops. In: Liu, Z., He, J. (eds.) ICFEM 2006. LNCS, vol. 4260, pp. 380–399. Springer, Heidelberg (2006)
20. Monniaux, D.: Abstract interpretation of probabilistic semantics. In: Palsberg, J. (ed.) SAS 2000. LNCS, vol. 1824, Springer, Heidelberg (2000)
21. Morgan, C.: Private communication. The Lamington model: a probabilistic model with miracles (1995)
22. Morgan, C.C.: The specification statement. ACM Transactions on Programming Languages and Systems 10(3), 403–419 (1988)
23. Morgan, C.C.: Programming from Specifications, 2nd edn. Prentice-Hall, Englewood Cliffs (1994)
24. PRISM. Probabilistic symbolic model checker, www.cs.bham.ac.uk/~dxp/prism

25. Rabin, M.O.: N-process mutual exclusion with bounded waiting by $4 \log 2n$-valued shared variable. Journal of Computer and System Sciences 25(1), 66–75 (1982)
26. Schneider, S., Hoang, T.S., Robinson, K.A., Treharne, H.: Tank monitoring: a case study in $pAMN$. Formal Aspects of Computing 18(3), 308–328 (2006)
27. Sere, K., Troubitsyna, E.: Probabilities in action systems. In: Proc. of the 8th Nordic Workshop on Programming Theory (1996)

Model Checking in Practice: Analysis of Generic Bootloader Using SPIN

Kuntal Das Barman[1] and Debapriyay Mukhopadhyay[2,*]

[1] Honeywell Technology Solutions Lab (HTSL),
151/1, Doraisanipalya, Bannerghatta Road, Bangalore 560 076, India
kuntal.dasbarman@honeywell.com
[2] TOR ANUMANA Technologies Pvt Ltd,
12, Lee Road, Kolkata 700020, India
debapriyay.mukhopadhyay@gmail.com

Abstract. This work presents a case study of the use of model checking for analyzing an industrial software, the Generic Bootloader. Analysis of the software have been carried out using the automated verification system SPIN. A model of the software has been developed using the specification language PROMELA, and the properties expressed in the LTL have been verified against the model. We propose a new modeling technique that helps to model communication protocols efficiently. Formal analysis has also helped us to reveal a flaw in the implementation of the software which otherwise remain undetected through testing process.

1 Introduction

Model checking ensures the correctness of a safety critical system in a rigorous manner. Formally specified models, written in the constrained language of the model checkers, are fed to the model checkers, along with the formally written formulas describing the desired properties of the specified model. Model checkers then automatically generate the state space that the model will traverse in its original run. Verifying any property of that model reduces to state space graph traversal and finding a bad state in the path. A common problem faced by explicit state model checkers is the combinatorial blow up of the state space, known as state space explosion.

Extensive study of formal verification of communication protocols using model checkers can be found in the literature [2,3,4,5]. Formal verification of communication protocols are becoming very significant as they become an important part of safety critical systems or security protocols. The Spin model checker [1] is a well proven explicit state model checker for distributed software systems.

The Spin Model checker provides a specification language Promela. It provides a way for making abstractions of distributed systems. Among the basic features, the Promela syntax has a special data type to model communication channels,

---

* Author was a member of Honeywell Technology Solution Lab, Bangalore, India, when we were carrying out this work.

M. Butler, M. Hinchey, M.M. Larrondo-Petrie (Eds.): ICFEM 2007, LNCS 4789, pp. 232–245, 2007.
© Springer-Verlag Berlin Heidelberg 2007

called chan. This data type allows to specify two different type of communications, asynchronous (point to point) and synchronous (handshake). Essentially, the difference between them is in the channel length. In case of synchronous communications channel length should be zero.

Modeling broadcast or multicast communication using only one channel has never been done. In literature, broadcast or multicast communication was modeled using shared variable. We do not find any reference where all four types of communication, viz. point to point, broadcast, multicast and handshake, were modeled using the same channel. However, in a practical scenario, all four types of communication do take place over the same channel.

In literature [2,3,4,5] we find that attempts were made to model broadcast communication. In [2] the authors modeled the broadcast communication using as many channels as the number of processes. Thus the common bus was replaced by several point to point channels, and then a broadcast packet is sent synchronously through all the channels. This specification is not close to the practical scenario and significantly increases the state space.

In fact the earliest attempt were made by Jensen et. al. In [3] they considered a similar model like [1] with a separate process for the bus. That process ensures different types of communications using different flags. Again this implementation is not close to the practical scenario, as one more extra process is needed. The bus is replaced by several point to point channels, therefore common shared bus is not modeled in its true sense.

In [5] the authors modeled the broadcast communication using a shared variable for the bus. This specification does not blow the state space, but it does not use the channels. Therefore this specification can not be used to model handshake communication.

In this article we model the communication protocol between Generic Bootloader, that lies in every line replacement modules of a switching network and Quickloader, which is also a part of this network. This switching network is an important part of the A380 Aircraft's Secondary Electrical Power Distribution System. Each module is connected to a shared RS432 bus. The line replacement modules need to upload the required software from the Quickloader. This process of uploading the required software consists of complex communication protocol, involving various type of communications.

We claim to provide an easier and efficient way of specification technique to model a common shared bus for different type of communications, viz. multicast, broadcast, point to point and handshake. This technique models the bus more closely to a practical scenario, like CAN bus, RS485 etc, in the Promela language of SPIN model checker. The generated state space using our technique is also minimum compared to other known techniques.

We also show that our formal analysis of the model could find out a serious bug, which was otherwise overlooked by common industrial software testing processes.

The rest of the paper is organized as follows. Section 2 provides a brief description of the communication pattern between Generic Bootloader and Quickloader.

Section 3 gives an overview of the Promela model of the communication of the system. In Section 4 we describe what are the desired properties of the model described in the previous section and in Section 5 we describe verification results and give explanations of our findings. Section 6 contains the concluding remarks.

2   Generic Bootloader

In a commercial aircraft, electric power system has two major tasks, viz. power generation and power distribution. Power generation is classified in three categories, viz. AC generation, DC generation and External power. AC generator is the main power generation system serving almost every component of an aircraft. DC power supply is provided to cater the emergency purpose in case the AC power supply fails and External power is needed to start the engine at airport. Electric power distribution system is also categorised in three components based on their purpose. Standby electric power distribution system provides power supply for flight essential loads. Primary electric power distribution system provides power supply in most of the components with requirements 5 to 100 KVA, either in AC or in DC or as a combination of both. Secondary electric power distribution system provides power supply with requirements 25A or less, mainly to relay panels or circuit breaker panels.

In Airbus A380 aircraft, the Secondary Electric Power Distribution System (SEPDS), acts as the main power distribution system. The switching software that runs on SEPDS has a shared bus architecture, as given in Figure 1. Several components are connected to a shared RS432 bus. These components are also called as Line Replacement Modules or LRMs because they are replaced as a whole module to correct faultiness. In the network, AC/DC component delivers power supply to loads. There could be more than one such component. GATE-WAY component acts as a gateway for outside signals and GFI component takes care of ground fault interrupts. Any such network contains only one GATEWAY component and one GFI component.

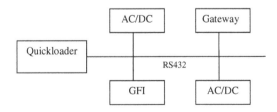

Fig. 1. SEPDS network switch architecture

When the power is switched on in the network, each of the LRMs verifies that the correct software is loaded in them. Now this software is different for different LRMs. If the correct software is not present in the LRM or the software is not

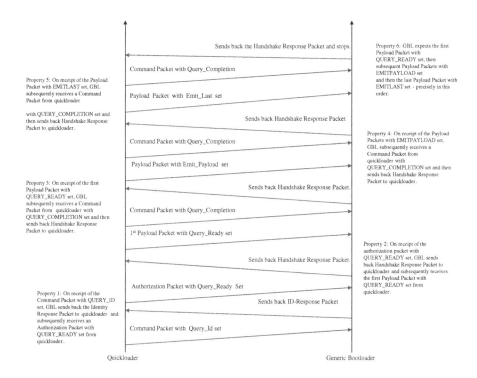

Fig. 2. Communication protocol between Generic Boot Loader and Quickloader

properly present, then the corresponding LRM uploads the correct software from the Quickloader, another module connected to the same RS432 bus. To upload the software each of the LRMs communicates with the Quickloader Module. All kinds of communication, viz. point to point, handshake, multicast and broadcast take place between them. The communication protocol between the Generic Bootloader and the Quickloader can be best described using Figure 2.

Quickloader starts the communication with each Generic Bootloader. In a point to point communication Quickloader sends a *command packet* with opcode QUERY_ID. Generic bootloader replies back to Quickloader by sending *ID_Response* packet in another point to point communication. Quickloader responds by sending an *authorization packet* with opcode QUERY_READY set using point to point communication. Generic bootloader acknowledges by sending a *response packet* using handshake communication. Quickloader then starts broadcasting *payload packets* containing the required software for a particular type of LRM. After sending each payload packet Quickloader broadcasts a command packet with QUERY_COMPLETION set signalling that it had completed the sending of *that payload packet*. Following which the concerned Generic Bootloader acknowledges the receipt of the payload packet and the command packet by sending a response packet in a handshake communication with Quickloader. Payload packets are categorized into three different types of packets. First payload packet has opcode "QUERY_READY" set. This signals that this is the first payload packet. The last payload packet has opcode "EMIT_LAST" set, which says that complete software has been sent. Receiving the command packet following this packet the concerned Generic Bootloader sends handshake response packet and stops its uploading process. The intermediate payload packets contains opcode "EMIT_PAYLOAD". Essentially the process of uploading software should follow the above mentioned ordered steps. The properties mentioned in the Figure 2 are described in detail in Section 4, and these are the properties which we intend to verify for this uploader communication protocol.

3   Description of the Model

We try to model the communication protocol, described in the previous section, close to its original implementation. In fact our model for the communication protocol is based on its original implementation in approximately 5K LOC of C++. We manually abstracted the model from the original implementation.

In our model we consider different LRMs and the Quickloader as different processes. The LRMs ac and dc behave in the same way in the communication protocol and in our model we did not differentiate them. Thus we have four different processes ACDC, GFI, GATEWAY and Quickloader. Our interest is primarily in the complexity of interaction involved between these LRMs and therefore we modeled only the relevant parts of each of these LRMs and not their complete state machine.

Each of the above mentioned processes communicate with each other by sending packets using a shared bus. These packets are defined in the following way.

```
typedef packet   {
    byte TYPE;
    byte ID;
    byte OPCODE;
    bit  EMIT_LAST;
};
```

where the field TYPE describes the type of packet, in other words whether it is a command packet or an authorization packet or a handshake response packet etc. The ID field describes the recipient or the sender. In practice, in the network there will be one Quickloader, one GFI and one GATEWAY. But AC or DC LRMs could be more than one in numbers. We need a mechanism to differentiate between two AC/DC LRMs. Using the ID field we can identify a particular LRM. In this work we kept only one ACDC process and kept this option as a future extension of this work. The differentiation mechanism is described in the documentation with the Promela code given below. OPCODE describes the opcode we mentioned in the previous section, viz., EMIT_PAYLOAD, EMIT_LAST,

QUERY_COMPLETION etc. To ease the verification process we kept one more separate bit for EMIT_LAST opcode. Below we present the fragment of the specification that describes the packet in detail.

```
/* IDs to decide
   1) who is recipient
   2) who is sender

Numbers here represent sender identifiers

Ac/Dc 1, 2, 3, 4  are marked as 11, 12, 13, 14
GFI - 25, Gateway - 36, Quickloader - 47

In other words, ID mod 10 ->    0  for Invalid
 (1 - 4) for AcDc 1-4, 5 for GFI
 6 for Gateway and 7 for Quickloader,

And,
ID div 10 ->    0    Invalid
                1    AcDc
                2    GFI
                3    Gateway
                4    Quickloader

ID = 0 means empty packet

TYPE to assert that LRMs are receiving right set of packets

TYPE  0    Invalid/Empty packet
      1    Command packet
      2    ID_RESPONSE packet
      3    Authorization packet
      4    Handshake packet
      5    Payload packet

OPCODEs to denote different kinds of "queries"

OPCODE  0    Invalid
        1    QUERY_ID
        2    QUERY_READY for Payload packet
        3    QUERY_COMPLETION
        4    EMIT_PAYLOAD
        5    EMIT_LAST
        6    QUERY_READY for Authorization packet

EMIT_LAST to denote whether this is the last packet or not
```

```
EMIT_LAST   0   not LAST PACKET
            1   LAST PACKET
```

```
*/
```

We need to model different type of communication over a shared channel. SPIN provides data type *chan* to describe the communication channel between two processes. This channel allows only two type of communications viz., asynchronous or "point to point" and synchronous or "handshake" communication. In our case we also need to model broadcast communication using the same channel. Using a shared variable for broadcast communication can not essentially model handshake communication. On the other hand having more than one channel not only increases the complexity of the model but also significantly increases the state space size.

We have 4 processes who communicate with each other using a shared bus. All the four types of communications, mentioned earlier, are possible in between them. We keep one shared bit for each of these processes. Each time a packet is sent to the channel (representing the bus), these 4 extra bits are added at the end of the packet. Each of these extra bits represents one process. In other words, for every process we add an extra bit at the end of each packet.

A bit is on, if the packet is meant for the corresponding process. Otherwise the bit is off. For example, in case of broadcast, all the bits except the one representing the sender will be on. We also keep one more extra flag (or shared bit), say bus_empty, to show that the channel (or bus) is empty or not. In case of handshake response, as the communication is synchronous we do not need to off this bit. In case of other communications, as soon as a packet is sent to the channel the bus_empty flag will be set to off. This flag will remain off until all the receivers receive the packet. No communication is possible over a channel if its bus_empty flag is off.

A receiver receives a packet from the bus if the packet is destined for it. After receiving the packet the receiver checks whether the packet has to be received by some other receivers. If yes, it sends back the same packet to the bus. Otherwise, it sets on the bus_empty flag. In either case it sets off its representing bit, which comes at the end of the packet. Below we provide a fragment of the specification, where the bits for_acdc, for_gfi, for_gateway and for_quickloader are used for the purposes we just described.

```
chan bus = [0] of {packet, bit, bit, bit, bit};

bit bus_empty = 1;

packet  bus_queue, acdc_packet, gfi_packet,
        gateway_packet, quickloader_packet;
bit for_acdc, for_gfi, for_gateway, for_quickloader;
```

```
bit quickloader_stops = 0;
bit acdc_uploaded = 0;
bit gfi_uploaded = 0;
bit gateway_uploaded = 0;


inline send_to_bus (pack, bit1, bit2,bit3,bit4) {
    bus_empty = 0;

    bus!pack,bit1,bit2,bit3,bit4;
}

inline acdc_receive_from_bus () {
  !(bus_empty) ->
   bus?bus_queue,for_acdc,for_gfi,for_gateway,for_quickloader;
    !(bus_empty) -> acdc_packet.TYPE = bus_queue.TYPE;
        acdc_packet.ID = bus_queue.ID;
        acdc_packet.OPCODE = bus_queue.OPCODE;
        acdc_packet.EMIT_LAST = bus_queue.EMIT_LAST;
        for_acdc = 0;  to_acdc = 0;
    if
    :: for_gfi | for_gateway | for_quickloader ->
    bus!bus_queue,for_acdc,for_gfi,for_gateway,for_quickloader;
    :: else -> bus_empty = 1;
    fi;
}
```

Similarly we have defined the packet receiving function for each of the processes. Specification of the processes are then straightforward and follows the original C++ implementation. In our simulation we tried with four processes communication with each other in all different combinations. We could easily verify the properties without any state space explosion. One simulation message sequence chart showing all the different type of communications is in Figure 3.

In Figure 3, we have four processes, viz. ACDC, GFI, GATEWAY and Quickloader, indicated by four vertical lines from left to right respectively. The arrows denote the communication between processes. For example the first arrow from the top is a point to point communication from the process Quickloader to the process GATEWAY. The second and third arrows as well are point to point communications. The fourth arrow from the top is a handshake communication from GATEWAY to Quickloader. The fifth, sixth and seventh arrow in together represents the broadcast communication from Quickloader to ACDC, GFI and GATEWAY.

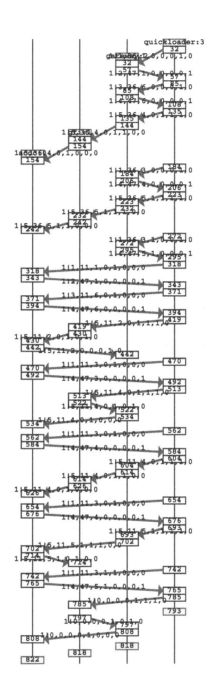

Fig. 3. Simulation results

4   Properties

As mentioned in the earlier sections we aim to formally analyze Generic Boot-loader (GBL) software, which communicates with the Quickloader following Uploader Communication Protocol. In this study, we have modeled GBL in SPIN (using the specification language PROMELA) taking into account only the uploader communication protocol. We then express the response properties of the uploader communication protocol in LTL and can be verified against the GBL model. The response properties of the uploader communication protocol and how the properties can be expressed in LTL are described as under.

Property 1: On receipt of the Command Packet with QUERY_ID set, GBL sends back the Identity Response Packet to Quickloader and subsequently receives an Authorization Packet with QUERY_READY set from Quickloader.
Property 2: On receipt of the authorization packet with QUERY_READY set, GBL sends back Handshake Response Packet to Quickloader and subsequently receives the first Payload Packet with QUERY_READY set from Quickloader.
Property 3: On receipt of the first Payload Packet with QUERY_READY set, GBL subsequently receives a Command Packet from Quickloader with QUERY_COMPLETION set and then sends back the Handshake Response Packet to Quickloader.
Property 4: On receipt of the Payload Packets with EMIT_PAYLOAD set, GBL subsequently receives a Command Packet from Quickloader with QUERY_COMPLETION set and then sends back the Handshake Response Packet to Quickloader.
Property 5: On receipt of the Payload Packet with EMIT_LAST set, GBL subsequently receives a Command Packet from Quickloader with QUERY_COMPLETION set and then sends back the Handshake Response Packet to Quickloader.
Property 6: GBL expects the first Payload Packet with QUERY_READY set, then subsequent Payload Packets with EMITPAYLOAD set and then the last Payload Packet with EMIT_LAST set - precisely in this order.

From the description of the properties, it is now apparent that the LTL forms of these properties will be similar. So, we do not make it a point to describe LTL expressions of all these properties, rather we only describe how Property 1 can be expressed in LTL. A closer look of all these properties show that all of them are comprised of three events as can be seen that for Property 1 to Property 5, two of these events are receiving a packet and the third one is sending a packet. For Property 6 all these events correspond to receiving a packet. We now turn our attention in describing Property 1, for each of its events we have a Boolean expression. We thus have the following.

p1 = ((bus_empty == 0) & (for_acdc == 1)) & ((acdc_packet.ID == 11) & (acdc_packet.TYPE == 1) & (acdc_packet.OPCODE == 1))

p2 = ((bus_empty == 0) & (for_quickloader == 1)) & (quickloader_pack et.TYPE == 2) p3 = ((bus_empty == 0) & (for_acdc == 1)) & ((acdc_packet.ID == 11) & (acdc_packet.TYPE == 3) & (acdc_packet.OPCODE == 2))

p1 corresponds to the receipt of the Command packet with Query_Id set and p3 denotes that an authorization packet with QUERY_READY set is being received by GBL. p2 symbolizes that GBL sends back an Identity Response Packet to Quickloader. Property 1 can now be expressed as,

```
( <> p1) & (![]<> p1 ) & (<>p1 U <>p2 )
        & (![](<>p1 U <>p2) ) & ((<>p1 U <> p2) U <>p3 ).
```

Eventually, GBL will receive a Command Packet with QUERY_ID set and hence we have $<> p1$ as first term in the above expression. The third term in the above expression $(<> p1 \bigcup <> p2)$ signifies that on receipt of the Command packet with QUERY_ID set, GBL eventually sends back the Identity Response Packet to Quickloader. But, this can be true in a way that $<> p1$ is globally true and $<> p2$ is false, which in other words can be said as GBL always waits for the Command packet with QUERY_ID set, but never receives. To prevent this from happening, we have the second term $(![] <> p1)$, i.e., $<> p1$ is not globally true. The first three terms in the above expression thus model the fact that, on receipt of the Command packet with QUERY_ID set, GBL sends back the Identity Response packet to Quickloader. The fourth and the fifth term of the expression can be analogously explained.

5   Verification and Results

We have carried out the verification of the LTL properties using SPIN. What has been attempted here is to verify the individual terms of the property. If each of the terms gets verified in affirmative then the property holds in the model. Verification result as has been obtained from our experiment is captured in Table 1. The columns in the table are labeled as Term 1, Term 2, to Term 5. For Property 1, Term 1 is $(<> p1)$, Term 2 is $(![] <> p1)$, Term 3 is $(<> p1 U <> p2)$, Term 4 is $(![](<> p1 U <> p2))$, and Term 5 is $((<> p1 U <> p2) U <> p3)$. In order for the property to be true, all the terms are required to be true in the model, and the validity results of these terms are shown separately in the table. The terms for other properties can be similarly identified. From the table, we can see that, only property 1 is valid in the model, whereas all other properties are invalid. Row that corresponds to property 1 shows that, the depths reached in verifying Term 1, Term 3 and Term 5 are respectively 27, 56 and 87. This monotonically increasing order in depths reached is expected. For these three terms correspond to three events comprising Property 1 and as has been also evident from the description that they should also happen in this order.

Depths reached in verifying Term 2 and Term 4 have achieved the maximum value of 864 and this can also be explained, for these two terms have to be true over the entire state space. Verification of Property 2 can also be explained in a similar way, with the only exception that Term 5 has been found to be

Table 1. Verification results

Properties	Term 1	Term 2	Term 3	Term 4	Term 5	Results
Property 1	27	864	56	864	87	Valid
Property 2	87	864	118	864	761	Not valid
Property 3	761	N.A.	N.A.	N.A.	N.A.	Not valid
Property 4	761	N.A.	N.A.	N.A.	N.A.	Not valid
Property 5	761	N.A.	N.A.	N.A.	N.A.	Not valid
Property 6	761	N.A.	N.A.	N.A.	N.A.	Not valid

invalid in the model. SPIN thus have found one error while verifying Term 5 and have provided with us one counter example of how this can be invalid. This has helped us to find a bug in the GBL software, which is mainly because of a switch statement. The parameter of this switch statement is the type of the payload packet that the GBL software expects and for each of the values of its types, it has separate blocks. Thus, it looks like the following.

```
switch ( Payload Packet Type){
    case QUERY_READY:    ...
                         break;
    case EMIT_PAYLOAD:   ...
                         break;
    case EMIT_LAST:      ...
                         break;
}
```

The correctness of the GBL expects the payload packets to arrive in order, i.e, first payload packet with QUERY_READY set, the payload packets with EMIT_PAYLOAD set, and lastly to mark the end of uploading the software the payload packet with EMIT_LAST set. But the problem with the switch statement it doesn't guarantee this order. Thus, because of this bug, GBL either can enter into a faulty state or can erroneously flag that it has successfully completed uploading the software.

Property 2 says that on receipt of the authorization packet with QUERY_READY set, GBL sends back Handshake Response Packet to Quickloader and subsequently receives the first Payload packet with QUERY_READY set from Quickloader. But, instead of sending the first payload packet with QUERY_READY set, if Quickloader sends either a payload packet with EMIT_PAYLOAD or EMIT_LAST set, then the GBL enters into an erroneous state. Because of the same reason all the other properties are also invalid in the model. For the properties Property 3 to Property 6, SPIN reports this error for the first term of the corresponding LTL expression and hence we havent carried our verification process for the remaining terms as marked in the table by N.A.

6   Conclusion

In this work we have shown a modeling technique that provides an easier way to model the practical channels which are of use in industry, like CAN bus, RS485 etc. This will help to model a lot more similar channels or communications in between processes without blowing up the state space.

Our technique specifies the common shared bus between several processes for different types of interprocess communications using only one channel. In case of Spin Model Checker this channel can be specified using the already available data type chan in Promela. Broadcast, multicast, point to point and handshake communications are then modeled by adding one extra shared bit per process, representing each process and sent across at the end of each packet. If the bit corresponding to a process is on, the packet is meant for that process. One more shared bit makes sure that the channel is not used simultaneously for two communicating processes.

Let us compare our technique with the already available techniques in literature to model different communications. Replacing a broadcast channel by point to point channels, as many as the number of processes, increases the number of channels to four in our example. That too only if we have a single sender acting as broadcaster. If we have senders where each of them can act as broadcaster then the number of channels will increase even further. In our case only four bits were enough to model the broadcast communication.

Again having a separate process taking care of broadcasting faces similar problems. That process has to have as many channels as the processes. Therefore it remains expensive. Since in this case, there will be no direct channel between two processes handshake communications can not be modeled easily, if possible. Another way of modeling the broadcast communication is to have a shared variable. This way of modeling does not need to have any channel. Messages are copied to the shared variable and receivers read from them. Modeling other type of communications needs extra information about the sender and receiver. In other words our technique of adding extra bits representing the processes will model different communications. The state space size will be nearly equal when compared with our technique. Since channels have an internal representation in the tool, our technique will build the state space with smaller size, as in the shared variable technique the shared variable has to be explicitly kept in the state space. Also the modeling of a common bus using a channel is more close to the practical scenario than modeling the bus using a shared variable. In other words our technique is easier and better than the techniques available in the literature.

We hope that our technique will be helpful to the researchers from industry to formally verify communication protocols. As a future extension of this work we would like to try the network with more than one ACDC processes and implementing the multicast communication between Quickloader and these ACDC processes.

References

1. SPIN Model Checker. http://www.spinroot.com/
2. de Renesse, R., Aghvami, A.H.: Formal verification of ad-hoc routing protocols using spin model checker. In: IEEE MELECON, IEEE Computer Society Press, Los Alamitos (2004)
3. Jensen, H., Larsen, K., Skou, A.: Modelling and analysis of a collision avoidance protocol using spin and uppaal. In: The Second Workshop on the SPIN Verification System, American Mathematical Society. Discrete Mathematics and Theoretical Computer Science, vol. 32 (1996)
4. Pike, L.: Formal verification of time triggered systems. PhD thesis, Indiana University (2005)
5. van Osch, M.J.P., Smolka, S.A.: Finite-state analysis of the can bus protocol. In: HASE 2001, p. 42. IEEE Computer Society, Washington, DC, USA (2001)

Model Checking Propositional Projection Temporal Logic Based on SPIN[*]

Cong Tian and Zhenhua Duan

Institute of Computing Theory and Technology
Xidian University, Xi'an, 710071, P.R. China
{ctian,zhhduan}@mail.xidian.edu.cn

Abstract. This paper investigates a model checking algorithm for Propositional Projection Temporal Logic (PPTL) with finite models. To this end, a PPTL formula is transformed to a Normal Form Graph (NFG), and then a Nondeterministic Finite Automaton (NFA). The NFA precisely characterizes the finite models satisfying the corresponding formula and can be equivalently represented as a Deterministic Finite Automaton (DFA). When the system to be verified can be modeled as a DFA A_s, and the property of the system can be specified by a PPTL formula P, then $\neg P$ can be transformed to a DFA A_p. Thus, whether the system satisfies the property or not can be checked by computing the product automaton of A_s and A_p, and then checking whether or not the product automaton accepts the empty word. Further, this method can be implemented by means of the verification system SPIN.

Keywords: Model Checking, Propositional Projection Temporal Logic, Automaton, SPIN, Verification.

1 Introduction

Model checking is an important approach for verification of the properties of hardware, softwares, multi-agent systems, communication protocols, embedded systems and so forth. In the last two decades, several model checkers such as SPIN [15] and SMV [16] were developed with success. In particular, as a software verification system, SPIN has attracted a fairly broad group of users in both academia and industry. SPIN can be used as a full Propositional Linear Temporal Logic (PLTL) [2] model checking system, supporting checks of all correctness requirements expressible in linear time temporal logic. However, PLTL is not powerful enough to describe all the ω-regular properties which can be verified in SPIN [15]. For instance, it is impossible to describe the property that proposition p must hold at even states regardless of odd states over a run (sequence of states) [20,15]. Thus, to capture a property that is not expressible in PLTL we need encode it directly into a Never Claim, but this is an error-prone process. Fortunately, it has been proved that these properties can be specified by more

---

[*] This research is supported by the NSFC Grant No. 60373103 and 60433010.

M. Butler, M. Hinchey, M.M. Larrondo-Petrie (Eds.): ICFEM 2007, LNCS 4789, pp. 246–265, 2007.
© Springer-Verlag Berlin Heidelberg 2007

powerful logics with chop operator [20]. Within Propositional Projection Temporal Logic (PPTL) [6,7] and Propositional Interval Temporal Logic (PITL) [3], chop and projection operators are introduced. Thus, the above property can be specified. It has also been proved that the logic with chop operator has the expressive power of full regular expressions [20,2]. Therefore, we are motivated to investigate a model checking algorithm and the corresponding verification technique based on SPIN for PPTL. Note that PPTL is an extension of PITL [6,7,9], our method can also be applied to PITL.

Within PPTL, many logic laws have been formalized and proved [6,7], and a decision procedure for checking satisfiability of PPTL formulas with infinite models has been given in [9]. Thus, model checking PPTL is decidable. The method presented in this paper is mainly inspired by our previous work [9]. For simplicity, we consider only PPTL formulas defined over finite intervals. The full logic will further be studied in the near future.

With our method, the model of the system to be verified is specified by a DFA A_s, and the property of the system is described by a PPTL formula P. Further, $\neg P$ is transformed to a Normal Form Graph (NFG), and then a Nondeterministic Finite Automaton (NFA). The NFA precisely characterizes the finite models satisfying P and can be equivalently represented as a Determined Finite Automaton (DFA) A_p. Thus, whether the system satisfies property P or not can be checked by computing the product automaton of A_s and A_p, and then checking whether or not the product automaton accepts the empty word. When implemented in SPIN, the system is described in terms of PROMELA which produces the automaton A_s when executed by the PROMELA interpreter within SPIN. The automaton A_p of $\neg P$ is also described as Never Claim in the syntax of PROMELA. Thus, SPIN can be employed to implement the model checking procedure.

Our method has several advantages. For instance, first, the method is based on the verification tool SPIN. As known, SPIN is a successful and widely used software model checking tool. So we can benefit from SPIN; secondly, our method extends the function of SPIN since specification language PPTL can be used in SPIN. This enables us to verify systems with properties specified in PLTL and PPTL; finally, all the properties which can be verified in SPIN can now be specified by PPTL, since logic with chop operator has the expressive power of full regular expressions.

The rest of the paper is organized as follows. The next section briefly presents the syntax and semantics of PPTL. Section 3 introduces the normal form of PPTL formulas. In Section 4, the definition of NFG and the algorithm for constructing NFG are given. Further, the upper bound of the number of nodes in NFGs is proved in details. Section 5 is devoted to the transformation from NFG to NFA. Further, in Section 6, the model checking method for PPTL is illustrated and how the method can be implemented in SPIN are presented. In addition, simple examples are given to show how our method works. Finally, conclusions are drawn in Section 7.

2   Propositional Projection Temporal Logic

Our underlying logic is Propositional Projection Temporal Logic (PPTL) [6,7];
it is an extension of Propositional Interval Temporal Logic (PITL) [3].

2.1   Syntax

Let *Prop* be a countable set of atomic propositions. The formula P of PPTL is
given by the following grammar:

$$P ::= p \mid \bigcirc P \mid \neg P \mid P_1 \vee P_2 \mid (P_1, ..., P_m) \; prj \; P$$

where $p \in Prop$, P_1 ,..., P_m and P are all well-formed PPTL formulas. $\bigcirc$
(next) and prj (projection) are basic temporal operators. The abbreviations
$true$, $false$, $\wedge$, $\rightarrow$ and $\leftrightarrow$ are defined as usual. In particular, $true \overset{def}{=} P \vee \neg P$
and $false \overset{def}{=} P \wedge \neg P$ for any formula P. Also we have the following derived
formulas:

$$\varepsilon \overset{def}{=} \neg \bigcirc true \qquad\qquad more \overset{def}{=} \neg \varepsilon$$
$$\bigcirc^0 P \overset{def}{=} P \qquad\qquad \bigcirc^n P \overset{def}{=} \bigcirc(\bigcirc^{n-1}P)$$
$$len\ n \overset{def}{=} \bigcirc^n \varepsilon \qquad\qquad skip \overset{def}{=} len\ 1$$
$$\odot P \overset{def}{=} \varepsilon \vee \bigcirc P \qquad\qquad P; Q \overset{def}{=} (P, Q) \; prj \; \varepsilon$$
$$\diamond P \overset{def}{=} true\ ;\ P \qquad\qquad \square P \overset{def}{=} \neg \diamond \neg P$$
$$halt(P) \overset{def}{=} \square(\varepsilon \leftrightarrow P) \qquad\qquad fin(P) \overset{def}{=} \square(\varepsilon \rightarrow P)$$
$$keep(P) \overset{def}{=} \square(\neg \varepsilon \rightarrow P)$$

where $\odot$ (weak next), $\square$ (always), $\diamond$ (sometimes), and ; (chop) are derived
temporal operators; ε (empty) denotes an interval with zero length, and *more*
means the current state is not the final one over an interval; $halt(P)$ is true over
an interval if and only P is true at the final state, $fin(P)$ is true as long as P
is true at the final state and $keep(P)$ is true if P is true at every state ignoring
the final one.

Also with projection construct $(P_1, ..., P_m) \; prj \; Q$, in some circumstances,
there may exist some parts, such as $(P_i, ...,P_j)$, that can repeatedly appear in
$P_1, ..., P_m$ for several times. In this case, for concise, the projection construct can
be described as follows:

$$(P_1, ..., (P_i, ..., P_j)^k, ..., P_m) \; prj \; Q$$
$$\overset{def}{=} (P_1, ..., \underbrace{(P_i, ..., P_j), ..., (P_i, ..., P_j)}_{k \text{ times}}, ..., P_m) \; prj \; Q$$

where $1 \leq i \leq j \leq m, k \geq 0$. When $i = 1$ and $j = m$, we have,

$$(P_1, ..., P_m)^k \; prj \; Q \overset{def}{=} (\ \underbrace{(P_1, ..., P_m), ..., (P_1, ..., P_m)}_{k \text{ times}}\ ) \; prj \; Q$$

Further, the following formulas can be derived,

$$\varepsilon \; prj \; Q \stackrel{def}{=} (P_1, ..., P_m)^k \; prj \; Q \quad \text{if } k = 0$$
$$(P_1, ..., P_m)^+ \; prj \; Q \stackrel{def}{=} (P_1, ..., P_m)^k \; prj \; Q \quad \text{if } k > 0$$
$$(P_1, ..., P_m)^* \; prj \; Q \stackrel{def}{=} (P_1, ..., P_m)^k \; prj \; Q \quad \text{if } k \geq 0$$

In particular, when $m = 1$, let $P_1 \equiv P$, we have,

$$\varepsilon \; prj \; Q \stackrel{def}{=} P^k \; prj \; Q \quad \text{if } k = 0$$
$$P^+ \; prj \; Q \stackrel{def}{=} P^k \; prj \; Q \quad \text{if } k > 0$$
$$P^* \; prj \; Q \stackrel{def}{=} P^k \; prj \; Q \quad \text{if } k \geq 0$$

Accordingly, in PITL, if $P \; proj \; Q$ [3] holds for some P and Q, then we can express it using prj construction in PPTL,

$$(P^* \; prj \; (Q; r \wedge \varepsilon)) \wedge halt(r)$$

where $r \in Prop$ does not appear in P and Q.

2.2   Semantics

Following the definition of Kripke's structure [1], we define a state s over $Prop$ to be a mapping from $Prop$ to $B = \{true, false\}$, $s : Prop \longrightarrow B$. We will use $s[p]$ to denote the valuation of p at the state s.

An interval σ is a non-empty sequence of states, which can be finite or infinite. The length, $|\sigma|$, of σ is ω if σ is infinite, and the number of states minus 1 if σ is finite. To have a uniform notation for both finite and infinite intervals, we will use extended integers as indices. That is, we consider the set N_0 of non-negative integers and ω, $N_\omega = N_0 \cup \{\omega\}$, and extend the comparison operators, $=, <, \leq$, to N_ω by considering $\omega = \omega$, and for all $i \in N_0$, $i < \omega$. Moreover, we define $\preceq$ as $\leq -\{(\omega, \omega)\}$. To simplify definitions, we will denote σ as $< s_0, ..., s_{|\sigma|} >$, where $s_{|\sigma|}$ is undefined if σ is infinite. With such a notation, $\sigma_{(i..j)}$ $(0 \leq i \preceq j \leq |\sigma|)$ denotes the sub-interval $< s_i, ..., s_j >$ and $\sigma^{(k)}$ $(0 \leq k \preceq |\sigma|)$ denotes $< s_k, ..., s_{|\sigma|} >$. The concatenation of a finite σ with another interval (or empty string) σ' is denoted by $\sigma \cdot \sigma'$.

Let $\sigma =< s_0, s_1, ..., s_{|\sigma|} >$ be an interval and $r_1, ..., r_h$ be integers $(h \geq 1)$ such that $0 \leq r_1 \leq r_2 \leq ... \leq r_h \preceq |\sigma|$. The projection of σ onto $r_1, ..., r_h$ is the interval (named projected interval)

$$\sigma \downarrow (r_1, ..., r_h) =< s_{t_1}, s_{t_2}, ..., s_{t_l} >$$

where $t_1, ..., t_l$ is obtained from $r_1, ..., r_h$ by deleting all duplicates. That is, $t_1, ..., t_l$ is the longest strictly increasing subsequence of $r_1, ..., r_h$. For instance,

$$< s_0, s_1, s_2, s_3, s_4 > \downarrow (0, 0, 2, 2, 2, 3) =< s_0, s_2, s_3 >$$

An interpretation is a quadruple $\mathcal{I} = (\sigma, i, k, j)[1]$, where σ is an interval, i, k are integers, and j an integer or ω such that $i \leq k \preceq j \leq |\sigma|$. We use the notation $(\sigma, i, k, j) \models P$ to denote that formula P is interpreted and satisfied over the subinterval $< s_i, ..., s_j >$ of σ with the current state being s_k. The satisfaction relation ($\models$) is inductively defined as follows:

$\mathcal{I} \models p$ iff $s_k[p] = true$, for any given atomic proposition p

$\mathcal{I} \models \neg P$ iff $\mathcal{I} \not\models P$

$\mathcal{I} \models P \vee Q$ iff $\mathcal{I} \models P$ or $\mathcal{I} \models Q$

$\mathcal{I} \models \bigcirc P$ iff $k < j$ and $(\sigma, i, k+1, j) \models P$

$\mathcal{I} \models (P_1, ..., P_m) \, prj \, Q$ if there exist integers $k = r_0 \leq r_1 \leq ... \leq r_m \leq j$
    such that $(\sigma, 0, r_0, r_1) \models P_1$, $(\sigma, r_{l-1}, r_{l-1}, r_l) \models P_l, 1 < l \leq m$, and
    $(\sigma', 0, 0, |\sigma'|) \models Q$ for one of the following σ' :
    (a) $r_m < j$ and $\sigma' = \sigma \downarrow (r_0, ..., r_m) \cdot \sigma_{(r_m+1..j)}$ or
    (b) $r_m = j$ and $\sigma' = \sigma \downarrow (r_0, ..., r_h)$ for some $0 \leq h \leq m$

2.3   Satisfaction and Validity

A formula P is satisfied by an interval σ, denoted by $\sigma \models P$, if $(\sigma, 0, 0, |\sigma|) \models P$. A formula P is called satisfiable if $\sigma \models P$ for some σ. A formula P is valid, denoted by $\models P$, if $\sigma \models P$ for all σ.

Two formulas, P and Q, are equivalent, denoted by $P \equiv Q$, if $\models \Box(P \leftrightarrow Q)$. A formula P is called a state formula if it contains no temporal operators, a terminal formula if $P \equiv P \wedge \varepsilon$, a non-local formula if $P \equiv P \wedge more$, and a local formula if P is a state or terminal formula.

3   Normal Form of PPTL

Definition 1. Let Q be a PPTL formula and Q_p denote the set of atomic propositions appearing in Q. The normal form of Q is defined as follows,

$$Q \equiv \bigvee_{j=1}^{n_0}(Q_{ej} \wedge \varepsilon) \vee \bigvee_{i=1}^{n}(Q_{ci} \wedge \bigcirc Q'_i)$$

where $Q_{ej} \equiv \bigwedge_{k=1}^{m_0} \dot{q}_{jk}$, $Q_{ci} \equiv \bigwedge_{h=1}^{m} \dot{q}_{ih}$, $l = |Q_p|$, $1 \leq n$ (also n_0) $\leq 3^l$, $1 \leq m$ (also m_0) $\leq l$; $q_{jk}, q_{ih} \in Q_p$, for any $r \in Q_p$, $\dot{r}$ denotes r or $\neg r$; Q'_i is an arbitrary PPTL formula[2].

In some circumstances, for convenience, we write $Q_e \wedge \varepsilon$ instead of $\bigvee_{j=1}^{n_0}(Q_{ej} \wedge \varepsilon)$ and $\bigvee_{i=1}^{r}(Q_i \wedge \bigcirc Q'_i)$ instead of $\bigvee_{i=1}^{n}(Q_{ci} \wedge \bigcirc Q'_i)$. Thus,

$$Q \equiv (Q_e \wedge \varepsilon) \vee \bigvee_{i=1}^{r}(Q_i \wedge \bigcirc Q'_i)$$

where Q_e and Q_i are state formulas or $true$.

---

[1] Parameter i is used to handle past operators and redundant with the current version of the underlying logic. However, to be consistent with previous expositions, it is kept in the interpretation.

[2] It is an exercise to prove $n, n_0 \leq 3^l$.

Definition 2. In a normal form, if $\bigvee_i Q_i \equiv true$ and $\bigvee_{i \neq j}(Q_i \wedge Q_j) \equiv false$, then this normal form is called a complete normal form.

The complete normal form plays an important role in transforming the negation of a PPTL formula into its normal form. For example, if P has been rewritten to its complete normal form:

$$P \equiv P_e \wedge \varepsilon \vee \bigvee_{i=1}^r (P_i \wedge \bigcirc P_i')$$

then we have,

$$\neg P \equiv \neg P_e \wedge \varepsilon \vee \bigvee_{i=1}^r (P_i \wedge \bigcirc \neg P_i')$$

The normal form enables us to rewrite the formula into two parts: the terminating part $\bigvee_{j=1}^{n_0}(Q_{ej} \wedge \varepsilon)$ and the future part $\bigvee_{i=1}^n (Q_{ci} \wedge \bigcirc Q_i')$. For any PPTL formula P, P can be rewritten into its normal form and complete normal form. The details of the proofs and the algorithms for transforming PPTL formulas into normal forms and complete normal forms can be found in [8,9].

4   Normal Form Graph of PPTL

To transform a PPTL formula to an automaton that accepts precisely the sequences of sets of propositions satisfying the formula, we first construct a directed graph, called a Normal Form Graph (NFG), for the formula according to the normal form.

4.1   Definition of NFG

For a PPTL formula P, the NFG of P is a labeled directed graph, $G = (CL(P), EL(P))$, where $CL(P)$ denotes the set of nodes and $EL(P)$ denotes the set of edges in the graph. In $CL(P)$, each node is specified by a formula in PPTL, while in $EL(P)$, each edge is identified by a triple (Q, Q_e, R). Where Q and R are nodes and Q_e is the label of the directed arc from Q to R. $CL(P)$ and $EL(P)$ of G can be inductively defined below.

Definition 3. For a PPTL formula P, set of nodes, $CL(P)$, and set of of edges, $EL(P)$, connecting nodes in $CL(P)$ are inductively defined as follows:

1. $P \in CL(P)$;
2. For all $Q \in CL(P) \setminus \{\varepsilon, false\}$, if $Q \equiv \bigvee_{j=1}^h(Q_{ej} \wedge \varepsilon) \vee \bigvee_{i=1}^k(Q_{ci} \wedge \bigcirc Q_i')$, then $\varepsilon \in CL(P)$, $(Q, Q_{ej}, \varepsilon) \in EL(P)$ for each j, $1 \leq j \leq h$; $Q_i' \in CL(P)$, $(Q, Q_{ci}, Q_i') \in EL(P)$ for all i, $1 \leq i \leq k$;

$CL(P)$ and $EL(P)$ are only generated by 1 and 2. The NFG of formula P is the directed graph $G = (CL(P), EL(P))$.

In the NFG of P, the root node P is denoted by a double circle, ε node by a small black dot, and each of other nodes by a single circle. Each of the edges is denoted by a directed arc connecting two nodes. Fig.1 shows an example of NFG.

4.2   Constructing NFG

In the following, algorithm NFG for constructing the NFG of a PPTL formula is presented. It is actually a sketch of the implementation of Definition 3. The

---

function NFG(P):
/* precondition: P is a PPTL formula*/
/* postcondition: NFG(P) computes NFG of P, $G = (CL(P), EL(P))$*/

begin function
  Create root node P;
  $Mark(P)=0$; AddE = AddN =0;
  while there exists node Q (not ε and $false$) in the NFG and $Mark(Q) == 0$
      Mark(Q)=1;   /*marking R is decomposed*/
      Rewrite Q to its normal form;
      case
        Q is $\bigvee_{j=1}^{h} Q_{ej} \wedge \varepsilon$: AddE=1;   /*need to add first part of NF*/
        Q is $\bigvee_{i=1}^{k} Q_i \wedge \bigcirc Q_i'$: AddN=1;   /*second part of NF needs added*/
        Q is $\bigvee_{j=1}^{h} Q_{ej} \wedge \varepsilon \vee \bigvee_{i=1}^{k} Q_i \wedge \bigcirc Q_i'$: AddE=AddN=1;
                                      /*both parts of NF needs added*/
      end case
      if AddE == 1   /*add first part of NF*/
        if there exists no ε node
          create node ε;
        for $1 \leq j \leq h$,
          create edge (Q, Q_{ej}, ε);
        end for
        AddE=0;
      if AddN == 1   /*add second part of NF*/
        for $1 \leq i \leq k$
          if $Q_i' \notin CL(P)$
            create node Q_i';
            if Q_i' is $false$
              $mark(Q_i')=1$;   /*Q_i' not decomposed*/
            else $mark(Q_i')=0$;   /*Q_i' needs to be considered*/
          create edge (Q, Q_i, Q_i');
        end for
        AddN=0;
  end while
  return G;
end function

---

algorithm uses $mark[]$ to indicate whether or not a formula needs to be decomposed. If $mark[P] == 0$ (unmarked), P needs further to be decomposed, otherwise $mark[P] == 1$ (marked), thus P has been decomposed or needs not to be precessed. Note that algorithm NFG employs algorithm NF [8] to transform a formula into its normal form. Further, in the algorithm, two global boolean variables AddE and AddN are employed to indicate whether or not terminating and future parts in the normal form are encountered respectively. Note also that the algorithm only deals with formulas in a pre-prepared form in which only $\vee$, $\wedge$ and $\neg$, as well as temporal operators $\bigcirc$, ; and prj are contained. Others such as $\rightarrow$, $\leftrightarrow$, $\Diamond$, $\Box$, $\neg\neg$ etc. can be eliminated since they can be expressed by the basic operators. Algorithm NFG is slightly different from the one we gave in [9], since only finite models are considered in this paper.

Example 1. Construct the NFG of formula $\neg(true; \neg\bigcirc q) \vee p \wedge \bigcirc q$ by algorithm NFG.

As depicted in Fig.1, initially, the root node $\neg(true; \neg\bigcirc q) \vee p \wedge \bigcirc q$ is created and denoted by v_0; rewrite $\neg(true; \neg\bigcirc q) \vee p \wedge \bigcirc q$ to its normal form, $\neg(true; \neg\bigcirc q) \vee p \wedge \bigcirc q \equiv \bigcirc(q \wedge \neg(true; \neg\bigcirc q)) \vee p \wedge \bigcirc q$, nodes $q \wedge \neg(true; \neg\bigcirc q)$ and q

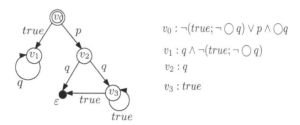

$$v_0 : \neg(true; \neg\bigcirc q) \vee p \wedge \bigcirc q$$
$$v_1 : q \wedge \neg(true; \neg\bigcirc q)$$
$$v_2 : q$$
$$v_3 : true$$

Fig. 1. NFG of formula $\neg(true; \neg\bigcirc q) \vee p \wedge \bigcirc q$

are created and denoted by v_1 and v_2 respectively; also edges $(v_0, true, v_1)$ and (v_0, p, v_2) are created; further, rewrite $q \wedge \neg(true; \neg\bigcirc q)$ to its normal form, $q \wedge \neg(true; \neg\bigcirc q) \equiv q \wedge \bigcirc(q \wedge \neg(true; \neg\bigcirc q))$, edge (v_1, q, v_1) is created; subsequently, rewrite q to its normal form, $q \equiv q \wedge \varepsilon \vee q \wedge \bigcirc true$, node $true$, denoted by v_3 and ε node are created, also edges (v_2, q, ε) and (v_2, q, v_3) are created; finally, rewrite $true$ to its normal form, $true \equiv \varepsilon \vee \bigcirc true$, edges $(v_3, true, \varepsilon)$ and $(v_3, true, v_3)$ are created.

4.3   Upper Bound of NFGs

For an arbitrary PPTL formula Q, if Q is rewritten into its normal form as follows,

$$Q \equiv (Q_e \wedge \varepsilon) \vee \bigvee_{i=1}^{r}(Q_i \wedge \bigcirc Q_i')$$

then ε or each of Q_i' is called a succ-formula of Q. The set of succ-formulas of Q is denoted by $succ(Q)$.

The length of a PPTL formula Q is denoted by $length(Q)$ (or $|Q|$), and is inductively defined in Definition 4. Note that we need consider only the operators $\neg$, $\bigcirc$, $\vee$, $\wedge$, ; and prj supported in algorithm NFG.

Definition 4. Let θ be an atomic proposition, or derived formula $true$, $false$ or ε, $length(\theta)=1$. Suppose P_i, $1 \leq i \leq m$, and Q are PPTL formulas, $length(P_i) = n_i$ and $length(Q) = n$, then

- For unary operators $\neg$ or $\bigcirc$ denoted by Θ_1, $length(\Theta_1 Q) = n + 1$
- For binary operators $;$, $\vee$ or $\wedge$ denoted by Θ_2, $length(P_1 \Theta_2 P_2) = n_1 + n_2 + 1$
- For operator prj, $length((P_1, ..., P_m)\ prj\ Q) = n_1 + ... + n_m + n + m$

Roughly speaking, the length of a formula P is the number of the symbols appearing in P.

Lemma 1. Suppose for each formula P_i and Q, $0 \le i \le m$, the length of each succ-formula of P_i (or Q) is not larger than the length of P_i (or Q), then the length of each succ-formula of $(P_1, ..., P_m)\ prj\ Q$ is not larger than the length of $(P_1, ..., P_m)\ prj\ Q$.

Proof. The proof proceeds by induction on m. Suppose P_1 and Q are rewritten into their normal forms,

$$P_1 \equiv P_{1e} \wedge \varepsilon \vee \bigvee_{i=1}^{n}(P_{1i} \wedge \bigcirc P'_{1i})$$
$$Q \equiv Q_e \wedge \varepsilon \vee \bigvee_{k=1}^{n'}(Q_k \wedge \bigcirc Q'_k)$$

By hypothesis, $|\varepsilon| \le |P_1|$, $|\varepsilon| \le |Q|$, for each i, $1 \le i \le n$, $|P'_{1i}| \le |P_1|$, and for each k, $1 \le k \le n'$, $|Q'_k| \le |Q|$. Since,

$$P_1\ prj\ Q \equiv P_{1e} \wedge Q_e \wedge \varepsilon \vee \bigvee_{i=1}^{n}(P_{1i} \wedge Q_e \wedge \bigcirc P'_{1i})$$
$$\vee \bigvee_{i=1}^{n}\bigvee_{k=1}^{n'}(P_{1i} \wedge Q_k \wedge \bigcirc(P'_{1i};Q'_k))$$
$$\vee \bigvee_{k=1}^{n'}(P_{1e} \wedge Q_k \wedge \bigcirc Q'_k)$$

So, $succ(P_1\ prj\ Q) = \{\varepsilon\} \cup \bigcup_{i=1}^{n}(P'_{1i}) \cup \bigcup_{i=1}^{n}\bigcup_{k=1}^{n'}(P'_{1i};Q'_k) \cup \bigcup_{k=1}^{n'}(Q'_k)$. Obviously, $|\varepsilon| \le |P_1\ prj\ Q|$; for each P'_{1i} and Q'_k, $|P'_{1i}| \le |P_1| \le |P_1\ prj\ Q|$ and $|Q'_k| \le |Q| \le |P_1\ prj\ Q|$; for each $P'_{1i};Q'_k$, $|P'_{1i};Q'_k| = |P'_{1i}\ prj\ Q'_k| \le |P_1\ prj\ Q|$. Suppose $(P_2, ..., P_m)\ prj\ Q$ has been rewritten to its normal form,

$$(P_2, ..., P_m)\ prj\ Q \equiv R_e \wedge \varepsilon \vee \bigvee_{j=1}^{t}(R_j \wedge \bigcirc R'_j)$$

And for ε and each R'_j, $|\varepsilon| \le |(P_2, ..., P_m)\ prj\ Q|$, $|R'_j| \le |(P_2, ..., P_m)\ prj\ Q|$. Since,

$$(P_1, ..., P_m)\ prj\ Q$$
$$\equiv P_{1e} \wedge R_e \wedge \varepsilon \vee \bigvee_{j=1}^{t}(P_{1e} \wedge R_j \wedge \bigcirc R'_j)$$
$$\vee \bigvee_{i=1}^{n}\bigvee_{k=1}^{n'}(P_{1i} \wedge Q_k \wedge \bigcirc(P'_{1i};((P_2, ..., P_m)\ prj\ Q'_k)))$$
$$\vee \bigvee_{i=1}^{n}(P_{1i} \wedge Q_e \wedge \bigcirc(Q'_{1i};P_2;...;P_m))$$

So, $succ((P_1, ..., P_m)\ prj\ Q) = \{\varepsilon\} \cup \bigcup_{j=1}^{t}(R'_j) \cup \bigcup_{i=1}^{n}\bigcup_{k=1}^{n'}(P'_{1i};((P_2, ..., P_m)\ prj\ Q'_k)) \cup \bigcup_{i=1}^{n}(Q'_{1i};P_2;...;P_m)$. Obviously, $|\varepsilon| \le |(P_1, ..., P_m)\ prj\ Q|$; for each R'_j, $|R'_j| \le |(P_2, ..., P_m)\ prj\ Q| \le |(P_1, ..., P_m)\ prj\ Q|$; for each $P'_{1i};((P_2, ..., P_m)\ prj\ Q'_k)$, $|P'_{1i};((P_2, ..., P_m)\ prj\ Q'_k)| \le |(P_1, ..., P_m)\ prj\ Q|$; for each $Q'_{1i};P_2;...;P_m$, $|Q'_{1i};P_2;...;P_m| \le |(P_2, ..., P_m)\ prj\ Q| \le |(P_1, ..., P_m)\ prj\ Q|$. Thus, the lemma holds.

Lemma 2. For any PPTL formula P, when rewritten into its normal form, the length of each succ-formula of P is not larger than the length of P.

Proof. The proof proceeds by induction on the structure of PPTL formulas composed of the operators $\neg$, $\bigcirc$, $\wedge$, $\vee$, ; and prj which are supported in algorithm NFG.

Base case: P is an atomic proposition p. Rewrite p to its normal form, $p \equiv p \wedge \varepsilon \vee p \wedge \bigcirc true$. For the succ-formulas ε and $true$, $|\varepsilon| \leq |p|$, $|true| \leq |p|$.

Induction step: Suppose for each formula P_i (or Q), $0 \leq i \leq m$, when rewritten into its normal form, the length of each succ-formula of P_i (or Q) will be not larger than the length of P_i (or Q). Then,

(1) $P \equiv \bigcirc P_1$: $|P_1| < 1 + |P_1| = |P|$.

(2) $P \equiv \neg P_1$: If the complete normal form of P_1 is as follows,

$$P_1 \equiv (P_{1e} \wedge \varepsilon) \vee \bigvee_{i=1}^{r}(P_{1i} \wedge \bigcirc P'_{1i})$$

then,

$$\neg P_1 \equiv (\neg P_{1e} \wedge \varepsilon) \vee \bigvee_{i=1}^{r}(P_{1i} \wedge \bigcirc \neg P'_{1i})$$

By hypothesis, $|\varepsilon| \leq |P_1|$, $|P'_{1i}| \leq |P_1|$, $1 \leq i \leq r$. Thus, we have $|\varepsilon| \leq |P_1| < 1 + |P_1| = |\neg P_1|$, $|\neg P'_{1i}| = 1 + |P'_{1i}| \leq 1 + |P_1| = |\neg P_1|$, $1 \leq i \leq r$.

(3) $P \equiv P_1 \vee P_2$: Let

$$P_1 \equiv (P_{1e} \wedge \varepsilon) \vee \bigvee_{i=1}^{r}(P_{1i} \wedge \bigcirc P'_{1i})$$
$$P_2 \equiv (P_{2e} \wedge \varepsilon) \vee \bigvee_{j=1}^{k}(P_{2j} \wedge \bigcirc P'_{2j})$$

Then,

$$P_1 \vee P_2 \equiv (P_{1e} \vee P_{2e}) \wedge \varepsilon \vee \bigvee_{i=1}^{r}(P_{1i} \wedge \bigcirc P'_{1i}) \vee \bigvee_{j=1}^{k}(P_{2j} \wedge \bigcirc P'_{2j})$$

By hypothesis, $|\varepsilon| \leq |P_1|$, $|\varepsilon| \leq |P_2|$, $|P'_{1i}| \leq |P_1|$, $1 \leq i \leq r$, and $|P'_{2j}| \leq |P_2|$, $1 \leq j \leq k$. Thus, we have $|\varepsilon| \leq |P_1| < |P_1| + |P_2| + 1 = |P_1 \vee P_2|$, $|P'_{1i}| \leq |P_1| < |P_1| + |P_2| + 1 = |P_1 \vee P_2|$, $1 \leq i \leq r$, and $|P'_{2i}| \leq |P_2| < |P_1| + |P_2| + 1 = |P_1 \vee P_2|$.

(4) $P \equiv P_1 \wedge P_2$: Let

$$P_1 \equiv (P_{1e} \wedge \varepsilon) \vee \bigvee_{i=1}^{r}(P_{1i} \wedge \bigcirc P'_{1i})$$
$$P_2 \equiv (P_{2e} \wedge \varepsilon) \vee \bigvee_{j=1}^{k}(P_{2j} \wedge \bigcirc P'_{2j})$$

Then,

$$P_1 \wedge P_2 \equiv (P_{1e} \wedge P_{2e}) \wedge \varepsilon \vee \bigvee_{i=1}^{r} \bigvee_{j=1}^{k}(P_{1i} \wedge P_{2j} \wedge \bigcirc(P'_{1i} \wedge P'_{2j}))$$

By hypothesis, $|\varepsilon| \leq |P_1|$, $|\varepsilon| \leq |P_2|$, $|P'_{1i}| \leq |P_1|$, $1 \leq i \leq r$, and $|P'_{2j}| \leq |P_2|$, $1 \leq j \leq k$. Thus, we have $|\varepsilon| \leq |P_1| < |P_1| + |P_2| + 1 = |P_1 \wedge P_2|$, $|P'_{1i} \wedge P'_{2j}| = |P'_{1i}| + |P'_{2j}| + 1 \leq |P_1| + |P_2| + 1 = |P_1 \wedge P_2|$, $1 \leq i \leq r$ and $1 \leq j \leq k$.

(5) $P \equiv P_1; P_2$: Let

$$P_1 \equiv (P_{1e} \wedge \varepsilon) \vee \bigvee_{i=1}^{r}(P_{1i} \wedge \bigcirc P'_{1i})$$
$$P_2 \equiv (P_{2e} \wedge \varepsilon) \vee \bigvee_{j=1}^{k}(P_{2j} \wedge \bigcirc P'_{2j})$$

Then,

$$P_1; P_2 \equiv P_{1e} \wedge P_{2e} \wedge \varepsilon \vee P_{1e} \wedge \bigvee_{j=1}^{k}(P_{2j} \wedge \bigcirc P_{2j}') \vee \bigvee_{i=1}^{r}(P_{1i} \wedge \bigcirc(P_{1i}'; P_2))$$

By hypothesis, $|\varepsilon| \leq |P_1|$, $|\varepsilon| \leq |P_2|$, $|P_{1i}'| \leq |P_1|$, $1 \leq i \leq r$, and $|P_{2j}'| \leq |P_2|$, $1 \leq j \leq k$. Thus, we have $|\varepsilon| \leq |P_1| < |P_1| + |P_2| + 1 = |P_1; P_2|$, $|P_{2j}'| \leq |P_2| < |P_1| + |P_2| + 1 = |P_1; P_2|$, $1 \leq i \leq r$, $|P_{1i}'; P_2| = |P_{1i}'| + |P_2| + 1 \leq |P_1| + |P_2| + 1 = |P_1; P_2|$.

(6) $P \equiv (P_1, ..., P_m) \, prj \, Q$: The conclusion has been proved in Lemma 1.

Theorem 3. For any PPTL formula Q, let $|Q| = n$, and Q_p denote the set of atomic propositions appearing in Q, and $|Q_p| = l$. Let the NFG of Q be $G = (CL(Q), EL(Q))$. Then we have $|CL(Q)| \leq (10 + l)^n$.

Proof. By algorithm NFG, the nodes of the NFG of Q are generated by repeatedly rewriting the new generated succ-formulas into their normal forms. Further, Lemma 2 confirms that when written into the normal form, the length of each succ-formula of Q is not larger than the length of Q. Moreover, each node (formula) in the NFG of Q is composed of basic connectives, $\neg, \wedge, \vee, \bigcirc, ;, prj$, and comma $(,)^3$ brought forth by prj, atomic propositions appearing in Q, as well as $true$ and $false$. Accordingly, there are at most $(9 + l)$ symbols possibly appearing in a formula. In addition, each formula is no longer than n. Hence, by the principle of permutation and combination, at most $(10 + l)^n$ formulas (as nodes) can appear in the NFG of Q, leading to $|CL(Q)| \leq (10 + l)^n$.

In the NFG constructed by algorithm NFG for formula Q, a finite path, $\Pi = \langle Q, Q_e, Q_1, Q_{1e}, ..., \varepsilon \rangle$, is an alternating sequence of nodes and edges from the root to ε node. Actually, a finite path in the NFG of formula Q corresponds to a finite model of Q. The fact is concluded in [9].

5   Nondeterministic Finite Automata of PPTL

In this section, we show how to build a Nondeterministic Finite Automaton from an NFG. First, let us recall the definition of Nondeterministic Finite Automaton [12].

5.1   Nondeterministic Finite Automata

Definition 5. A Nondeterministic Finite Automaton is a quintuple $A = (Q, \Sigma, \delta, q_0, F)$, where,

- Q is a finite set of states
- Σ is a finite set of input symbols
- $q_0 \in Q$, is the start state
- $F \subseteq Q$, is the set of final (or accepting) states
- δ, a transition function $\delta : Q \times \Sigma \to 2^Q$

---

[3] Here , is used in the prj construct.

For an NFA, the transition function δ is extended to a function $\hat{\delta}$ that takes a state q and a string of input symbols w as its input, and returns the set of states in Q if it starts in state q and successfully processes the string w. The NFA accepts a string w if it is possible to make any sequence of choices of next state, while reading the characters of w, and go from the start state to any accepting state. The fact that other choices using the input symbols of w lead to a non-accepting state, or do not lead to any state at all (i.e., the sequence of states "dies"), doses not prevent w from being accepted by the NFA as a whole. Formally, for an NFA $A = (Q, \Sigma, \delta, q_0, F)$, then

$$L(A) = \{w \mid \hat{\delta}(q_0, w) \cap F \neq \phi\}$$

That is, $L(A)$ is the set of strings w in Σ^* such that $\hat{\delta}(q_0, w)$ contains at least one accepting state.

5.2   Constructing NFAs from NFGs

For a PPTL formula P, let P_p be the set of atomic propositions appearing in P, and $|P_p| = l$. Further, we define sets A_i $(1 \leq i \leq l)$ as follows,

$$A_i = \{\{\dot{q}_{j_1}, ..., \dot{q}_{j_i}\} \mid q_{j_k} \in P_p, 1 \leq k \leq i\}$$

Thus, the alphabet Σ for the DFA of formula P can be defined as follows,

$$\Sigma = \bigcup_{i=1}^{l} A_i \cup \{true\}$$

It can be proved that $|\Sigma| = 3^l$.

Let q_k be an atomic proposition, we define a function $atom(\bigwedge_{k=1}^{m_0} \dot{q}_k)$ for picking up atomic propositions or their negations appearing in $\bigwedge_{k=1}^{m_0} \dot{q}_k$ as follows,

$$atom(true) = \{true\}$$
$$atom(\dot{q}_1) = \begin{cases} \{q_1\}, & \text{if } \dot{q}_1 \equiv q_1 \\ \{\neg q_1\}, & \text{otherwise} \end{cases}$$
$$atom(\bigwedge_{k=1}^{m_0} \dot{q}_k) = atom(\dot{q}_1) \cup atom(\bigwedge_{k=2}^{m_0} \dot{q}_k)$$

Accordingly, algorithm NFG-NFA is given for obtaining an NFA from the NFG, $G = (CL(P), EL(P))$, of PPTL formula P. In the algorithm, each node in the NFG is transformed as a state in the corresponding NFA; each edge (P_i, P_e, P_j) forms a transition in the NFA, $P_j \in \delta(P_i, atom(P_e))$; the root node P and ε node forms the start state q_0 and the accepting state respectively. Alphabet Σ is defined as above. Further, as proved, the number of the nodes in the NFG of P meets $|CL(P)| \leq (10+l)^n$, so does the number of states in NFA, $|Q| \leq (10+l)^n$.

Example 2. (Continue Example 1) Construct NFA of formula $\neg(true; \neg \bigcirc q) \vee p \wedge \bigcirc q$.

Function NFG-NFA(G)
/* precondition: $G = (CL(P), EL(P))$ is an NFG of PPTL formula $P*/$
/* postcondition: NFG-NFA(G) computes an NFA $A = (Q, \Sigma, \delta, q_0, F)$ from G*/

---

begin function
    $Q = \phi$; $F = \phi$; $q_0 = \{P\}$; $\delta = \phi$;
    for each node $P_i \in CL(P)$,
        add a state P_i to Q, $Q = Q \cup \{P_i\}$;
        if P_i is ε, $F = F \cup \{P_i\}$;
    end for
    for each edge $(P_i, P_e, P_j) \in EL(P)$,
        $P_j \in \delta(P_i, atom(P_e))$;
    end for
    return $A = (Q, \Sigma, \delta, q_0, F)$
end function

By algorithm NFG-NFA, the NFA $A = (Q, \Sigma, \delta, q_0, F)$ for formula $\neg(true; \neg \bigcirc q) \vee p \wedge \bigcirc q$ can be obtained from the NFG G built with Example 1 as follows,

- $Q = \{q_0, q_1, q_2, q_3, q_4\}$ is obtained from the set of nodes in G, $\{v_0, v_1, v_2, v_3, \varepsilon\}$
- q_0 is v_0 in G
- $F = \{q_4\}$, since q_4 is the ε node in G
- $a_0 = atom(ture) = \{true\}$, $a_1 = atom(q) = \{q\}$, $a_2 = atom(p) = \{p\}$; $\delta(q_0, a_0) = \{q_1\}$, $\delta(q_0, a_2) = \{q_2\}$, $\delta(q_1, a_1) = \{q_1\}$, $\delta(q_2, a_1) = \{q_3\}$, $\delta(q_2, a_0) = \{q_4\}$, $\delta(q_3, a_0) = \{q_3, q_4\}$

Thus, A is depicted in Fig.2.

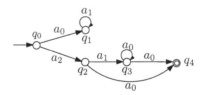

Fig. 2. NFA for $\neg(true; \neg \bigcirc q) \vee p \wedge \bigcirc q$

Given a PPTL formula P, let $M(P)$ denote the set of finite models of P, $G(P)$ the NFG of P, and $A(P)$ the DFA of P. According to algorithm NFG-NFA, for each finite path $\Pi = \langle P, P_e, P_1, P_{1e}, ..., P_{ie}, \varepsilon \rangle$ in $G(P)$, there exists a word $w = atom(P_e)atom(P_{1e})... atom(P_{ie})$ accepted by $A(P)$. Further, for an arbitrary word $w = a_0a_1...a_i$ accepted by $A(P)$, there exists a finite model $\sigma = < s_0, s_1, ..., s_i >$ in $M(P)$, where if atomic proposition $q \in a_0$, $s_i[q] = true$, otherwise if $\neg q \in a_0$, $s_i[q] = false$. Moreover, in [9], we have proved that for any finite model in $M(P)$, there exists a finite path in $G(P)$, and also for any finite path in $G(P)$, there exists a corresponding model in $M(P)$. So the relationship among $M(P)$, $G(P)$ and $A(P)$ is shown in Fig.3. Thus, we can conclude that

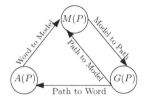

Fig. 3. Relationship among models, NFGs and DFAs

the DFA of formula P precisely characterizes the finite models of P. In a sense, the $M(P)$, $G(P)$ and $A(P)$ are equivalent.

6   Model Checking PPTL Based on SPIN

6.1   Model Checking PPTL Based on SPIN

Similar to the traditionally automata based model checking algorithm for PLTL [13], with our approach, the system M is modeled as a DFA, while the property is specified by a PPTL formula P. To check whether M satisfies P or not, $\neg P$ is transformed into an NFG, and further an NFA. The NFA can be equivalently represented as a DFA. Thus, the model checking procedure can be done by computing the product of the two automata and then deciding whether the words accepted by the product automaton is empty or not as shown in Fig. 4. If

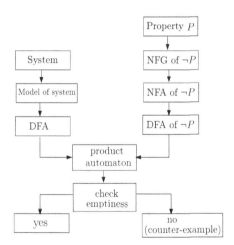

Fig. 4. Model checking PPTL

the words accepted by the product automaton is empty, the system can satisfy the property, otherwise the system cannot satisfy the property, and counter-examples are found.

To implement our method with SPIN, the model of the system is still specified in PROMELA. The property of the system is expressed by a PPTL formula. The negation of the formula is transformed into an NFG and then an NFA. Further, we transform the NFA to a DFA. By describing the DFA in terms of Never Claim, SPIN can be employed to complete the model checking procedure.

6.2   Case Studies

Example 3. The property "p is true at every odd position" is a typical example for showing the limitation of the expressive power of PLTL. Here, we present a simple system which has this property first; then specify the property by PPTL; finally illustrate how the system can be checked with our method. In Fig.5, a

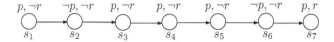

Fig. 5. Model of the system

system is shown as a Kripke structure, where p holds at states s_1, s_3, s_4, s_5 and s_7; $\neg p$ holds at states s_2 and s_6; $\neg r$ holds over the sequence except for the final state s_7. The system has a property that p holds at every odd state. The property can be specified by the following PPTL formula,

$$(len(2)^* \ prj \ (\Box p; r \wedge \varepsilon)) \wedge halt(r)$$

Accordingly, the NFG of formula $\neg((len(2)^* \ prj \ (\Box p; r \wedge \varepsilon)) \wedge halt(r))$ can be constructed as shown in Fig.6. And the corresponding NFA and DFA are shown

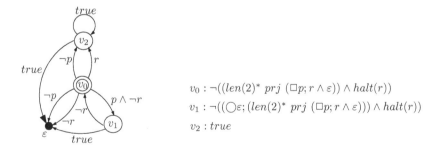

$v_0 : \neg((len(2)^* \ prj \ (\Box p; r \wedge \varepsilon)) \wedge halt(r))$

$v_1 : \neg((\bigcirc \varepsilon; (len(2)^* \ prj \ (\Box p; r \wedge \varepsilon))) \wedge halt(r))$

$v_2 : true$

Fig. 6. NFG of $\neg((len(2)^* \ prj \ (\Box p; r \wedge \varepsilon)) \wedge halt(r))$

in Fig.7 (a) and (b) respectively.

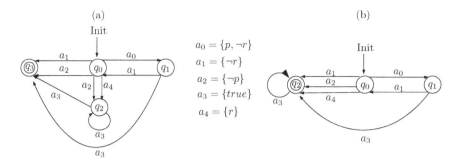

Fig. 7. NFA and DFA of $\neg((len(2)^* \ prj \ (\Box p; r \wedge \varepsilon)) \wedge halt(r))$

Further, the DFA can be expressed in Never Claim as shown in Fig.8. When implemented in SPIN, it outputs that the system satisfies the property.

```
Never{/*¬((len(2)* prj (□p;r)) ∧ halt(r))*/
       T0_init:
             if
             ::((!r)||(!p)||(r)) → goto accept_all
             ::((p) && (!r))→ goto T0_S2
             fi;
       T0_S2:
             if
             ::(!r)→ goto T0_init
             ::(1)→ goto accept_all
             fi
       accept_all:
             if
             ::skip
             ::(1)→ goto accept-all
             fi
       }
```

Fig. 8. Never Claim of $\neg((len(2)^* \ prj \ (\Box p; r \wedge \varepsilon)) \wedge halt(r))$

Example 4. This example shows how Needham-Schroeder protocol [18] can be verified by our method. In the protocol, two agents A(lice) and B(ob) try to establish a common secret over an insecure channel in such a way that both are convinced of each other's presence and no intruder can get hold of the secret without breaking the underlying encryption algorithm. The protocol is pictorially represented in Fig.9. It requires the exchanges of three messages between the participating agents. Notation such as $\langle M \rangle_C$ denotes the message M is encrypted using C's public key. Throughout, we assume the underlying encryption algorithm to be secure and the private keys of the honest agents to be uncompromised. Therefore, only agent C can decrypt $\langle M \rangle_C$ to learn M.

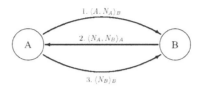

Fig. 9. Needham-Schroeder public-key protocol

1. Alice initiates the protocol by generating a random number N_A and sending the message $\langle A, N_A \rangle_B$ to Bob (numbers such as N_A are called *nonces* in cryptographic jargon, indicating that they should be used only once by any honest agent). The first component of the message informs Bob of the identity of the initiator. The second component represents one half of the secret.
2. Bob similarly generates a nonce N_B and responds with the message $\langle N_A, N_B \rangle_A$. The presence of the nonce N_A generated in the first step, which only Bob could have decrypted, convinces Alice of the authenticity of the message. She therefore accepts the pair $\langle N_A, N_B \rangle$ as the common secret.
3. Finally, Alice responds with the message $\langle N_B \rangle_B$. By the same argument as above, Bob concludes that this message must originate with Alice, and therefore also accepts $\langle N_A, N_B \rangle$ as the common secret.

We assume all messages to be sent over an insecure medium. Attackers may intercept messages, store them, and perhaps replay them later. They may also participate in ordinary runs of the protocol, initiate runs or respond to runs initiated by honest agents, who need not be aware of their partners true identity. However, even an attacker can only decrypt messages that were encrypted with his own public key.

The purpose of the protocol is to ensure mutual authentication (of honest agents) while maintaining secrecy. In other words, whenever both A and B have successfully completed a run of the protocol, then A should believe her partner to be B if and only if B believes to talk to A. Moreover, if A successfully completes a run with B then the intruder should not have learnt A's nonce, and similarly for B. These properties can be expressed in PPTL as follows:

$$\Box((statusA = ok \wedge statusB = ok) \rightarrow ((partnerA = B) \leftrightarrow (partnerB = A)))$$
$$\Box(statusA = ok \wedge partnerA = B \rightarrow \neg knows - nonceA)$$
$$\Box(statusB = ok \wedge partnerB = A \rightarrow \neg knows - nonceB)$$

We focus on the first formula. To present it in a standard way, P, Q and R are employed to denote $statusA=ok \wedge statusB=ok$, $partnerA=B$ and $partnerB=A$ respectively. Thus, we have

$$\Box(P \rightarrow (Q \leftrightarrow R))$$

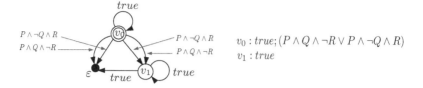

$v_0 : true; (P \wedge Q \wedge \neg R \vee P \wedge \neg Q \wedge R)$

$v_1 : true$

Fig. 10. NFG of formula $\neg\Box(P \rightarrow (Q \leftrightarrow R))$

Accordingly, $\neg\Box(P \rightarrow (Q \leftrightarrow R))$ is transformed to NFG (see Fig.10), NFA and then DFA subsequently (the NFA and DFA are depicted in Fig.11 (1) and (2) respectively). Note that, to transform the NFG of $\neg\Box(P \rightarrow (Q \leftrightarrow R))$ by Algorithm NFG, the formula is equivalently rewritten as $true; (P \wedge Q \wedge \neg R \vee P \wedge \neg Q \wedge R)$. Further, the DFA can be expressed in Never Claim as shown in Fig.12

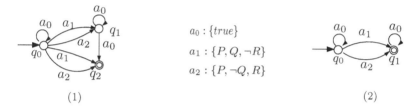

$a_0 : \{true\}$

$a_1 : \{P, Q, \neg R\}$

$a_2 : \{P, \neg Q, R\}$

(1)   (2)

Fig. 11. NFA and DFA of formula $\neg\Box(P \rightarrow (Q \leftrightarrow R))$

```
Never{/*□(P → (Q ↔ R))*/
        T0-init:
            if
            ::((P&&Q&&!R)||(P&&!Q&&R)) → goto accept-all
            ::(1)→ goto T0-init
            fi
        accept-all:
            if
            ::skip
            ::(1)→ goto accept-all
            fi
}
```

Fig. 12. Never Claim of formula $\neg\Box(P \rightarrow (Q \leftrightarrow R))$

Providing the PROMELA specification of the protocol and the Never Claim of $\neg\Box(P \rightarrow (Q \leftrightarrow R))$, SPIN declares the property violated and outputs a run that contains the attack. The run is visualized as a message sequence of chart, shown in Fig.13. Alice initiates a protocol run with Intruder who in turn (but masquerading as A) starts a run with Bob, using the nonce received in the first message. Bob replies with a message of type 2 that contains both A's and B's nonces, encrypted for A. Although agent I cannot decrypt that message itself, it forwards it to A. Unsuspecting, Alice finds her nonce, returns the second nonce to her partner I, and declares success. This time, agent I can decrypt the message, extracts B's nonce and sends it to B who is also satisfied. As a result, we have reached a state where A correctly believes to have completed a run with I, but B is fooled into believing to talk to A.

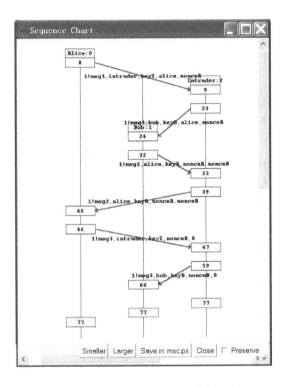

Fig. 13. Checking result of Needham-Schroeder protocol

7   Conclusions

In this paper, we have presented a model checking approach for PPTL with finite models. This enables us to verify properties of concurrent systems with PPTL by means of SPIN. To support our approach, we have developed a tool, a translator from PPTL formulas to Never Claim in C++, in which all of the algorithms presented in the paper have been implemented. The tool works well with SPIN. However, we are only concerned with finite models in this paper. In the near future, we will further investigate both finite and infinite models with our approach. Furthermore, we are motivated to develop a practical verification environment for the verification of Web services and hardware systems with a set of supporting tools based on the model checker for PPTL.

References

1. Kripke, S.A.: Semantical analysis of modal logic I: normal propositional calculi. Z. Math. Logik Grund. Math. 9, 67–96 (1963)
2. Rosner, R., Pnueli, A.: A choppy logic. In: LICS, pp. 306–314. IEEE Computer Society Press, Los Alamitos (1986)
3. Moszkowski, B.: Reasoning about digital circuits. Ph.D Thesis, Department of Computer Science, Stanford University. TRSTAN-CS-83-970 (1983)
4. Moszkowski, B.: An Automata-Theoretic Completeness Proof for Interval Temporal Logic. In: Welzl, E., Montanari, U., Rolim, J.D.P. (eds.) ICALP 2000. LNCS, vol. 1853, pp. 223–234. Springer, Heidelberg (2000)
5. Zhou, C., Hoare, C.A.R., Ravn, A.P.: A calculus of duration. Information Processing Letters 40(5), 269–275 (1991)
6. Duan, Z.: An Extended Interval Temporal Logic and A Framing Technique for Temporal Logic Programming. PhD thesis, University of Newcastle Upon Tyne (May 1996)
7. Duan, Z.: Temporal Logic and Temporal Logic Programming. Science Press, China (2006)
8. Duan, Z., Zhang, L.: A Decision Procedure for Propositional Projection Temporal Logic. Technical Report No.1, Institute of computing Theory and Technology, Xidian University, Xi'an P.R.China (2005), http://www.paper.edu.cn/process/download.jsp?file=200611-427
9. Duan, Z., Tian, C.: Decidability of Propositional Projection Temporal Logic with Infinite Models. In: TAMC 2007. LNCS, vol. 4484, pp. 521–532. Springer, Heidelberg (2007)
10. Duan, Z., Yang, X., Koutny, M.: Semantics of Framed Temporal Logic Programs. In: Gabbrielli, M., Gupta, G. (eds.) ICLP 2005. LNCS, vol. 3668, pp. 256–270. Springer, Heidelberg (2005)
11. Manna, Z., Pnueli, A.: The temporal logic of reactive and concurrent systems. Springer, Heidelberg (1992)
12. Hopcroft, J., Motwani, R., Ullman, J.: Introduction to Automata Theory, Languages and Computation, 2nd edn. Addison-Wesley, Reading (2001)
13. Vardi, M.Y., Wolper, P.: An automata-theoretic approach to automatic program verification. In: LICS 1986, pp. 332–344. IEEE CS Press, Los Alamitos (1986)
14. Dutertre, B.: Complete proof systems for first order interval temporal logic. In: Proc. 10th LICS, pp. 36–43. IEEE Computer Soc. Press, Los Alamitos (1995)
15. Holzmann, G.J.: The Model Checker Spin. IEEE Trans. on Software Engineering 23(5), 279–295 (1997)
16. McMillan, K.L.: Symbolic Model Checking. Kluwer Academic Publishers, Dordrecht (1993)
17. Lowe, G.: Breaking and fixing the Needham-Schroeder public key protocol using FDR. In: Margaria, T., Steffen, B. (eds.) TACAS 1996. LNCS, vol. 1055, pp. 147 166. Springer, Heidelberg (1996)
18. Needham, R., Schroeder, M.: Using encryption for authentication in large networks of computers. Communications of the ACM 21(12), 993–999 (1978)
19. Merz, S.: Model Checking: A Tutorial Overview. In: Cassez, F., Jard, C., Rozoy, B., Dermot, M. (eds.) MOVEP 2000. LNCS, vol. 2067, pp. 3–38. Springer, Heidelberg (2001)
20. Wolper, P.L.: Temporal logic can be more expressive. Information and Control 56, 72–99 (1983)

A Denotational Semantics for Handel-C Hardware Compilation

Juan Ignacio Perna and Jim Woodcock

Computer Science Department
The University of York
York - United Kingdom
{jiperna,jim}@cs.york.ac.uk

Abstract. Handel-C is a hybrid language based on C and CSP for the high level description of hardware components. Several semantic models for the language and a non-rigorous compilation mechanism have been proposed for it. The compilation has been empirically validated and used in commercial tools, but never formally verified. This work presents a semantic model of the generated hardware and establishes the foundations for the formal verification of correctness of the transformation approach.

1 Introduction

Handel-C [18] is a Hardware Description Language (HDL) based on the syntax of the C language extended with constructs to deal with parallel behaviour and process communications based on CSP [16]. As an example, the Handel-C source code of a two-place queue implemented with two parallel data containers is shown in figure 1.

The language is designed to target synchronous hardware components with multiple clock domains, usually implemented in Field Programmable Gate Arrays (FPGAs). Operational [9] and denotational [8,6,7] semantics have been proposed for Handel-C, providing interpretations for most constructs, ranging from simple assignments to prioritised choices (priAlts).

A model for the translation into gate-level components has also been proposed [26,25] and later applied in the implementation of commercial tools [19]. Despite the existence of formal algebraic rules to handle hardware compilation [4,2,3], the proposed translation is based on netlist graphs representing the higher level constructs. This more informal approach is justified, essentially, because of its efficiency (as a translation process) and because of the complexity of the algebraic rules.

The compilation is based on the fact that the control of the generated circuits is handled by a pair of handshake signals (*start* and *finish*). The semantics is intuitively given by the assumption that the *start* signal will be given to a circuit only if all the previous circuits have already finished. Then, the translation mechanism is designed in a way that ensures the validity of this assumption, leading to the satisfaction of a system-level assumption: "the environment will start the hardware program running just once and will not attempt to start it again before the program has completed".

M. Butler, M. Hinchey, M.M. Larrondo-Petrie (Eds.): ICFEM 2007, LNCS 4789, pp. 266–285, 2007.

```
void main(void) {
  chan unsigned int link;
  chanin unsigned int 8 input;
  chanout unsigned int 8 output;
  unsigned int state[2];

  par {
    // First queue location
    while (1) {
      input ? state[0]; link ! state[0];
    }

    // Second queue location
    while (1) {
      link ? state[1]; output ! state[1];
    }
  }
}
```

Fig. 1. Handel-C source code for a two place queue

In this context, it is relevant to provide a formal model of the translation approach and denotational semantics for the generated hardware in order to validate the whole approach. In particular, a semantic model will allow the proof of the semantic equivalence (or a *refinement* relationship) between the original source code and the generated hardware, ensuring the correctness of the compilation process.

This paper presents the first results towards the goal of formally verifying the compilation of Handel-C. In particular, we first introduce a syntax to capture the information that was graphically provided in [26,25,19] by means of a deep embedding in Higher Order Logic (HOL). Then we provide an encoding of the basic actions performed by the generated hardware and a semantic domain (an extension of sequences) that is able to describe parallel behaviour in a shared-variable environment. Finally, we present a denotational semantics for the generated hardware, including fixpoint proofs in order to ensure the existence of solutions to constructs involving control loops, such as while and communications (modelled as recursive calls in the semantics).

2 The Language

In order to abstract essential features and treat their translation in detail we present a simplified form of the original Handel-C. In particular, prioritised choice (priAlt) and multi-way synchronisation or communication are left aside from this work. The priAlt construct has been excluded because the purpose of this work is to formalise the compilation of Handel-C into hardware and this feature is not covered by published work describing this translation. Multi-way operators are simplified into their binary counterparts (the same effect can be achieved by means of nesting the binary versions as deeply as needed).

The input language consists of the following constructs:

$$c \in Circ ::=$$

$$\delta_{start,finish}$$
$$\mid v :=_{start,finish} e$$
$$\mid c_1 \|_{start,finish} c_2$$
$$\mid c_1;_{start,finish} c_2$$
$$\mid c_1 \lhd cond \rhd_{start,finish} c_2$$
$$\mid cond *_{start,finish} c$$
$$\mid ch?_{start,finish} var$$
$$\mid ch!_{start,finish} e$$

As we are focusing this work on the translation mechanism, the input language needs to account not only for the high level constructs but also the wires used in the handshaking synchronisation protocol. In particular, we have chosen to show the pair of wires associated with each construct as part of the syntax. It would also be possible to achieve the same means by having a unique identifier for each occurrence of the syntactic constructs in the program text, together with a function mapping identifiers into the corresponding pair of wire names. We have decided to include the wire identifiers in the syntax in order to have simpler semantic expressions (the alternative implies a heavy usage of the mapping to obtain the wire names every time they are needed, making the semantics more difficult to follow).

The delay construct δ propagates the signal on its start to its finish wire one clock cycle after receiving it[1]. The assignment construct propagates the start signal as delay does but updates the store location v according to the expression e just before the end of the clock cycle.

The sequential composition operator (;) achieves its usual semantics by firstly linking its start wire to the start wire of c_1. Then it wires the end wire of c_1 to the start one of c_2. Finally, it connects the finish wire of c_2 to its own finish signal. The parallel composition operator ($\|$) behaves as expected and it achieves this behaviour by wiring its start wire to the start wires of c_1 and c_2. Its finish signal is the logical-and of the finish signals of c_1 and c_2 (it memorises the individual finish signals of c_1 and c_2 to handle uneven execution times in the parallel branches).

The selection construct (if-then-else) evaluates its condition and transfers control (by setting the appropriate start signal) to the circuit on its left or right depending on the truth value of the condition. Its finish signal is set by a logical-or operation between the finish signals of both circuits.

The while construct evaluates its condition and, if true, transfers control to its body. After the completion of the body, its finish signal is looped back and used to trigger another evaluation of the whole while construct. In case the condition

---

[1] The language described in this section is a formalisation of the building blocks for the translation presented graphically in [26].

evaluates to false, the finish signal is set to true and the construct's execution finishes in the same cycle (i.e., it reduces to a form of skip).

Finally, the communication primitives (input and output), signal their presence over the communication channel and, if their counterpart is also present in the same clock cycle, the value is transferred to the variable associated with the input command. In case the communication is not possible (because the other end of the communication is not ready), the side that is trying to communicate will wait for a whole clock cycle and re-start (by setting the start signal to true through a feedback loop).

3 Translation Semantics

The input language denoted by $Circ$ defined in the previous section denotes a set of values whose structure mirrors the way in which Handel-C constructs are translated into hardware. In order to be able to analyse the validity of this translation approach, we need to define formally what we mean by the syntactic constructs defined in the previous section. The aim of this section is to present the semantic domain and denotational semantics for the approach used in the translation from Handel-C into netlists.

As pointed out in [7] the presence of a global clock synchronising all the hardware components preempts the usage of standard trace models (such as prefix-closed sets or event sequences) as the domain for the semantics. On the other hand, the absence of prioritised communication (by the exclusion of priAlts) would allow the usage of CSP-like semantic domains. However, as we intend to extend this framework to analyse prioritised choice in the future, we exclude this choice in order to guarantee the extensibility of the approach[2].

From the problem's domain, it is possible to extract five possible actions to be performed while the hardware is executing the translated code.

- *Skip*. Represents the action that consumes no time and does not modify the state of the system (neither wires nor store).
- *Wire signal transfer (WST)*. Represents the action of transmitting the value from a wire (high or low) to another one. This action is modelling a system's invariant: the linking of the end of a wire with the beginning of another one.
- *Wire set (WS)*. Models the idea of a wire in the "true" state.
- *Bus value (BV)*. Models a value being transmitted over a bus. This type of action will be used to model the value being communicated through a channel.
- *Conditional (CND)*. Stands for boolean expressions that may involve relational operators, values of the store and presence/absence of current on a given set of wires.
- *Store update (SU)*. Represents the change of value of one of the system registers (i.e., variable assignment).

---

[2] As mentioned in [17], the notion of priorities in communication guards cannot be modelled in CSP-like models.

As we are modelling Handel-C constructs and their hardware counterparts, we need a suitable formalism to express both the translation process and hardware components. In this context, Higher Order Logic (HOL) has been shown to be a very powerful framework for describing and reasoning about hardware devices [20,23,12,14]. Several HDL languages have been given semantics using HOL as the semantic domain [1]. Several approaches have been used, and they can be grouped by the kind of embedding of the syntax into HOL that they have used (shallow or deep embedding).

In our case, a deep embedding seems to be the most appropriate approach because we are interested in the translation from Handel-C into netlists and it is not clear how to encode this kind of information in a shallow approach. Also, we aim at reasoning about equivalences between the original Handel-C program and its compiled code. A deep embedding will allow us to do this by means of quantifying over syntactic structures [21], permitting us to reason about classes of programs and their translations.

In the context of HOL, it is possible to model the semantics of our "actions" as boolean predicates over a given environment (the predicates represent a particular restriction that should hold true in the current environment). This approach has been successfully applied in [23] to provide denotational semantics to CMOS circuits. Following this idea, we can define our basic set of actions as HOL boolean predicates involving wire names and store locations.

Within this framework, skip is captured by *true* (i.e., there is no additional restriction over the state) and the linking of wires is captured by the predicate $w_1 = be$, where w_1 is a wire name and be stands for a boolean relation (see [18] for a complete list of the boolean operations allowed by Handel-C) involving wire names and, possibly, some boolean operator. Similarly, the action of setting a wire is captured by $w_1 = T$, setting a bus's value by $ch = expr$, and conditionals by the appropriate boolean predicates.

The semantics of the translation is then defined based on the idea that an environment is a function that maps wire names and store locations to their corresponding values. In particular, the environment is an n-tuple of functions:

$$e \in Env ::= \langle| \; wire : String \rightarrow Bool,$$
$$store : String \rightarrow storeVal,$$
$$busVal : String \rightarrow storeVal,$$
$$time : Nat \; |\rangle$$

The *wire* function in the environment is meant to hold the current status of each wire at any given time. The information contained in this function is not only of the individual start/finish wires but also the wires signalling the presence of channel writers (c!) and readers (c?) for any given channel c.

On the other hand, the *store* component models the state space of the program, which is known to be static (because Handel-C does not support procedure names) and known at compile-time. *busVal* is a function from channel names into the value being transmitted through them (or an undefined value if the channel is not being used). Finally, the field *time* holds the current time of the system.

Having presented a way of describing the individual actions performed at the hardware level, we need to account for the advance of time and the persistence of the changes on the environment. Taking into account the synchronous nature of Handel-C (that gets reflected as well in the hardware generated from it) it is possible to group basic actions into three sets: *combinatorial actions*, *combinatorial tests* and *sequential actions*. Combinatorial actions and tests are essentially actions performed within a clock cycle. In particular, combinatorial actions will modify the state of the system in the current clock cycle (the modifications they produce on the system are not propagated further than the current clock cycle). On the other hand, combinatorial tests will not modify the state, but will deadlock the system if they do not hold (i.e., it is an error to try to "execute" a circuit without giving it the start signal). This is the way in which we capture the invariant associated with the handshaking protocol used in the compilation.

Sequential actions, on the contrary, produce changes expected to be preserved further than the current clock cycle (usually involving bi-stable components, such as flip-flops or latches). As expected, the SU action is the only action (plus skip) belonging to the sequential set while all the remaining actions belong to the combinatorial category. With this classification in mind and making use datatypes in HOL [22] we provide the class of actions used in our denotational semantics:

$$
\begin{aligned}
e \in \textit{Action} ::= \quad &\texttt{CombAction} \ \ ca \quad &&\text{where } ca \in \{\text{WST}, \text{WS}, \text{BV}, \text{Skip}\} \\
&| \ \texttt{CombTest} \ \ ct \quad &&\text{where } ct \in \{\text{CND}\} \\
&| \ \texttt{SeqAction} \ \ sa \quad &&\text{where } sa \in \{\text{SU}, \text{Skip}\}
\end{aligned}
$$

With this, we have defined the basic actions of the system. We now need to focus on the sequencing of these actions. From partial correctness analysis, it is well known [15,24] that in a language including parallel composition and shared variables it is not possible to reason semantically about partial correctness of a statement in isolation. In this sense, we need a semantic domain that allows us to account for actions happening in parallel and to describe their effects when executed in this way.

With this idea in mind we interpret our actions (i.e., the *boolean predicates*) as *state transformers* following the ideas presented in [5,7]. In this way, actions can be seen as functions partially modifying the environment (instead of returning a whole new updated environment) and the effects of parallel actions can be composed together (in our case, conjoined together).

The problem of this approach, however, is that the semantics are expressing the way in which the execution may (or may not) modify the state, so we need to be able to explicitly represent different alternative "execution" paths in our semantic domain. To cope with this, we define a branching sequences semantic domain with the following constructors:

$$e \in BSeq ::= \quad \texttt{Empty}$$
$$\mid \texttt{LNode } Action \rightarrow BSeq$$
$$\mid \texttt{BNode } Action \rightarrow BSeq \rightarrow BSeq$$
$$\mid \texttt{SmNode } Circ \rightarrow BSeq$$
$$\mid \texttt{ParNode } BSeq \rightarrow Action \rightarrow BSeq \rightarrow Action \rightarrow BSeq$$

The first two constructors correspond directly to the standard constructors for lists (the empty list and the "linear" sequence). $\texttt{BNode}$ stands for control flow decisions: its first element is meant to hold the logical condition that determines the execution flow, while its second and third elements are placeholders for the paths to be followed if the branching condition is true or false respectively.

The $\texttt{SmNode}$ constructor models the loop-back of control signals used to define iteration and communication and it is, essentially, a deep embedding of tail recursion (the following section will go further into details about this constructor).

On the other hand, $\texttt{ParNode}$, is meant to capture actions being performed in parallel. Its first and third arguments are placeholders for the semantic expressions of each of the two parallel branches. The actions in its second and fourth arguments, on the other hand, are meant for expressing combinatorial circuitry in order to hold the finish signal (for as many cycles as needed) of the circuit running in parallel with the shortest execution time (all parallel branches must synchronise at the end of the parallel construct).

Based on its three first constructors and its general idea, our approach resembles the branching sequences domain presented in [7] but we present two new constructors: $\texttt{SmNode}$ and $\texttt{ParNode}$. Both are a consequence of the usage of a deep-embedding. In previous related works [6,8,7,10], the notion captured by $\texttt{SmNode}$ in our semantics was just expressed by tail-recursive or fixpoint equations. On the other hand, the presence of nodes that may expand into further sequences (i.e., several nodes of the $\texttt{SmNode}$ kind), preempts the usage of a parallel-flattening operator and this forces the explicit representation of parallel behaviour by means of the $\texttt{ParNode}$ constructor.

Having defined the domain for our denotational semantics, we just need to define an operator to concatenate elements of type Seq. We do so by defining:

$$concat : BSeq \rightarrow BSeq \rightarrow BSeq$$
$$(concat \ a \ \texttt{Empty}) = a = (concat \ \texttt{Empty} \ a)$$
$$(concat \ (\texttt{SmNode } c \ r) \ a) = (\texttt{SmNode } c \ (concat \ r \ a)))$$
$$(concat \ (\texttt{LNode } ac \ r) \ a) = (\texttt{LNode } ac \ (concat \ r \ a)))$$
$$(concat \ (\texttt{BNode } ct \ b_1 \ b_2) \ a) = (\texttt{BNode } ct \ (concat \ b_1 \ a) \ (concat \ b_2 \ a)))$$
$$(concat \ (\texttt{ParNode } b_1 \ a_1 \ b_2 \ a_2 \ r) \ a) = (\texttt{ParNode } b_1 \ a_1 \ b_2 \ a_2 \ (concat \ r \ a))$$

3.1   The Semantics

Using the branching sequences domain defined in the previous section, a denotational semantics can be given to elements of type $Circ$ by defining a semantic function $Sm : Circ \rightarrow Env \rightarrow Seq$ that maps circuit terms and an environment to branching sequences of boolean predicates.

In order to keep the presentation compact, we adopt some shorthands for the actions and constructors in the domain. In particular, we represent applications of $(\texttt{CombAction}\ a)$ just by a; $(\texttt{CombTest}\ ct)$ as $(ct)^{\perp}$ and $(\texttt{SeqAction}\ sa)$ as $\lfloor sa \rfloor$.

Regarding Seq elements, $\texttt{Empty}$ will be modelled as $[]$, the application of $\texttt{LNode}$ to an action a and a sequence s will be modelled $a : s$. The branching constructor $\texttt{BNode}$ applied to a condition c and with alternative branches b_1 and b_2 will be expressed as $c \rightarrow b_1 \mid b_2$. Occurrences of the $\texttt{SmNode}$ constructor applied to a circuit c followed by the sequence s will be presented as $[\![c]\!] : s$. On the other hand, applications of the type $(\texttt{ParNode}\ b_1\ a_1\ b_2\ a_2\ r)$ will be expressed as $(b_1 \Rightarrow a_1) \parallel (b_2 \Rightarrow a_2) : r$. Finally, applications of the type $(\texttt{concat}\ s_1\ s_2)$ will be expressed as $s_1 \boxplus s_2$, where $\boxplus$ is just the infix, left-associative version of the $\texttt{concat}$ function.

The semantics for the constructor $\texttt{Delay}$ can, then, be stated as follows:

$$(\texttt{Sm}\ \delta_{start,finish}) \equiv (start)^{\perp} : \lfloor skip \rfloor : finish : []$$

It states that if properly started (by means of the assertion over the $start$ wire), its operation ends one clock cycle later by releasing the control (by signaling a high pulse on $finish$).

On the other hand, the assignment is a delay block plus the proper modification over the store.

$$(\texttt{Sm}\ v :=_{start,finish}\ ex) \equiv (start)^{\perp} : \lfloor v = ex \rfloor : finish : []$$

In order to describe the semantics of sequential and parallel composition, it is necessary to define a projection operator. Projection over circuits of type $Circ$ is defined as the function $\pi_{x \in \{start,finish\}} : Circ \rightarrow String$ where, for example, $\pi_{start}(\delta_{start,finish}) = start$.

With the projection operator, it is possible to define the semantics of the sequential composition as:

$$(\texttt{Sm}\ c_1\ {}^{\circ}_{\mathfrak{s}start,finish}\ c_2) \equiv (\pi_{start}\ c_1) = start : (\texttt{Sm}\ c_1) \boxplus$$
$$(\pi_{start}\ c_2) = (\pi_{finish}\ c_1) : (\texttt{Sm}\ c_2) \boxplus finish = (\pi_{finish}\ c_2) : []$$

The semantics of the sequential composition initially transfers its start signal to the first circuit. Then it expands its semantics and turns its finish signal into the start signal of the second circuit. The process is then repeated with the second circuit but turning its finish signal into the composition's finish signal.

Regarding the semantics of the parallel composition operator, it first transfers its start signal to its parallel components. Then, each branch expands the appropriate semantic sequence (of the circuit being placed in parallel) and holds at the end a combinatorial action to preserve the finish signal (in case a parallel branch finishes earlier than the other).

$$(\texttt{Sm}\ c_1 \|_{start,finish} c_2) \equiv (\pi_{start}\ c_1) = start \land (\pi_{start}\ c_2) = start :$$
$$((\texttt{Sm}\ c_1) \Rightarrow (\pi_{finish}\ c_1)) \parallel ((\texttt{Sm}\ c_2) \Rightarrow (\pi_{finish}\ c_2)) :$$
$$finish = (\pi_{finish}\ c_1) \land (\pi_{finish}\ c_2) : []$$

Note that the flip-flop used in the actual translation to hardware from Handel-C is not directly stated in the semantics. In the hardware translator, it is necessary to store the *finish token* produced by each individual circuit in order to make sure that the finish signal of the parallel composition represents that all the parallel circuits have finished. In the case of the semantics, the same result is achieved by means of explicitly signaling the finish of each branch at the end of the parallel composition.

The semantics of the selection (`if-then-else`) construct is given by the conditional expansion of the proper circuit depending on the boolean expression guarding the conditional. The selected circuit is then expanded and the start/finish signals of the whole selection are bound to those of the selected circuit.

$$(\text{Sm } c_1 \vartriangleleft cond \vartriangleright_{start,finish} c_2) \equiv cond \rightarrow$$
$$((\pi_{start} \ c_1) = start : (\text{Sm } c_1) \boxplus finish = (\pi_{finish} \ c_1) : []) \ |$$
$$((\pi_{start} \ c_2) = start : (\text{Sm } c_2) \boxplus finish = (\pi_{finish} \ c_2) : [])$$

In the case of the guarded iteration (`while`), the semantics are provided by means of a deep embedding of a tail recursive equation. In particular, the evaluation of the boolean guard to true yields the expansion of the circuit in the body of the while (setting the value of the start signal appropriately). Then, the whole while construct should be expanded again, using the finish signal of the current body's execution as start signal. In case the evaluation of the boolean guard fails, the while circuit finishes reducing to skip.

In our approach, we combine the deep embedding with a *lazy* approach: we don't expand the re-invocation of the while construct, but we denote it with a particular constructor (`SmNode`). The prune operator (see section 3.3) will do the actual expansion if it is needed. This approach simplifies the mechanisation of our semantics and it is easily proven to be semantically equivalent.

$$(\text{Sm } (cond *_{start,finish} b) \ e) \equiv (start)^{\perp} : cond \rightarrow$$
$$((\pi_{start} \ b) = start : (\text{Sm } b) \boxplus$$
$$start = (\pi_{finish} \ b) : [\![cond *_{start,finish} b]\!]) : [] \ |$$
$$(finish : [])$$

Notice that in the translation to hardware, the activation of the while's body (b) depends on the conjunction of the boolean condition and a second signal. This second signal is the disjunction of the start signal of the while circuit with the output of b's previous execution. The main reason for this activation logic is to preempt the execution of b by the sole fact of having the while's condition set to true (i.e., without the start signal). Given the fact that the start signal is set to true only at the activation time of the while, either the start signal of the while or the feedback from a previous b's execution are used to control the current activation of b. We achieve the same effect by setting the start signal of the next recursive expansion of the whole while to the finish signal of the current instance of b.

Finally, the semantics for the **Input** and **Output** operations over channels, are based on two special wires ($ch?$ and $ch!$) and one bus ch. The elements in the pair of wires represent, respectively, the presence of a reader and writer over channel ch. The bus ch, on the other hand, is meant to hold the value being transmitted when the communication is successful. It is also important to point out that the (channel-wise) centralised arbitration mechanism described in the actual translation has been distributed into guards on both the Input and Output circuits' semantics.

$$(\text{Sm } ch?_{start,finish} \ var) \equiv (start)^{\perp} :$$
$$ch? : (ch! \rightarrow (\lfloor var = ch \rfloor : finish : []) \ | $$
$$(\lfloor skip \rfloor : start : \llbracket ch?_{start,finish} \ var \rrbracket) : [])$$

From the semantics for the Input command it is possible to see that the first action of the circuit is to check for the start token and to flag the presence of the reader over the channel at the moment of execution. Then, the control flow splits depending on the presence or absence of the writer over the channel. If the communication counterpart is present and ready to communicate, the Input command updates the store according to the value being transmitted over the bus and then emits the finish signal. In case that there is no writer willing to communicate, a clock cycle is spent *waiting*, the start signal re-established and the Input command re-initiated.

$$(\text{Sm } ch!_{start,finish} \ ex) \equiv (start)^{\perp} :$$
$$ch! : (ch? \rightarrow (ch = ex : \lfloor skip \rfloor : finish : []) \ | $$
$$(\lfloor skip \rfloor : start : \llbracket (ch!_{start,finish} \ ex) \rrbracket) : [])$$

The Output command semantics behaves similarly to the Input one. The main difference is after engaging in the communication: the Input command will first set the value being transmitted in the appropriate bus. After that, it will reduce to a one-clock cycle delay (the rest of the actions take place on the readers' side of the communication).

3.2 Fixpoints

As the semantic definitions of While, Input and Output involve (tail) recursive equations, it is necessary to assure the existence of an appropriate semantic domain with fixpoint guaranteeing the existence of solutions for them.

The idea is to establish a semantic domain with an associated *complete partial order* (cpo), this is, a set with a partial-ordering v, a least element $\perp$, and limits of all non-empty chains [11]. In turn, the semantics are described in terms of continuous functions, i.e., functions between cpos that preserve the partial-order and limit structure.

We firstly extended Seq with a bottom element $\perp$ to get $Seq_{\perp} ::= Seq \cup \perp$ and defined our ordering over $Seq_{\perp}$ as the smallest relation $\preceq$ satisfying:

$$\bot \preceq \sigma$$

$$a : \sigma \preceq a : \tau \Leftrightarrow \sigma \preceq \tau$$

$$cond(\sigma_1 \mid \sigma_2) \preceq cond(\tau_1 \mid \tau_2) \Leftrightarrow \sigma_i \preceq \tau_i$$

$$[\![circ]\!] : \sigma \preceq circ : \tau \Leftrightarrow \sigma \preceq \tau$$

$$(\sigma_i \Rightarrow a) \parallel (\tau_i \Rightarrow a) : \gamma \preceq (\eta_i \Rightarrow a) \parallel (\theta_i \Rightarrow a) : \gamma \Leftrightarrow \sigma_i \preceq \eta_i \wedge \tau_i \preceq \theta_i$$

Then we used the HOL system [13] to prove that the relation $\preceq$ is a partial order. After defining the types $Circ$, $Action$ and $Seq_\bot$ in HOL, we defined the relation $\preceq$ and proved it is a partial order. In particular, the proofs of all the properties follow from inductively applying the definition of $\preceq$. We only show here the proof for the transitive property, the other ones follow a similar approach.

```
val ord_trans = store_thm("ord_trans",
  ``!s1 s2 s3. (ord s1 s2) /\ (ord s2 s3) ==> (ord s1 s3)``,
  (Induct_on 's1') THEN (Induct_on 's2') THEN (Induct_on 's3')
  THEN PURE_REWRITE_TAC [ord_def] THEN PROVE_TAC []);
```

In order to establish the existence of fixpoints, we also need to show that the constructors in Seq and the concatenation operator are monotonic regarding the relation $\preceq$.

The proofs for `Bottom` and `Empty` are trivial from the definition of order so we omit them. The proof for `LNode` and `SmNode` are similar and straightforward from their definition:

```
val LNode_mono = store_thm("LNode_mono"
  ``!x seq1 seq2. (ord seq1 seq2) ==>
  (ord (LNode x seq1) (LNode x seq2))``, REWRITE_TAC [ord_def]);
```

For the rest of the constructors, we need to prove they are monotonic on all of their arguments. The proof for the `BNode` constructor is almost immediate by the order's definition and its reflexivity.

```
val BNode_left_mono = store_thm("BNode_left_mono",
  ``!cond seq seq1 seq2. (ord seq1 seq2) ==>
    (ord (BNode cond seq1 seq) (BNode cond seq2 seq))``,
  REWRITE_TAC [ord_def] THEN PROVE_TAC [ord_refl]);

val BNode_right_mono = store_thm("BNode_right_mono",
  ``!cond seq seq1 seq2. (ord seq1 seq2) ==>
    (ord (BNode cond seq seq1) (BNode cond seq seq2))``,
  REWRITE_TAC [ord_def] THEN PROVE_TAC [ord_refl]);
```

In the case of the `ParNode` constructor we need to prove that the order is preserved not only on both of the parallel branches, but also in the sequence that follows it. Here we present the proof of monotonicity on the left parallel branch (the remaining ones follow the same pattern).

```
val ParNode_left_mono = store_thm("ParNode_left_mono",
  ``!ia aa s0 s1 s2 s3. (ord s1 s2) ==>
    (ord (ParNode s1 ia s0 aa s3) (ParNode s2 ia s0 aa s3))``,
  REWRITE_TAC [ord_def] THEN PROVE_TAC [ord_refl]);
```

Finally, we have to verify that the concatenation function preserves the order as well. Firstly, we extend it in order to handle $\perp$ by adding the clause (*concat* $\perp$ *a* = $\perp$) to its definition ($\perp$ is a left zero for the function). With the extended definition, we prove that concat is monotonic on its first argument (by structural induction on its arguments).

```
val concat_left_mono = store_thm("concat_left_mono",
  ``!s1 s2 s.(ord s1 s2) ==>
        (ord (concat s1 s) (concat s2 s))``,
  (Induct_on 's1') THEN (Induct_on 's2') THEN (Induct_on 's')
  THEN PURE_REWRITE_TAC [ord_def, concat_def]
  THEN RW_TAC std_ss [ord_def,ord_refl]);
```

In order to prove monotonicity on concat's second argument, we first need to prove two results: (a) that concat preserves the order when handling $\perp$ and (b) that concat preserves $\preceq$'s reflexivity. The proof for (a) follows by induction on the sequence being concatenated with $\perp$ and from $\preceq$'s and concat's definitions.

```
val lemma1 = store_thm("lemma1",
  ``!s. (ord (concat s Bottom) s)``,
  Induct_on 's' THEN PURE_REWRITE_TAC [ord_def, concat_def]
  THEN RW_TAC std_ss [ord_def,ord_refl]);
```

The proof for (b) is by induction on sequences being concatenated, the definitions concat and by of $\preceq$'s definition and reflexivity.

```
val lemma2 = store_thm("lemma2",
  ``!s1 s2. (ord (concat s1 s2) (concat s1 s2))``,
  Induct_on 's1' THEN Induct_on 's2'
  THEN PURE_REWRITE_TAC [ord_def, concat_def, ord_refl]
  THEN RW_TAC std_ss [ord_def,ord_refl]);
```

Using the previous results, the proof of right monotonicity follows by induction on the sequences being concatenated and by the definitions of $\preceq$ and concat, and their properties.

```
val concat_right_mono = store_thm("concat_right_mono",
  ``!s1 s2 s.(ord s1 s2) ==>
        (ord (concat s s1) (concat s s2))``,
  (Induct_on 's1') THEN (Induct_on 's2') THEN (Induct_on 's')
  THEN PURE_REWRITE_TAC [ord_def, concat_def, lemma1, lemma2]
  THEN TRY (RW_TAC std_ss [ord_def,ord_refl,prop])
  THEN TRY (METIS_TAC [ord_def]));
```

3.3 Getting the Actual Execution Path's Semantics

So far we have described the semantics of the translation from Handel-C into netlists as branching sequences and proved the existence of fixpoint solutions to our recursive semantic equations. In particular, the semantics is providing a tree of actions that captures all possible execution paths of the circuit being analysed. In order to complete the semantic description of the generated circuit, we need to flatten the structure of the execution tree and provide the actual execution path and outcome of the program.

In order to keep the presentation compact, we define two auxiliary functions: $updateEnv : Env \rightarrow Action \rightarrow Env$ and $flattenEnv : Env \rightarrow Env$. As expected, the former updates the environment according to the action passed as argument by means of rewriting the appropriate function using λ-abstractions. On the other hand, $flattenEnv$ is meant to be used to generate a new environment after a clock cycle edge. In particular, it flattens all wire values (to the logical value false), resets the bus values to the undefined value and advances the timestamp in one unit.

With our auxiliary functions, we define the *flattening* operator $prune : Env \rightarrow BSeq \rightarrow (Env, BSeq) \cup \checkmark \cup \perp$ that advances one step at a time over the sequence of possible actions and updates the environment accordingly. With the updated environment information available, $prune$ is also able to select the appropriate path when a condition branches the control flow of the program. Given an environment e, we define $prune$ over $s \in Seq$ as follows:

If the empty branching sequence of actions is reached, then the execution is successful $\left(\overline{(prune\ e,\ [])\longrightarrow\checkmark}\right)$.

Pruning a sequence of actions starting with the combinatorial action a modifies the state according to this first action and leaves the rest of actions pending for execution $\left(\overline{(prune\ e,\ a{:}s)\longrightarrow((updateEnv\ e\ a),\ s)}\right)$.

On the contrary, a sequence of actions starting with an assertion *cond* will proceed and leave the state unchanged if the condition holds in the current environment $\left(\dfrac{cond(e)}{(prune\ e,\ (cond)^{\perp}{:}s)\longrightarrow(e,\ s)}\right)$. On the other hand, if *cond* does not hold, the system deadlocks $\left(\dfrac{\neg cond(e)}{(prune\ e,\ (cond)^{\perp}{:}s)\longrightarrow\perp}\right)$.

Pruning a sequence starting with a sequential action $\lfloor a \rfloor$ will flatten the environment (i.e., set all wires and buses to the low value and advance the clock count in one) and perform the action a on the new environment $\left(\overline{(prune\ e,\ \lfloor a \rfloor{:}s)\longrightarrow((updateEnv\ (flattenEnv\ e)\ a),\ s)}\right)$.

A branching node depending on the condition *cond* will select its left or right sequence depending on the truth value of the condition in the current environment. If the condition holds, then the left sequence is chosen $\left(\left(\dfrac{cond(e)}{(prune\ e,\ cond\rightarrow(s_1)\ |\ (s_2))\longrightarrow(e,\ s_1)}\right)\right)$; in case the condition does not hold, the right sequence is chosen instead $\left(\dfrac{\neg cond(e)}{(prune\ e,\ cond\rightarrow(s_1)\ |\ (s_2))\longrightarrow(e,\ s_2)}\right)$.

Pruning a SmNode leads to its evaluation (using the semantic function Sm) and the SmNode itself being replaced by the result of this evaluation $\left(\dfrac{(Sm\ c)=s_c}{(prune\ e,\ [\![c]\!]{:}s)\longrightarrow(e,\ s_c \boxplus s)}\right)$.

The remaining constructor, `ParNode`, is not straightforward to be handled and increases the complexity of the *prune* function. This is so because it is possible to have nested parallel constructors and we need to keep the execution of all the parallel branches while preserving the original semantics of Handel-C. To achieve this we need to define how the basic actions in our semantics are going to be executed when found in parallel with other actions. In particular, we have defined three classes of actions in our semantics: *combinatorial actions*, *combinatorial tests* and *sequential actions*. In order to preserve the semantics, we need our prune operator to account for these categories and to treat them accordingly. In particular, we want:

- To prioritise *combinatorial actions* over *combinatorial tests*. Combinatorial tests will either branch the control flow (in the case of a *BNode* selector) or validate/stop the system's execution (in the case of an assertion). In order to be able to select the right action, we need as much information as possible, justifying the priorities of combinatorial actions over tests.
- To order the evaluation of combinatorial tests. The class of combinatorial tests collects three kinds of conditions: *assertions* (ASRs) (referring to verifications over control signals), *control flow decisions* (CFDs) (control flow changes due to `while` and `selection` constructs) and *communication conditions* (CCs) (verifications of the presence of both sides in a communication event).

  In particular, ASRs verify the "sanity" of the the execution's control system. As we want to detect flaws of this kind at the earliest possible stage, we give them the highest priority among conditionals.

  CFDs, on the other hand, depend only on the current environment and are independent of other actions being performed in parallel with them provided that all the pertinent combinatorial actions have been already performed before them.

  Finally, as the evaluation of CCs depend on the presence (over another parallel branch) of the counterpart over a channel, we need defer their evaluation after all other conditions. A clear example of the reason for this choice arises, for example, in (`while b {ch?a} || ch!val`). In this case, we eventually reach a point in the execution where we have a CFD (the evaluation of `b`) in parallel with a CC (the verification of the presence of the reader in the semantics of `ch!val`). If we allow the CC to be evaluated first, it will (wrongly) assume that there is no reader to synchronize with in the current clock cycle and turn the output command into a delay. On the other hand, the evaluation of the while's condition first, produces the right result.
- To give priority to all combinatorial fragments (actions and tests) over *sequential actions*. As sequential actions signal the end of the current clock cycle, any combinatorial fragment left for execution after the sequential actions will belong to the next clock cycle, leading to erroneous results.
- To synchronise the parallel execution of all actions at the same level of priority. If not done in this way, an action a_1 may not be chosen for execution at its priority level (another action a_0 of the same kind is selected for execution) and never get to be executed again because the actions following a_0 are of higher

priority than a_1. In the case of *sequential actions*, this is as well fundamental to achieve the synchronous behaviour reinforced by Handel-C's semantics.

With these considerations in mind, we define a priority system over our semantic actions implemented by a function *priority* : $Action \rightarrow \mathbb{N}$ that implements the following ordering over actions: $\texttt{CombActions} \prec ASRs \prec CFDs \prec CCs \prec \texttt{SeqActions}$.

In order to make the semantics clearer, we define three auxiliary functions: *getPriority*, *colActions* and *doActions*. The first one, *getPriority* : $Seq \rightarrow \mathbb{N}$, traverses the branching structure of the parallel node(s) (probably nested) getting the priority of the first available action on each of them. The highest collected priority is returned.

The second function, *colActions* : $Seq \rightarrow \mathbb{N} \rightarrow (\{Action\}, Seq)$, looks in the head of the branching sequence passed as argument and collects all available actions that match the priority level given as second argument. It returns the set of collected actions together with an updated sequence (the original argument without the actions that have been selected for execution).

Finally, *doActions* : $\{Action\} \rightarrow Env \rightarrow Env$, will perform the set of selected actions and update the the current environment appropriately.

With the priority system and the auxiliary functions, the *prune* function will, on each step, select the current priority level p from all the actions ready to be executed (i.e., the highest priority among the first actions of each of the parallel branches) and execute all the available actions at level p in parallel. The following rules describe the way *prune* handles the $\texttt{ParNode}$ constructor (symmetric cases ommited):

$$\frac{p_1 = (priority\ s_1) \wedge p_2 = (priority\ s_2) \wedge p_1 \geq p_2}{(e,\ (s_1{:}ss_1 \Rightarrow r_1) \| (s_2{:}ss_2 \Rightarrow r_2){:}r) \longrightarrow \textbf{let}\ (ac_1,\ ns_1) = (colActions\ p_1\ s_1),\ (ac_2,\ ns_2) = (colActions\ p_1\ s_2)\ \textbf{in}\ ((doActions\ (ac_1 \cup ac_2),\ e),\ (ns_1 \boxplus ss_1 \Rightarrow r_1) \| (ns_2 \boxplus ss_2 \Rightarrow r_2){:}r)}$$

$$\frac{p_1 = (priority\ s_1)}{(e,\ (s_1{:}ss_1 \Rightarrow r_1) \| ([]\Rightarrow r_2){:}r) \longrightarrow \textbf{let}\ (ac_1,\ nf_1) = (colActions\ p_1\ f_1)\ \textbf{in}\ ((doActions\ ac_1,\ e),\ (nf_1 \boxplus ss_1 \Rightarrow r_1) \| ([]\Rightarrow r_2){:}r)}$$

$$\frac{}{(e,\ ([] \Rightarrow r_1) \| ([] \Rightarrow r_2){:}r) \longrightarrow ((doActions[r_1 + {+}r_2],\ e),\ r)}$$

4   Testing the Semantics

In this section we present some examples to illustrate the way the semantics are generated by the $\texttt{Sm}$ function and how *prune* flattens the branching structure.

Firstly we present the case of two threads sharing global variables:

$$((x :=_{s_1, f_1} 1)\ \S_{s_5, f_5}\ (x :=_{s_2, f_2} x + y)\ \|_{s_7, f_7}\ (y :=_{s_3, f_3} 2))\ \S_{s_6, f_6}\ (y :=_{s_4, f_4} y - x)$$

We apply $\texttt{Sm}$ to get the sequence of semantic actions and obtain:

$$s_7 = s_6 :$$ sequential composition start

$$s_5 = s_7 \wedge s_3 = s_7 :$$ parallel start signal propagation

$$(s_1 = s_5 : (s_1)^{\perp} : \lfloor x = 1 \rfloor : f_1 :$$ $$x := 1$$

$$s_2 = f_1 : (s_2)^{\perp} : \lfloor x = x + y \rfloor : f_2 :$$ $$x := x + y$$

$$f_5 = f_2$$ sequential composition finishes

$$\Rightarrow f_5)$$

$$\|$$

$$((s_3)^{\perp} : \lfloor y = 2 \rfloor : f_3 :$$ $$y = 2$$

$$\Rightarrow f_3) :$$

$$f_7 = (f_5 \wedge f_3)$$ parallel composition finishes

$$s_2 = f_7 : (s_2)^{\perp} : \lfloor y = y - x \rfloor : f_2 :$$ $$y = y - x$$

$$f_6 = f_2$$ sequential composition finishes

In order to make the presentation clearer, we introduce $\mathcal{W}, \mathcal{S}$ and τ to represent the *wire*, *store* and *time* components of the environment respectively. We also introduce two function shorthands: Ξ (that flattens all wires and buses to the logical value false) and $\oplus$ (function overriding). With this compact notation and an initial environment $e = \langle |wire = \lambda x.\ \text{if } x = s_6 \text{ then } T \text{ else } F,\ store = \lambda s.\ ?,\ busVal = \lambda b.\ ?,\ time = 0| \rangle$, we apply the *prune* operator to obtain:

Now we present two parallel processes trying to communicate over a channel (c) but one of the sides has to wait:

$$((y :=_{s_4, f_4} 10;_{s_6, f_6} c!_{s_5, f_5} y) \|_{s_7, f_7} (c?_{s_1, f_1} x;_{s_3, f_3} c =_{s_2, f_2} c + 1))$$

$(prune\ e, s_6 = s_7 \wedge s_3 = s_7 : ...)$	$\mathcal{W} \oplus \{s_6 = T, s_3 = T\}$
$(prune\ e, (s_4 = s_6 : ...) \| (s_1 = s_3 : ...))$	$\mathcal{W} \oplus \{s_4 = T, s_1 = T\}$
$(prune\ e, ((s_4)^{\perp} : ...) \| ((c_1)^{\perp} : ...))$	e
$(prune\ e, (...) \| (c?...))$	$\mathcal{W} \oplus \{c? = T\}$
$(prune\ e, (...) \| ((c!) \rightarrow ...))$	e (false branch selected)
$(prune\ e, (\lfloor y = 10 \rfloor : ...) \| (\lfloor skip \rfloor : ...))$	$\mathcal{S} \oplus \{y \rightarrow 10\} \wedge \tau - 1 \wedge \Xi(e)$
$(prune\ e, (f_4 : ...) \| (s_1 : ...))$	$\mathcal{W} \oplus \{f_4 = T \wedge s_1 = T\}$
$(prune\ e, (s_5 = f_4 : ...) \| (...))$	$\mathcal{W} \oplus \{s_5 = T\}$
$(prune\ e, (...) \| (\llbracket c?_{s_1, f_1} x \rrbracket : ...))$	e
$(prune\ e, ((s_5)^{\perp} : ...) \| ((s_1)^{\perp}...))$	e
$(prune\ e, (c! : ...) \| (c? : ...))$	$\mathcal{W} \oplus \{c! = T \wedge c? = T\}$

$$(prune\ e, s_7 = s_6 : ...) \qquad \mathcal{W} \oplus \{s_7 = T\}$$
$$(prune\ e, s_5 = s_7 \wedge s_3 = s_7 : (...) \parallel (...)) \qquad \mathcal{W} \oplus \{s_5 = T, s_3 = T\}$$
$$(prune\ e, (s_1 = s_5 : ...) \parallel (...)) \qquad \mathcal{W} \oplus \{s_1 = T\}$$
$$(prune\ e, ((s_1)^{\perp} : ...) \parallel ((s_3)^{\perp}...)) \qquad e$$
$$(prune\ e, (\lfloor x = 1 \rfloor : ...) \parallel (\lfloor y = 2 \rfloor : ...)) \qquad \mathcal{S} \oplus \{x \to 1, y \to 2\} \wedge \tau = 1 \wedge \Xi(e)$$
$$(prune\ e, (f_1 : ...) \parallel (f_3 : ...)) \qquad \mathcal{W} \oplus \{f_1 = T, f_3 = T\}$$
$$(prune\ e, (s_2 = f_1 : ...) \parallel (\lfloor \rfloor \Rightarrow ...)) \qquad \mathcal{W} \oplus \{s_2 = T\}$$
$$(prune\ e, ((s_2)^{\perp} : ...) \parallel (\lfloor \rfloor \Rightarrow ...)) \qquad e$$
$$(prune\ e, (\lfloor x = x + y \rfloor : ...) \parallel (\lfloor \rfloor \Rightarrow ...)) \qquad \mathcal{S} \oplus \{x \to 1 + 2\} \wedge \tau = 2 \wedge \Xi(e)$$
$$(prune\ e, (f_2 : ...) \parallel (\lfloor \rfloor \Rightarrow ...)) \qquad \mathcal{W} \oplus \{f_2 = T\}$$
$$(prune\ e, (f_5 = f_2 : ...) \parallel (\lfloor \rfloor \Rightarrow ...)) \qquad \mathcal{W} \oplus \{f_5 = T\}$$
$$(prune\ e, (\lfloor \rfloor \Rightarrow f_5) \parallel (\lfloor \rfloor \Rightarrow f_3)) \qquad \mathcal{W} \oplus \{f_5 = T \wedge f_3 = T\}$$
$$(prune\ e, f_7 = (f_5 \wedge f_3) : ...) \qquad \mathcal{W} \oplus \{f_7 = T\}$$
$$(prune\ e, s_2 = f_7 : ...) \qquad \mathcal{W} \oplus \{s_2 = T\}$$
$$(prune\ e, (s_2)^{\perp} : ...) \qquad e$$
$$(prune\ e, (\lfloor y = y - x \rfloor : ...)) \qquad \mathcal{S} \oplus \{y \to 2 - 3\} \wedge \tau = 3, \Xi(e)$$
$$(prune\ e, f_2 : ...) \qquad \mathcal{W} \oplus \{f_2 = T\}$$
$$(prune\ e, f_6 = f_2 : ...) \qquad \mathcal{W} \oplus \{f_6 = T\}$$

Using the same conventions described in the previous example plus $\mathcal{B}$ for the bus component in the environment, the *prune* function processes flattens the semantics of this construct as follows.

5   Conclusions and Future Work

We have presented a suitable semantic domain and used it to provide denotational semantics to the translation from Handel-C into hardware-level descriptions. The main contribution of this work is the formalisation of the translation approach that has been validated and applied in several academic and industrial projects but has not been, yet, formally verified.

In particular, our semantic domain is an extension of the branching sequences presented in [7,10] that is able to cope with low level hardware actions and that captures the control-flow structure that is used in the current translation approach. We have modelled the semantics by means of a deep embedding into Higher Order Logic and mechanically verified the existence of fixpoint solutions to the semantic equations involving recursion using the HOL system.

As the main goal of this work is to provide a formal verification of the translation from Handel-C into hardware components, we still need to prove that the

$$s_6 = s_7 \wedge s_3 = s_7 \qquad\qquad\qquad \text{parallel composition start propagation}$$
$$(s_4 = s_6 : \qquad\qquad\qquad\qquad \text{sequential composition starts}$$
$$(s_4)^\perp : \lfloor y = 10 \rfloor : f_4 : \qquad\qquad\qquad\qquad y := 10$$
$$s_5 = f_4 : \qquad\qquad\qquad\qquad \text{sequential link}$$
$$(s_5)^\perp : c! : (q?) \to \qquad\qquad\qquad\qquad \text{is the reader ready?}$$
$$(c = y : \lfloor skip \rfloor : f_5) \mid \qquad\qquad\qquad\qquad \text{communication successful}$$
$$(\lfloor skip \rfloor : s_5 : [\![c!_{s_5, f_5} y]\!] : \qquad\qquad\qquad\qquad \text{wait one cycle and retry}$$
$$f_6 = f_5) \qquad\qquad\qquad\qquad \text{sequential composition finishes}$$
$$\Rightarrow f_6)$$
$$\|$$
$$(s_1 = s_3 : \qquad\qquad\qquad\qquad \text{sequential composition starts}$$
$$(s_1)^\perp : c? : (c!) \to \qquad\qquad\qquad\qquad \text{is the writer ready?}$$
$$(\lfloor x = c \rfloor : f_1) \mid \qquad\qquad\qquad\qquad \text{communication successful}$$
$$(\lfloor skip \rfloor : s_1 : [\![c?_{s_1, f_1} x]\!] : \qquad\qquad\qquad\qquad \text{wait one cycle and retry}$$
$$s_2 = f_1 : \qquad\qquad\qquad\qquad \text{sequential link}$$
$$(s2)^\perp : \lfloor x = x + 1 \rfloor : f_2 \qquad\qquad\qquad\qquad x := x + 1$$
$$f_3 = f_2) \qquad\qquad\qquad\qquad \text{sequential composition finishes}$$
$$\Rightarrow f_3)$$
$$f_7 = (f_6 \wedge f_3) \qquad\qquad\qquad\qquad \text{parallel composition finishes}$$

$$(prune\ e, ((c?) \to ...) \| ((c!) \to ...)) \qquad e\ \text{(true branch on both sides)}$$
$$(prune\ e, (c = y : ...) \| (...)) \qquad \mathcal{B} \oplus \{c = 10\}$$
$$(prune\ e, (\lfloor skip \rfloor : ...) \| (\lfloor x = c \rfloor ...)) \qquad \mathcal{S} \oplus \{x \to 10\} \wedge \tau = 2 \wedge \Xi(e)$$
$$(prune\ e, (f_5 : ...) \| (f_1 : ...)) \qquad \mathcal{W} \oplus \{f_5 = T \wedge f_1 = T\}$$
$$(prune\ e, (f_2 = f_5 : ...) \| (s_2 = f_1 : ...)) \qquad \mathcal{W} \oplus \{f_2 = T \wedge s_2 = T\}$$
$$(prune\ c, ([] \Rightarrow ...) \| ((s_2)^\perp)) \qquad e$$
$$(prune\ e, ([] \Rightarrow ...) \| (\lfloor x = x + 1 \rfloor)) \qquad \mathcal{S} \oplus \{x \to 11\} \wedge \tau = 3 \wedge \Xi(e)$$
$$(prune\ e, ([] \Rightarrow ...) \| (f_2)) \qquad \mathcal{W} \oplus \{f_2 = T\}$$
$$(prune\ e, ([] \Rightarrow ...) \| (f_3 = f_2)) \qquad \mathcal{W} \oplus \{f_3 = T\}$$
$$(prune\ e, ([] \Rightarrow f_6) \| ([] \Rightarrow f_3)) \qquad \mathcal{W} \oplus \{f_6 = T \wedge f_3 = T\}$$
$$(prune\ e, (f_6 \wedge f_3) \qquad \mathcal{W} \oplus \{f_6 = T\}$$

hardware generated by the compilation rules is *correct* (i.e., semantically equivalent to its original Handel-C code). Towards this end, the next step will be to prove the existence of an equivalence relationship using the semantic models for Handel-C [6,10] and the semantics for the generated hardware presented in this paper. We are also interested in extending the compilation approach in order to include priAlts and formally verify the correctness of the extension.

References

1. Boulton, R., et al.: Experience with embedding hardware description languages in HOL. In: Proc. of the International Conference on Theorem Provers in Circuit Design: Theory, Practice and Experience, pp. 129–156 (1992)
2. Bowen, J.: Hardware compilation of the ProCoS gas burner case study using logic programming. In: ProCoS-US Hardware Synthesis and Verification Workshop (1996)
3. Bowen, J., Jifeng, H.: Hardware compilation: Verification and rapid-prototyping. Technical report, The University of Reading (1999)
4. Bowen, J., Jifeng, H., Page, I.: Hardware compilation, pp. 193–207. Elsevier, Amsterdam (1994)
5. Brookes, S.: On the axiomatic treatment of concurrency. In: Brookes, S.D., Winskel, G., Roscoe, A.W. (eds.) Seminar on Concurrency. LNCS, vol. 197, pp. 1–34. Springer, Heidelberg (1985)
6. Butterfield, A.: Denotational semantics for prialt-free Handel-C. Technical report, The University of Dublin, Trinity College (December 2001)
7. Butterfield, A., Woodcock, J.: Semantic domains for Handel-C. Electronic Notes in Theoretical Computer Science, vol. 74 (2002)
8. Butterfield, A., Woodcock, J.: Semantics of prialt in Handel-C. In: Concurrent Systems Engineering, IOS Press, Amsterdam (2002)
9. Butterfield, A., Woodcock, J.: Prialt in handel-c: an operational semantics. International Journal on Software Tools Technology Transfer 7(3), 248–267 (2005)
10. Butterfield, A., Woodcock, J.: A Hardware Compiler Semantics for Handel-C. In: MFCSIT 2004. ENTCS, vol. 161, pp. 73–90 (2006)
11. Davey, B., Priestley, H.: Introduction to Lattices and Order. Cambridge University Press, Cambridge (2002)
12. Gordon, M.: Why higher-order logic is a good formalism for specifying and verifying hardware. In: Formal Aspects of VLSI Design, pp. 153–177 (1986)
13. Gordon, M., Melham, T. (eds.): Introduction to HOL: a theorem proving environment for higher order logic. Cambridge University Press, Cambridge (1993)
14. Hanna, F., Daeche, N.: Specification and verification using higher-order logic: A case study. In: Formal Aspects of VLSI Design, pp. 179–213 (1986)
15. Hennessy, M., Plotkin, G.: Full abstraction for a simple parallel programming language. Math. Foundations of Computer Science 74, 108–120 (1979)
16. Hoare, C.A.R.: Communicating sequential processes. Commun. ACM 26(1), 100–106 (1983)
17. Lawrence, A.: CSPP and Event Priority. In: Communicating Process Architectures 2001, pp. 67–92 (2001)
18. Celoxica Ltd. DK3: Handel-C Language Reference Manual (2002)
19. Celoxica Ltd. The Technology behind DK1, Application Note AN 18 (August 2002)

20. Melham, T.: Abstraction mechanisms for hardware verification. In: VLSI Specification, Verification, and Synthesis, pp. 129–157 (1988)
21. Melham, T.: Using recursive types to reason about hardware in higher order logic. In: The Fusion of Hardware Design and Verification, pp. 27–50 (1988)
22. Melham, T.: Automating recursive type definitions in higher order logic. In: Current trends in hardware verification and automated theorem proving, pp. 341–386. Springer, New York (1989)
23. Melham, T.: Higher Order Logic and Hardware Verification. Cambridge Tracts in Theoretical Computer Science, vol. 31. Cambridge University Press, Cambridge (1993)
24. Milner, R.: Fully abstract models of typed lambda-calculi. Theoretical Computer Science 4(1), 1–22 (1977)
25. Page, I.: Constructing hardware-software systems from a single description. Journal of VLSI Signal Processing 12(1), 87–107 (1996)
26. Page, I., Luk, W.: Compiling Occam into field-programmable gate arrays. In: FPGAs, Oxford Workshop on Field Programmable Logic and Applications, pp. 271–283 (1991)

Automatic Generation of Verified Concurrent Hardware

Marcel Oliveira[1] and Jim Woodcock[2]

[1] Departamento de Informática e Matemática Aplicada, UFRN, Brazil
[2] Department of Computer Science, University of York, UK

Abstract. The complexity inherent to concurrent systems can turn their development into a very complex and error-prone task. The use of formal languages like CSP and tools that support them simplifies considerably the task of developing such systems. This process, however, usually aims at reaching an executable program: a translation between the specification language and a practical programming language is still needed and is usually rather problematic. In this paper we present a translation framework and a tool, csp2hc, that implements it. This framework provides an automatic translation from a subset of CSP to Handel-C, a programming language that is similar to standard C, but whose programs can be converted to produce files to program an FPGA.

Keywords: concurrency, refinement, program development, tool support, Handel-C, FPGA, CSP, automatic compilation.

1 Introduction

The development of large-scale distributed systems is very complex, error-prone and time-consuming. This is because concurrent applications can be very complicated since they normally consist of many components running in parallel.

The use of formal methods like Hoare's CSP [13], an algebra designed for describing and reasoning about synchronisations and communications between processes, may simplify this task because it provides a way to explicitly specify the required synchronisation among processes. Furthermore, phenomena that are exclusive to the concurrent world, since they arise from the combination of components and not from the components alone, like deadlock and livelock, can be much more easily understood and controlled using such formalisms.

Tool support is another reason for the success of CSP. For instance, FDR [9] provides an automatic analysis of correctness and of properties like deadlock and divergence. It accepts a machine-processable subset of CSP, called CSP_M [20], which combines an ASCII representation of CSP with a functional language.

Using CSP, we may capture systems descriptions at the levels of specifications, design, and implementation. This allows a stepwise development in a single framework from a specification to an implementation. Nevertheless, in reality, the final product of a program development is an executable program. Hence, we still need to translate the CSP implementation into a practical programming language. Preferably, languages that directly support the CSP style of concurrency

M. Butler, M. Hinchey, M.M. Larrondo-Petrie (Eds.): ICFEM 2007, LNCS 4789, pp. 286–306, 2007.

through channels, such as occam-2 [14] and Handel-C [8], or other languages using packages that add CSP features, such as CTJ [12] and JCSP [22] for Java, CCSP [16] for C, and C++CSP [5] for C++, should be used as target languages.

Unfortunately, this translation may not be trivial and usually, it is rather problematic. In the presence of a large number of processes with a reasonably complex pattern of communications, the implementation of a program that behaves like the CSP specification is quite error-prone. By providing an automatic translation into a programming language, we achieve a comprehensive methodology for developing concurrent applications as illustrated in Fig. 1: first, we specify the system's desired concurrent behaviour; next, we gradually refine it into a CSP implementation and verify the correctness of each refinement and other properties using tools like FDR. Finally, we automatically translate the CSP_M implementation into a practical programming language. We target Handel-C code, which can itself be converted to produce files to program FPGAs.

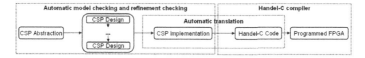

Fig. 1. Methodology using an Automatic CSP Translator

We present csp2hc, an automatic translator from CSP_M to Handel-C. Using csp2hc, we apply our methodology, which provides a development path for hardware generated from a high-level description of a system. The subset of supported CSP_M includes SKIP, STOP, sequential composition, recursion, prefixing, external choice, internal choice, concurrency, datatypes, constants, functions, expressions, alternation, and guarded processes. Besides the CSP_M constructors that are accepted by csp2hc, there are some other restrictions that are specific to the translation of some constructs; they are summarised in Table 1. These restrictions are automatically verified by csp2hc.

Sections 2 and 3 contain an introduction to both CSP_M and Handel-C, respectively. In Sect. 4, we present the translations done by csp2hc, which is briefly described in Sect. 5. We draw our conclusions and discuss future work in Sect. 6.

1.1 Related Work

Other researchers have already considered the translation of process algebras into programming languages. For instance, in [15], the refinement of CSP_M specifications into occam-2 and Ada 9X [1] code was presented. The intention, however, is to illustrate the translation; no tool support is available.

The translation of CSP_M into imperative and object-oriented programming languages is also the subject of [19], where Raju *et al.* present a tool that translates a small subset of CSP_M into Java and C, with the help of libraries that provide models for processes and channels and allows programmers to abstract

Table 1. Restrictions Summary

CSP$_M$	Restrictions
Datatypes, constants, functions, and expressions	Sets/constants cannot be used as datatypes constructors arguments; no recursive datatypes; restricted syntax.
`SKIP`, `STOP`, `;`, `|~|`, `[]`, guarded process, synchronisation, and tail recursion	
Output/Input Prefix	Single output/input; not before projections; the name of the input variable is not repeated in the next process.
Projection	Consistent use of projections.
Mutual Recursion	Parallel composition only in the main behaviour
External choice	Only between prefixing processes; no two input variables with the same name.
Parallel composition	Shared channels are in the synchronisation channel set; no multi-synchronisation.
`P \ CS`	Under certain conditions.

from basic constructs of these languages (i.e., JCSP [22] for Java and CCSP [16] for C). Using this approach, we have an automatic translation into software.

In [17], we extend this work and provide a translation from a subset of *Circus*, a combination of CSP with Z [23] and Dijkstra's command language that has an associated refinement theory [7], into JCSP. In [10], that authors extended [17] and implemented a tool that automatically applies this translation strategy.

Most of the translations between CSP$_M$ and a programming language available in the literature target the generation of software. In [15], occam-2, which is the native programming language for a line of transputer microprocessors, is the target language. Unfortunately, it is not supported by any tool.

Handel-C's approach differs from BlueSpec's one [2]. The later is based on Verilog, a hardware description language that is useful for developing complex, bespoke hardware, exploiting a hardware engineer's skill and knowledge of circuits. The former is a programming language for compiling programs into hardware images of FPGAs or ASICs; it provides fast development and rapid prototyping, without hardware skills, and allows massive parallelism to be easily exploited.

In this paper, we achieve an automatic generation of verified hardware. In the literature, as far as we know, only [18](probably based on [21]) present tools that convert a subset of CSP$_M$ into Handel-C code. Their methodology is very similar to ours, but the subset of CSP$_M$ considered is relatively small.

2   CSP$_M$

CSP [13] is a process algebra that can be used to describe systems composed by interacting components, which are independent self-contained processes with interfaces that are used to interact with the environment. Most of the CSP tools, like FDR, accepts a machine-processable subset of CSP, called CSP$_M$.

The two basic CSP$_M$ processes are STOP (deadlock) and SKIP (successful termination). The prefixing a -> P is initially able to perform only the event a; afterwards it behaves like process P. A boolean guard may be associated with a process: given a predicate g, if the condition g is true, the process g & P behaves like P; it deadlocks otherwise. The sequence operator P1;P2 combines processes P1 and P2 in sequence. The external choice P1[]P2 initially offers events of both processes. The performance of the first event resolves the choice in favour of the process that performs it. The environment has no control over the internal choice P1|~|P2. The sharing parallel composition P1[|cs|]P2 synchronises P1 and P2 on the channels in the set cs; events that are not listed occur independently. In the alphabetised parallel composition P1[cs1||cs2]P2, the processes synchronise on the channels in cs1 ∩ cs2; the remaining events occur independently. Processes composed in interleaving P1|||P2 run independently. The event hiding operator P\cs encapsulates the events that are in the channel set cs, which become no longer visible to the environment. Some other constructors are available in CSP$_M$ but omitted here; they are not accepted by csp2hc.

Figure 2 presents the specification of a parking spot. It contains special comments called directives (--!!), which gives extra information to csp2hc, such as: information on whether simple synchronisation channels are input channels or output channels within a process; the types of processes arguments; the main behaviour of the system; the length of the integers used within the system; and the moment internal choices should be made. The directives are either mandatory or optional; csp2hc will raise an error describing missing mandatory directives.

The abstract specification PARKING only requires that, after entering, a customer must leave before the next customer enters. Process PAID_PARKING describes a parking spot with a pay and display machine that accepts cash, and issues tickets and change.

First, we declare a datatype ALPHA: variables of this type can assume either value a or b. The next datatype, ID, represents identifications: the constructor Letter receives an ALPHA value and returns a value of ID (for example, Letter.a); another possibility is the unknown ID. After receiving the cash, the machine issues tickets and change. The process CUST models a customer: after entering the parking spot, a customer interacts with the ticket machine: he inserts the cash, picks the ticket and the change in any order, and finally, leaves the parking spot. Customers have unique identification that guarantees that tickets and changes are only issued to the right customer. The paid parking spot is modelled by PAID_PARKING. For simplification purposes, it is a parallel composition of only one customer and a machine; they synchronise on cash, ticket and change, which are encapsulated. Finally, a CAR interacts with the parking spot; the main behaviour of the system, SYSTEM, is the parallel composition between the CAR and the parking spot.

```
--!!mainp SYSTEM
--!!int_bits 2
datatype ALPHA = a | b
datatype ID = Letter.ALPHA | unknown
channel enter, leave
channel cash, ticket, change : ID

--!!channel enter in within PARKING
--!!channel leave in within PARKING
PARKING = enter -> leave -> PARKING
--!!channel cash in within MACHINE
--!!channel ticket out within MACHINE
--!!channel change out within MACHINE
MACHINE = cash?id -> ticket.id ->
            change.id -> MACHINE
 --!!channel enter in within CUST
 --!!channel leave in within CUST
 --!!channel cash out within CUST
```

```
--!!channel ticket in within CUST
--!!channel change in within CUST
--!!arg id ID within CUST
CUST(id) =
 (enter -> cash!id ->
  (ticket.id -> change.id -> SKIP
   []change.id -> ticket.id -> SKIP
  )); leave -> CUST(id)
PAID_PARKING =
 (CUST(Letter.a)
 [| {|cash,ticket,change|} |]
 MACHINE) \ {|cash,ticket,change|}
--!!channel enter out within CAR
--!!channel leave out within CAR
CAR = enter -> leave -> CAR
SYSTEM = CAR
        [| {| enter,leave |} |]
        PAID_PARKING
```

Fig. 2. CSP$_M$ Example

3   Handel-C

Handel-C is a procedural language, rather like occam, but with a C-like syntax. It was designed by Celoxica and has as its main purpose the compilation into netlists to configure FPGAs or ASICs. Although targeting hardware, it is a programming language with hardware output rather than a hardware description language. This makes Handel-C different from VHDL [3]. A hardware design using Handel-C is more like programming than hardware engineering; this language is developed for programmers who have no hardware knowledge at all.

Basically, Handel-C contains a small subset of C that includes common expressions that can be used to describe complex algorithms. However, it does not include processor-oriented features like floating point arithmetic, which is supported through external libraries. Handel-C extends C by providing constructs that facilitate the description of parallel behaviour based on CSP concepts. For instance, using the parallel construct PAR, we can execute instructions in parallel; the parallel branches can communicate values via channels. The prialt statement can be used to select one of the channels that are ready to communicate, and that channel is the only one that will be allowed to communicate. The only data type allowed in Handel-C is int, which can be declared with a fixed size, hence avoiding unneeded bits that would lead to an inefficient hardware

By way of illustration, we present a simple BUFFER that receives an integer value through a channel input and outputs it through channel output.

```
#define integer int 8
set clock = external "clock1";
chan integer input, output, middle;
```

```
void IN(){ integer v; while(1) { input?v; middle!v; } }
void OUT(){ integer v; while(1) { middle?v; output!v; } }
void BUFFER(){ par{ IN(); OUT(); } }
void main(){ BUFFER(); }
```

This buffer can be decomposed into a process IN that receives an integer value and passes it through channel middle to another process OUT that finally outputs this value. A possible CLIENT can interact with the BUFFER by sending an integer value via channel input and receiving it back via channel output. The Handel-C code presented at the end of the previous page implements such a buffer.

We define a constant integer that represents the 8-bit integers, an external clock named clock1, and declare the channels used in the system. The Handel-C function IN implements the process of same name. It declares a local variable v and starts an infinite loop: in each iteration, it receives a value via channel input, assigns it to v, and writes the value of v on middle. The function OUT is very similar; however, it receives a value via channel middle and writes this value on output. The BUFFER is defined as the parallel composition of both functions IN and OUT. We declare the main function as the process BUFFER.

The development process we propose, from an abstract CSP_M specification to its Handel-C implementation was presented in Fig. 1. An automatic translation from CSP_M to Handel-C is straightforward for some CSP_M constructs because Handel-C provides constructs that facilitate the description of parallel behaviour based on CSP concepts. Nevertheless, for many of the CSP_M constructs an automatic translation into Handel-C is not trivial. In the next section, we present the translation that is done by csp2hc from a useful subset of CSP_M into Handel-C.

4   Translating CSP_M into Handel-C

Our tool mechanises the translation of a subset of CSP_M to Handel-C, which includes SKIP, STOP, sequential composition, recursion, prefixing, external choice, internal choice, concurrency, datatypes, constants, expressions, and alternation. Although they represent a subset of CSP_M, using these constructors, we are already able to automatically translate some of the classical CSP_M examples in the literature. A more interesting application of our results has been the case studies elaborated by our industrial partner.

In what follows, we describe the details of the translation adopted by csp2hc; it assumes that the original CSP_M specification has already been loaded and checked by FDR. Besides, csp2hc does not deal directly with the system's clock. Since every Handel-C program must have a clock related to it, we use a dummy clock, called clock1 as the only clock of our programs. Besides, in CSP_M, we can have communications on channels with no value being carried; this, however, is not reflected in Handel-C where every communication must carry a value. For this reason, we declare a type SYNC. It is used as the type of a dummy constant value syncout, which is written on the channels in such communications, and as the type of a dummy input variable syncin. For this reason, every Handel-C code generated by csp2hc starts as follows.

```
set clock = external "clock1";
typedef unsigned int 1 SYNC; const SYNC syncout = 0; SYNC syncin;
```

Afterwards, the resulting Handel-C program contains the following items (declared in this order): constants related to the types used in the CSP$_\mathsf{M}$ specification; constants and functions declared in the CSP$_\mathsf{M}$ specification; channels used in the CSP$_\mathsf{M}$ specification; constants related to sets of channels and parallel branches; functions that implement the CSP$_\mathsf{M}$ processes; and the main function.

4.1   Types

We start by describing the constants that are related to the types used in the CSP$_\mathsf{M}$ specification. This includes the constants related to the CSP$_\mathsf{M}$ types Int, Bool, and all existing datatypes. For every type T, we calculate all possible values $v_0, v_1, \ldots, v_n$ that are in T. For instance, for the boolean type we have that $v_0 = false$ and $v_1 = true$. This calculation is possible because csp2hc supports only bounded (hence enumerable) types. This approach restricts the datatypes that are accepted by csp2hc; recursive datatypes are not allowed, but they can be removed from the specification using the same strategy as in Z [23], which could be applied either by hand or automatically by csp2hc.

We start by defining the type T as an unsigned int of length l, which is the number of bits needed to represent $n + 1$ values. For example, the declaration of the boolean is #define boolean unsigned int 1. Next, for each value v_i in T, we declare a constant v$_i$ with a value i. The constants related to false and true are declared as #define false 0 and #define true 1, respectively.

The cardinality of T (for instance, #define boolean_card 2) is also part of the code. csp2hc uses a bitwise representation of sets: a set of type T, called T_set, is a bit value of same length as the cardinality T_card of T.

```
#define boolean_set unsigned int boolean_card
```

In this representation, a set contains a value v_n if the n-th bit (from left to right) of the bit word (preceded by 0b in Handel-C) is one. Hence, the empty set has all the bits equals to zero: #define boolean_set_nil 0b00.

For every value v_n in the type T, we declare a singleton containing v_n. It is represented as a bit word of length T_card, with all bits but the n-th one set to zero. For instance, the constant #define true_set 0b10 and the constant #define false_set 0b01 represent the sets that contains only false and true, respectively. Finally, we have a look-up table T_set_LUT that is used to access the representation of every singleton set. It is a static array of type T_set and size T_card, and whose elements are the singleton sets previously declared.

```
static boolean_set boolean_set_LUT[boolean_card] = {false_set,true_set};
```

Using this approach we will be able to translate set values and expressions. For instance, boolean_set_LUT[false] | boolean_set_LUT[true] corresponds to the set {false,true}; in Handel-C, | is bitwise logical or.

The first directive we present is optional; it gives to csp2hc the number of bits used to represented integer numbers in the system (the default value is 1).

The directive --!!int_bits 2 tells csp2hc that integers need at most 2 bits to be represented; hence, they are signed integers ranging from -2 to 1. We present below the declaration of the constants related to the type integer in the translation of Figure 2. In the access to arrays like the look-up tables we cast signed integers into unsigned ones. The look-up table for the integers implements the transformation which is implicitly done by the Handel-C casting.

```
#define integer int 2
#define integer_card 4
#define integer_set unsigned int integer_card
#define integer_neg_1_set 0b1000
#define integer_neg_2_set 0b0100
#define integer_1_set 0b0010
#define integer_0_set 0b0001
#define integer_set_nil 0b0000
static integer_set integer_set_LUT[integer_card] =
    {integer_0_set,integer_1_set,integer_neg_2_set,integer_neg_1_set};
```

The number of bits declared by this directive must be sufficient to include the evaluation of all integer expressions within the specification. Otherwise, the generated code may be inconsistent: turning a signed number that is out of the range of the valid integers specified by the directive into an unsigned number may have the same bitwise representation as some valid signed numbers. For instance, given 2-bit integers, (unsigned)2 is the same as -2. In the future, we intend to provide csp2hc with a dataflow analysis on the Handel-C code that could identify overflows; such technique is already used by the Spark-ADA compiler [6].

In the translation of both simple and complex datatypes, we use the same strategy used for the boolean type, which is simply based on the set of values $v_0, v_1, \ldots, v_n$ that compose the type. For the simple datatypes, the calculation of these values is trivial; they are simply all the constants used in the declaration of the datatype (a and b for ALPHA). For complex datatypes T, the used constructors C are interpreted as functions: for each element e in the domain of C there is a corresponding value C_e in the datatype. For example, the constructor Letter is used is the definition of ID in Fig. 2; hence the values Letter_a and Letter_b are possible values of type ID. Furthermore, another sort of look-up table is created for each one of the constructors used in the specification: it returns the corresponding value in the datatype for each element in the domain of the constructor. By way of illustration, ID_Letter_LUT[ALPHA_card] is the look-up table for the constructor Letter used in the definition of the datatype ID. Its length is ALPHA_card because the domain of this constructor is the type ALPHA. These look-up tables are used in the translation of such values. For example, the translation of Letter.b is ID_Letter_LUT[b]; this corresponds to the first (b is a constant equals to 0) element of the array, Letter_b. In The translation of ALPHA is very similar to the translation of boolean; just replace false by b and true by a. In what follows, we present the translation of ID. Currently, csp2hc does not allow constants and sets to be given to datatype constructors.

```
#define ID unsigned int 2        #define ID_set unsigned int ID_card
#define unknown 0                 #define unknown_set 0b001
#define Letter_a 1                #define ID_set_nil 0b000
#define Letter_b 2                static ID_set ID_set_LUT[ID_card]=
#define ID_card 3                   {unknown_set,Letter_a_set,Letter_b_set};
#define Letter_b_set 0b100        static ID ID_Letter_LUT[ALPHA_card]=
#define Letter_a_set 0b010          {Letter_b ,Letter_a};
```

4.2   Constants and Functions

Constants and functions are translated into Handel-C macro expressions, whose definition and compilation have the same behaviour as in ANSI-C. Nevertheless, Handel-C provides additional macro support that allows more powerful (for example, recursive) macros. By translating them into expressions, instead of functions, we avoid some restrictions that Handel-C has for function invocations. For instance, the condition of an alternation cannot contain a function call.

As in C, Handel-C also has function prototypes as a means of providing type checking and parameter checking for function calls. Hence, we declare macros and function in two blocks: the first one declares the prototypes of all constants and functions, and the second one defines the constants and functions.

4.3   Channels

Every channel used in a Handel-C program must be declared. The general syntax for a channel declaration is `chan type csp_id`. csp2hc uses the channel declarations from the CSP_M specification in order to infer the types used to declare the channels in the resulting Handel-C code. We translate synchronisations like `c1.e`, where `c1` is declared as `channel c1:T1`, into an access to the e-th element of an array of channels `c1`. Hence, for channels used in such way, we declare an array of channels instead of a single channel. The length of this array is defined by the number of values in the channel type. In our example, we would have `chan SYNC c1[T1_card]`; the type communicated is SYNC because there is no value actually being communicated. Because of some restrictions imposed by our translation and discussed in more details later in this section, if a channel is declared with more than one type, the type communicated by that channel is the right-most one; the remaining types are synchronisation types. For example, a channel declared as `channel c1:T1.T2` communicates values of type T2; its Handel-C declaration is `chan T2 c1[T1_card];`.

Channel sets are commonly used in a CSP_M specification and have a major influence in the behaviour of constructs like parallel composition. Hence, we need a notation to represent them. In order to reuse the implementation done for types, we consider a datatype CHANNEL: for each channel c used in the system, there is a branch chan_c. For example, if an input CSP_M specification uses channels c1, c2, and c3, the translator includes a code that corresponds to the translation of `datatype CHANNEL = chan_c1 | chan_c2 | chan_c3;`.

4.4   Processes

Each process is translated to an `inline` function in Handel-C. The declaration of functions as `inline` causes their expansion where they are called; this ensures that they are not accessed at the same time by parallel branches of the code. This would lead to an interference between different instances of the same process running in parallel. For instance, the process `PARKING = ...` is translated to a function `inline void PARKING(){ ... }` in Handel-C. For the same reasons as for the constants and functions, we prototype all the processes declared in a specification before their actual definition. For instance, let us consider our CSP_M specification of a parking spot presented in Fig. 2. The generated Handel-C code presented below is composed of four functions, which correspond to each one of the processes in the original CSP_M specification.

```
inline void PARKING();              inline void PARKING() { ... }
inline void MACHINE();              inline void MACHINE() { ... }
inline void CUST(ID id);            inline void CUST(ID id) { ... }
inline void PAID_PARKING();         inline void PAID_PARKING() { ... }
inline void CAR();                  inline void CAR() { ... }
inline void SYSTEM();               inline void SYSTEM() { ... }
```

CSP_M processes can be parametrised; the parameters, however, are not typed. For this reason, csp2hc requires this information in order to be able to correctly translate the process; another directive is needed. The mandatory directive `--!!arg id ID within CUST` informs csp2hc that the type of the argument `id` of process `CUST` is `ID`. Using this information, the translator is able to correctly declare and define the function `CUST` as we presented above.

Simple Processes. The translations of `SKIP` and `STOP` are trivial: the former is ignored and the latter is translated to an input communication on a channel we assume is not used anywhere in the specification because its name is a csp2hc reserved word. The code `if(g){ P1(); } else { P2();}` is given as the translation of the process `if g then P else Q`. The process `g & P` is translated in the same way as the process `if g then P else STOP`.

Sequential composition is also trivially translated using the Handel-C `seq` constructor. For example, `P1; P2` is translated into `seq { P1(); P2() }`; it invokes both `P1` and `P2` in sequence. The process `P1; P2` could also have been translated into `P1(); P2()`. Nevertheless, Handel C's parallel operator (`par`) has the same syntax as the sequence operator. If we translate sequence as `P1(); P2()`, then the translation of `(P1;P2) || P3` could lead, as we will present later in this section, to `par { P1(); P2(); P3() }`, which does not have the desired behaviour, since it executes the three processes in parallel.

Communication. We consider that the use of channels first declare possible synchronisation of the form `.csp_exp`, and finally possible communications of the form `?csp_id` or `!csp_exp`. Our translation also constrains the channels to have only one input or output value; multiple inputs and outputs must be encapsulated in datatypes. For example, c.0, c.0!true, c are valid communications for csp2hc, but c!1.0 and c?x!1 are not; the former has a synchronisation value after an output, and the later has both an input and an output.

For single output communications, the mapping is straightforward because the syntax of both is the same. Nevertheless, we make use of the Handel-C seq constructor; this makes the translation more generic because it allows the translation of parallel composition of nameless process as we present later in this section. For example, a CSP$_M$ output communication cash!id -> ... is translated into seq { cash!id; ... }.

The translation of single input communications declares the input variable, which is in the scope of the translation of the CSP$_M$ process that follows; its type is retrieved from the channel declaration in the CSP$_M$ specification. For instance, the input communication cash?id -> ... from our example is translated to seq{ ID id; cash? id; ... }. In both cases, it is trivial to conclude if the channel is either an input or an output channel. For simple synchronisations, however, csp2hc gets this information from the user: the directive --!!channel c in within P informs csp2hc that the channel c is an input channel within process P; for output, we replace in with out. This directive simplifies the work of csp2hc because it does not need to enforce the direction of these communications.

Because every Handel-C communication must carry a value, we communicate a dumb value on the channel: a dumb value syncout is written on output communications and a dumb variable is used on input communications. In our example, the first communication of process CUST is a simple synchronisation on channel enter. Using the directive presented below, csp2hc is able to translate the synchronisation to seq { enter?syncin; ... } .

```
--!!channel enter in within CUST
```

Projections c.e are translated to an access to the e-th element of an array c of channels. The declaration of channel c in the CSP$_M$ is used to get the array dimensions and use this information in the declaration of the array of channels. For each type T used in a channel projection, we add an extra dimension to the array with size T_card. If after the projection, no value is communicated, as for the simple synchronisations, we need a directive to inform if it is an input or an output synchronisation. For instance, in Fig. 2, the channel ticket is declared to have type ID and used as ticket.id within process CUST. First, the source CSP$_M$ must have the directive --!!channel ticket in within CUST. As a result, the translated Handel-C code declares this channel as chan SYNC ticket[ID_card];. Because no value is communicated, the type of the channel is the value of the dumb value, SYNC; otherwise, the type of the value communicated would be used. Next, the communication ticket.id -> ... within CUST is translated into seq{ ticket[id]!syncout; ... }. In this case, the type ID is used and, as previously described, it is declared as an unsigned integer. If, however, the CSP$_M$ type Int is used in a projection, csp2hc includes a casting to an unsigned integer that is required by the Handel-C compiler in order to guarantee that we do not have access to negative indexes of an array. For example, a synchronisation `c.v` is translated to `c[(unsigned)v]`.

This approach imposes a restriction to our source CSP_M specifications: projections must be consistently used. This means that if a channel is used as `c.e`, it cannot be used as `c!e` elsewhere in the specification.

Recursion. In Handel-C, functions may not be recursive; however, recursive processes can be defined in CSP_M. Our translation allows tail recursive processes and mutually recursive processes. Tail recursive processes may be translated to a loop that iterates while a special boolean variable is **true**. Initially, each iteration sets this variable to **false** and only the recursive call sets this variable back to **true**. This causes the loop to stop or not. For instance, the translation of the tail recursive process `PARKING` used in our example is presented below.

```
inline void PARKING(){
    boolean KEEP_LOOPING; KEEP_LOOPING = true;
    while(KEEP_LOOPING){
        KEEP_LOOPING = false;
        seq{ seq{ enter?syncin; seq{ leave?syncin;
                                KEEP_LOOPING = true; } } } }
```

It declares a variable `KEEP_LOOPING` and initialises it with **true**. This variable is used as the condition of the loop that follows. The first action of the loop is to set `KEEP_LOOPING` to **false**; the recursive invocation of `PARKING` is translated into the code `KEEP_LOOPING = true`.

Process arguments are declared as local copies, which are initialised before the beginning of the loop with the given value and are updated before the end of each iteration. In our example, the process `CUST` is a parametrised tail recursive process. Its translation presented below omits the translation of the external choice (this will be presented later in this section). In the declaration part, we also declare a local copy `CUST_local_id` of the process argument `id`, which is initialised with the given real argument and updated with the argument used in the recursive invocation before setting the variable `KEEP_LOOPING` to **true**.

```
inline void CUST(ID id){
    boolean KEEP_LOOPING; ID CUST_local_id;
    CUST_local_id = id; KEEP_LOOPING = true;
    while(KEEP_LOOPING){
        KEEP_LOOPING = false;
        seq{ seq{ seq{ enter?syncin;
                    seq{ cash! CUST_local_id;
                        // translation of external choice
                        seq{ leave?syncin;
                            CUST_local_id = CUST_local_id;
                            KEEP_LOOPING = true; } } } } } }
```

This translation for tail recursive processes does not allow parallel composition in the tail recursion. This could lead to infinite expansion, which would be impossible to map into hardware. Furthermore, this solution for tail recursive processes is valid only for specifications that contain no mutually recursive processes. If, however, mutually recursive processes are present in the specification,

csp2hc uses a different translation, which transforms the whole model into an
action-system-like model [4]. It declares all the processes parameters as global
variables and uses a single function parametrised by a process counter to represent the whole system. As for tail recursive processes, the body of this single
function is a loop controlled by a boolean variable KEEP_LOOPING. The parameter of the function is used as a program counter and indicates the behaviour that
the function must have in each iteration. Because we are mapping the behaviour
of the system into an action-system-like, this solution can only be applied to
CSP$_M$ specification in which parallel composition is present only in the process
given as the main behaviour of the system.

Our example does not present mutual recursion; the example in Fig. 3 shows
the translation of a CSP$_M$ specification of two mutually recursive processes. They
represent a lamp that can be switched on and off and that memorises the number
of times it has been switched on. In the CSP$_M$ specification presented below
we have the declaration of a datatype that represents the status on which a
lamp can be: it is either ON or OFF. This type is used to synchronise with the
processes L_ON and L_OFF, which represent a lamp that is switched on and off,
respectively. Besides, as we can see in the information given by the directives,
both their arguments are integers and in both processes, the channel switch is
an input channel. If the lamp is OFF, it can only be switched ON and vice-versa;
if the lamp is switched ON, it increments the counter.

```
--!!mainp L_OFF(0)                        L_OFF(x) = switch.ON -> L_ON(x+1)
datatype STATUS = ON | OFF                --!!arg y integer within L_ON
channel switch:STATUS                     --!!channel switch in within L_ON
--!!arg x integer within L_OFF            L_ON(y) = switch.OFF -> L_OFF(y)
--!!channel switch in within L_OFF
```

A directive that declares the main behaviour of the specification can also be
given to csp2hc. In our example, we have that initially the system behaves like
L_OFF and has a counter set to zero. For conciseness, we omit the preamble of
the resulting translation presented in Fig. 3. It declares two constants L_ON and
L_OFF they represent each one of the processes. The arguments of each process
are declared as global variables: for every argument x of a process P, we name
a global variable P_local_x (i.e., L_OFF_local_x for argument x of L_OFF).
The system is implemented by the function MUTUAL_REC that is parametrised
by a PROGRAM_COUNTER. In each iteration, it falsifies KEEP_LOOPING. Next, it
checks the current value of the program counter and behaves accordingly: if
PROGRAM_COUNTER indicates that we are in L_OFF, the process waits to synchronise on channel switch[ON]. Afterwards, it sets the value of the global variable
that represents the argument of process L_ON, L_ON_local_y. The main method
implements the behaviour of the system: it sets the value of the global variable
that represents the argument of L_OFF and invokes the mutual recursion giving
the initial value of the program counter, L_OFF, as argument.

External and Internal Choice. The translation of external choice uses Handel-
C's prialt, which makes a prioritised choice between the channels that are in the

```
...
#define L_ON 2
#define L_OFF 1
integer L_OFF_local_x; integer L_ON_local_y;
inline void MUTUAL_REC(int 2 PROGRAM_COUNTER){
  boolean KEEP_LOOPING; KEEP_LOOPING = true;
  while(KEEP_LOOPING){
    KEEP_LOOPING = false;
    switch(PROGRAM_COUNTER){
      case L_OFF :{ seq{ switch[ON]?syncin;
                         L_ON_local_y = L_OFF_local_x+1;
                         PROGRAM_COUNTER = L_ON; KEEP_LOOPING = true; }
                  break; }
      case L_ON :{ seq{ switch[OFF]?syncin;
                         L_OFF_local_x = L_ON_local_y;
                         PROGRAM_COUNTER = L_OFF; KEEP_LOOPING = true; }
                  break; }
      default: KEEP_LOOPING = false; } } }
void main(){ L_OFF_local_x = 0; MUTUAL_REC(L_OFF); }
```

Fig. 3. Translation of Mutually Recursive Processes

choice. Currently, only choices between prefixed processes can be translated by csp2hc. Furthermore, to avoid name clashes, if two input communications are in an external choice, their input variables must have different names.

In our example, CUST has an external choice. After giving the cash to the machine, it either receives the ticket or the cash. The following code, which is the part of the translation of process CUST indicated as a commentary in Page 297, is the translation of this external choice.

```
prialt{ case ticket[CUST_local_id]?syncin :{
          seq{ change[CUST_local_id]?syncin; } }; break;
        case change[CUST_local_id]?syncin :{
          seq{ ticket[CUST_local_id]?syncin; } }; break; };
```

It is a choice between ticket and change; the local copy of the customer id is used to access the corresponding channel in the array. Any other input variable is declared before the Handel-C prioritised choice that implements the choice.

Using another directive, the user can choose the time he wants internal choices to be carried out. Using the directive --!!int_choice at compiletime, for instance, we request csp2hc to resolve the internal choice P |~| Q at translation returning P(); as result. If, however, runtime is used, the translation is random(random_var); if((random_var % 2) == 0) P(); else Q();. The global variable random_var is an integer; it is given to the macro procedure random that updates its value to a random value. Next, if this new value is an even number, the process behaves like P; it behaves like Q, otherwise. This directive is optional: the default value is compiletime.

Parallel Composition. Handel-C provides the command par { P() ; Q() } that executes the methods P and Q in parallel; they may interact via channel communications, but it is not possible to explicitly declare the synchronisation channel set. As a side effect, the direct translation into a parallel composition using par is only valid for processes with no interleaved events in the synchronisation set. Formally, for every two processes P and Q composed in parallel in a channel set CS (P [| CS |] Q), the intersection of their alphabets (the set of events performed by a process) must be a subset of CS. Similar restrictions also apply to alphabetised parallel: in P [CS1 || CS2] Q, the intersection of the alphabets of P and Q must be a subset of the intersection of CS1 and CS2. Furthermore, only interleave of processes with no events in common can be directly translated into a simple parallel composition using Handel-C's par.

For example, consider PAID_PARKING in Fig. 2. It is a parallel composition between a customer and a machine; they interact on cash, ticket, and change. Analysing CUST, we see that it also has enter and leave in its alphabet, which, since they are not in the synchronisation channel set, must be interleaved. Nevertheless, the MACHINE does not mention these channels and, as result, csp2hc translates the process PAID_PARKING as follows.

```
inline void PAID_PARKING(){ par{ CUST(ID_Letter_LUT[a]); MACHINE(); } }
```

It accesses the look-up table corresponding to the constructor Letter in order to pass the right value as argument to the function CUST.

In Fig. 4 we present the resulting Handel-C code of our example in Fig. 2. For conciseness, we omit some parts of the code like the typing related constants. Currently, synchronisation channel sets must be explicit; no constant reference, functions on sets, set productions, or set comprehension are accepted as the synchronisation channel set. Furthermore, csp2hc does not support multi-synchronisation and, to some extent, neither does Handel-C. We may, though, using the DK Design Suite, change the settings of a project in order to be allowed to have multiple channels reading and writing. In this case, the debugger requires only two processes to be willing to synchronise on an event in order to make the communication happen. In a CSP$_M$ multi-synchronisation, however, the communication happens only if all parts are willing to synchronise.

Hiding. In our example, the definition of process PAID_PARKING hides some channels from the environment, but its translation simply ignores the hiding. Fortunately, under certain conditions, which are automatically checked (starting from the main process), the translation of P \ cs may ignore the hiding; all these conditions are met by the main process in our example. The first two conditions guarantee that for every channel c in cs that is visible in P, there is some communication on c in P: a process that is not in parallel with any other process cannot have a communication on a given channel that is being hidden; and for every parallel composition P [| CS |] Q, the set of the hidden channels that are also visible in both P and Q must be a subset of the set of channels that are in CS and are either written to and visible in P and read from and visible in Q or vice-versa. The third condition guarantees that communications on hidden

```
...
chan SYNC INEXISTENT_CHANNEL;
chan SYNC change[ID_card]; chan SYNC ticket[ID_card];
chan ID cash; chan SYNC enter; chan SYNC leave;
...
inline void PARKING(){ ... }
inline void CUST(ID id){ ... }
inline void PAID_PARKING(){ ... }
inline void MACHINE(){
    boolean KEEP_LOOPING; KEEP_LOOPING = true;
    while(KEEP_LOOPING){
        KEEP_LOOPING = false;
        seq{ seq{ ID id; cash? id;
                seq{ ticket[id]!syncout;
                    seq{ change[id]!syncout;
                        KEEP_LOOPING = true; }; }; }; } } }
inline void CAR(){
    boolean KEEP_LOOPING; KEEP_LOOPING = true;
    while(KEEP_LOOPING){
        KEEP_LOOPING = false;
        seq{ seq{ enter!syncout;
                seq{ leave!syncout; KEEP_LOOPING = true; }; } } } }
inline void SYSTEM(){ par{ { CAR(); };{ PAID_PARKING(); } } }
void main(){ SYSTEM(); }
```

Fig. 4. Complete Translation of our CSP$_M$ Example

channels do not happen outside the hiding: given P [| CS |] Q, there cannot be any channel that is a member of CS, hidden in P and mentioned in Q, or hidden in Q and mentioned in P.

The examples presented in this section have been automatically translated by csp2hc, whose design and architecture is the subject of the next section.

5 csp2hc: Design and Architecture

csp2hc is simple to use: the user opens the original CSP$_M$ file and, if the translation is successful, saves the result in a Handel-C file. Non-successful translations are displayed to the user as error messages, which are detailed in the log window. In such cases, the user can correct the file and translate it again.

Internally, csp2hc uses a CSP$_M$ parser and type checker that has been developed by our collaborators in UFPE/Brazil. This parser is strongly based in the visitor design pattern [11] and for this reason our implementation is based on a small number of visitors; most of them collect information about the specification (directives, constants, functions, types, processes, parallelism, channels, and recursion). This information is used by the main visitor, the translator, that actually translates the specification into Handel-C. We believe that the information needed by the translator and some of the ordering in which this information

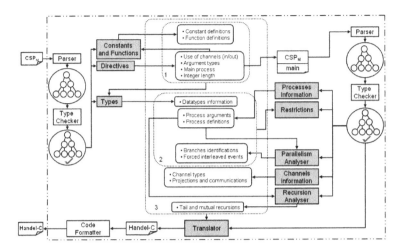

Fig. 5. The Internal Behaviour of csp2hc

is retrieved is significant not only to translate CSP_M into Handel-C, but in other translations from a process algebra to a programming language.

Figure 5 illustrates the internal behaviour of csp2hc. We identify the visitors with grey boxes and the information processed by them with soft-edged boxes. The arrows indicate the generation (from generator to information) and the usage (from information to user) of this information, which is grouped using dotted soft-edged boxes (identified with a number in the bottom left corner).

First, csp2hc receives the CSP_M specification, which is parsed. The result is a concrete tree that is given to the directives visitor who retrieves the information given by the directives. This information is used by the next visitor that retrieves information about the constants and functions in the specification. Then, the types visitor uses the information retrieved so far (grouped in box 1 in Fig. 5) to retrieve the information about the datatypes used in the system.

The next stage of the translation needs to access the directives information to append the definition of the main process to the original CSP_M specification code. This extended specification is also parsed and type checked. The resulting concrete tree is the one that is analysed by the visitors that follows. The first one is the visitor that retrieves the information about the channels: types, projections, and communications. The next one retrieves the processes' information, which includes their arguments and definitions. This information is used by the parallelism analyser, the next visitor, which gives unique identifications to each of the parallel branches (starting from the main process) and stores information that is used to identify the events on which the branches cannot synchronise on. Only then, csp2hc can check the specification against the csp2hc restrictions previously described. The restrictions visitor uses the information on the datatypes, processes, and parallelism that are grouped in box 2 in Fig. 5. All the restrictions described in this paper, including identifying unsupported CSP_M constructors and keywords, are automatically checked by csp2hc.

The last visitor before the actual translation, the recursion visitor, analyses possible recursions and stores information about them. Finally, the translator visitor is invoked; it uses all the information retrieved by the previous visitors to translate the CSP$_M$ into an unformatted Handel-C code. This code is formatted by the csp2hc code formatter and output to the user.

The automatic translations of the examples presented in this paper were fairly quick. For instance, the 38 lines of the parking spot's specification were translated into 268 lines of Handel-C code in 1359ms. Optimization of this code can still be achieved automatically and manually and is the topic of future research.

6   Conclusions

We presented a translation approach from CSP$_M$ to Handel-C and a tool that automates this translation. With this tool, we achieve a method for developing concurrent applications in hardware. Starting from an abstract CSP$_M$ specification of system, we gradually refine this specification into a CSP$_M$ implementation. Using CSP$_M$'s analysis tools like FDR, we can verify the correctness of each refinement and some other properties. Finally, csp2hc translates the CSP$_M$ implementation into Handel-C code that can be used to program a FPGA. Testing should also be contemplated in this method; nevertheless, using our method, the time spent in this stage can be considerably reduced.

During the implementation of the translation of the remaining CSP$_M$ operators, we faced some interesting problems that are inherent in targeting hardware from a specification language like CSP$_M$. The solutions to some of them are presented in this paper: we could not translate all recursive structures, but only those who would not create infinite recursion; deadlock was implemented as process reading from a fresh new channel to simulate deadlock; we needed to create a bit representation for sets; although not directly related to the CSP$_M$ semantics, we implemented a synchronisation like c.e as accesses to the e-th element of an array of channels c; finally, integer representations for datatypes, parallel branches, and channel identification had also to be used.

Some information was either impossible or not trivial to retrieve from the CSP$_M$ specification and yet was needed in the translation process. For instance, csp2hc needed information about the types of the processes' arguments and about writers and readers in the translation of a synchronisation c. This extra information is given in the form of special CSP$_M$ comments called directives.

Finally, because the concurrency model on which Handel-C is based is slightly different from that of CSP, the translation of CSP$_M$ parallel composition into Handel-C's par construct has some restrictions; a protocol is needed and is being currently implemented. It must guarantee that, if two processes should not synchronise on a channel, this will not happen. There are some further consequences from this difference on the concurrency model. For instance, in CSP$_M$, if three processes should synchronise on c and only two processes are ready to do so, the synchronisation should not happen. This is not what happens in Handel-C; in the near future we intend to introduce support for multi-synchronisation to csp2hc, which will be a simple extension of the protocol mentioned above.

csp2hc has already been able to translate some of the classical CSP_M problems (including a quarter of the examples provided with the FDR distribution) and parts of a very complex CSP_M specification provided by our industrial partner. Nevertheless, there is still a long road ahead of us. Some of the CSP_M constructs have restrictions that could be removed. For instance, prefixed processes guarded by boolean conditions could take part in the external choice and is not yet considered in csp2hc. Furthermore, there is still a large subset of CSP_M constructs that have not yet been included in csp2hc: nametypes, local definitions, chase, linked parallelism, constrained inputs (c?x:S), iterated operators, local definitions, renaming, and hiding are some of them. Most of the specifications that cannot be currently translated because they contain some of these operators must be changed by hand into a corresponding specification that is csp2hc compatible. This substitution is possible in most of the cases, but can prove to be fairly difficult sometimes; it can, however, be proven correct using FDR.

We intend to translate part of FDR's functional language: set expressions, set comprehension, functions on sets, integer ranges, sequence expressions and functions on sequences, tuple expressions, and pattern matching are among the elements we intend to automatically translate into Handel-C. With this result, csp2hc could translate a large set of CSP_M specifications, which includes a fairly complex specification used by our industrial partner that motivated the start up of our project and all the examples provided in the FDR distribution. A full automatic translation from CSP_M to Handel-C still requires the translation of interruptions, pipping, untimed time out, external, and the remaining of FDR's functional language; these translations are also in our agenda.

The performance of the code generated by csp2hc was not considered so far. We believe optimisation is possible and should be implemented. Currently, we may implement these by hand and use the automatic optimisation provided by the DK Design Suite. Nevertheless, we intend to investigate and to automatise part of this optimisation in order to achieve smaller and faster programs. For instance, in Handel-C, each assignment takes one clock cycle; hence, executing these assignments in parallel would be faster than the current solution.

Correctness of the translation approach was not considered in this paper. We currently rely on the validation of the implementation of our examples and on the fairly direct correspondence of CSP_M and Handel-C. We intend to formalise the translation as translation rules, and then prove these rules.

We intend to integrate our tool with FDR, creating a complete framework that will support the full development of verified hardware. It would consist of a powerful tool that is of much interest not only to academia but also to industry.

Acknowledgements

CNPq supports the work of Marcel Oliveira: grant 551210/2005-2. The work was partially supported by QinetiQ. We are grateful to Andrew Butterfield for helpful discussions on the finer details of the Handel-C language and its compilation. The work benefited from discussions between the authors and Juan Ignacio Perna.

We are grateful to Ana Cavalcanti for comments on earlier drafts of this paper. The anonymous referees also contributed to the final version of this paper.

References

1. Burns, A., Wellings, A.: Concurrency in Ada, 2nd edn. Cambridge University Press, Cambridge (1997)
2. Arvind: Bluespec: A language for hardware design, simulation, synthesis and verification invited talk. In: MEMOCODE 2003, p. 249. IEEE Computer Society Press, Washington, DC, USA (2003)
3. Augustin, L.M., Luckham, D.C., Gennart, B.A., Huh, Y., Stanculescu, A.G.: Hardware Design and Simulation in VAL/VHDL. Kluwer Academic Publishers, Dordrecht (1991)
4. Back, R.-J., Sere, K.: Stepwise Refinement of Action Systems. In: Proceedings of the International Conference on Mathematics of Program Construction, 375th Anniversary of the Groningen University, pp. 115–138. Springer, London, UK (1989)
5. Brown, N., Welch, P.: An Introduction to the Kent C++CSP Library. In: Broenink, J.F., Hilderink, G.H. (eds.) Communicating Process Architectures 2003, pp. 139–156 (September 2003)
6. Carré, B., Garnsworthy, J.: Spark-an annotated ada subset for safety-critical programming. In: TRI-ADA 1990, pp. 392–402. ACM Press, New York (1990)
7. Cavalcanti, A.L.C., Sampaio, A.C.A., Woodcock, J.C.P.: A refinement strategy for *Circus*. Formal Aspects of Computing 15(2–3), 146–181 (2003)
8. Celoxica. Handel-C language reference manual, v3.0 (2002)
9. Formal Systems Ltd. FDR: User Manual and Tutorial, version 2.82 (2005)
10. Freitas, A., Cavalcanti, A.L.C.: Automatic Translation from *Circus* to Java. In: Misra, J., Nipkow, T., Sekerinski, E. (eds.) FM 2006. LNCS, vol. 4085, pp. 115–130. Springer, Heidelberg (2006)
11. Gamma, E., Helm, R., Johnson, R., Vlissides, J.: Design patterns: elements of reusable object-oriented software. Addison-Wesley, Reading (1995)
12. Hilderink, G., Broenink, J., Vervoort, W., Bakkers, A.: Communicating Java threads. In: Andr{\'e} Bakkers, W.P. (ed.) A Concurrent Pascal Compiler for Minicomputers, University of Twente, Netherlands, vol. 50, pp. 48–76. IOS Press, Netherlands (1997)
13. Hoare, C.A.R.: Communicating Sequential Processes. Prentice-Hall, Englewood Cliffs (1985)
14. Jones, G., Goldsmith, M.: Programming in occam 2. Prentice-Hall, Englewood Cliffs (1988)
15. Hinchey, M.G., Jarvis, S.A.: Concurrent Systems: Formal Development in CSP. McGraw-Hill, New York (1995)
16. McMillin, B., Arrowsmith, E.: CCSP-A Formal System for Distributed Program Debugging. In: Proceedings of the Software for Multiprocessors and Supercomputers, Theory, Practice, Experience, Moscow, Russia (September 1994)
17. Oliveira, M.V.M., Cavalcanti, A.L.C.: From *Circus* to JCSP. In: Davies, J., Schulte, W., Barnett, M. (eds.) ICFEM 2004. LNCS, vol. 3308, pp. 320–340. Springer, Heidelberg (2004)
18. Phillips, J.D., Stiles, G.S.: An Automatic Translation of CSP to Handel-C. In: East, I.R., Duce, D., Green, M., Martin, J.M.R., Welch, P.H. (eds.) Communicating Process Architectures 2004, pp. 19–38 (September 2004)

19. Raju, V., Rong, L., Stiles, G.S.: Automatic Conversion of CSP to CTJ, JCSP, and CCSP. In: Broenink, J.F., Hilderink, G.H. (eds.) Communicating Process Architectures 2003, pp. 63–81 (September 2003)
20. Roscoe, A.W.: The Theory and Practice of Concurrency. Prentice-Hall Series in Computer Science. Prentice-Hall, Englewood Cliffs (1998)
21. Stepney, S.: CSP/FDR2 to Handel-C translation. Technical Report YCS-2002-357, Department of Computer Science, University of York (June 2003)
22. Welch, P.H.: Process oriented design for Java: concurrency for all. In: Arabnia, H.R. (ed.) Proceedings of the International Conference on Parallel and Distributed Processing Techniques and Applications, pp. 51–57. CSREA Press (June 2000)
23. Woodcock, J.C.P., Davies, J.: Using Z—Specification, Refinement, and Proof. Prentice-Hall, Englewood Cliffs (1996)

Modeling and Verification of Master/Slave Clock Synchronization Using Hybrid Automata and Model-Checking

Guillermo Rodriguez-Navas[1], Julián Proenza[1], and Hans Hansson[2]

[1] Departament de Matemàtiques i Informàtica,
Universitat de les Illes Balears, Spain
guillermo.rodriguez-navas@uib.es, julian.proenza@uib.es
[2] Malardalen Real Time Research Center,
Dept. of Computer Science and Electronics,
Malardalen University, Sweden
hans.hansson@mdh.se

Abstract. An accurate and reliable clock synchronization mechanism is a basic requirement for the correctness of many safety-critical systems. Establishing the correctness of such mechanisms is thus imperative. This paper addresses the modeling and formal verification of a specific fault-tolerant master/slave clock synchronization system for the Controller Area Network. It is shown that this system may be modeled with hybrid automata in a very natural way. However, the verification of the resulting hybrid automata is intractable, since the modeling requires variables that are dependent. This particularity forced us to develop some modeling techniques by which we translate the hybrid automata into single-rate timed automata verifiable with the model-checker UPPAAL. These techniques are described and illustrated by means of a simple example.

1 Introduction

This paper addresses the formal verification of a specific solution for fault-tolerant clock synchronization over the Controller Area Network (CAN) field-bus [1]. This solution is called OCS-CAN, which stands for *Orthogonal Clock Subsystem for the Controller Area Network* [2,3]. The aim of this formal verification is to use model checking in order to determine whether the designed fault tolerance mechanisms guarantee the desired precision in the presence of potential channel and node faults.

OCS-CAN can be naturally described with the formalism of hybrid automata [4] by assuming that clocks are continuous variables. Unfortunately, the resulting automata cannot be directly verified with model checking. The main difficulties are caused by two specific characteristics of the adopted clock synchronization algorithm: the existence of clocks of various rates, and the fact that neither the rates nor the values of the clocks are independent.

Without the second characteristic, the first one would not be a real problem. It is known that a system with clocks of different rates, also known as *multirate*

M. Butler, M. Hinchey, M.M. Larrondo-Petrie (Eds.): ICFEM 2007, LNCS 4789, pp. 307–326, 2007.
© Springer-Verlag Berlin Heidelberg 2007

clock system, can be translated into a verifiable single-rate timed automata as long as the rates of the clocks are independent [5,6]. But the second characteristic —the lack of independence— poses a real challenge to model checking, as it actually relates to a more general issue in the field of hybrid systems: the undecidability of the reachability problem in hybrid automata where variables are not decoupled [4], also called *non-rectangular hybrid automata*.

Despite this limitation, we were able to translate our non-rectangular hybrid automata into a network of timed automata verifiable with UPPAAL [7], and thus model check the precision guaranteed by OCS-CAN, as shown in [3,8]. The essence of this translation is twofold: 1) the behavior of the system is expressed over a single timeline, and 2) the lack of precision (the offset) between the clocks is converted into the corresponding delays over that timeline. The techniques developed to perform these tasks, which are closely related to the notion of *perturbed timed automata* [6], are discussed in this paper.

The contribution of this paper is relevant in many senses. First, it concerns the application of model checking to a realistic, and relatively complex, system. Second, it addresses a very important topic in the context of dependable embedded systems: formal verification of clock synchronization; and proposes a novel approach, since to the authors' best knowledge, model checking has not been previously applied to master/slave clock synchronization. Third, it shows that despite the theoretical limitation of verifying non-rectangular hybrid automata, the model of OCS-CAN can be translated into timed automata to allow model checking of certain properties. The discussed translation techniques may inspire other researchers willing to model check hybrid systems with dependent variables.

The rest of the paper is organized as follows. Sect. 2 introduces the notion of perturbed time automaton and relates it to the problem of clock synchronization. In Sect. 3, the main characteristics of OCS-CAN are discussed, paying special attention to the properties of its clock synchronization algorithm. In Sect. 4, the basic notation of OCS-CAN is defined, and the aim of the formal verification is stated in terms of this notation. Sect. 5 describes the modeling of OCS-CAN as a network of non-rectangular hybrid automata. In Sect. 6, the translation of such hybrid automata into a network of timed automata verifiable with UPPAAL is addressed. Some verification results are presented in Sect. 7, whereas Sect. 8 summarizes the paper.

2   Perturbed Timed Automata

Timed automata are, in principle, a very useful formalism to model systems with clocks. However, timed automata exhibit an important limitation: although they allow definition of multiple clocks, all clocks must evolve at the same pace [9]. This represents a limitation because real systems often work with *drifting clocks*, i.e. clocks that evolve at a slightly different rate, and therefore such systems cannot be directly modeled as timed automata. This limitation may, however, be overcome by adopting certain modeling techniques. One of such techniques,

Fig. 1. An example of two perturbed timed automata

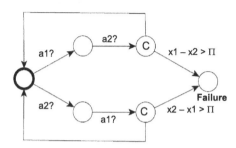

Fig. 2. An external observer to check precision between clock x1 and clock x2

which is known as perturbed timed automata [6], proposes to move the un-
certainty caused by the drifting clocks into the guards and invariants of the
automata. A similar technique is also used in [5].

The usefulness of perturbed timed automata is illustrated by the example
in Fig. 1. This example shows two automata which exhibit the same behavior:
they both use a clock (x1 and x2, respectively) to trigger a periodical action
(signaled through channel a1 and a2, respectively)), with period R. Both clocks
are assumed to start simultaneously and to have the same maximum drift (ρ)
with respect to real time. Due to this drift, they actually do not trigger the
periodical actions at an exact point of time, but they may trigger it within a
time interval $[R - \rho R, R + \rho R]$, as defined by the guard and invariant expressions.

When using such a model, the lack of synchronism between the clocks can
be easily checked by an external observer, which just measures the time elapsed
between the signaling over channel a1 and the signaling over channel a2. This
observer is depicted in Fig. 2. Notice that location **Failure** can only be reached
when one of the automata has performed the periodical signaling at least Π
time units later than the other one. Assuming that exceeding such threshold is
undesirable for some reason, the following safety property should be defined for
the system: A[ ] not Observer.Failure, stating that location **Failure** should
never be reached.

Note that according to the automata of Fig. 1, the location **Failure** is reachable, regardless of the value of Π, because the clocks are never resynchronized.
Therefore, behaviors in which they continuously diverge are possible. This per-
fectly matches the behavior of a real system with unsynchronized clocks.

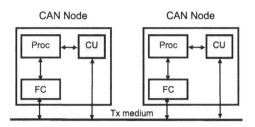

Fig. 3. Architecture of an OCS-CAN system

Nevertheless, the aim of this work is to model check the clock error of a system (OCS-CAN) where clock resynchronization is periodically performed, and where the effect of resynchronization is to dynamically change the values and drifts of the clocks. For instance, we wish to specify actions such as x2:= x1, which means that clock x2 takes the value of clock x1 (i.e. x2 synchronizes to x1). This requires more complex modeling than just perturbed automata. The techniques we have developed for this modeling are described in Sect. 6.

3   System Under Verification

OCS-CAN is designed to be incorporated into a CAN-based distributed embedded system. The role of OCS-CAN within such a system is to provide a common time view, which the processors of the nodes can rely on in order to perform coordinated actions [2,3].

3.1   Architecture of OCS-CAN

OCS-CAN is made up of a set of specifically designed hardware components, named *clock units*, which are interconnected through a CAN bus. When OCS-CAN is used, a clock unit is attached to every node of the system, as depicted in Fig. 3, along with the processor and the fieldbus controller (FC). Notice that the clock unit has its own connection to the CAN bus.

The clock unit is provided with a discrete counter, the so-called *virtual clock*, which is intended to measure real time. The clock units execute a master/slave clock synchronization algorithm, which aims at keeping all virtual clocks within a given interval of tolerance, which is called precision. In principle, only one of the clock units (the *master*) is allowed to spread its time view, and the rest of clock units (the *slaves*) synchronize to this time view.

In order to spread its time view, the master periodically broadcasts a specific message, which is called the *Time Message* (TM). Fig. 4 shows the transmission pattern of the TM when the resynchronization period is R time units.

The function of the TM is twofold: it signals the resynchronization event, which coincides with the first bit (the Start of Frame bit) of the TM, and also contains a timestamp that indicates the occurrence time of that event. This is

Fig. 4. Transmission pattern of the TM in the absence of faults

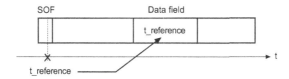

Fig. 5. The Time Message contains a timestamp of the Start of Frame bit

depicted in Fig. 5. Thanks to such timestamp mechanism, after receiving the TM, every slave can adjust the value and the rate of its virtual clock to take the value and the rate of the master's virtual clock [2].

3.2 Fault Tolerance Issues

Concerning the fault model, it is important to remark that the failure semantics of the clock unit is restricted to *crash failure semantics* by means of internal duplication with comparison. With respect to channel faults, OCS-CAN assumes the CAN bus to provide timely service but not reliability nor data consistency. This means that a TM broadcast by a master clock unit at time t is expected to be delivered to some clock unit within the interval $(t, t + wcrt]$ or not delivered at all, where $wcrt$ is the worst-case response time of the message [10]. Both inconsistent duplicates and inconsistent omissions of the TM, as defined in [11,12], may occur. Permanent failures of the bus, such as bus partition or stuck-at-dominant failures, are not addressed by OCS-CAN.

In order to provide tolerance to faults of the master, OCS-CAN defines a number of backup masters, one of which should take over upon failure of the active master. The mechanism for master replacement assumes that masters are organized hierarchically. The priority of a master is defined with two parameters. The first parameter is the identifier of the TM broadcast by the master; following the common convention in CAN, a lower identifier implies higher priority. The second parameter is the *release time* of the TM, which for every round indicates to every master when it is allowed to broadcast its corresponding TM. The *release time* of master m in the resynchronization round k, is calculated as follows:

$$T_{rls_m} = k \cdot R + \Delta_m$$

Where R is the resynchronization period (the same for all masters) and Δ_m (the *release delay*) is a small delay —in the order of a few ms— whose length is inversely proportional to the priority of the master.

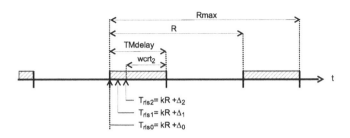

Fig. 6. Order of events within a synchronization round

The release time, combined with the assignment of identifiers discussed above, must guarantee that in a round, a master may broadcast its TM before a master of higher priority only if the latter is faulty. This is depicted in Fig. 6, for the case of three masters. In the absence of faults, the second and third TM are usually not broadcast, and if any of them is broadcast (for instance because one backup master could not timely abort a just-requested TM broadcast) then it is ignored by the slaves. The spare TMs are only taken into account if master 0 fails and is not able to broadcast its TM. Thanks to the master redundancy, in such situation the system will recover after a very short delay.

Nevertheless, in a CAN network it may happen that a message is not consistently received by all the nodes, as discussed in [11,12]. In such cases, the clock units might not receive a TM to synchronize with, or even worse, in the same round different clock units may synchronize to TMs broadcast by different masters. These scenarios, although being rather unlikely, may jeopardize clock synchronization and should be carefully studied.

A fundamental property of the CAN protocol states that, regardless of being consistent or not, a CAN broadcast always finishes within a bounded time interval, so the worst-case response time of any broadcast can be calculated, as discussed in [10]. In OCS-CAN this property implies that whenever a master clock units requests a TM broadcast, this request causes a reception of the TM in some other clock units before $wcrt$ time units, or it does not cause any reception at all.

This property also means that for every resynchronization round, receptions of the TM may only happen within a bounded temporal interval. This is shown in Fig. 6 by means of a shadowed window, which is called TMdelay. In an OCS-CAN system, the length of TMdelay is equal to $\Delta_l + wcrt_l$, where l is the master of lowest priority in the system. Since clock synchronization may only happen after reception of a TM, this implies that the maximum distance between two consecutive synchronizations of a clock unit is Rmax = R + TMdelay. Although it is not properly represented in Fig. 6, R is always much greater than TMdelay.

3.3 Master and Slave Finite State Machines

This section describes the algorithms executed by the clock units, as they are fundamental to understand the model used for formal verification. Every clock unit may behave either as a master or a slave. A non-faulty master clock unit executes the finite state machine in Fig. 7, whereas a non-faulty slave clock unit executes the finite state machine in Fig. 8. Both algorithms are built upon five primitives: TM.Request, TM.Indication, TM.Confirm, TM. Abort and Sync.

TM.Request. A master executes TM.Request to broadcast its TM as soon as it reaches the corresponding release time. This primitive is denoted TM.Req(n), where n is the identifier of the TM broadcast. Further information about the low-level actions triggered by TM.Req, such as timestamping, is available in [3].

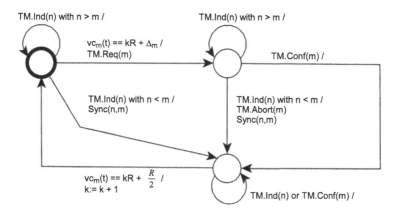

Fig. 7. Behavior of a non-faulty master m

TM.Indication. This primitive is executed when a TM is received. It is denoted TM.Ind(n), where n indicates the identifier of the received TM. Every master compares the value of n with its own identifier (m) to determine whether this TM comes from a higher priority master (case n < m) or not. Masters may only synchronize to masters of higher priority.

TM.Confirm. This primitive indicates to the transmitting master that a previously requested TM broadcast has been successful. It is denoted TM.Conf(n), where n indicates the identifier of the successfully broadcast TM.

TM.Abort. A master uses this primitive to abort the broadcast of a TM whose transmission was previously requested. It is denoted TM.Abort(n), where n is the identifier of the TM to be aborted. This action is caused by the reception of a higher priority TM, and has some associated latency so it may be the case that the TM broadcast is not timely aborted.

Sync. This primitive is executed by any clock unit (either master or slave) that receives a *valid* TM and wants to adjust its own virtual clock to the value conveyed by the TM. For the slaves, a valid TM is the first TM received in any resynchronization round (first TM.Ind(n)). For the masters, a valid TM is the first TM *of higher priority* received in any resynchronization round (the

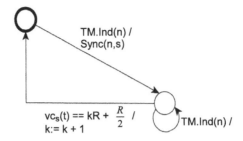

Fig. 8. Behavior of a non-faulty slave s

firstTM.Ind(n) with n < m), provided that the master did not successfully broadcast its own TM in that round. This primitive is denoted Sync(n, a), where a indicates the clock unit that is adjusting its virtual clock, and n is the identifier of the TM which clock unit a is using as a reference.

Concerning the Sync primitive, it is important to remark that the clock adjustment can never be exact. Even with the very accurate timestamping mechanism of OCS-CAN [3], certain imprecision remains, for instance due to small system latencies or to fixed-point arithmetics.

Note that a clock unit can only synchronize once per round. This is ensured by entering a waiting state after execution of the Sync primitive, in which further receptions of TM are ignored. Given that $\frac{R}{2}$ > TMdelay (as already indicated in Sect. 3.2), we ensure that TM duplicates and non-aborted TMs cannot cause duplicated resynchronizations.

4   Aim of Our Formal Verification

In this section, the basic notions of OCS-CAN, such as clock unit or virtual clock, are formally defined. These definitions are specially useful for describing the aim of our formal verification, which is to model check the precision guaranteed by OCS-CAN under diverse fault assumptions.

4.1   Basic Definitions

The synchronization algorithm is characterized by the resynchronization period R, and two parameters ϵ_0 and γ_0, which indicate the "quality" of the mechanism for clock adjustment. The failure assumptions are defined with two values *OD* (the *omission degree*) and *CD* (the *crash degree*), which indicate the maximum number of consecutive rounds affected by inconsistent message omissions and the maximum number of faulty masters, respectively.

Definition 1. *An OCS-CAN system is a set:*

$$OCSS = \{A, R, \epsilon_0, \gamma_0, OD, CD\}$$

such that:

- *A is a set of clock units.*
- *R ∈ $\mathbb{R}^+$ is the resynchronization period of the clock synchronization algorithm.*
- *ϵ_0 ∈ $\mathbb{R}^+$ is the maximum offset error after synchronization.*
- *γ_0 ∈ $\mathbb{R}^+$, $\gamma_0 \ll 1$, is the maximum drift error after synchronization.*
- *OD ∈ $\mathbb{N}$ is the omission degree.*
- *CD ∈ $\mathbb{N}$ is the crash degree.*

In an OCS-CAN system, the state of a clock unit is defined at any instant by the three following variables: the value of its virtual clock $vc(t)$, the rate of its virtual clock $\dot{vc}(t)$, and its operational state $f(t)$. Furthermore, every clock unit is characterized by the following three additional parameters, which indicate how the clock unit executes the clock synchronization algorithm: the relative priority (p) of the TM that the clock unit broadcasts, the release delay (Δ) of the TM that the clock unit broadcasts, and the worst case response time ($wcrt$) of the TM that the clock unit broadcasts.

Definition 2. *A clock unit a ∈ A is a 6-tuple:*

$$a = (vc_a, \dot{vc}_a, f_a, p_a, \Delta_a, wcrt_a)$$

such that:

- *$vc_a(t)$ ∈ $\mathbb{R}^+$ is the value of the virtual clock of a at time $t, \forall t \in \mathbb{R}^+$.*
- *$\dot{vc}_a(t)$ ∈ $\mathbb{R}^+$ is the instantaneous rate (or speed) of the virtual clock of a at time $t, \forall t \in \mathbb{R}^+$.*
- *$f_a : \mathbb{R}^+ \to \{0,1\}$ is the operational state of clock unit a. $f_a(t) = 1$ when a is faulty at time t, otherwise $f_a(t) = 0$.*
- *p_a ∈ $\mathbb{N}$ is the relative priority of the TM that clock unit a broadcasts, where $p_a = 0$ means that the clock unit never broadcasts the TM.*
- *Δ_a ∈ $\mathbb{R}^+$ is the release delay of the TM that clock unit a broadcasts.*
- *$wcrt_a$ ∈ $\mathbb{R}^+$ is the worst case response time of the TM that clock unit a broadcasts.*

Note that although the virtual clock of a clock unit is actually implemented as a discrete counter, and therefore it may take only values over $\mathbb{N}$, we define it over $\mathbb{R}^+$ for compatibility with the definition of time in timed automata. Also note that the values of Δ_a and $wcrt_a$ are irrelevant for slaves.

4.2   Offset and Precision

In OCS-CAN, each clock unit supplies its corresponding processor with a local view of real time. Therefore, the consistency in the perception of time depends on the difference (or *offset*) exhibited by the virtual clocks.

Definition 3. *Let A be a set of clock units. The maximum offset of set A at time t is:*

$$\Phi_A(t) = \max_{a,b \in A} \{|\Phi_{ab}(t)|\}$$

where:
$\Phi_{ab}(t) = vc_a(t) - vc_b(t)$ *is the offset between clock units $a, b \in A$ at time t.*

When the maximum offset between the clock units is always bounded, then the OCS-CAN system is said to be synchronized.

Definition 4. *An OCS-CAN system is Π-synchronized when there exists a constant $\Pi \in \mathbb{R}^+$, which is called the* precision, *such that $\Phi_A(t) \leq \Pi, \forall t \in \mathbb{R}^+$.*

The extent to which the system is synchronized depends on the value of Π. The lower the value of Π, the higher is the achieved precision.

Last, we define the concept of *consonance* between two clock units, as this concept turns out to be very important when modeling drifting clocks.

Definition 5. *Let $a, b \in A$ be two clock units. The consonance between them at time t is:*

$$\gamma_{ab}(t) = \dot{vc}_a(t) - \dot{vc}_b(t)$$

5   Modeling OCS-CAN as a Network of Hybrid Automata

The first step of model checking is to specify a formal model of the system under verification. Whenever a system combines both continuous components, which evolve over time as expressed by a differential equation, and discrete components, expressed by finite state machines, hybrid automata are very suitable for the modeling [13]. This is the case of OCS-CAN, since the virtual clocks can be easily modeled as continuous variables that are modified by the (discrete) synchronization actions performed by the clock units.

In this section, we discuss how the behavior of OCS-CAN can be specified by means of hybrid automata. It is shown that the resulting model includes variables that are not independent. Although this characteristic makes, in principle, the verification of our model unfeasible by model checking, in Sect. 6 we show that the model can still be translated into timed automata. Thanks to this, some safety properties, such as the guaranteed precision, can be verified.

5.1   Channel Abstraction

The communication channel is abstracted by means of an additional process channel_control, together with a global variable msg_id and a *broadcast channel* [7] called tx_msg. This abstraction is shown in Fig. 9. The function of the automaton channel_control is to enforce the worst-case response time of the TM broadcasts. A full description of channel_control is available in [3].

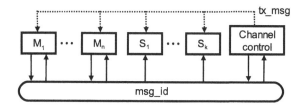

Fig. 9. Abstraction of the communication channel in OCS-CAN

The variable `msg_id` represents the identifier of the TM being broadcast. TM.Request is modeled as a write operation over `msg_id`, and CAN arbitration [1] is modeled by allowing the masters to overwrite the value of `msg_id` only whenever they have higher priority that the TM being transmitted. Therefore, TM.Req(m) is modeled with the following assignment: `msg_id:= min{m,msg_id}`. However, and for compatibility with the UPPAAL model checker, we hereafter use the C-like assignment: `msg_id:= m <? msg_id`, which is equivalent.

The broadcast channel `tx_msg` is used by `channel_control` to signal the instant at which the TM is delivered. Therefore, TM.Confirm and TM.Indication primitives are both signaled through `tx_msg`. For a master, a signaling through `tx_msg` is a TM.Confirm if the value of `msg_id` is equal to the identifier written by the master. Otherwise, it is a TM.Indication.

5.2   Abstraction of Clock Correction

In [2], we provide some details about the way virtual clocks are corrected (or adjusted) in OCS-CAN, and we highlight that clock correction is never performed immediately, but it is gradually carried out. This is called clock amortization.

Nevertheless, for the purpose of modeling and formal verification, we assume instantaneous clock correction instead of clock amortization. We make this abstraction because including clock amortization would cause an unnecessary complexity in the modeling. We are interested in assessing the maximum error (the achievable precision) between virtual clocks, and to do this we *only* have to examine the value of the virtual clocks a long time after the last resynchronization action. At these time instants, and provided that clock amortization is properly implemented [14], there is no difference between considering either instantaneous clock correction or clock amortization.

When instantaneous clock correction is assumed, executing the Sync(n,a) primitive is equivalent to assigning the value and the rate of the virtual clock of master n to the virtual clock of the synchronizing clock unit a. Since this assignment is never exact, the value and the rate assigned are always within an error interval. The width of this interval is determined by the maximum offset error ϵ_0, in the case of clock value assignments, and by the maximum drift error γ_0, in the case of clock rate assignments.

Since the Sync(n,a) primitive may cause discontinuities of the virtual clock values as well as discontinuities of the virtual clock rates, it makes sense to define the following notation.

$$f(t_0^+) = \lim_{t \searrow t_0} f(t)$$

$$f(t_0^-) = \lim_{t \nearrow t_0} f(t)$$

After that, the points of discontinuity can be characterized.

Definition 6. *Let $a \in A$ be a clock unit and $m \in M$ be a master. Then both $\dot{v}c_a(t)$ and $vc_a(t)$ are piecewise linear functions such that:*

- $\dot{v}c_a(t^+) = \bar{B}(\dot{v}c_m(t^-), \gamma_0)$ *when clock unit a executes Sync(m, a) at time t.*
- $vc_a(t^+) = \bar{B}(vc_m(t^-), \epsilon_0)$ *when clock unit a executes Sync(m, a) at time t.*

where $\bar{B}(x, \epsilon) = [x - \epsilon, x + \epsilon]$.

Remark 1. Let $m \in M$ be a master and $a \in A$ be a clock unit. If clock unit a executes Sync(m,a) at time t then $|\Phi_{ma}(t^+)| \leq \epsilon_0$ and $|\gamma_{ma}(t^+)| \leq \gamma_0$.

5.3   Master and Slave Hybrid Automata

When using the discussed abstractions for the communication channel and for clock correction, the hybrid automaton of a master corresponds to the one in Fig. 10.

Notice that in the transitions where the Sync(n, a) primitive should be executed, which were described in Sect. 3.3, this model includes assignments to the virtual clock's value and to the virtual clock's rate, as specified in Sect. 5.2 (Definition 6). Particularly, these assignments occur in the transitions from location 1 to location 4 and from location 2 to the committed location right before locations 3 and 4.

Furthermore, this automaton models three additional characteristics of OCS-CAN masters: the inconsistent reception of the TM, the possible non-abortion of the TM, and the possibility of master crash. A full description of these characteristics can be found in [3].

Inconsistent receptions of the TM are modeled at the receiver's side, by ignoring TM.Indications. For this reason, in locations 1 and 2, it is possible that a transition fired by a valid TM (tx_msg? with msd_id < m) does not cause any modification of the virtual clock.

When describing the management of the TM in Sect. 3.3, it was mentioned that a TM broadcast may not be timely aborted. This is modeled with a committed location, between locations 2 and 3, which is reached when the master has performed a TM.Request, but receives a TM.Indication of a higher priority master. From this location, the master may either overwrite again the variable msg_id or not. The first behavior would represent a non-aborted message.

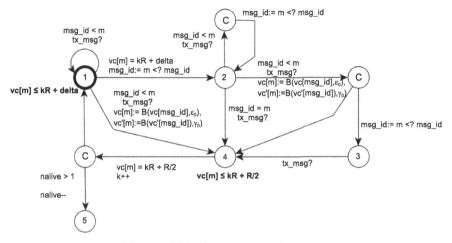

Fig. 10. Hybrid automaton of master m

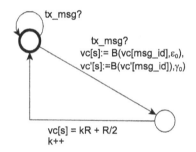

Fig. 11. Hybrid automaton of slave s

The master hybrid automaton includes a location that represents the *crash* failure (location 5). Notice that a master may nondeterministically step into this state as long as there is another non-faulty master in the system (condition `nalive > 1`).

The hybrid automaton of a slave is depicted in Fig. 11. This automaton also models the synchronization as an assignment to the virtual clock's value and to the virtual clock's rate, according to Definition 6. The possibility of inconsistent receptions of the TM is modeled by having transitions that are fired by TM.Indications but do not cause any clock correction.

Crash failures are not modeled for slaves, as such failures do not have any consequence for the rest of the system.

6   Translating the Model into Timed Automata

As discussed in Sect. 4, the aim of our formal verification is to determine whether an OCS-CAN system is Π-synchronized under certain fault hypotheses or not.

This formal verification is addressed by translating our hybrid automata into a network of timed automata verifiable with UPPAAL.

The main challenge of such translation is that, as a consequence of the Sync actions, clock and rate assignments exist. Although these assignments cannot be directly specified in timed automata notation, we circumvent this limitation in the following way: 1) the behavior of the system is expressed over a single timeline, and 2) the offset between the virtual clocks is converted into delays over that timeline.

Therefore, the first step is to decide what this single timeline represents. In our model, time corresponds to the clock of the highest priority master, which is called *reference clock* hereafter. For the rest of clock units, we use the consonance (γ_i) with respect to this clock in order to calculate the delays over the reference timeline. Furthermore, four additional aspects need special consideration:

- The instant when the offset is to be checked has to be properly defined. This instant is called the *observance instant*.
- Updates of the value of a virtual clock, as defined in the equations of Sect. 5.2, must be modeled.
- Updates of the rate of a virtual clock need to be modeled as well. Particularly, it is important to model how a rate change may affect the consonance with respect to the reference clock.
- The model must include changes of the reference clock when the master of highest priority crashes.

In the following, these aspects are described in detail. A model of a simplified OCS-CAN system, which is made up of two masters and an arbitrary number of slaves, is used to illustrate the main points. The modeling of the failure assumptions of OCS-CAN is not included to reduce the complexity of the model and help reader's understanding. The complete UPPAAL model can be found in [8].

6.1   Definition of the Observance Instant

In order to adopt the verification technique described in Sect. 2 (the `precision observer`), the observance instant must be known a priori, and it must be signaled by all of the clock units. Since we are interested in knowing the precision of OCS-CAN, we should check it at the instant with the maximum offset. This instant must be located before a Sync(n,a) primitive because the involved clocks converge immediately after this primitive is executed.

Although it is not possible to know the exact instant of execution of any Sync(n,a) primitive, it is possible to determine the maximum distance between the synchronization instants of two consecutive rounds. In Sect. 3.3 it was shown that the maximum distance is given by Rmax= R + TMdelay. This value can be used to upper bound the offset accumulated during one synchronization round, as described next.

Fig. 12 depicts the `virtual clock` automaton, which models the behavior of virtual clock i. Although one `virtual clock` is included for each clock unit

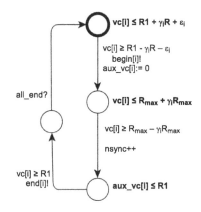

Fig. 12. Virtual clock of clock unit i

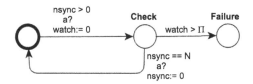

Fig. 13. Precision observer

in the system, this automaton does not describe the behavior of a master or a slave; what it actually models is the passage of time as measured by clock unit i, and represents it with the clock vc[i]. According to the value of vc[i] certain events are signaled, so the clock units (either master or slave) can execute the clock synchronization algorithm discussed in Sect. 3.3. This means that in every round, every master and slave automaton chooses which virtual clock it uses, which is equivalent to having clock assignments.

As shown in Fig. 12, the **virtual clock** automaton signals three events: the instant to broadcast the TM (through channel begin[i]); the observance instant; and the instant for resetting the virtual clocks (through channel end[i]). Notice that the first two events are signaled within time intervals whose lengths depend on the consonance (γ_i) with respect to the reference clock.

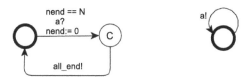

Fig. 14. Auxiliary automata

In the second event, the integer variable nsync is incremented. This variable is monitored by the observer depicted in Fig. 13, in order to detect the first virtual clock to reach this point. This observer resets clock watch after that event. If watch exceeds a given value Π before all nodes increment nsync then location Failure will be reached, expressing that the system is *not* Π-synchronized. Note that the observer makes use of the synchronization channel a, which is activated by the dummy automaton shown in Fig. 14.

6.2   Modeling of Virtual Clock Value Assignments

Once the observance instant and the precision observer have been defined, the model must ensure that, for each virtual clock, the delay in reaching this instant really corresponds to the offset between the virtual clock and the reference clock.

According to the hybrid automata of Sect. 5.3, the Sync(n,a) primitive causes an update on the value of the synchronizing virtual clock. This kind of clock assignments may be indirectly modeled with the simultaneous restart of the clocks involved in the synchronization action. However, in our model virtual clocks cannot be restarted immediately after the Sync(n,a) primitive because this would interfere the role of the observer. Instead, virtual clocks have to continue until they reach the observance instant and signal it.

This forces us to delay the simultaneous restart. In this manner, the Sync(n,a) primitive does not cause a clock assignment (which is not possible in a timed automaton) nor an immediate restart (which would make the measurement of the precision impossible). Instead, Sync(n,a) causes an assignment to a *clock pointer*, the variable ref_id, which is used later on to detect when to restart vc[i]. This is shown in Fig. 15 for master 2, and in Fig. 16 for slave j.

In these automata, the channel abstraction of Sect. 5.3, based on the variable msg_id and the channel tx_msg, is further simplified to reduce the complexity of the automata and improve legibility. In fact, Sync(1,j) is signaled through channel s1 whereas Sync(2,j) is signaled through channel s2.

In both automata it can be observed that vc[i] is restarted when the corresponding virtual clock automaton signals —through channel end[ref_id]— that the pointed clock has reached a certain value R1= R/2 (third event in Fig. 12). This modeling technique guarantees that all the clocks that have synchronized to the same master are restarted simultaneously, thus fulfilling Remark 1 in Sect. 5.2. In contrast, whenever two clocks do not synchronize to the same master, the offset that these two clocks have accumulated in the round is kept for the next round.

Channel all_end, which appears in the automaton of Fig. 12, is used in order to avoid violation of time invariants. The left auxiliary automaton of Fig. 14 uses this channel to make every virtual clock automaton wait until all masters and slaves have reset vc[i].

6.3   Modeling of Virtual Clock Rate Assignments

Clock rate assignments can be easily modeled with a variable γ_i that keeps the consonance with respect to the reference clock. This variable is used by

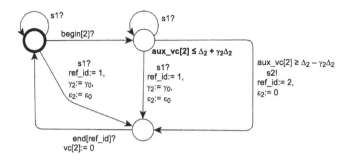

Fig. 15. Automaton of master 2

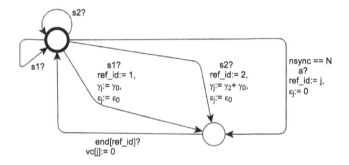

Fig. 16. Automaton of slave j

the virtual clock automata in order to define the interval of occurrence of any relevant event. In Fig. 15 and 16 it can be seen that the value of γ_i is updated in every synchronization action. Whenever a clock unit does not synchronize to any master within a synchronization round, the value of γ_i remains unchanged.

It is important to remark that whenever a clock unit synchronizes to a master that is not the current reference clock, the clock unit "inherits" the drift error of that master. In this case, the consonance after synchronization may be worse than before synchronization. This can be observed in one of the transitions fired by s2 in the slave automaton of Fig. 16.

6.4   Change of the Reference Clock Due to Master Crash

Whenever the reference clock crashes, the timeline of the model needs be redefined. Although it is not shown in the automata, this recalculation is implicitly performed if in every round the value of γ_i is assigned as follows:

- If master i is the current reference clock: $\gamma_i := 0$.
- If clock unit i synchronizes to the current reference clock: $\gamma_i := \gamma_0$.

- If clock unit i synchronizes to a master n that is not the current reference clock: $\gamma_i := \gamma_0 + \gamma_n + \gamma_{ref}$; where γ_{ref} is the consonance between the current reference clock and the reference clock of the previous synchronization round.

7   Some Verification Results

By applying the transformations described above, an OCS-CAN system can be modeled as a network of timed automata and the guaranteed precision can be model checked. In a previous paper we provided some results that were achieved with the complete UPPAAL model of OCS-CAN [8]. These verification results were obtained in the following situations:

- Fault-free scenario.
- Only master faults (no channel faults).
- Only channel faults (no master faults), assuming *data consistency* and without assuming *data consistency*.
- Master faults and channel faults, assuming *data consistency* and without assuming *data consistency*.

Concerning the precision guaranteed by the clock synchronization service, Table 1 shows the precision that was verified under diverse fault assumptions. These results were obtained with the following parameters: N= 4 masters, R= 1s, $\Delta_0 = 0$, $\Delta_1 = 1$ ms, $\Delta_2 = 2$ ms, $\Delta_3 = 3$ ms. Regarding the network load, it was assumed that no other messages were sent on the bus, so wcrt= 1.04 ms was used in those scenarios without channel faults whereas wcrt= 6 ms was used in those scenarios with channel faults.

The first cell in Table 1 shows the precision guaranteed in the fault-free scenario. This precision equals to 2 μs. The first row of Table 1 corresponds to the scenarios in which only master's faults were assumed. Note that the number of faulty masters does not affect significantly the precision guaranteed. This is due to the fact that master replacement takes place in a very short time, which is negligible compared to R.

The first column of Table 1 corresponds to the scenarios in which only channel's faults were assumed. OD= 0 indicates that no inconsistent omissions can occur, which is a common assumption in other clock synchronization protocols

Table 1. Fault assumptions and precision guaranteed (in μs) with R = 1 sec

# Channel faults	# Faulty masters			
	0	1	2	3
No faults	2	2.1	2.1	2.1
OD = 0	2.1	2.1	2.1	2.1
OD = 1	6.1	6.1	6.1	6.1
OD = 2	10.1	12.1	12.1	12.1
OD = 3	14.1	16.1	16.1	16.1

for CAN. The rest of cells in Table 1 correspond to the scenarios where a combination of node and channel faults is assumed. In particular, the right bottom cell corresponds to the most severe fault scenario.

8   Conclusions

In this paper, the formal verification of OCS-CAN has been discussed. OCS-CAN is a solution for clock synchronization over CAN that adopts a fault-tolerant master/slave clock synchronization. It has been shown that this system can be naturally described with hybrid automata, by modeling the virtual clocks as variables that evolve over time with certain rates.

An important particularity of these hybrid automata is that they are not rectangular, because of the inevitable dependencies that the clock synchronization actions cause among the clocks. This lack of independence makes, in principle, the verification of these timed automata intractable by model checking. However, we have shown that it is possible to translate the hybrid automata into a timed automata verifiable with the UPPAAL model checker. Thanks to this, the precision guaranteed by OCS-CAN has been successfully model checked under diverse fault assumptions.

The techniques developed in order to carry out such translation have been presented, and they have been illustrated in a simple example. These techniques somehow extend the notion of perturbed timed automata, by allowing drifting clocks whose rates may change dynamically as a consequence of discrete actions. Our modeling may be useful for other researchers that aim at model checking hybrid systems in which variables are dependent.

Acknowledgments. This work is partially supported by DPI 2005-09001-C03-02 and FEDER funding. Authors would like to thank Mercè Llabrés and Antonio E. Teruel for their useful remarks on the mathematical notation.

References

1. ISO: ISO11898. Road vehicles - Interchange of digital information - Controller area network (CAN) for high-speed communication (1993)
2. Rodríguez-Navas, G., Bosch, J., Proenza, J.: Hardware Design of a High-precision and Fault-tolerant Clock Subsystem for CAN Networks. In: FeT 2003, Portugal (2003)
3. Rodríguez-Navas, G., Proenza, J., Hansson, H.: Using UPPAAL to Model and Verify a Clock Synchronization Protocol for the Controller Area Network. In: Proc. of the 10th IEEE International Conference on Emerging Technologies and Factory Automation, Catania, Italy (2005)
4. Henzinger, T.A., Kopke, P.W., Puri, A., Varaiya, P.: What's decidable about hybrid automata? Journal of Computer and System Sciences 57(1), 94–124 (1998)
5. Daws, C., Yovine, S.: Two examples of verification of multirate timed automata with KRONOS. In: RTSS 1995, Pisa, Italy, pp. 66–75. IEEE Computer Society Press, Los Alamitos (1995)

6. Alur, R., Torre, S.L., Madhusudan, P.: Perturbed Timed Automata. In: Morari, M., Thiele, L. (eds.) HSCC 2005. LNCS, vol. 3414, pp. 70–85. Springer, Heidelberg (2005)
7. Behrmann, G., David, A., Larsen, K.G.: A tutorial on UPPAAL. In: Bernardo, M., Corradini, F. (eds.) SFM-RT 2004. LNCS, vol. 3185, pp. 200–236. Springer, Heidelberg (2004)
8. Rodriguez-Navas, G., Proenza, J., Hansson, H.: An UPPAAL Model for Formal Verification of Master/Slave Clock Synchronization over the Controller Area Network. In: Proc. of the 6th IEEE International Workshop on Factory Communication Systems, Torino, Italy, IEEE Computer Society Press, Los Alamitos (2006)
9. Alur, R., Madhusudan, P.: Decision problems for timed automata: A survey. In: Bernardo, M., Corradini, F. (eds.) SFM-RT 2004. LNCS, vol. 3185, pp. 200–236. Springer, Heidelberg (2004)
10. Tindell, K., Burns, A., Wellings, A.J.: Calculating Controller Area Network (CAN) Message Response Time. Control Engineering Practice 3(8), 1163–1169 (1995)
11. Rufino, J., Veríssimo, P., Arroz, G., Almeida, C., Rodrigues, L.: Fault-tolerant broadcasts in CAN. In: The 28th IEEE International Symposium on Fault-Tolerant Computing, Munich, Germany (1998)
12. Proenza, J., Miro-Julia, J.: MajorCAN: A modification to the Controller Area Network to achieve Atomic Broadcast. In: IEEE Int. Workshop on Group Communication and Computations, Taipei, Taiwan (2000)
13. Henzinger, T.A., Pei-Hsin, H., Wong-Toi, H.: Algorithmic analysis of nonlinear hybrid systems. IEEE Transactions on Automatic Control 43(4), 540–554 (1998)
14. Schmuck, F., Cristian, F.: Continuous clock amortization need not affect the precision of a clock synchronization algorithm. In: PODC 1990, pp. 133–143. ACM Press, New York (1990)

Efficient Symbolic Execution of Large Quantifications in a Process Algebra

Benoît Fraikin and Marc Frappier

Département d'informatique, Université de Sherbrooke, Québec, Canada
{Benoit.Fraikin,Marc.Frappier}@Usherbrooke.CA

Abstract. This paper describes three optimization techniques for a process algebra interpreter called EB^3PAI. This interpreter supports the EB^3 method, which was developed for the purpose of automating the development of information systems using *efficient symbolic execution* of abstract specifications. The proposed optimizations allow an interpreter to execute actions on a quantified choice in constant time and on a quantified parallel composition in logarithmic time with respect to the number of entities in a quantified entity type. This time complexity is comparable to that of programmer-derived implementation of process expressions and significantly better than the time complexity of common process algebra simulators, which execute quantifications by computing their expansion into binary expressions.

1 Introduction

Process algebras have now been recognized has excellent modelling notations for specifying system behavior. They are used in various areas such as telecom systems, control systems, business processes and web services. In the APIS project [1,2], they are used to specify information systems (IS). The APIS platform supports the EB^3 method [3], which was designed for the specification of IS. This platform includes a symbolic interpreter, called EB^3PAI, to efficiently execute process expressions of IS specifications. Its goal is to reach a level of efficiency comparable to hand-made implementations, thereby avoiding the implementation of these process expressions, which represents a significant increase in software development productivity.

In developing an efficient interpreter for IS process expressions, one has to deal with quantified (also called indexed or replicated) process expressions, mainly for choice quantification and parallel composition quantification. For example, the process expression

$$||| \, x \in 1..m \, : \, \mathbf{P} \, (\, x \,)$$

denotes the expanded process expression

$$\mathbf{P} \, (\, 1 \,) \, ||| \, \ldots \, ||| \, \mathbf{P} \, (\, m \,).$$

Existing process algebras simulators like PROBE [4] and CIA [5] for CSP, the simulator in the μCRL tool set [6], and CADP's OCIS [7] for LOTOS, are executing quantifications (or an equivalent feature) by expanding them. Code generators like JCircus [8,9] translates a Circus [10] specification into a Java program

M. Butler, M. Hinchey, M.M. Larrondo-Petrie (Eds.): ICFEM 2007, LNCS 4789, pp. 327–344, 2007.

using JCSP [11]. A quantification is also expanded and each interleaved process is implemented by a separate thread.

Expansion of quantifications is not acceptable for the execution of IS process specifications, because the size of the quantification set is typically huge (e.g., $m \geq 10^{10}$). Constant m denotes the maximum value of a key of an entity in an IS (e.g., a book id in a library system).

In this paper we propose techniques, called κ-optimization, to efficiently execute quantifications in a process expression. These techniques apply to several recurrent patterns of IS specifications which are found in EB^3 specifications and defined in [3]. Let n denote the number of entities in an entity type (e.g., the number of books in a library system). When the sufficient conditions are met, our algorithms can execute choice quantifications in constant time and quantified parallel composition in $\mathcal{O}(log(n))$ or in constant time, depending on the implementation used for a map (B-tree or hash table). A programmer derived (i.e., hand-made) implementation of these process expressions has a comparable time complexity, although it is more efficient since there is less overhead than for symbolic execution. Our algorithms are more efficient than existing process algebra simulators, since they expand quantifications, which means that their time complexity is linear ($\mathcal{O}(m)$) for both quantified choice and quantified parallel composition. Note that usually m is quite greater than n, since m denotes the upper bound for the value of an entity key, hence it denotes the maximum number of entities, whereas n denotes the number of entities currently existing in the system. Our algorithms are also more efficient than code generation in JCircus, since it requires m threads to implement a quantification.

The proposed algorithms are defined for the EB^3 process algebra, but they could probably be adapted for other process algebras like CSP, μCRL, FSP and Circus, which include quantified operators. LOTOS does not include quantification; it must be simulated using recursion.

Our algorithms are suitable for process algebra *simulators*, but not for *model checkers*. A simulator executes actions as requested by the environment. It explores only the execution path that the environment commands during execution. Simulators are typically used for specification animation and validation with users. The objective of EB^3PAI is to increase the efficiency of simulators to use them as an implementation of a specification.

Model checkers are addressing another issue for which our algorithms are not relevant. They are used to verify that a process expression satisfy a given property. The property is checked by exploring the entire transition system of the process expression; hence expansion of quantification is necessary since each individual process may have to be checked. Typical examples of model checkers include FDR2 [12] for CSP, the Concurrency Workbench [13] for CCS, ProB [14] for a combination of CSP and B, the model checking tools in the μCRL tool set [6], LTSA [15] for FSP, and CADP's EVALUATOR [7] for LOTOS.

This paper is structured as follows. Section 2 provides a brief overview of the EB^3 process algebra method and describes the general idea of symbolic execution with EB^3PAI. Section 3 is the main part of this paper. It describes the optimization of large quantified expressions. Finally, Section 4 analyzes the space and time complexity of the symbolic execution algorithm and provides some experimental results showing the actual performance of its implementation, EB³PAI. Section 5 concludes with some remarks and future work on improvements to EB³PAI.

2   The EB³ Process Algebra and Symbolic Execution

The EB³ process algebra is inspired from regular expressions, CSP [16], CCS [17], ACP [18] and LOTOS [19]. Its syntax has been simplified in order to streamline IS specification. The reader may consult [3,20,21] for additional details and a thorough comparison with these process algebras.

2.1   Syntax

A process expression is defined over a set of symbols Σ, called the *action set*, whose elements are denoted by $a(t_1, \ldots, t_n)$, where a is an action label and t_i denotes a constant or a variable. Set Σ_e is the set of ground actions from Σ, i.e., those with no variable; it is called the *input event set*. Set Σ_l denotes the set of labels of actions in Σ.

The process expressions over Σ are defined recursively as follows. Elements of $\Sigma \cup \{\lambda\}$ represent *elementary* process expressions over Σ. The symbol $\square$, called "box", is an elementary process expression denoting successful completion. Let E, E_1, and E_2 be process expressions over Σ, $n \in \mathbb{N}$, $\Delta \subseteq \Sigma_l$ and Φ be a formula. The expressions E^*, E^+, E^n, $E_1 \cdot E_2$, $E_1 \mid E_2$, $E_1 |[\Delta]| E_2$, $E_1 \parallel E_2$, $E_1 \parallel\mid E_2$, $\Phi \Longrightarrow E$, and $([x := t_1, \ldots, x := t_n])E$ are process expressions over Σ. Operations $*$, $+$, n, and $\cdot$ denote the usual Kleene closure, positive closure, and concatenation of regular expressions. Operation $\mid$ is a choice between E_1 and E_2; it is drawn from regular expressions and CSP [16]. Operation $|[\Delta]|$ is the parameterized parallel composition of E_1 and E_2 with synchronization on actions whose labels belong to Δ; it is drawn from LOTOS. Intuitively, the composition $E_1 |[\Delta]| E_2$ is a process that can execute actions of either E_1 or E_2 without constraint, but actions in Δ must be executed by both E_1 and E_2. Actions in Δ are said to be synchronized. Operations $\parallel\mid$ and $\parallel$ are the interleave and parallel composition of CSP [16], respectively; they are special variants of $|[\ ]|$: $E_1 \parallel\mid E_2$ is equivalent to $E_1 |[\emptyset]| E_2$ and $E_1 \parallel E_2$ is a synchronized composition of E_1 and E_2 on shared actions of E_1 and E_2, i.e., $E_1 |[\alpha(E_1) \cap \alpha(E_2)]| E_2$, where the operator α denotes the alphabet (set of labels) of a process expression. The operator α is defined recursively on the structure and returns the set of all the action labels occurring in a process expression but λ. The process expression $\Phi \Longrightarrow E$ is the guard of E by Φ: it means that E can execute an action if and only if Φ is true. The process expression $([x_1 := t_1, \ldots, x_n := t_n])E$ is called an environment and it denotes the simultaneous substitution of $x_1, \ldots, x_n$ by $t_1, \ldots, t_n$ in E. The special symbol λ denotes an internal action that a process may execute without requiring input from the system's environment. It plays a role similar that of the empty word ϵ in regular expressions or the unobservable action τ in

CCS and i in LOTOS. The EB^3 process algebra also allows *quantification* (also called *indexing* or *replication* in CSP) over operators $|, |[\Delta]| , |||$. For instance, the process expression $| x \in 1..n : \mathbf{P}(x)$ denotes $\mathbf{P}(1) | \mathbf{P}(2) | \cdots | \mathbf{P}(n)$. Quantifications are restricted to finite sets.

For the sake of readability, we sometimes write a instead of a( ). We use the following precedence of operators from highest to lowest, enclosing between "(" and ")" operators with the same precedence: $(^{*}, \ ^{+})$, ., $|$, $(|[ ]|, |||, \|$ as binary operators), $(|[ ]|, |||, |$ as quantified operators).

2.2   An Example

To illustrate our optimizations, consider the specification provided by Figure 1. It shows the process **main** and auxiliary process definitions for a simple library system. The rest of the EB^3 specification is omitted, since it is not relevant to illustrate our optimization techniques. Figure 2 provides the entity-relationship diagram of this specification.

There are two entity types (book and member) and one association (loan), each modelled by a process expression. A book must be acquired in order to be used in the library, and a member must join it. Books and members are identified by a number (bId and mId). A member can borrow a book, renew it as many times as he wants and, finally, return it to the library. While a member is borrowing a book, no other member can borrow it. Other usual properties of loans are represented by this specification. The behavior of each single entity or

---

main ( )=
      $(||| \ bId \in$ BOOKID $: \mathbf{book}(bId)^{*})$
    $\|$
      $(||| \ mId \in$ MEMBERID $: \mathbf{member}(mId)^{*})$

book (bId : BOOKID) =
    Acquire(bId).
    $(| \ mId \in$ MEMBERID $: \mathbf{loan}(mId, bId))^{*}$.
    Sell(bId) ;

loan (mId : MEMBERID, bId : BOOKID) =
    Lend(mId, bId).
    Renew(bId)*.
    Return(bId) ;

member (mId : MEMBERID) =
    Join(mId).
    $(||| \ bId \in$ BOOKID $: \mathbf{loan}(mId, bId))^{*}$.
    Leave(mId) ;

Process expression **main** and process definitions

Fig. 1. EB^3 specification example

Fig. 2. Entity-relationship diagram of the library system

association (a book, a member, or a loan) is defined by the corresponding process definition. The system is defined using quantifications that, on the one hand, allow for multiple entities (quantified interleave), and on the other hand, model the cardinality of the association (quantified choice for $0..1$ and a quantified interleave for $*$). In the following, an *entity* is an instance of a process that models an IS entity like **book** or **member**. An *association* is an instance of a process that models an IS association like **loan**. An entity type is represented in EB^3 by a quantification over all possible entities. For example,

$$||| \, mId \in \text{MEMBERID} \; : \; \mathbf{member} \, (\, mId \,)^*$$

represents the entity type member. Process **member** (1) represents the member entity with $mId = 1$. Additional explanations and a more complex example of a library can be found in [22].

It is important to note that quantification is a crucial operator in IS specification. This constitutes a major difference from other problem domains where process algebras are typically used (protocol specification for example). Since the main aim of EB^3 is to provide an executable specification, the specification style used to achieve this goal is also different.

2.3 Symbolic Execution of EB^3 Process Expressions

EB^3PAI is a symbolic interpreter. It executes the inference rules of an operational semantics defined in the CCS style [17]. The original semantics of the EB^3 process algebra has been defined in [3]. A new operational semantics, optimized for symbolic execution, has been defined in [20,21]. EB^3PAI is based on this semantics. We provide below an outlook of the symbolic execution strategy. For more details, the reader may consult [20,21].

Given a process expression P and an action σ, one can compute the possible transitions and resulting process expressions (PEs) using the inference rules. This involves a proof search that determines which inference rules are applicable, by matching the structure of P with E_1 in an inference rule of the form $\frac{E_2 \xrightarrow{\sigma} E_2'}{E_1 \xrightarrow{\sigma} E_1'}$. When a match is found, the rule's premiss, which are themselves transitions (e.g., $E_2 \xrightarrow{\sigma} E_2'$), induce a recursive search. Ultimately, the search reaches a rule which doesn't have a transition in its premiss. Then, the resulting process expression Q is constructed by backtracking over the inference rules through termination of recursive search calls.

In summary, EB^3PAI executes a specification by simply evaluating the inference rules. We do not generate code per se; EB^3PAI can be considered as a virtual machine and each specification becomes a high-level program. The implementation is the combination of EB³PAI and the specification.

3   Optimizations for Symbolic Execution

3.1   Optimizing Quantification Execution Time: Direct κ-Optimization

The Problem of Large Quantification. The EB³ language allows the use of quantification operators. For example,

$$| x \in 1..10^{10} \; : \; ||| \, y \in 1..10^{10} \; : \; \mathsf{a}(\, x, y \,) \cdot \mathsf{b}(\, y, x \,) \tag{1}$$

A basic approach to executing quantification operators is to iterate over the values of the quantification set to determine whether a transition is feasible. It is clear that such a linear search through a large set is too ineffective to be acceptable. Moreover, the execution of a quantified interleave generates large interleave expressions. For instance, if the process defined by (1) has executed $\mathsf{a}(\, 2, 1 \,), \ldots, \mathsf{a}(\, 2, 10^9 \,)$, the resulting PE is

$$(\![y := 1, x := 2]\!)\mathsf{b}(\, y, x \,)$$
$$|||$$
$$\cdots$$
$$|||$$
$$(\![y := 10^9, x := 2]\!)\mathsf{b}(\, y, x \,)$$
$$|||$$
$$(\,||| \, y \in 1..10^{10} - 1..10^9 \; : \; \mathsf{a}(\, x, y \,) \cdot \mathsf{b}(\, y, x \,)).$$

When action $b(10^9, 2)$ must be executed, another linear search must be done over the interleave composition, which is also too inefficient.

To optimize these executions, we determine by static analysis of each quantified expression which value of the quantified set must be selected based on the parameters of the action to execute. We call these values κ-**values**, the positions of the values in the action parameters κ-**positions**, and this method direct κ-**optimization.**

For instance, in process expression (1), we can determine that when

$$| x \in 1..10^{10} \; : \; \ldots$$

must execute $\mathsf{a}(\, t_1, t_2 \,)$, the only execution feasible is with $x = t_1$; similarly, the only execution feasible for

$$||| \, y \in 1..10^{10} \; : \; \ldots$$

is with $y = t_2$. Hence, whenever possible, we determine a map $\Pi : \Sigma \to T$ for each quantified expression $\Phi x \in T : E$ such that $(\![x := \Pi(\sigma)]\!)E$ is the only candidate to execute a transition with σ. Specifically, we determine the position of the quantification variable within the parameters of each action.

These positions, called κ-positions, are determined by static analysis before the execution of a specification. Let $\kappa(\chi, E)$ be the κ-position of χ-labelled actions in E, where E is a quantified interleave operator or a quantified choice operator. Then, if we need to optimize the quantification E for any event σ,

$$\Pi(\sigma) \triangleq \pi_{\kappa(\alpha(\sigma),E)}(param(\sigma))$$

where $\pi_i((x_1,\ldots,x_i,\ldots,x_n)) = x_i$, $\alpha(\sigma)$ is the label of σ and $param(\sigma)$ is the tuple of the parameters of σ.

This approach is sufficient to optimize a choice quantification, since the quantification disappears after the transition. In the case of a quantified interleave, the quantification remains in the result process expression, since it can spawn one interleave process for each value in the quantification set. For example, the execution of $a(1)$ from the process expression

$$| \, x \in [1..3] \; : \; a(x) \, \centerdot \, b(x)$$

returns $(\![x := 1]\!)b(x)$. The execution of the same event on

$$||| \, x \in [1..3] \; : \; a(x) \, \centerdot \, b(x)$$

returns

$$\big(\, (\![x := 1]\!)b(x) \, \big) \; ||| \; \big(\, ||| \, x \in [2..3] \; : \; a(x) \, \centerdot \, b(x) \, \big).$$

The interleave of the instantiated process expressions (i.e., $P(t_1) \; ||| \; \ldots \; ||| \; P(t_n)$) is represented by a function $K : T \to \mathcal{PE}$ such that $K(\Pi(\sigma))$ is the only process expression that can execute σ.

Figure 3 describes the function $find_\kappa(E, x, \text{EP})$, which determines a κ-position for a variable x in a process E. The parameter EP is used to keep track of the process definitions that have been parsed so far over recursive calls; it is set to $\emptyset$ on the initial call. The function $find_\kappa$ returns a relation between action labels and $\mathbb{N} \cup \{\bot\}$. The symbol $\lrcorner$ is used as a marker to detect overlapping quantifications on the same variable; the algorithm returns $\bot$ for actions within the scope of these overlapping quantifications. When an action does not contain x in its parameters, $\bot$ is also returned. A quantification is κ-optimizable if the result of $find_\kappa$ is a deterministic relation and does not include $\bot$ in its codomain (i.e., x occurs in the same position for each occurrence of an action in E). A choice quantification is also partially κ-optimizable when the image set of the action to execute is a singleton; for other actions which include either $\bot$ or several κ-positions, κ-optimization is not applicable.

This algorithm, which is part of a static analysis of the specification prior to its execution, is applied on every quantified process expression. Its algorithmic complexity is $\mathcal{O}(N_E)$, where N_E is the number of nodes in the syntax tree of E. This number is usually small ($N_E < 100$). It does not depend on the number of entities involved in E. At runtime, the algorithmic complexity of retrieving the instantiated interleave process depends on the implementation chosen for map K; databases usually offer either hash tables or B-trees, which means constant or logarithmic access time. As for space complexity, a process

$find_\kappa(E, x, \text{EP}) \triangleq$ match E with

$$(\![z_1 := y_1 \ldots z_n := y_n]\!)E_0 \;\text{-> if } \exists_i\,(y_i = x)\text{ then } t := z_i \text{ else } t := x \text{ endif};$$
$$\text{return } find_\kappa(E_0, t, \text{EP}),$$

$$\lambda \;\text{-> return } \emptyset,$$

$$\text{a}(y_1, \ldots, y_n) \;\text{-> if } \exists_i\,(y_i = x)\text{ then } j = i \text{ else } j = \perp \text{ endif};$$
$$\text{return } \{\,(\text{a}, j)\,\},$$

$$E_1\Phi E_2 \;\text{-> return } find_\kappa(E_1, x, \text{EP})\;\cup\;find_\kappa(E_2, x, \text{EP}),$$

$$\varphi \Longrightarrow E_0 \;\text{-> return } find_\kappa(E_0, x, \text{EP}),$$

$$\Phi(E_0) \;\text{-> if } \Phi \text{ is a quantification on } x$$
$$\text{then } t := \lrcorner \text{ else } t := x \text{ endif};$$
$$\text{return } find_\kappa(E_0, t, \text{EP}),$$

$$Q(y_1, \ldots, y_n) \;\text{-> if } Q \in \text{EP then return } \emptyset \text{ else}$$
$$\text{let } E_0 \text{ be the definition of } Q(x_1, \ldots, x_n)\;;$$
$$\text{return } find_\kappa((\![x_1 := y_1 \ldots x_n := y_n]\!)E_0, x, \text{EP} \cup \{Q\})$$
$$\text{endif}.$$

Fig. 3. An algorithm that computes κ-positions

expression $\||x \in T : E$ requires a map and only one instance of E for all map entries, because the environment $(\![x := \Pi(\sigma)]\!)$ is represented by a map entry. Each process expression E' reachable from E by transition execution is also instantiated only once, which is very efficient.

Example. Consider the library specification in Figure 1. The algorithm of Figure 3 has to be applied on four quantified process expressions:

1. $find_\kappa(\textbf{book}\,(\,bId\,)^*,\,bId,\,\emptyset)$ in the **main** process definition;
2. $find_\kappa(\textbf{loan}\,(\,mId, bId\,)^*,\,mId,\,\emptyset)$ in the **book** process definition;
3. $find_\kappa(\textbf{loan}\,(\,mId, bId\,)^*,\,bId,\,\emptyset)$ in the **member** process definition;
4. and $find_\kappa(\textbf{member}\,(\,mId\,)^*,\,mId,\,\emptyset)$ in the **main** process definition.

Once the computation is done, we obtain the following results:

1. $\{\;(\text{Acquire}, 1), (\text{Lend}, 2), (\text{Renew}, 1),$
   $(\text{Return}, 1), (\text{Sell}, 1)\;\}$

2. $\{\;(\text{Lend}, 1), (\text{Renew}, \perp), (\text{Return}, \perp)\;\}$

3. $\{\;(\text{Lend}, 2), (\text{Renew}, 1), (\text{Return}, 1)\;\}$

4. $\{\;(\text{Join}, 1), (\text{Lend}, 1), (\text{Renew}, \perp),$
   $(\text{Return}, \perp), (\text{Leave}, 1)\;\}$

The first and third quantifications are κ-optimizable. Therefore, to execute the action $\text{Lend}(\,1, 2\,)$ from $\||\,bId \in \text{BOOKID} : \textbf{loan}\,(\,mId, bId\,)$, we can directly try to execute $\text{Lend}(\,1, 2\,)$ from the process expression $(\![bId := 2]\!)\textbf{loan}\,(\,mId, bId\,)$, instead of trying every value of BOOKID for bId until $bId = 2$ is found. The fourth quantification is not κ-optimizable since it is an interleave and the codomain of the result contains two occurrences of $\perp$ (for Renew and Return), because mId is not a parameter of these actions. The second quantification is a choice. It is partially κ-optimizable: κ-optimization can be used for a Lend, but not for a Renew or a Return. Hence, the κ-optimization is not totally satisfactory. The next section addresses this issue.

3.2   Extending Quantification Optimization: Indirect κ-Optimization

We have found conditions under which a quantification can be optimized when the algorithm in Figure 3 fails to find a single κ-position for each action. These conditions cover a large number of IS specification patterns described in [3]. Hence, our interpreter can optimize the execution of quantified interleaves in most common IS specifications. Let us start by providing the intuition behind this second optimization.

Example. Consider the example in Figure 1 and the action Renew, which cannot be optimized by the algorithm in Figure 3. Intuitively, one can see that when a loan is initiated, the action (Lend(mId, bId)) binds book bId to member mId. Since a book can only be borrowed by one member at a time, and since a renew can only occur after a book is borrowed, bId is sufficient to deduce mId; hence, actions Renew and Return do not need to include mId as a parameter, because of this binding between a borrowed book and its borrower. In entity-relationship data modeling, we say that loan is a one-to-many relationship between members and books: a member can borrow several books concurrently, but a book is borrowed by at most one member at any given time. Hence, there is a functional dependency from entity type book to entity type member.

The first question that must be raised is how exactly one can deduce, solely by static analysis of the process expression, that there exists a functional dependency between book and member. Next, we have to determine under what conditions such a dependency can be found.

In our example, one can deduce the functional dependency between a book and a member from the position of the choice quantification in the process **book**:

book (bId : BOOKID) =
    Acquire(bId) **.**
    (| $mId \in$ MEMBERID : **loan** (mId, bId))* **.**
    Sell(bId)

Indeed, the choice quantifier implies that one book (with the number bId) can be borrowed by only one member at a time. To be lent to another member, the execution of process **loan** has to be completed. If we closely examine the **loan** process expression,

loan (mId : MEMBERID, bId : BOOKID) =
    Lend(mId, bId)**.** Renew(bId)***.** Return(bId)

we see that it is made of three parts : a producer (Lend), a modifier (Renew) and a consumer (Return). This is a classical IS pattern described in [3]. The producer is the action that binds mId and bId. The consumer is the action that tells us that the bond is no longer active. Since the interleave quantification to optimize for action Renew and Return is synchronized over actions of **loan** with this quantified choice expression, we know which mId can execute Renew and Return from the process expression **loan** (mId, bId).

Using this example, we can summarize the general idea of indirect κ-optimization, as follows.

During static analysis:

1. Find the quantified choice operators to deduce the possible functional dependencies (below we refer to choice quantified variables occurring in the scope of other quantifications (interleave or choice) as the *dependent variables* and the enclosing quantified variables as the *keys*).
2. For all actions not optimized with the algorithm in Figure 3, identify the producer that binds the keys (bId in the example) to the dependent variable (mId in the example) under the condition that the choice and interleave quantifications to optimize are synchronized on these actions.

At runtime:

1. When a producer is executed, store the value of the functional dependency between the set of keys and the dependent variable.
2. Store the value of the new process expression for the operand of the quantified interleave in a mapping K, as for direct κ-optimization.
3. When a consumer is executed, delete the stored value of the functional dependency between the keys and the dependent variable.
4. Accept or reject an action using the value of the functional dependency and mapping K. If the value of the functional dependency is not initialized, then reject the modifier or the consumer; if it is initialized, then check if the corresponding process expression in mapping K can execute the action.

Functional Dependencies. The first part of the optimization process is a search for the functional dependencies. In a recursive search on the structure of the process expression of each entity type, the algorithm stores the *candidate* functional dependencies: a function from $\mathcal{P}(\mathcal{V}ar)$ to $\mathcal{V}ar$, where $\mathcal{V}ar$ is the set of all variables used in the entity types and $\mathcal{P}(\mathcal{V}ar)$ is the set of all subsets of $\mathcal{V}ar$. We say candidates, because a functional dependency will be selected only when it is required to optimize an interleave.

Algorithm in Figure 4 computes the functional dependencies for a process expression E. The function $FD(E, \text{KS}, wait?, \text{EP})$ is called initially with $\text{KS} = \emptyset$, $\text{EP} = \emptyset$ and $wait? = false$, since the parameter KS represents the set of keys that will be mapped to the dependent variable and EP represents the process definitions already parsed. The variable $wait?$ is used to avoid the creation of the next dependency.

$$FD(E, \text{KS}, \textit{wait?}, \text{EP}) \; \triangleq \; \texttt{match } E \texttt{ with}$$

$$\Gamma E_0 \; \texttt{-> return } FD(E_0, \text{KS}, \textit{wait?}, \text{EP}),$$

$$\lambda \; \texttt{-> return } \emptyset,$$

$$a() \; \texttt{-> return } \emptyset,$$

$$a(y_1, \ldots, y_n) \; \texttt{-> return } \emptyset,$$

$$E_1 \,\textbf{.}\, E_2 \; \texttt{-> return } FD(E_1, \text{KS}, \textit{wait?}, \text{EP}) \cup FD(E_2, \text{KS}, \textit{wait?}, \text{EP}),$$

$$E_1 \mid E_2 \; \texttt{-> return } FD(E_1, \text{KS}, \textit{wait?}, \text{EP}) \cup FD(E_2, \text{KS}, \textit{wait?}, \text{EP}),$$

$$E_1 \parallel E_2 \; \texttt{-> return } FD(E_1, \text{KS}, \textit{wait?}, \text{EP}) \cup FD(E_2, \text{KS}, \textit{wait?}, \text{EP}),$$

$$E_1 \mathbin{|\!|\!|} E_2 \; \texttt{-> return } FD(E_1, \text{KS}, \textit{true}, \text{EP}) \cup FD(E_2, \text{KS}, \textit{true}, \text{EP}),$$

$$E_1 |[\Delta]| \, E_2 \; \texttt{-> return } FD(E_1, \text{KS}, \textit{true}, \text{EP}) \cup FD(E_2, \text{KS}, \textit{true}, \text{EP}),$$

$$\varphi \Longrightarrow E_0 \; \texttt{-> return } FD(E_0, \text{KS}, \textit{wait?}, \text{EP}),$$

$$E_0{}^* \; \texttt{-> return } FD(E_0, \text{KS}, \textit{wait?}, \text{EP}),$$

$$\mid x \in \text{S} : E_0 \; \texttt{-> if } \textit{wait?} \texttt{ then } \textit{add} := \emptyset \texttt{ else } \textit{add} := \{(\text{KS}, x)\} \texttt{ endif;}$$
$$\texttt{return } \textit{add} \cup FD(E_0, \text{KS} \cup \{x\}, \textit{false}, \text{EP})$$

$$\Phi x \in \text{S} : E_0 \; \texttt{-> where } \Phi \; \texttt{ either a quantification } |\!|\!| \texttt{ or } |[]| \texttt{ on } x$$
$$\texttt{then } \text{KS}' := \text{KS} \cup \{x\} \texttt{ else } \text{KS}' := \text{KS} \texttt{ endif;}$$
$$\texttt{return } FD(E_0, \text{KS}', \textit{false}, \text{EP}),$$

$$Q(y_1, \ldots, y_n) \; \texttt{-> if } Q \in \text{EP} \texttt{ then return } \emptyset \texttt{ else}$$
$$\texttt{let } E_0 \texttt{ be the definition of } Q(z_1, \ldots, z_n) \texttt{ ;}$$
$$\texttt{return } FD(E_0, \text{KS}, \textit{wait?}, \text{EP} \cup \{Q\})$$
$$\texttt{endif.}$$

Fig. 4. An algorithm that computes functional dependencies

For example, if we analyze the process expression

$$\mathbin{|\!|\!|} x \in \text{X} : \big((\mid y \in \text{Y} : E') \mathbin{|\!|\!|} (\mid y \in \text{Y} : E') \big)$$
$$\parallel \tag{2}$$
$$\mathbin{|\!|\!|} y \in \text{Y} : \mathbin{|\!|\!|} x \in \text{X} : E'$$

we don't know whether it associates one x to one or two y, because of the combination of two choice quantifications of $\mid y$ with $|\!|\!|$. Since these cases can associate more than one value of y to a value of x, the existence of a functional dependency is not guaranteed. Even after excluding these cases, we can still successfully identify the functional dependencies for the process expressions that fit the patterns in [3]. The function call $FD(E, \text{KS}, \textit{wait?}, \text{EP})$ returns a map that is associated to E.

$$(\cdots E \cdots) \parallel (\cdots E' \cdots) \quad \text{where} \quad E = \mathbin{|\!|\!|} x \cdots \mathbin{|\!|\!|} \overrightarrow{y} \cdots \mathbf{A}(\overrightarrow{y}, x) \cdots$$
$$\text{and} \quad E' = \mathbin{|\!|\!|} \overrightarrow{y} \cdots \mid x \cdots \mathbf{A}(\overrightarrow{y}, x) \cdots .$$

Fig. 5. Example of structure for the κ-optimization

The Complete κ-optimization of an Action. Consider the example of a general process expression structure illustrated in Figure 5. The process definition **A** can be a simple pattern (Figure 6), or there could also be several producers and consumers with an arbitrary combination of $b_i(\overrightarrow{y})$, which we denote by $\Xi_i b_i(\overrightarrow{y})$ (Figure 7).

$$\mathbf{A}(\overrightarrow{y} : \overrightarrow{T}, x : T') = (\mathsf{a}(\overrightarrow{y}, x) \cdot \mathsf{b}(\overrightarrow{y})^* \cdot \mathsf{c}(\overrightarrow{y}))^*$$

Fig. 6. First pattern for the κ-optimization

The execution of an action $\mathsf{b}(\overrightarrow{y})$ for a quantifier $||| x$ in the entity E can be optimized under the following conditions:

1. Entity E is synchronized with an entity E' over a binding process expression **A** such that there is a functional dependency from $\overrightarrow{y}$ to x in E'. A binding expression is a process expression under the quantified choice scope that defined the functional dependency.
2. The binding process expression **A** enforces the following ordering constraints:
   (a) An event $\mathsf{b}(\overrightarrow{y})$ can only occur between a producer $\mathsf{a}(\overrightarrow{y}, x)$ and a consumer $\mathsf{c}(\overrightarrow{y})$
   (b) A consumer $\mathsf{c}(\overrightarrow{y})$ must be preceded by one producer $\mathsf{a}(\overrightarrow{y}, \_)$ (i.e., the producer occurs before the consumer).
   (c) A consumer $\mathsf{c}(\overrightarrow{y})$ must occur between each pair of producers $\mathsf{a}(\overrightarrow{y}, \_)$.
   (d) A producer $\mathsf{a}(\overrightarrow{y}, \_)$ must occur between each pair of consumers $\mathsf{c}(\overrightarrow{y})$.
   Hence, a trace of $\mathbf{A}(\overrightarrow{y}, x)$ is of the form

$$\mathsf{a}(\overrightarrow{y}, x) \cdot \cdots \cdot \mathsf{b}(\overrightarrow{y}) \cdot \cdots \cdot$$
$$\mathsf{c}(\overrightarrow{y}) \cdot \mathsf{a}(\overrightarrow{y}, x') \cdot \cdots \cdot$$
$$\mathsf{b}(\overrightarrow{y}) \cdot \cdots \cdot \mathsf{c}(\overrightarrow{y}) \cdot \cdots$$

A consumer c can also be optimized under these conditions. Condition 1 is satisfied by the general structure of the expression in Figure 5. The patterns for **A** in Figures 6 and 7 satisfy condition 2 above.

$$\mathbf{A}(\overrightarrow{y} : \overrightarrow{T}, x : T') =$$
$$($$
$$(\mathsf{a}_1(\overrightarrow{y}, x) | \cdots | \mathsf{a}_n(\overrightarrow{y}, x)) \cdot$$
$$(\Xi_i \mathsf{b}_i(\overrightarrow{y}))^* \cdot$$
$$(\mathsf{c}_1(\overrightarrow{y}) | \cdots | \mathsf{c}_m(\overrightarrow{y}))$$
$$)^*$$

Fig. 7. Second pattern for the κ-optimization

When a producer $a(\overrightarrow{y}, x)$ is executed, the pair $\overrightarrow{y} \mapsto x$ is stored in a map f which represents the functional dependency $\overrightarrow{y} \rightarrow x$. When action $b(\overrightarrow{y})$ must be executed, the only value of x in $|||x$ of E (i.e., quantification to optimize) that can execute $b(\overrightarrow{y})$ is $f(\overrightarrow{y})$. This can be proved by contradiction. Suppose there are two values of x, v_1 and v_2 that can execute $b(\overrightarrow{w})$. By condition 2a, each execution of $b(\overrightarrow{y})$ is preceded by a producer in $\mathbf{A}$, which means that $|||x$ of E has spawned two interleaved processes, one for v_1 and one for v_2; each one has executed a producer, $a(\overrightarrow{w}, v_1)$ and $a(\overrightarrow{w}, v_2)$, respectively, and no consumer yet, by condition 2a. But since E and E' are synchronized over $\mathbf{A}$ by condition 1, the $|||\overrightarrow{y}$ of E' has spawned a single process for $\overrightarrow{w}$, and this process has executed two producers, $a(\overrightarrow{w}, v_1)$ and $a(\overrightarrow{w}, v_2)$, without a consumer in between, which contradicts condition 2c above.

The only candidate to execute a consumer $c(\overrightarrow{w})$ is also the spawned process for $x = f(\overrightarrow{w})$ in $|||x$ of E. This can be proved as follows. Suppose there are two values of x, v_1 and v_2 that can execute $c(\overrightarrow{w})$. By condition 2b, $|||x : T$ of E has spawned two interleaved processes, one for v_1 and one for v_2; each one has executed a producer, $a(\overrightarrow{w}, v_1)$ and $a(\overrightarrow{w}, v_2)$, respectively. Consider the last occurrences of these two actions. Since E and E' are synchronized over $\mathbf{A}$ by condition 1, the $|||\overrightarrow{y}$ of E' has spawned a single process for $\overrightarrow{w}$, and this process has now executed two producers, $a(\overrightarrow{w}, v_1)$ and $a(\overrightarrow{w}, v_2)$. By condition 2c, exactly one consumer $c(\overrightarrow{w})$ must have been executed in between. Hence, only the last producer can execute $c(\overrightarrow{w})$.

3.3   Generality of κ-optimization

Complete κ-optimization is not effective for all specifications that can be written. Actually, it is not effective for all IS specifications. However, our aim is to optimize all specifications written with the patterns described in [3]. There are seven patterns:

1. the producer-modifier-consumer pattern;
2. the one-to-many association pattern;
3. the multiple association pattern;
4. the n-ary association pattern;
5. the weak entity type pattern;
6. the recursive association pattern;
7. the inheritance association pattern.

For the sake of conciseness, the complete description of these patterns is omitted. It is straightforward to check that the first four patterns satisfy the conditions for κ-optimization. The first pattern describes the structure of an entity type. The producers of the association in the second pattern are exactly the producers of the functional dependency needed. These producers contain all the key variables, and the dependent variables, since they build an instance of the association. Each association also has consumer actions. The second pattern is same as the one used to illustrate indirect κ-optimization (i.e., a one-to-many association). The third and fourth patterns can use either direct or indirect κ-optimization, depending on the cardinality of the association. An important point is that when an entity participates in several associations, these associations are combined with a parallel operator ($\|$). Therefore the problem of the process expression 2 (page 337) does not occur. This point justifies the use of the *wait?* predicate in the algorithm of Figure 4: if these patterns are used, there is no loss of generality. The last three patterns also fit our conditions for κ-optimization. They are special cases of the first four: a weak entity is just an instance of a simple association for our purpose; a recursive association is just an association between the entities of the same entity type; an inheritance association is decomposed into many process definitions, but it still has a behavior similar to that of simple entity types.

4   Implementation and Performance

EB^{3}PAI is implemented with Java 1.4 and an OODB ObjectStore PSE Pro for Java 6.0. The parser was built with ANTLR 2.7.1. Indirect κ-optimization is not implemented, but direct κ-optimization is. The performance for indirect κ-optimization should be very close to that of direct κ-optimization, because it uses the same data structures plus an additional hash table to store the functional dependencies.

4.1   Complexity Analysis

Let E_i, $1 \leq i \leq m_E$, denote an entity type and A_j, $1 \leq j \leq m_A$, denote an association. An association links two or more entity type E_i. The size $|E_i|$ of an entity types E_i is the maximal number of entities in the entity type. The size $|A_j|$ of an association A_j is a product of all $|E_k|$, where E_k is an entity type involved in A_j. Let n denote the sum of all $|X|$, where X is either an entity type or an association of an EB^3 specification. Let s denote the number of nodes in the tree representing a process expression, excluding the nodes of a κ-optimized quantification (they will be computed with n). Note that for most ISs, s is usually smaller, whereas n can be quite larger. Therefore, the number of nodes s can be considered negligible with respect to the number of entities and associations n. The search for a proof using the inference rules requires inspection (in the worst case) of all the nodes (i.e., s nodes). The space complexity is $\mathcal{O}(s + n)$, which corresponds to the size of a process expression, including instances of quantified process expressions. But, since s is negligible with respect to n, the space complexity is $\mathcal{O}(n)$. Without κ-optimization, the algorithmic complexity is impractical since the number of nodes s is multiplied by the number n of entities and associations involved. So a transition computation has a complexity of $\mathcal{O}(s\,n)$. With the κ-optimization, only one node is inspected for quantified expressions. The execution of a κ-optimized quantification depends on the implementation chosen for a map K. ObjectStore offers hash tables, which yield constant time in an average case, or B-trees, which yield logarithmic time. Hence, the algorithmic complexity of a transition computation is $\mathcal{O}(s + log(n))$

on average. The space complexity is still $\mathcal{O}(n)$. For indirect κ-optimization, we also need to store the functional dependencies (*cf.* 3.2). The total size of the tables needed for these optimizations is bounded by the number of quantifications involved multiplied by the number of actions involved. Theorically, this number could be an overwhelming difficulty to tackle. However, practicably, it is still negligible with respect to n. Therefore, the space complexity is the same as that of direct κ-optimization. The algorithmic complexity is also the same because the small tables needed can be implemented with hash tables which yield constant time. Typically, the algorithmic complexity of a manual implementation of an IS specification is $\mathcal{O}(log(n))$, since it will access several records from the database, each access usually being backed by an index which yields $log(n)$ access time using B-trees; its space complexity is $\mathcal{O}(n)$ on average. All of these complexities are summarized in Figure 8, under the hypothesis of IS domain. Thus, for κ-optimizable specifications, EB^{3}PAI has an overhead of $\mathcal{O}(s)$

	Algorithmic complexity	Space complexity
EB^{3}PAI with no optimization	$\mathcal{O}(s.n)$	$\mathcal{O}(n)$
EB^{3}PAI with direct κ-optimization	$\mathcal{O}(log(n) + s)$	$\mathcal{O}(n)$
EB^{3}PAI with indirect κ-optimization	$\mathcal{O}(log(n) + s)$	$\mathcal{O}(n)$
manual implementation	$\mathcal{O}(log(n))$	$\mathcal{O}(n)$

Fig. 8. Algorithmic and space complexity of EB^{3}PAI for IS specifications

compared with manual implementation of an IS. With no κ-optimization, the difference is substantial and EB^{3}PAI becomes impractical as a tool, but it can still be useful for specification animation for validation purposes.

4.2 Performance for Direct κ-optimization

Performance tests were conducted with a specification of a library management system on an Intel Core Duo 1.66GHz with 1GB of DDR2 SDRAM, running Mac OSX 10.4. Indirect κ-optimization has not been implemented yet; only direct κ-optimization. Figure 9 provides some statistics on these experiments. The column titled "Without DB" corresponds to the execution time without the use of a database; the column titled "With DB" corresponds to the time of executions with the use of an Object Store PSEPro as database. The experiment consists of the execution of actions creating 9,000 books and 9,000 members, followed by the execution of 30,000 actions which were randomly generated; 9,899 of these actions were valid and 20,101 were invalid. Figure 9 only shows information for valid actions. Invalid actions (actions which must be rejected by the interpreter) are less expensive in time than valid actions: they require approximately half the time of a valid action. We also manually implemented the

	Without DB	With DB
Time	1 m 52 s	8 m 27 s
Mean	4 ms	81 ms
Median	1 ms	10 ms

Fig. 9. EB³PAI execution times for the library system

library specification in Java using an Oracle database. The average transaction processing time is 10 ms, which is 8 times faster than EB³PAI with a database. Nevertheless, 80 ms is still acceptable for many IS systems where the transaction rate is low (e.g., a library management system). The results are good, but the median is quite low in comparison to the mean time. This is because some executions are rather slow (more than 2 s). These executions occur periodically. We are currently investigating the reason for these anomalies in order to correct this behavior. We also intend to implement indirect κ-optimization and validate its real performance.

5 Conclusion

In this paper, we have presented two optimization techniques to efficiently execute quantified process expressions in the EB³ process algebra. Their space and algorithmic complexities are comparable to those of a manual implementation for a large number of IS specifications which are determined by a set of classical specification patterns. Direct κ-optimization was implemented in the EB³PAI interpreter. It performs 8 times slower than a manual implementation of the specification for the library system, but its average response time is acceptable for a large class of IS with low transaction rates, which demonstrates that symbolic execution is a viable way of implementing IS.

The performance of EB³PAI is largely dependent on the OO database used to the store the object representation of the specification. It seems quite feasible to implement a dedicated persistence manager for EB³PAI to reduce the number of disk IOs.

We are currently looking at other optimizations for EB³PAI. Tail-recursive deterministic process expressions can be represented by an extended labelled-transition system (ELTS) [23], which basically takes less space and avoids the computation of a proof at each transition. Preliminary experimentation has shown us that ELTS coupled with κ-optimization could cut computation time by as much as 40%. We are working on a complete definition of ELTS and the algorithms to translate an EB³ process expression into an ELTS.

Future work also includes techniques for issuing meaningful error messages when an action is not executed. For instance, if a Lend(bId, mId) is rejected by the interpreter, we must tell the user why; it could be that the book or the member does not exist, the book is on loan to another member, or the member has reached his loan limit. This problem is similar to the determination of error messages by a compiler. Finally, we wish to investigate how parallelism could be used for symbolic execution.

References

1. Frappier, M., Fraikin, B., Laleau, R., Richard, M.: Automatic Production of Information Systems. In: AAAI Symposium on Logic-Based Program Synthesis, p. 7. AAAI, Stanford University, Stanford, CA (2002)
2. Fraikin, B., Gervais, F., Frappier, M., Laleau, R., Richard, M.: Synthesizing Information Systems: the APIS Project. In: Rolland, C., Pastor, O., Cavarero, J.L. (eds.) First International Conference on Research Challenges in Information Science (RCIS), Ouarzazate, Morocco, p. 12 (2007)
3. Frappier, M., St-Denis, R.: EB^3: an Entity-Based Black-Box Specification Method for Information Systems. Software and Systems Modeling 2, 134–149 (2003)
4. Formal Systems (Europe) Ltd.: Process Behaviour Explorer (ProBE) User Manual (2003)
5. Leuschel, M.: Design and Implementation of the High-Level Specification Language CSP(LP) in Prolog. In: Ramakrishnan, I.V. (ed.) PADL 2001. LNCS, vol. 1990, pp. 14–28. Springer, Heidelberg (2001)
6. Wooters, A.G.: Manual for the CRL tool set (version 2.8.2). Report SEN-R0130, CWI, Amsterdam, the Netherlands (2001)
7. Garavel, H., Lang, F., Mateescu, R.: An Overview of CADP 2001. European Association for Software Science and Technology (EASST) Newsletter 4, 13–24 (2002)
8. Freitas, A., Cavalcanti, A.: Automatic Translation from *Circus* to Java. In: Misra, J., Nipkow, T., Sekerinski, E. (eds.) FM 2006. LNCS, vol. 4085, pp. 115–130. Springer, Heidelberg (2006)
9. Freitas, A.: From Circus to Java: Implementation and Verification of a Translation Strategy. Master's thesis, Department of Computer Science, The University of York (2005)
10. Oliveira, M.: Formal Derivation of State-Rich Reactive Programs using Circus. PhD thesis, Department of Computer Science - University of York, UK (2005)
11. Welch, P.H.: Process oriented design for java: Concurrency for all. In: Priss, U., Corbett, D.R., Angelova, G. (eds.) ICCS 2002. LNCS (LNAI), vol. 2393, Springer, Heidelberg (2002)
12. Formal Systems (Europe) Ltd.: Failures-Divergence Refinement (FDR2) User Manual (2005)
13. Moller, F., Stevens, P.: (Edinburgh Concurrency Workbench user manual (version 7.1))
14. Butler, M., Leuschel, M.: Combining CSP and B for Specification and Property Verification. In: Fitzgerald, J.A., Hayes, I.J., Tarlecki, A. (eds.) FM 2005. LNCS, vol. 3582, pp. 221–236. Springer, Heidelberg (2005)
15. Magee, J., Kramer, J.: Concurrency: State Models & Java Programs. Wiley, Chichester (2006)
16. Hoare, C.A.R.: Communicating Sequential Processes. Prentice-Hall, Englewood Cliffs, NJ (1985)
17. Milner, R.: Communication and Concurrency. International Series in Computer Science. Prentice-Hall, Englewood Cliffs (1989)
18. Bergstra, J.A., Klop, J.W.: Process Algebra for Synchronous Communication. Information and Control 60, 109–137 (1984)

19. Bolognesi, T., Brinksma, E.: Introduction to the ISO Specification Language LO-TOS. Computer Networks and ISDN Systems 14, 25–59 (1987)
20. Fraikin, B.: Interprétation efficace d'expression de processus EB^3. PhD thesis, Département d'informatique, Université de Sherbrooke, Sherbrooke, Québec, Canada (2006)
21. Fraikin, B., Frappier, M.: Efficient Execution of Process Expressions Using Symbolic Interpretation. Technical Report 8, Université de Sherbrooke, Département d'informatique, Sherbrooke, Québec, Canada (2005)
22. Fraikin, B., Frappier, M., Laleau, R.: State-Based versus Event-Based Specifications for Information System Specification: a comparison of B and EB^3. Software and System Modeling 4, 236–257 (2005)
23. Frappier, M., Laleau, R.: Verifying Event Ordering Properties for Information Systems. In: Bert, D., Bowen, J.P., King, S. (eds.) ZB 2003. LNCS, vol. 2651, pp. 421–436. Springer, Heidelberg (2003)

Formalizing SANE Virtual Processor in Thread Algebra[*]

Thuy Duong Vu[1] and Chris Jesshope[2]

[1] Sectie Software Engineering,
[2] Computer Systems Architecture Group,
University of Amsterdam,
The Netherlands
{tdvu,jesshope}@science.uva.nl

Abstract. *The SANE Virtual Processor* (SVP) is a fine-grain, thread-based model of concurrent program composition developed and used at the University of Amsterdam as a basis for designing and programming many-core chips. Its design goal was to support dynamic concurrency and hence support self-adaptive systems within the AETHER collaborative European project. It provides an effective solution for programming chip multiprocessor systems [1,2,3]. In this paper, we take thread algebra [4], a semantics for recent object-oriented programming languages such as C# and Java, as a theoretical framework to the verification and evaluation of SVP. We show how a SVP program behavior can be determined in TA_{svp}, an extension of thread algebra with the features of SVP, and prove that SVP programs satisfy the determinism property, i.e. the programs always give the same result, a key property of the sequential paradigm that SVP will replace.

Keywords: SANE Virtual Processor, microthreading, thread algebra.

1 Introduction

The SANE Virtual Processor (SVP) was defined as a concurrent programming model with two broad requirements. Firstly, that it provide a suitable substitute for the ubiquitous sequential model of program composition while retaining the latter's properties of safe composition of programs. The required properties in this case are freedom from deadlock under composition and determinism of results under whatever schedule is used to execute the equivalent concurrent program. The second broad requirement of the model is that it should have scalable implementations in silicon as many-core chips. The model is defined by a small number of actions used to create and asynchronously manage the execution of concurrent SVP programs. These actions capture concurrency, implicit communication and resource management, and using these abstractions

---

[*] The work presented in this paper is supported by NWO (Netherlands Organisation for Scientific Research) in the "Foundations for Massively Parallel on-chip Architectures using Microthreading" project.

M. Butler, M. Hinchey, M.M. Larrondo-Petrie (Eds.): ICFEM 2007, LNCS 4789, pp. 345–365, 2007.
© Springer-Verlag Berlin Heidelberg 2007

we aim to develop an understanding of self-adaptive computational systems in the AETHER collaborative European project (http://www.aether-ist.org/).

Programs are composed in SVP by executing a *create* action on a fragment of code (a microthread), which dynamically creates a parameterized family of thread contexts based on that fragment and which may all execute concurrently, together with the creating thread. Every thread in a family is identified by a unique index value in its context. Further actions are defined to manage infinite families of threads and the termination of families, both destructively and by preempting the concurrent program defined by a family. The create action is used in place of the sequential composition actions of looping (both for and while loops) and function invocation.

This paper tackles the first broad requirement. However, it should be emphasized that this is not a theoretical exercise. Implementations of all of the above actions have been evaluated using an emulated many-core processor in which these actions are implemented as instructions in the processors' instruction set. Silicon implementations have also been investigated. This paper represents therefore, the application of theory to a very practical situation. This model will provide the issues of scalability and code compatibility that will be required for future generations of many-core processor chips. For more detail on this aspect of the research, the interested reader is directed towards the prior work dating back some ten years [1,5,6,2,3].

We aim to give a formal proof for the determinism property of SVP programs. We will need to define formally the semantics and the memory model of SVP. We take thread algebra [4], a semantics for recent object-oriented programming languages such as C# and Java, as a theoretical framework to the verification and evaluation of SVP. In particular, we extend thread algebra with the features of SVP to TA_{svp} (thread algebra for SVP), and show that TA_{svp} indeed is a formal semantics of SVP. To interpret the memory model of SVP, we adapt the concept of a Maurer machine [7], an extension of a Maurer computer [8,9], with the features of SVP. The reason to use Maurer computers is that they are closer to real computers than the well-known models such as register machines, multistack machines and Turing machines (see e.g. [10]). Threads in TA_{svp} can perform operations to transform states of a Maurer machine. The determinism property of SVP programs, i.e. concurrent SVP programs always give the same result as the result obtained when they are executed sequentially, therefore, can be proved as program behaviors and memory states are represented as threads in TA_{svp} and states of a Maurer machine.

Our work, like the previous works given in [7,11,12,13,14], is a part of a project investigating microthreading in a collaboration between the Computer Systems Architecture group and Sectie Software Engineering at the University of Amsterdam. We note that a denotational semantics and a structural operational semantics for TA_{svp} can be found in our other paper [14]. The other desired property of SVP programs, namely freedom from deadlock under composition, is also proven in that paper.

The structure of this paper as follows. Section 2 summaries the informal semantics of the SVP model. Section 3 defines TA_{svp} (thread algebra for SVP), a theoretical frame work for the verification and evaluation of SVP. Section 4 models the memory of SVP with the use of Maurer computers. Section 5 illustrates the programming language μTC (*microthreaded C*) [15], a realization of SVP, as a simple programming language $\mathcal{L}_{svp}$ and determines $\mathcal{L}_{svp}$ program behaviors in TA_{svp}. We also prove the determinism property of SVP programs in this section. The paper is ended with some concluding remarks in Section 6.

2   A Summary of the SVP Model

The SVP model provides five actions in order to create and manage concurrency. These actions replace those normally used to construct sequential programs, namely loops and function calls. Three of these actions are used to parallelize sequential programs and the other two are used for concurrency engineering, i.e. the self-adaptive aspects of the model.

The model is designed to capture the precise functionality of an equivalent sequential program, while relaxing as far as is practical the order of execution of the instructions. It captures a more relaxed partial order of instruction execution than the sequential program, although a more restricted partial order when compared to a dataflow representation of the same program. Because this paper is concerned with the determinacy of the results compared to the equivalent sequential program, only the parallelizing actions will be described. They include the *create, sync* and *break* actions.

The create action defines a *family* of threads based on a single fragment of code. The result of the create action is the creation of an ordered set of thread contexts defined by parameters to the action. These parameters define the code used, the size of the context required and the number of threads to be created. The latter is defined by a triple defining an index range and each thread has its context initialized with a unique value from this range. This provides an analogy to the limits defied within a loop in the sequential model. This family of threads is identified with a unique name so that it may be monitored and controlled by the other actions.

A thread's code may itself contain create actions and this provides for hierarchy in the composition of programs in the SVP model. Nested loops are just one example of a sequential construct that maps to nested creates. Function calls are another, as they are also translated into SVP create actions. A created function is a family with a singleton thread that executes concurrently and asynchronously with its creating thread. However, any thread creating a subordinate family of threads, be it a loop or a function equivalent, must wait for the entire family of threads to complete before any results the family has written to memory are fully defined. As a result, no two concurrent threads can read and write the same location in memory (nor both write to the same location). These constraints are enforced in the compilation of an SVP program. This model allows for significant concurrency without the cost associated with dataflow models. Unlike dataflow however, this constraint on concurrency allows for expressive stored-variable semantics on memory locations rather than the single assignment model of memory used in dataflow.

A thread creating a subordinate family can detect its termination using an SVP *sync* action. This identifies the family by name so that multiple concurrent families can be created and synchronized from within a single thread. The termination of the family also guarantees that all memory locations written to the shared memory by its threads have completed. Note that no guarantees are made on shared memory latency as it is deemed to be asynchronous and distributed. The sync action provides a return code that specifies how a family was terminated and can provide a return value in the case of a *break* action.

The break action is provided to allow for the creation of dynamically bounded families of threads. In such circumstances, a semi-infinite range of index values is specified in the family's parameters and any thread in the family may terminate the creation of new contexts using the break action and return a scalar value (e.g. an index or pointer) back to the creating thread via the sync action. This construct is the SVP concurrent equivalent of a while loop in a sequential program. Because of lack of space and simplicity, in this first report of our approach, we will ignore the existence of sync and break actions.

Communication between threads is achieved by two mechanisms. The first is the bulk synchronization on memory described above, where read after writes to asynchronous shared memory are synchronized by a sync action between the family that writes to memory and the family that reads from memory. The second mechanism uses a fine-grain synchronizing memory that stores the context of scalar variables for each thread created. This acts like a stack in a conventional sequential machine. Each word in this memory contains synchronization bits that identify whether the word has been written to, enabling threads to block on a read and to be rescheduled when data is written. This allows synchronization on operations within a thread, for example loading data from asynchronous shared memory and subsequently using it. It also provides blocking reads on communication between concurrently executing threads. The latter enables dependencies to be defined between the creating thread and the first thread it creates, as well as between a created thread and its successor in index sequence. It enables dataflow-like scheduling of instructions within a concurrently executing family of threads. Note that the sequential equivalent of this communication is a scalar value assigned within a loop body. This dependency chain is captured by defining a *shared* variable in each thread's context, where each thread has read only access to its predecessor's shared variable (the first thread in a family has access to an initializing variable defined in the creating thread).

The exact relationship between a sequential program and its SVP equivalent is outside of the scope of this paper, however the goal is to program multicores chips using code compiled from sequential languages and the goal of this paper is to ensure that the sequential program's determinism is retained by this model. A realization of the SVP model has been developed at the University of Amsterdam and called *microthreaded C* or μTC for short. More information, including program examples in μTC can be found in the following report [15].

3   Thread Algebra for SVP (TA$_{svp}$)

In this section, we introduce TA$_{svp}$, a theoretical framework for the verification and evaluation of SANE Virtual Processors.

3.1   Basic Thread Algebra for SANE Virtual Processors (BTA$_{svp}$)

BTA$_{svp}$ (*basic thread algebra for SVP*) is defined as a semantics for SVP sequential programs. It is based on *basic thread algebra* (BTA) [4], a semantics for sequential programming languages which was first introduced as *basic polarized process algebra* (BPPA) in [16].

We assume the existence of a fixed but arbitrary set $\mathcal{BA}$ of *basic actions* in BTA$_{svp}$. Each basic action $a \in \mathcal{BA}$ of a thread is taken as a command to the execution environment of the thread. This command is accepted or rejected depending on a boolean value $?a$ produced by the execution environment. If $?a = T$ (**true**) then the action a is *independent* and can be executed otherwise it is *blocked*. The execution environment cannot do anything with it. Here the term "independent" means that the execution of action a does not depend on any other actions. At completion of the processing of a basic action $a \in \mathcal{BA}$, the execution environment produces a reply value y_a. This reply is either T or F (**false**) and is returned to the thread concerned.

BTA$_{svp}$ (basic thread algebra for SVP) is the extension of BTA with the *independence* and *reply* [13] conditional operators. Hence, the set A of finite threads in BTA$_{svp}$ is defined inductively with the operators in BTA and additionally with the following operators:

- *Successful termination*: $S \in A$ yields successful terminating behavior.
- *Unsuccessful termination* or *deadlock*: $D \in A$ represents inactive behavior.
- *Postconditional composition*: $- \trianglelefteq a \trianglerighteq -$ with $a \in \mathcal{BA}$. The thread $p \trianglelefteq a \trianglerighteq q$, where $p, q \in A$, first performs a and then proceeds with p if T was returned and with q otherwise. In case $p = q$ we abbreviate this thread by the *action prefix* operator: $a \circ -$. In particular, $a \circ p = p \trianglelefteq a \trianglerighteq p$.
- The *independence* conditional operator: $- \vartriangleleft ?a \vartriangleright -$ with $a \in \mathcal{BA}$. The thread $p \vartriangleleft ?a \vartriangleright q$ behaves as p is a is independent ($?a = T$) and it behaves as q otherwise.
- The *reply* conditional operator: $- \vartriangleleft y_a \vartriangleright -$ with $a \in \mathcal{BA}$. The thread $p \vartriangleleft y_a \vartriangleright q$ behaves as p if the execution of a returns a positive reply T, and it behaves as q otherwise. In fact, $p \trianglelefteq a \trianglerighteq q = a \circ (p \vartriangleleft y_a \vartriangleright q)$.

We note that the reply conditional operator is needed for defining synchronous cooperation of threads. This operator and the independence conditional operator originate from the *conditional* operator [17] defined for process algebra, where the second argument must be T or F. Table 1 represents the axioms for these operators. The constants S and D are similar to the termination ϵ and the deadlock δ used in other process algebras such as CCS [18] and ACP [19].

The *concrete internal action* $\mathtt{tau} \in \mathcal{BA}$ [4] plays a special role. Its execution will never change any state and always produces a positive reply. The axiom for this action is given in Table 2.

We write $p.q$ for threads $p, q \in A$ with each occurrence of S of p replaced by q. This thread executes p and q sequentially.

Table 1. Axioms for conditions

$x \triangleleft T \triangleright y = x$	CO1
$x \triangleleft F \triangleright y = y$	CO2
$x \triangleleft c \triangleright x = x$	CO3
$(x \triangleleft c \triangleright y) \triangleleft c \triangleright z = x \triangleleft c \triangleright z$	CO4
$x \triangleleft c \triangleright (y \triangleleft c \triangleright z) = x \triangleleft c \triangleright z$	CO5
$(x \triangleleft c_1 \triangleright y) \triangleleft c_2 \triangleright z = (x \triangleleft c_2 \triangleright z) \triangleleft c_1 \triangleright (y \triangleleft c_2 \triangleright z)$	CO6
$x \triangleleft c_1 \triangleright (y \triangleleft c_2 \triangleright z) = (x \triangleleft c_1 \triangleright y) \triangleleft c_2 \triangleright (x \triangleleft c_1 \triangleright z)$	CO7
$x \trianglelefteq a \trianglerighteq y = a \circ (x \triangleleft \mathrm{y}_a \triangleright y)$	RC

Table 2. Axioms for the concrete internal action

$x \trianglelefteq \mathtt{tau} \trianglerighteq y = \mathtt{tau} \circ x$	IA1
$x \triangleleft ?\mathtt{tau} \triangleright y = x$	IA2
$x \triangleleft \mathrm{y}_{\mathtt{tau}} \triangleright y = x$	IA3

3.2 Approximation Induction Principle

An *infinite* thread in BTA_{svp} is represented by a *projective sequence* consisting of its finite approximations. These finite approximations are defined inductively by means of the approximation operators $\pi_n(-)$ of depth n of threads with $n \in \mathbb{N}$ whose axioms on finite threads are given as P0-P5 in Table 3. Note that axioms P4 and P5 makes use of the assumption that $\mathcal{BA}$ is finite.

A *projective sequence* is a sequence $(p_n)_{n \in \mathbb{N}}$ such that $\pi_n(p_{n+1}) = p_n$ for all $n \in \mathbb{N}$.

The *Approximation Induction Principle* (AIP) in Table 3 states that two threads are considered identical if their finite approximations at every depth are identical. We write A^∞ for the set of (finite and infinite) threads, and $\pi_n(p)$ for the projection at depth n of a thread $p \in A^\infty$. A^∞ is called a *projective limit model*. For infinite threads $p_1, \ldots, p_n \in A^\infty$, we define for all $n \in \mathbb{N}$ that

$$\pi_n(p_1 \ldots p_n) = \pi_n(\pi_n(p_1) \ldots \pi_n(p)).$$

3.3 The Current Thread Persistence with Blocking Strategy in TA_{svp}

We now extend BTA_{svp} with the basic interleaving strategy that is used in SVP, called the *current thread persistence with blocking* and written as $\|_{ctpb}$.

Table 3. Axioms for approximation operators and induction principle

$\pi_0(x)=D$	P0
$\pi_{n+1}(S)=S$	P1
$\pi_{n+1}(D)=D$	P2
$\pi_{n+1}(x \trianglelefteq a \trianglerighteq y)=\pi_n(x) \trianglelefteq a \trianglerighteq \pi_n(y)$	P3
$\pi_{n+1}(x \vartriangleleft y_a \trianglerighteq y)=\pi_{n+1}(x) \vartriangleleft y_a \trianglerighteq \pi_{n+1}(y)$	P4
$\pi_{n+1}(x\vartriangleleft?a \trianglerighteq y)=\pi_{n+1}(x)\vartriangleleft?a \trianglerighteq \pi_{n+1}(y)$	P5
If $\pi_n(x) = \pi_n(y)$ for all $n \in \mathbb{N}$ then $x = y$	AIP

Table 4. Axioms for approximation operators with thread creation

$x \trianglelefteq \mathtt{NT}(\langle\langle z_1 \rangle\rangle \frown \ldots \frown \langle z_n \rangle) \trianglerighteq y= \mathtt{NT}(\langle z_1 \rangle \frown \ldots \frown \langle z_n \rangle) \circ x$	PerfectNT
$\pi_{n+1}(\mathtt{NT}(\langle z_1 \rangle \frown \ldots \frown \langle z_k \rangle) \circ x) = \mathtt{NT}(\langle \pi_n(z_1) \rangle \frown \ldots \frown \langle \pi_n(z_k) \rangle) \circ \pi_n(x)$	PNT

Thread Creation. First of all, we will explain how a family of threads in SVP is created. We assume that there is no resource deadlock in thread creation. Hence thread creation considered here is a perfect forking.

Let $\langle\rangle$ denote the empty sequence, $\langle p \rangle$ the sequence having p as sole element, and $\alpha \frown \beta$ the concatenation of finite sequences α and β.

The creation of a family of threads in TA_{svp} is given by the *forking postconditional composition* operator $- \trianglelefteq \mathtt{NT}(\alpha) \trianglerighteq -$ where α is a sequence of threads. The thread $r = p \trianglelefteq \mathtt{NT}(\alpha) \trianglerighteq q$ for some threads p, q is called the *creating* thread of the threads in α. $\mathtt{NT}(\alpha)$ is considered as a *thread forking action*. Like a real action, its execution also produces a reply. Since we only deal with perfect forking in this paper, this reply is always T. The axioms for thread creation are given in Table 4. We note that thread creation has been considered for thread algebra in [4,13] with perfect forking and imperfect forking (forking off a thread may be blocked and/or fail). Our axiom PNT coincides with the axiom for thread creation in [4,13] in the case that the sequence of threads to be created is of length one.

In the thread creation $\mathtt{NT}(\langle p_1 \rangle \frown \ldots \frown \langle p_n \rangle)$, we say that $p_1, \ldots, p_n$ are the threads in the same family, and are also in the same family with the creating thread. Moreover, p_i is a *predecessor* of p_j for all $1 \le i < j \le n$, and p_n is a predecessor of its creating thread. If $r \ne p_n$ is a predecessor of the creating thread then r is also a predecessor of $p_1, \ldots, p_n$.

In SVP, the blocking of a thread in a sequence of concurrent threads is allowed in a very restricted manner, depending only on its predecessors. In other words, a thread may only be waiting for some data produced by its predecessors. Hence, dependencies between threads in SVP can be represented as an acyclic graph, which in turn ensures freedom from *communication-deadlock* in the model SVP (see [14]).

The Current Thread Persistence with Blocking. We assume the existence of a special action $\mathtt{swch} \in \mathcal{BA}$ to switch off the current thread to another thread in the sequence of concurrent threads. Like the concrete internal action $\mathtt{tau}$, the execution of $\mathtt{swch}$ will never change any state and always produces a positive reply. The switching off may speed up processors in some cases. The axiom for the $\mathtt{swch}$ action is given in Table 5.

Table 5. Axioms for swch

$x \triangleleft \text{swch} \, \triangleright \, y = \text{swch} \circ x$	SWCH1
$x \triangleleft ? \text{swch} \, \triangleright \, y = x$	SWCH2
$x \triangleleft y_{\text{swch}} \, \triangleright \, y = x$	SWCH3

Table 6. Axioms for current thread persistence with blocking. Here $a \in \mathcal{BA}$.

$\|_{ctpb} (\alpha) = \|^0_{ctpb} (\alpha)$	Ctpb0
$\|^{\text{length}(\alpha)}_{ctpb} (\alpha) = D$	Ctpb1
$\|^k_{ctpb} (\langle\rangle) = S$	Ctpb2
$\|^k_{ctpb} (\langle S \rangle \frown \alpha) = \|^k_{ctpb} (\alpha)$	Ctpb3
$\|^k_{ctpb} (\langle D \rangle \frown \alpha) = D$	Ctpb4
$\|^k_{ctpb} (\langle x \trianglelefteq a \, \trianglerighteq y \rangle \frown \alpha) =$	
$\quad (\|^0_{ctpb} (\langle x \rangle \frown \alpha) \trianglelefteq a \trianglerighteq \|^0_{ctpb} (\langle y \rangle \frown \alpha)) \triangleleft ? a \, \triangleright \, (\text{tau} \circ \|^{k+1}_{ctpb} (\alpha \frown \langle x \trianglelefteq a \, \trianglerighteq y \rangle))$	Ctpb5
$\|^k_{ctpb} (\langle x \trianglelefteq \text{swch} \, \trianglerighteq y \rangle \frown \alpha) = \text{tau} \circ \|^0_{ctpb} (\alpha \frown \langle x \rangle)$	Ctpb6
$\|^k_{ctpb} (\langle x \trianglelefteq \text{NT}(\beta) \, \trianglerighteq y \rangle \frown \alpha) = \text{tau} \circ \|^k_{ctpb} (\beta \frown \langle x \rangle \frown \alpha)$	Ctpb7
$\|^k_{ctpb} (\langle x \triangleleft ? a \, \triangleright \, y \rangle \frown \alpha) = \|^k_{ctpb} (\langle x \rangle \frown \alpha) \triangleleft ? a \, \triangleright \, \|^k_{ctpb} (\langle y \rangle \frown \alpha)$	Ctpb8

The axioms for current thread persistence with blocking $\|_{ctpb}$ are given in Table 6. Initially, $\|_{ctpb} (\alpha) = \|^0_{ctpb}$. The superscript k used in $\|^k_{ctpb} (\alpha)$ denotes the number of the blocked threads in α. If all the threads are blocked then communication-deadlock occurs. The composition of an empty sequence of threads will terminate successfully. If the first thread of the sequence is terminated then the execution proceeds with the subsequent threads. If the first thread is in deadlock then whole system is in deadlock. In the remaining case, the system will execute the actions of the first thread until there is a blocked action, or the action swch. The control flow then proceeds with the next thread in the sequence. The first thread meanwhile is put to the end of the sequence in a round-robin fashion. When creating a new family of threads or switching off to another thread, the action tau will arise as a residue to keep pace with other threads in the sequence. We note that the threads are supposed initially not to contain any guards.

The axioms in Table 6 are defined for finite threads only. For a sequence of arbitrary (finite or infinite) threads $\alpha = \langle p_1 \rangle \frown \ldots \frown \langle p_m \rangle$, $\|_{ctpb} (\alpha)$ is determined by its projective sequence where $\pi_n(\|_{ctpb} (\alpha)) = \pi_n(\|_{ctpb} (\langle \pi_n(p_1) \rangle \frown \ldots \frown \langle \pi_n(p_m) \rangle))$.

3.4 Synchronous Cooperation of Threads in TA$_{svp}$

In this section, we extend TA$_{svp}$ with a form of synchronous cooperation of threads in SVP.

Atomic Actions and Concurrent Actions. Like [13], we assume a fixed but arbitrary set $\mathcal{AA}$ of *atomic actions* (tau $\in \mathcal{AA}$), a fixed but arbitrary set $\mathcal{CA} \supseteq \mathcal{AA}$ of *concurrent actions*, and a fixed but arbitrary synchronization function $| : \mathcal{CA} \times \mathcal{CA} \to \mathcal{CA}$ satisfying that:

Table 7. Conditions on the synchronization function. Here $\xi, \xi', \xi'' \in \mathcal{CA}$.

$$
\begin{aligned}
\mathsf{tau}|\xi &= \xi \\
(\xi|\xi')|\xi'' &= \xi|(\xi'|\xi'') \\
(\xi|\xi')|\xi'' &= (\xi'|\xi)|\xi'' \\
x \lhd ?(\xi|\xi') \rhd y &= x \lhd ?\xi' \rhd y \\
x \lhd \mathsf{y}_{\xi|\xi'} \rhd y &= x \lhd \mathsf{y}_{\xi'} \rhd y
\end{aligned}
$$

Table 8. Axioms for synchronous cooperation with blocking

$\|_{scb} (\langle\rangle)=S$	Scb1
$\|_{scb} (\alpha \frown \langle S \rangle \frown \beta)=\|_{scb} (\alpha \frown \beta)$	Scb2
$\|_{scb} (\alpha \frown \langle D \rangle \frown \beta)=D$	Scb3
$\|_{scb} (\langle x_1 \unlhd \xi_1 \unrhd y_1 \rangle \frown \ldots \frown \langle x_n \unlhd \xi_n \unrhd y_n \rangle)=\psi_0^\emptyset$	Scb4
$\|_{scb} (\alpha \frown \langle x \unlhd \mathtt{NT}(\langle z_1 \rangle \frown \ldots \frown \langle z_n \rangle) \unrhd y \rangle \frown \beta)=$	
$\quad \|_{scb} (\alpha \frown \langle \mathtt{tau} \circ z_1 \rangle \frown \ldots \frown \langle \mathtt{tau} \circ z_n \rangle \frown \langle \mathtt{tau} \circ x \rangle \frown \beta)$	Scb5
$\|_{scb} (\alpha \frown \langle x \lhd c \rhd y \rangle \frown \beta)= \|_{scb} (\alpha \frown \langle x \rangle \frown \beta) \lhd c \rhd \|_{scb} (\alpha \frown \langle y \rangle \frown \beta)$	Scb6

- $\mathsf{tau} \in \mathcal{AA}$;
- for an action $\xi \in \mathcal{CA}$ if and only if $\xi \in \mathcal{AA}$ or there exist ξ', ξ'' such that $\xi = \xi'|\xi''$;
- for an action $\xi \in \mathcal{CA}$ there is a boolean value $?\xi$ stating that ξ is independent or blocked.

Hence, each concurrent action can be reduced to one of the following form:

- a with $a \in \mathcal{AA}$;
- $a_1|\ldots|a_n$ with $a_1, \ldots a_n \in \mathcal{AA}$ for $n > 1$;

The axioms for concurrent actions are given in Table 7. We assume that the independence of a concurrent action and its reply depend only on its last atomic action. The set $\mathcal{BA}$ of basic actions is extended with this set $\mathcal{CA}$ of concurrent actions.

The Synchronous Cooperation with Blocking Strategy. The synchronous cooperation of threads in SVP is dynamic. We intend to perform simultaneously the maximum number of independent actions from concurrent threads. This might speed up processors [20]. We call this interleaving strategy the *synchronous cooperation with blocking*, denoted by $\|_{scb}$.

The axioms for synchronous cooperation with blocking $\|_{scb}$ are given in Table 8. The threads are supposed initially not to contain any guards. In this strategy, the composition of an empty sequence of threads is a termination. If a thread is in deadlock then the whole system is also in deadlock. If a thread is terminated then this thread is simply removed from the sequence. If all threads are blocked, deadlock will occur. If all threads are deadlock free, the synchronous cooperation strategy will execute simultaneously all and only independent threads. The indexes of these threads are contained in a set I. We note that the `tau` actions will arise when a family of thread is created in order to keep pace with other threads in the sequence. The auxiliary function ψ_i^I is defined by:

$$\psi_i^I = \psi_{i+1}^{I\cup\{i+1\}} \lhd ?\xi_{i+1} \rhd \psi_{i+1}^I$$
$$\psi_n^{\emptyset} = D$$
$$\psi_n^I = |_{i\in I}\xi_i \circ \|_{scb} (\langle\chi_i^I(x_1 \unlhd \xi_1 \unrhd y_1)\rangle \curvearrowright \ldots \curvearrowright \langle\chi_n^I(x_n \unlhd \xi_n \unrhd y_n)\rangle)) \quad (I \neq \emptyset)$$

where $\chi_i^I(x \unlhd \xi \unrhd y) = \begin{cases} x \lhd y_\xi \rhd y \text{ if } i \in I, \\ x \unlhd \xi \unrhd y \text{ otherwise.} \end{cases}$

For a sequence of arbitrary infinite threads $\alpha = \langle p_1\rangle \curvearrowright \ldots \curvearrowright \langle p_m\rangle$, $\|_{scb}(\alpha)$ is determined by its projective sequence where $\pi_n(\|_{scb}(\alpha)) = \pi_n(\|_{scb}(\langle\pi_n(p_1)\rangle \curvearrowright \ldots \curvearrowright \langle\pi_n(p_m)\rangle))$.

3.5   Basic Terms and Guarded Recursive Specifications in TA_{svp}

Basic Terms. We now denote $\mathcal{T}_{svp}$ as the set of all closed terms over the signature of TA_{svp}. The set $\mathcal{B}$ of *basic terms* is inductively defined by the following rules:

- $S, D \in \mathcal{B}$;
- if $p \in \mathcal{B}$ then $\text{tau} \circ p \in \mathcal{B}$;
- if $p, q \in \mathcal{B}$ and $a \in \mathcal{BA}$ then $p \unlhd a \unrhd q \in \mathcal{B}$;
- if $p, q \in \mathcal{B}$ then $p \unlhd \text{swch} \unrhd q \in \mathcal{B}$;
- if $p, r_1, \ldots, r_n \in \mathcal{B}$ then $\text{NT}(\langle r_1\rangle \curvearrowright \ldots \curvearrowright \langle r_n\rangle) \circ p \in \mathcal{B}$;
- if $p, q \in \mathcal{B}$ and $a \in \mathcal{BA}$ then $p \lhd y_a \rhd q \in \mathcal{B}$;
- if $p, q \in \mathcal{B}$ and $a \in \mathcal{BA}$ then $p\lhd?a \rhd q \in \mathcal{B}$;

We write $\mathcal{B}^0$ for the set of all terms from $\mathcal{B}$ in which no subterm of the form $p \unlhd \text{NT}(\alpha) \unrhd q$ occurs.

Lemma 1. *For all $p_1, \ldots, p_n \in \mathcal{B}$, there is a term $q \in \mathcal{B}^0$ such that $\|_{ctpb}^k (\langle p_1\rangle \curvearrowright \ldots \curvearrowright \langle p_n\rangle) = q$ is derivable from the axioms of TA_{svp}.*

Theorem 1. (Elimination). *For all $p \in \mathcal{T}_{svp}$, there is a term $q \in \mathcal{B}$ such that $p = q$ is derivable from the axioms of TA_{svp}.*

The proofs of Lemma 1 and Theorem 1 are given in [14].

Guarded Recursive Specifications in TA_{svp}. We assume the existence of a fixed but arbitrary set of variables $\mathcal{X}$. Let $X \subseteq \mathcal{X}$. We write $\mathcal{T}_{svp}^X$ for the set of all terms from $\mathcal{T}_{svp}$ in which no other variables than the ones in X have free occurrences. The set $\mathcal{G}$ of *guarded* terms is defined inductively as follows:

- $S, D \in \mathcal{G}$;
- if $\xi \in \mathcal{BA}$ and $t_1, t_2 \in \mathcal{T}_{svp}$ then $t_1 \unlhd \xi \unrhd t_2 \in \mathcal{G}$;
- if $t_1, t_2, t_3 \in \mathcal{T}_{svp}$ then $t_1 \unlhd \text{NT}(t_3) \unrhd t_2 \in \mathcal{G}$;
- if $\xi \in \mathcal{BA}$ and $t_1, t_2 \in \mathcal{G}$ then $t_1 \lhd y_\xi \rhd t_2 \in \mathcal{G}$;
- if $\xi \in \mathcal{BA}$ and $t_1, t_2 \in \mathcal{G}$ then $t_1\lhd?\xi \rhd t_2 \in \mathcal{G}$;

Table 9. Axioms for the constants $\langle X|E \rangle$

$\langle x_i|E \rangle = t_i(\langle x_1|E \rangle, \ldots, \langle x_n|E \rangle)$ $(i \in [1, n])$	RDP
If $y_i = t_i(y_1, \ldots, y_n)$ for $i \in [1, n]$ then $y_i = \langle x_i|E \rangle$ $(i \in [1, n])$	RSP

- if $t_1, \ldots, t_n \in \mathcal{G}$ then $\|_{ctpb} (\langle t_1 \rangle \curvearrowright \ldots \curvearrowright \langle t_n \rangle) \in \mathcal{G}$.
- if $t_1, \ldots, t_n \in \mathcal{G}$ then $\|_{scb} (\langle t_1 \rangle \curvearrowright \ldots \curvearrowright \langle t_n \rangle) \in \mathcal{G}$.

A *finite recursive specification* E is a finite set $\{x_i = t_i | i \in [1, n]\}$ of recursive equations where t_i, for all $1 \leq i \leq n$, are terms in $\mathcal{T}_{svp}^{\{x_1, \ldots, x_n\}}$. The finite recursive specification E is *guarded* if for all $1 \leq i \leq n$, t_i are guarded.

Theorem 2. *A guarded recursive specification determines a unique solution.*

The proof of the previous theorem can be obtained in the same line as the proof of Theorem 5 in [13]. If E is a guarded recursive specification and x a recursive variable in E, then $\langle x|E \rangle$ denotes the thread that has to be substituted for x in the solution for E. This thread is called *regular*. The axioms for guarded recursive specifications are given in Table 9, where RDP and RSP refer to *Recursive Definition Principle* and *Recursive Specification Principle* as in other process algebras (see e.g. [21]).

In [14], we have given both a denotational semantics [22] and a structural operational semantics [23,24] for TA$_{svp}$, and shown that threads in TA$_{svp}$ are communication-deadlock free. In Section 5.3, we will see how a SVP program behavior is represented as a thread in TA$_{svp}$. This means that SVP programs are communication-deadlock free, a desired property for the SVP model.

4   Memory Model for SVP

This section interprets the memory of the SVP model with the use of Maurer computers [8].

4.1   Maurer Computer

A Maurer computer has a memory and operations. The contents of all memory elements construct a state of the computer. This state can be transformed to another state when a certain operation is performed. We recall the definition of Maurer computers from [9,7]. A *Maurer computer* C consists of the following components:

- a set M;
- a set B with $|B| \geq 2$;
- a set $\mathcal{S}$ of functions $s : M \to B$;
- a set $\mathcal{O}$ of functions $O : \mathcal{S} \to \mathcal{S}$;

and satisfies the following conditions:

- $s_1, s_2 \in \mathcal{S}$, $M' \subseteq M$ and $s_2 : M \to B$ is such that $s_3(x) = s_1(x)$ if $x \in M'$ and $s_3(x) = s_2(x)$ if $x \notin M'$, then $s_3 \in \mathcal{S}$;
- if $s_1, s_2 \in \mathcal{S}$ then the set $\{x \in M | s_1(x) \neq s_2(x)\}$ is finite.

M is called the *memory*; the elements of M are called the *locations*; B is called the *base set*; the elements of $\mathcal{S}$ are called the *states*; the elements of $\mathcal{O}$ are called the *operations*. The first condition is satisfied if C is *complete*, i.e. if $\mathcal{S}$ is the set of all functions $s : M \to B$, and the second condition is satisfied if C is *finite*, i.e. M and B are finite sets.

Let $(M, B, \mathcal{S}, \mathcal{O})$ be a Maurer computer, and $O \in \mathcal{O}$. Then the *input region* of O, written IR, and the *output region* of O, written OR, are the subsets of M defined as follows:

$$
\begin{aligned}
\text{IR}(O) &= \{x \in M \mid \exists s_1, s_2 \in \mathcal{S} : \forall z \in M : s_1(z) = s_2(z) \wedge \\
&\qquad \exists y \in \text{OR}(O) : O(s_1)(y) \neq O(s_2)(y)\}, \\
\text{OR}(O) &= \{y \in M \mid \exists s \in \mathcal{S} : s(y) \neq O(s)(y)\}
\end{aligned}
$$

$\text{OR}(O)$ is the set of all memory elements (or locations) that are possibly affected by O; and $\text{IR}(O)$ is the set of all memory elements that possibly affects elements of $\text{OR}(O)$.

4.2   Maurer Machines

Threads in TA_{svp} can be used to direct a Maurer machine [7,13], an extension of a Maurer computer, in performing operations on its states. In this section, we define Maurer machines with the features of memory and synchronization of the SVP model.

We extend Maurer computers $(M, B, \mathcal{S}, \mathcal{O})$ with a set Act, a function $?_- : \text{Act} \to M$ and a function $[\![_-]\!] : \text{Act} \to (\mathcal{O} \times M)$ to obtain Maurer machines. For each $a \in \text{Act}$, we write $m_a^?$ for the unique $m \in M$ such that $?a = m$. Furthermore, we write O_a and m_a for the unique $O \in \mathcal{O}$ and $m' \in M$, respectively, such that $[\![a]\!] = (O, m')$.

A *Maurer machine* is a tuple $H = (M, B, \mathcal{S}, \mathcal{O}, \text{Act}, ?_-, [\![_-]\!])$ where $(M, B, \mathcal{S}, \mathcal{O})$ is a Maurer computer, and:

- $?_- : \text{Act} \to$ is such that for all $a \in \text{Act}$, $s(m_a^?) \in \{T, F\}$.
- $[\![_-]\!] : \text{Act} \to (\mathcal{O} \times M)$ is such that for all $a \in \text{Act}$ and $s \in \mathcal{S}$, $s(m_a) \in \{T, F\}$; $O_a(s)$ is defined if $s(m_a^?) = T$ otherwise it is *undefined*, denoted by $\uparrow$;

The elements of Act are the *actions*, and $?_-$ is the *request function*, and $[\![_-]\!]$ is the *action interpretation function* of H.

We assume that $\text{Act} = \mathcal{AA} \cup (\mathcal{BA} \setminus \mathcal{CA})$. Let $\sigma(p)$ denote the set of actions $a \in \text{Act}$ occurring in a thread p. We define that

$$
\text{IR}(O_p) = \cup_{a \in \sigma(p)} \text{IR}(O_a) \text{ and } \text{OR}(O_p) = \cup_{a \in \sigma(p)} \text{OR}(O_a)
$$

The SVP model supports two kinds of memory namely *asynchronous shared memory* and *synchronizing memory*.

- *Asynchronous shared memory* supports bulk synchronization between families of threads and provides the permanent state of a computation. There are two simple rules that can be identified for writing deterministic programs, e.g.:
  - no two concurrently executing threads write to the same location in asynchronous shared memory;
  - no two concurrently executing threads read and write to the same location in asynchronous shared memory.
- *Synchronizing memory* supports communication and synchronization between threads in a family. A location in synchronizing memory accessed by a thread in a family is available in read-only form to the other threads in the family.

We then impose two restrictions on threads in TA_{svp} as follows:

- no two concurrently executing threads write to the same location in the memory, i.e. for two threads p and q that are in the same family or in different families executing concurrently, $\text{OR}(O_p) \cap \text{OR}(O_q) = \emptyset$.
- no two concurrently executing threads from different families of threads read and write to the same location in the memory, i.e. for two concurrent threads p and q that are not in the same family, $\text{IR}(O_p) \cap \text{OR}(O_q) = \emptyset$.

We say that an action a is *independent from* a thread p if a is not waiting for any data produced by p, and p is not waiting for the data produced by a either, i.e. $\text{IR}(O_a) \cap \text{OR}(O_p) = \emptyset$ and $\text{IR}(O_p) \cap \text{OR}(O_a)$.

The request function $?a$ is to request the execution of an action a. This action a can be executed if it is *independent*, acknowledged by $s(m_a^?) = T$. In case $s(m_a^?) = F$, a is *blocked* and cannot be executed.

As mentioned earlier, the dependency of a thread in the SVP model is allowed in a very restricted manner, depending only on its predecessors. In particular, a thread may only be waiting for a data produced by its predecessors. Hence, if thread p is not a predecessor of thread q then $\text{IR}(p) \cap \text{OR}(q) = \emptyset$.

We now say that an action a of a thread p in a sequence of concurrent threads is *independent* if it is not waiting for any data produced by the predecessors of p, i.e. for all predecessors q of p, $\text{IR}(O_a) \cap \text{OR}(O_q) = \emptyset$. This also means that a is independent from all predecessors of p.

The actions tau and swch are always independent and have no effect on the state space. That is, for all $s \in S$, $s(m_{\text{tau}}^?) = T$, $s(m_{\text{swch}}^?) = T$, $O_{\text{tau}}(s) = s$, $s(m_{\text{tau}}) = T$, $O_{\text{swch}}(s) = s$, and $s(m_{\text{swch}}) = T$.

For a concurrent action $\xi \in \mathcal{CA}$, where $\xi = a_1 | \ldots | a_n$ with $n > 1$ and $a_i \in \mathcal{AA}$ for $i \in [1, n]$, we define that $s(m_\xi^?) = s(m_{a_n}^?)$ and $s(m_\xi) = s(m_{a_n})$ for all $s \in S$. Furthermore, $O_\xi(s) = O_{a_n}(\ldots O_{a_1}(s) \ldots)$,

$$\text{IR}(O_\xi) = \cup_{i \in [1,n]} \text{IR}(O_{a_i}) \text{ and } \text{OR}(O_\xi) = \cup_{i \in [1,n]} \text{OR}(O_{a_i}).$$

In TA_{svp}, the simultaneously performing act $\xi = a_1 | \ldots | a_n$ occurs only in the case that all actions a_i ($i \in [1, n]$) are independent. Since the dependency of an

Table 10. Axioms for the apply operator. Here $\xi \in \mathcal{BA}$.

$$
\begin{aligned}
x \bullet \uparrow &= \uparrow \\
S \bullet s &= s \\
D \bullet s &= \uparrow \\
(x \triangleleft ?\xi \, \triangleright y) \bullet s &= x \bullet s && \text{if } s(m_\xi^?) = T \\
(x \triangleleft ?\xi \, \triangleright y) \bullet s &= y \bullet s && \text{if } s(m_\xi^?) = F \\
(x \trianglelefteq \xi \trianglerighteq y) \bullet s &= x \bullet O_\xi(s) && \text{if } s(m_\xi^?) = T \text{ and } O_\xi(s)(m_\xi) = T \\
(x \trianglelefteq \xi \trianglerighteq y) \bullet s &= x \bullet O_\xi(s) && \text{if } s(m_\xi^?) = T \text{ and } O_\xi(s)(m_\xi) = F \\
(x \trianglelefteq \xi \trianglerighteq y) \bullet s &= \uparrow && \text{if } s(m_\xi^?) = F \\
(x \trianglelefteq \mathtt{NT}(\alpha) \trianglerighteq y) \bullet s &= \uparrow \\
(x \triangleleft \mathtt{y}_\xi \, \triangleright y) \bullet s &= x \bullet s && \text{if } s(m_\xi) = T \\
(x \triangleleft \mathtt{y}_\xi \, \triangleright y) \bullet s &= y \bullet s && \text{if } s(m_\xi) = F \\
\wedge_{n \geq 0} \pi_n(x) \bullet s = \uparrow &\Rightarrow x \bullet s = \uparrow
\end{aligned}
$$

action depends only on the predecessors of the thread containing that action, there cannot be two actions a_i and a_j for $i, j \in [1, n]$ with $i \neq j$ such that they write to the same location in the memory, or they read and write to the same location in the memory. Therefore, $s(m_\xi^?) = T$ and $O_\xi(s) = O_{a_{i_n}}(\ldots O_{a_{i_1}}(s)\ldots)$ where $i_1..i_n$ is a permutation of $1..n$.

4.3   Applying Threads in TA_{svp} to Maurer Machines

The *apply* operator $\_ \bullet \_$ [7,13] allows threads to transform states of the Maurer machine H by means of it operations. Such state transformations produce either a state of H or the undefined state $\uparrow$.

Let $p \in \mathrm{TA}_{svp}$ and $s \in \mathcal{S}$, then $p \bullet s$ is the state that results if all actions performed by thread p are processed by the Maurer machine H from initial state H. The processing of an action $\xi \in \mathcal{BA}$ is allowed by the boolean value produced by H contained in memory element $m_\xi^?$. This processing amounts to a state change according to the operation O_ξ. In the resulting state, the reply produced by H is contained in memory element m_ξ. If p is S, then there will be no state change. If p is D, then the result is $\uparrow$. If the current action of p is a thread forking action, then the resulting is also $\uparrow$, since thread forking is carried into effect only if it is put in the context of concurrency. Table 10 represents axioms for the apply operator.

We say that $p \bullet s$ is *convergent* if $\exists n \in \mathbb{N} : \pi_n(p) \bullet s \neq \uparrow$. If $p \bullet s$ is convergent then the *length of the computation* of $p \bullet s$, written $\|p \bullet s\|$, is the least $n \in \mathbb{N}$ such that $\pi_n(s) \bullet S \neq \uparrow$.

Two threads p and q are *state transformer equivalent*, written $p \approx q$, if for all $s \in \mathcal{S}$, $p \bullet s = q \bullet s$.

Lemma 2. *If an action ξ is independent from a thread p then for all $s \in \mathcal{S}$,*
$$p \bullet O_\xi(s) = O_\xi(p \bullet s).$$

Proof. Straightforward.

5   TA$_{svp}$ as a Formal Semantics of SVP

This section intends to determine the behaviors of programs (or threads) in μTC, a programming language that realizes the model SVP [15], in the setting of TA$_{svp}$. In order to illustrate our approach, we construct a simple programming language $\mathcal{L}_{svp}$, a subset of the language μTC, with a least collection of primitive statements, but rich enough for important applications. We will show that $\mathcal{L}_{svp}$ threads have a desired property, the determinism property, i.e. the threads should always give the same result as the result obtained when they are executed sequentially.

5.1   The Program Notation $\mathcal{L}_{svp}$

We assume the existence of a set Var of *variables* ranged over $x, y, \ldots$. The program notation $\mathcal{L}_{svp}$ is generated from five kinds of constructs and two composition mechanisms. The constructs used in $\mathcal{L}_{svp}$ are as follows:

- assignment $x{=}e$;
- the constant swch, used to switch off the current thread to another thread in the sequence of concurrent threads;
- thread creation create$(X_1, \ldots, X_n)$;
- conditional statement if$(e)\{X\}\{Y\}$;
- while-loop statement while$(e)\{X\}$.

Here x is a variable and e stands for a boolean or an arithmetic expression, whose syntax we do not describe here. The semantics of conditional statements and while-loops is given as in other programming languages. Two composition mechanisms of $\mathcal{L}_{svp}$ are:

1. sequential composition $X; Y$; and
2. concurrent composition $\| (\langle X_1 \rangle \curvearrowright \ldots \curvearrowright \langle X_n \rangle)$ where $\| \in \{\|_{ctpb}, \|_{scb}\}$.

Let X, Y, X_i denote the programs (or threads) in $\mathcal{L}_{svp}$. Then

$$X, Y := x{=}e \mid \text{if}(e)\{X\}\{Y\} \mid \text{while}(e)\{X\} \mid \text{swch} \mid \text{create}(X_1, \ldots, X_n) \mid$$
$$X; Y \mid \| (\langle X_1 \rangle \curvearrowright \ldots \curvearrowright \langle X_n \rangle).$$

Threads X and Y in the sequential composition $X; Y$ must be sequential. Furthermore, thread creation create$(X_1, \ldots, X_n)$ must be put in the context of concurrency initially. In μTC, the threads $X_1, \ldots, X_n$ in create$(X_1, \ldots, X_n)$ are identical. However, in the verification and evaluation of SVP, it is not necessary to impose this restriction to programs in $\mathcal{L}_{svp}$. Thus, the threads in a created family in $\mathcal{L}_{svp}$ can be different.

5.2   Communication Between Threads with Shared Variables in $\mathcal{L}_{svp}$

A variable occurring in a thread can be a *local* variable (defined by the thread itself) or a *global* variable (defined by the creating threads of that thread). A

Table 11. Example of μTC programs

```
thread main()
{
    int *a;
    int fid, t=0, n=3;
    create(fid;0;n-1)
        {
        index int i;
        shared int s=t; /*initializes s in first thread only*/
        s = s + a[i];
        }
    sync(fid);
}
```

local variable can be *shared*. Every local variable of a thread corresponds to a location in the memory. The set of the locations of all local variables of a thread is called the *working* memory of that thread. A thread can manipulate the values in its working memory, which is inaccessible to other threads from a different family. However, this working memory will be available in read-only form to the subthreads created by the thread itself, and to other threads in the same family if the variable is a shared variable. The communication between threads, as described in Section 2, happens via shared variables. In other words, shared variables define dependency between threads. This dependency depends only on the predecessors of a thread. In particular, if a shared variable s occurs as an input of an assignment or a conditional in a thread then its value is taken as the last value of s produced by the thread and its predecessors.

Example 1. A typical μTC program is given in Table 11. The thread in this table sums the values of array a. Here i for $i \in [0, n-1]$ are the indexes of the subthreads. The instruction $s = s + a[0]$ is never blocked, and the instruction $s = s + a[i]$ of thread i for $i > 0$ will be blocked until the value of s is produced by thread $i - 1$.

Without loss of generality, we can assume that all local variables of concurrently executing threads in $\mathcal{L}_{svp}$ are distinct. Furthermore, a shared variable of a thread does not occur in the predecessors of that thread. Since a thread can write only to its working memory, there cannot be an assignment $x = e$ occurring in that thread where x is not defined by the thread itself.

Example 2. The thread given in Example 1 can be formulated as program X in $\mathcal{L}_{svp}$ below.

$$X_0 := s_0 = t; s_0 = s_0 + a[0]$$
$$X_1 := s_1 = s_0 + a[1]$$
$$X_2 := s_2 = s_1 + a[2]$$
$$X := \| \, (t = 0; \mathtt{create}(X_0, X_1, X_2))$$

where $\| \in \{\|_{ctpb}, \|_{scb}\}$. We note that the sum of the array a is stored in s_2.

Table 12. Axioms for thread extraction operation

$\|\langle\rangle\|$	$= S$
$\|a\|$	$= a \circ S$
$\|a; X\|$	$= a \circ \|X\|$
$\|\texttt{swch}; X\|$	$= \texttt{swch} \circ \|X\|,$
$\|\texttt{create}(X_1, \ldots, X_n); X\|$	$= \texttt{NT}(X_1, \ldots, X_n) \circ \|X\|$
$\|\texttt{if}(a)\{X\}\{Y\}; Z\|$	$= \|X; Z\| \trianglelefteq a \trianglerighteq \|Y; Z\|$
$\|\texttt{if}(T)\{X\}\{Y\}; Z\|$	$= \|X; Z\|$
$\|\texttt{if}(F)\{X\}\{Y\}; Z\|$	$= \|Y; Z\|$
$\|\texttt{while}(a)\{X\}; Z\|$	$= \|X; \texttt{while}(a)\{X\}; Z\| \trianglelefteq a \trianglerighteq \|Z\|$
$\|\texttt{while}(T)\{X\}; Z\|$	$= \|X; \texttt{while}(T)\{X\}\|$
$\|\texttt{while}(F)\{X\}; Z\|$	$= \|Z\|$
$\| \, \|_{ctpb} (\langle X_1 \rangle \curvearrowright \ldots \curvearrowright \langle X_n \rangle)\|$	$= \|_{ctpb} (\langle \|X_1\| \rangle \curvearrowright \ldots \curvearrowright \langle \|X_n\| \rangle)$
$\| \, \|_{scb} (\langle X_1 \rangle \curvearrowright \ldots \curvearrowright \langle X_n \rangle)\|$	$= \|_{scb} (\langle \|X_1\| \rangle \curvearrowright \ldots \curvearrowright \langle \|X_n\| \rangle)$

5.3   The Thread Extraction Operation

We now consider instructions $x = e$ and e of $\mathcal{L}_{svp}$ as the actions in $\mathcal{BA}$, written as $[x = e]$ and $\langle e \rangle$. The behaviors of programs in $\mathcal{L}_{svp}$ are determined by means of the *thread extraction operation* $|_-|$, which assigns a thread in TA_{svp} to a program (or thread) in $\mathcal{L}_{svp}$. Table 12 represents axioms for thread extraction operation. If the behavior of a thread in $\mathcal{L}_{svp}$ cannot be computed according to the thread extraction operation, then it is identified with D. For instance, the behavior of a non-trivial loop in which no action occurs can be identified with D.

Example 3. The behavior of program X in Example 2 can be determined as a thread in TA_{svp} as follows.

$$
\begin{aligned}
|X_0| &= \ [s_0 = t] \circ [s_0 = s_0 + a[0]] \circ S \\
|X_1| &= \ [s_1 = s_0 + a[1]] \circ S \\
|X_2| &= \ [s_2 = s_1 + a[2]] \circ S \\
|X| &:= \ \| \, (\langle [t = 0] \circ \texttt{NT}(\langle |X_0| \rangle \curvearrowright \langle |X_1| \rangle \curvearrowright \langle |X_2| \rangle) \circ S \rangle) \text{ with } \| \in \{\|_{ctpb}, \|_{scb}\}.
\end{aligned}
$$

Lemma 3. *Let X, Y be two sequential programs in $\mathcal{L}_{svp}$. Then $|X; Y| = |X|.|Y|$.*

Theorem 3. *The behaviors of programs in $\mathcal{L}_{svp}$ are regular threads in TA_{svp}.*

The proof of Lemma 3 is straightforward, and Theorem 3 can be proven by induction on the structure of the programs using Lemma 3.

5.4   Determinism

For each program $X \in \mathcal{L}_{svp}$, we write $\overline{X}$ for the sequential form of X, obtained from X by replacing any subterm of the forms $\texttt{create}(X_1, \ldots, X_n)$, $\|_{ctpb} (\langle X_1 \rangle \curvearrowright \ldots \curvearrowright \langle X_n \rangle)$ and $\|_{scb} (\langle X_1 \rangle \curvearrowright \ldots \curvearrowright \langle X_n \rangle)$ with $X_1; \ldots; X_n$.

Theorem 4. *(Determinism). Let X be a program in $\mathcal{L}_{svp}$. Then $|X| \approx |\overline{X}|$.*

Proof. See Appendix A.

6   Concluding Remarks

In this paper, we have given a formal proof for the determinism property of SANE Virtual Processors (SVP). We taken thread algebra (TA) [4] as a theoretical framework for the verification and evaluation of SVP. In particular, TA has been extended with the features of SVP to TA_{svp} (thread algebra for SVP). We have shown that TA_{svp} indeed is a formal semantics of SVP by assigning a thread in TA_{svp} to a program in $\mathcal{L}_{svp}$, a simple programming language that illustrates the realization $\mu\mathrm{TC}$ of SVP. We have interpreted the memory of SVP with the use of Maurer computers [8,9], and considered the interaction between threads in TA_{svp} and Maurer machines. Finally, we have proven that $\mathcal{L}_{svp}$ programs always give the same result as the result obtained when they are executed sequentially. Our work together with the work presented in [14] show that the SVP model has the desired properties, namely determinism and freedom from deadlock.

Acknowledgments. We thank Jan Bergstra for the fruitful discussions.

References

1. Bolychevsky, A., Jesshope, C., Muchnick, V.: Dynamic sheduling in rics architectures. IEE Proceedings Computers and Digital Techniques 143(5), 309–317 (1996)
2. Bousias, K., Hasasneh, N., Jesshope, C.: Instruction-level parallelism through Microthreading-a scalable Approach to chip multiprocessors. The Computer Journal 49 (2), 211–233 (2006)
3. Jesshope, C.: Microthreading a model for distributed instruction-level concurrency. Parallel Processing Letters 16 (2), 209–228 (2006)
4. Bergstra, J., Middelburg, C.: Thread algebra for strategic interleaving. Formal Aspects of Computing. Preliminary version: Computer Science Report PRG0404: Sectie Software Engineering, University of Amsterdam (to appear, 2007)
5. Jesshope, C., Luo, B.: Micro-threading: A new approach to future risc. In: ACAC 2000, pp. 31–41. IEEE Computer Society Press, Los Alamitos (2000)
6. Jesshope, C.: Multithreaded microprocessors evolution or revolution. In: Omondi, A.R., Sedukhin, S. (eds.) ACSAC 2003. LNCS, vol. 2823, pp. 21–45. Springer, Heidelberg (2003)
7. Bergstra, J., Middelburg, C.: Maurer computers with single-thread control. Fundamenta Informaticae (to appear, 2007)
8. Maurer, W.: A theory of computer instructions. Journal of ACM 13(2), 226–235 (1966)
9. Maurer, W.: A theory of computer instructions. Science of Computer Programming 55(1/2), 1–19 (2006)
10. Hopcroft, J., Motwani, R., Ullman, J.: Introduction to Automata Theory, Languages and Computation, 2nd edn. Addition-Wesley, Reading, MA (2001)
11. Bergstra, J., Middelburg, C.: Simulating turing machines on maurer machines. CS-Report 05-28, Department of mathematics and computer science, Technische Universiteit Eindhoven (2005)
12. Bergstra, J., Middelburg, C.: Maurer computers for pipelined instruction processing. CS-Report 06-12, Department of mathematics and computer science, Technische Universiteit Eindhoven (2006)

13. Bergstra, J., Middelburg, C.: Synchronous cooperation for explicit multi-threading. CS-Report 06-29, Department of mathematics and computer science, Technische Universiteit Eindhoven (2006)
14. Vu, T., Jesshope, C.: Thread algebra for SANE virtual processors (2007), available at http://staff.science.uva.nl/~jesshope
15. Jesshope, C.: SVP and μTC-A dynamic model of concurrency and its implementation as a compiler target (2006), http://staff.science.uva.nl/~jesshope/Papers/uTC-paper.pdf
16. Bergstra, J., Loots, M.: Program algebra for sequential code. J. of Logic and Algebraic Programming 51, 125–156 (2002)
17. Baeten, J., Bergstra, J.: Process algebra with signals and conditions. In: Broy, M. (ed.) Programming and Mathematical Methods. NATO ASI Series, vol. F88, pp. 1–21 (1992)
18. Milner, R.: Communication and Concurrency. Prentice-Hall, Englewood Cliffs (1989)
19. Bergstra, J., Klop, J.: Process algebra for synchronous communication. Inform. and Control 60 (1-3), 109–137 (1984)
20. Ungerer, T., Robič, B., Šilc, J.: A survey of processors with explicit multithreading. ACM Computing Surveys 35 (1), 29–63 (2003)
21. Fokkink, W.: Introduction to Process Algebra. EATCS Series. Springer, Heidelberg (2000)
22. Bakker, J., Zucker, J.: Processes and the denotational semantics of concurrency. Information and Control 54(1/2), 70–120 (1982)
23. Plotkin, G.: A structural approach to operational semantics. Aarhus DAIMI FN-19, Computing Science Department (1981)
24. Aceto, L., Fokkink, W., Verhoef, C.: Structural operational semantics. In: Bergstra, J., Ponse, A., Smolka, S. (eds.) Handbook of Process Algebra, pp. 197–222. Elsevier, Amsterdam (2001)

A   Proofs

In this section, we provide a proof for Theorem 4. We will use some supporting results. The first result states that the execution of concurrent finite threads in TA_{svp} gives the same result as the result obtained when they are executed sequentially.

Lemma 4. *Let $p_1, \ldots, p_n$ be terms in B, and $\| \in \{\|_{ctpb}, \|_{scb}\}$. By Lemma 1 and Theorem 1, there are $q_i \in \mathcal{B}^0$ such that $\| (\langle p_i \rangle) = q_i$ for all $i \in [1, n]$. Then*

1. *If for all $1 \leq i < j \leq n$, p_j is not a predecessor of p_i, and $i_1 .. i_n$ is a permutation of $1..n$ then $\| (\langle p_{i_1} \rangle \curvearrowright \ldots \curvearrowright \langle p_{i_n} \rangle) \approx q_1 \ldots q_n$.*
2. *$\| (\langle p_1 \ldots p_n \rangle) \approx q_1 \ldots q_n$.*

Proof. We prove (1) only. The proof of (2) can be obtained in the same way. We consider the case $\|=\|_{ctpb}^{k}$. The case $\|=\|_{scb}$ is similar. We note that in the interleaving strategy $\|_{ctpb}^{k}$, the case $k \geq n$ never happens since the threads in

TA_{svp} are communication-deadlock free (see [14]). Let $p = \|_{ctpb}^k (\langle p_{i_1} \rangle \curvearrowright \ldots \curvearrowright \langle p_{i_n} \rangle)$. We prove by induction on $(L(p), n - k)$ where $L(p)$ is defined by

$$
\begin{aligned}
L(S) &= 1, \\
L(D) &= 1, \\
L(p \lhd c \rhd q) &= \max\{L(p), L(q)\} + 1, \\
L(p \trianglelefteq a \trianglerighteq q) &= \max\{L(p), L(q)\} + 1, \\
L(\mathtt{NT}(\langle r_1 \rangle \curvearrowright \ldots \curvearrowright \langle r_n \rangle) \circ p) &= \max\{L(p), L(r_1), \ldots, L(r_n)\} + 1, \\
L(\| (\langle q_1 \rangle \curvearrowright \ldots \curvearrowright \langle q_n \rangle)) &= \max\{L(q_1), \ldots, L(q_n)\} + 1.
\end{aligned}
$$

Let $q = q_1 \ldots q_n$. We show that $p \approx q$. Let $q' = q_1 \ldots q_{i_1 - 1}$ and $q'' = q_{i_1+1} \ldots q_n$. We consider the following possibilities:

- $p_{i_1} = S$. Then $p \approx \|_{ctpb}^k (\langle p_{i_2} \rangle \curvearrowright \ldots \curvearrowright \langle p_{i_n} \rangle)$. By the induction hypothesis, $p \approx q'.q''$. Since $p_{i_1} = S$, $p \approx q$.
- $p_{i_1} = D$. Then $p \approx q \approx D$.
- $p_{i_1} = \mathtt{tau} \circ p'_{i_1}$. Then $p = \mathtt{tau} \circ p'$ where $p' = \|_{ctpb}^0 (\langle p'_{i_1} \rangle \curvearrowright \ldots \curvearrowright \langle p_{i_n} \rangle)$. By the induction hypothesis, $p' \approx q'.q'_{i_1}.q''$ where $q_{i_1} = \mathtt{tau} \circ q'_{i_1}$. Since $\mathtt{tau}$ has no effect on the state space $\mathcal{S}$, $p \approx p' \approx q' \approx q$.
- $p_{i_1} = \mathtt{swch} \circ p'_{i_1}$. Similar to the previous case, $p \approx q$.
- $p_{i_1} = p'_{i_1} \lhd c \rhd p''_{i_1}$. Then $p = p' \lhd c \rhd p''$ where $p' = \|_{ctpb}^k (\langle p'_{i_1} \rangle \curvearrowright \ldots \curvearrowright \langle p_{i_n} \rangle)$ and $p'' = \|_{ctpb}^k (\langle p''_{i_1} \rangle \curvearrowright \ldots \curvearrowright \langle p_{i_n} \rangle)$. By the induction hypothesis, we also have $p \approx q$.
- $p_{i_1} = p'_{i_1} \trianglelefteq a \trianglerighteq p''_{i_1}$. Then $p = (p' \trianglelefteq a \trianglerighteq p'') \lhd ?a \rhd \mathtt{tau} \circ p'''$ where $p' = \|_{ctpb}^0 (\langle p'_{i_1} \rangle \curvearrowright \ldots \curvearrowright \langle p_{i_n} \rangle)$, $p'' = \|_{ctpb}^0 (\langle p''_{i_1} \rangle \curvearrowright \ldots \curvearrowright \langle p_{i_n} \rangle)$ and $p''' = \|_{ctpb}^{k+1} (\langle p_{i_2} \rangle \curvearrowright \ldots \curvearrowright \langle p_{i_n} \rangle \curvearrowright \langle p_{i_1} \rangle)$. Hence for all $s \in \mathcal{S}$,

$$
p \bullet s = \begin{cases} p' \bullet O_a(s) \lhd O_a(s)(m_a) \rhd p'' \bullet O_a(s) & \text{if } s(m_a^?) = T \\ p''' \bullet s & \text{otherwise.} \end{cases}
$$

Let $q'_{i_1} = \|_{ctpb} (\langle p'_{i_1} \rangle)$ and $q''_{i_1} = \|_{ctpb} (\langle p''_{i_1} \rangle)$. By the induction hypothesis, $p' \approx q'.q'_{i_1}.q''$, $p'' \approx q'.q''_{i_1}.q''$, and $p''' \approx q$. If $s(m_a^?) = F$ then $p \bullet s = p''' \bullet s \approx q \bullet s$. If $s(m_a^?) = T$ then a is independent from all predecessors of p_{i_1}. This implies that a is independent from q'. Let $s' = q' \bullet s$. It follows from Lemma 2 that $q' \bullet O_a(s) = O_a(q' \bullet s) = O_a(s')$. Furthermore, $s'(m_a^?) = s(m_a^?) = T$. Therefore,

$$
\begin{aligned}
p \bullet s &= p' \bullet O_a(s) \lhd O_a(s)(m_a) \rhd p'' \bullet O_a(s) \\
&\approx (q'.q'_{i_1}.q'') \bullet O_a(s) \lhd O_a(s)(m_a) \rhd (q'.q''_{i_1}.q'') \bullet O_a(s) \\
&\approx (q'_{i_1}.q'') \bullet (q' \bullet O_a(s)) \lhd O_a(s)(m_a) \rhd (q''_{i_1}.q'') \bullet (q' \bullet O_a(s)) \\
&\approx q'_{i_1}.q'' \bullet (O_a(s')) \lhd O_a(s')(m_a) \rhd q''_{i_1}.q'' \bullet (O_a(s')) \\
&= (q'_{i_1} \trianglelefteq a \trianglerighteq q''_{i_1}.q'') \bullet s' \approx (q_{i_1}.q'') \bullet s' \approx q \bullet s.
\end{aligned}
$$

This implies that $p \approx q$.
- $p_{i_1} = \mathtt{NT}(\langle r_1 \rangle \curvearrowright \ldots \curvearrowright \langle r_m \rangle) \circ p'_{i_1}$. Then $p = \mathtt{tau} \circ \|_{ctpb}^k (\langle r_1 \rangle \curvearrowright \ldots \curvearrowright \langle r_m \rangle \curvearrowright \langle p'_{i_1} \rangle \curvearrowright \ldots \curvearrowright \langle p_{i_n} \rangle)$. By the induction hypothesis,

$$
p \approx q'.r'_1 \ldots r'_m.q'_{i_1}.q'' \approx q'.q_{i_1}.q'' \approx q.
$$

The following lemma extends Lemma 4 with the case of infinite threads.

Lemma 5. *Let $p_1, \ldots, p_n$ be infinite threads, and $\| \in \{\|_{ctpb}, \|_{scb}\}$. Then*

1. *If for all $1 \leq i < j \leq n$, p_j is not a predecessor of p_i, and $i_1..i_n$ is a permutation of $1..n$ then $\| \, (\langle p_{i_1} \rangle \curvearrowright \ldots \curvearrowright \langle p_{i_n} \rangle) \approx \| \, (\langle p_1 \rangle) \ldots \| \, (\langle p_n \rangle)$.*
2. *$\| \, (\langle p_1 \ldots p_n \rangle) \approx \| \, (\langle p_1 \rangle) \ldots \| \, (\langle p_n \rangle)$.*

Proof. We prove (1) only. The proof of (2) is similar. Let $p = \| \, (\langle p_{i_1} \rangle \curvearrowright \ldots \curvearrowright \langle p_{i_n} \rangle)$ and $q = \| \, (\langle p_1 \rangle) \ldots \| \, (\langle p_n \rangle)$. Since $\pi_k(p) = \pi_k(\| \, (\langle \pi_k(p_{i_1}) \rangle \curvearrowright \ldots \curvearrowright \langle \pi_k(p_{i_n}) \rangle))$, there is $N_p \in \mathbb{N}$ such that $p \approx \| \, (\langle \pi_k(p_{i_1}) \rangle \curvearrowright \ldots \curvearrowright \langle \pi_k(p_{i_n}) \rangle)$ for all $k \geq N_p$. Furthermore, for all $i \in [1, n]$, there are $N_i \in \mathbb{N}$ such that $p_i \approx \pi_k(p_i)$ for all $k \geq N_i$. Let $N = \max\{N_p, N_1, \ldots, N_n\}$. It follows from Lemma 4 that

$$p \approx \| \, (\langle \pi_N(p_{i_1}) \rangle \curvearrowright \ldots \curvearrowright \langle \pi_N(p_{i_n}) \rangle) \approx \| \, (\langle \pi_N(p_1) \rangle) \ldots \| \, (\langle \pi_N(p_n) \rangle)$$
$$\approx \| \, (\langle p_1 \rangle) \ldots \| \, (\langle p_n \rangle) \approx q.$$

Finally, we can prove our main result as follows.

Proof. (**The proof of Theorem 4**). If X is a sequential program then we are done. In the remaining case, we prove by induction on the structure of X.

- $X = \langle \rangle$. Then $\overline{X} = \langle \rangle$. Hence $|X| \approx |\overline{X}| \approx S$.
- $X = \| \, (\langle a \rangle)$. Then $\overline{X} = a$. Thus, $|X| \approx a \circ S = |\overline{X}|$.
- $X = \| \, (\langle \mathtt{if}(a)\{Y\}\{Z\} \rangle)$. Then $\overline{X} = \mathtt{if}(a)\{\overline{Y}\}\{\overline{Z}\}$. By the induction hypothesis, $|X| = \| \, (\langle |Y| \trianglelefteq a \trianglerighteq |Z| \rangle) \approx \| \, (\langle |Y| \rangle) \trianglelefteq a \trianglerighteq \| \, (\langle |Z| \rangle) \approx |\overline{Y}| \trianglelefteq a \trianglerighteq |\overline{Z}| = |\overline{X}|$.
- $X = \| \, (\langle \mathtt{while}(a)\{Y\} \rangle)$. Then $\overline{X} = \mathtt{while}(a)\{\overline{Y}\}$. Let $Z = \mathtt{while}(a)\{Y\}$. It follows from Lemma 3, Lemma 5 and the induction hypothesis that $|X| = \| \, (\langle |Y|.|Z| \trianglelefteq a \trianglerighteq S \rangle) \approx \| \, (\langle |Y|.|Z| \rangle) \trianglelefteq a \trianglerighteq S \approx \| \, (\langle |Y| \rangle).|X| \trianglelefteq a \trianglerighteq S$, $|\overline{X}| = |\overline{Y}|.|\overline{X}| \trianglelefteq a \trianglerighteq S$. This implies that $|X| \approx |\overline{X}|$.
- $X = \| \, (\langle \mathtt{create}(X_1, \ldots, X_n) \rangle)$. By Lemma 5 and the induction hypothesis, $|X| = \| \, (\langle |X_1| \curvearrowright \ldots \curvearrowright \langle |X_n| \rangle) \approx \| \, (\langle |X_1| \rangle) \ldots \| \, (\langle |X_n| \rangle) \approx |\overline{X_1}| \ldots |\overline{X_n}| = |\overline{X}|$.
- $X = \| \, (\langle X_1; \ldots; X_n \rangle)$. Similar to the previous case, we likewise get $|X| = \| \, (\langle |X_1| \ldots |X_n| \rangle) \approx \| \, (\langle |X_1| \rangle) \ldots \| \, (\langle |X_n| \rangle) \approx |\overline{X_1}| \ldots |\overline{X_n}| = |\overline{X}|$.
- $X = \| \, (\langle X_1 \curvearrowright \ldots \curvearrowright \langle X_n \rangle)$. Similarly, $|X| \approx \| \, (\langle |X_1| \rangle) \ldots \| \, (\langle |X_n| \rangle) \approx |\overline{X_1}| \ldots |\overline{X_n}| = |\overline{X}|$.

Calculating and Composing Progress Properties in Terms of the Leads-to Relation

Arjan J. Mooij

School of Computer Science and Information Technology,
The University of Nottingham, United Kingdom
Arjan.Mooij@cs.nott.ac.uk

Abstract. To facilitate the construction of concurrent programs based on progress requirements, we study an integration of the Owicki/Gries theory with UNITY's leads-to relation. In particular we investigate a set of calculational rules for leads-to, and we study the composition of programs regarding their effect on progress. Apart from parallel composition, we consider the less familiar notion of weak sequential composition. Our techniques are illustrated on two network initialisation protocols that are related to the protocol standard IEEE 1394.

1 Introduction

We study the construction of concurrent programs using formal derivation techniques, which is an approach that guarantees correctness by construction. In [FvG99], Feijen and van Gasteren have developed a method for deriving concurrent programs from their safety requirements. This method is based on the calculational method of Dijkstra [Dij76] and the axiomatic theory of Owicki and Gries [OG76]. It is applicable to shared-memory systems as well as to distributed systems that communicate using message passing. The resulting derivations are recognised to be elegant and insightful; see e.g. [FGR04].

Nevertheless, some concurrent programs are primarily motivated by their progress requirements, which makes it hard to derive them on the basis of safety alone. In [DG06], Dongol and Goldson integrated the progress logic of UNITY [CM88] into the theory of Owicki and Gries with its more conventional style of program description. In [DM06a, DM06b], Dongol and Mooij have started to develop a corresponding method for program derivation, such that both safety and progress requirements can be used.

The progress logic of UNITY is based on the leads-to relation $\leadsto$, for which usually a large collection of lemmas is provided. However, many of these are complicated and hard to remember; see also [Kna92]. In the present work we investigate a series of calculational rules with familiar algebraic shapes that are easy to remember. Apart from collecting some known properties, also some new properties are discovered.

In addition, to simplify the progress proofs of concurrent programs that can be decomposed into simpler concurrent programs, we develop some elementary rules

M. Butler, M. Hinchey, M.M. Larrondo-Petrie (Eds.): ICFEM 2007, LNCS 4789, pp. 366–386, 2007.

for the maintenance of progress properties under two kinds of program composition. The first kind of composition is the most natural kind of composition for concurrent programs, viz., parallel composition. Even though reasoning about parallelism is often considered to be difficult, we advocate the extensive use of parallelism for postponing design decisions and for decomposing specifications; see also [MW03, Moo06].

The second kind of composition is a kind of sequential composition. Usually *strong* sequential composition is studied, which imposes the requirement that the parallel components of the second program being composed can only start execution when *all* parallel components in the first program have terminated. However, implementing this kind of composition in a real concurrent system yields a considerable overhead for the additional synchronisation between the components. We study the more natural notion of *weak* sequential composition, which is the usual kind of sequential composition for scenario languages like Message Sequence Chart [ITU00]. This component-wise sequential composition allows more concurrency, and it is easy to implement in a real concurrent system.

To illustrate some of the techniques, we consider some network initialisation protocols. The basic purpose of such fundamental protocols is to get a distributed system into a desired initial state [Mis91]. In contrast to such protocols in [FvG99], we do not assume that all parallel components have access to one shared memory. The structure of the network protocols is closely related to the highly-concurrent architectures from the two protocol standards IEEE 1394 [IEE96] (see also [DGRV00]) and IEEE 1394.1 [IEE05] (see also [Moo06]).

Related work. In [MP91] a proof system for temporal logic is presented that is more general than UNITY, in particular including several kinds of fairness, and more kinds of temporal formulae. Nevertheless the UNITY logic continues to receive attention by focusing on a prevalent class of temporal formulae, for which the rules in [MP91] are similar to the usual definition of leads-to in UNITY. Moreover the emphasis in [MP91] is on completeness of a proof system, while we are looking for rules that support calculations on progress formulae.

Protocol composition is a very active area of research. In our study, the rely-guarantee method [Jon81, XdRH97] would be an obvious candidate framework, because it is considered to be a compositional reformulation of the theory from [OG76]. Furthermore, [Sto91, XdRH97] describe extensions to cover some progress properties. However, in contrast to strong sequential composition, the notion of weak sequential composition does not fit nicely within this framework, nor within UNITY-based frameworks like [CK97].

Instead of composing programs that interact, like in action refinement approaches [PVAS05], we focus on the composition of independent concurrent programs. This applies to proper modularisations of a program into simpler programs. The resulting composition rules seem to be useful and simple enough to be remembered easily and applied safely.

Overview. In Section 2 we summarise the basic theories on program construction that we use. Our collection of calculational rules is described in Section 3, and the composition rules are described in Section 4. In Section 5 we specify the initialisation protocol, and in Sections 6 and 7 we derive two distributed implementations. Finally some conclusions are provided in Section 8.

2 Preliminaries

In this section we summarise some basic material that we use in the remainder of this work. It is based on [FvG99, DG06, DM06a, DM06b].

2.1 Concurrent Programs

A *concurrent program* consists of a precondition *Pre* and a number of *components*, which are sequential programs with a unique identifier. The components are to be executed in parallel by interleaving their atomic statements, and they communicate via shared variables (which in turn can model message passing). The *control points* are the locations between the atomic statements in the components, and the *atomic statements* are typically the guard evaluations and the assignments.

Each control point is assigned a unique *label*, although we sometimes omit them. For each component X there is an auxiliary variable pc_X that represents the program counter of X in terms of the control-point labels. The program counters cannot explicitly be accessed by the statements, but they are implicitly updated and they can be used in the specification and proof of properties.

The programming language that we use is Dijkstra's Guarded Command Language [Dij76]. In this work we only use assignments, and guarded skips like **if** $b \rightarrow$ **skip fi**, with a boolean expression b as guard, which denotes a statement that is blocked as long as $\neg b$ holds. However, the approach equally applies to repetitions, selections, etc. The semantics of the statements follows from the weakest liberal precondition *wlp* and weakest precondition *wp* predicate transformers, where in particular the *wlp* does not require termination. The *wlp* of an atomic statement in component X and a predicate P is defined as:

$$[\; wlp.(x := E \; j\!:).P \qquad \equiv \quad (x, pc_X := E, j).P \;]$$
$$[\; wlp.(\textbf{if } b \rightarrow \textbf{skip fi } j\!:).P \quad \equiv \quad (b \; \Rightarrow \; (pc_X := j).P) \;]$$

Here $(x := E \; j\!:)$ denotes an assignment that terminates at program counter value j, $(x, pc_X := E, j)$ denotes a substitution, and $[\; \dots \;]$ denotes a universal quantifier binding all program variables.

As all atomic statements are assumed to be terminating, the *wp* and the *wlp* for the atomic statements are equal. The *guard* of a statement S, denoted $g.S$, is defined as $[\; g.S \equiv \neg wp.S.false \;]$. A statement S at control point i of component X is *enabled* whenever $pc_X = i \wedge g.S$ holds and *blocked* whenever $pc_X = i \wedge \neg g.S$ holds.

2.2 Owicki/Gries Theory

Safety properties are specified by annotating the program with assertions. An *assertion* is a predicate on the state of the system and it is located within brackets {...} at a control point. To prove partial correctness of the annotation, we use the classical Owicki/Gries theory [OG76] using the nomenclature of [FvG99]. An assertion P in a component is correct if it is both

- locally correct, i.e., it is established in the component:
  - if P is an initial assertion in the component: $[\ Pre \Rightarrow P\ ]$ holds;
  - if P is preceded by an atomic statement $\{Q\}\ S$, where Q is a pre-assertion of S, then $[\ Q \Rightarrow wlp.S.P\ ]$ holds.
- globally correct, i.e., it is maintained by all other components:
  - for each atomic statement $\{Q\}\ S$ in any other component, where Q is a pre-assertion of S, $[\ P \wedge Q \Rightarrow wlp.S.P\ ]$ holds.

Invariants are assertions that hold at every control point of a program. So an invariant is correct if it is both implied by the precondition, and maintained by each statement in any component. In turn, assertions could also be expressed in terms of invariants, possibly using some auxiliary variables. Hence, without loss of generality, we can assume the absence of either assertions or invariants, whenever appropriate.

2.3 Method from Feijen/Van Gasteren

The programming method from [FvG99] addresses the construction of concurrent programs hand-in-hand with a suitable annotation and correctness proof. Assertions play an important role, and in particular a *queried assertion* is an assertion whose correctness has not yet been proved. Usually a queried assertion Q is denoted as $\{?\ Q\}$.

Program construction starts with a specification in terms of a preliminary program and some queried assertions, like post-conditions. Program development consists of turning each queried assertion, one-by-one, into a correct assertion. The proof obligations for local correctness lead to a style in which programs are constructed from the required assertions towards the initial control point. When all assertions (which include those from the specification) are correct, the developed program is correct with respect to the specification.

If a queried assertion's correctness (in the current annotated program) cannot yet be proved, there are mainly two solutions (which can also be combined):

- introduce additional queried assertions in the current annotation;
- modify the program.

An important issue is whether these two steps can endanger the correctness of the other assertions. Introducing additional assertions cannot endanger the correctness of the other assertions, and typically the weakest possible strengthening of the annotation that serves the goal is calculated. However, modifying the program may transform all assertions into queried assertions again. The typical modification is inserting a statement for local correctness.

During the derivations we often omit the details of the proofs, in order to focus on program construction. Formal tool-support with an emphasis on the incremental nature of derivations has been developed in [MW05, Moo06, RWM07].

2.4   UNITY's Progress Logic

To prove progress properties of a program, we use the progress logic from [CM88] as proposed in [DG06]. The progress logic is based on the **un** relation, which captures the temporal notion of 'unless', which is also known as 'weak until'. The expression P **un** Q denotes that P continues to hold until Q becomes *true*, but it does not guarantee that Q will become *true*. For predicates P and Q, condition P **un** Q holds in an annotated program if

$$[\ P \wedge \neg Q \wedge U \ \Rightarrow \ wp.S.(P \vee Q)\ ]$$

holds for all atomic statements $\{U\}\ S$, where U is a pre-assertion of S. *Stability* of any predicate P is a special instance of the **un** relation, viz., P **un** *false*.

We use the term progress property to denote a property that can be expressed using the main operator in this progress logic, viz., the leads-to operator $\rightsquigarrow$, which is related to temporal logic using $(P \rightsquigarrow Q) \equiv \Box(P \Rightarrow \Diamond Q)$. Expression $P \rightsquigarrow Q$ for a program denotes that whenever an execution of the program reaches a state that satisfies P, each continuation of the execution will eventually reach a state that satisfies Q. A weakly fair scheduling regime is assumed such that in the interleaving, no component is neglected forever.

The progress properties include individual progress and termination. A program terminates if each component terminates. Termination of a component X can be expressed as the property *true* $\rightsquigarrow$ $pc_X = \tau_X$, for label τ_X the final control point of the component with identifier X. Possibly using extra auxiliary variables (e.g., to mimic the program counters), every property that refers to the program counters can be replaced by an equivalent property that does not refer to the program counters.

We use the following definition of the $\rightsquigarrow$ relation. For any predicates P and Q, condition $P \rightsquigarrow Q$ holds in an annotated program if it can be derived by a finite number of applications of the following rules:

- *Immediate-progress rule:* $P \rightsquigarrow Q$ holds in an annotated program whenever P **un** Q holds in the program and there exists an atomic statement S at a control point i of a component X such that $[\ P \wedge \neg Q \ \Rightarrow \ pc_X = i \wedge g.S \wedge wp.S.Q\ ]$ holds.
- *Transitivity rule:* $P \rightsquigarrow Q$ holds if there exists a predicate R such that $P \rightsquigarrow R$ and $R \rightsquigarrow Q$.
- *Disjunction rule:* $P \rightsquigarrow Q$ holds if there exist predicates $R.i$ such that $[\ P \equiv (\exists i :: R.i)\ ]$ and $(\forall i :: R.i \rightsquigarrow Q)$.

Usually we leave the program that we refer to implicit, but otherwise we use the notation $A \models P$ to denote that property P holds in concurrent program

A. An important result for maintaining progress under program modifications is the *Immediate Progress Preservation* theorem from [DM06a]. Let P and Q be predicates, and A be a program. Suppose that $A \models P \rightsquigarrow Q$ holds, and let K denote the set of instances of immediate progress that are used in a proof of it. Then $B \models P \rightsquigarrow Q$ holds for any program B in which each property from K is valid, i.e., $(\forall R: R \in K: B \models R)$.

3 Calculational Leads-to Rules

In this section we present our collection of calculational rules for the leads-to relation, independent of a particular program, and sometimes in relation to the notion of stability as defined in Section 2. In what follows, the bound variable x ranges over an arbitrary domain. Variables like P, Q and R denote predicates, and we typically omit the outer universal quantification over these predicates. The usual assumption is that there is at least one statement in any program, which makes the leads-to relation a pre-order (i.e., reflexive and transitive).

3.1 Basic Monotonicity Properties

In [DM06a], it has been shown that the leads-to relation is

– monotonic in its second argument:

$$[\, Q \Rightarrow R \,] \quad \Rightarrow \quad ((P \rightsquigarrow Q) \Rightarrow (P \rightsquigarrow R))$$

– anti-monotonic in its first argument:

$$[\, P \Rightarrow Q \,] \quad \Rightarrow \quad ((Q \rightsquigarrow R) \Rightarrow (P \rightsquigarrow R))$$

3.2 Distribution Properties

The leads-to relation distributes over

– disjunction as follows:

$$((\exists x:: \; P.x) \; \rightsquigarrow \; Q) \quad \equiv \quad (\forall x:: \; P.x \rightsquigarrow Q)$$

– conjunction as follows, if for all x, predicate $Q.x$ is *stable*:

$$(P \; \rightsquigarrow \; (\forall x:: \; Q.x)) \quad \equiv \quad (\forall x:: \; P \rightsquigarrow Q.x)$$

In addition there is the following rule:

– trading, if predicate Q is *stable*:

$$(P \; \rightsquigarrow \; Q \Rightarrow R) \quad \equiv \quad (P \wedge Q \; \rightsquigarrow \; R)$$

A proof of these three properties can be found in Appendix A.

3.3 More Monotonicity Properties

With respect to the leads-to relation,

- function $(\vee R)$ is monotonic:

$$(P \rightsquigarrow Q) \;\Rightarrow\; (P \vee R \;\rightsquigarrow\; Q \vee R)$$

- function $(\wedge R)$ is monotonic, if predicate R is *stable*:

$$(P \rightsquigarrow Q) \;\Rightarrow\; (P \wedge R \;\rightsquigarrow\; Q \wedge R)$$

We use $(\vee R)$ to denote a function that maps any predicate P to $(P \vee R)$. In [Mis94] the second property is called stable conjunction, and it is an instance of the progress-safety-progress theorem [CM88]. A proof of the first property can be found in Appendix A.

3.4 Closure Properties

Instead of these monotonicity properties, in calculations it is more effective to apply the following closure properties. Namely, by applying the equivalences from right to left the proof obligation just becomes simpler.

With respect to the leads-to relation,

- function $(\vee R)$ is an increasing closure:

$$(P \;\rightsquigarrow\; Q \vee R) \;\equiv\; (P \vee R \;\rightsquigarrow\; Q \vee R)$$

- function $(\wedge R)$ is a decreasing closure, if predicate R is *stable*:

$$(P \wedge R \;\rightsquigarrow\; Q) \;\equiv\; (P \wedge R \;\rightsquigarrow\; Q \wedge R)$$

A proof of these properties can be found in Appendix A.

3.5 Proof Techniques

The following is a series of rules that look like familiar proof techniques:

- proof by induction, for m a fresh variable and $\prec$ a well-founded order on the type of M, which is an expression over program variables:

$$(P \rightsquigarrow Q) \;\equiv\; (\forall m:: P \wedge M = m \;\rightsquigarrow\; (P \wedge M \prec m) \vee Q)$$

- proof by contradiction:

$$(P \rightsquigarrow Q) \;\equiv\; (P \wedge \neg Q \;\rightsquigarrow\; Q)$$

- proof by indirect inequality (two variants):

$$(P \rightsquigarrow Q) \;\equiv\; (\forall R:: (Q \rightsquigarrow R) \Rightarrow (P \rightsquigarrow R))$$

$$(Q \rightsquigarrow R) \;\equiv\; (\forall P:: (P \rightsquigarrow Q) \Rightarrow (P \rightsquigarrow R))$$

The first property is from [CM88], but extended with the equivalence observation from [DM06a]. The second property has been explicitly formulated in [DM06a], although it also appears somewhere in the middle of exercise 3.10 of [CM88]. The third property is less familiar, but it follows immediately from $\leadsto$ being a pre-order.

Using proof by indirect inequality, monotonicity of function $(\vee Q)$ is equivalent to the cancellation theorem from [CM88, DG06]:

$$(\forall D, Q, R :: (D \leadsto R) \;\Rightarrow\; (\forall P :: (P \leadsto D \vee Q) \;\Rightarrow\; (P \leadsto R \vee Q)))$$

4 Composition Rules

In this section we present the two elementary composition rules. Their proofs in terms of the UNITY-based framework from [DG06] can be found in Appendix B. We call two concurrent programs variable disjoint if the sets of variables that can be accessed by the programs are disjoint.

4.1 Parallel Composition

Given two concurrent programs A and B that use disjoint sets of component identifiers and disjoint sets of variables. The parallel composition $A \| B$ of the programs A and B yields a concurrent program with the union of the sets of components, and the conjunction of the preconditions.

Given a progress property $P \leadsto Q$ that holds in program A, i.e., $A \models P \leadsto Q$, and that does not refer to variables of program B. Then the property $P \leadsto Q$ also holds in the parallel composition of A and B, i.e., $A \| B \models P \leadsto Q$.

4.2 Weak Sequential Composition

Given two concurrent programs A and B that use identical sets of component identifiers and disjoint sets of variables, such that for each component identifier the sets of control-point labels are disjoint apart from the final control points in program A being identical to the initial control points in program B. The weak sequential composition $A \circ B$ of the programs A and B yields a concurrent program with components consisting of the sequential composition of the pairs of components with the same identifier, and the conjunction of the preconditions.

Given a progress property $P \leadsto Q$ that holds in program A, i.e., $A \models P \leadsto Q$, and that does not refer to variables of program B. Then the property $P \leadsto Q$ also holds in the weak sequential composition of A and B, i.e., $A \circ B \models P \leadsto Q$. Moreover, if program B is guaranteed to terminate (as defined in Section 2), then the property $P \leadsto Q$ also holds in the weak sequential composition of B and A, i.e., $B \circ A \models P \leadsto Q$.

5 Initialisation Protocol

In this section we introduce the specification of initialisation protocols, and we briefly discuss an implementation for two components.

5.1 Specification

The specification of an initialisation protocol for any number of components $C.x$, for any series of values x, is as follows:

$$
\boxed{
\begin{array}{l}
C.x: \quad \{Q.x\} \\
\qquad \cdots \\
\qquad \{?\ (\forall i::\ Q.i)\}
\end{array}
}
$$

So, if in every component $C.x$ the predicate $Q.x$ is established as a correct pre-assertion of the protocol (yet to be developed at the "..."), then the protocol has to establish as a post-assertion in every component $C.x$ that $Q.i$ holds for all i. Each predicate $Q.x$ is assumed (or, relied on) to be stable and does not contain any of the variables that will be used in the protocol. This specification resembles the rules of import and export that are sometimes used for asynchronous communication; see e.g. [Hoo06, Moo07].

In the original setting of an "initialisation protocol", predicate $Q.x$ is typically "the initialisation phase of component $C.x$ has terminated". In addition there is the restriction that the precondition must be a conjunction, such that the set of variables in each conjunct belongs to at most one component. Establishing such a precondition is a local affair that should be isolated from the main distributed protocol.

Initialisation protocols are in fact very general schemes. For any commutative and associative operator $\oplus$, they can usually be extended to compute in each component the value of $(\bigoplus i:: f.i)$, where $f.i$ is a constant value that initially resides in component $C.i$. In particular, for the addition operator a summation protocol is obtained, and for the minimum or maximum operator a deterministic consensus protocol is obtained from which in turn a deterministic leader election protocol can easily be built.

5.2 Two-Component Implementation

For derivations of a protocol for the two components $C.X$ and $C.Y$ we refer to [FvG99, DM06a], yielding for example the following solution:

$$
\boxed{
\begin{array}{l}
C.X: \quad c := \mathit{false} \\
\quad ;\ b := \mathit{true} \\
\quad ;\ \textbf{if}\ c \rightarrow \textbf{skip fi} \\
\quad ;\ b := \mathit{true}
\end{array}
}
\boxed{
\begin{array}{l}
C.Y: \quad b := \mathit{false} \\
\quad ;\ c := \mathit{true} \\
\quad ;\ \textbf{if}\ b \rightarrow \textbf{skip fi} \\
\quad ;\ c := \mathit{true}
\end{array}
}
$$

with the two fresh boolean synchronisation variables b and c. Freshness denotes that these variables are not used by the rest of the system. Notice that there is no assumption on the initial value of the booleans b and c. The annotation has been omitted, but it would include assertions like $b \Rightarrow Q.X$. The proved properties include individual progress, deadlock freedom and termination.

Without the restriction on the precondition, there are many more solutions. For example, based on two semaphores (both initialised at 0), or based on two unidirectional communication channels (both initialised with an empty buffer).

In Sections 6 and 7, we will discuss network protocols that use any such a two-component protocol as a building block. To this end we will abbreviate the protocol for each component as **sync** and assume that the synchronisation variables that are used for synchronisation, in this case b and c, do not occur anywhere else in the program.

6   Initialisation Protocol on Full Networks

In this section we discuss an implementation for a full network of nodes, in which each pair of nodes can communicate. A motivation for the composition rules in Section 4 is the desire to easily derive some progress properties of this implementation based on the properties of the implementation in Section 5.

6.1   Partial Correctness

Our starting point is the specification from Section 5, with a component for each node in the network. Considering the required post-assertion $(\forall j:: Q.j)$, it might be tempting to start determining for each component a sequential order to establish the conjuncts of the universal quantification, or inserting some repetition. Instead we propose to postpone this design decision by establishing them in parallel (see also [MW03, Moo06]), which is the key to success in this derivation. Notice that parallel composition can mimic sequential composition using some auxiliary variables, if this finally turns out to be necessary.

To model parallelism within the nodes, we introduce in each node x an additional component $S.x.y$ for each other node y. Then the requirement on the precondition of the program is that it is the conjunction of conditions that refer to the variables used in the components of at most one node.

To establish the required assertion, we synchronise the components in each node using a fresh series of variables b. That is, in each component $C.x$ we introduce a guarded skip with guard $(\forall j: j \neq x: b.x.j)$, which is valid if we require a pre-assertion $Q.x$ and an invariant $(\forall i, j:: b.i.j \Rightarrow Q.j)$. For correctness of this invariant, we require for any assignment $b.x.y := true$ the pre-assertion $Q.y$ as follows:

Pre: $(\forall i:: (\forall j:: \neg b.i.j))$

$C.x$: $\{Q.x\}$	$S.x.y$:
$\cdots$	
$; \{? \, Q.x\}$	
$\quad$ **if** $(\forall j: j \neq x: b.x.j) \to$ **skip fi**	$\cdots$
$\{(\forall j:: Q.j)\}$	$; \{? \, Q.y\}$
	$\quad b.x.y := true$

Inv: $(\forall i, j:: b.i.j \Rightarrow Q.j)$

Notice that the precondition is the conjunction of conditions that refer to the variables used in the components of at most one node. The b variables might be eliminated by implementing the guarded skip using a join construct that blocks until the execution of the corresponding S-components has terminated.

The new queried assertion $Q.y$ in component $S.x.y$ should be imported from a component in node y, for example from component $S.y.x$. This pair of components can be synchronised using a fresh copy of the initialisation protocol for two components (or any of the other solutions described in Section 5). The corresponding required pre-assertions in $S.x.y$ and $S.y.x$ are $Q.x$ and $Q.y$ respectively. Recall that the only requirement for partial correctness of this basic initialisation protocol is that the conditions $Q.x$ and $Q.y$ are stable.

Pre: $(\forall i:: (\forall j:: \neg b.i.j))$

$C.x$: $\{Q.x\}$	$S.x.y$: ...
$\quad$ ...	$\quad$; $\{?\ Q.x\}$
$\quad$; $\{?\ Q.x\}$	$\quad$ **sync** with $S.y.x$
$\quad$ **if** $(\forall j: j \neq x: b.x.j) \rightarrow$ **skip fi**	$\quad$; $\{Q.y\}$
$\quad$ $\{(\forall j:: Q.j)\}$	$\quad$ $b.x.y := true$

Inv: $(\forall i, j:: b.i.j \Rightarrow Q.j)$

What remains to establish in component $S.x.y$ is a pre-assertion $Q.x$. This can be established by synchronisation with component $C.x$ using a fresh series of variables a. That is, in each component $S.x.y$ we introduce a guarded skip with guard $a.x$, which is valid if we require an invariant $(\forall i:: a.i \Rightarrow Q.i)$. For correctness of this invariant, we need for any assignment $a.x := true$ the pre-assertion $Q.x$ as follows:

Pre: $(\forall i:: \neg a.i \ \wedge \ (\forall j:: \neg b.i.j))$

$C.x$: $\{Q.x\}$	$S.x.y$: **if** $a.x \rightarrow$ **skip fi**
$\quad$ $a.x := true$	$\quad$; $\{Q.x\}$
$\quad$; $\{Q.x\}$	$\quad$ **sync** with $S.y.x$
$\quad$ **if** $(\forall j: j \neq x: b.x.j) \rightarrow$ **skip fi**	$\quad$; $\{Q.y\}$
$\quad$ $\{(\forall j:: Q.j)\}$	$\quad$ $b.x.y := true$

Inv: $(\forall i, j:: b.i.j \Rightarrow Q.j)$
Inv: $(\forall i:: a.i \Rightarrow Q.i)$

Notice that the precondition is the conjunction of conditions that refer to the variables used in the components of at most one node. The a variables might be eliminated by implementing the assignment to variable a using a fork construct that explicitly starts the execution of the corresponding S-components.

6.2   Progress

The design so far has focussed on partial correctness; what remains to discuss is termination. This can easily be proved using the composition rules, since the protocol is the weak sequential composition of the following sub-protocols:

- simple protocol on the a variables;
- parallel composition of some independent copies of the initialisation protocol for two components (and some empty programs for the C-components);
- simple protocol on the b variables.

Since all sub-protocols are variable disjoint, and guaranteed to terminate in isolation, termination of the whole protocol is guaranteed as well. Notice that although the sub-protocols do not share any variables, the components in the final protocol share variables as they participate in several sub-protocols.

7   Initialisation Protocol on Acyclic Networks

In this section we discuss an implementation for an acyclic connected network of nodes, or phrased differently, an (undirected) tree-shape network. It shows the applicability of the rules from Section 4 in a more complicated setting. The irreflexive symmetric relation $\sim$ denotes the connected pairs of nodes.

7.1   Partial Correctness

Our starting point is the specification from Section 5, with a component for each node in the network. Splitting the required post-assertion $(\forall j:: Q.j)$ according to single nodes is not very effective in a network where some pairs of nodes are not directly connected. We introduce an auxiliary set $F.x.y$ for each two connected nodes x and y to denote the fragment of the nodes that can be reached from node y without using the edge (x, y). Thus in any network, the set of all reachable nodes from node x is:

$$\{x\} \cup (\textstyle\bigcup j: j \sim x: F.x.j)$$

In addition we have the following important recurrence relation:

$$F.y.x \;=\; \{x\} \cup (\textstyle\bigcup j: j \sim x \wedge j \neq y: F.x.j)$$

This is just a property for arbitrary networks, but for acyclic networks it is even a recursive definition. So although we have not yet used acyclicity of the network, the interest in these properties is inspired by the network being acyclic.

To model parallelism within the nodes, we introduce in each node x an additional component $I.x.y$ for each connected node $C.y$. To establish the required assertion, we synchronise them using a fresh series of variables b as follows:

Pre: $(\forall i:: (\forall j:: \neg b.i.j))$

```
C.x:  {Q.x}                          I.x.y:  ...
        ...                                  ; {? (∀k: k ∈ F.x.y:  Q.k)}
      ; {? Q.x}                                b.x.y := true
      if (∀j: j ∼ x: b.x.j) → skip fi
      {(∀j:: Q.j)}
```

Inv: $(\forall i, j:: b.i.j \;\Rightarrow\; (\forall k: k \in F.i.j: Q.k))$

Notice that the precondition is the conjunction of conditions that refer to the variables used in the components of at most one node.

The new queried assertion $(\forall k: k \in F.x.y: Q.k)$ in component $I.x.y$ should be imported from a component in node y. This time we propose to introduce an additional component $E.y.x$ within node y, which in general is less restrictive than re-using an existing component. These components can be synchronised using fresh copies of the initialisation protocol for two components (or any of the other solutions described in Section 5). Recall that the only requirement for partial correctness is that the condition $(\forall k: k \in F.x.y: Q.k)$ is stable.

Pre: $(\forall i:: (\forall j:: \neg b.i.j))$

$$
\begin{array}{|l|}
\hline
C.x: \quad \{Q.x\} \\
\qquad \cdots \\
\quad ; \{?\ Q.x\} \\
\quad \textbf{if } (\forall j:\ j \sim X:\ b.x.j) \rightarrow \textbf{skip fi} \\
\quad \{(\forall j::\ Q.j)\} \\
\hline
\end{array}
\qquad
\begin{array}{|l|}
\hline
I.x.y: \quad \textbf{sync with } E.y.x \\
\quad ; \{(\forall k: k \in F.x.y:\ Q.k)\} \\
\qquad b.x.y := true \\
\hline
\end{array}
$$

$$
\begin{array}{|l|}
\hline
E.x.y: \quad \cdots \\
\quad ; \{?\ (\forall k: k \in F.y.x:\ Q.k)\} \\
\quad \textbf{sync with } I.y.x \\
\hline
\end{array}
$$

Inv: $(\forall i, j::\ b.i.j \;\Rightarrow\; (\forall k: k \in F.i.j:\ Q.k))$

What remains to establish in component $E.x.y$ is a pre-assertion $(\forall k: k \in F.y.x:\ Q.k)$. This can be established by synchronisation with component $C.x$ using a fresh series of variables a, and re-using the variables b as follows:

Pre: $(\forall i::\ \neg a.i \;\wedge\; (\forall j::\ \neg b.i.j))$

$$
\begin{array}{|l|}
\hline
C.x: \quad \{Q.x\} \\
\qquad a.x := true \\
\quad ; \{Q.x\} \\
\quad \textbf{if } (\forall j:\ j \sim X:\ b.x.j) \rightarrow \textbf{skip fi} \\
\quad \{(\forall j::\ Q.j)\} \\
\hline
\end{array}
\qquad
\begin{array}{|l|}
\hline
I.x.y: \quad \textbf{sync with } E.y.x \\
\quad ; \{(\forall k: k \in F.x.y:\ Q.k)\} \\
\qquad b.x.y := true \\
\hline
\end{array}
$$

$$
\begin{array}{|l|}
\hline
E.x.y: \quad \textbf{if } a.x \wedge (\forall j:\ j \sim x \wedge j \neq y:\ b.x.j) \rightarrow \textbf{skip fi} \\
\quad ; \{(\forall k: k \in F.y.x:\ Q.k)\} \\
\quad \textbf{sync with } I.y.x \\
\hline
\end{array}
$$

Inv: $(\forall i, j::\ b.i.j \;\Rightarrow\; (\forall k: k \in F.i.j:\ Q.k))$
Inv: $(\forall i::\ a.i \;\Rightarrow\; Q.i)$

Notice that the precondition is the conjunction of conditions that refer to the variables used in the components of at most one node. The a variables might be eliminated by implementing each assignment $a.i := true$ using a fork construct that explicitly starts the execution of the E-components. Furthermore, in particular component $E.x.y$ is implementable, as the guard of the guarded skip refers to variables of node x only, and all its conjuncts are stable.

The leader election protocol for trees from the IEEE 1394 standard is similar to this initialisation protocol, although they elect the leader non-deterministically. This gives some additional troubles; the idea is that the last node that starts execution of its E-components becomes the root of the tree, but unfortunately it is not guaranteed that there is at most one such node. Unless probabilistic techniques are used, the usual models assume that this "root contention" situation is somehow solved in one step. In turn, the protocol from IEEE 1394 turns out to be essentially the same as an informally described protocol in [Lyn96], and in [DGRV00] it was presented as a challenge for the formal methods community.

7.2 Progress

The design so far has focussed on partial correctness; what remains to discuss is termination, for which we will need the acyclicity property, since cycles inevitably lead to deadlocks in this protocol.

Regarding each guarded skip we will exploit stability of the conjuncts of the guard (also within the universal quantification), which guarantees that it is equivalent to any sequential series of guarded skips with the required conjuncts as individual guards. In forward direction this relies on the guard conjunction lemma of [FvG99], and in backward direction it just corresponds to reducing the possible execution traces and the fact that the state in between cannot be detected by the other components.

To prove termination we will show how the protocol (without annotation) can be composed from simpler terminating programs using the composition rules. It is clear that the simple protocol on the a variables is terminating, and it can easily be isolated using weak sequential composition. In the remainder of the argument we do not consider this part of the protocol.

Notice that all remaining parts refer to connected pairs of nodes. We will use an induction principle based on a recursive definition of acyclic networks, namely any single node is an acyclic network, and recursively, connecting a single node to a node in an acyclic network results in a larger acyclic network.

For any single node, the concurrent program is empty since there are no edges. Then consider a terminating program for a tree that is extended with a single node Y connecting to node X. In this case the program must be extended with the parts that refer to the pairs (X, Y) and (Y, X).

The C-components do not impose restrictions on the order of these parts, while the I-components require that any $b.i.j$ occurs after synchronisation with $E.j.i$. The E-components require that any $b.i.j$ occurs before synchronisation with $I.k.i$ for any $j \neq k$. For the last requirement, the case $i = Y$ follows immediately from y being a new leaf. The other interesting case is $i = X$, for which we must consider the two special cases $j = Y$ and $k = Y$. Hence the extended program consists of the weak sequential composition of the following sub-protocols:

– synchronisation between $E.Y.X$ and $I.X.Y$;
– full simple protocol on the $b.X.Y$ variable;

- terminating protocol for the smaller tree;
- synchronisation between $E.X.Y$ and $I.Y.X$;
- full simple protocol on the $b.Y.X$ variable.

Since all sub-protocols are variable disjoint, and guaranteed to terminate in isolation, termination of the whole protocol is guaranteed as well.

8 Conclusions and Further Work

To facilitate the manipulation of leads-to formulae, we have investigated a set of calculational rules. The resulting rules look very similar to familiar algebraic properties, which makes them easier to remember and to apply. It is further work to investigate rules that address the unless relation, and combinations of the leads-to relation and the unless relation.

To construct progress arguments for programs that can be decomposed into programs with simpler progress arguments, we have developed some composition rules. Apart from parallel composition, we have considered a kind of sequential composition. In contrast to the usual strong sequential composition, we have imported the notion of weak sequential composition, which is more practical. It is further work to extend the applicability of the rules.

We have illustrated some of our techniques on two network initialisation protocols. By considering the initialisation protocol for two components as a building block, the derived protocols have a clean structure based on two levels of abstraction. The external synchronisation between the (physically distributed) nodes uses the binary initialisation protocol, while the internal synchronisation is performed using shared variables.

Although reasoning about concurrency is generally considered to be difficult, the derivations and descriptions of these protocols benefit from a massive use of concurrency. For a network consisting of N nodes and E edges, respectively $N + 2 \cdot E$ and $N + 4 \cdot E$ small components are used. Although the concurrency between the nodes is prescribed by the network, the concurrency within the nodes could be eliminated. Such an implementation would introduce a repetition with additional variables to record the state, but it would destroy the nice structure of the solution. Nodes that consist of a central component and some components for each incident edge, occur at least in the IEEE 1394 standard (nodes with a port for each bidirectional connection) and the recently approved IEEE 1394.1 standard (buses with a portal for each bidirectional bridge).

These protocols consist of arbitrary numbers of components, in contrast to the examples in [DG06, DM06a, DM06b] that consist of only two components. In the present work progress was a concern that was mainly discussed after the whole derivation for safety, like in [FvG99]. It is further work to obtain a closer integration with the derivation, like in [DM06a, DM06b]. For example, in the challenging context of non-blocking algorithms, whose progress properties can also be expressed using the leads-to relation [Don06]. Also the tool-support from [MW05, Moo06, RWM07] needs to be extended to cover the progress logic.

Acknowledgements. The author thanks the other members of the Eindhoven Tuesday Afternoon Club for their contributions to the safety-based derivations of these network initialisation protocols, and for the informal discussions about their problematic progress argument. The author also likes to thank Judi Romijn for suggesting the relation with the leader election protocol from IEEE 1394, and the anonymous referees for their suggestions for improvement.

References

[CK97]   Collette, P., Knapp, E.: A foundation for modular reasoning about safety and progress properties of state-based concurrent programs. Theoretical Computer Science 183, 253–279 (1997)

[CM88]   Chandy, K.M., Misra, J.: Parallel Program Design: A Foundation. Addison-Wesley Longman Publishing Co. Inc., Reading (1988)

[DG06]   Dongol, B., Goldson, D.: Extending the theory of Owicki and Gries with a logic of progress. Logical Methods in Computer Science 2(1), 1–25 (2006)

[DGRV00]   Devillers, M.C.A., Griffioen, W.O.D., Romijn, J.M.T., Vaandrager, F.W.: Verification of a leader election protocol – formal methods applied to IEEE 1394. Formal methods in system design 16(3), 307–320 (2000)

[Dij76]   Dijkstra, E.W.: A Discipline of Programming. Prentice-Hall, Englewood Cliffs (1976)

[DM06a]   Dongol, B., Mooij, A.J.: Progress in deriving concurrent programs: emphasizing the role of stable guards. In: Uustalu, T. (ed.) MPC 2006. LNCS, vol. 4014, pp. 140–161. Springer, Heidelberg (2006)

[DM06b]   Dongol, B., Mooij, A.J.: Streamlining progress-based derivations of concurrent programs. Technical Report SSE-2006-06, School of Information Technology and Electrical Engineering, The University of Queensland, 2006. Accepted for publication in the Formal Aspects of Computing journal (2006)

[Don06]   Dongol, B.: Formalising progress properties of non-blocking programs. In: Liu, Z., He, J. (eds.) ICFEM 2006. LNCS, vol. 4260, pp. 284–303. Springer, Heidelberg (2006)

[FGR04]   Fokkink, W., Groote, J.F., Reniers, M.A.: Process algebra needs proof methodology. In: Aceto, L. (ed.) The concurrency column. Bulletin of the EATCS, vol. 82, pp. 108–125 (February 2004)

[FvG99]   Feijen, W.H.J., van Gasteren, A.J.M.: On a method of multiprogramming. Springer, Heidelberg (1999)

[Hoo06]   Hoogerwoord, R.R.: A formal derivation of a sliding window protocol. Computer Science Report 06-31, Technische Universiteit Eindhoven (2006)

[IEE96]   Institute of Electrical and Electronics Engineers. IEEE standard for a high performance serial bus, IEEE Std 1394-1995 (August 1996)

[IEE05]   Institute of Electrical and Electronics Engineers. IEEE standard for high performance serial bus bridges, IEEE Std 1394.1-2004 (July 2005)

[ITU00]   International Telecommunication Union - Telecom Standardization. Message Sequence Chart, ITU-T Recommendation Z.120 (2000)

[Jon81]   Jones, C.B.: Development methods for computer programs including a notion of interference, Oxford University Computing Laboratory. Dphil. thesis (1981)

[Kna92]   Knapp, E.: Derivation of concurrent programs: two examples. Science of Computer Programming 19(1), 1–23 (1992)

[Lyn96]   Lynch, N.: Distributed Algorithms. Morgan Kaufmann, San Francisco (1996)

[Mis91]   Misra, J.: Phase synchronization. Information Processing Letters 38(2), 101–105 (1991)

[Mis94]   Misra, J.: A logic for concurrent programming. Technical report, The University of Texas at Austin (April 1994)

[Moo06]   Mooij, A.J.: Constructive formal methods and protocol standardization, Technische Universiteit Eindhoven, PhD thesis (October 2006)

[Moo07]   Mooij, A.J.: Constructing and reasoning about security protocols using invariants. In: REFINE 2007. ENTCS (to appear, 2007)

[MP91]   Manna, Z., Pnueli, A.: Completing the temporal picture. Theoretical Computer Science 83(1), 91–130 (1991)

[MW03]   Mooij, A.J., Wesselink, J.W.: A formal analysis of a dynamic distributed spanning tree algorithm. Computer Science Report 03-16, Technische Universiteit Eindhoven (2003)

[MW05]   Mooij, A.J., Wesselink, J.W.: Incremental verification of Owicki/Gries proof outlines using PVS. In: Lau, K.-K., Banach, R. (eds.) ICFEM 2005. LNCS, vol. 3785, pp. 390–404. Springer, Heidelberg (2005)

[OG76]   Owicki, S., Gries, D.: An axiomatic proof technique for parallel programs I. Acta Informatica 6, 319–340 (1976)

[PVAS05] Prasetya, I.S.W.B., Vos, T.E.J., Azurat, A., Swierstra, S.D.: A UNITY-based framework towards component based systems. In: Higashino, T. (ed.) OPODIS 2004. LNCS, vol. 3544, pp. 52–66. Springer, Heidelberg (2005)

[RWM07]   Romijn, J., Wesselink, W., Mooij, A.: Assertion-based proof checking of Chang-Roberts leader election in PVS. In: Namjoshi, K.S., Yoneda, T., Higashino, T., Okamura,Y. (eds.) ATVA 2007. LNCS, vol. 4762. Springer, Heidelberg (2007)

[Sto91]   Stolen, K.: A method for the development of totally correct shared-state parallel programs. In: Groote, J.F., Baeten, J.C.M. (eds.) CONCUR 1991. LNCS, vol. 527, pp. 510–525. Springer, Heidelberg (1991)

[XdRH97] Xu, Q., de Roever, W.-P., He, J.: The rely-guarantee method for verifying shared variable concurrent programs. Formal Aspects of Computing, 149–174 (1997)

A   Proofs of Our Calculational Rules

Lemma 1 (Distribution over existential quantification). *For any predicates $P.x$, for any x, and Q, $\rightsquigarrow$ distributes over disjunction as follows:*

$$((\exists x:: P.x) \rightsquigarrow Q) \quad \equiv \quad (\forall x:: P.x \rightsquigarrow Q)$$

Proof. Implication $\Leftarrow$ follows from the disjunction rule in the definition of $\rightsquigarrow$. For implication $\Rightarrow$ we calculate:

$$((\exists x:: P.x) \rightsquigarrow Q) \quad \Rightarrow \quad (\forall x:: P.x \rightsquigarrow Q)$$
$$\equiv \quad \{\text{logic: } (\ldots \Rightarrow) \text{ distributes over } \forall\}$$

$$(\forall x :: \ ((\exists x :: \ P.x) \ \leadsto \ Q) \ \Rightarrow \ (P.x \ \leadsto \ Q)\ )$$
$\Leftarrow \quad \{\text{anti-monotonicity of } \leadsto\}$
$$(\forall x :: \ [\ P.x \ \Rightarrow \ (\exists x :: \ P.x)\ ]\ )$$
$\equiv \quad \{\text{logic: } (\ldots \Rightarrow) \text{ distributes over non-empty } \exists\}$
$\quad true$

$\hfill \square$

Lemma 2 (Distribution over *stable* universal quantification). *For any predicate P and stable predicates $Q.x$, for any x, $\leadsto$ distributes over conjunction as follows:*

$$(P \ \leadsto \ (\forall x :: \ Q.x)) \quad \equiv \quad (\forall x :: \ P \ \leadsto \ Q.x)$$

Proof. Implication $\Leftarrow$ follows from the completion theorem [CM88], using stability of $Q.i$ for each i. For implication $\Rightarrow$ we calculate:

$$(P \ \leadsto \ (\forall x :: \ Q.x)) \quad \Rightarrow \quad (\forall x :: \ P \ \leadsto \ Q.x)$$
$\equiv \quad \{\text{logic: } (\ldots \Rightarrow) \text{ distributes over } \forall\}$
$$(\forall x :: \ (P \ \leadsto \ (\forall x :: \ Q.x)) \ \Rightarrow \ (P \ \leadsto \ Q.x)\ )$$
$\Leftarrow \quad \{\text{monotonicity of } \leadsto\}$
$$(\forall x :: \ [\ (\forall x :: \ Q.x) \ \Rightarrow \ Q.x\ ]\ )$$
$\equiv \quad \{\text{logic: } (\Rightarrow \ldots) \text{ distributes over non-empty } \forall\}$
$\quad true$

$\hfill \square$

Lemma 3 (Monotonicity under disjuncts). *For any predicates P, Q and R, $\leadsto$ has the following monotonicity property:*

$$(P \leadsto Q) \quad \Rightarrow \quad (P \vee R \ \leadsto \ Q \vee R)$$

Proof. We calculate:

$\quad P \vee R \ \leadsto \ Q \vee R$
$\equiv \quad \{\text{distribution of } \leadsto \text{ over disjunction in its first argument}\}$
$\quad (P \ \leadsto \ Q \vee R) \ \wedge \ (R \ \leadsto \ Q \vee R)$
$\Leftarrow \quad \{\text{monotonicity of } \leadsto \text{ (twice), reflexivity}\}$
$\quad P \leadsto Q$

$\hfill \square$

Lemma 4 (Closure under disjuncts). *For any predicates P, Q and R, $\leadsto$ has the following closure property:*

$$(P \ \leadsto \ Q \vee R) \quad \equiv \quad (P \vee R \ \leadsto \ Q \vee R)$$

Proof. Implication $\Leftarrow$ follows from anti-monotonicity of $\leadsto$. For implication $\Rightarrow$ we calculate:

$\quad P \vee R \ \leadsto \ Q \vee R$
$\equiv \quad \{\text{idempotence of } (\vee R)\}$
$\quad P \vee R \ \leadsto \ (Q \vee R) \vee R$
$\Leftarrow \quad \{\text{monotonicity of } (\vee R)\}$
$\quad P \ \leadsto \ Q \vee R$

$\hfill \square$

Lemma 5 (Closure under stable conjuncts). *For any predicates P and Q, and* stable *predicate R, $\leadsto$ has the following closure property:*

$$(P \wedge R \ \leadsto \ Q) \quad \equiv \quad (P \wedge R \ \leadsto \ Q \wedge R)$$

Proof. Implication $\Leftarrow$ follows from monotonicity of $\leadsto$. For implication $\Rightarrow$ we calculate:

$$
\begin{aligned}
& P \wedge R \ \leadsto \ Q \wedge R \\
\equiv \quad & \{\text{idempotence of } (\wedge R)\} \\
& (P \wedge R) \wedge R \ \leadsto \ Q \wedge R \\
\Leftarrow \quad & \{\text{monotonicity of } (\wedge R) \text{ for stable } R\} \\
& P \wedge R \ \leadsto \ Q
\end{aligned}
$$

$\square$

Lemma 6 (Trading). *For any predicates P and R, and* stable *predicate Q, $\leadsto$ has the following closure property:*

$$(P \ \leadsto \ Q \Rightarrow R) \quad \equiv \quad (P \wedge Q \ \leadsto \ R)$$

Proof. The two implications $\Leftarrow$ and $\Rightarrow$ are proved separately:

$$
\begin{aligned}
& P \ \leadsto \ Q \Rightarrow R \\
\equiv \quad & \{\text{contradiction}\} \\
& P \ \wedge \ Q \ \wedge \ \neg R \ \leadsto \ Q \Rightarrow R \\
\Leftarrow \quad & \{\text{monotonicity of } \leadsto\} \\
& P \wedge Q \ \leadsto \ R
\end{aligned}
\qquad
\begin{aligned}
& P \wedge Q \ \leadsto \ R \\
\Leftarrow \quad & \{\text{monotonicity of } \leadsto\} \\
& P \wedge Q \ \leadsto \ (Q \Rightarrow R) \ \wedge \ Q \\
\Leftarrow \quad & \{\text{monotonicity of } (\wedge Q) \text{ for stable } Q\} \\
& P \ \leadsto \ Q \Rightarrow R
\end{aligned}
$$

$\square$

B   Proofs of the Composition Rules

B.1   Parallel Composition (Section 4.1)

Let K denote the instances of immediate progress that are used in a proof of $A \models P \leadsto Q$. Using the Immediate Progress Preservation theorem, property $A\|B \models P \leadsto Q$ follows from $(\forall R: R \in K: A\|B \models R)$. Consider such an instance of immediate progress R: $R \in K$, including the unless condition and all the invariants that are used in a proof of $A \models R$. We will show that $A\|B \models R$.

We will show that R is an instance of immediate progress in $A\|B$. The invariants and the unless condition from program A are valid in program $A\|B$, since the precondition of $A\|B$ implies the precondition of program A, and since the statements from program B are orthogonal to A. Since the statements in A are contained in those from $A\|B$, the immediate progress proof of property R from program A is also valid in $A\|B$. $\square$

B.2   Weak Sequential Composition, First Part (Section 4.2)

Let K denote the instances of immediate progress that are used in a proof of $A \models P \leadsto Q$. Using the Immediate Progress Preservation theorem, property

$A \circ B \models P \rightsquigarrow Q$ follows from $(\forall R \colon R \in K \colon A \circ B \models R)$. Consider such an instance of immediate progress $R \colon R \in K$, including the unless condition and all the invariants that are used in a proof of $A \models R$. We will show that $A \circ B \models R$.

As the immediate progress rule refers to program counters, the invariants may need to refer to program counters. Since the program counters are shared between A and B, we restrict their use as follows. In program A, introduce in the component X that is referred to in the immediate progress proof of R, a fresh auxiliary variable v that mimics pc_X both in the precondition and in the statements, and replace every occurrence of pc_X by v. To maintain the immediate progress proof in program A, we introduce for the relevant non-final label i in component X the invariant $v = i \Rightarrow pc_X = i$.

Thus the program counters only occur in one invariant, which is correct in program $A \circ B$ as i is not the final label of component X in program A. The other invariants and the unless condition from program A are valid in program $A \circ B$, since the precondition of $A \circ B$ implies the precondition of program A, and since the statements from program B are orthogonal to program A. Since the statements in A are contained in those from $A \circ B$, the immediate progress proof of property R from program A is also valid in $A \circ B$. □

B.3 Weak Sequential Composition, Second Part (Section 4.2)

Let K denote the instances of immediate progress that are used in a proof of $A \models P \rightsquigarrow Q$. Using the Immediate Progress Preservation theorem, property $B \circ A \models P \rightsquigarrow Q$ follows from $(\forall R \colon R \in K \colon B \circ A \models R)$. Consider such an instance of immediate progress $R \colon R \in K$, including the unless condition and all the invariants that are used in a proof of $A \models R$. We will show that $B \circ A \models R$.

As the immediate progress rule refers to program counters, the invariants may need to refer to program counters. Since the program counters are shared between A and B, we restrict their use as follows. In program A, introduce in the component X that is referred to in the immediate progress proof of R, a fresh auxiliary variable v that mimics pc_X both in the precondition and in the statements, and replace every occurrence of pc_X by v. To maintain the immediate progress proof in program A, we introduce for the relevant non-final label i in component X the invariant $v = i \Rightarrow pc_X = i$.

Thus the program counters only occur in one invariant, which is correct in program $B \circ A$ once component X has terminated program B, using that until then v has its initial value. The other invariants and the unless condition from program A are valid in program $B \circ A$, since the precondition of $B \circ A$ implies the precondition of program A, and since the statements from program B are orthogonal to program A. Refining R into $S \rightsquigarrow T$, we would obtain the weaker immediate progress property $B \circ A \models S \wedge$ "X terminated program B" $\rightsquigarrow T$, by using S **un** T, stability of "component X terminated program B", and the set of statements only being extended.

To conclude the required property $S \rightsquigarrow T$, we can use S **un** T again and the assumption that program B terminates (which is maintained under composition), based on the following lemma:

$$(A \rightsquigarrow B) \wedge (C \text{ \bf un } D) \wedge (B \wedge C \rightsquigarrow D) \Rightarrow (A \wedge C \rightsquigarrow D)$$

for any predicates A, B, C and D. The particular instance is $A := true$, $B :=$ "X terminated program B", $C := S$ and $D := T$. The general lemma can be proved as follows:

$$A \wedge C \rightsquigarrow D$$
$$\Leftarrow \quad \{\text{use } B \wedge C \rightsquigarrow D, \text{ monotonicity of } (\vee D)\}$$
$$A \wedge C \rightsquigarrow (B \wedge C) \vee D$$
$$\Leftarrow \quad \{\text{progress-safety-progress [CM88], use } C \text{ \bf un } D\}$$
$$A \rightsquigarrow B$$

$\square$

Erratum to: Challenges in Software Certification

Tom Maibaum

Software Quality Research Laboratory and Department of Computing and Software
McMaster University
1280 Main St West, Hamilton ON, Canada L8S 4K1
tom@maibaum.org

M. Butler, M. Hinchey, M.M. Larrondo-Petrie (Eds.): ICFEM 2007, LNCS 4789, pp. 4–18, 2007.
© Springer-Verlag Berlin Heidelberg 2007

DOI 10.1007/978-3-540-76650-6_22

'The author of the paper 'Challenges in Software Certification' on pages 4-18 of this volume, is grateful to his former student, Mr. Marwan Abdeen, for the considerable content quoted from his thesis entitled, 'A Model for the FDA: General Principles of Software Validation', and from a joint paper entitled, 'FDA: Between Process and Product Evaluation', co-authored by Mr. Abdeen, Dr. Maibaum and Dr. Kahl.'

The original online version for this chapter can be found at
http://dx.doi.org/10.1007/978-3-540-76650-6_2

Author Index

Abrial, Jean-Raymond   1
Adler, Rasmus   76

Bryans, Jeremy W.   37

Cavalcanti, Ana   151
Chen, Chunqing   96
Chen, Jessica   171

Das Barman, Kuntal   232
de Groot, Martin   19
Dong, Jin Song   57, 96
Duan, Lihua   171
Duan, Zhenhua   246

Feng, Yuzhang   57
Fitzgerald, John S.   37
Fraikin, Benoît   327
Frappier, Marc   327

Gaudel, Marie-Claude   151
Gonzalia, Carlos   212

Hansson, Hans   307

Jesshope, Chris   345
Julliand, Jacques   116

Leung, Ho-fung   57
Liu, Shaoying   136

Maibaum, Tom   4, E1
McIver, Annabelle   212
Mooij, Arjan J.   366
Mountassir, Hassan   116
Mukhopadhyay, Debapriyay   232

Oliveira, Marcel   286
Oudot, Emilie   116

Perna, Juan Ignacio   266
Proenza, Julián   307

Rodriguez-Navas, Guillermo   307

Schaefer, Ina   76
Schuele, Tobias   76
Sun, Jun   96

Tian, Cong   246

Vecchié, Eric   76
Vu, Thuy Duong   345

Woodcock, Jim   266, 286

Zhang, Wenhui   191